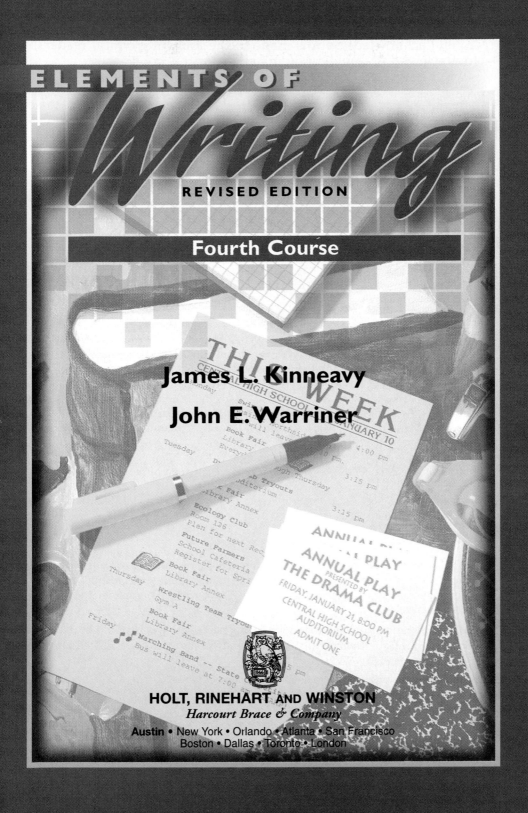

ELEMENTS OF
Writing
REVISED EDITION
Fourth Course

James L. Kinneavy
John E. Warriner

HOLT, RINEHART AND WINSTON
Harcourt Brace & Company

Austin • New York • Orlando • Atlanta • San Francisco
Boston • Dallas • Toronto • London

Critical Readers

Grateful acknowledgment is made to the following critical readers who reviewed pre-publication materials for this book:

John Algeo
University of Georgia
Athens, Georgia

David England
Louisiana State University
Baton Rouge, Louisiana

Mary McFarland-McPherson
Chicago Public Schools
Chicago, Illinois

Anthony Buckley
East Texas State
  University
Commerce, Texas

Elaine A. Espindle
Peabody Veterans Memorial
  High School
Peabody, Massachusetts

Linda E. Sanders
Jenks High School
Tulsa, Oklahoma

Ken Spurlock
Covington Independent
  Public Schools
Covington, Kentucky

Norbert Elliot
New Jersey Institute
  of Technology
Newark, New Jersey

William McCleary
Monroe Community College
Rochester, New York

Staff Credits

Associate Director: Mescal K. Evler
Executive Editors: Kristine E. Marshall, Robert R. Hoyt
Editorial Staff: Managing Editor, Steve Welch; *Editors,* Cheryl Christian, A. Maria Hong, Constance D. Israel, Kathryn Rogers Johnson, Karen Kolar, Christy McBride, Laura Cottam Sajbel, Patricia Saunders, Michael L. Smith, Suzanne Thompson, Katie Vignery; *Copyeditors,* Michael Neibergall, Katherine E. Hoyt, Carrie Laing Pickett, Joseph S. Schofield IV, Barbara Sutherland; *Editorial Coordinators,* Amanda F. Beard, Rebecca Bennett, Susan G. Alexander, Wendy Langabeer, Marie H. Price; *Support,* Ruth A. Hooker, Christina Barnes, Kelly Keeley, Margaret Sanchez, Raquel Sosa, Pat Stover
Permissions: Catherine J. Paré, Janet Harrington
Production: Pre-press, Beth Prevelige, Simira Davis; *Manufacturing,* Michael Roche
Design: Richard Metzger, *Art Director;* Lori Male, *Designer*
Photo Research: Peggy Cooper, *Photo Research Manager;* Tim Taylor, Sherrie Cass, *Photo Research Team*

Portions of this work were published in previous editions.

Acknowledgments: See pages 1075–1082, which are an extension of the copyright page.

Printed in the United States of America

ISBN 0–03–050867–3

3 4 5 6 7 043 00 99 98

James L. Kinneavy, the Jane and Roland Blumberg Centennial Professor of English at The University of Texas at Austin, directed the development and writing of the composition strand in the program. He is the author of *A Theory of Discourse* and coauthor of *Writing in the Liberal Arts Tradition*. Professor Kinneavy is a leader in the field of rhetoric and composition and a respected educator whose teaching experience spans all levels—elementary, secondary, and college. He has continually been concerned with teaching writing to high school students.

John E. Warriner developed the organizational structure for the Handbook of Grammar, Usage, and Mechanics in the book. He coauthored the *English Workshop* series, was general editor of the *Composition: Models and Exercises* series, and editor of *Short Stories: Characters in Conflict*. He taught English for thirty-two years in junior and senior high school and college.

Writers and Editors

Ellen Ashdown has a Ph.D. in English from the University of Florida. She has taught composition and literature at the college level. She is a professional writer of educational materials and has published articles and reviews on education and art.

Phyllis Goldenberg has an A.B. in English from the University of Chicago. She has been a writer and editor of educational materials in literature, grammar, composition, and critical thinking for over thirty-five years.

Elizabeth McCurnin majored in English at Valparaiso University. A professional writer and editor, she has over twenty-five years' experience in educational publishing.

John Roberts has an M.A. in English Education from the University of Kentucky. He has taught English in secondary school. He is an editor and a writer of educational materials in literature, grammar, and composition.

Alice M. Sohn has a Ph.D. in English Education from Florida State University. She has taught English in middle school, secondary school, and college. She has been a writer and editor of educational materials in language arts for seventeen years.

Raymond Teague has an A.B. in English and journalism from Texas Christian University. He has been children's book editor for the *Fort Worth Star-Telegram* for more than fifteen years and has been a writer and editor of educational materials for twelve years.

Carolyn Calhoun Walter has an M.A.T. in English Education from the University of Chicago. She has taught English in grades nine through twelve. She is a professional writer and editor of educational materials in composition and literature.

Acknowledgments

We wish to thank the following teachers who participated in field testing of pre-publication materials for this series:

Susan Almand-Myers
Meadow Park
Intermediate School
Beaverton, Oregon

Theresa L. Bagwell
Naylor Middle School
Tucson, Arizona

Ruth Bird
Freeport High School
Sarver, Pennsylvania

Joan M. Brooks
Central Junior High
School
Guymon, Oklahoma

Candice C. Bush
J. D. Smith Junior High
School
N. Las Vegas, Nevada

Mary Jane Childs
Moore West Junior High
School
Oklahoma City,
Oklahoma

Brian Christensen
Valley High School
West Des Moines, Iowa

Lenise Christopher
Western High School
Las Vegas, Nevada

Mary Ann Crawford
Ruskin Senior High
School
Kansas City, Missouri

Linda Dancy
Greenwood Lakes
Middle School
Lake Mary, Florida

Elaine A. Espindle
Peabody Veterans
Memorial High School
Peabody, Massachusetts

Joan Justice
North Middle School
O'Fallon, Missouri

Beverly Kahwaty
Pueblo High School
Tucson, Arizona

Lamont Leon
Van Buren Junior High
School
Tampa, Florida

Susan Lusch
Fort Zumwalt South High
School
St. Peters, Missouri

Michele K. Lyall
Rhodes Junior High
School
Mesa, Arizona

Belinda Manard
McKinley Senior High
School
Canton, Ohio

Nathan Masterson
Peabody Veterans
Memorial High School
Peabody, Massachusetts

Marianne Mayer
Swope Middle School
Reno, Nevada

Penne Parker
Greenwood Lakes Middle
School
Lake Mary, Florida

Amy Ribble
Gretna Junior-Senior High
School
Gretna, Nebraska

Kathleen R. St. Clair
Western High School
Las Vegas, Nevada

Carla Sankovich
Billinghurst Middle
School
Reno, Nevada

Sheila Shaffer
Cholla Middle School
Phoenix, Arizona

Joann Smith
Lehman Junior High
School
Canton, Ohio

Margie Stevens
Raytown Middle School
Raytown, Missouri

Mary Webster
Central Junior High
School
Guymon, Oklahoma

Susan M. Yentz
Oviedo High School
Oviedo, Florida

We wish to thank the following teachers who contributed student papers for the Revised Edition of *Elements of Writing, Fourth Course.*

Janet G. Anderson
Carson High School
Carson City, Nevada

Patricia Attri
Bret Harte Junior High
School
Oakland, California

Amy C. Holley
Enterprise Senior High
School
Enterprise, Alabama

Contents in Brief

PART ONE

WRITING

INTRODUCTION TO WRITING

Secret Forces 2

WRITING HANDBOOK

1 Writing and Thinking 16
2 Understanding Paragraph Structure 62
3 Understanding Composition Structure 108

AIMS FOR WRITING

4 Expressive Writing: Narration 138
5 Using Description 174
6 Creative Writing: Narration 212
7 Writing to Inform: Exposition 248
8 Writing to Explain: Exposition 288
9 Writing to Persuade 324
10 Writing About Literature: Exposition 362
11 Writing a Research Paper: Exposition 400

LANGUAGE AND STYLE

12 Writing Complete Sentences 446
13 Writing Effective Sentences 461
14 English: Origins and Uses 484

PART TWO

HANDBOOK

GRAMMAR

15 The Parts of Speech 512
16 The Sentence 543
17 The Phrase 572
18 The Clause 595

USAGE

19 Agreement 616
20 Using Pronouns Correctly 647
21 Using Verbs Correctly 676
22 Using Modifiers Correctly 712
23 A Glossary of Usage 736

MECHANICS

24 Capitalization 762
25 End Marks and Commas 787
26 Semicolons and Colons 814
27 Italics and Quotation Marks 829
28 Apostrophes, Hyphens, Dashes, Parentheses 846
29 Spelling 870
30 Correcting Common Errors 896

PART THREE

RESOURCES

31 Speaking 928
32 Listening and Viewing 941
33 The Library/Media Center 952
34 The Dictionary 959
35 Vocabulary 963
36 Letters and Forms 973
37 Reading, Studying, and Test Taking 983

Table of Contents

PART ONE **WRITING**

Secret Forces

An Introduction to Writing by James L. Kinneavy 2

WRITING HANDBOOK

▶ CHAPTER *1* **WRITING AND THINKING**   16

Reading About One Writer's Process 18
from *A Fire in My Hands* by Gary Soto

Aim—The "Why" of Writing 22

Process—The "How" of Writing 22

PREWRITING 24
Finding Ideas for Writing 24
  Keeping a Writer's Journal 25
  Freewriting 26
  Brainstorming 27
  Clustering 28
  Asking Questions 30
  Using Your Five Senses 31
  Reading with a Focus 32
  Listening with a Focus 33
  Imagining 34
Thinking About Purpose, Audience, and Tone 35
Critical Thinking Analyzing Purpose and Audience 36
Arranging Ideas 39
Critical Thinking Arranging Information 40
Critical Thinking Classifying Information 43

WRITING A FIRST DRAFT 45

EVALUATING AND REVISING 47
Critical Thinking Evaluating 49

PROOFREADING AND PUBLISHING 55
Critical Thinking Reflecting on Your Writing 58

MAKING CONNECTIONS 61
  BRAINSTORMING WITH A COMPUTER

WRITING HANDBOOK

▶ **CHAPTER 2** UNDERSTANDING PARAGRAPH STRUCTURE   62

Reading a Model of Paragraph Form 64

from *Nisei Daughter*
Monica Sone

What Makes a Paragraph 67

The Main Idea 67
The Topic Sentence 68
Supporting Sentences 71
   Sensory Details 71
   Facts and Statistics 71
   Examples 73
   Anecdotes 74
The Clincher Sentence 76
Unity 77
Coherence 82
   Order of Ideas 82
   Connections Between Ideas 88
Strategies of Development 93
   Description 94
   Narration 95
   Classification 97
   Evaluation 100

MAKING CONNECTIONS 102

WRITING PARAGRAPHS FOR DIFFERENT PURPOSES 102
   Writing a Paragraph to Express Yourself 102
   Writing a Paragraph to Inform 103
   Writing a Paragraph to Persuade 104
   Writing a Paragraph That Is Creative 106

▶ **CHAPTER 3 UNDERSTANDING COMPOSITION STRUCTURE** 108

Reading a Model of Composition Form 110

"Quasi-Humans"
R. A. Deckert

What Makes a Composition 112

The Thesis Statement 113
Early Plans and Formal Outlines 117
A Writer's Model 120
The Introduction 122
Techniques for Writing Introductions 123
The Body 128
Unity 128
Coherence 128
The Conclusion 130
Techniques for Writing Conclusions 130

MAKING CONNECTIONS 135
WRITING AN INFORMATIVE COMPOSITION

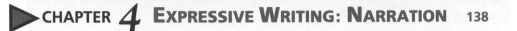

Reading a Model of Personal Expression 140

from *Black Elk Speaks*
As told through John G. Neihardt (Flaming Rainbow)

Writing a Personal Narrative 145

PREWRITING 145
Choosing a Personal Experience 145
Planning Your Personal Narrative 147
    Thinking About Purpose, Audience, and Tone 147
    Recalling Details 148
    Reflecting on the Meaning of the Experience 151
Critical Thinking Interpreting Meaning 152
    Organizing Your Ideas 154

WRITING YOUR FIRST DRAFT 155
    The Structure of Your Personal Narrative 155
    A Passage from an Autobiography 156
    from *An American Childhood*, Annie Dillard

    A Writer's Model 159

EVALUATING AND REVISING 163
Grammar Hint Using Action Verbs 166

PROOFREADING AND PUBLISHING 167
    A Student Model 168
    "The Current," Hilary Hutchinson

WRITING WORKSHOP 169

IMAGINING A UTOPIA • from *A Modern Utopia*, H. G. Wells • Describing
a Personal Utopia

MAKING CONNECTIONS 172

SELF-EXPRESSION ACROSS THE CURRICULUM Science • "Sky Dance," Aldo
Leopold

Reading a Model of Descriptive Writing 176
from "Date with Dracula," *American Way*
Daniel D. Morrison

Writing a Description 181

PREWRITING 181
Focusing Your Description 181
  Choosing a Subject 181
  Thinking About Purpose and Audience 181
  Deciding on Tone 183
Planning Your Description 186
  Collecting Details 186
  Identifying an Emphasis 187
  Organizing Details 189

WRITING YOUR FIRST DRAFT 191
  Using Descriptive Language 191
Critical Thinking Making Comparisons 195
  A Passage from a Novel 196
  from *The Street*, Ann Petry

  A Writer's Model 199

EVALUATING AND REVISING 200
Grammar Hint Using Participles 202

PROOFREADING AND PUBLISHING 204
  A Student Model 205
  "The Wise Lady," Alissa Bird

WRITING WORKSHOP 207
  A FREE VERSE POEM • "Tumbleweed,"
David Wagoner • Writing a Free Verse Poem

MAKING CONNECTIONS 209
  COMBINING DESCRIPTION WITH NARRATION from *Ernie's War: The Best of Ernie Pyle's World War II Dispatches*, Ernie Pyle 209
  DESCRIPTION ACROSS THE CURRICULUM Objective Description in Science 210

► CHAPTER 6 CREATIVE WRITING: NARRATION   212

Reading a Short Story 214
"The Scholarship Jacket"
Marta Salinas

Writing a Short Story 221

PREWRITING 221
Exploring Story Ideas 221
Planning Your Story 223
  Thinking About Purpose, Audience, and Tone 223
Critical Thinking Analyzing Point of View 223
  Thinking About Characters and Setting 225
  Developing the Plot 226

WRITING YOUR FIRST DRAFT 229
  The Basic Elements of Stories 229
  A Short Story 231
  "Mushrooms in the city" from "Spring,"
  Italo Calvino
  A Basic Framework for a Story 236
  A Writer's Model 236

EVALUATING AND REVISING 239

PROOFREADING AND PUBLISHING 241
Mechanics Hint Punctuating Dialogue 241
  A Student Model 243
  from "Memoirs of an Adolescent," Noah Kramer-Dover

WRITING WORKSHOP 244
  A NEWS STORY • "Tornadoes Damage School" • Writing a News Story

MAKING CONNECTIONS 247
  SPEAKING AND LISTENING Creating a Fable
  SHORT STORY WRITING ACROSS THE CURRICULUM History

CHAPTER 7 WRITING TO INFORM: EXPOSITION 248

Reading a Model of Informative Writing 250
from *Moncrief: My Journey to the NBA*
Sidney Moncrief with Myra McLarey

Writing a Comparison/Contrast Essay 256

PREWRITING 256
Choosing Subjects 256
Critical Thinking Classifying Objects and Ideas 257
Thinking About Purpose and Audience 258
Gathering and Arranging Information 260
Developing a Thesis Statement 265

WRITING YOUR FIRST DRAFT 266
The Elements of a Comparison/Contrast Essay 266
A Newspaper Article 267
"Time out! Is baseball Finnished?," Bob Secter from *The Miami Herald*
A Basic Framework for a Comparison/Contrast Essay 271
A Writer's Model 271

EVALUATING AND REVISING 274

PROOFREADING AND PUBLISHING 278
Grammar Hint Using the Degrees of Comparison 279
A Student Model 280
"Football and Cyberball," Chris Chavis

WRITING WORKSHOP 282
AN EXTENDED DEFINITION Writing an Extended Definition

MAKING CONNECTIONS 285
TEST TAKING Writing for an Essay Test Question 285
COMPARISON ACROSS THE CURRICULUM
Literature • "The Eagle-Feather Fan,"
N. Scott Momaday 286

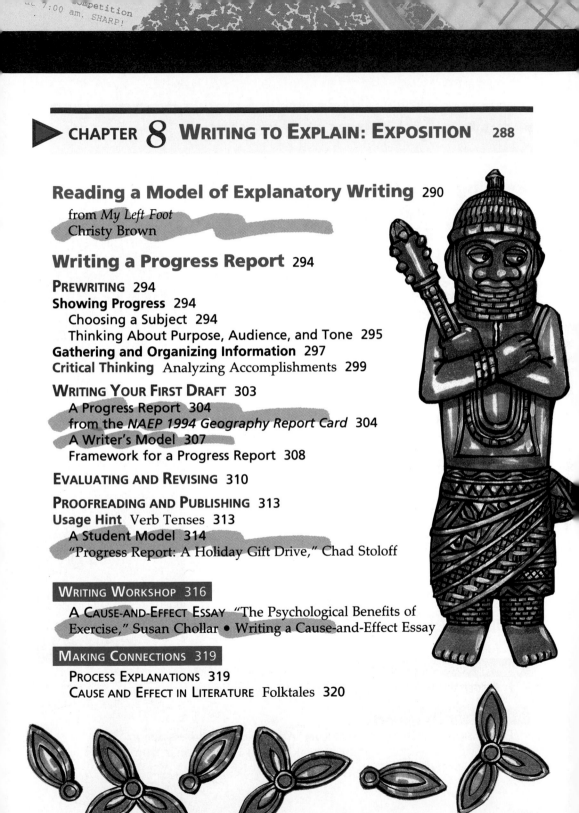

▶ CHAPTER 8 WRITING TO EXPLAIN: EXPOSITION 288

Reading a Model of Explanatory Writing 290
from *My Left Foot*
Christy Brown

Writing a Progress Report 294

PREWRITING 294
Showing Progress 294
Choosing a Subject 294
Thinking About Purpose, Audience, and Tone 295
Gathering and Organizing Information 297
Critical Thinking Analyzing Accomplishments 299

WRITING YOUR FIRST DRAFT 303
A Progress Report 304
from the *NAEP 1994 Geography Report Card* 304
A Writer's Model 307
Framework for a Progress Report 308

EVALUATING AND REVISING 310

PROOFREADING AND PUBLISHING 313
Usage Hint Verb Tenses 313
A Student Model 314
"Progress Report: A Holiday Gift Drive," Chad Stoloff

WRITING WORKSHOP 316
A CAUSE-AND-EFFECT ESSAY "The Psychological Benefits of
Exercise," Susan Chollar • Writing a Cause-and-Effect Essay

MAKING CONNECTIONS 319
PROCESS EXPLANATIONS 319
CAUSE AND EFFECT IN LITERATURE Folktales 320

Reading a Model of Persuasive Writing 326
"A Letter to the Duke of Milan"
Leonardo da Vinci

Writing a Persuasive Essay 332
PREWRITING 332
Choosing a Topic 332
   An Opinion Statement 333
Thinking About Purpose, Audience, and Tone 335
Supporting Your Opinion 337
   Logical Appeals 337
   Emotional Appeals 339
Critical Thinking Evaluating Your Reasoning 340

WRITING YOUR FIRST DRAFT 343
   The Basic Elements of Persuasive Essays 343
   A Magazine Editorial 343
   "Can Bicycles Save the World?,"
   Jane Bosveld from *Omni*
   A Simple Framework for a Persuasive Essay 347
   A Writer's Model 347

EVALUATING AND REVISING 351
Grammar Hint Changing Sentence Length
   for Emphasis 354

PROOFREADING AND PUBLISHING 355
   A Student Model 355
   "Uniforms Reduce Problems," Katie Baker

WRITING WORKSHOP 357
   A **LETTER TO THE EDITOR** Writing a Letter to the Editor

MAKING CONNECTIONS 359
   PERSUASION ACROSS THE CURRICULUM Advertising and Persuasion 359
   SPEAKING AND LISTENING Public Speaking and Persuasion • from *My Life
   with Martin Luther King, Jr.*, Coretta Scott King 360

© 1998, The Boston Globe Newspaper
Co./Washington Post Writers Group.
Repinted with permission.

CHAPTER 10 WRITING ABOUT LITERATURE: EXPOSITION 362

Reading a Model of Literary Analysis 364

from *The Best, Worst, and Most Unusual: Horror Films*
Darrell Moore

Writing a Critical Analysis 369

PREWRITING 369
Reading and Responding to Stories 369
  Responding to Stories as an Active Reader 369
  A Short Story 370
  "An Astrologer's Day," R. K. Narayan
  Understanding and Using Literary Elements 376
Critical Thinking Analyzing a Short Story 379
Planning a Critical Analysis 381
  Thinking About Purpose and Audience 381
  Finding a Focus and Developing a Main Idea 381
  Collecting Support and Organizing
  Your Ideas 382

WRITING YOUR FIRST DRAFT 384
  A Writer's Model 385

EVALUATING AND REVISING 387

PROOFREADING AND PUBLISHING 390
Mechanics Hint Denoting Titles 390
  A Student Model 391
  "The Big Picture," Matt Sanders

WRITING WORKSHOP 393
  A CRITICAL REVIEW A Mini-Review of *Driving Miss Daisy*
  by Pauline Kael for *The New Yorker* • Writing a
  Mini-Review of a Movie or Television Program

MAKING CONNECTIONS 396
  RESPONDING TO LITERATURE "The Bean Eaters," Gwendolyn Brooks 396
  CRITICAL ANALYSIS ACROSS THE CURRICULUM from "CD & Videodisc
  Players," *Consumers Digest* 398

CHAPTER 11 WRITING A RESEARCH PAPER: EXPOSITION 400

Reading a Model of Reporting 402
from "America's Ancient Skywatchers" by Robert B. Carlson

Writing a Research Paper 407

PREWRITING 407
Finding and Limiting a Subject 407
  Choosing a Subject 407
  Limiting Your Subject to a Specific Topic 408
  Selecting a Suitable Topic 408
  Thinking About Purpose, Audience, and Tone 410
  Developing Research Questions 412
Finding and Evaluating Sources of Information 414
  Preparing Source Cards 416
Planning, Recording, and Organizing Information 420
  Drafting an Early Plan 420
  Taking Notes 421
  Developing a Thesis Statement 423
Critical Thinking Analyzing Your Topic 423
  Preparing an Outline 424

WRITING YOUR FIRST DRAFT 426
  Combining the Basic Elements of a Research Report 426
Mechanics Hint Using Quotations 427
  Giving Credit to Your Sources 428
  A Writer's Model 430

EVALUATING AND REVISING 436

PROOFREADING AND PUBLISHING 439
  A Student Model "A Moving Tune," Lam Votran 440

WRITING WORKSHOP 441
  A BOOK REPORT THAT EVALUATES Writing a Book Report

MAKING CONNECTIONS 443
  RESEARCH ACROSS THE CURRICULUM The Visual Arts 443
  SPEAKING AND LISTENING Public Opinion Polls 444

▶ CHAPTER *12* **WRITING COMPLETE SENTENCES** 446

Sentence Fragments 446

Phrase Fragments 449
  Verbal Phrases 449
  Appositive Phrases 450
  Prepositional Phrases 450
Subordinate Clause Fragments 451

Run-on Sentences 456

Revising Run-on Sentences 456

> MAKING CONNECTIONS 460
>   FILL IN THE MISSING PIECES

▶ CHAPTER *13* **WRITING EFFECTIVE SENTENCES** 461

Combining Sentences 461

Inserting Words 462
Inserting Phrases 465
  Prepositional Phrases 465
  Participial Phrases 465
  Appositive Phrases 465

Book Signing
Thursday, 2:30
Amy Tan, author of
The Joy Luck Club

Using Compound Subjects and Verbs 467
Grammar Hint Checking for Subject-Verb Agreement **468**
Creating a Compound Sentence 468
Creating a Complex Sentence 470
  Adjective Clauses 470
Mechanics Hint Punctuating Adjective Clauses **471**
  Adverb Clauses 471
  Noun Clauses 472

Improving Sentence Style 474

Using Parallel Structure 474
Revising Stringy Sentences 475
Revising Wordy Sentences 477
Varying Sentence Beginnings 478
Varying Sentence Structure 481

MAKING CONNECTIONS 483
  ENTER A CONTEST

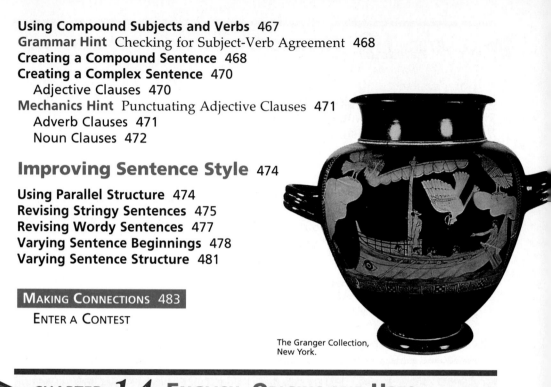

The Granger Collection, New York.

► CHAPTER *14* ENGLISH: ORIGINS AND USES 484

Where English Comes From 484

Old English (450–1100) 486
  Old English Gains New Words 487
Middle English (1100–1500) 487
  English Triumphs 489
Modern English (1500–Present) 490
  The Great Vowel Shift 490
  London Sets the Standard 491
  English Travels Abroad 492
American English 493
English Around the World 494
A Changing Language 495

How English Is Used 496

Dialects of American English 496
   Regional Dialects 497
   Ethnic Dialects 498
Standard American English 498
Standard English—Formal to Informal 500
Uses of Informal English 501
   Colloquialisms 501
   Slang 502

How to Say What You Mean 503

Synonyms 503
Denotation and Connotation 504
Loaded Words 505
Euphemisms 505
Jargon 506

Handle with Care 507

Mixed Figures of Speech 507
Tired Words 507
Clichés 508

MAKING CONNECTIONS 509
   WRITING A TRAVEL AD

PART TWO HANDBOOK

▶ CHAPTER 15 THE PARTS OF SPEECH 512

Their Identification and Function

DIAGNOSTIC TEST A. Identifying the Parts of Speech in Sentences 512
B. Identifying the Parts of Speech in a Paragraph 513

Nouns 514
Proper Nouns and Common Nouns 515
Concrete Nouns and Abstract Nouns 515

Pronouns 516
Personal Pronouns 517
Other Commonly Used Pronouns 517

Adjectives 518
Articles 519
Pronoun or Adjective? 520
Nouns Used as Adjectives 521
Writing Application Using Adjectives to Describe
an Imagined Self 521

Verbs 524
Action Verbs 524
Transitive Verbs 524
Intransitive Verbs 524
Linking Verbs 525
The Verb Phrase 527

Adverbs 529
Adverbs Modifying Verbs 529
Adverbs Modifying Adjectives 530
Adverbs Modifying Other Adverbs 531
Picture This 532

Prepositions 534

Conjunctions 536
Coordinating Conjunctions 536
Correlative Conjunctions 536

Interjections 537

Determining Parts of Speech 538

REVIEW: POSTTEST 1 Determining the Parts of Speech of Words 540

REVIEW: POSTTEST 2 Writing Sentences with Words Used as Different Parts of Speech 541

SUMMARY OF PARTS OF SPEECH 542

▶ CHAPTER 16 THE SENTENCE 543

Subjects, Predicates, Complements

DIAGNOSTIC TEST A. Identifying Subjects, Verbs, and Complements 543
B. Classifying Sentences as Declarative, Interrogative, Imperative, or Exclamatory 544

Sentences and Sentence Fragments 544

Subject and Predicate 546
The Simple Subject 548
The Simple Predicate 548
How to Find the Subject of a Sentence 549
Sentences Beginning with *There* or *Here* 553
Sentences That Ask Questions 553
The Understood Subject 554
Compound Subjects and Verbs 554
Picture This 557

Complements 557
The Subject Complement 560
Objects 562

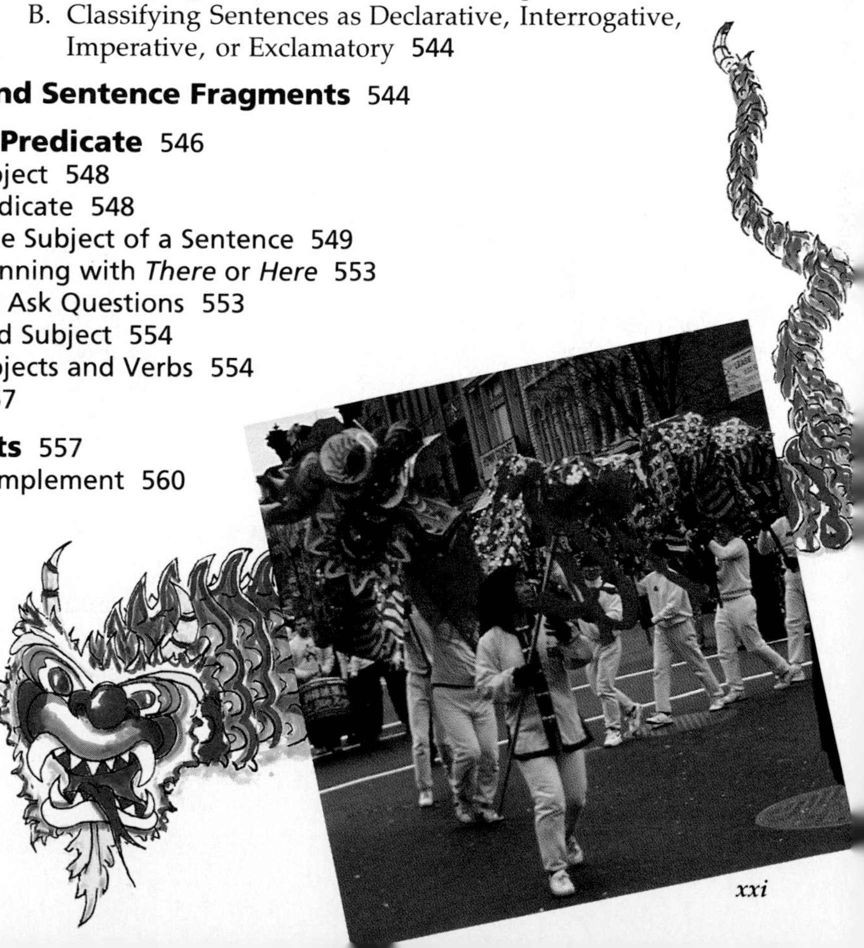

Sentences Classified by Purpose 565

Writing Application Catching a Reader's Interest with Appropriately Varied Sentences 567

REVIEW: POSTTEST 1 A. Identifying Subjects, Verbs, and Complements 570
  B. Classifying Sentences as Declarative, Interrogative, Imperative, or Exclamatory 570

REVIEW: POSTTEST 2 Writing Sentences 571

▶ CHAPTER 17 THE PHRASE 572

Prepositional, Verbal, and Appositive Phrases

DIAGNOSTIC TEST A. Identifying Phrases in Sentences 572
  B. Identifying Phrases in a Paragraph 573

Prepositional Phrases 574
Adjective Phrases 574
Adverb Phrases 576
Writing Application Using Prepositional Phrases to Write Clear Directions 578

Verbals and Verbal Phrases 579
The Participle 579
The Participial Phrase 582
The Gerund 584
The Gerund Phrase 585
The Infinitive 586
The Infinitive Phrase 587
The Infinitive Without *to* 588

Appositives and Appositive Phrases 590
Picture This 591

REVIEW: POSTTEST 1 Identifying Prepositional, Verbal, and Appositive Phrases 593

REVIEW: POSTTEST 2 Writing Sentences with Phrases 594

▶ CHAPTER 18 THE CLAUSE 595

Independent and Subordinate Clauses

DIAGNOSTIC TEST A. Identifying and Classifying Clauses 595
                B. Classifying Sentences According to Structure 596

Kinds of Clauses 597
Independent Clauses 597
Subordinate Clauses 598
   Complements and Modifiers in Subordinate Clauses 599

The Uses of Subordinate Clauses 600
The Adjective Clause 600
   Relative Pronouns 601
The Adverb Clause 603
   Subordinating Conjunctions 603
The Noun Clause 606
Writing Application Using Subordination to Reflect Your Thoughts 608

Sentences Classified According to Structure 610
Picture This 612

REVIEW: POSTTEST 1 A. Identifying Independent and Subordinate Clauses;
                Classifying Subordinate Clauses 613
                B. Classifying Sentences According to Structure 614
REVIEW: POSTTEST 2 Writing Sentences with Varied Structures 615

▶ CHAPTER 19 AGREEMENT 616

Subject and Verb, Pronoun and Antecedent

DIAGNOSTIC TEST A. Selecting Verbs That Agree with Their Subjects **616**
B. Identifying Verbs That Agree with Their Subjects and
Pronouns That Agree with Their Antecedents **617**

Number 618

Agreement of Subject and Verb 619
Intervening Phrases 620
Indefinite Pronouns 622
Picture This 626
Compound Subjects 627
Other Problems in Agreement 628

Agreement of Pronoun and Antecedent 637
Writing Application Using Agreement to Make Meaning Clear **644**

REVIEW: POSTTEST A. Selecting Verbs That Agree with Their Subjects and
Pronouns That Agree with Their Antecedents **645**
B. Selecting Verbs That Agree with Their Subjects and
Pronouns That Agree with Their Antecedents **646**

▶ CHAPTER 20 USING PRONOUNS CORRECTLY 647

Nominative and Objective Case

DIAGNOSTIC TEST A. Using Pronouns Correctly in Sentences **647**
B. Identifying Correct Pronoun Forms in a Paragraph **648**

Case Forms of Personal Pronouns 649
The Nominative Case 651
The Objective Case 655
Picture This 659

Special Problems in Pronoun Usage 661
Who and *Whom* 661
Appositives 664
Pronouns in Incomplete Constructions 668
Inexact Pronoun Reference 668
Writing Application Using Pronouns Correctly in a Letter 671
REVIEW: POSTTEST A. Determining the Proper Case of Pronouns in
                        Sentences 674
                     B. Proofreading Sentences for the Correct Use of
                        Pronouns 675

▶ CHAPTER *21* **USING VERBS CORRECTLY** 676

Principal Parts, Tense, Voice

DIAGNOSTIC TEST A. Writing the Past or Past Participle Form of Verbs 676
                  B. Revising Verb Tense or Voice 677
                  C. Determining Correct Use of *Lie* and *Lay, Sit* and *Set,*
                     and *Rise* and *Raise* in Sentences 677

The Principal Parts of Verbs 678
Regular Verbs 679
Irregular Verbs 679

Tense 684
Picture This 691
Consistency of Tense 692

Active Voice and Passive Voice 694
Using the Passive Voice 696

Six Troublesome Verbs 697
Lie and *Lay* 697
Sit and *Set* 700
Rise and *Raise* 704
Writing Application Using Verb Tense to Establish Time of Action 706

REVIEW: POSTTEST A. Writing the Past and Past Participle Form of Verbs 709
                  B. Revising Verb Tense or Voice 710
                  C. Determining Correct Use of *Lie* and *Lay, Sit* and *Set,*
                     and *Rise* and *Raise* in Sentences 711

Forms, Comparison, and Placement

DIAGNOSTIC TEST A. Correcting Errors in the Use of the Comparative and
Superlative Forms 712
B. Revising Sentences by Correcting Dangling and Misplaced
Modifiers 713

Adjective and Adverb Forms 714
Three Troublesome Pairs 716
Bad and *Badly* 716
Well and *Good* 717
Slow and *Slowly* 717

Comparison of Modifiers 719
Regular Comparison 720
Irregular Comparison 721
Use of Comparative and
Superlative Forms 722
Writing Application Using Comparative
and Superlative Degrees to Make
Comparison Clear 726

Dangling Modifiers 728
Correcting Dangling Modifiers 728

Misplaced Modifiers 730
Misplaced Phrase Modifiers 730
Misplaced Clause Modifiers 732

REVIEW: POSTTEST A. Revising Sentences by Correcting Errors
in the Use of Modifiers 734
B. Revising a Paragraph by Correcting Errors
in the Use of Modifiers 734

► CHAPTER **23** **A GLOSSARY OF USAGE** 736

Common Usage Problems

DIAGNOSTIC TEST Revising Expressions by Correcting Errors in Usage 736
Writing Application Using Standard English to Make a Good Impression 752
The Double Negative 756
Picture This 758
REVIEW: POSTTEST A. Revising Expressions by Correcting Errors in Usage 760
B. Proofreading Paragraphs to Correct Usage Errors 761

The Granger Collection, New York.

► CHAPTER **24** **CAPITALIZATION** 762

Standard Uses of Capitalization

DIAGNOSTIC TEST Correcting Sentences by Using Capitalization Correctly 762
Picture This 775
Writing Application Using Capital Letters Correctly 782
REVIEW: POSTTEST A. Capitalizing Sentences Correctly 783
B. Capitalizing a Paragraph Correctly 784
SUMMARY STYLE REVIEW 785

► CHAPTER **25** PUNCTUATION 787

End Marks and Commas

Diagnostic Test Correcting Sentences by Adding End Marks and Commas 787

End Marks 789

Commas 793
Items in a Series 793
Independent Clauses 796
Nonessential Clauses and Phrases 797
Introductory Elements 800
Writing Application Using Commas in Writing Instructions for a Game 803
Interrupters 805
Conventional Situations 808
Picture This 808
Unnecessary Commas 809
Review: Posttest A. Correcting Sentences by Adding End Marks and Commas 811
B. Correcting Paragraphs by Adding End Marks and Commas 812
Summary of the Uses of the Comma 813

► CHAPTER **26** PUNCTUATION 814

Semicolons and Colons

Diagnostic Test Correcting Sentences by Using Semicolons and Colons 814

Semicolons 816

Colons 821
Picture This 822
Writing Application Using Semicolons and Colons in a Business Letter 825
Review: Posttest Correcting Sentences by Adding Semicolons and Colons 827

► CHAPTER **27** PUNCTUATION   829

Italics and Quotation Marks

DIAGNOSTIC TEST Correcting Sentences by Adding Italics and Quotation
Marks **829**

Italics 831

Quotation Marks 834
Picture This 839
Writing Application Writing an Interior Dialogue **843**
REVIEW: POSTTEST Correcting Sentences by Adding Italics or
Quotation Marks **844**

► CHAPTER **28** PUNCTUATION   846

Apostrophes, Hyphens, Dashes, Parentheses

DIAGNOSTIC TEST A. Using Apostrophes and Hyphens Correctly **846**
B. Using Dashes and Parentheses Correctly **847**

Apostrophes 848
Possessive Case 848
  Nouns in the Possessive Case 848
  Pronouns in the Possessive Case 850
  Compounds in the Possessive Case 851
Contractions 854
Picture This 857
Plurals 857

Hyphens 859
Word Division 859
Compound Words 860

Dashes 862

Parentheses 863

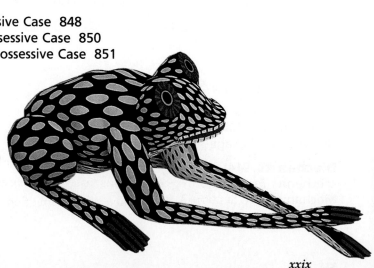

Writing Application Using Dashes in Poetry **866**
REVIEW: POSTTEST A. Correcting Sentences by Using Apostrophes and
                          Hyphens **868**
                      B. Correcting Sentences by Using Dashes and Parentheses **869**

CHAPTER **29** SPELLING   **870**

Improving Your Spelling

Good Spelling Habits 870

Spelling Rules 872
ie and *ei* 872
–cede, –ceed, and *–sede* 872
Adding Prefixes 873
Adding Suffixes 873
Forming Plurals of Nouns 877
Spelling Numbers 881

Words Often Confused 882
100 Commonly Misspelled Words 893
300 Spelling Words 893

CHAPTER **30** CORRECTING COMMON ERRORS   **896**

Key Language Skills Review

Grammar and Usage 897
Grammar and Usage Test: Section 1 910
Grammar and Usage Test: Section 2 911

Mechanics 914
Mechanics Test: Section 1 922
Mechanics Test: Section 2 923

PART THREE RESOURCES

▶ CHAPTER *31* SPEAKING 928

Skills and Strategies

The Communication Cycle 928
Nonverbal Communication 929

Speaking Informally 929

Speaking Formally 930
Preparing a Speech 930
Gathering Material 932
Giving Your Speech 933
Special Speaking Situations 934

Group Discussions 934
Establishing a Purpose 934
Assigning Roles for a Discussion 935
Parliamentary Procedure 935

Oral Interpretation 936
Adapting Material 936
Presenting an Oral Interpretation 937

Review 938

▶ CHAPTER 32 **LISTENING AND VIEWING** 941

Strategies for Listening and Viewing
Listening with a Purpose 941

Listening for Information 942
Listening for Details 942
Using the LQ2R Method 942
Listening to Instructions 942
Listening and Responding Politely 943
Conducting an Interview 943

Critical Listening 944
Taking Lecture Notes 945

Understanding the Impact of Mass Media 946
Persuasive Techniques 947

Viewing for Information 948
Sources of Information 948
Evaluating What You See 949
What You Can Do 950

Review 950

▶ CHAPTER 33 **THE LIBRARY/MEDIA CENTER** 952

Finding and Using Information
Classifying and Arranging Information 952
Dewey Decimal Arrangement of Fiction 953
Types of Card Catalogs 953

Using Reference Materials 955
The *Readers' Guide* 955
Special Information Sources 956
Reference Sources 956

Review 958

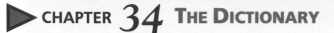

► CHAPTER 34 THE DICTIONARY   959

Types and Contents

Types of Dictionaries 959
A Sample Entry 960

Review 961

► CHAPTER 35 VOCABULARY   963

Learning and Using New Words

Creating a Word Bank 963

Using Context Clues 964
Determining Meanings from the General Context 965
Choosing the Right Word 965

Using Word Parts 966
Roots 966
Prefixes 968
Suffixes 969

Review 970

► CHAPTER 36 LETTERS AND FORMS 973

Style and Contents
The Appearance of a Business Letter 973

Writing Business Letters 974
The Parts of a Business Letter 974
Types of Business Letters 976
   Request or Order Letter • Complaint or Adjustment Letter • Appreciation
   or Commendation Letter • Letter of Application

Writing Informal or Personal Letters 980
   Thank-you Letters • Invitations • Letters of Regret

Addressing an Envelope 980

Completing Printed Forms 981

Review 981

▶ CHAPTER **37** READING, STUDYING, AND TEST TAKING   983

Using Skills and Strategies

Planning a Study Routine 983

Strengthening Reading and Study Skills 984
Reading and Understanding 984
   Writing to Learn 984
   Using Word-Processing Tools for Writing 985
   Using the SQ3R Reading Method 986
Interpreting and Analyzing What You Read 987
   Stated Main Idea • Implied Main Idea
   Reading to Find Relationships Among Details 987
   Reading Passage and Sample Analysis 988
Applying Reasoning Skills to Your Reading 989
Reading Graphics and Illustrations 990
Applying Study and Reading Strategies 992
   Taking Notes • Classifying • Organizing Information
   Visually • Outlining • Paraphrasing • Summarizing
   • Memorizing

Improving Test-Taking Skills 1000
Preparing Yourself 1000
Preparing for Standardized Tests 1000
Objective Tests 1001
   Taking Different Kinds of Objective Tests 1002
Essay Tests 1008
   Taking Essay Tests 1008

Review 1011

APPENDIX: DIAGRAMING SENTENCES 1017

GLOSSARY OF TERMS 1032

GLOSSARY 1043

INDEX 1047

ACKNOWLEDGMENTS 1075

PHOTO CREDITS 1080

ILLUSTRATION CREDITS 1082

Fiction

Gwendolyn Brooks, "Home," *Maud Martha*

Italo Calvino, "Spring," *Marcovaldo, or the Seasons in the City*

Harold Courlander with Ezekiel A. Eshugbayi, "Why No One Lends His Beauty," *Olode the Hunter and Other Tales from Nigeria*

Umberto Eco, *The Name of the Rose*

Edith Hamilton, *Mythology*

David Low, "Winterblossom Garden," *Ploughshares*

Lucy Maud Montgomery, *Anne of Green Gables*

R. K. Narayan, "An Astrologer's Day"

Tim O'Brien, "Where Have You Gone, Charming Billy?" *Going After Cacciato*

Ann Petry, *The Street*

Marta Salinas, "The Scholarship Jacket"

Ntozake Shange, *Sassafrass, Cypress, and Indigo*

John Steinbeck, *The Pearl*

Carl Stephenson, "Leiningen Versus the Ants"

Nonfiction

Emily R. Alling, "Letter to the Editor," *Newsweek*

Sandra R. Arbetter, "Introverts and Extroverts," *Current Health*

Sherry Baker, "Pioneers Underfoot," *Omni*

Robert D. Ballard, *Exploring the Titanic*

Stanley Bing, "The Most Beautiful Girl in the World," *Esquire*

Jane Bosveld, "Can Bicycles Save the World?" *Omni*

Albert Britt, *Great Indian Chiefs*

Christy Brown, *My Left Foot*

Malcolm W. Browne, "3 Scientists Say Travel in Time Isn't So Far Out," *The New York Times*

Robert B. Carlson, "America's Ancient Skywatchers," *National Geographic*

"CD & Videodisc Players," *Consumer Digest*

James R. Chiles, "To break the unbreakable codes," *Smithsonian*

Susan Chollar, "The Psychological Benefits of Exercise," *American Health*

John Ciardi, "bits," *A Browser's Dictionary*

Michael D. Coe, "Olmec and Maya: A Study in Relationships," *The Origins of Maya Civilization*

Mason Crum, *Gullah*

Leonardo da Vinci, "Leonardo da Vinci to the Duke of Milan: 'certain of my secrets,'" *A Treasury of the World's Great Letters*

R. A. Deckert, "Quasi-Humans," *Omni*

Annie Dillard, *An American Childhood*

Roger Ebert, *The Chicago Sun-Times*

Timothy Egan, "School for Homeless Children: A Rare Experience," *The New York Times*

John Elkington, et al., *Going Green: A Kid's Handbook to Saving the Planet*

Betty Lou English, *Behind the Headlines at a Big City Paper*

Lawrence M. Fisher, "A Thirsty California Is Trying Desalination," *The New York Times*

Lisa W. Foderaro, "At Rye High, Students Not Only Must Do Well, They Must Do Good," *The New York Times*

Billie Follensbee, "Olmec Heads: A Product of the Americas"

Roy A. Gallant, *Private Lives of the Stars*

Ellen Goodman, *On Being a Writer*, ed. Bill Strickland

John Steele Gordon, "Financial Folklore," *American Heritage*

Evan and Janet Hadingham, *Garbage! Where It Comes From, Where It Goes*

Helen Hayes, "Hayes: There Is So Much to Do"

Jesse L. Jackson, "We Need Power, Program, and Progress," *The Progressive*

Suzanne Jurmain, *Once Upon a Horse*

Pauline Kael, review—"Driving Miss Daisy," *The New Yorker*

Coretta Scott King, *My Life with Martin Luther King, Jr.*

Maxine Hong Kingston, "White Tigers," *The Woman Warrior*

Doris G. Kinney, "Reopening the Gateway to America," *Life*

Kwei-li, *Golden Lilies*

William Least Heat-Moon, *Blue Highways*

Aldo Leopold, "Sky Dance," *A Sand County Almanac*

Charles Mann and Gwenda Blair, "Juan's Place," *Geo*

Milton Meltzer, ed., *Voices from the Civil War*

Sidney Moncrief, *Moncrief: My Journey to the NBA*

Darrell Moore, "Frankenstein," *The Best, Worst, and Most Unusual: Horror Films*

Daniel D. Morrison, "Date with Dracula," *American Way*

"Mourning Dove (Hum-ishu-ma)," *The Norton Anthology of Literature by Women*

John G. Neihardt, "Black Elk Speaks," *Black Elk Speaks: Being the Life Story of a Holy Man of the Oglala Sioux*

George Plimpton, "Neil Armstrong's Famous First Words," *Esquire*

Joyce Pope, *Do Animals Dream?*

"A Progress Report from the NAEP 1994 Geography Report Card," *NAEP 1994 Geography Report Card*

Ernie Pyle, "North Africa: November 1942–June 1943," *Ernie's War: The Best of Ernie Pyle's World War II Dispatches*

Bob Secter, "Time out! Is baseball Finnished?" *Miami Herald*

Ellen Ruppel Shell, "Seeds in the bank could stave off disaster on the farm," *Smithsonian*

Monica Sone, *Nisei Daughter*

Gary Soto, "Foreword," *A Fire in My Hands*

Sharon Stocker, "Stretchbreak: Good-Morning Wake-Up Stretch," *Prevention*

Kathleen Teltsch, "For Young and Old, A Pocket Paradise," *The New York Times*

Paul Theroux, *Riding the Iron Rooster*

Susan Allen Toth, "Nothing Happened," *Blooming: A Small Town Girlhood*

Mark Twain, "A Genuine Mexican Plug"

"Two tornadoes damage airport, Miami school," *The Ledger*

Ed Ward, et al., *Rock of Ages: The Rolling Stone History of Rock & Roll*

Geoffrey C. Ward and Ken Burns, *Baseball: An Illustrated History*

H. G. Wells, *A Modern Utopia*

Tom Wolfe, "Clean Fun at Riverhead"

Rick Wolff, "A Yen for Baseball Cards," *Sports Illustrated*

Arthur Zich, "Japanese Americans: Home At Last," *National Geographic*

Poetry

Gwendolyn Brooks, "The Bean Eaters," *Blacks*

N. Scott Momaday, "The Eagle-Feather Fan," *The Gourd Dancer*

David Wagoner, "Tumbleweed," *Collected Poems 1945–1976*

The Granger Collection, New York.

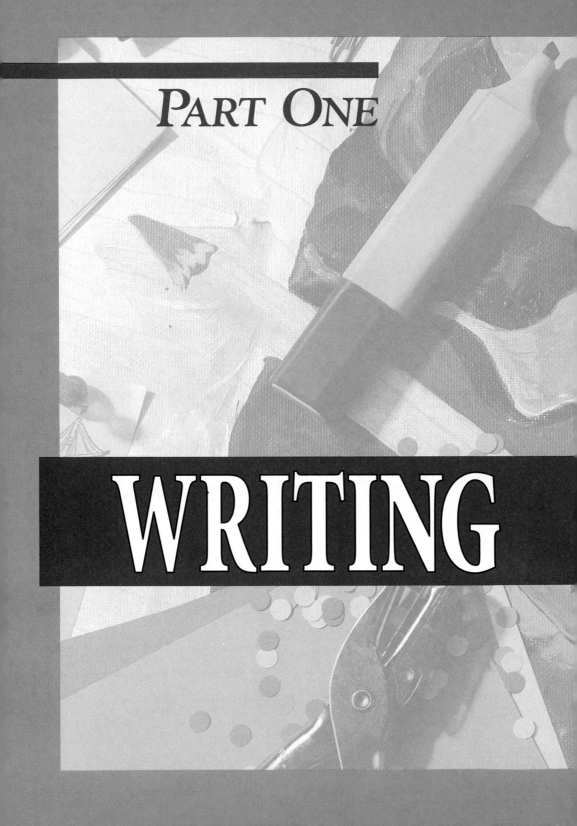

PART ONE

WRITING

INTRODUCTION TO WRITING
Secret Forces

WRITING HANDBOOK
1 Writing and Thinking
2 Understanding Paragraph Structure
3 Understanding Composition
  Structure

AIMS FOR WRITING
4 Expressive Writing: Narration
5 Using Description
6 Creative Writing: Narration
7 Writing to Inform: Exposition
8 Writing to Explain: Exposition
9 Writing to Persuade
10 Writing About Literature: Exposition
11 Writing a Research Paper: Exposition

LANGUAGE AND STYLE
12 Writing Complete Sentences
13 Writing Effective Sentences
14 English: Origins and Uses

1

SECRET FORCES

James L. Kinneavy

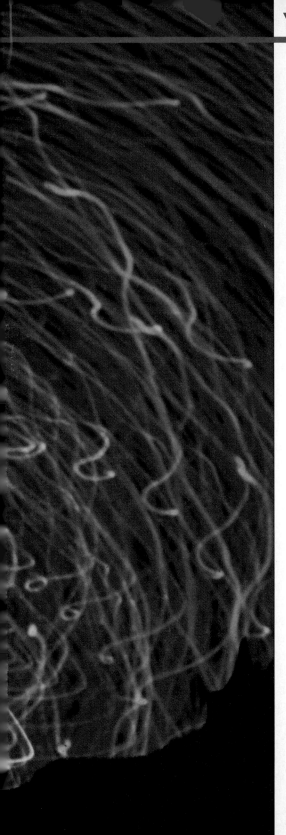

The world is not always what it seems. Even now you are surrounded by unseen forces. These powerful forces influence your life in many ways. They educate and entertain and connect. They make possible marvelous things like talking computers, telephones for people who are deaf, and manned space stations.

These forces are everywhere. You read about and see the results of them every day. In fact, you may become one of the **secret forces** yourself someday.

Have you guessed who these forces are? Do you know what gives them their power?

Who Are These Forces ?

These forces are often unseen, but they aren't really mysterious. In fact, the secret forces are all around you. They're the writers, planners, and communicators of the world. They're hard at work in every office, factory, museum, and laboratory.

They're political leaders, scientists, environmentalists, and city planners who determine what your world will be like someday. They're advertising people, song writers, and cartoonists who affect how you look at the world today. They're Nobel and Pulitzer Prize winners, dynamic public speakers, or famous generals. They're unknown speechwriters for government figures who change the world. They're scriptwriters whose works delight you or move you or thrill you. They're newspaper or magazine writers who tell you about the world around you. The secret forces are people who see a need and set out to meet it.

Whether you see them or not, these forces are an important part of your life. They wield the power that shapes the world you live in.

What Is Their Power ?

Whether they're in the spotlight or behind the scenes, all writers and planners have in common the power of communication. *Writers* have something to say (a *subject*), someone to say it to (an *audience*), and a way to say it (a *language*). You can think of these elements as a communications triangle with language—both written and spoken—at its very center.

How Do They Communicate?

The Writing Process

Powerful communication comes from presenting ideas effectively. Good writers use a general method for developing their ideas and communicating them clearly. The method is called the *writing process.* Different writers use the process differently—there's no right way or wrong way to go through it. But there are several steps, or stages, writers usually work through.

Prewriting	Thinking and planning; deciding what subject to write about and for what purpose and audience; gathering ideas and details; building a plan for presenting ideas
Writing	Writing a first draft; following some kind of plan to put ideas into sentences and paragraphs; including new ideas as they occur to you
Evaluating and Revising	Rereading the draft to decide about strengths and weaknesses; making changes to improve it
Proofreading and Publishing	Finding and fixing errors; making a final copy and sharing it with an audience

Why Do They Communicate?

The Aims of Writing

Writers who are secret forces always have an *aim*—a purpose—in mind when they write. Sometimes they have more than one. But they know what they want to accomplish. There are four basic aims of writing: to inform, to persuade, to express oneself, and to create literature.

To Inform	Sometimes writers want to give information or to explain something to readers.
To Persuade	Writers may want to convince people to change their minds about something, or to stir people into action.
To Express Themselves	Sometimes writers want simply to explore their thoughts and feelings about something.
To Create Literature	Writers may use their talents to create literature—stories, poems, songs, and plays.

On the following pages, you'll read four models. They all have the same topic—home loan foreclosures—but each model exemplifies a different aim for writing. Notice how the writing changes when the aim changes.

INFORMATIVE WRITING

Mayor Asks for Federal Help

At a press conference earlier today, Mayor Jane Wing announced that she is asking for the federal government's help in dealing with the city's financial crisis.

Wing said that the closing of Resticon Corporation last fall caused the city's unemployment rate to triple. She added that sales tax revenues declined nearly fifty percent this quarter because the unemployed ex-Resticon workers had little or no money to spend. Property tax payments are late or unpaid for the same reason, adding to the city's financial crisis.

Wing said that her major concern is that many local homeowners can no longer meet their mortgage payments. She is requesting a federally backed program that will allow local banks to offer low-interest loans to people needing to refinance their homes.

"Such a loan program," she said, "will help prevent foreclosure and enable people to keep their homes while they seek other employment. By keeping our work force, we have a good chance of attracting another major employer like Resticon. The loan program will benefit the people now, and the city in the long run."

READER'S RESPONSE

1. If your family lived in Mayor Wing's city and were faced with foreclosure, would you be interested in the information in this article? What else might you want to know about the low-interest mortgage program?
2. What information does the article give about the reasons for the city's financial problems?

PERSUASIVE WRITING

Fellow Representatives, as you know, I represent the people of the fifth district of my state. It is an honor and a privilege. The people of the fifth district are a special group of people. Honest, hard-working, and self-reliant, they know the true value of the American life. They have dreamed the American dream and found it within their grasp. Now they are in danger of having it taken from them.

Recently, the fifth district has fallen on hard times. Resticon, the major employer, closed shop last fall, leaving more than 2,000 people unemployed. Such massive unemployment has affected the economic well-being of the entire area. Now, the people of my district are struggling to hang on. Their homes, the shining examples of their American dreams, are in danger of foreclosure.

Ladies and gentlemen, these good people are the backbone of America. Their dream is our dream. They work hard, they pay their taxes, they support their country in peace and war, they struggle to educate their children and pass on the dream to them. They need a chance to salvage that dream from the hard times surrounding them. They need our help.

Let's make it possible for them to hang on to their dreams. Please vote for this program that will allow these wonderful people to refinance their homes at low interest rates. Don't turn the best of America out into the street. I thank you, and the people of the fifth district thank you.

READER'S RESPONSE

1. If you were a member of Congress, would this speech persuade you to vote for the special legislation? Explain why or why not.
2. What ideas does this persuasive speech include that the informative article on page 8 does not?

EXPRESSIVE WRITING

Dear Angie,
 I wanted to drop you a note to let you know I really miss
you. The old neighborhood just isn't the same since you left.
Since the plant closed, <u>For Sale</u> signs have gone up all over
town. Dino and his family just left and let their house go
back to the bank. They couldn't make their mortgage payments any more. He didn't even say good-bye, but he left a
school picture and a rose from his mama's garden on our
front porch. I cried for a long time.
 We don't know how long we can keep up the payments on
our house. Dad says we may be able to refinance the house
if the low-interest loan program goes through. He's working,
and so is Mama, but they don't make near as much as they
did at the plant. Our savings are almost gone. There's a rumor
that a big company might start up in the old plant next
spring. I'm scared that we won't be able to hang on till then.
 Write to me about life in sunny California. I can't imagine
a year without winter. To tell the truth, it seems like winter
all the time here since you and Dino left. Write me. Write me.
       Love,
       Celina

READER'S RESPONSE

1. Suppose you were Celina and watched your friends lose
their homes. What would you think and feel?
2. In expressive writing, the writer explores or expresses
thoughts and feelings. What thoughts and feelings does
Celina express in this letter?

HOME

by Gwendolyn Brooks

What had been wanted was this always, this always to last, the talking softly on this porch, with the snake plant in the jardiniere in the southwest corner, and the obstinate slip from Aunt Eppie's magnificent Michigan fern at the left side of the friendly door. Mama, Maud Martha, and Helen rocked slowly in their rocking chairs, and looked at the late afternoon light on the lawn and at the emphatic iron of the fence and at the poplar tree. These things might soon be theirs no longer. Those shafts and pools of light, the tree, the graceful iron, might soon be viewed possessively by different eyes.

Papa was to have gone that noon, during his lunch hour, to the office of the Home Owners' Loan. If he had not succeeded in getting another extension, they would be leaving this house in which they had lived for more than fourteen years. There was little hope. The Home Owners' Loan was hard. They sat, making their plans.

"We'll be moving into a nice flat somewhere," said Mama. "Somewhere on South Park, or Michigan, or in Washington Park Court." Those flats, as the girls and Mama knew well, were burdens on wages twice the size of Papa's. This was not mentioned now.

"They're much prettier than this old house," said Helen. "I have friends I'd just as soon not bring here. And I have other friends who wouldn't come down this far for anything, unless they were in a taxi."

Yesterday, Maud Martha would have attacked her. Tomorrow she might. Today she said nothing. She merely gazed at a little hopping robin in the tree, her tree, and tried to keep the fronts of her eyes dry.

"Well, I do know," said Mama, turning her hands over and over, "that I've been getting tireder and tireder of doing that firing. From October to April, there's firing to be done."

"But lately we've been helping, Harry and I," said Maud Martha. "And sometimes in March and April and in October, and even in November, we could build a little fire in the fireplace. Sometimes the weather was just right for that."

She knew, from the way they looked at her, that this had been a mistake. They did not want to cry.

But she felt that the little line of white, sometimes ridged with smoked purple, and all that cream-shot saffron would never drift across any western sky except that in back of this house. The rain would drum with as sweet a dullness nowhere but here. The birds on South Park were mechanical birds, no better than the poor caught canaries in those "rich" women's sun parlors.

"It's just going to kill Papa!" burst out Maud Martha. "He loves this house! He *lives* for this house!"

"He lives for us," said Helen. "It's us he loves. He wouldn't want this house, except for us."

"And he'll have us," added Mama, "wherever."

"You know," Helen sighed, "if you want to know the truth, this is a relief. If this hadn't come up, we would have gone on, just dragged on, hanging out here forever."

"It might," allowed Mama, "be an act of God. God may just have reached down and picked up the reins."

"Yes," Maud Martha cracked in, "that's what you always say—that God knows best."

Her mother looked at her quickly, decided that the statement was not suspect, looked away.

Helen saw Papa coming. "There's Papa," said Helen.

They could not tell a thing from the way Papa was walking. It was that same dear little staccato walk, one shoulder down, then the other, then repeat, and repeat. They watched his progress. He passed the Kennedys', he passed the vacant lot, he passed Mrs. Blakemore's. They wanted to hurl themselves over the fence, into the street, and shake the truth out of his collar. He opened his gate—the gate—and still his stride and face told them nothing.

"Hello," he said.

Mama got up and followed him through the front door. The girls knew better than to go in too.

Presently Mama's head emerged. Her eyes were lamps turned on.

"It's all right," she exclaimed. "He got it. It's all over. Everything is all right."

The door slammed shut. Mama's footsteps hurried away.

"I think," said Helen, rocking rapidly, "I think I'll give a party. I haven't given a party since I was eleven. I'd like some of my friends to just casually see that we're homeowners."

READER'S RESPONSE

1. How did you feel about the problems with home loan payments when you read the article on page 8? How are your feelings different now?
2. The basic aim of literary writing is to create a work of art. What other aims might Gwendolyn Brooks have had in writing this story? Explain.

Writing and Thinking Activities

1. Meet with two or three classmates to discuss the following questions about the four models you've read.
   a. Which model tries to convince people to do something? How?
   b. Which model explains the problems facing the city?
   c. Which model most dramatically shows the human emotions triggered by the financial crisis?
   d. Which model is mostly about what the writer feels and thinks about the situation?
2. Consider your own communication techniques. During a two-hour stretch of a typical day, make a list of all the different ways you communicate—writing, reading, speaking, and listening. Keep track of how much of your communication is informative, persuasive, self-expressive, or literary. Then, sit down with two or three classmates and discuss your communication patterns. Are they similar?

3. Notice how professional writers communicate. Bring a magazine or newspaper to class. Work with two or three classmates to find examples of these four kinds of writing: informative, persuasive, self-expressive, and creative writing. Which type of writing is used most often? Does each magazine and newspaper have about the same percentage of each type of writing?

4. When you hear the words *creative writing*, what do you think of—short stories? poems? novels? plays? What about other kinds of writing? Can letters to the editor, speeches, editorials, or journal entries also be creative? In what way? What other kinds of writing would you call original or creative?

1 WRITING AND THINKING

Looking at the Process

Being a good writer starts with being a good thinker and planner. The writing comes later, as part of the entire writing **process.**

Writing and You. Is writing easy for you? Or do you often find yourself sitting and staring at a blank sheet of paper? Do you enjoy writing or is it a pain that you'd rather live without? All writers, even professional writers, get frustrated. They have trouble getting started, finding information, thinking up ideas, and then putting their ideas on paper. Which of these parts of the writing process cause you the greatest trouble?

As You Read. As you read the following foreword from Gary Soto's book of poems, think about the difficulties he faced and how he dealt with them.

Henri Matisse, *Interior with Etruscan Vase* (1940). Oil on canvas, 29" × 39 1/2". Collection of The Cleveland Museum of Art, Gift of the Hanna Fund, 52.153. © 1993 Succession H. Matisse, Paris/ Artist Rights Society (ARS), New York.

FROM

A FIRE IN MY HANDS

BY GARY SOTO

I began writing poems fifteen years ago while I was in college. One day I was in the library, working on a term paper, when by chance I came across an anthology of contemporary poetry. I don't remember the title of the book or any of the titles of the poems except one: "Frankenstein's Daughter." The poem was wild, almost rude, and nothing like the rhyme-and-meter poetry I had read in high school. I had always thought that poetry was flowery writing about sunsets and walks on the beach, but that library book contained a direct and sometimes shocking poetry about dogs, junked cars, rundown houses, and TVs. I checked the book out, curious to read more.

Soon afterward, I started filling a notebook with my own poems. At first I was scared, partly because my poetry teacher, to whom this book is dedicated, was a stern man who could see the errors in my poems. Also, I realized the seriousness of my dedication. I gave up geography to study poetry, which a good many friends said offered no future. I ignored them because I liked working with words, using them to reconstruct the past, which has always been a source of poetry for me.

When I first studied poetry, I was single-minded. I woke to poetry and went to bed with poetry. I memorized poems, read English poets because I was told they would help shape my poems, and read classical Chinese poetry because I was told that

"...that library book contained a direct and sometimes shocking poetry about dogs, junked cars, rundown houses, and TVs."

it would add clarity to my work. But I was most taken by Spanish and Latin American poets, particularly Pablo Neruda. My favorites of his were the odes—long, short-lined poems celebrating common things like tomatoes, socks, scissors, and artichokes. I felt joyful when I read these odes; and when I began to write my own poems, I tried to remain faithful to the common things of my childhood—dogs, alleys, my baseball mitt, curbs, and the fruit of the valley, especially the orange. I wanted to give these things life, to write so well that my poems would express their simple beauty.

I also admired our own country's poetry. I saw that our poets often wrote about places where they grew up or places that impressed them deeply. James Wright wrote about Ohio and West Virginia, Philip Levine about Detroit, Gary Snyder about the Sierra Nevadas and about Japan, where for years he studied Zen Buddhism. I decided to write about the San Joaquin Valley, where my hometown, Fresno, is located. Some of my poems are stark observations of human violence—burglaries, muggings, fistfights—while others are spare images of nature—the orange groves and vineyards, the Kings River, the bogs, the Sequoias. I fell in love with the valley, both its ugliness and its beauty, and quietly wrote poems about it to share with others.

READER'S RESPONSE

1. Are you, like Soto, ever scared to write because you don't want others to criticize your writing? How can you overcome this fear?
2. When Soto became interested in writing poetry, he started reading more poetry. Do you agree that reading the writing of others can help a writer? Why?
3. Soto says that he wants to write about common things like dogs, fistfights, and orange groves. Have you ever read poetry about such everyday events and objects? Do you think such things make good subjects for poetry? Why?

LOOKING
AHEAD

In this chapter, you'll learn a general approach to writing that you can apply to all types of writing. You'll go through the stages of the writing process from choosing a topic to publishing. As you work through the chapter, remember that

- writing and thinking are both part of the process
- the writing process is flexible: you can adapt it to your own writing style and situation
- your topic, audience, and purpose emerge together when you write for yourself

"I start at the beginning, go on to the end, then stop."

Anthony Burgess

• • • •

"I always know the ending; that's where I start."

Toni Morrison

Aim—The "Why" of Writing

Why do people write?—usually for the same reason they talk. They have something to say, someone to say it to, and some purpose for saying it. Of course, that's a general *why*. But what are a few *why's*, or basic purposes, people have for writing?

WHY PEOPLE WRITE	
To express themselves	To get to know themselves, to discover meaning in their own lives
To share information	To give other people information they want or need; to share some special knowledge they have
To persuade	To convince other people to do something or believe something
To create literature	To be creative, to say something in a unique way

Process—The "How" of Writing

Anything people say or write has one of the four basic purposes you've just read about—sometimes even has more than one purpose at a time. For example, a writer may want to persuade as well as to share information. Like all the other speakers and writers in the world, you'll be writing for one or more of these four purposes.

As Gary Soto's experience shows, writing doesn't just happen. A great deal of thought goes into writing, using a whole *process* or series of stages. The process begins with a prewriting stage that is mostly thinking. It moves through other stages that focus more on writing and then on to more thinking after the writing occurs. That's why some sections of this chapter focus more on thinking and other sections focus more on writing.

The following diagram shows the stages that usually take place during the writing process. As the diagram shows, you can go back to an earlier stage, or even start over again, at any point in the process.

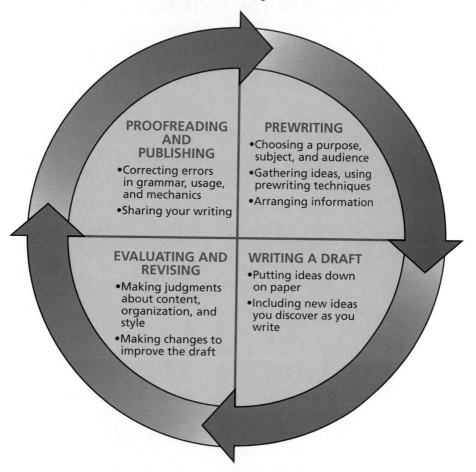

PROOFREADING AND PUBLISHING
- Correcting errors in grammar, usage, and mechanics
- Sharing your writing

PREWRITING
- Choosing a purpose, subject, and audience
- Gathering ideas, using prewriting techniques
- Arranging information

EVALUATING AND REVISING
- Making judgments about content, organization, and style
- Making changes to improve the draft

WRITING A DRAFT
- Putting ideas down on paper
- Including new ideas you discover as you write

For example, you're writing a report for art class on the life and work of artist Vincent van Gogh. You have gathered information from various books and have seen an exhibit featuring some of his works. You have your first draft almost finished. However, you read in a newspaper story that a long-lost van Gogh painting has been found, and you find another book that contains some important facts about his life that you didn't have. You go back to the prewriting stage and take more notes. Then you start writing again by adding the new information to your first draft.

Prewriting

Finding Ideas for Writing

"Write about anything you want" and "write about one of the assigned topics" are opposite instructions—but you may have the same reaction to both: a big blank. Where *do* professional writers get their ideas for writing? How do they get started on an assignment? Every writer might say something different (even "I don't know—I just do it"), but there are definite ways to get your brain moving when you want (or need) to write. This section will give you practical help—summarized in the following chart—for finding ideas.

PREWRITING TECHNIQUES		
Writer's Journal	Recording personal experiences and observations	Page 25
Freewriting	Writing for a few minutes about whatever comes to mind	Page 26
Brainstorming	Listing ideas as quickly as they come	Page 27
Clustering	Using circles and lines to show connections between ideas	Pages 28–29
Asking Questions	Using the reporter's *5W–How?* questions	Page 30
Using Your Five Senses	Observing details of sight, hearing, smell, taste, touch	Page 31
Reading with a Focus	Reading to find specific information	Page 32
Listening with a Focus	Listening to find specific information	Page 33
Imagining	Imagining details for creative writing	Page 34

As the chart shows, you have many prewriting techniques to choose from and many ways to use them. You'll often use more than one technique at a time. You'll use some more than others because of your own thinking style. And you'll use different techniques for different writing situations. For example, if you're writing a personal narrative about a hiking trip, you might use all five senses to recall vivid details about the adventure. But if you're searching for details about the subject "American railroads," you might use clustering or reading with a focus.

Keeping a Writer's Journal

If you aren't already doing so, start keeping a *writer's journal.* Use it to record thoughts, feelings, opinions, and great ideas—for example, things that bug you, song lyrics, and notes about famous people you wish you knew. Your journal can be small enough to carry around or big enough for drawing and pasting in cartoons and photos. Before you know it, you'll have a surprising source book of ideas for writing.

Here are some suggestions for getting started.

1. Make a habit of writing every day, and date your entries. Some people like to set a special time for writing—others like to be spontaneous and write when the mood (or an event) hits.
2. Write for yourself—which may mean messy and misspelled. Journals don't have "mistakes."
3. Be creative (even zany). Let your imagination go in songs, drawings, movie ideas, or poems.
4. React, reflect, explore random thoughts: Record some response to anything you include (like a quotation, an ad, a newspaper editorial). Why did you choose it?

E X E R C I S E **1**▶ **Keeping a Writer's Journal**

If you're not already keeping a journal, start one now. And don't worry if nothing glamorous or dramatic happened to you lately: Your personal thoughts, feelings, and experiences are unique—and that's what makes journals fun and fascinating. To get started, try writing about one *event* or *emotion* that sticks in your mind from yesterday.

Freewriting

To *freewrite,* just let your mind go and write.

1. Use a watch or clock, set a time limit (three to five minutes is good), and keep writing until the time's up.
2. Start with a word, phrase, or topic that's important to you—like *gymnastics* or *animal rights.*
3. Write any ideas, images, or details that come to you, without stopping to think about grammar, spelling, or punctuation. Just let the words flow.
4. If the flow stops, copy the last word until something new appears, or talk to yourself: *I'm stuck—what can I say after "competition"—maybe maybe maybe "judges". . .*
5. To vary freewriting, choose one word or phrase from your freewriting, and use it as a starting point for more writing. This process is called *focused freewriting,* or *looping,* because it allows you to make a "loop" from what you've already written and then continue writing.

Here's a sample of a few minutes of freewriting on the word *recycling.*

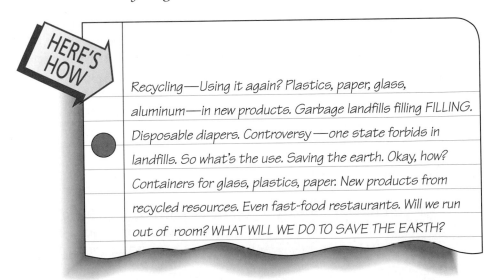

HERE'S HOW

Recycling—Using it again? Plastics, paper, glass,

aluminum—in new products. Garbage landfills filling FILLING.

Disposable diapers. Controversy—one state forbids in

landfills. So what's the use. Saving the earth. Okay, how?

Containers for glass, plastics, paper. New products from

recycled resources. Even fast-food restaurants. Will we run

out of room? WHAT WILL WE DO TO SAVE THE EARTH?

EXERCISE 2 ▶ **Using Freewriting**

What's your concern about the environment? Write down a phrase that describes your thoughts and freewrite about it for three or four minutes. Then choose one phrase from your freewriting and do some focused freewriting or looping.

Brainstorming

Brainstorming generates ideas by free association. You can brainstorm alone, with a partner, or in a group.

1. Write any subject, word, or phrase at the top of a sheet of paper (or on the chalkboard).
2. Jot down *every* idea that comes to your mind. (In a group, brainstorm out loud and appoint one person to record all of the ideas.)
3. Don't stop to evaluate; just keep going until you run out of ideas.

   Here are a group's brainstorming notes on electric cars. They're not all serious, but off-the-wall associations can always be cut or changed later.

HERE'S HOW

electric cars	speed? problems?
when first used?	probably dinky
need <u>long</u> cords	not dependent on gasoline
Who invented them?	high cost now, low later
car of the future	models: the Sparky,
no pollution	the Shocker
little pollution—	Who's building them?
what kind?	they're ready now—
how far on one charge?	just read <u>Road and Track</u>

EXERCISE 3 ▶ **Using Brainstorming**

Practice brainstorming with a partner or a small group so that you'll hear ideas besides your own (which will probably spark more of your own). Together, list ideas about one of the following topics, or choose your own.

1. the funniest TV shows
2. compact discs
3. the American flag
4. slang
5. life in the year 2010
6. today's heroines

Clustering

Clustering is similar to brainstorming, but it is more visual and shows connections between ideas. Like brainstorming, clustering generally breaks a subject down into smaller parts, so it's good both for finding topics and gathering information.

1. Begin by writing a subject in the middle of your paper, and circle or box it.
2. Around the subject, write related ideas that you think of, circle them, and connect them with lines to your subject (and maybe to each other).
3. Let your new ideas lead to others. Just keep associating, circling, and connecting until you're ready to stop.

Clustering is also called *webbing*, a good name as the example shows. Even though your cluster or web may not make complete sense to someone else, you've made the connections and can follow your own thinking.

kinds of horses

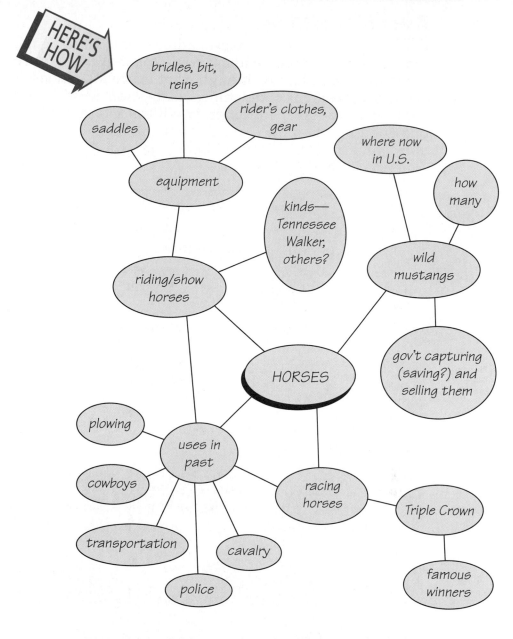

HERE'S HOW

bridles, bit, reins

saddles

rider's clothes, gear

where now in U.S.

how many

equipment

kinds— Tennessee Walker, others?

wild mustangs

riding/show horses

HORSES

gov't capturing (saving?) and selling them

plowing

uses in past

cowboys

racing horses

Triple Crown

transportation

cavalry

police

famous winners

EXERCISE 4 **Using Clustering**

Create a cluster diagram using one of the topics you *didn't* use in Exercise 3 or another topic of your own choice. Use the clustering hints and Here's How diagram as guides.

Asking Questions

One to-the-point way of investigating a topic is asking the reporter's *5W-How?* questions: *Who? What? When? Where? Why? How?* You'll find, though, that every topic doesn't equal six questions. Sometimes a question word won't apply to your topic, and often you'll think of more than one good question for a word. Here are some questions you could ask for a paper about one group of Native Americans, the Creeks.

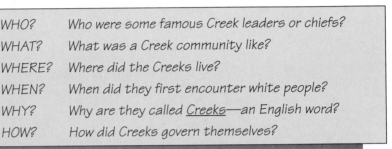

HERE'S HOW

WHO?	Who were some famous Creek leaders or chiefs?
WHAT?	What was a Creek community like?
WHERE?	Where did the Creeks live?
WHEN?	When did they first encounter white people?
WHY?	Why are they called <u>Creeks</u>—an English word?
HOW?	How did Creeks govern themselves?

Tecumseh, Opothleyahola, Jerome Tiger, Angie Debo

EXERCISE 5 ▶ **Asking the *5W-How?* Questions**

You're a reporter covering a hot story for the school paper: the school board's proposal to require students to attend school year-round. Working in teams, list as many good *5W-How?* questions for digging out information about the proposal as you can, and then compare lists.

Using Your Five Senses

Wherever you are, whatever you're doing, sensations of hearing, touch, smell, and taste are zinging into your brain right along with visual images. Pay attention to them, and you can improve your writing with vivid sensory details.

For example, here are details you could record about an experience that's probably familiar: a night football game.

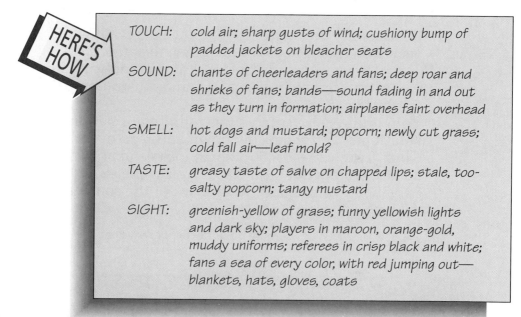

TOUCH:	cold air; sharp gusts of wind; cushiony bump of padded jackets on bleacher seats
SOUND:	chants of cheerleaders and fans; deep roar and shrieks of fans; bands—sound fading in and out as they turn in formation; airplanes faint overhead
SMELL:	hot dogs and mustard; popcorn; newly cut grass; cold fall air—leaf mold?
TASTE:	greasy taste of salve on chapped lips; stale, too-salty popcorn; tangy mustard
SIGHT:	greenish-yellow of grass; funny yellowish lights and dark sky; players in maroon, orange-gold, muddy uniforms; referees in crisp black and white; fans a sea of every color, with red jumping out—blankets, hats, gloves, coats

---

EXERCISE 6 ▶ **Using Your Five Senses**

If you really focus on your sensations, in any situation, you'll surprise yourself with life's sensory details—and your own sensitivity to them. Choose one of the following places, if possible *go to it* (if not, imagine it), and write down the sensory details you observe. You can make a column on your paper for each sense.

1. the lobby of a movie theater
2. inside your family's or a friend's car
3. the gymnasium during any kind of game or event
4. your school lunchroom at noon on a school day
5. a yogurt shop or any store

Reading with a Focus

How much do you know about the ancient Mayas of Central America? If you choose a topic you haven't experienced or can't observe firsthand, you'll probably use magazines and newspapers for ideas and information. Reading for a specific purpose—to find information about your topic—is very different from reading a novel for pleasure or browsing through a magazine. When you've found a possible source of information, follow these steps.

1. "Check out" the source first; don't start reading on page 1. Look for key words in the index (*Mayas, Central America*), study the table of contents, and in the text check headings, charts, and illustrations. Be on alert for your topic.

2. Skim until you're sure you've found information on your topic, and then slow down and read every word. Take notes on both main ideas and specific details, using your own words unless the exact quotation is important. Keep track of the sources you use.

☞ REFERENCE NOTE: For more on using library resources, see pages 952–957.

EXERCISE 7▶   **Reading with a Focus**

In Florida, the manatee, an aquatic mammal, is in danger of extinction. In California, the condor, a large vulture, faces similar problems. What animals in your state are on the endangered species list or may soon be put there? Find some information about an endangered animal, and read to find answers to the following questions. If you work in a group, each person could find a different source and compare your answers.

1. What are the animal's habitat and feeding habits?
2. Why is the animal in danger of becoming extinct? (Look for multiple reasons.)
3. How long has the animal been in trouble?
4. What efforts to date have been made to save the animal? How successful have these efforts been?

Listening with a Focus

Printed words aren't your only outside source of information. You can also listen—to radio and television programs, to video and audio tapes from the library, to people (anyone knowledgeable about your topic) in personal or telephone interviews. Good listening means focused listening, so prepare in advance.

1. Brainstorm or cluster what you already know about your topic, and reread any of your reading notes.
2. Make a list of the information you're looking for about your topic (in question form, if you want). Keep it by you as you listen.
3. Think ahead about note taking. You can't record every word, and you can't always "rewind" and rehear. Get the main points and supporting details by writing in phrases and using abbreviations.

☞ REFERENCE NOTE: For information on interviewing, see pages 943–944.

EXERCISE 8 ▶ **Listening for Specific Information**

Listen to an evening sportscast on your local television station. If there is more than one sportscast, divide the class so that some of you listen to each program. Listen for answers to the following questions.

1. What's the top sports story? Why is it ranked most important? Does it, for example, involve an outstanding sports performance, or does it involve the amount of money a player has signed for?
2. What sport is given the most time in the broadcast—football, baseball, soccer, or some other sport?

3. What's the most interesting story in the sportscast? What makes it interesting?
4. Based on the time devoted to each, whose sport seems more important—men's or women's?

Imagining

When you write creatively—stories, poems, plays, and so on—you usually write about people, places, and events that aren't real. You may begin with what you've observed, but many of the details have to come from your imagination. One way to spark your imagination for these kinds of details is to ask yourself "What if?" questions. Filmmakers and other creative people often use these kinds of questions to produce unusual ideas. The question *What if a family went on vacation and forgot to take one of the children along?* resulted in *Home Alone*—one of the biggest moneymaking movies of the early 1990s.

Here are some general questions that can help get you in a creative mode.

1. *What if I could change one thing in the past?* (What if my family had moved to a lighthouse off the coast of Maine? What if I had been born the greatest genius the world had ever seen?)
2. *What if something we take for granted were totally different?* (What if all the electricity all across the country went off at once and stayed off? What if everyone looked exactly alike?)
3. *What if I could create something new?* (What if I designed an invention that could move people through time as well as space? What if I could write music that would make everyone feel happy?)

EXERCISE 9 ▶ **Using the "What if?" Questions**

The movie moguls are in trouble. They've got to come up with a dynamite movie idea, or the studio will go broke. Working with several of your classmates, brainstorm a series of "What if?" questions that might result in a movie idea for the studio. When you've finished, choose the idea you think would make the best movie.

 *Prewriting*

Thinking About Purpose, Audience, and Tone

Purpose. Any piece of writing—even the most personal, that no one will ever see—has a *purpose*, a reason for being. You write in many different forms, but you always write for some end result: to express feelings, to be creative, to explain or inform, or to persuade. (You may even combine two or more purposes in a single piece of writing.) This chart shows the different forms you may use for each of the main purposes.

MAIN PURPOSE	FORMS OF WRITING
To express yourself	Journal, letter, personal essay
To be creative	Short story, poem, play, novel
To explain or inform	Science and history writing, newspaper and magazine articles, biography, autobiography, travel essay
To persuade	Persuasive essay, letter to editor, advertisement, political speech

Audience. It's also true that your *audience*—your readers—affect what you say and how you say it. To consider the needs of your audience, you can use these questions.

- Why am I writing for this audience? Do I want to inform or persuade them? to share a personal experience, amuse them, or stir their emotions?
- What does my audience already know about my topic? (You want to help readers, not bore them!)
- What will this particular audience be looking for or find interesting?
- What level of language is appropriate for this audience? A simple or more complex vocabulary? Short sentences, long sentences, or both?

Tone.   You can think of *tone* as the personality of your writing. You can sound outraged, sarcastic, serious, or funny. You can sound casual and personal or more distant and formal. How you sound—your tone—comes from the language you use. To create the tone you want, pay attention to

- choice of details (facts? sensory words? personal thoughts?)
- choice of words (slang? conversational style? figurative language? formal wording?)
- the rhythms and sounds of language (short, brisk sentences? long, leisurely ones?)

A word that's closely related to tone is voice. *Voice* simply means writing in a way that sounds like you. You can do this even when you're writing with a formal, serious tone by making your writing sound as natural as possible. Avoid using words or phrases just because they sound pretentious or knowledgeable. Use the precise word, but keep your writing as simple as possible. Let your own voice come through.

CRITICAL THINKING

Analyzing Purpose and Audience

You already tailor your writing to different situations even though you may not always stop and think about it. You don't write the same way in journal entries, reports, funny letters to friends, and thank-you letters to your aunt. Making that tailoring conscious simply makes your writing better.

Adjust your writing for both your purpose and your audience. To see how this works, read the following excerpt of a review of *Once Upon a Time . . . When We Were Colored*, a film by Tim Reid. The author's main purpose is to evaluate the film and thus to persuade others to see it.

It is almost impossible to express the cumulative power of *Once Upon a Time . . . When We Were Colored.* It isn't a slick, tightly packaged docudrama, but a film from the heart, a film that is not a protest against the years of segregation so much as a celebration of the human qualities that endured and overcame. Although the movie is about African Americans, its message is about the universal human spirit. I am aware of three screenings it has had at film festivals: before a largely black audience in Chicago, a largely white audience in Virginia, and a largely Asian audience in Honolulu. All three audiences gave it a standing ovation. There you have it.

Roger Ebert, *Chicago Sun-Times*

What guesses would you make about the audience for this review? Notice that, in addition to evaluating the film, the reviewer is careful to give enough information for readers who haven't seen the film. The audience consists of general readers, who may or may not have seen the film.

Now read a short passage that has a different purpose and a slightly different audience. The purpose of these paragraphs is to inform readers about the movie and about the actor Tim Reid's involvement with it.

Tim Reid's *Once Upon a Time . . . When We Were Colored* has been lauded as a movie all Americans should see. Set in 1946 in the Mississippi Delta, the movie chronicles the life of Cliff, who is African American, and, likewise, the period of history and the community in which he grows up. The three actors who play Cliff at age five (Charles Earl Taylor, Jr.), age twelve (Willis Norwood, Jr.), and age sixteen (Damon Hines) are supported by strong performances from Phylicia Rashad, Richard Roundtree, Iona Morris, Nila Fontaine, Isaac Hayes, and Al Freeman, Jr.

Reid based the movie on the best-selling book by Clifton L. Taulbert; Paul W. Cooper wrote the screenplay. After reading the book, Reid, a television actor, was determined to produce the film, despite the fact that the story was not easily packaged as a box-office hit. He and the cast shot on location in North Carolina, capturing authentically—in 111 minutes of film—the feel of the era.

Notice how, in this second piece, the writer gives much more information about the film than the reviewer whose purpose is to evaluate the film.

 CRITICAL THINKING EXERCISE:
Writing for a Different Purpose and Audience

What will the car of the future be like? Write a short, informative piece for readers who haven't seen the car that you plan to be driving in twenty years. Then, write an evaluation (an ad) of the same car. This time your purpose is to persuade readers to buy the car. These readers may or may not already have seen the car.

Arranging Ideas

By now you've gathered a ton of information. You could gather still more, but you really think you've had enough. Before writing, though, you need to think about arranging your prewriting ideas. This chart shows four common ways of ordering, or arranging, ideas.

ARRANGING IDEAS		
TYPE OF ORDER	**DEFINITION**	**EXAMPLES**
Chronological	Narration: Order that presents events as they happen in time	Story; narrative poem; explanation of a process; history
Spatial	Description: Order that describes objects according to location	Description (near to far; left to right; top to bottom; and so on)
Importance	Evaluation: Order that gives details from least to most important or the reverse	Persuasive writing; description; explanation (main idea and supporting details); evaluative writing
Logical	Classification: Order that relates items and groups	Definition; classifications; comparison and contrast

☞ **REFERENCE NOTE:** For more information on arranging ideas, see pages 82–85.

CRITICAL THINKING

Arranging Information

When you're deciding how to arrange ideas, once again think about purpose, audience, and subject. Sometimes purpose and audience lead to a particular arrangement. If you're writing about a typical school day in a letter to a foreign exchange student who'll soon be attending your school, you'll probably describe events in the order they happened (chronological order). But if you're writing about your own day in a journal entry, you might start with the highlights and move to the more insignificant incidents (order of importance).

Often the subject itself suggests the order of ideas. For example, this paragraph contrasts how American colonists paid for large items with how they made small transactions. It's natural for this writer to use logical order.

> Colonial America, lacking an official mint, suffered a constant shortage of small coins. Large transactions could be handled with letters of credit, but how did a traveler pay for a meal or for a drink? Coins of all nations were used in making change, the commonest being the Spanish silver piece of eight, very like the later U.S. silver dollar, and so called because it was stamped with a large Arabic 8 to signify a value of eight Spanish *reals,* a *real* having a value of about 12 1/2¢. (There was a Mexican *real* of that value [later a peso], but there is no evidence that the coin had a general circulation in the early colonies.) A whole piece of eight, however, was a coin of substantial value. To provide small change, these coins were regularly cut into halves and quarters called "bits."
>
> John Ciardi, *A Browser's Dictionary*

CRITICAL THINKING EXERCISE:
Analyzing the Order of Details

Using the chart on page 39, decide which type of order each of these passages uses.

1.   The first native-American woman to write and publish a novel, Mourning Dove (a translation of Hum-ishu-ma) was a member of the Okanogan tribe, whose communities were located in British Columbia and north-central Washington state. Born near Bonner's Ferry, Idaho, she was given the English name Christal Quintasket but raised in part by a grandmother who taught her to respect the rapidly vanishing traditions of her people. Although she had little formal education—three years at the Sacred Heart Convent in Ward, Washington, and brief periods at government Indian schools—Mourning Dove began early to collect and transcribe Okanogan tribal legends. In 1912, she enrolled in a business school to study English and typing so that she could improve her work on Indian tales and on the novel-in-progress which was to become her *Cogewea the Half Blood: A Depiction of the Great Montana Cattle Range* (1927).

> Sandra M. Gilbert and Susan Gubar,
> *The Norton Anthology of Literature by Women: The Tradition in English*

2.   In the 1990s, as in the past, there will be conservatives, liberals, and progressives. Conservatives want to maintain the status quo or turn back the clock. Liberals want to change things a little, incrementally. Progressives want rapid, significant change. Too often, progressives focus almost exclusively on ends (programs) and not enough on means (power). We need power, program, and progress—in that order. Progressives need power in order to implement their program, in order to make progress.

Jesse L. Jackson, "We Need Power,
Program, and Progress"

3.   I said before that at this point you pushed a wooden door and found yourself in the kitchen, behind the fireplace, at the foot of the circular staircase that led to the scriptorium. And just as we were pushing that door, we heard to our left some muffled sounds within the wall. They came from the wall beside the door, where the row of niches with skulls and bones ended. Instead of a last niche, there was a stretch of blank wall of large squared blocks of stone, with an old plaque in the center that had some worn monograms carved on it. The sounds came, it seemed, from behind the plaque, or else from above the plaque, partly beyond the wall, and partly almost over our heads.

Umberto Eco, *The Name of the Rose*

Using Charts

As visual organizations of information, charts are often a helpful technique for arranging your prewriting notes. They help you see "blocks" of information, and their relationships, clearly. Here's a chart about two minerals and their effects on our health. The writer organizes the information into three categories: each mineral's sources, its function, and deficiency symptoms.

HERE'S HOW

	Sources of Mineral	Uses by the Body	Deficiency Symptoms
Calcium	milk, cheese, whole grains, meat, leafy vegetables, peas, and other legumes	bone and tooth development, muscular and nervous system functioning, blood clotting	soft bones, poor teeth, failure of blood to clot
Iron	liver, red meat, egg yolk, whole grains, prunes, nuts	healthy red blood cells	anemia

CRITICAL THINKING

Classifying Information

When you make a chart, you're *classifying*, grouping together related information. And this takes thinking— deciding on the headings, or categories, to cover your information. Here's a way to approach the task.

1. Read through your notes. When you find items that seem to go together, rewrite them in a new list.
2. Look at each list, and decide what the items have in common. Why do they belong together? Your answer is a heading or category for the list.

⚡ CRITICAL THINKING EXERCISE:
Making a Chart to Organize Information

With a small group, make a chart of the following information about the planets Saturn and Earth. Remember: first group similar information and then decide on headings. Compare your chart with another group's.

Earth—one of terrestrial planets
   (Mercury, Venus, Earth, and Mars)
Earth—third planet from sun
Earth's orbit (once around sun) 365 days
Saturn's almost 30 years
Saturn—one of giant planets
   (Jupiter, Saturn, Uranus, Neptune)
Saturn—sixth planet from sun
Giant planets—large, much less dense, and cold (because far from sun)
Terrestrial planets—small, dense, and warm
Earth—one moon
Saturn—at least 18 named satellites

A time line is a chart of chronological information. It helps you (and your readers) organize dated information by clearly showing the sequence of actions or events. Here is a time line of important events in American independence.

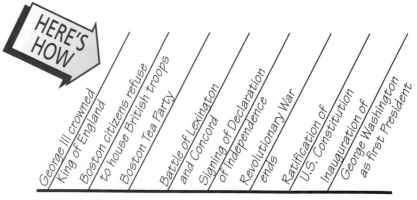

HERE'S HOW

George III crowned King of England
Boston citizens refuse to house British troops
Boston Tea Party
Battle of Lexington and Concord
Signing of Declaration of Independence
Revolutionary War ends
Ratification of U.S. Constitution
Inauguration of George Washington as first President

1760 1768 1773 1775 1776 1783 1788 1789

Writing a First Draft

It would be easy to keep prewriting . . . until your paper's due. That's not the idea. At some point, you have to dive in and start a draft.

There's no single right way to write a draft. You may feel comfortable writing a first draft based on scribbled notes only you could interpret. Or you may need a detailed outline before you begin. You may write quickly, trying just to get your ideas down on paper. Or you may shape each sentence carefully, trying to connect ideas with exactly the right word. As you write your first draft, try these suggestions.

- Use your prewriting plans to guide your draft.
- Write freely, but try to express your ideas clearly.
- Don't hesitate to add new ideas and details. Writing *is* discovery.
- Don't worry about errors in grammar, usage, and mechanics. You can find and fix them later.

COMPUTER NOTE: To avoid the urge to correct mechanical errors as you write, type with your monitor dimmed. Turn it back up to review what you've written.

Here is the first draft of a brief paper on a sport called lacrosse. Notice how the writer makes a change (a revision) even while drafting and also writes personal notes and questions that will lead back to prewriting.

Lacrosse is a team sport that Native Americans invented a long time ago. French explorers named it lacrosse because its long, curved playing stick looked like a bishop's staff, [what's French word?]. It's really a long-handled racket, with a mesh head like a pocket.

The ball is passed and received in this stick, and players score points by kicking or ~~throwing~~ hurling the ball into the goal.

Lacrosse is a rough game, but it's an ancient, formal sport. Since 18?? [check date] it's been the official national sport of Canada. Oren Lyons, on the Iroquois Nationals team [chief too—Onandagas?], has said, "We were playing team sports here when in Europe, they were still knocking people off horses, clubbing each other, fencing for keeps, all those so-called sports."

| EXERCISE 10▶ | **Writing a First Draft** |

Here are some prewriting notes about a very modern sport, in-line skating. Work alone or with a partner to turn the notes into an interesting paragraph. You can add or drop details if you want. Then, arrange the information and start drafting.

In-line skates—roller skates similar to ice skates—four wheels in a single file down the middle of the skate

1980 first appeared—for professional ice hockey players to practice off-season

Can perform stunts— similar to skateboarding; most skaters just cruise

Expensive—$180 to $250 pair

Cheryl Rowars, Miami Beach, sells one to three pairs every day: "They sell because it's something fun to do. It's not replacing the skateboard, though."

Requires a strong sideways stroke—"A great workout" Sara Kendall, age 15

"It's a super athletic sport without contact"—Rick Carlson, South Miami

Beginning in 1981—bought by ordinary people

Evaluating and Revising

Although they often occur at the same time, evaluating and revising are two separate steps in your writing.

Evaluating—deciding on your paper's strengths and weaknesses
Revising—making improvements

Evaluating

You have something to say about how good (or bad) things are every day. You evaluate your friend's new shirt and the food at a party. You evaluate your options for work: lifeguarding or tutoring. Evaluating your own writing, though, is more personal—and that means much harder.

Self-Evaluation. Three strategies can help you evaluate your writing.

READING CAREFULLY. Read your paper several times, concentrating each time on something different. First, read for *content* (what you say), then for *organization* (how you've arranged your ideas), and then for *style* (how you've used words and sentences).

LISTENING CAREFULLY. Read your draft aloud to yourself and try to "hear" what you've written. Using a different sense—hearing instead of reading—may help you notice awkward sentences and foggy ideas.

TAKING TIME. Set your first draft aside for several hours or overnight. You usually see your writing more clearly—as if it's someone else's—if you put it out of your mind for a while.

Peer Evaluation. All professional writers expect—and even rely on—other people to read their work: friends, family, editors. Other people are simply more objective, and, after all, writers write for *readers*.

You can have the help of outside readers by working with your classmates in peer-evaluation groups, which can be just two people or as many as four or five. Remember that in peer evaluation you have two roles: Sometimes you're the writer whose work is being evaluated, and sometimes you're the evaluator of other students' writing.

EVALUATING

Guidelines for the Writer

1. List some specific questions or concerns. What part of your paper do you think needs work?
2. Keep a positive attitude. Think of the evaluator's comments as real help for you. Don't get defensive or depressed about them.

Guidelines for the Peer Evaluator

1. Always look for strengths as well as weaknesses. Writers not only need encouragement, but they also need to know what's good in their writing and build on it.
2. Be serious and thorough about the evaluation, but also be sensitive. For example, ask the writer a question about a weakness instead of just pointing it out.
3. Make specific, positive suggestions for improvement. A criticism of a weakness without any ideas for fixing it is negative.
4. Look at content, organization, and style. Don't comment on mistakes in spelling, usage, and mechanics unless they make the meaning unclear. Proofreading comes later.

CRITICAL THINKING

Evaluating

You know that evaluating means making a judgment about whether something is good, bad, or somewhere in between. You evaluate things all the time—movies, CDs, the latest styles of jeans. When you evaluate anything, you measure it against a set of established criteria, or standards. Here are some criteria for evaluating effective writing.

1. The writing gets and holds your attention—it's interesting.
2. The meaning is clear.
3. There is a main idea.
4. There are enough supporting details for the main idea in the piece of writing.
5. The ideas are connected smoothly—no gaps or jumps to cause confusion.
6. The ideas are arranged well; their order makes sense.
7. The writing has no clichés (trite words or phrases) or unnecessary repetition and details.

CRITICAL THINKING EXERCISE:
Evaluating a Paragraph

Try out your peer-evaluation skills, using the seven criteria given above. With a partner or small group, discuss the following paragraph and write at least three comments about what can be improved in the paragraph. As you work, keep in mind the Guidelines for the Peer Evaluator on page 48.

Ludwig van Beethoven lived from 1770 to 1827. He was born in Bonn, Germany. What's most amazing about Beethoven is that he composed some of his greatest music when he was totally deaf. Beethoven was from a musical family. He showed his genius early. Some of his music was published when he was twelve. When he was seventeen, he met Wolfgang Amadeus Mozart. Mozart said of Beethoven: "Keep your eyes on him. Someday, he will give the world something to talk about." Beethoven moved to Vienna. He stayed there for the rest of his life and is buried there too. He became deaf gradually but for the last nine years of his life was totally deaf. He completed his last symphony, the Ninth Symphony, in 1824. The Ninth Symphony is called the Choral Symphony because of its "Ode to Joy" chorus in the last movement. He was completely deaf then. He directed the symphony when it was first performed. He couldn't hear the music or the applause.

Peanuts reprinted by permission of United Feature Syndicate, Inc.

Revising

After your classmates evaluate your paper, you'll need some time to think about their comments and suggestions and to combine them with your own ideas of what's wrong. Which comments about problems really seem on target? Which suggested changes seem like good solutions? (Remember your purpose and audience—they'll help you make decisions.)

Once you've decided what *needs* to be done, you move on to *doing* it: revising, or making the actual changes that will fix the problems you've found. There are four basic revision techniques—adding, cutting, replacing, and reordering—that you can use to make changes. In this stage, look at your first draft as just what it is—a beginning—and don't be shy about marking it up. Handwrite your corrections on the paper, using the revising and proofreading symbols on page 60, and then make a new copy by rewriting, retyping, or making the changes on the computer and printing the new version.

REVISING TECHNIQUES	
TECHNIQUE	EXAMPLE
1. **Add.** Add new information and details. Add words, phrases, sentences, whole paragraphs.	*⌃ or chain of islands⌃* The Japanese archipelago is made up of four large islands and many smaller ones.
2. **Cut.** Take out information, details, examples, or words. Cut repetition, wordiness, and details unrelated to the main idea.	From 1904 to 1914 the United States built the Panama Canal, ~~a canal~~ which connects ~~two bodies of water,~~ the Atlantic and Pacific oceans.
3. **Replace.** Take out weak words, clichés, awkward-sounding sentences, unnecessary information or details. Replace with more precise words, more relevant details.	Sydney, Australia, was founded in 1788 and was the first ~~place~~ *penal colony* for British *convicts* ~~troublemakers~~.
4. **Reorder.** Move phrases, details, examples, or paragraphs for variety and an order that makes sense.	The Galapagos Islands are in the Pacific Ocean off South America, known for their giant tortoises and other unique species.

Here are the paragraphs on lacrosse (pages 45–46), revised by using the four revision techniques. To understand the changes, you may want to refer to the chart of symbols for revising and proofreading on page 60. Notice how the writer has answered the questions noted on the first draft.

HERE'S HOW

Lacrosse is a team sport that
Native Americans invented ~~a long time~~ (more than a thousand years)   **replace**

ago. French explorers named it lacrosse
because (they thought) its long, curved playing stick   **add**

looked like a bishop's staff, ~~what's French~~ a crosier⊙   **replace**

~~word?~~ It's really a long-handled racket, This stick is   **cut/replace**

with a mesh head like a pocket. The ball is
passed and received (carried) in this stick, and   **add/reorder/ add**

players score points by kicking or ~~throwing~~   **cut**

hurling the ball into the goal.
Like hockey, Lacrosse is a ~~rough~~ game, (with a lot of physical contact,) but it's an   **add/cut/add**
ancient, formal sport (that Indian players are proud of.) Since 18⁶⁷ ~~[check~~   **add/replace**

~~date]~~ it's lacrosse has been the official national sport of   **cut/replace**

Canada. Oren Lyons, ~~on~~ Onandaga chief and leader of the Iroquois   **replace**

Nationals ~~team [chief too—Onandagas?]~~   **cut**

has said, "We were playing team sports

here when in Europe, they were still

knocking people off horses, clubbing each

other, fencing for keeps, all those so-called

sports."   **reorder**

When you evaluate and revise, you're focusing on three different, important aspects of your paper—content, organization, and style—so plan to read through it at least three times. Some overall guidelines for evaluating and revising follow. In later chapters, you'll find similar charts that focus on a particular type of writing.

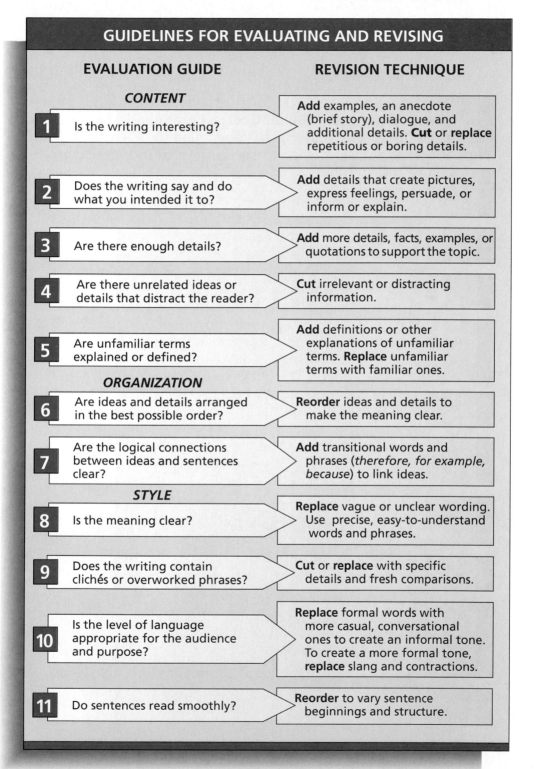

GUIDELINES FOR EVALUATING AND REVISING

EVALUATION GUIDE

REVISION TECHNIQUE

CONTENT

1 Is the writing interesting?

Add examples, an anecdote (brief story), dialogue, and additional details. **Cut** or **replace** repetitious or boring details.

2 Does the writing say and do what you intended it to?

Add details that create pictures, express feelings, persuade, or inform or explain.

3 Are there enough details?

Add more details, facts, examples, or quotations to support the topic.

4 Are there unrelated ideas or details that distract the reader?

Cut irrelevant or distracting information.

5 Are unfamiliar terms explained or defined?

Add definitions or other explanations of unfamiliar terms. **Replace** unfamiliar terms with familiar ones.

ORGANIZATION

6 Are ideas and details arranged in the best possible order?

Reorder ideas and details to make the meaning clear.

7 Are the logical connections between ideas and sentences clear?

Add transitional words and phrases (*therefore, for example, because*) to link ideas.

STYLE

8 Is the meaning clear?

Replace vague or unclear wording. Use precise, easy-to-understand words and phrases.

9 Does the writing contain clichés or overworked phrases?

Cut or **replace** with specific details and fresh comparisons.

10 Is the level of language appropriate for the audience and purpose?

Replace formal words with more casual, conversational ones to create an informal tone. To create a more formal tone, **replace** slang and contractions.

11 Do sentences read smoothly?

Reorder to vary sentence beginnings and structure.

| EXERCISE 11▶ | **Evaluating and Revising a Paragraph** |

Work with a partner to evaluate and revise the following first draft of a paragraph. Be sure to focus on content, organization, and style for this activity, using the guidelines on page 53. (You may correct grammatical errors that you find, but that's not your main task.) Check with another revision team to see if they found similar problems and solutions.

It often seems important to wear just the right outfit. Yet we rarely stop to think about the origins of clothing. Originally, clothing was designed for protection from the elements and probably for decoration. Clothing can tell you something about the person wearing it. People in different parts of the world used the materials they had to create their clothing. For example, Japanese silk and Australian wool. Most people made their own clothes until the 1700s. When weaving and sewing machines were invented and started the ready-to-wear industry. However, in some places in the world, handmade care still goes into each garment, especially in countries that do not rely on New York's Fifth Avenue or the fashion shows in Paris for their sense of style or culture. It has become a major industry, employing designers, weavers, models, sewing-machine operators, and advertising executives. For something that is a basic need, it has gotten out of hand.

Proofreading and Publishing

Just as you take one final look in the mirror to fix whatever isn't "just right" before going out, you'll take a last look at your paper to be sure it's ready to face your readers. This final touching up—getting details and appearance just right—is called *proofreading*.

Proofreading

When you *proofread,* you carefully reread your revised draft to correct mistakes in grammar, usage, and mechanics (spelling, capitalization, and punctuation). Remember that your goal is to find and correct any errors. You've worked hard on your paper, and you don't want any mistakes to distract your audience from what you have to say.

To proofread, put your paper aside for a while. You've been reading it so much during revision that you're probably not noticing every word and comma. Distance can make mistakes jump out clearly.

When you proofread, slow down and read each word carefully. These techniques will make proofreading easier.

1. Focus on one line at a time. Use a sheet of paper to cover all the lines below the one you are proofreading. Some writers proofread backwards—beginning with the bottom line and moving to the top.
2. Try peer proofreading. Exchange papers with a classmate (or group of classmates) and check each other's paper for errors.
3. When in doubt, look it up. Use a college dictionary for spelling and a handbook like the one on pages 510–895 for grammar, usage, and punctuation.
4. Use the revising and proofreading symbols on page 60 to mark changes.

The following guidelines apply to almost all of the writing you'll do for school. Read them before proofreading. They'll remind you of typical errors you're looking for.

GUIDELINES FOR PROOFREADING

1. Is every sentence a complete sentence? (See pages 446–457.)
2. Does every sentence end with the appropriate punctuation mark? Are other punctuation marks correct? (See pages 787–864.)
3. Does every sentence begin with a capital letter? Are all proper nouns and appropriate proper adjectives capitalized? (See pages 762–779.)
4. Does every verb agree in number with its subject? (See pages 618–634.)
5. Are verb forms and tenses used correctly? (See pages 678–704.)
6. Are subject and object forms of personal pronouns used correctly? (See pages 649–658.)
7. Does every pronoun agree with its antecedent in number and in gender? Are pronoun references clear? (See pages 637–639.)
8. Are frequently confused words (such as *lie* and *lay, fewer* and *less*) used correctly? (See pages 661–662, 697–704, 716–717, 738–756.)
9. Are all words spelled correctly? (See pages 870–895.)
10. Is the paper neat and in correct manuscript form? (See page 59.)

EXERCISE 12 **Proofreading a Paragraph**

See if you can find all ten mistakes in the following paragraph. Look for errors in grammar, usage, spelling, capitalization, and punctuation. Use the handbook at the back of the book or a dictionary to be sure you've found an error and to correct it.

How would you like to design a car that runs only on the suns power? That's what college students from universitys done in a 1,600-mile car race from Florida to Michigan. The thirty-one cars was desinged by engineering students, they had solar batterys that could be recharged only twice a day. On the first day the cars

traveled 75 miles. At speeds up to 52 miles an hour.
Unfortunatly, heavy rains and cloudy
skies slowed the cars.
rains caused the
drivers' cockpits
to leak.

Publishing

Early in prewriting, your thoughts about an audience
helped shape your writing. Now it's time to let some of
these readers actually share the final result. Besides
sharing your writing with your teacher, here are some
other suggestions.

- Submit your writing for publication. Try the school
  newspaper or yearbook or magazine. Your local
  newspaper may be interested in publishing a letter
  to the editor or a feature article.
- Make a class anthology. Have each student
  contribute one piece of writing, a drawing, or a
  favorite cartoon. Exchange anthologies with other
  classes. You could donate your class anthology to
  a school library or children's floor in a hospital.
- Make an anthology of your best writing for your
  family and yourself. You can save it in a folder or
  notebook and add to it throughout high school.
- Enter a writing contest. Some of these have cash
  prizes; others award certificates. Ask your teacher
  or counselor for information.
- Make a video. If you can find a video camera (try
  your public or school library), work with a partner.
  While you take pictures to illustrate your writing,
  ask a good reader to read your writing aloud.
  Show your video to the class.
- Post movie and book reviews on a school bulletin
  board or in a library.

CRITICAL THINKING

Reflecting on Your Writing

Photograph albums and scrapbooks help people keep track of their past accomplishments. Similarly, a **portfolio,** a collection of your work, can help you to maintain a record of your writing accomplishments and measure your continuing progress. Reflecting on pieces you have written gives you a chance to improve your writing as you complete new assignments: Old topics may prompt ideas for new papers, or you may notice that a certain style is particularly effective. Keeping a portfolio may be especially helpful if college or job applications require a writing sample. Review your work to analyze what you do well and where you would like to refine your writing.

Each paper you save has something to teach you. Date each piece of writing that you include in your portfolio, and write a brief reflection about your work. Which part of the paper is your favorite? What was the most difficult part of the assignment? How did you pick a topic? What revisions made the paper better? Would the writing be clear and interesting to an audience?

CRITICAL THINKING EXERCISE:
Reflecting on Your Writing

Reread some of your recent writing assignments. Then, using the following questions, reflect on your work. Date your written observations, and include them in your **portfolio** to keep as records to gauge your progress.

1. Which part of the writing process do you find easiest? most difficult? Why?
2. What passages of your papers would you handle differently? What passages do you like best? Why?
3. What did you learn about yourself as you wrote? What did you learn about the writing process?

When someone else reads your paper (your teacher, another student, or some adult outside of school), appearance is important. If you follow these guidelines for your final copy, your papers will look better.

GUIDELINES FOR MANUSCRIPT FORM

1. Use only one side of a sheet of paper.
2. Type, use a word processor, or write in blue or black ink.
3. If you type, double-space the lines. If you write, don't skip lines.
4. Leave margins of about one inch at the top, sides, and bottom of a page.
5. Indent the first line of each paragraph.
6. Number all pages (except the first page) in the upper right-hand corner.
7. All pages should be neat and clean. You may use correction fluid to make a few changes, but they should be barely noticeable.
8. Follow your teacher's instructions for placement of your name, the date, your class, and the title of your paper.

EXERCISE 13 ▶ **Publishing Your Writing**

Working with your classmates, brainstorm some other ideas for publishing your writing. Assign committees to follow up on all suggestions, including those listed above. Find out the specific information a writer would need to carry out each suggestion.

Frank & Ernest reprinted by permission of Newspaper Enterprise Association, Inc.

SYMBOLS FOR REVISING AND PROOFREADING

SYMBOL	EXAMPLE	MEANING OF SYMBOL
≡	Maple High school	Capitalize a lowercase letter.
/	the First person	Lowercase a capital letter.
∧	the first ₒf May	Insert a missing word, letter, or punctuation mark.
∧	sep^aerate	Change a letter.
∧—	in the East ^South	Replace a word.
⌐	Tell me the the plan.	Leave out a word, letter, or punctuation mark.
⟋	an unussual idea	Leave out and close up.
⌒	a water fall	Close up space.
∽	recieve	Change the order of the letters.
(tr)	the last Saturday of September in the month	Transfer the circled words. (Write (tr) in nearby margin.)
¶	¶"Help!" someone cried.	Begin a new paragraph.
⊙	Please don't go⊙	Add a period.
∧	Well what's new?	Add a comma.
#	birddog	Add a space.
⊙	the following ideas⊙	Add a colon.
∧	Houston, Texas; St. Louis, Missouri; and Albany, New York	Add a semicolon.
=	at half=mast	Add a hyphen.
∨	Sally's new job	Add an apostrophe.
(stet)	An extremely urgent	Keep the crossed-out material. (Write (stet) in nearby margin.)

MAKING CONNECTIONS

BRAINSTORMING WITH A COMPUTER

Prewriting usually requires brainstorming and time. A partner can really help you brainstorm during prewriting, and a computer may be the next best thing. Computers let you quickly access large amounts of thought-provoking information, and some computer programs can even generate questions like the ones a partner might ask.

All of the computer software described below can help you generate ideas. Some of the programs can even make the prewriting stage a little more fun.

- **Thesaurus and Word-Association Programs.** These programs help you find synonyms and other terms or phrases related to words you type in. Some allow you to compare words and to find new ideas associated with combinations of words.
- **Text-Based Outliners and Visual Outliners.** These programs make it easy to expand and refine your ideas by helping you create and change outlines, cluster diagrams, and other visual organizers.
- **Questioning Programs.** These programs take the place of a brainstorming partner by asking you questions about your subject and by allowing you to type your responses and to save them.
- **World Wide Web Search Engines.** These Internet-based programs help you search the millions of documents on the Web for keywords related to your topic. Web searches can often reveal surprising links between your subject and other information.

If you have a computer and a brainstorming program, use them to generate a list of ideas for a paper. Show your list to a partner, and discuss how the software helped you. If you don't have brainstorming software, interview some people who do and ask how they use their programs. Write a short summary of your findings.

2 UNDERSTANDING PARAGRAPH STRUCTURE

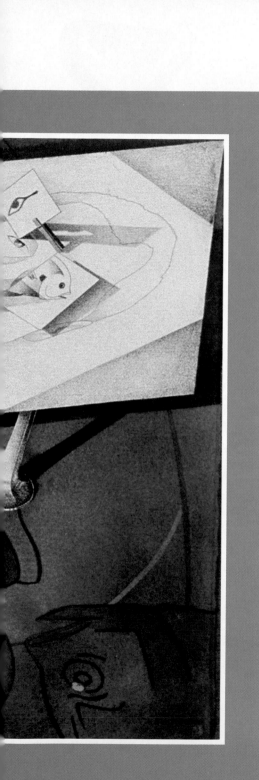

Looking at the Parts

Can you name all the parts in a computer? It has a processor, disc drives, a keyboard, and a monitor. But not all computers are alike. Some are faster or bigger or have more **parts** than others. The same is true of paragraphs. They all have certain things in common, but they are not all alike.

Writing and You.   You see paragraphs all the time—in letters, books, and magazines. Some have only one word or sentence, but some go on for pages. Some paragraphs stand alone, but most of them work with others like links in a chain. What else have you noticed about paragraphs?

As You Read.   As you read the following paragraphs from *Nisei Daughter,* notice how Monica Sone separates, yet links together, fond memories of her childhood.

Mark Hartman, *Relative Realities #2* (1989). Charcoal & watercolor on paper, 22" × 30". Collection of the artist.

Nisei Daughter

YES, life to us children was a wonderful treat—especially during hot summer nights when Father slipped out to a market stand down the block and surprised us with an enormous, ice-cold watermelon. It was pure joy when we first bit into its crisp pink succulence and let the juice trickle and seeds fall on old newspapers spread on the round table in the parlor. Or sometimes on a wintry evening, we crowded around the kitchen table to watch Father, bath towel-apron draped around his waist, whip up a batch of raisin cookies for us. It wasn't everybody's father who could turn out thick, melting, golden cookies. We were especially proud that our father had once worked as a cook on romantic Alaska-bound freighters.

Life was hilarious whenever Mother played *Jan-ken-pon! Ai-kono-hoi!* with us. This was the game played by throwing out paper, scissors, and rock symbols with our hands, accompanied by the chant. The winner with the stronger symbol had the privilege of slapping the loser's wrist with two fingers. Mother pretended to cry whenever our small fingers came down on her wrist. With her oval face, lively almond-shaped eyes, and slender aquiline nose, Mother was a pretty, slender five feet of youth and fun.

I thought the whole world consisted of two or three old hotels on every block. And that its population consisted of families like mine who lived in a corner of the hotels. And its other inhabitants were customers—fading, balding, watery-eyed men, rough-tough bearded men, and good men like Sam, Joe, Peter, and Montana who worked for Father, all of whom lived in these hotels.

It was a very exciting world in which I lived.

from

NISEI

DAUGHTER

by

MONICA

SONE

READER'S RESPONSE

1. Some of Monica Sone's fondest memories are connected with eating—watermelon juice trickling onto newspapers and her father making cookies. Get together with a partner and share the eating experiences (funny or serious) that stand out in your mind.
2. As a child, Sone thought the whole world was exactly like the neighborhood she lived in. In your journal, write about some of the impressions you had of the world when you were a young child.

WRITER'S CRAFT

3. Although all of Sone's paragraphs are about her memories from childhood, each paragraph makes a slightly different point. What is the main idea of each paragraph?
4. Sone's longest paragraph has five sentences, and the shortest has only one sentence. Is one paragraph more effective than the other? What do you think determines the length of the paragraphs?

LOOKING AHEAD

In this chapter, you'll study the form and structure of paragraphs. Keep in mind that

- most paragraphs are a part of a longer piece of writing
- most paragraphs have a main idea
- a main idea may be supported or explained in several ways
- there are four basic strategies for developing paragraphs

What Makes a Paragraph

The Main Idea

Paragraphs, especially those that stand alone, usually are organized around one main idea. All the sentences in the paragraph make the *main idea* clear. For paragraphs that are part of longer pieces of writing, the other paragraphs help you understand the main idea.

Read the following paragraph from the selection by Monica Sone (page 65). What is its main idea?

> Life was hilarious whenever Mother played *Jan-ken-pon! Ai-kono-hoi!* with us. This was the game played by throwing out paper, scissors, and rock symbols with our hands, accompanied by the chant. The winner with the stronger symbol had the privilege of slapping the loser's wrist with two fingers. Mother pretended to cry whenever our small fingers came down on her wrist. With her oval face, lively almond-shaped eyes, and slender aquiline nose, Mother was a pretty, slender five feet of youth and fun.
>
> Monica Sone, *Nisei Daughter*

The first sentence of this paragraph states the main idea: that the author remembers her childhood as a time of great happiness. The other sentences support that idea by giving specific details about how the children played a game with their mother and how she looked and acted.

In the longer passage on page 65, you'll find that the other paragraphs help you understand this idea by giving details about other interesting experiences the author remembers from her childhood.

"IF IT SOUNDS LIKE WRITING, I REWRITE IT."

Elmore Leonard

The Topic Sentence

The main idea of a paragraph is often expressed in a single sentence, called the *topic sentence.* In writing, whether for school or for the workplace, you'll find that using a topic sentence helps the reader to identify your main idea.

Location of a Topic Sentence. The topic sentence often appears as the first or second sentence of a paragraph. You'll recall that the first sentence of Sone's paragraph on page 67—the one about playing a game with her mother—states the main idea of the paragraph.

It's easier to understand what a paragraph is about if the topic sentence appears at the beginning. However, a topic sentence can occur at any place in a paragraph. In fact, you'll sometimes find topic sentences at or near the end of a paragraph. Writers sometimes place topic sentences there to create surprise or to summarize ideas.

Here's a paragraph about the success of Japanese Americans after they were released from camps where many of them were held during World War II. As you read, notice how the writer draws all the details together and sums up the information with a topic sentence at the end.

> Twenty-five years after the camps were closed, the average personal income of Japanese Americans was 11 percent above the national average; average family income was 32 percent higher. A higher proportion of Japanese Americans were engaged in professional occupations than were whites. By 1981, an astonishing 88 percent of Sansei (third generation) children were attending college, and of these, 92 percent planned professional careers. In California, where more than a third of the nation's 720,000 Japanese Americans reside (88 percent of them U.S. born), family income remains 15 percent above the statewide average. Wrote sociologist William Petersen: "Even in a country whose patron saint is Horatio Alger, there is no parallel to this success story."
> Arthur Zich, "Japanese Americans: Home at Last"

Importance of a Topic Sentence.   Many paragraphs don't have a topic sentence. Some paragraphs, especially those that relate a sequence of events or actions, may not even seem to have a main idea. But topic sentences are useful, both to readers and to writers. They help readers know what they might find in the rest of the paragraph. And topic sentences help you as a writer to focus your paragraphs. They keep you from wandering off the main idea.

EXERCISE 1▶   **Identifying Main Ideas and Topic Sentences**

Each of the following paragraphs develops a main idea. Two of the paragraphs have topic sentences, and one does not. In your own words, state the main idea of each paragraph. Then identify the topic sentences of the two paragraphs that have them.

1.   Disease took more victims in the Civil War than the bullet did, and the toll from both was enormous. In the Federal forces four men died of sickness for every one killed in battle. In the early period almost one out of every four soldiers fell sick. It was just as bad or worse for the Confederates. At least half the men in a regiment could not fight for sickness, and often more. One authority on Confederate medicine estimated that on the average each Southern soldier was sick or wounded six times during the war. But five times as many fell sick as were injured.

Milton Meltzer, *Voices from the Civil War*

2. The first step on American soil for 12 million immigrants was no patch of warm, welcoming earth but a wooden ramp at Ellis Island. More than 100 million living Americans trace their U.S. roots to a man, woman or child who came through Ellis Island between 1892 and 1954. America's gateway reopens this month with a new National Park Service museum commemorating four centuries of U.S. immigration. Privately funded, the $156 million restoration has been the work of the Statue of Liberty–Ellis Island Foundation, which also dressed up Miss Liberty for her 1986 birthday centennial.

Doris G. Kinney, "Reopening the Gateway to America"

3. Pontiac had a great idea in his intertribal league against the whites. Tecumseh had a similar idea, backed by an unusual humanity toward captives and an exalted concept of a divine purpose embodied in him. Sitting Bull nourished an implacable hatred and suspicion of the whites and showed unusual power in intrigue. Chief Joseph exhibited an ability in the conduct of a losing war that Napoleon might have envied in his retreat from Moscow. . . . These were all individual differences, basic differences in individual capacity, and it was these differences alone that set the Indian leaders off from the rest of their people.

Albert Britt, *Great Indian Chiefs*

Supporting Sentences

The topic sentence of a paragraph states a general idea. To make that idea clear and interesting to the reader, you develop it with details in sentences that support the topic sentence. The kinds of details you'll use depend upon the subject. You might use *sensory details, facts or statistics, examples,* or an *anecdote.*

Sensory Details

Sensory details are details you observe through your five senses—sight, sound, smell, touch, taste. You use them to help create a picture or image in the reader's mind. If you describe the color of a snazzy new car, how the cold misty air feels, or how your favorite pizza tastes, you're using sensory details.

In this paragraph, notice how the writer uses details of sight, sound, smell, and touch to describe a train in China. In the first sentence, for example, the writer uses both sight and sound details to help you see and hear the train.

> The train pulled in, steaming and gasping, just as the sun came up. It had come from Dalian, 600 miles away, and it stopped everywhere. So it was sensationally littered with garbage—peanut shells, apple cores, chewed chicken bones, orange peels and greasy paper. It was very dirty and it was so cold inside the spit had frozen on the floor into misshapen yellow-green medallions of ice. The covering between coaches was a snow tunnel, the frost on the windows was an inch thick, the doors had no locks and so they banged and thumped as a freezing draft rushed through the carriages.
>
> Paul Theroux, *Riding the Iron Rooster*

Facts and Statistics

You can also support a main idea with facts and statistics. A *fact* is something that can be proven true by concrete information: in 1981, Sandra Day O'Connor became the first woman U.S. Supreme Court justice. A *statistic* is a fact based on numbers: according to the Motion Picture Association of America, more new films were released in the United States in 1920 (796) than in 1987 (478). You can look in reference materials to check that these facts and statistics are true.

In the following paragraph, facts and statistics support and prove the main idea that the enormous amount of trash Americans throw away today is a big problem: "2,460 pounds of paper," for example, is a statistic; "that we are running out of landfill space" is a fact.

Every year, the typical American family throws out:
2,460 pounds of paper
540 pounds of metals
480 pounds of glass
480 pounds of food scraps
All told, each of us throws away more than 1,200 pounds of trash per year, far more than people in most other countries. About 80 percent of that garbage ends up in landfills—dumps, as they are more commonly known. (Of the remaining 20 percent, about half is recycled and half is incinerated.) One big problem is that we are running out of landfill space—more than half of the nation's landfills will be full within ten years.

John Elkington, Julia Hailes, Douglas Hill, and Joel Makower, *Going Green*

Examples

Another good way for you to support a main idea is to give *examples,* which are specific instances or illustrations of a general idea. An apartment is an example of a type of housing. Getting a scholarship is an example of what can happen if your grades are good.

This paragraph uses specific examples to show the extent of Japan's longtime recycling program. As you read, look for three specific examples the writer uses to support the main idea. The first example is about containers in city parks.

> In Japan, recycling has been practiced for hundreds of years. In public places such as city parks, you'll see separate containers for paper and cans. Recycling centers are more than just the temporary storage places they are in the U.S.A. In Japan, retired or disabled people work in these centers, repairing old furniture or household appliances and then selling them again. And in Machida City, not far from Tokyo, they have a program called *chirigami kokan* ("tissue-paper exchange") in which you receive free recycled paper products, such as tissue paper, napkins, and toilet paper, in exchange for your old newspapers.
>
> Evan and Janet Hadingham, *Garbage! Where It Comes From, Where It Goes*

Anecdotes

An *anecdote* is an extended example, or story, that can be used to support a main idea. In this paragraph, for example, the main idea is stated in the first sentence. An anecdote about President William Howard Taft then supports the main idea about one of baseball's opening-day rituals.

April 14, 1910, was opening day at National Park, the home of the Washington Senators and, for the first time in history, a president of the United States was on hand to throw out the first ball. That fact alone was something of a logistical triumph: President William Howard Taft weighed better than 300 pounds and, just to hold him, a specially reinforced, broad-seated chair had to be found and imported into the newly named Presidential Box next to the first-base dugout. Taft genuinely liked baseball (he had played catcher on a sandlot team in his hometown of Cincinnati). He spoke for most of the country when he said it was "a clean, straight game, [which] summons to its presence everybody who enjoys clean, straight athletics," and he wanted to identify himself with it, setting a precedent that has been followed by every subsequent president.

Geoffrey C. Ward and Ken Burns, *Baseball: An Illustrated History*

Notice the details that develop the anecdote, such as the type of role President Taft undertakes and how he handles the role. These details help readers understand the main idea the anecdote supports.

EXERCISE 2 ▶   **Collecting Supporting Details**

Here's your chance to write about a monument that has meaning for every American—the Statue of Liberty. Below are four main ideas that you might use in writing a paragraph about Miss Liberty. With each idea, a type of support—sensory details, facts or statistics, examples, or an anecdote—is suggested. Think up at least two ideas to support each main idea. You may have to do a little research to find support, especially facts or statistics.

EXAMPLE   **1.** The Statue of Liberty, which itself is a symbol of liberty, is adorned with symbolism. (examples)

               1. *The crown on the Statue of Liberty has seven spikes, representing the world's seven seas and seven continents. A broken chain at the statue's feet and the statue's left foot thrust forward represent freedom from bondage.*

1. The dimensions of the Statue of Liberty are impressive. (facts and statistics)
2. The Statue of Liberty has special meaning for many American citizens. (examples)
3. I took a boat close to the statue one evening at sunset. (sensory details)
4. In America, we often take our liberty and the historic symbols that represent it for granted. (anecdote)

The Clincher Sentence

Novels and short stories have snappy endings that emphasize or summarize the authors' main ideas. You may want to add zing to the end of some of your paragraphs, especially long ones, by emphasizing or summarizing the main idea in your final sentence. This concluding sentence is called a *clincher sentence.* It pulls all your information together or emphasizes your main idea. The following paragraph uses a clincher to restate and emphasize the author's opening declaration of his determination to have a horse.

I resolved to have a horse to ride. I had never seen such wild, free, magnificent horsemanship outside of a circus as these picturesquely clad Mexicans, Californians, and Mexicanized Americans displayed in Carson streets every day. How they rode! Leaning just gently forward out of the perpendicular, easy and nonchalant, with broad slouch-hat brim blown square up in front, and long riata swinging above the head, they swept through the town like the wind! The next minute they were only a sailing puff of dust on the far desert. If they trotted, they sat up gallantly and gracefully, and seemed part of the horse; did not go jiggering up and down after the silly Miss Nancy fashion of the riding schools. I had quickly learned to tell a horse from a cow, and was full of anxiety to learn more. *I resolved to buy a horse.*

Mark Twain, "A Genuine Mexican Plug"

WRITING NOTE   Clincher sentences shouldn't be overused. Be sure your clinchers emphasize or effectively restate the main idea. Don't use weak and unnecessary clinchers such as "Those are the reasons I dislike snow."

Unity

A paragraph should have ***unity;*** that is, it should be about one main idea. Unity is created when all the sentences support the main idea, whether the main idea is stated in a topic sentence or is implied. (*Implied* means "understood but not directly stated.") In paragraphs that relate a series of actions or events, unity is achieved by the sequence of the actions or events. The unity is spoiled by any detail that doesn't relate to the main idea or to the sequence of events or actions.

All Sentences Relate to the Main Idea Stated in the Topic Sentence.   In the following paragraph, the topic sentence states the main idea—that horse-drawn chariots, though useful in battles, were a problem. As you read, notice how each of the supporting sentences includes a detail related to a problem involved in using the chariot. In the second sentence, for example, one problem is that a soldier driving alone had to wrap the reins around his waist to keep his arms free for fighting.

> By 1000 B.C. horse-drawn chariots were standard equipment in most armies, and soldiers had discovered that the world's greatest weapon was also the world's greatest nuisance. In the first place, the chariot was hard to use. A two-man chariot team could manage nicely if one man drove while the other bombarded the enemy with spears or arrows. But when a soldier

The Granger Collection, New York.

drove alone, he had to tie the reins around his waist and control the horses with his body in order to keep his hands free for fighting. Since most chariots had no seats, the passengers and driver had to stand. They struggled to keep their balance as the little cart careened across country like a crazy roller coaster car and fought to keep their tempers when the chariot came to a sudden, unexpected halt. Such stops occurred frequently because chariots had to be carried across rivers and hoisted over hedges. They fell into ruts and wouldn't roll over rocks. They were too wide to squeeze through narrow mountain passes and so fragile that they broke down regularly.

Suzanne Jurmain, *Once Upon A Horse*

All Sentences Relate to an Implied Main Idea.   The following paragraph doesn't have a topic sentence. But all the sentences work together to support an implied main idea—that the *Titanic*'s two radio operators were too tired or busy to heed the last warnings before the luxury ship hit an iceberg in 1912. In the first sentence, for example, the fact that the radio operator was exhausted kept him from listening to the radio and hearing the warnings about the iceberg.

In the radio room, Harold Bride was exhausted. The two operators were expected to keep the radio working twenty-four hours a day, and Bride lay down to take a much-needed nap. Phillips was so busy with the passenger messages that he actually brushed off the final ice warning of the night. It was from the *Californian*. Trapped in a field of ice, she had stopped for the night about nineteen miles north of the *Titanic*. She was so close that the message literally blasted in Phillips' ears. Annoyed by the loud interruption, he cut off the *Californian's* radio operator with the words, "Shut up, shut up. I'm busy."

Robert D. Ballard, *Exploring the Titanic*

All Sentences Relate to a Sequence of Events. Although the following paragraph doesn't actually state a main idea, it does have purpose and unity. The purpose is to narrate a series of events that happen at a demolition derby. The paragraph's unity comes from the sequence of events described. Each action detail is part of a sequence that begins when the second driver for the finals has to be selected. This paragraph, like all other narrative paragraphs, is actually a cause-and-effect paragraph. One action in the demolition derby (cause) results in the next action (effect), and so on.

After each trial or heat at a demolition derby, two drivers go into the finals. One is the driver whose car was still going at the end. The other is the driver the crowd selects from among the 24 vanquished on the basis of his courage, showmanship, or simply the awesomeness of his crashes. The numbers of the cars are read over loudspeakers, and the crowd chooses one with its cheers. By the same token, the crowd may force a driver out of competition if he appears cowardly or merely cunning. This is the sort of driver who drifts around the edge of the battle avoiding crashes with the hope that the other cars will eliminate one another. The umpire waves a yellow flag at him and

he must crash into someone within 30 seconds or run the risk of being booed off the field in dishonor and disgrace.

Tom Wolfe, "Clean Fun at Riverhead"

EXERCISE 3 ▶ **Identifying Sentences That Destroy Unity**

One of the following paragraphs has unity, and the other doesn't. Try to figure out which sentence destroys the unity of that paragraph.

1.　A lot of wizardry went into the special effects in the 1939 MGM movie classic *The Wizard of Oz*. Perhaps the picture's most famous special effect is the tornado that carries Dorothy and her dog, Toto, to Oz. Legend has it that L. Frank Baum got the idea for the name of Oz from a file cabinet drawer labeled O–Z. The tornado was created by using fans, a crane, and a muslin cone rotated by a motor. Another famous special effect is the melting of the Wicked Witch. She melted away by disappearing through the floor on a hydraulic lift. Her costume was fastened to the floor, and dry ice or liquid smoke created the melting effect. The Winged Monkeys "flew" by means of support wires. The Wicked Witch's skywriting was achieved by using black liquid released from a hypodermic needle to which was fastened a small profile of the witch.

2. Gloria put her head farther down and pumped harder. The three leading competitors were not as far ahead as they had been only moments ago. Perhaps they were tiring. The last section of the race was five miles of steeply rising uphill. She geared down once and pushed herself, willing herself not to waste her time by checking positions. She passed one cyclist without even glancing at him, concentrating on keeping her pace smooth and strong. She had three miles left and two riders ahead of her. "Maybe I can go faster," she thought. Gritting her teeth, she forced the pace. "I can go faster. I can. I *will*," she persuaded herself. She pushed herself harder. With less than a mile left, she passed another rider. Concentrating, willing herself to victory, she passed the last competitor and pumped victoriously across the finish line, winner of the Annual 120-Mile Bike Marathon.

Coherence

A paragraph has *coherence* when the ideas are clearly connected and arranged in an order that makes sense to readers. This coherence helps readers follow your ideas easily.

Order of Ideas

You can help your readers follow your ideas by the way you arrange, or order, them. Often, the subject you're writing about will suggest the order of ideas.

Chronological Order.   In a story, the actions or events are usually arranged according to the order in which they occur. This is *chronological,* or time, *order.* (*Chrono-* means "time.") Chronological order works because it often shows the cause-and-effect relationship between events: one action (cause) results in another action (effect). You'll also use chronological order to explain a process, with steps in the process listed in the (time) order they are to be carried out. In the following paragraph, the writer uses chronological order to arrange the events in a story told by adults to young Chinese girls.

When we Chinese girls listened to the adults talking-story, we learned that we failed if we grew up to be but wives or slaves. We could be heroines, swordswomen. Even if she had to rage across all China, a swordswoman got even with anybody who hurt her family. Perhaps women were once so dangerous that they had to have their feet bound. It was a woman who invented white crane boxing only two hundred years ago. She was already an expert pole fighter, daughter of a teacher trained at the Shao-lin temple, where there lived an order of fighting monks. She was combing her hair one morning when a white crane alighted outside her window. She teased it with her pole, which it pushed aside with a soft brush of its wing. Amazed, she dashed outside and tried to knock the crane off its perch. It snapped her pole in two. Recognizing the presence of great power, she asked the spirit of the white crane if it would teach her to fight. It answered with a cry that white crane boxers imitate today. Later the bird returned as an old man, and he guided her boxing for many years. Thus she gave the world a new martial art.

> Maxine Hong Kingston, *The Woman Warrior: Memoirs of a Girlhood Among Ghosts*

Spatial Order. When you describe something, you usually arrange the details according to their location in space. *Spatial order* allows you to show where objects are in relation to each other (such as from left to right, from near to far, from front to back). In the following paragraph, spatial order helps you picture what a girl observes, from left to right and from near to far, during a buggy ride on Canada's Prince Edward Island. In the second sentence, for example, your attention is directed to "the right hand." What other words and phrases in the paragraph help you follow the girl's observations?

> The shore road was "woodsy and wild and lonesome." On the right hand, scrub firs, their spirits quite unbroken by long years of tussle with the gulf winds, grew thickly. On the left were the steep red sandstone cliffs, so near the track in places that a mare of less steadiness than the sorrel might have tried the nerves of the people behind her. Down at the base of the cliffs were heaps of surf-worn rocks or little sandy coves inlaid with pebbles as with ocean jewels; beyond lay the sea, shimmering and blue, and over it soared the gulls, their pinions flashing silvery in the sunlight.
>
> Lucy Maud Montgomery, *Anne of Green Gables*

Order of Importance. If your paragraph were to give information or persuade, you usually would arrange ideas or details in *order of importance.* You could begin with the least important idea or detail and move to the most important, or begin with the most important and move to the least important. Readers usually are more aware of what they read first or what they read last.

In this paragraph the actress Helen Hayes gives reasons why she thinks older people should write an "autobiography." She begins with the least important reason—the therapeutic value—and moves to the most important reason—the preservation of personal history.

> I also like to see older folks write an "autobiography." Writing is very therapeutic. In fact, experts say it promotes self esteem and personal integration. Personally, I think it also clears away the cobwebs and stimulates a fresh way of thinking and looking back at your life. Most important, perhaps, it leaves a private history of yourself and your family. Don't you wish your grandmother and her grandmother before her had done that?
>
> Helen Hayes, "Hayes: 'There Is So Much to Do' "

Logical Order. *Logical order* simply means the grouping of related ideas together. If your paragraph classifies, divides, defines, compares, or contrasts, you might choose logical order to arrange your ideas. The writer of the following paragraph, for example, compares selling teenagers new singing idols with selling them other fads. Notice that details about the singing idols are grouped together, followed by the details about the other fads.

> It was the industry's consensus that Tin Pan Alley had missed the boat, and that if the traditional songwriting industry was to survive, rock and roll would have to be factored in. It wasn't enough for rockers to cut the occasional standard; they would have to be given well-crafted, professionally written pop songs that had a rock-and-roll feeling. And this, it

was beginning to occur to some of the brains on Tin Pan Alley, would mean that the kids would have to be fed some new pop idols—which didn't seem that hard, really. It was already a truism that kids would buy anything, and the Wham-0 company had proved it. Late in 1958 they had started a craze for a length of plastic tubing stapled into a circle, marketed under the name Hula-Hoop. Millions sold, and then Hula-Hoops vanished as quickly as they came, but Wham-0 had learned a valuable lesson to be applied to its other products, Silly Putty and the redoubtable Frisbee.

Ed Ward, Geoffrey Stokes, and Ken Tucker, *Rock of Ages: The Rolling Stone History of Rock & Roll*

EXERCISE 4 ▶   **Choosing an Order of Ideas**

Try to figure out what order—chronological order, spatial order, order of importance, or logical order—would be best to develop each of the following topics in a paragraph. (You might use more than one type of order for some of the topics.)

1. accomplishments of Dr. Martin Luther King, Jr.
2. description of the Oval Office in the White House
3. five health reasons in favor of a vegetarian diet
4. how to make your own camera
5. comparing blues and jazz music

| EXERCISE 5 ▶ | **Identifying Order of Ideas** |

Following are three paragraphs. Two of the paragraphs follow the types of order you've just studied, but in one paragraph the ideas have no sensible order. Identify that paragraph and rewrite it so that the flow of ideas makes sense. Then identify the type of order followed by each of the other paragraphs.

1.   W.E.B. Du Bois and Booker T. Washington were two of this century's most influential black writers. Washington wrote most of his works between 1900 and 1911. With a longer career, Du Bois wrote between 1896 and the 1960s. Their educations were not alike, although both had more education than was average for the time. Washington graduated from the Hampton Institute, a vocational school, almost twenty years before Du Bois received a Ph.D. from Harvard in 1895. Both writers were very interested in education, although they looked at it differently. Washington founded the Tuskegee Normal and Industrial Institute, which stressed vocational training as the first step in upward mobility. Du Bois believed in classical education, teaching for a time at Atlanta University. Their educational beliefs were revealed in their works, Washington's in *The Future of the American Negro* and *Up from Slavery* and Du Bois's in *The Education of Black People.*

Booker T. Washington

W.E.B. Du Bois

2.   Sitting Bull was a mighty Sioux who distinguished himself early in life. At fourteen, he won his first honor in battle. At ten, he killed his first buffalo. He was born in 1834 in what is now South Dakota. He became known as a brave warrior and was named a chief of his nation. He acted as the main medicine man before the victorious Native American attack against Lieutenant Colonel George Armstrong Custer's regiment at the famous Battle of Little Bighorn on June 25, 1876. In 1866 he led raids against U.S. army troops moving into his people's land. The government agreed to peace talks by 1868, but Sitting Bull refused to participate.

3.   The Sun Dance of the Plains Indians, also called the Medicine Dance or Thirst Lodge, is an annual event. This spring dance is held in a large circular open frame lodge representing the world's creation. A sacred cottonwood tree is placed in the center of the lodge. This tree acts as the focus of the dance and links sky and earth. On the tree is attached one or more sacred objects. A sacred object may be an eagle head or skull or a bison head or skull. The dancers move from the outside edge of the lodge to the tree at the center and back again. Each dancer always faces the tree. Each dancer concentrates on the tree or on one of the objects attached to the tree.

Connections Between Ideas

To give a paragraph coherence, you should do more than arrange the ideas in an order that makes sense; you should also show how the ideas are connected. There are two ways to show connections: (1) make *direct references* to something else in the paragraph or (2) use words that make a *transition*, or bridge, from one idea to another.

Direct References. A natural way to link ideas in a paragraph is to refer to a noun or pronoun that you've used earlier. You can make ***direct references*** in these three ways:

1. Use a noun or pronoun that refers to a noun or pronoun used earlier.
2. Repeat a word used earlier.
3. Use a word or phrase that means the same thing as one used earlier.

This paragraph, from a famous adventure story, has several direct references. The numbers above the references show you the type of reference.

> That same evening, however, Leiningen assembled *his*[1] workers. *He*[1] had no intention of waiting till the news reached *their*[1] ears from other sources. *Most*[1] of *them*[1] had been born in the district; the cry "The ants are coming!" was to *them*[1] an imperative signal for instant, panic-stricken flight, a spring for life itself. But so great was the *Indians'*[1] trust in *Leiningen,*[2] in *Leiningen's*[2] word, and in *Leiningen's*[2] wisdom, that *they*[1] received *his*[1] curt *tidings,*[3] and *his*[1] orders for the imminent struggle, with the calmness with which *they*[1] were given. *They*[1] waited, unafraid, alert, as if for the beginning of a new game or hunt which *he*[1] had just described to *them.*[1] The *ants*[2] were indeed mighty, but not so mighty as the *boss.*[1] Let *them*[1] come!
>
> Carl Stephenson, "Leiningen Versus the Ants"

Transitional Words and Phrases.   Words and phrases that indicate the relationships between ideas are called *transitional expressions.* Prepositions that show chronological or spatial order and conjunctions are also transitions. In the chart that follows, notice the relationships shown by the different types of transitions and the types of writing to which they're related.

TRANSITIONAL WORDS AND PHRASES		
Comparing Ideas/Classification and Definition		
also	besides	similarly
and	in addition	too
another	other	
Contrasting Ideas/Classification and Definition		
although	instead	otherwise
but	nevertheless	still
however	on the other	yet
in spite of	hand	
Showing Cause and Effect/Narration		
as a result	for	therefore
because	since	thus
consequently	so	
Showing Time/Narration		
after	eventually	meanwhile
at last	finally	then
at once	first	when
before	for a time	
Showing Place/Description		
above	from	on
across	here	over
around	in	there
before	nearby	to
beyond	next	under
Showing Importance/Evaluation		
first	mainly	then
last	more important	to begin with

In the following paragraph, transitional words, which are underlined, are used to strengthen the connections and show relationships in time and place.

> <u>Then from</u> the corner of the house came a sound so soft that it might have been simply a thought, a little furtive movement, a touch of a foot <u>on</u> earth, the almost inaudible purr of controlled breathing. Kino held his breath to listen, <u>and</u> he knew that whatever dark thing was <u>in</u> his house was holding its breath <u>too,</u> to listen. <u>For a time</u> no sound at all came <u>from</u> the corner of the brush house. <u>Then</u> Kino might have thought he had imagined the sound. <u>But</u> Juana's hand came creeping <u>over to</u> him <u>in</u> warning, <u>and then</u> the sound came again! the whisper of a foot <u>on</u> dry earth <u>and</u> the scratch of fingers <u>in</u> the soil.
>
> John Steinbeck, *The Pearl*

EXERCISE 6 ▶ **Identifying Direct References and Transitions**

The following paragraph uses both direct references and transitions to connect ideas. Label two columns "Direct References" and "Transitions." Then identify each direct reference and transition in the paragraph. Remember to refer to the chart of commonly used transitions on page 89, and to think about conjunctions and prepositions telling *when* and *where*.

EXAMPLE   Moreover, Mayor Mary Rodríguez made a promise to balance the city budget. When election day arrived, her pledge proved popular, and she won. Few people, however, realized how painful carrying out her commitment would be.

Direct References	Transitions
her	moreover
pledge	when
she	and
her	however
commitment	

Although the popular cartoon *The Far Side* by Gary Larson had extraordinary success, its beginnings were modest. Larson says he always loved to draw, but he never took art lessons. Also, Larson says he always liked science. His famous panel, consequently, combined those two loves. In 1979, Larson started drawing a cartoon in the *Seattle Times* called *Nature's Way*. Before long, his drawings moved to the *San Francisco Chronicle* as *The Far Side*. Syndication began, and *The Far Side* became a household name. Larson says he frequently is asked, "Where did you get your ideas?" The artist answers that he doesn't know; most ideas came from thinking and doodling. Because people enjoyed the cartoon so much, Larson decided to write a book about his work. That volume is *The PreHistory of The Far Side*.

Courtesy of Universal Press Syndicate.

EXERCISE 7 ▶ **Using Transitions**

There's little wonder that the ideas in this paragraph are confusing—there are few transitions to make ideas clear to readers. Revise the paragraph by adding the transitions that help readers follow the order of ideas. (You may also decide to make other changes to improve the paragraph.)

Angie was very interested in the Seven Wonders of the Ancient World. She decided to write a report on them. She went to Egypt last year. She saw the pyramids, the only existing wonder. To write her report, Angie went to the library. She checked out books on the ancient wonders. She read about them in encyclopedias. Angie talked to her history teacher. Angie found conflicting information. Most of the old books said that the Colossus of Rhodes stood over the harbor entrance on the Greek island of Rhodes. More modern research indicates that the huge bronze statue was not at the harbor. Angie located pictures of all the seven wonders. She wrote her report. She had seen the pyramids. That's why she wrote most about them.

Zeus at Olympia

Lighthouse of Alexandria

Temple of Artemis at Ephesus

Pyramids at Giza

Colossus of Rhodes

Mausoleum at Halicarnassus

Hanging Gardens of Babylon

Strategies of Development

Description, narration, classification, and evaluation are four strategies for developing a main idea. The strategy, or method, you choose to develop a paragraph depends upon your specific purpose and audience for writing. The strategy determines what kind of supporting details you will use, such as facts or examples, and affects the order of your ideas. These four strategies of development are basically different ways of looking at a topic or subject.

STRATEGIES OF DEVELOPMENT	
Description	Looking at individual features of a particular subject
Narration	Looking at changes in the subject over a period of time
Classification	Looking at a subject in relation to other subjects
Evaluation	Looking at the value of the subject (judging)

Each paragraph or each piece of longer writing you create should have a purpose and a strategy that develops that purpose. You may use description to write a friend about your dream car. Or you may use narration to write in your journal about what happened during the last football game. In school you might use classification to compare and contrast the sciences of biology and zoology. And you would choose evaluation to tell your theater teacher your opinion of a play you saw.

WRITING NOTE Frequently, paragraphs and longer pieces of writing have more than one purpose, so they use more than one strategy of development. For example, description and narration are often combined in reports, stories, and even poetry.

Description

What does your state flag look like? How will you recognize Gothic architecture?

To tell what something is like or what it looks like, you need to examine its particular features. Then you choose description as a strategy of development, using sensory details for support and spatial order. The following paragraph, for example, describes the brightly dressed Gullah women of the Carolina Sea Islands.

> All day long they travel the highways in twos, threes, and dozens. Dressed in their best bibs and tuckers, they present a varicolored procession, moving leisurely over shell and sand roads. Every color of the rainbow is presented in their dresses, calicoes of blue, red, yellow, and green—garments simply made, and mostly homemade. They chat and laugh and enjoy the holiday spirit. Like the ancient Hebrews they have learned the happy art of combining religion and social life. A woman comes by with her large pocketbook balanced on her head—why, I do not know. A proud mother carries her baby in her arms, dressed in brilliant yellow.
>
> Mason Crum, *Gullah*

EXERCISE 8 ▶   **Using Description as a Strategy**

"It's a really economical and smooth car," she says. "What kind is it? What does it look like?" her friend asks. Description adds information about a subject. Choose two of the following subjects and list at least five features—sensory details—to describe each one. Remember to use a technique like brainstorming or freewriting to think up sensory details (see pages 24–34).

1. a school dance
2. a favorite musician or musical group
3. your neighborhood on a winter's day
4. yourself when you have a bad cold
5. the busiest, most crowded place you've ever been

Narration

What happened when young Arthur tried to pull the sword from the stone? How does a video recorder work? What economic and political events caused the Berlin Wall to come down?

To answer these questions, you use the strategy of narration, looking at events or actions in time. And to find the answers to these questions, you have to look at changes over a period of time. Since you're looking at a subject from a time perspective, you usually use chronological (or time) order. You may use narration *to tell a story or incident* (what happened when Arthur tried the sword), *to explain a process* (how a video recorder works), or *to explain cause and effect* (why the Berlin Wall came down).

Telling a Story. Storytellers use the strategy of narration to tell a story (what happened over time). The story may be either true or imaginary (fiction). In the following paragraph, the writer tells a story about a contest between the Greek gods Athena and Poseidon for the city of Athens.

> In one story of this contest between the two deities, woman's suffrage plays a part. In those early days, we are told, women voted as well as men. All the women voted for the goddess, and all the men for the god. There was one more woman than there were men, so Athena won. But the men, along with Poseidon, were greatly chagrined at this female triumph; and while Poseidon proceeded to flood the land the men decided to take the vote away from the women. Nevertheless, Athena kept Athens.
>
> Edith Hamilton, *Mythology*

Explaining a Process. Telling how something works or how to do something is *explaining a process.* You use narration to explain a process because you look at your subject as it changes over time. In the following paragraph, the writer explains how he helps his mother close the family restaurant. (The steps in the process are the changes over time.)

> At night I help my mother close the restaurant. I do what she and my father have done together for the past forty-three years. At ten o'clock I turn off the illuminated white sign above the front entrance. After all the customers leave and the last waiter says goodbye, I lock the front door and flip over the sign that says "Closed." Then I shut off the radio and the back lights.
>
> David Low, "Winterblossom Garden"

Explaining Cause and Effect. To explain what causes something or what the effects of something are, you also look at the way things have changed over the course of time. You use narration again. In this paragraph, the writer reveals the two effects of her realization that she was growing up and wouldn't always be at Ames High School. One effect is that she felt a sense of sadness. The other is that she "nestled" into familiar surroundings.

> As I grew older, I began to realize that this quiet was not going to last. Time was speeding up; at some sharply definable point I would grow up and leave Ames. At odd moments in those last years I would be surprised by sadness, a strange feeling that perhaps I had missed something, that maybe life was going to pass me by. At the same time I nestled securely in the familiar landscape of streets whose every bump and jog I knew, of people who smiled and greeted me by name wherever I went, of friends who appeared at every movie, store, or swimming pool.
>
> Susan Allen Toth, "Nothing Happened"

EXERCISE 9 ▶ **Using Narration as a Strategy**

You've read about the different times you can use narration to develop a paragraph—to explain causes and effects, to explain a process, and to tell a story. Now, use the following instructions for using that strategy.

1. List the effects of poor nutrition and lack of exercise on your health as an adult.
2. List the steps in the process for getting a learner's driving permit in your state.
3. List the actions in a story about what might happen if an alien spacecraft landed on the White House lawn.

EXERCISE 10▶ **Speaking and Listening: Explaining a Process**

Think about a simple process that you could explain to the class or a smaller group—perhaps how to make tortillas or how to hook up a stereo system with tape deck, CD player, receiver, and so on. Then, make a list of the major steps in the process. Using your list as an outline, explain the process to your audience. If you like, use props or visual aids to make your process clearer.

COMPUTER NOTE: If you are writing your list on a computer, remember to save your work every ten to fifteen minutes. Use automatic Save if you have it.

Classification

What are the sizes and depths of the world's oceans? What is a laser? What are the differences between hurricanes and tornadoes?

To answer these questions, you need to *classify,* or look at a subject as it relates to other subjects in a group. There are three ways to classify: divide a subject into its parts (the oceans), define it (a laser), or compare and contrast it with something else (hurricanes and tornadoes).

Dividing.   With some subjects, the best way to explain them as a whole is to look at their parts. For example, to explain what the United Nations is, you may have to divide it into the parts that make up the overall organization known as the United Nations, such as the General Assembly, the Security Council, and the International Court of Justice. This paragraph uses the strategy of dividing in order to explain the makeup of the news department at the *New York Times*.

> In the news department at *The Times* there are some 570 people who assign, gather, and edit the news. Under the executive editor, A. M. Rosenthal, are managing editor Seymour Topping and his deputy and assistants, among them the news editor. There are nine news desks, and of these, the metropolitan, national, and foreign are the best-known. Each is headed by an editor who, with a deputy and assistants, supervises a staff of reporters or correspondents and oversees the flow of news to the respective copy desk and from there to the composing room. The other news desks—business and financial, culture, family/ style, science, real estate, and sports—operate in much the same way.
>
> Betty Lou English, *Behind the Headlines*

Defining.   When you *define* a subject, you first identify it as a part of a larger group or class. Then you discuss features that make the subject unique in its class. In the following paragraph, the first sentence defines "stars" and identifies the larger group to which they belong (gas). The remaining sentences give details about stars that distinguish them from other types of gases.

> Stars are hot, glowing globes of gas that emit energy. Nearly all of a star's gas is hydrogen. Because the Sun is a hot ball of hydrogen that emits huge amounts of energy, it is a star, and the star

closest to us. The next closest star is one called Alpha Centauri, more than 270,000 times farther away than the Sun.

Roy A. Gallant, *Private Lives of the Stars*

Comparing and Contrasting. Another way to classify subjects is by comparing them (telling how they are alike), contrasting them (telling how they are different), or by both comparing and contrasting. The following paragraph contrasts the characteristics of spiders and insects.

Spiders are not insects. Although they are often confused with them, they differ from them in many ways. Most adult insects, for example, have wings; spiders never do. All insects have bodies divided into three major parts: head, thorax and abdomen, the latter two divided into smaller segments. The thorax carries four or six legs, never more. A spider's body is in two main parts. Attached to the front one of these are eight legs, never fewer.

Joyce Pope, *Do Animals Dream?*

EXERCISE 11 ▶ Using Classification as a Strategy

How can you divide it, define it, compare it, or contrast it? Follow the directions to develop each of the main ideas given below.

Main Idea	Classification Strategy
1. There's a car on the market to appeal to every type of individual taste.	Examine the subject of cars by dividing them into types. List details for each type to support the main idea.
2. Take the teachers and books away, and would it still be a school?	Define the subject "school." What larger group does it belong to—political organization, an institution for learning, or some other group? Now, list some features that make it different from other groups.
3. If you're good at one computer game, will you be good at another?	Compare and contrast two computer games by listing their likenesses and differences.

Evaluation

Should our schools use suspension as a punishment for students who create discipline problems? Is Morgan Freeman's latest movie as good as his last one?

   To answer such questions, you look at the value of the subject, or make a judgment about it. There are two main reasons for evaluating a subject: to inform other people or to persuade them to think or act differently. Of course, an evaluation often has both purposes at once. For example, movie reviewers tell you their opinions in order to persuade you to see or to avoid movies. When you evaluate, it's important to give some reasons to support your evaluation (that is, tell *why* you have this judgment about the subject). The following paragraph is part of a review of the television series *Frasier.* What is the reviewer's evaluation of the program? Does she make you want to see it? How does the reviewer support her evaluation?

> My favorite television series this season has to be *Frasier.* It just keeps getting better and better. In only a few seasons the show has established its place among the pantheon of prime time comedies, as its writers and actors have learned how to play the quirky characters off each other to maximum comic effect. The blustery arrogance of Kelsey Grammer's Frasier is counterbalanced by both the superrefined nervousness of David Hyde Pierce's Niles and the persistent grumpiness of John Mahoney's Dad. Offsetting the quarrelsome interactions of the three male characters is Jane Leeves as the sweet-tempered, no-nonsense Daphne, the British housekeeper. Each week, the talented cast brings this mix of oddly appealing characters to life with surprising and convincing ingenuity.

EXERCISE 12▶   **Using Evaluation as a Strategy**

What's your evaluation? Why do you feel that way? Evaluate each of the following broad subjects by making a positive or negative judgment about it. Then give two or three reasons to support your judgment.

1. the latest movie you've seen
2. the latest book you've read
3. the most current fad around school (in clothes, hairstyles, or language)

MAKING CONNECTIONS

WRITING PARAGRAPHS FOR DIFFERENT PURPOSES

In this chapter you studied the form and structure of paragraphs. Now you can apply that knowledge by writing paragraphs for different purposes: to express yourself, to inform, to persuade, and to create.

Writing a Paragraph to Express Yourself

Do you ever find yourself thinking about things that you want to understand more? Do you have feelings that you would like to explore? Writing about your thoughts and feelings can help you learn more about yourself, whether or not you share such writing with anyone else.

A diary or a writer's notebook—or any sheet of paper—is a good place to write an expressive paragraph. Use one of the following sentences to start an expressive paragraph.

Starter Sentences for Expressive Writing
It's so great that ____.
What really frustrates me is ____.
Happiness would be understanding ____.
The person I most admire is ____.
To improve the world, each person should ____.

Prewriting. Begin by identifying your thoughts and feelings about your topic, perhaps by simply listing them. Or make a cluster diagram to help you focus on the topic (see pages 28–29). You can also ask yourself a series of questions or review old journal entries for ideas.

Writing, Evaluating, and Revising. If you're writing only for yourself, write a first draft and leave it. If you'll share your paragraph, look more carefully at what you wrote and how you wrote it. Does the paragraph make sense and express what you want it to?

Proofreading and Publishing. Review your paragraph to correct errors in usage and mechanics. You could "publish" your paragraph by reading it aloud to the class. Or you and your classmates might make a booklet of your expressive paragraphs.

Writing a Paragraph to Inform

Information is constantly available—from other people, television, radio, newspapers, books, the World Wide Web, and many other sources. People get information from you, too. When you write to inform, your purpose is to present clear, useful information.

The chart below gives some information about the impact of the Olympic Games on employment in the host city. Use the information in the chart and the following topic sentence to write an informative paragraph. If you want, research more information about the job growth in a city hosting the Olympics. Assume that your audience (classmates) knows nothing about the subject.

Topic Sentence: The Olympic Games create temporary job growth in the host city.

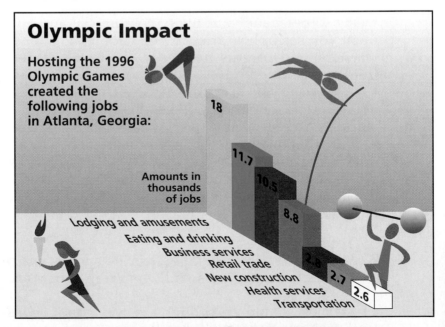

Olympic Impact

Hosting the 1996 Olympic Games created the following jobs in Atlanta, Georgia:

Amounts in thousands of jobs

Lodging and amusements 18
Eating and drinking 11.7
Business services 10.5
Retail trade 8.8
New construction 2.8
Health services 2.7
Transportation 2.6

Sources: The Atlanta Committee for the Olympic Games and the University of Georgia

Prewriting and Writing. Study the chart carefully to understand the various new job opportunities. Next, write the topic sentence on your paper. Then, support the topic sentence with three or four sentences based on information from the chart or your own research. Be sure to arrange the information in order of importance. You may want to include a clincher sentence, too.

Evaluating and Revising. Does each supporting sentence give information (facts and statistics) about the topic sentence? If not, rewrite or cut any sentences that break the unity of your paragraph. Have you arranged the information in order of importance? If not, reorder the sentences so that you start with either your most important or least important point.

Proofreading and Publishing. Review your paragraph to correct any errors in grammar, usage, and mechanics. Share your paragraph to inform someone about the job opportunities created by the Olympics.

Writing a Paragraph to Persuade

Even though you may not realize it, people are constantly trying to persuade you. Every commercial and advertisement you see or hear tries to persuade you. Your friends, teachers, and parents frequently try to persuade you to think or act differently.

Likewise, you may find yourself in situations where you want to persuade others. Suppose you are taking sides in a controversy over whether whales should be moved from the ocean to the confinement of a local aquarium. Write a paragraph in which you try to persuade people to support or not to support having a whale tank in the local aquarium. If you want, use one of the following topic sentences.

Topic Sentences:
Whales are an ecologically delicate species and should not be moved to a small, confining aquarium.

Whales should be brought to the local aquarium so that everyone can enjoy them.

Prewriting. Which side of the controversy are you on? To decide, make two lists of reasons: one telling why you feel whales should be brought to the aquarium and another telling why they should not be brought. Suggestions: How do you feel about animals' being taken from their natural habitats? about the amount of money and resources needed to provide for them in a large aquarium? After reviewing your own beliefs, decide which side to take. (You may want to do some research to gather support for your opinion.)

Writing, Evaluating, and Revising. For your paragraph, list three or four persuasive reasons to back up your position. Be sure to state your position clearly in a topic sentence. After you write your draft, look at the reasons you have given. Do you have enough reasons? Are they persuasive? Revise your paragraph to make it more persuasive.

Proofreading and Publishing. Correct any errors in grammar, usage, and mechanics. To see if someone else would be persuaded, read your paragraph aloud to the class or to a small group.

Writing a Paragraph That Is Creative

Stories and poems are writers' attempts to use situations, characters, and/or language in a particular way. Look at the painting *High Tide: The Bathers,* by Winslow Homer, and write a paragraph that begins a story suggested by Homer's painting. In your paragraph, give your readers some idea about who the characters are, and describe the setting. Also, establish a conflict—a struggle of some kind—for the characters. These questions may help you imagine a scene that involves a conflict.

- Who are the bathers? What is their relationship to each other?
- Where are the bathers? What are they doing there? What do they plan to do next?
- What feelings do you get from the characters? Why do you see only one face clearly? What is the expression of the girl sitting on the beach?
- What part does the dog play in the bathers' story? Is the dog with them or with someone else?

Winslow Homer, *Eaglehead, Manchester, Massachusetts. (High Tide: The Bathers.)* Oil on canvas, 26″ × 38″. The Metropolitan Museum of Art, Gift of Mrs. William F. Milton, 1923. (23.77.2) Photograph © The Metropolitan Museum of Art 1980.

Prewriting. Study the painting to see what details you think would enrich your story. Jot down the details, along with sensory descriptions such as the color of the sky and water, the sounds, and the smells.

Writing, Evaluating, and Revising. Write a paragraph that describes the scene at the beginning of your story, introduces the characters and situation, and prepares your readers for the conflict to come. Then, exchange your paragraph with a classmate. Is the beginning of your story clear to your reader? Does your reader understand the situation and conflict? If not, add or change details.

 Proofreading and Publishing. Correct any errors in grammar, usage, and mechanics. Share your paragraph by reading it aloud to the class or to a small group. You may even want to finish writing the whole story.

Reflecting on Your Writing

If you decide to include any of your paragraphs in your **portfolio,** attach to your paper a brief reflection answering the following questions.

- How did you decide whether to state your main idea in a topic sentence?
- Was it harder to collect supporting details or to cut unrelated ideas? Why?
- Which paragraph did you most enjoy writing— expressive, informative, persuasive, or creative? Why?

"A sentence should contain no unnecessary words, a paragraph no unnecessary sentences, for the same reason that a drawing should have no unnecessary lines and a machine no unnecessary parts."

William Strunk, Jr.

3 UNDERSTANDING COMPOSITION STRUCTURE

Looking at the Whole

Have you ever overheard just the punch line of a joke? Although everyone else is laughing, it doesn't seem funny to you—you didn't hear the whole joke. That's the way it is with a composition. All of the parts work together to make a **whole** composition.

Writing and You. A movie review in *Rolling Stone* . . . an article in *Life* magazine about space . . . a newspaper story about rising taxes. These are all compositions. If you look at them closely, you'll see that they have a certain form: an introduction, a body, and a conclusion. Besides magazines and newspapers, where else might you find compositions?

As You Read. As you read the following article from *Omni* magazine, notice how the writer uses composition form to tell about cyborgs.

Ben Shahn, *Still Music* (1948). Casein on fabric, 48" × 83½".
Collection of The Phillips Collection, Washington, D.C. © 1998
Estate of Ben Shahn/Licensed by VAGA, New York, N.Y.

109

QUASI-HUMANS

by R. A. Deckert

The Six Million Dollar Man and the Bionic Woman were TV's first cyborgs—part human, part technowizardry. We may soon live in a world populated by these beings, futurist Jerome Glenn believes, because we are evolving into them.

Cyborgs, says Glenn, are the inevitable result of two trends about to merge into one. The first trend—the increasing use of technology to correct physical disabilities—can be seen in the progression from eyeglasses to contact lenses to surgically implanted lenses. The second trend—the tendency for technology to become more humanlike—is continuing to evolve rapidly. The ability to associate ideas as well as the ability to speak and to recognize voices are all within the range of today's computer chips.

Glenn says that the two trends will usher in an age of "conscious technology" in which "robots will get biochips to become more human and humans will become cyborgs" within the first half of the twenty-first century.

By then technology won't be limited to simply correcting disabilities but will increasingly be used to enhance the human body's performance. "Contact lenses with zoom vision, miniature hearing aids to hear selected sounds at greater distances, or miniature transceivers to reach out and touch someone are just some of the ways future cyborgs will go beyond our inherited biology," Glenn says.

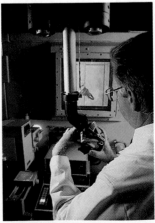

While he is confident that he has seen the future that lies ahead for humanity, Glenn acknowledges there is a certain amount of resistance to be overcome. "As [Isaac] Asimov says, 'All new technology is rejected and then accepted.' I don't see any difference with this."

READER'S RESPONSE

1. What do you think of Jerome Glenn's theory? Do any of your own experiences and observations support his theory? Which ones?
2. Do you think it's true that people at first always reject new technology? If so, why?

WRITER'S CRAFT

3. What is the thesis statement—the sentence that tells the main idea—in this article?
4. In the body of the article, the author discusses two trends. What are they? How does this discussion reflect and support the main idea?

LOOKING AHEAD

In this chapter, you'll learn about the parts of a composition. You'll learn that

- most compositions have an introduction that attracts the reader's attention, sets the tone, and gives the thesis statement
- each body paragraph is unified and clearly connected to the surrounding paragraphs
- most compositions have a conclusion that reinforces the main idea and brings the composition to a definite close

What Makes a Composition

Not only do you read compositions for information and enjoyment—you also write them yourself for the same purposes. For instance, in school you write compositions, also called *essays*, both for assigned papers and for tests. And you'll also write compositions when you apply for college admission and scholarships and for jobs. Many colleges and businesses often ask applicants to write compositions about themselves, their interests, and their goals.

   In other chapters, you'll learn how to use the composition form when writing persuasive essays and research papers, when writing about literature, or when explaining a process. In this chapter you'll concentrate on the basic principles of composition form.

"Provoke the reader.

Astonish the reader.

Writing that has no surprises

is as bland as oatmeal."

Anne Bernays

The Thesis Statement

A *thesis statement* gives the composition's main, or unifying, idea about a topic. It's a sentence or two in the introduction that "tells your readers what you're going to tell them." It announces your limited topic and your main idea about it, just as a topic sentence does in a paragraph.

Some thesis statements simply identify the limited topic, for example: "Californians are facing a water shortage resulting from several years of drought."

But most thesis statements, including the ones you'll be asked to write, do more. They identify a main idea the writer is actually trying to prove to the reader. Here's an example of this kind of thesis statement.

> Facing a possible fifth year of sustained drought, communities along the California coast are looking to desalinated ocean or bay water as a way to quench their thirst and water their lawns.
>
> Lawrence M. Fisher, "A Thirsty California Is Trying Desalination"

Hints for Writing and Using a Thesis Statement

1. **Develop your thesis statement from information you've gathered.** Review your prewriting material—the ton of facts and details you've gathered. Ask yourself: *What main, or unifying, idea do the facts and details suggest?*
2. **Include both a limited topic and your main idea about it.** Most thesis statements answer these two questions: *What's my topic? What am I saying about my topic?* To make sure you've included both parts, underline the limited topic and circle the main idea.

   For example, notice this thesis statement: "If you're interested in bicycle touring, you need to make some specific preparations involving your bike, yourself, your clothing, and your route." It's clear that this writer is going to discuss bicycle touring (topic) and specific preparations for your bike, yourself, your clothing, and your route (main idea).

3. **Be clear and specific.** Keep your language and ideas sharp and definite. Compare this vague and fuzzy thesis statement with the actual one you've just read: "So if you're interested in bicycle touring, you need to do some things before you leave."

4. **Keep your thesis statement in front of you as you plan and write.** It will help keep you on track. Every idea and detail should directly support your thesis statement, so be tough and get rid of any that don't.

WRITING NOTE Your preliminary thesis statement, the one you develop before you actually write your composition, is probably direct and straightforward. You may even think it's a little dull. Later on, you can revise it to give it more punch and zing, as professional writers do. Here's an example of how one writer revised a thesis statement.

PRELIMINARY The opening day of the baseball season marks the beginning of a long, dramatic conflict for the pennant for both individual players and teams.

REVISED "Play ball!" For baseball fans everywhere, the umpire's opening-day cry begins another season of high drama for individual players and teams.

EXERCISE 1 ▶ Analyzing Thesis Statements

Do these thesis statements meet the two-part test? Does each one have a topic and a main idea? Identify the limited topic and the writer's main idea in each one.

EXAMPLE   **1.** Hundreds of highly trained and motivated disabled athletes compete each year in the Paralympics, the World Championships, and Games for the Disabled.

1. *Limited topic: athletes who have disabilities*
Main idea: compete in the Paralympics, the World Championships, and Games for the Disabled

1. "No more helium-filled balloons!" Environmentalists and animal rights groups are boycotting balloons because they are concerned about wild animals that die from eating balloons.
2. If you call 911 in Darien, Connecticut, your ambulance crew will include at least one teenager, trained as a skilled volunteer emergency medical technician.
3. Mount McKinley is Denali, and Greenland has become Kalaallitt Nunaat. Dozens of geographical features and countries have had their names changed during the past decade.
4. The holiday of Kwanzaa, beginning on December 26 and lasting for seven days, is a celebration of African American history, culture, and values.

EXERCISE 2 ▶ Writing a Thesis Statement

Work with a partner or small group to develop a thesis statement for each of the sets of prewriting details on the next page. Make your thesis statement interesting, specific, clear, and lively. Also check to see that your thesis statement meets the two-part test of stating both the topic and a main idea. Your group may want to compare these thesis statements with the ones other groups write.

COMPUTER NOTE: If you have computers at your school that are arranged in a network, you may be able to use them to do collaborative prewriting or drafting.

1. Limited topic: regulating public school clothing
   Ideas and details
   - goal—create an environment supportive of learning
       uniforms as option in public schools
       students and parents in favor
       ties for boys on Fridays
       sense of unity from wearing uniforms
   - banned items
       T-shirts
       cut-off or torn jeans
       shorts
       expensive jewelry

2. Limited topic: world's declining whale population
   Ideas and details
   - whales severely overhunted
   - from the 1930s to the present, the number of blue, right, humpback, bowhead (kinds of whales) has severely declined
   - some whales, such as the northern right whale, are close to becoming extinct
   - International Whaling Commission supposed to manage whaling, but whaling nations resist controls
   - members of Greenpeace organization fight whaling—say that continued whaling threatens existence of whale
   - some countries, such as Norway, have been allowed to sell whale meat to Japan
   - nations allowed to kill whales for scientific research

Early Plans and Formal Outlines

Some people are naturally neat and tidy—but most aren't. Here's your chance to clean house. Throw out every bit of information that doesn't directly support your thesis statement, and pull together every bit that does. *Early plans* and *formal outlines* help you do this.

The Early Plan

An *early plan* is also called a rough, or informal, outline. It looks like a set of orderly notes, with each group of details arranged under a heading. The first step in making an early plan is to group your ideas and information; the next step is to order, or arrange, them.

Grouping.   Use these three questions to sort and group information: *Which details belong together? What do they have in common? Which details don't fit in any group?* (Discard these details.) Also think of a heading—a word or phrase—that identifies what the details have in common. For example, here's how one writer grouped and labeled information for a composition on bicycle touring.

> *bicycle helmet, water bottle, tire repair kit—SAFETY ITEMS*
>
> *mountain bike, sport/touring bike, racing bike—TYPES OF BICYCLES*

Ordering.   You have two kinds of ordering to think about: (1) order of details within each group; (2) order of groups within the composition. In both cases, arrange your information in a way that will make sense to your readers.

Sometimes your topic suggests an order. For example, if you're explaining a step-by-step process, such as how to change an automobile's flat tire, you'd use *chronological (time) order*. You'd use *spatial order* to describe the layout of your school. You may use *classification* to describe three types of school athletes, or *order of importance* (from most important reason to least important, or vice versa) to persuade eighteen-year-olds to register to vote.

But sometimes none of these orders apply. Then you just have to figure out an arrangement that will let your reader follow your ideas easily. "First things first" is a good rule for organizing information. For instance, if you're writing about unrest in the former Soviet republics, you'll first need to give a paragraph of background information about what led up to the problems.

 REFERENCE NOTE: For more on arranging ideas, see pages 82–85.

The Formal Outline

A *formal outline* has a format that shows the order and relationship of ideas, using letters and numbers to label headings. A *sentence outline* uses complete sentences for all main headings and subheadings, while a *topic outline* uses single words or phrases.

 REFERENCE NOTE: For more information on formal outlines, see pages 424–425.

Here's the first part of a topic outline for the composition on pages 120–121. Notice that the outline lists the ideas in the paper's second and third paragraphs.

Title: Bicycle Touring
Thesis statement: If you're interested in bicycle touring, you need to make some specific preparations involving your bike, yourself, your clothing, and your route.

 I. Your bike
  A. Type of bike
  B. Condition of bike
  C. Equipment
   1. Map
   2. Light
   3. Kits
    a. Bicycle repair kit
    b. First-aid kit
   4. Saddlebags
   5. Water container
 II. Your physical condition
  A. Exercise program
   1. Muscles
   2. Endurance
  B. Goal: 10–15 miles

| EXERCISE 3 ▶ | **Making an Early Plan or an Outline** |

Here are some notes for a composition about how to avoid getting hit by lightning. Work with a partner to organize this jumble of notes into an early plan or a formal outline for a composition. [Hint: The advice on what to do is different if you're indoors or outdoors.]

Surviving Lightning Storms
swimmers--get out of water immediately
in a small boat--get to shore
if you're inside, don't use telephone
before storm hits, unplug electric appliances
if outdoors, find shelter in a building, cave,
    canyon, thick growth of low trees
stay away from isolated trees, metal fences
if no shelter outdoors, keep low--away from high
    places, tall trees
if you're in car, stay there--a safe shelter
indoors, stay away from metal pipes, appliances,
    open doors, and windows
don't shower or take bath during electrical storm
number of deaths each year from lightning
people hit by lightning more frequently in summer
    and fall

A WRITER'S MODEL

Following is the final draft of a composition based on the outline on page 118. As you read, try to think about a good title for the composition. (See the Writing Note on page 133.)

INTRODUCTION

Automobiles speed along highways about fifty-five miles an hour. Bullet trains rocket down their tracks at nearly two hundred miles an hour. And if that's not fast enough for you, the Concorde jet carries passengers faster than the speed of sound! Yet more and more people are choosing to take day trips, overnights, or extended tours the slow way--by bicycle. But don't pedal away yet. If you're interested in bicycle touring, you'll need to make some specific preparations involving your bike, yourself, your clothing, and your route.

Thesis statement

BODY
Main topic: Your bike

The first thing to consider is your bicycle. With so many types to choose from--road bikes, off-road bikes, mountain bikes, and all-terrain bikes--you can pick one that's appropriate for the kind of terrain you'll be traveling on. Whichever bike you choose, it should be in excellent condition. Equip it with a map, a light, a bicycle-repair kit, a first-aid kit, saddlebags for food and clothing, and a water carrier.

Main topic: Your physical condition

Your bike may be in good shape, but what about you? Whether your trip is a few miles to the next town or across country, you need to get yourself in good physical condition. Start an exercise program and build up your muscles and endurance gradually. You should be able to easily cycle ten to fifteen miles a day.

Main topic: Your clothing

Now think about clothing. What you pack will depend on the season, but always prepare for possible bad weather. Pack rain gear and clothing that allows freedom of movement as it protects you from strong winds, wet, and cold. In general, avoid clothing that might interfere with

**Main topic:
Choosing
your route**

your mobility or comfort, and be sure to wear a helmet. Head injuries are a cyclist's biggest worry.

Finally, talk to experienced cyclists and read books and magazines to plan your route. You may want to join the American Youth Hostels (AYH), which offers its members inexpensive lodging and group rides. Bicycling magazines appear each month with information and special features about bicycle touring. And an organization called the Adventure Cycling Association publishes guidebooks, maps of the U.S. National Bicycle Trails Network, and a list of bicycle tour operators.

CONCLUSION

If you plan your trip well, you'll discover that bicycle touring--alone or with a group--is more fun than faster ways of travel. Before you go, give yourself enough time to get your bike, your body, your clothing, and your route in top condition. Careful advance planning practically guarantees a safe trip.

The Introduction

If you didn't have to, would you read a composition that begins like this: "In this composition I plan to tell you about some of the things I've learned about how scientists are studying human genes"? You probably wouldn't want to read it. It sounds too dull. An effective introduction will catch the reader's interest, set the tone of the composition, and present the thesis statement.

Catching the Reader's Interest. The introduction may be the most important paragraph in your composition. If the introduction isn't well written, your reader might not bother reading the rest of your paper. On pages 123–126 you'll find six strategies for grabbing the reader's attention.

Setting the Tone. As you introduce your topic, the words you choose and what you say set the composition's tone, the feeling you reveal about your topic. The tone of a composition may be serious, humorous, formal, informal, critical—even outraged.

For example, what can you tell about the writer's attitude from the two-sentence introduction to "Quasi-Humans" (page 110)? Its tone is definitely serious; there's nothing to indicate that this is a humorous piece. But it's also informal because a scholarly, technical discussion wouldn't refer to television shows or use the term *technowizardry*.

Presenting the Thesis Statement. You can be as clever as you want in order to catch the reader's interest, but somewhere you need to include a thesis statement that clearly summarizes the composition's main idea. Often, but not always, the thesis statement comes at the end of the introduction.

Techniques for Writing Introductions

Following are six techniques for writing effective introductions. You can also try combining techniques.

1. **Begin with a question.** Some introductions begin with a question that contradicts the thesis. Others use a rhetorical question, one with no answer expected. But any question that applies to the reader can be intriguing, as in this long introduction.

> If you could design your own personality, would you rather be lively, outgoing, and the center of attention, or quiet, thoughtful, and private?
>
> It would not be surprising if you opted for the first description. You would have lots of company. According to some estimates, there are three times as many lively extroverts in the United States as reflective introverts. Our society prefers fun-loving, friendly people with "good personalities" over quiet, private types.
>
> Is one style really better than the other? Do we have a choice?
>
> Sandra R. Arbetter, "What's Your Type? Introverts and Extroverts"

2. **Begin with an anecdote or example.** An anecdote is a little story, or incident, that may be humorous or just intriguing. This introduction begins with an example.

> The rhubarb is ready for picking in Julie Kirkpatrick's garden patch on East Fourth Street and Avenue C, and Francisco Ortiz is giving away snippets of sage and tarragon. This is El Jardin del Paraiso, a lofty name for a community garden that grows upon the rubble of long-gone tenements on the Lower East Side. The fenced space where tulips and fruit trees bloom had been a dump for garbage and old bedsprings. The neighborhood is dotted with boarded-up buildings.
>
> Kathleen Teltsch, "For Young and Old, a Pocket Paradise"

3. **State a startling fact or an unusual opinion.** The article "Quasi-Humans" (page 110) uses this technique. Here's another example of an introduction designed to arouse the reader's curiosity.

> Juan de la Cruz Briceño may be the only man on earth to have an ancient Mayan city under construction in his backyard. Six days a week, a large open truck rumbles through the dawn fog behind Juan's home, scattering a flock of outraged chickens and disgorging a score of men. Behind them rise the ruins of Becan, a cluster of pyramids ringed by a destroyed canal, magnificent in their lonely desolation. The men from the truck quickly overrun the structures, swarming over rickety wooden scaffolding, working with stone and sweat to bring back the glories of this long vanished civilization. . . .
>
> Charles Mann and Gwenda Blair, "Juan's Place"

4. **Begin with background information.** Facts and other specific details not only help your reader understand your main idea but may also create interest in your topic.

> Arising spontaneously from the people, folktales are little windows into the collective human psyche. Most people think of them as stories concerning the long ago and the faraway. In fact, all times and places have produced them, and modern times are no exception. Instead of dealing with dragons, wolves, and other menaces to the medieval world order, however, present-day folktales often revolve around modern technology and the attempts of human beings to come to terms with it.
>
> John Steele Gordon, "Financial Folklore"

5. **Set the scene.** Just as a short story may begin with a description of the setting (when and where the events take place), you might describe the setting of your topic. This introduction entices the reader with a vivid description of place that has little to do with the topic—storing seeds.

> It's barely 7 o'clock on a brisk spring morning, but the campus of Colorado State University in Fort Collins is already bustling with activity. On the track, joggers trot, runners sprint, while couples stroll and skateboarders glide nearby. Casting a feeble shadow over these proceedings is an undistinguished structure of tan-colored concrete and sandstone. This is the U.S. Department of Agriculture's National Seed Storage Laboratory (NSSL)—Fort Knox to our agricultural heritage. There are no bars on the windows, no security guards at the door, yet the billions of seeds stored here are beyond price—they are said to be our last line of defense against agricultural bankruptcy.
>
> Ellen Ruppel Shell, "Seeds in the bank could stave off disaster on the farm"

6. **Begin with a simple statement of your thesis.** You don't always have to be clever. You can be direct and straightforward and get right to your main ideas.

> Chinatown is as much a San Francisco landmark as the Golden Gate Bridge. Little is known, however, about the people who originally settled that part of the city. Now Berkeley, California, archaeologist Allen Pastron thinks his recent discovery of one of Chinatown's original buildings reveals how the unsung Chinese pioneers lived.
>
> Sherry Baker, "Pioneers Underfoot"

WRITING NOTE Professional writers often write two- or even three-paragraph introductions. But since you're writing a brief composition, limit your introduction to a single paragraph. A long-winded introduction—even if it's funny or fascinating—can get you way off track.

EXERCISE 4 ▶ **Analyzing Introductions**

Sharpen your skills by analyzing the introductions of professional writers. Read the two introductions below and answer the following questions about each one.

- What technique does the writer use in the introduction? (Look back over the techniques on pages 123–126.)
- How well do you think the technique works? (Would you read the article?)
- How would you describe the tone—the writer's attitude toward the topic? What words and details in the introduction reveal the tone?

1.   Could some advanced civilization devise a tunnel that would open shortcuts through space between distant regions of the universe or through time into the past?

   The traditional reaction of most scientists to such notions is to dismiss them as naïve science fiction. But three theoretical astrophysicists have published a suggestion that the laws of physics might not prohibit such "wormhole" travel through space and time.

   Malcolm W. Browne, "3 Scientists Say Travel in Time Isn't So Far Out"

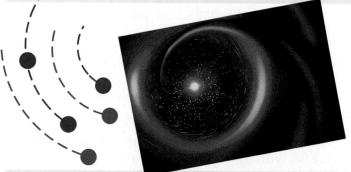

2.   At Rye High School, only do-gooders get diplomas. And virtually everyone is a do-gooder. To graduate, students are required to perform 60 hours of community service over their four years.

   Lisa W. Foderaro, "At Rye High, Students Not Only Must Do Well, They Must Do Good"

The Body

Your composition would read like a telegram if you simply stated your main ideas. And who would believe you? An effective composition consists mostly of a *body* of paragraphs. Each paragraph supports or proves a main point by developing it with supporting details.

 REFERENCE NOTE: See pages 93–101 for information on strategies of paragraph development.

Unity

It's a strain to try to follow someone whose thoughts leap illogically from topic to topic. When a composition has *unity,* the separate paragraphs work smoothly together to support a single main idea—your thesis. Drop all details and statements that detract from this sense of "oneness."

Coherence

Coherence means that ideas are woven together so they're strongly connected. In a coherent composition, the ideas are easy to follow and the writing seems to flow smoothly from beginning to end. The reader doesn't have to agonize over what something means; nothing sounds awkward or disjointed. You can make your composition coherent by arranging ideas in an order that makes sense and by using words and phrases—either direct references or transitional words and phrases—that show how ideas are connected.

Direct References. One way to connect ideas is to make direct references to something you've already mentioned. Here are three ways to use direct references.

1. Use pronouns to refer to nouns or ideas. For example, by using *she, they,* or *this,* you can avoid awkwardly repeating nouns.
2. Repeat key words or phrases. Tie paragraphs together by reminding the reader of what's important. In "Quasi-Humans" (page 110) for example, the key words *cyborgs, technology,* and *human* appear in almost every paragraph.
3. Use synonyms or slight rewordings of previous ideas and key words. Too much repetition sounds awkward.

Transitional Words and Phrases. *For example, therefore, of course, on the other hand*—these words and phrases connect ideas and make relationships clear.

 REFERENCE NOTE: See pages 88–90 for more about using direct references and transitional words and phrases.

EXERCISE 5 ▶ **Analyzing a Paragraph**

Do professional writers follow the rules? Here's a paragraph from *Sports Illustrated* magazine. With two or three classmates, look for direct references and transitional words and phrases. Find the key word(s) and pronouns, and explain what words or ideas the pronouns refer to. What's the main idea? Does every detail support it?

Japanese baseball cards were introduced in the '30s and '40s on a limited basis, and like the original U.S. cards, they continue to be used as a come-on for other products. For example, the country's leading card-maker, Calbee, attaches individually wrapped baseball cards to bags of potato chips. Because the card is on the outside of the package, someone could easily remove it without shelling out the 40 yen (31 cents) for the potato chips. "But that's not a problem in Japan," says Fuhrmann. "Kids just don't do that kind of thing."

Rick Wolff, "A Yen for Baseball Cards"

The Conclusion

Imagine seeing a movie that stops just before the ending or reading a novel with the last few pages missing. The conclusion of your composition is just as important as the introduction. A composition that lacks a strong conclusion leaves the reader feeling puzzled.

Techniques for Writing Conclusions

1. **Restate your main idea.** Say it again, but use different words. This is probably the easiest kind of conclusion to write. When you use this technique, it works well to put the reworded version of your thesis statement at the beginning of the last paragraph. (See the bicycle composition, pages 120–121.)

2. **Summarize the main points you've developed in the body.** Use different wording to sum up your main points. This type of conclusion emphasizes and reinforces your main points, leading right into your final words about the subject.

   "When it comes to maintaining the flexibility in connective tissue like ligaments and tendons around the joints, you use it or lose it," says Dr. Findley. "If you don't take these connective tissues through their maximum range daily, eventually the range will shrink and you'll lose mobility." In addition to the long-term

> flexibility benefits, I find that doing this stretch each morning gets my blood flowing, jumpstarts my brain and expands my chest so I can breathe deeper. Within minutes, I feel energized to greet the coming day.
>
> Sharon Stocker, "Stretchbreak: Good-Morning Wake-Up Stretch"

3. **End with a final comment or example.** Your last word may be a thoughtful observation, a personal reaction, or a look to the future or to larger issues. The writer of "Quasi-Humans" (page 110) ends by saying that a "certain amount of resistance" will have to be overcome before his vision of the future becomes a reality.

4. **End with a call to action.** Persuasive essays often end by asking the reader to take a specific action. This makes an effective ending for other kinds of compositions, too.

> Alan Tiger, director of the Y.W.C.A. here, says he would like to see the program applied on a national level. "This school came up through the grass roots," he said. "It's a simple enough idea that any city can pull it off. You need the school district to get out front on it, but don't forget community support. People want to help."
>
> Timothy Egan, "School for Homeless Children: A Rare Experience"

5. **Refer to the introduction.** Bring the reader back full circle by referring to something in your introduction. George Plimpton begins "Neil Armstrong's Famous First Words" by comparing Armstrong and Charles Lindbergh. He doesn't mention Lindbergh again until the conclusion:

> Charles Lindbergh is supposed to have said, "Well, I made it!" when he touched down at Le Bourget. What he actually said, leaning out, with the crowd surging around his plane, was: "Are there any mechanics here?" And then, "Does anyone here speak

English?" So it is apparent that however self-deprecatory Armstrong is about his own contributions, he is certainly a giant leap ahead of Lindbergh in the immortal-words department.

> George Plimpton, "Neil Armstrong's
> Famous First Words"

(By the way, Neil Armstrong's "famous first words"—delivered when he first stepped on the moon on July 20, 1969—were: "That's one small step for a man, one giant leap for mankind.")

6. **Use a quotation.** A quotation that's startling or moving works just as well to end a composition as it does to begin one.

> The gardeners still have nagging worries they could lose El Jardin to developers. "I don't think there is another place where our neighborhood people could go," said Ms. Kirkpatrick. "You need a ray of hope and you find it seeing what can grow out of rubble."
>
> Kathleen Teltsch, "For Young and Old,
> a Pocket Paradise"

WRITING NOTE You can wait until you've finished writing your composition before you worry about its title. Use your thesis statement—and your imagination—to think of a brief, catchy way to describe what your readers are about to encounter.

Try writing several titles until you find one you like. Here are some suggestions for the bicycle touring composition (pages 120–121). Which one do you like best? Can you think of others?

EXAMPLES   Seeing the Country on Two Wheels
              Advice for Beginning Bicycle Trippers
              Bicycle Touring: Muscle, Sweat, and Gears

E X E R C I S E 6 ▶   **Improving a Conclusion**

Here's the first draft of a conclusion for a composition about uniforms in public schools. Get together with a partner to answer these questions: *What's wrong with this conclusion? How can it be improved?* Then, write a better conclusion. You can change it any way you like, make up details, or even start over completely. (For some ideas, refer to the techniques on pages 130–132.)

> Someday all public school students--both boys and girls--may wear uniforms. Will uniforms make schools better or worse than the way things are today? No one knows.

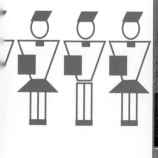

EXERCISE 7 ▶ Writing a Conclusion

Use your imagination to write a different conclusion for the composition about bicycle touring (pages 120–121). Use one technique or some combination of the techniques on pages 130–132. Feel free to make up quotations and additional details. (It's a good idea to read the composition again before you begin.)

WRITING NOTE The two models of composition form you've read in this chapter are written in different points of view. The first one, "Quasi-Humans" (page 110), is written in the third-person point of view (*he, she, it, they*). Since a third-person point of view keeps the writer at a distance from the reader, it's the point of view you'll need to use when you're writing a formal composition. The second composition, the one on bicycle touring (pages 120–121), is written in the second-person point of view (*you, your*). Since the second-person point of view brings the writer closer to the reader, you may use it when your composition is more informal.

FRAMEWORK FOR A COMPOSITION

Introduction	■ Arouses the reader's interest
	■ Sets the tone
	■ Presents the thesis statement
Body	■ States the main points
	■ Provides support for the main points
Conclusion	■ Reinforces the main idea
	■ Leaves the reader with a final impression and a sense of completeness

MAKING CONNECTIONS

WRITING AN INFORMATIVE COMPOSITION

A useful formula for writing an informative composition is *introduction + body + conclusion = composition*. Remember that to explain and inform is only one of the purposes for writing. Others are to express yourself, to be creative, and to persuade others. The composition form can also be adapted to these purposes.

In this assignment, you'll apply this three-part formula to write an informative essay about the President's Council on Physical Fitness and Sports. Since you are writing for a high school audience, your purpose will be to explain how students can qualify for awards. Imagine that the following list of facts and the following chart are the prewriting information that you've gathered so far.

Information About President's Council on Physical Fitness and Sports

1. Florence Griffith Joyner and Tom McMillen, cochairs: "Schools can nurture children's love of physical activity, laying the foundation for a healthy life."

2. a nation of young couch potatoes: nearly half don't get enough exercise; only a quarter of high school students participate in physical education daily
3. Council founded in 1956: President's Challenge awards program for boys and girls 6 through 17 that recognizes achievement in physical fitness
4. more than two million students earned awards in recent years
5. students in 85th percentile in all five events get emblem and Certificate of Achievement signed by president
6. students in 50th percentile get National Physical Fitness Award emblems and certificates
7. students who have disabilities also participate
8. five events: curl-ups (sit-up with bent knees, arms crossed on chest); shuttle run (30-foot run picking up and moving blocks); 1-mile combined run and walk; pull-ups or push-ups; V-sit reach (reaching with hands through legs in sitting position)
9. free booklet *Get Fit*—from President's Council on Physical Fitness and Sports, 701 Pennsylvania Avenue, N.W., Suite 250, Washington, DC 20004

	AGE	CURL-UPS (Limited one min.)	SHUTTLE RUN (seconds)	V-SIT REACH (inches)	ONE-MILE RUN (min./sec.)	PULL-UPS
BOYS	6	33	12.1	+3.5	10:15	2
	7	36	11.5	+3.5	9:22	4
	8	40	11.1	+3.0	8:48	5
	9	41	10.9	+3.0	8:31	5
	10	45	10.3	+4.0	7:57	6
	11	47	10.0	+4.0	7:32	6
	12	50	9.8	+4.0	7:11	7
	13	53	9.5	+3.5	6:50	7
	14	56	9.1	+4.5	6:26	10
	15	57	9.0	+5.0	6:20	11
	16	56	8.7	+6.0	6:08	11
	17	55	8.7	+7.0	6:06	13
GIRLS	6	32	12.4	+5.5	11:20	2
	7	34	12.1	+5.0	10:36	2
	8	38	11.8	+4.5	10:02	2
	9	39	11.1	+5.5	9:30	2
	10	40	10.8	+6.0	9:19	3
	11	42	10.5	+6.5	9:02	3
	12	45	10.4	+7.0	8:23	2
	13	46	10.2	+7.0	8:13	2
	14	47	10.1	+8.0	7:59	2
	15	48	10.0	+8.0	8:08	2
	16	45	10.1	+9.0	8:23	1
	17	44	10.0	+8.0	8:15	1

Prewriting. Add or subtract from the data bank given above. You don't have to use all the information given, and you can do some research to find additional facts. (Suggestions: If your school participates, what are the statistics? Interview a physical education teacher or a coach.)

Narrow your topic to one you can cover in a brief composition. Express your main idea in a preliminary thesis statement. Then, arrange the information into an early plan.

Writing, Evaluating, and Revising. Follow your early plan as you draft your composition, and try one of the introduction techniques suggested on pages 123–126. As you draft the body, concentrate on unity and coherence. Each paragraph should develop one main point directly related to your thesis statement. When you get to the conclusion, review the techniques for writing conclusions on pages 130–132.

Proofreading and Publishing. When you're satisfied with your revisions, change your focus, and search for errors in grammar, usage, and mechanics. Exchange papers with a partner, and proofread each other's compositions. (See the proofreading guidelines on pages 55–56.) Find a way to share your composition with an audience. If your school isn't participating in the program of the President's Council on Physical Fitness and Sports, you might use your compositions to try to get the program under way.

Reflecting on Your Writing

Date your paper, to include it in your **portfolio,** and attach a brief reflection that answers the following questions.

- What is most appealing about your introduction?
- How did you make sure that your body paragraphs maintained unity and coherence?
- Which part of the paper do you think is strongest?

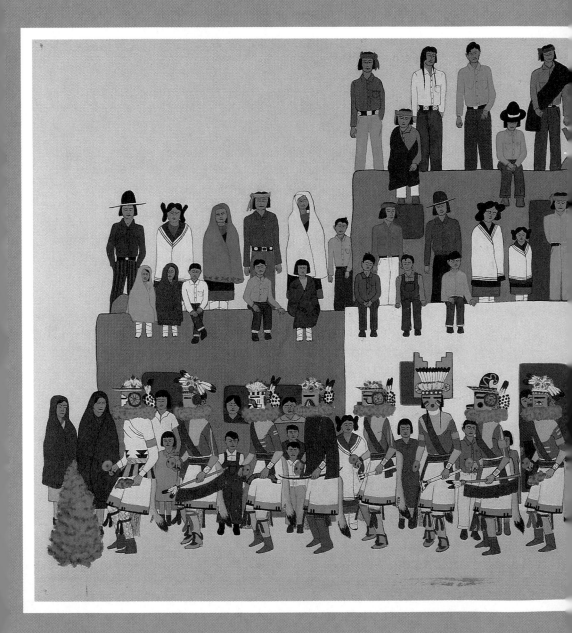

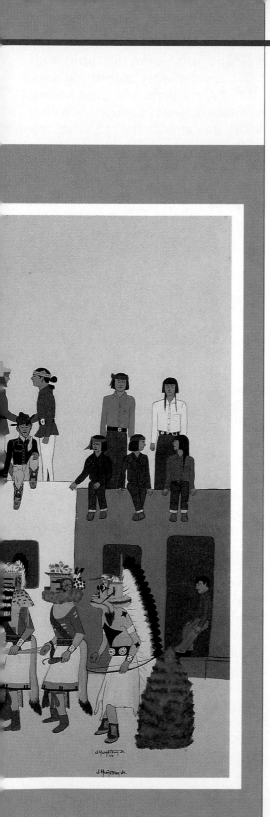

Discovering Yourself

What do you really know about yourself? What can you **discover** about **yourself?** One way you can find out more about your inner feelings is to write about them.

Writing and You. "I'll never forget the time when . . . " "I felt so good the day that . . . " You probably think or talk this way often. Many writers take these thoughts further by writing them down. Doing so helps us explore our deepest feelings, our fears, hopes, and dreams. You may want to write just for yourself. Or you might share your feelings with others in a personal narrative. Can you think of an emotional experience you would like to write about?

As You Read. As you read the following narrative, notice how Black Elk, an Oglala Sioux, looks inside himself to tell about the hardships of his people.

James Humetawa, *Kachina Dance* (1944). Hopi, born 1926. Watercolor. 1946.29.4. The Philbrook Museum of Art, Tulsa, Oklahoma.

from

Black Elk Speaks

as told through

JOHN G. NEIHARDT

(Flaming Rainbow)

The wind came up again with the daylight, and we could see only a little way ahead when we started west in the morning. Before we came to the ridge, we saw two horses, dim in the blowing snow beside some bushes. They were huddled up with their tails to the wind and their heads hanging low. When we came closer, there was a bison robe shelter in the brush, and in it were an old man and a boy, very cold and hungry and discouraged. They were Lakotas and were glad to see us, but they were feeling weak, because they had been out two days and had seen nothing but snow. We camped there with them in the brush, and then we went up on the ridge afoot. There was much timber up there. We got behind the hill in a sheltered place and waited, but we could see nothing. While we were waiting, we talked about the people starving at home, and we were all sad. Now and then the snow haze would open up for a little bit and you could see quite a distance, then it would close again. While we were talking about our hungry people, suddenly the snow haze opened a little, and we saw a shaggy bull's head coming out of the blowing snow up the draw that led past us below. Then seven more appeared, and the snow haze came back and shut us in there. They could not see us, and they were drifting with the wind so that they could not smell us.

We four stood up and made vows to the four quarters of the world, saying: "Haho! haho!" Then we got our horses from the brush on the other side of the ridge and came around to the mouth of the draw where the bison would pass as they drifted with the wind.

The two old men were to shoot first and then we two boys would follow the others horseback. Soon we saw the bison coming. The old people crept up and shot, but they were so cold, and maybe excited, that they got only one bison. They cried "Hoka!" and we boys charged after the other bison. The snow was blowing hard in the wind that sucked down the draw, and when we came near them the bison were so excited that they backtracked and charged right past us bellowing. This broke

"...when we came near them the bison were so excited that they backtracked and charged right past us bellowing."

the deep snow for our horses and it was easier to catch them. Suddenly I saw the bison I was chasing go out in a big flurry of snow, and I knew they had plunged into a snow-filled gulch, but it was too late to stop, and my

National Museum of American Art, Washington, D.C./Art Resource.

horse plunged right in after them. There we were all together—four bison, my horse and I all floundering and kicking, but I managed to crawl out a little way. I had a repeating rifle that they gave me back at the camp, and I killed the four bison right there, but I had thrown my mittens away and the gun froze to my hands while I was shooting, so that I had to tear the skin to get it loose.

When I went back to the others, the other boy had killed three, so we had eight bison scattered around there in the snow. It was still morning, but it took till nearly dark for my father and the other old man to do the butchering. I could not help, because my hands were frozen. We finally got the meat all piled up in one place, and then we made a camp in a fine shelter behind a big rock with brush all around it and plenty of wood. We had a big fire, and we tied our tanned robes on our horses and fed them plenty of cottonwood bark from the woods by the stream. The raw robes we used for the shelter. Then we had a big feast and we sang and were very happy.

READER'S RESPONSE

1. What images in Black Elk's narrative are most vivid in your mind? Why do you think these details or mental pictures made a strong impression on you?
2. Black Elk's experience shows the physical hardships he faced. Can you imagine what it would be like to have to chase bison through the snow for food for your family? In your journal, write about your own life as compared with this experience of Black Elk.

WRITER'S CRAFT

3. Black Elk uses many details that help readers feel the bitter cold. How do the details about Black Elk's hands in the last two paragraphs help you feel the awful cold?
4. Black Elk uses many transitional words and phrases to help readers follow the order of events. In the first sentence, for example, he says, "The wind came up *again* . . . *when* we started west in the morning." What are some other transition words and phrases in the first paragraph?

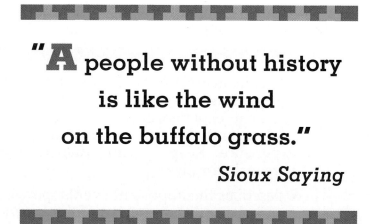

"A people without history
is like the wind
on the buffalo grass."

Sioux Saying

Ways to Express Yourself

Like anyone who does expressive writing, Black Elk wants to present his own thoughts and feelings. But he's also writing to inform readers about the terrible conditions faced by the Oglala Sioux and to persuade readers that tragic changes are occurring in the lives of his people. Expressing yourself is your main reason for writing a personal narrative. Here are some examples of the ways you can develop an expressive message.

- in your journal, writing about a funny event at school
- in a letter, telling a friend about getting lost on the subway
- in a postcard, describing your fellow camp counselors
- in a poem, describing your dog's funny habits
- in a team newsletter, comparing last year's soccer team with this year's
- in a conversation with a co-worker, defining the word *enthusiasm* and explaining what it means to you
- in your school newspaper, evaluating your volunteer work at the animal shelter
- in a focus group, discussing what you think of a company's product

LOOKING
AHEAD

In the main assignment in this chapter, you'll use narration to tell about an important personal experience. As you write, you'll explore and discover the meaning of your experience. Keep in mind that an effective personal narrative

- describes the important events, people, and places that were part of the experience
- includes your thoughts and feelings
- uses specific sensory details
- explains what the experience meant to you

Writing a Personal Narrative

Choosing a Personal Experience

Some experiences stand out in your memory—and not just the "big occasions." You may never forget the first time your band played in public (absolute terror and then relief when everybody danced).

But you may also remember—vividly—your first walk on a beach, when all that happened was watching sandpipers and gathering shells, but you decided you were *determined* never to live in the city.

Your experience for a personal narrative may be simple and ordinary instead of unusual or surprising, but if it passes these three tests, it's a good topic.

1. The experience seems important to you: it has personal meaning.
2. The experience is clear in your memory: you remember details.
3. The experience is not too private: you're willing to share it with others.

The first test is one to think about a bit. Unlike most other papers you write, the focus of a personal narrative is **you.** That's why the word *experience*, not *event*, is significant. You won't write about celebrations for the Chinese New Year just to describe what your neighborhood does, but because those celebrations made an impression on you. What counts is what you saw, heard, did, felt, and thought.

| EXERCISE 1▶ | **Tapping Your Memory for Personal Experiences** |

How did you meet your best friend? Have you ever had to think fast in an emergency? Did your favorite aunt give you the world's ugliest sweater to wear to a party? All of these events could be topics for a personal narrative. The subjects and suggestions below can help trigger your memories. Choose two or three of the general topics below and try to remember specific, important experiences about them.

- **People:** family, coaches, friends, neighbors
- **Places:** a treehouse, the gym, a pool, a place to be alone
- **Experiences:** secrets, surprises, borrowing and lending, disappointments, graduations
- **Values:** loyalty, friendship, honesty, maturity

EXAMPLES   People: Neighbors
"I remember the time the baby in the apartment next door wandered off and I helped find her."
Places: The gym
"I remember the time when I shot the winning basket against our biggest rivals."

PART 1:
Choosing an Experience for a Personal Narrative

Now put the experiences you've remembered to the test. Ask yourself: Was this experience somehow significant to me? Can I recall details to bring it alive? Do I want to make it public? Choose one personal experience as a topic to write about.

Prewriting

Planning Your Personal Narrative

The narrative you'll write is personal, but it's not a diary or journal entry meant for you alone. It's an essay written for others—a way to share your experience. This means planning and shaping your narrative for maximum effect, to communicate what you want.

Thinking About Purpose, Audience, and Tone

Purpose. Your purpose in this paper is to express yourself. You're telling about something that happened to you and exploring your thoughts and feelings about it. In this remembering and exploring, you'll make some discovery—about yourself, others, or the world around you—and share it with an audience.

Audience. Making your experience real and alive to an audience calls for details: Solid descriptions of both events and feelings that let your readers live through the experience with you. Think about your particular audience: teacher and classmates? family? Sometimes readers will need background to understand your topic. If you're writing for classmates about a chess competition, they'll probably want to know where and when it occurred, how it was organized, and some basic facts about the game.

Tone. Since this is a personal expression paper, your voice should come through—as though you're talking directly to readers. You may feel happy or angry or sad about the experience, but you'll sound honest to your readers. Personal expression is informal, which means using everyday vocabulary and sentence structure. And you'll write in the first person, using *I, me, our,* and *we.*

COMPUTER NOTE: If you store your prewriting in files on a diskette, you won't have to worry about keeping track of scraps or bundles of paper.

| EXERCISE 2 ▶ | **Speaking and Listening: Creating a Natural Tone** |

You have a unique style of expressing yourself—a way of talking that is only yours. If you want your writing to sound more like talking, why not try talking it out—with good listeners? To improve tone, try this method with a small group.

1. Think about your topic, write down a few sentences about it, and give them to the group to read.
2. Now *tell* your partners the same information out loud. Just talk—but don't repeat your written words.
3. Ask the listeners to pinpoint differences in your speaking and writing (words, expressions, sentence length), and discuss how to make the written sentences more natural.

Recalling Details

Have you ever had the experience of a certain smell or sound suddenly exploding a whole memory in your head? One whiff of a strong, old-fashioned soap, and you're right back in your grandfather's workshop.

In a way, that's what you need to do in your narrative: provide concrete, sensory details that will *re-create* your experience for readers.

Lively, Specific Details.   Don't just state, for example, that you stood on a diving board. Say instead that your knees had turned to mashed potatoes and that noises from the pool were a blurred roar. Readers will share in your experience if you use details that are specific, not vague, and that appeal to all the senses. See what details you can come up with now, and then add others later when you're writing your first draft.

Helps to Memory.   While some details will leap out of your memory, as fresh as when they happened, others may be cloudy or lost. If so, you can use brainstorming or freewriting to uncover them. You can also talk to other people who were involved (use *their* memories as well as your own) and even revisit places for a firsthand refresher of details.

Events, People, and Places. Begin with exactly what happened—first, second, third. Events are the "bones" of your narrative, its framework. First you remember main events: (1) you watched divers at a pool, (2) the lifeguard taught you some dives, and so on. Then you reach back for details about each event: You watched other kids do swan dives but you would only try plain dives from the pool's edge.

Recalling events will lead you to people. Who—besides yourself—played a part in your experience? What did they look like? What did they say? Telling that your grandfather smelled of a certain after-shave puts your readers right beside him. Use all your senses to describe yourself, another person, even crowds or animals.

Give the same all-five-senses attention to describing place details in your narrative. After all, a place can be a key part of your experience—like a white-water river on a canoe trip. But even if everything takes place somewhere ordinary—like your bedroom—put readers there. Make them *see* your posters, *smell* a candle, *feel* the cold floor.

WRITING NOTE You're telling a story, so use dialogue to add variety and bring people to life. You could write *My mother shouted at us to stop the rehearsal.* But her own words emphasize her mood: *Mother shouted, "Unplug those guitars now—or I will!"* Dialogue should fit the speaker and can be informal, including the use of slang and sentence fragments.

Thoughts and Emotions.   Don't forget yourself in this living picture you're creating. What's going on *inside* you? (Look inside other people, too, if their reactions make a difference.) Use specific words to record your feelings (*furious, delighted*), and use actions, appearance, and dialogue to tell readers how you feel. ("Mashed-potato" knees show fear.) Use a chart like this one to recall and record details.

HERE'S HOW

WHO OR WHAT?	DETAILS
Events	
1. Watching divers at swim center	Kids practicing jackknives, swan dives. I dive (plain ones) from side.
2. Brian offers to help me	He says, "Why not off the board?" Try—really scared—pull it off.
3. Practice and make team	Hard work—lots of bad "landings." Water in face. Keep it a secret.
4. In first meet	Mom, Dad, Gerald, Elizabeth having picnic. My name over loudspeaker. Me on high board (shock). Picture in paper, swan dive.
People	
Me	Shy (not like G. & E.), 12—athletic, always at pool.
Brian	College student, swims like a fish, friendly smile, called me "a natural."
Gerald and Elizabeth	Older, popular, good grades, in clubs ("Oh, you're E & G's sister!")
Mom and Dad	At center a lot with us. Running (terrified I'm drowned). Amazed then proud.
Places	
Center	Pool, activity room, picnic place—really <u>hot</u>.
Pool	Diving boards, lots of kids—noisy.
Thoughts and Feelings	
Envy divers	Imagine being graceful, cutting water cleanly. Afraid to use board.
Surprise and fear!	Don't remember going up on board. Knees soft, roar in head.
Relief	Praise great!
I am a diver!	On high board, seeing family, feeling confident. No medal—but their pride.

Reminder

When recalling details about your experience

- look for specific details and sensory details
- use brainstorming or clustering, interviewing, and observing to help your memory
- focus on events, people, places, thoughts, and feelings

WRITING ASSIGNMENT

PART 2:
Recalling Details

Sometimes relaxing is the best way to unlock memory. Make a chart like the one on page 150 to record details, and try closing your eyes and imagining yourself back in time, going through the experience again. Gather as many details as you can. "Replay" the experience in your mind as many times as you need to so you can gather the details you need.

Reflecting on the Meaning of the Experience

As you've recalled details, especially thoughts and feelings, the meaning of your experience has probably become clearer. Now is a good time to try to bring it into focus. Don't be surprised, however, if your understanding of your experience changes as you write your draft.

To reflect on (think about) why the experience was important to you, use these questions.

1. Were you somehow different at the end of the experience? If so, what were you like at the beginning? How exactly did you change?
2. Did you learn something new about yourself? What?
3. Did you learn something new about other people, human nature, or life in general? What was it?

Some unusual insight (never before thought or felt!) isn't what's necessary here. It can be as simple as "I realized that my grandfather would soon be gone. I should spend time with him *now*."

CRITICAL THINKING

Interpreting Meaning

When you *interpret,* you bring out meaning: you explain something, make it understandable. You're used to doing this in literature. For example, a character in a story competes fiercely for a scholarship but in the end turns it down to stay at home with her mother. It's up to you to interpret her action, and you decide the girl just can't bear to leave her mother alone in her last years.

An experience may have more than one interpretation (perhaps the girl also sees that she competed mainly to beat a rival), so—whether in literature or your narrative—you aren't trying to uncover the "correct" meaning. You're trying to state a meaning that makes the facts and details understandable.

CRITICAL THINKING EXERCISE:
Interpreting the Meaning of an Experience

The following notes give the main events of an experience, along with a person's thoughts and feelings about it. With others, read and discuss the statements, put yourself in the person's place, and suggest a possible meaning for the experience. What could be its importance? Write the meaning in one or two sentences. (You can give more than one interpretation if you want.)

- A Korean boy, Jae Rhee, and his family moved to neighborhood (last year). Not in U.S. long, but Jae's English pretty good.
- Jae and I partners for science experiments so get to know him a little. Jae's shy but tries to do his part in everything. Like him, try to be friendly.
- The Rhees open small store. I go in, Jae's unpacking fruit, says hi. When I pay for milk, Jae's mother looks away (I'm smiling at her), puts change on counter, not in my hand. Feels odd, but forget it.

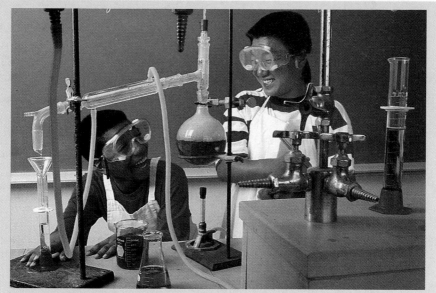

- Happens more (with Mr. Rhee too). Other people—kids *and* parents—start to talk. "Rhees unfriendly. Rude. Think they're better." Feel funny around Jae; just do experiments, don't talk.
- Rhees' store not doing well. One day Jae's not in school—they've moved, new people in store. Surprised, mixed-up feelings.
- Social studies class this year, unit on "cultural differences." Teacher talks about how gestures, feelings about personal space, and respectful behavior differ from one culture to another.

WRITING
ASSIGNMENT

PART 3:
Stating the Meaning of Your Experience

What you've just done for the experience about Jae Rhee, now do for your own experience. Look closely at your notes about main events, thoughts, and feelings, and write one statement of meaning. You can use a simple framework like "I realized that ___," or "At first, I ___, but afterward I ___."

Organizing Your Ideas

The natural order for the events of a narrative is *chronological:* what happened first, second, third, and so on. The notes you've made should already be in chronological order, but check to be sure. Do all the events follow in sequence, so that a reader can move easily from one to another?

 **REFERENCE NOTE:** For more help with chronological order, see pages 82–83.

WRITING NOTE
Are there exceptions to the rule of chronological order? Yes. You might start at the end of your experience and then "flash back" to its beginning. For example, in a narrative about losing your ring, you could first describe yourself on hands and knees, under the bleachers, searching for it. After painting that interesting scene for readers, you could explain—in chronological order—how you got there.

"And so you just threw everything together? ... Mathews, a posse is something you have to *organize*."

Writing Your First Draft

The Structure of Your Personal Narrative

Like other essays, personal narratives have three parts: *introduction, body,* and *conclusion.* You use the introduction—one or two paragraphs—to grab your readers' attention (usually with specific details) and to supply background information: What do readers need to know about people, places, or events to understand your experience? Your introduction may also let your readers know the experience you're going to tell about has a certain importance. It's not just another story.

In the body, you present events in chronological order. To connect these events clearly for readers, you can use transitional words like *at first, then,* and *finally.*

In the conclusion (again, maybe only one paragraph), you bring your essay to a close by explaining the meaning of your experience. But that doesn't mean tacking on a moral—"I learned never to lie"—at the end. It means that the meaning should be obvious to the reader because of the way you've portrayed the experience.

☞ REFERENCE NOTE: For more help on writing the introduction, body, and conclusion, see pages 122–132.

As you write, remember that—to have a strong impact on readers—a personal narrative

- relates an experience that meant something to you
- describes in specific, sensory detail the events, people, and places important to the experience
- explores your thoughts and feelings
- explains the experience's meaning for you

These elements are basic, but in the hands of different writers, they still produce unique results. In the following narrative, Annie Dillard recalls a childhood incident that still moves her as an adult. As you read, remember that the writer wants you to live through the experience with her. Do you?

A PASSAGE FROM AN AUTOBIOGRAPHY

from An American Childhood
by Annie Dillard

INTRODUCTION
Feelings/ Meaning of experience

Summary of experience

BODY
Event 1
Sensory details

Thoughts and feelings
Sensory details

Event 2

Background details

At school I saw a searing sight. It turned me to books; it turned me to jelly; it turned me much later, I suppose, into an early version of a runaway, a scapegrace. It was only a freshly hatched Polyphemus moth crippled because its mason jar was too small.

The mason jar sat on the teacher's desk; the big moth emerged inside it. The moth had clawed a hole in its hot cocoon and crawled out, as if agonizingly, over the course of an hour, one leg at a time; we children watched around the desk, transfixed. After it emerged, the wet, mashed thing turned around walking on the green jar's bottom, then painstakingly climbed the twig with which the jar was furnished.

There, at the twig's top, the moth shook its sodden clumps of wings. When it spread those wings — those beautiful wings — blood would fill their veins, and the birth fluids on the wings' frail sheets would harden to make them tough as sails. But the moth could not spread

Detail

its wide wings at all; the jar was too small. The wings could not fill, so they hardened while they were still crumpled from the cocoon. A smaller moth could have spread its wings to their utmost in that mason jar, but the Polyphemus moth was big. Its gold furred body was almost as big as a mouse. Its brown, yellow, pink, and blue wings would have extended six inches from tip to tip, if there had been no mason jar. It would have been big as a wren.

Sensory details

Event 3

Details

The teacher let the deformed creature go. We all left the classroom and paraded outside behind the teacher with pomp and circumstance. She bounced the moth from its jar and set it on the school's asphalt driveway. The moth set out walking. It could only heave the golden wrinkly clumps where its wings should have been; it could only crawl down the school driveway on its six frail legs. The moth crawled down the driveway toward the rest of Shadyside, an area of fine houses, expensive apartments, and fashionable shops. It crawled down the driveway because its shriveled wings were glued shut. It crawled down the driveway

Sensory details

Details

Sensory details

Background details

toward Shadyside, one of several sections of town where people like me were expected to settle after college, renting an apartment until they married one of the boys and bought a house. I watched it go.

CONCLUSION

Thoughts

Details

Feelings

Event 4

Feelings

Meaning of experience

I knew that this particular moth, the big walking moth, could not travel more than a few more yards before a bird or a cat began to eat it, or a car ran over it. Nevertheless, it was crawling with what seemed wonderful vigor, as if, I thought at the time, it was still excited from being born. I watched it go till the bell rang and I had to go in. I have told this story before, and may yet tell it again, to lay the moth's ghost, for I still see it crawl down the broad black driveway, and I still see its golden wing clumps heave.

EXERCISE 3 ▶ **Analyzing a Personal Narrative**

Read the essay about the crippled moth (pages 156–158), and then meet with two or three classmates to discuss these questions.

1. In this experience, the main actor is the moth, and the writer is an observer. What are the events that Annie Dillard describes?
2. Dillard is known for using precise, fresh words to describe both things and feelings. Find a sensory detail about the moth and a detail about feelings that you especially liked—or were surprised by.
3. Where does Dillard work background, or helpful explanations, into her essay? What do you learn?
4. Dillard tells us the importance of the experience in her first paragraph. What do you think the moth meant to her?
5. Dillard reveals the meaning of the experience again at the end of the narrative. How does she do that without tacking on a moral?

A Basic Framework for a Personal Narrative

Annie Dillard is a professional writer, and as you saw, she's experienced enough to make her writing more than a little bit out of the ordinary. But when you're learning to write a personal narrative, a simpler model may help. The following narrative shows a good framework for your writing.

A WRITER'S MODEL

The Diving Lesson

INTRODUCTION   Without admitting it to myself, I always seemed to live in the shadows of my older brother and sister. After all, they were "A" students, popular leaders in every club. Whenever I met new people, they'd say, "Oh, you're Elizabeth and Gerald's younger sister!" I liked the attention, but it had a bad side, too. You see, I made average grades, had a few friends instead of hundreds, and was too shy even to join a club. Secretly, I always suspected people wondered how in the world we could be from the same family.

Background information

Feelings

Details

Thoughts

BODY
Event 1   But something magical happened when I turned twelve. That June, my parents began taking the family to a local community center. We could swim, play games, and visit with other families. Actually, though, I'm not sure what my brother and sister did during those hot summer days at the center, because for the first time in my life I was too busy doing my own thing.

Foreshadowing of meaning

Details

Sensory detail

Every day I watched three or four kids practice their dives: jackknives, swan dives, half gainers. I memorized all the names, studied all their moves, and imagined I was the one springing high in

Details

Thoughts

the air, twisting gracefully, cutting into the water without a splash. Instead I did plain dives from the pool's edge. The board was for pros.

Sensory details

Event 2

Then one day it happened. The lifeguard and diving coach, a college student who swam like he'd been born in the water, called to me just as I surfaced from a dive. "Why don't you do that off the board?" he asked. "I could teach you some others." If Brian hadn't been so friendly, I might have tried to escape. But instead I found myself on the board, knees like mashed potatoes, the pool noises just a roar in my head. There was no place to go but in--head first.

Details

Feelings

Sensory details

Event 3

"See?" Brian said afterward. "You're a natural." That was the right thing to say, then, because I needed praise. But this "natural" never worked so hard in her life. At first instead of perfect, splashless dives, I took a lot of water slaps in the face. Eventually, though, I was not just graceful but good enough for the center's team. Meanwhile my parents thought I was "playing at the pool."

Thoughts

Feelings

Sensory details

Thoughts

Event 4

My mother still likes to tell the next part of this story. One Saturday, she and Dad and my brother and sister were eating lunch at the center's picnic area when they heard my name blared over a loudspeaker. Here Mother always says, "We thought you had drowned!" But by the time they ran to the pool, the announcements were about a diving and swimming meet. However, their shock wasn't over: There was their younger daughter, poised confidently on the board, waiting to execute her first competition dive.

Details

Sensory detail

Feelings

Details

CONCLUSION

And what a dive it was! I didn't win any medals in that meet, but I did get my picture in the newspaper (a clean swan dive from the <u>high</u> board) and had the reward of my parents' amazed and proud faces. Looking back, I realize now that my

Details

Feelings
Thoughts

Meaning of experience

parents didn't need "proof" to think I was worth something. I did. I needed an accomplishment all my own, and diving was it. From then on, I felt like a person, not a shadow.

As you begin to write your first draft, you may find it helpful to model your essay on "The Diving Lesson." It uses the following pattern, or framework. (Notice how the framework allows you to add both events and details about these events according to what's most important in your experience.)

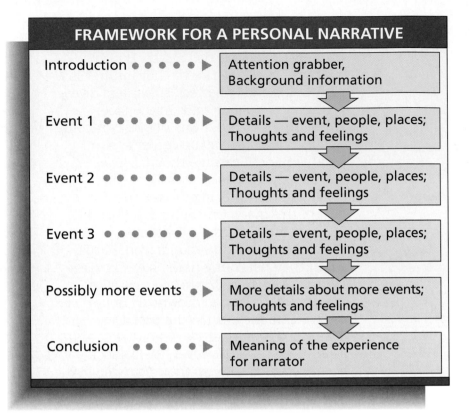

FRAMEWORK FOR A PERSONAL NARRATIVE

Introduction • • • • • ▶	Attention grabber, Background information
Event 1 • • • • • • • ▶	Details — event, people, places; Thoughts and feelings
Event 2 • • • • • • • ▶	Details — event, people, places; Thoughts and feelings
Event 3 • • • • • • • ▶	Details — event, people, places; Thoughts and feelings
Possibly more events • ▶	More details about more events; Thoughts and feelings
Conclusion • • • • • ▶	Meaning of the experience for narrator

WRITING ASSIGNMENT

PART 4:
Writing a Draft of Your Personal Narrative

You have events, you have details, you have a meaning. Now put them all together, sentence by sentence, so that readers can share your experience with you. Using your prewriting notes and following the framework above, write a rough draft.

"A writer's material is what he cares about."

John Gardner

Evaluating and Revising

You've just been the writer. Now you have to be a reader. A help in making this about-face is to set your draft aside for a while (to rest from your writer role). Doing this isn't so unusual. Many writers—including some famous ones—rely on reading their drafts as a start on revising them. Ernest Hemingway, for example, says this about rereading and revising (what he calls "editing") his work:

> I rise at first light and I start by rereading and editing everything I have written to the point I left off. That way I go through a book I'm writing several hundred times. Most writers slough off the toughest but most important part of their trade—editing their stuff, honing it and honing it until it gets an edge like a bullfighter's killing sword. One time my son Patrick brought me a story and asked me to edit it for him. I went over it carefully and changed one word. "But, Papa," he said, "you've only changed one word." I said: "If it's the right word, that's a lot."
>
> Ernest Hemingway, *Writers on Writing*

To evaluate and revise your own work, you can use the following chart. If you find a problem indicated in the left-hand column, use the revision technique suggested in the right-hand column.

The Granger Collection, New York.

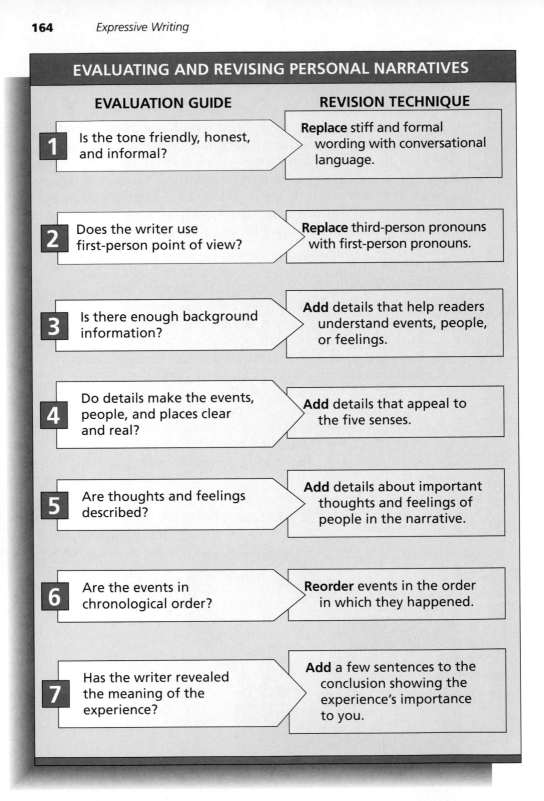

EVALUATING AND REVISING PERSONAL NARRATIVES

EVALUATION GUIDE	REVISION TECHNIQUE
1 Is the tone friendly, honest, and informal?	**Replace** stiff and formal wording with conversational language.
2 Does the writer use first-person point of view?	**Replace** third-person pronouns with first-person pronouns.
3 Is there enough background information?	**Add** details that help readers understand events, people, or feelings.
4 Do details make the events, people, and places clear and real?	**Add** details that appeal to the five senses.
5 Are thoughts and feelings described?	**Add** details about important thoughts and feelings of people in the narrative.
6 Are the events in chronological order?	**Reorder** events in the order in which they happened.
7 Has the writer revealed the meaning of the experience?	**Add** a few sentences to the conclusion showing the experience's importance to you.

Reminder

When you evaluate and improve your narrative, make sure it

- begins with an attention-grabbing introduction
- includes clear transitions between events and paragraphs
- uses a variety of sentences

EXERCISE 4 ▶ **Analyzing a Writer's Revisions**

Study the writer's revision of the fifth paragraph in "The Diving Lesson" (pages 159–161). Then answer the questions that follow the paragraph.

"See?" Brian said afterward. "You're a

natural." That was the right thing to say,

⌊*because I needed praise.*⌋

then, but this "natural" never worked so   **add**

hard in her life. Eventually, though, ~~she~~ *I*   **replace**

was not just graceful but good enough for   **reorder**

the center's team. At first instead of perfect   **add** ⌈*splashless*⌉

took a lot of water slaps in the face., *Meanwhile*

dives, I ~~did pretty bad ones.~~ My parents   **replace/add**

thought I was "playing at the pool."

1. Why did the writer add *because I needed praise* in the third sentence? Do you think breaking this sentence into two sentences is a good idea? Why or why not?
2. Why did the writer move the sentence beginning *Eventually, though . . .*? How does this help the meaning?
3. In the same sentence, what's the reason for replacing *she* with *I*?
4. Why did the writer replace *did pretty bad ones* with *took a lot of water slaps in the face*? What's the effect of the change?
5. Why did the writer add *splashless* to the next-to-the-last sentence and *meanwhile* to the last sentence?

EXERCISE 5 ▶ **Evaluating a Personal Narrative**

The following paragraph ends a narrative about losing a ring—a gift from the writer's grandmother. In a small group, evaluate the paragraph and suggest changes to improve it. Use the guidelines on page 164.

> I thought seeing my grandmother's sorrowful face would be the hardest part of the whole experience. What the guilty girl learned was different. My grandmother, gentle and soft-voiced, wasn't upset about her nice ring. She got it when she was nineteen. What she said made a big impression on me. My fear was really hardest.

GRAMMAR HINT

Using Action Verbs

Action verbs express action, both physical and mental: *She **dances** like a pro and **knows** the new styles.* Action verbs are important in a personal narrative because your whole subject is action of one kind or another: events, thoughts, and feelings. Make them as precise and vivid as possible.

EXAMPLES   I **sprang** high in the air, **twisted** gracefully, and **cut** into the water without a splash.

☞ REFERENCE NOTE: For more information on action verbs, see pages 524–525.

WRITING ASSIGNMENT

PART 5:
Evaluating and Revising Your Personal Narrative

Now, judge and improve your own paper. Use the chart on page 164 to evaluate and revise your narrative.

Proofreading and Publishing

Carefully proofread your essay for mistakes in grammar, punctuation, and spelling, and publish it in some way. Here are two suggestions.

- Read your paper to the class. Practice reading out loud beforehand, so that you can read with expression and look up from the page.
- Make a performing script from your narrative for a readers' theater, a class skit, or a video.

WRITING ASSIGNMENT

PART 6:
Proofreading and Publishing Your Personal Narrative

Read your paper for errors, fix them, and then publish your essay, using the ideas listed above or your own.

 Reflecting on Your Writing

To include your essay in your **portfolio,** date your paper and attach a reflection answering the following questions.

- How did you decide which details to include?
- How did you make the meaning of the essay clear?
- What was the easiest part of writing this essay? Why?

"Most of the basic material a writer works with is acquired before the age of fifteen."

Willa Cather

A STUDENT MODEL

Hilary Hutchinson, a student from Enterprise, Alabama, thought it was hard to decide what to write about in her personal narrative but says that "after I started writing, it got easier to finish the paper."

The Current
by Hilary Hutchinson

It was a beautiful day at Panama City Beach. The gulf was like a huge lake. No waves were to be seen. My brother Blair and I had our floats and were ready to relax in the calm water. My mom sat in the sand while Blair and I ran to the water.

We were floating in the sun when I noticed we were drifting out too far. I saw that I could not touch the bottom. With Blair holding on to my foot, I tried to paddle with my arms, but we were not going anywhere. A current was taking us out to sea!

My mom motioned for us to come closer, but when I was too busy paddling to wave back, she knew something was wrong. With all her clothes on, she jumped into the water to swim to us.

Finally she got there. Blair fell off his float and luckily landed on the edge of mine. His float was swept away by the strong current. With all the energy my mom and I had left, we pulled the float with Blair on it back to shore. Sitting in the sand, we looked out onto the water. Blair's float was a little dot where the sky meets the water. A chill went down me as I thought that Blair and I would have been that far out.

Blair and I are very careful now when we swim. We are also thankful. The week after our incident two men drowned in that same current. People need to learn to be careful and watch what they are doing. I just hope they do not have to learn the hard way as Blair and I did.

Imagining a Utopia

You've looked at the personal narrative as a form of expressive writing. Another form of expressive writing is creating a **utopia.** Long before Sir Thomas More coined the word *utopia* in 1516 (it means "no place" in Greek), people have imagined and expressed in writing their personal, perfect places or worlds. Sometimes they propose a model for the future, and sometimes their utopias are expressed in stories.

One early believer in a utopia was the writer H. G. Wells. (He also wrote *The War of the Worlds* that so terrified Americans when Orson Welles broadcast it on the radio in 1938.) In 1905, Wells described his version of utopia in the book *A Modern Utopia.* In this excerpt, Wells describes transportation in the ideal society. As you read, think about Wells's predictions of his future utopia. How right or wrong was he?

from A Modern Utopia
by H. G. Wells

Such great tramways as this will be used when the Utopians wish to travel fast and far; thereby you will glide all over the land surface of the planet; and feeding them and distributing from them, innumerable minor systems, clean little electric tramways I picture them, will spread out over the land in finer reticulations, growing close and dense in the urban regions and thinning as the population thins. And running beside these lighter railways, and spreading beyond their range, will be the smooth minor high roads such as this one we now approach, upon which independent vehicles, motorcars, cycles, and what not, will go. I doubt if we shall see any horses upon this fine, smooth, clean road; I doubt if there will be many horses on the high roads of Utopia, and, indeed, if they will use draught horses at all upon that planet. Why should they? Where the world gives turf or sand, or along special tracts, the horse will perhaps be ridden for exercise and pleasure, but that will be all the use for him; and as for the other beasts of burthen, on the remoter mountain tracks the mule will no doubt still be a picturesque survival, in the desert men will still find a use for the camel, and the elephant may linger to play a part in the pageant of the East. But the burthen of the minor traffic, if not the whole of it, will certainly be mechanical. This is what we shall see even while the road is still remote, swift and shapely motorcars going past, cyclists, and in these agreeable mountain regions there will also be pedestrians upon their way. Cycle tracks will abound in Utopia, sometimes following beside the great high roads, but oftener taking their own more agreeable line amidst woods and crops and pastures; and there will be a rich variety of footpaths and minor ways. There will be many footpaths in Utopia. There will be pleasant ways over the scented needles of the mountain pinewoods, primrose-strewn tracks amidst the budding thickets of the lower country, paths running beside rushing streams, paths across the wide spaces of the corn land, and, above all, paths through the flowery garden spaces amidst which the houses in the towns will stand. And everywhere about the world, on road and path, by sea and land, the happy holiday Utopians will go.

1. How accurate was Wells's prediction about "clean little electric tramways" that would spread out over the country?
2. In 1905, most transportation was provided by the horse. What was Wells's prediction about the horse? How accurate was he?
3. What role does Wells visualize nature playing in Utopia? Would Utopians be more or less a part of nature than people are today?

Describing a Personal Utopia

Prewriting. Think of something that really matters to you about life in your community or city, the United States, or the world. (You may want to brainstorm about education, environment, government, transportation, male/female roles, or art to find a specific focus.) Then, concentrating on your topic, imagine the utopia, or perfect world, you would want to see one hundred years from now. Use any comfortable prewriting technique to generate details. (See pages 24–34 for more information on prewriting techniques to use.)

Writing, Evaluating, and Revising. There's no set form or length for a personal expression of a utopia. But in this exercise, write informally and describe the utopia in the present tense, as if it actually exists ("No cars clog the streets as electric monorails speed by high overhead.") If possible, have someone read your draft. Can the reader picture your world? make sense of how it works or what it contains? Look for changes that will make the utopia more "real."

Proofreading and Publishing. After you check for errors and correct them, see if you and your classmates can combine your utopias into a single society. Give it a name; find or draw pictures of places, vehicles, and people; write the music that people listen to. Then, through a skit or practiced readings of your papers, present what life is like in your utopia.

Date your paper to add it to your **portfolio,** and attach a brief written reflection that summarizes how you selected appropriate details to illustrate your utopia.

MAKING CONNECTIONS

SELF-EXPRESSION ACROSS THE CURRICULUM

Science

Animals fascinate people. Whether the setting is a swamp where scientists observe the rare Florida crocodile, or the backyard where your sister watches a nest of wrens, human beings spend some important moments with their furred, feathered, slippery, and hard-shelled friends.

Aldo Leopold was an observer of nature. In this excerpt from *A Sand County Almanac*, he narrates the performance of a male woodcock. As you read, notice the specific details that make the bird's flight seem real.

Sky Dance
by Aldo Leopold

I owned my farm for two years before learning that the sky dance is to be seen over my woods every evening in April and May. Since we discovered it, my family and I have been reluctant to miss even a single performance.

The show begins on the first warm evening in April at exactly 6:50 P.M. The curtain goes up one minute later each day until 1 June, when the time is 7:50. This sliding scale is dictated by vanity, the dancer demanding a romantic light intensity of exactly 0.05 foot-candles. Do not be late, and sit quietly, lest he fly away in a huff.

The stage props, like the opening hour, reflect the temperamental demands of the performer. The stage must be an open amphitheater in woods or brush, and in its center there must be a mossy spot, a streak of sterile sand, a bare outcrop of rock, or a bare roadway. Why the male woodcock should be such a stickler for a bare dance floor puzzled me at first, but I now think it is a matter of legs. The woodcock's legs are short, and his struttings cannot be executed to advantage in dense grass or weeds, nor could his lady see them there. I have more woodcocks than most farmers because I have more mossy sand, too poor to support grass.

Knowing the place and the hour, you seat yourself under a bush to the east of the dance floor and wait, watching against the sunset for the woodcock's arrival. He flies in low from some neighboring thicket, alights on the bare moss, and at once begins the overture: a series of queer throaty *peents* spaced about two seconds apart, and sounding much like the summer call of the nighthawk.

Suddenly the peenting ceases and the bird flutters skyward in a series of wide spirals, emitting a musical twitter. Up and up he goes, the spirals steeper and smaller, the twittering louder and louder, until the performer is only a speck in the sky. Then, without warning, he tumbles like a crippled plane, giving voice in a soft liquid warble that a March bluebird might envy. At a few feet from the ground he levels off and returns to his peenting ground, usually to the exact spot where the performance began, and there resumes his peenting.

It is soon too dark to see the bird on the ground, but you can see his flights against the sky for an hour, which is the usual duration of the show. On moonlight nights, however, it may continue, at intervals, as long as the moon continues to shine.

At daybreak the whole show is repeated. In early April the final curtain falls at 5:15 A.M.; the time advances two minutes a day until June, when the performance closes for the year at 3:15. Why the disparity in sliding scale? Alas, I fear that even romance tires, for it takes only a fifth as much light to stop the sky dance at dawn as suffices to start it at sunset.

What animal has made a strong impression on you? Write a personal narrative about your encounter(s) with that animal. What was the importance of what happened? What can you generalize from it? Write one paragraph or more, using details to make this animal, what happened, and what you felt come alive for readers.

5 USING DESCRIPTION

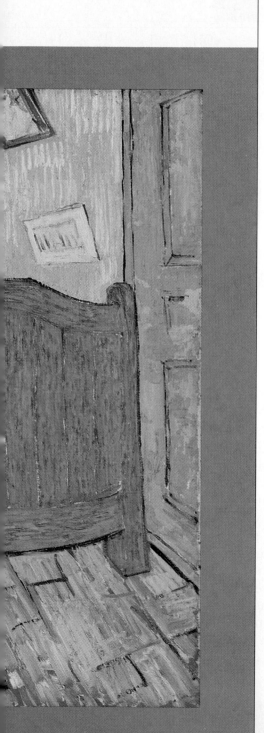

Creating Pictures and Images

One way to explain what something looks like is to show a picture of it. Another way is to **create a picture or image** with words.

Writing and You. When you read a novel, you feel closer to the main character when you picture what he or she looks like. When you read about the sea, a foreign land, or a mysterious setting, images begin to form in your head. Like painters—Van Gogh, for example—writers help you form these images by appealing to your senses. They bring them to life with their words. Have you ever tried to describe your room to someone who has never seen it?

As You Read. In the following selection, Daniel D. Morrison describes a castle in Romania. As you read, notice how he uses sensory details to bring the scene to life.

Vincent van Gogh, *The Bedroom at Arles* (1888). Oil on canvas, 29 1/2" × 37". The Art Institute of Chicago, Helen Birch Bartlett Memorial Collection, 1926.417. Photograph © 1996, The Art Institute of Chicago. All rights reserved.

from

"DATE WITH DRACULA"

by Daniel D. Morrison

racula once stood on the steps where I was now standing. I backed slowly away from the castle door and sat on a large rock overlooking the castle grounds. It was nearly dark now. The trees glared silently but shook their branches with malevolent intent; the rocks all around me squatted like black gnomes. A mist began to fall down upon the valley, wrapping the mountains in a dirty gray shroud. Below me, on the hillside, the leaves rustled; someone, or something walked toward me. Then it stopped. Was it watching, waiting?

My fears now rising uncontrollably, I decided to return to the shop below to join Monique. But as I turned to walk down the trail, I could hear someone coming up the trail toward me, so I called out, no more than a whisper. "Monique?" There was no answer, but the steps continued their steady advance on the gravel trail. I called again; again, no answer. I backed up to where the hilltop ended in a precipice. I could retreat no farther.

"There was nothing I could do, nowhere to run, no one to help me."

Whoever it was—whatever it was—continued to approach, hidden from view by the boulders strewn among the trees. I stood waiting, the sound of my heart competing with the excited voices in the forest.

Slowly, steadily, a low dark form rounded a boulder and crested the hill. A dog, all broad shoulders and massive muscles, walked toward me, its head hung low to the ground, its eyes staring directly at me. It had thick, black fur, with a wide muzzle, lips curled back just slightly with the hint of a snarl. It walked with purpose in its steps, the stare malicious. The animal blocked my only avenue of escape. There was nothing I could do, nowhere to run, no one to help me.

As the dog neared, I could hear its labored breath, could see the drool on its jowls, the white of its pointed canine fangs. Its eyes locked onto mine and never blinked. This, I thought, has to be a nightmare. The voices in the trees grew louder, then hushed as if in anticipation of what was about to happen. The creature walked to within a few feet of where I stood, and it seemed I could feel the heat of its moist breath on my face, on my neck. Then it stopped.

READER'S RESPONSE

1. Do Morrison's descriptions seem real and believable to you? Why? How do they make you feel?
2. Like Morrison, have you ever been frightened by your own imagination? (Why not swap stories with your classmates?)

WRITER'S CRAFT

3. What are five specific details from the description that appeal to your senses of sight or hearing?
4. Descriptive writers sometimes use personification— giving human qualities to nonhuman objects—to help tell about a scene or an incident. How does Morrison use personification to describe trees and rocks?
5. Connotations—the emotional overtones—of words are often important in descriptions. In Morrison's description of the dog, what are some words that especially make you see and feel the author's terror?

Uses of Description

Descriptive writing usually has a primary purpose. This is true whether the author is trying to present an accurate description of something real or a picture that reveals his or her feelings or beliefs. The author carefully chooses details that support the primary purpose. There are many uses of description. Here are some examples.

- in a newspaper article, describing the grand opening of a music store with a high-tech interior
- in a report for an archaeologist, describing the landscape and finds at a dinosaur dig in Colorado
- in your journal, writing about a school or community event that particularly affected you
- in a letter to the editor, describing the success of a fund-raising dinner
- in an article for a city magazine, describing the effects of pollution on a specific lake or river to persuade people to clean up the environment in the region
- in a letter to the city council, describing a neglected area of town to convince council members to improve conditions
- in a short story, creating the setting and describing the characters
- in a poem, re-creating the sights and sounds of a storm that caused boats to break loose from their moorings
- in a memorandum to your supervisor, describing the tasks that need to be accomplished on a new project

If you pick up a brochure at a travel agency, you'll find a description of faraway lands. If you read the sports section of your local newspaper, you'll find descriptions of specific plays made by the players of various sports. If you look for them, you'll find descriptions around you everywhere—in novels, in encyclopedias, in news stories, in poems, in biographies, even in textbooks. Descriptions, if they are effective, have one thing in common—they "paint a picture" in the mind of the reader.

LOOKING AHEAD

In the main part of this chapter, you'll write a description that is subjective. Your primary purpose will be expressive or creative. Keep in mind that descriptive writing

- uses precise words
- provides sensory details that re-create in the mind of your reader a person, place, thing, or event
- is organized in a manner that is easy to follow

"*Don't describe it. Show it. That's what I try to teach all young writers – take it out! Don't describe a purple sunset, make me see that it is purple.*"

James Baldwin

Writing a Description

Prewriting

Focusing Your Description

Have you ever been in a movie audience when the picture became fuzzy, and the audience began to chant "Focus! Focus!"? Like a clear, sharp movie image, a good description also needs a focus. Before you write, bring your description into focus by thinking about your subject, your purpose and audience, and your attitude toward the subject.

Choosing a Subject

Many times outside circumstances decide the subject of your description for you. For example, if you were involved in an accident, you'd need to describe the damage for an insurance claim. Or, your history teacher might ask you to describe conditions that led up to the French Revolution.

But if the choice of a subject is yours, it's a good idea to think of a specific person, object, or place that you already know well or that you can observe directly.

Thinking About Purpose and Audience

At times, good description stands on its own. For instance, you may just want to recapture a specific moment for your journal. More often, however, good description is used for a specific *purpose,* as an important part of other types of writing. For example, if you're writing to inform your chemistry teacher about the results of your lab experiment, part of your report might be a description of the color, texture, and odor of the resulting solution. Or, if you're writing a letter to the editor urging an all-school, anti-litter campaign, your most convincing support might be a detailed description of the bleachers after last Saturday's game.

Your *audience* for a description is usually very closely tied to your purpose. As you think about why you're writing your description, consider your readers by asking:

- Who is going to read this?
- Why are they reading it?
- What do I want my audience to think, feel, do, or know after reading my description?

Once you know why you're writing a description and who your audience is, you'll also know whether your description should be *objective* or *subjective*.

Objective Description. An *objective description* creates an accurate, thorough picture without revealing a particular judgment or feeling about the subject. You write this kind of description when your purpose is to inform and sometimes to persuade. Objective description consists mostly of realistic, or factual, details, as this short description of a starfish shows.

A typical starfish has five arms, one of which is slightly bent. Its surface is etched with small nodules. Many starfishes are a uniform color, a pale mustard yellow.

Subjective Description. A *subjective description* creates a selective picture that reveals the writer's thoughts and feelings about the subject. When your purpose is to express yourself, to be creative, and sometimes to persuade, you will probably write a subjective description. Subjective description consists mostly of sensory details and figurative language (see pages 191–194), as this second starfish description on the next page shows.

> When I look at the starfish skeleton on the table, it almost seems alive. It's like a little man, his head bent slightly as he looks at me and points with one hand back to the sea where I found him.

Deciding on Tone

You also focus your description by deciding on an appropriate tone. In an objective description, you usually use a more formal, impersonal tone. To remain more distant from your subject, you usually use the ***third-person point of view***—pronouns such as *it, she, he,* and *they.* Like the writer of the objective description about the starfish, you aren't in the picture at all—you remain separate from it, never revealing your own thoughts and feelings.

In a subjective description, you often use an informal, personal tone to bring yourself close to the subject. Like the writer of the subjective starfish description, you put yourself in the picture by including your own thoughts and feelings. In this case, you use first-person pronouns such as *I* and *we*—the ***first-person point of view.*** (In some instances, such as writing a description to persuade an audience, you may choose a third-person point of view instead.)

Charting the decisions you make now can help you focus your description as you continue developing it. For example, if your subject is the black-necked crane of Asia, you might record your decisions this way.

HERE'S HOW

SUBJECT:	black-necked crane of Asia
PURPOSE:	for a news editorial; to persuade others to help save the crane
AUDIENCE:	students, teachers, general public
POINT OF VIEW:	third person
TONE:	personal
TYPE:	subjective

Saving the
Black-necked Crane

EXERCISE 1 ► **Analyzing Purpose, Audience, and Tone**

Read this description about an unusual dog named Elizabeth. Then answer the questions that follow.

I named the dog Elizabeth. Height: about thirty inches. Weight: thirty-five pounds. Eyes: brown. Tongue: red. Tail: rich and plumy. A coat of pure china white, so thick and lustrous and profuse that people would later suggest that I shear her and turn the output into a serape. In the summer she shed badly. In the winter, worse. All my clothes and furniture were coated with a fine layer of white flax. When she was young, her tummy was as pink as a baby's bottom, and she had a marvelous, doggy smell, clean, pungent, yet sweet. Her personality? All I can say is that when the Lord made her, he forgot to add any malice, guile, or aggressiveness. Didn't chase squirrels, even. If another dog attacked her, she would roll over on her back immediately and expose her soft underbelly, clearly conveying the message: "Go ahead and kill me. I don't mind, but I think it would be a totally unnecessary waste of energy. But hey, just my opinion." Not once in her life was she hurt by any living creature.

> Elizabeth was not smart, but she made the most of it. "She's the sweetest dog in the world," said a friend about her. "But she's got an IQ somewhere between a brick and a house-plant." . . . For all intents and purposes, she was mute: Not a bark, yelp, nor whimper escaped her. In fourteen years, I heard her voice maybe three times. It was always a shock.
>
> Stanley Bing, "The Most Beautiful Girl in the World"

Illustration by
Blair Drawson.

1. What is the author's purpose: to express himself, to inform, or to persuade the reader to do or believe something? How can you tell?
2. Who do you think is the writer's audience? Why would they be reading this description?
3. What is the writer's tone? How does he feel about his subject?
4. What point of view does the writer use?
5. Is the description objective or subjective? How can you tell?

WRITING ASSIGNMENT

PART 1:
Developing a Subject for Your Description

The writer of the description you've just read wrote about his dog. Now, choose a specific person, place, or object as the subject for your own subjective description. Then, fill out a chart like the one on page 183, recording your ideas about your subject, purpose, audience, point of view, tone, and type.

Prewriting

Planning Your Description

Have you ever arrived at the library without your library card or shown up for a test without a pencil? Anyone making an extra trip to retrieve the library card or to find a pencil probably has vowed to plan ahead next time. In writing a description, planning ahead means collecting details, determining an emphasis for your description, and organizing details. It will be time well spent.

Collecting Details

An effective description is made up of specific details. You can collect these details in several ways.

Observing Directly.   If you're writing about something you can observe firsthand, go directly to the source and study your subject carefully. For example, if you're describing your bicycle for a newspaper classified ad, look at the bike carefully. What is the exact color? Is the seat leather or vinyl—smooth or textured? How tall is it?

Recalling.   Sometimes your description may be about a subject you've seen before but can't observe directly now. Then, you have to tap into all the little details stored in your memory. Imagine yourself back in the time when

you were actually observing your subject. For example, you might describe your experience last year at the Indianapolis 500 auto race. To re-create the scene, you would try to remember the sights (mobs of people), the sounds (loud roar of engines), and the smells (oil and grease).

Researching.   Sometimes you may have to describe a subject you haven't experienced directly. In this case, you can gather details from other sources: books, magazines, pictures, audiovisual materials, or interviews. For example, you might collect details about undersea sights and sounds by watching a Jacques Cousteau film. You might collect details on George Washington's life and appearance by reading an encyclopedia article, biography, or collection of letters and by observing his portraits.

Imagining.   Description can move beyond the boundaries of reality. To create a description of an imaginary person, place, or object, begin with what you know. For example, you know the features you'd identify in describing a real person. To create an imaginary one, just create the details in your mind—for a man, you'd decide on the color of his hair, the shape of his nose, the way he walks, stands, sits, talks, and so on.

Identifying an Emphasis

At times you may want to describe all parts of your subject. At other times you may want to create a special *emphasis,* or impression. For example, if you're trying to persuade your classmates to save the sandhill crane, you may want to emphasize its beauty. In this case, you would probably gather details about how the sandhill crane looks in majestic flight. However, you'd probably omit the loud penetrating noise that the crane makes. Or, in describing your dog, you may want to emphasize its friendliness. Details such as "sparkling eyes" and "thumping tail" would support this impression, but "muddy paws" or "matted fur" would not.

Decide whether you want your description to convey a particular impression, and, if so, what it will be. Then evaluate the details you've gathered to decide which ones support that impression.

EXERCISE 2 ▶ **Collecting Details**

Using the following steps, exercise your collecting skills on the subject of shoes.

1. Observe one of the shoes you're wearing now.
2. Recall how your shoe looked when it was new.
3. Research a shoe. Read up on high-button shoes or the latest trends in athletic shoes.
4. Imagine the "perfect" shoe: design and describe the "perfect" shoe for a specific purpose or for a special outfit.

On your paper, make a copy of the following chart. Use it as a guide for collecting as many kinds of details about shoes as you can. You probably won't fill in all the spaces.

HERE'S HOW

	Sight	Hearing	Smell	Touch
Observing				
Recalling				
Researching				
Imagining				

EXERCISE 3 ▶ Speaking and Listening: Collecting Details

Another way to gather details when you can't observe directly is to interview someone who has. To gather details about shoes teenagers once wore, interview a parent or an older friend or relative about their shoes when

they were your age. Ask questions about style and appearance, but also ask for details related to other senses as well. For example, how did the shoes sound when the person walked down the sidewalk?

WRITING ASSIGNMENT ✏

PART 2:

Collecting Details and Finding an Emphasis

Now that you're experienced in collecting details, concentrate on details for the subject you selected in Writing Assignment, Part 1 (page 185). List as many details about your subject as you can, using any of the techniques for gathering details: observing, recalling, researching, and imagining. If you feel it's appropriate, decide on an emphasis or impression you'd like to convey, too.

Organizing Details

You can create a vivid picture and highlight your emphasis by presenting details in a clear order. Spatial order, order of importance, and chronological order are three possibilities for doing this. The order that you actually use will depend on your purpose for writing and how you want your readers to feel or think.

TYPE OF ORDER	WHEN TO USE	EXAMPLE
spatial (from top to bottom, from side to side, from near to far)	primarily for sight details; to show how details are located in space	describe how a building looks from top to bottom or from left to right
importance (from least to most important, from most to least important)	for all types of details; to identify emphasis or to convey an idea or impression	describe sounds in the woods on a dark night, loudest to softest
chronological (time order)	for all types of details; to show the order in which events or actions occur	describe a crying child as she begins to cry and then gets louder and louder

👉 REFERENCE NOTE: For more information on the types of order, see pages 82–85.

Reminder

To plan your description

- observe, recall, research, or imagine your subject
- identify an emphasis or impression you want to convey
- arrange your details in a clear order

WRITING ASSIGNMENT

PART 3:
Organizing Details

Look carefully at the list of details you gathered in Writing Assignment, Part 2 (page 189). Thinking about your purpose, audience, and emphasis, decide on the best way to present your details. Add, subtract, or change any details that don't fit your plan. When you've finished, number the details in the order you think you'll be using them in your description.

Writing Your First Draft

Now that you've collected and organized details for your description, it's time to write your first draft.

To create a clear image of your subject, you need to select specific words. For example, when the writer William Least Heat-Moon describes a room lighted by "three fifty-watt bulbs," you know exactly how much and what kind of light there was. When you describe how the sun reflects off a new car, *glinted* gives your readers a more specific picture than *shone*.

Good descriptions include specific adjectives, adverbs, nouns, and verbs that appeal to your senses. They may also include comparisons that help you understand the subject and give you new insights. When Virginia Woolf describes sea anemones "stuck like lumps of jelly to the side of the rock," you understand how a sea anemone looks even if you haven't seen one firsthand.

Using Descriptive Language

Sensory Words. When you write, words and phrases that appeal to the senses make your observations come alive for your readers. Whenever possible, use the precise sound—*roared*, or *twittered*, or *cawed*; or touch—*icy* or *slimy*; or taste—*bitter* or *sour*; or smell—*rotten* or *sweet*. If you don't have a name for a smell, or a taste, or a touch, just name the source of the observation—"the scent of freshly baked bread."

Using a Word Bank. Sometimes writers keep lists of words, or word banks, to refer to when they're looking for just the right word. It's a little like having their own specialized thesaurus. Here's a word bank of sensory words you might refer to when you're writing descriptions.

A SENSORY WORD BANK		
SIGHT WORDS		
Appearance		
frail	glossy	flushed
sturdy	slender	muscular
pale	portly	angular
tapered	swollen	shapely
Color		
ivory	ebony	crimson
rose	hazel	canary
bronze	raven	pearl
milky	bleached	azure
SOUND WORDS		
boom	roar	rasp
whine	shriek	screech
hum	mutter	sigh
growl	snort	whimper
SMELL WORDS		
fragrant	earthy	spoiled
stench	piney	musty
flowery	stale	fresh
TOUCH WORDS		
cool	icy	fuzzy
oily	silky	velvety
gritty	sandy	slippery
TASTE WORDS		
sweet	tart	salty
tangy	sour	bittersweet
spicy	bitter	mellow

William Least Heat-Moon wrote a book about his travels on America's side roads. As you read this paragraph, notice how he re-creates what he observed through his senses.

> The old store, lighted only by three fifty-watt bulbs, smelled of coal oil and baking bread. In the middle of the rectangular room, where the oak floor sagged a little, stood an iron stove. To the right was a wooden table with an unfinished game of checkers and a stool made from an apple-tree stump. On shelves around the walls sat earthen jugs with corncob stoppers, a few canned goods, and some of the two thousand old clocks and clockworks Thurmond Watts owned. Only one was ticking; the others he just looked at.
>
> William Least Heat-Moon, *Blue Highways*

Although William Least Heat-Moon's description appeals most to his readers' sense of sight, it also includes details of sound ("ticking") and smell ("coal oil" and "baking bread"). The sensory words you use will vary depending upon your subject and emphasis. But remember that for both you and your readers, your five senses usually work together in creating an impression.

Figurative Language.   To describe a person or object, you often make a comparison: "He acts just like his older brother." When you use *figurative language* (sometimes called figures of speech), you are also comparing. But, instead of comparing similar things, you're comparing *unlike* things that share one basic feature. Because the comparison is so unusual, it catches your audience's attention. Here's an example:

> A tightly smoothed *quilt* of brown, green, and gold blanketed *South Dakota*.

The basic feature South Dakota and a quilt have in common is that they are flat and have alternating colors. Otherwise, they are very unlike things and make for an unusual comparison.

Used wisely, figurative language can help your readers' understanding by linking a familiar image with an unfamiliar one: *"Looking like a harmless drifting log, a crocodile can float unnoticed toward its prey."* As the following chart shows, figurative language may express comparisons in several ways.

TYPE OF FIGURATIVE LANGUAGE	EXAMPLE
A **simile** uses the words *like* or *as* to make the comparison.	The loud music shielded me like a crash helmet.
A **metaphor** makes a direct comparison.	The loud music was my crash helmet, protecting me from outside forces.
Personification gives human characteristics to things.	The fist of loud music pounded all thought from my mind.

CRITICAL THINKING

Making Comparisons

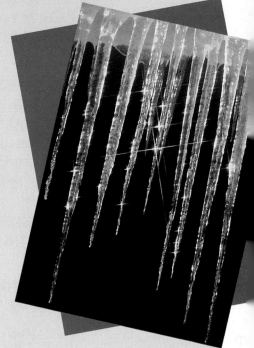

If you're lucky, a fresh, creative comparison may occur to you as a sudden inspiration. Usually, though, you have to devote some effort to looking at reality in a new way.

To create a unique figure of speech, analyze the parts of your subject carefully. If you're describing a melting icicle, the drip may remind you of tears: *The dripping icicles were crying over their own departure.* Or, the icicle's shape may remind you of a sword: *The icicle is winter's sword.*

CRITICAL THINKING EXERCISE:
Making Comparisons

Stretch your imagination. Create at least three original metaphors or similes by comparing an item from Column A with an item from Column B. Write a sentence expressing your comparison, adding descriptive words or phrases as you wish.

EXAMPLE *The frightened child clung like a stamp to its mother.*

Column A	Column B
fog	sand
puppy	stamp
sailboat	leaf
bicycle	ball
child	tablecloth

With overuse, figurative language loses all its freshness and originality and becomes stale and worn out. These worn-out expressions (for example, "cool as a cucumber" or "busy as a bee") are called *clichés.* Try to avoid them in your writing.

A Model for Description

Ann Petry created the following description for the opening of a novel. As you read, notice the specific words that appeal to various senses and emphasize a harsh, desolate feeling. Look for the writer's use of figurative language as she makes the wind seem human.

A PASSAGE FROM A NOVEL

from The Street
by Ann Petry

Personification

There was a cold November wind blowing through 116th Street. It rattled the tops of garbage cans, sucked window shades out through the top of opened windows and set them flapping back against the windows; and it drove most of the people off the street in the block between Seventh and Eighth Avenues except for a few hurried pedestrians

Sight detail

who bent double in an effort to offer the least possible exposed surface to its violent assault.

Specific details

It found every scrap of paper along the street—theater throwaways, announcements of dances and lodge meetings, the heavy waxed paper that loaves of bread had been wrapped in, the thinner waxed paper that had enclosed sandwiches, old envelopes, newspapers. Fingering its way along the curb, the wind set the bits of paper to dancing high in the air, so that a barrage of paper swirled into the faces of the people on the street. It even took time to rush into doorways and areaways and find chicken bones and pork-chop bones and pushed them along the curb.

It did everything it could to discourage the people walking along the street. It found all the dirt and dust and grime on the sidewalk and lifted it up so that the dirt got into **Touch detail** their noses, making it difficult to breathe; the dust got into their eyes and blinded them; and the grit stung their skins. It wrapped newspaper around their feet entangling them **Sound details** until the people cursed deep in their throats, stamped their feet, kicked at the paper. The wind blew it back again and again until they were forced to stoop and dislodge the paper with their hands. And then the wind grabbed their hats, pried their scarves from around their necks, stuck its fingers inside their coat collars, blew their coats away from their bodies.

> The wind lifted Lutie Johnson's hair away from the back of her neck so that she felt suddenly naked and bald, for her hair had been resting softly and warmly against her skin. She shivered as the cold fingers of the wind touched the back of her neck, explored the sides of her head. It even blew her eyelashes away from her eyes so that her eyeballs were bathed in a rush of coldness and she had to blink in order to read the words on the sign swaying back and forth over her head.

EXERCISE 4 ▶   **Analyzing a Description**

1. Where does Petry announce the subject of her description?
2. Petry uses many details that emphasize the wind's violent nature. What are some of these details?
3. From the second sentence on, Petry *personifies* the wind—making it seem human—when she says that "it rattled the tops of garbage cans." What are other examples where the writer personifies the wind?
4. Petry uses many sight details in this description. What are three or four sound details that she uses? Touch details?
5. Have you ever been in a heavy, violent wind like the one Petry describes? Do you think her description is accurate? Would you add or change anything in her description?

A Writer's Model for You

Ann Petry is a professional writer who imagines specific details right down to two different types of wax paper—"heavy" and "thinner." Most of the time you'll be observing or recalling details from experience. But like Ann Petry, you can also create a specific word picture by using figurative language and sensory details. As you write your own description, you might follow this shorter model—it describes a place like one you might know.

A WRITER'S MODEL

Subject
Emphasis

Sound detail
Sight detail

Simile

Touch detail

Smell details

Sight details

Writer's feeling

Whenever I'm hungry for a snack, I head for Angela's Pizza Place, just around the corner from school. Angela's is quite a place. It looks as though it's been there forever. On the outside, there's an ancient neon sign that buzzes and flickers against the peeling white paint on the red brick wall. Inside, an antique espresso machine sits like a brass robot guarding the front door. And on the shiny dining room walls, bright colors reflect off the fake Tiffany lamps hanging over every booth.

Each time I turn the greasy doorknob to open Angela's front door, the first thing that greets me is a wonderful warm cloud of pizza odors. My mouth starts to water as the cheese and garlic aromas embrace me. While I wait for my order, I usually watch the chef in the kitchen, tossing dough, pouring sauces, putting pies in the oven, and cutting slices. As entertaining as the airborne saucers of dough are, though, no one comes to Angela's for the sights alone. My first bite of hot melted cheese always reminds me of exactly why I come here.

WRITING
ASSIGNMENT

PART 4:
Writing Your First Draft

Remember that the two models above have been revised and proofread. No one expects your first draft to be perfect. Write a paragraph or two on the subject you've been developing. Include details you've gathered, but don't hesitate to include details that occur to you as you write.

COMPUTER NOTE: If you're writing on a computer, use bold-face, italics, or underlining to mark words you plan to revise.

Evaluating and Revising

Evaluating. Now that you've drafted your description, it's time to evaluate it—to judge it for both strengths and weaknesses, to see what works and what doesn't.

Revising.   If you identify any problems, revise by making the changes that will improve your paper. To do so, ask yourself the questions in the left-hand column in the chart on the next page. Then, if you identify a particular problem, use the suggestions in the right-hand column as a guide for revising.

Shoe reprinted by permission: Tribune Media

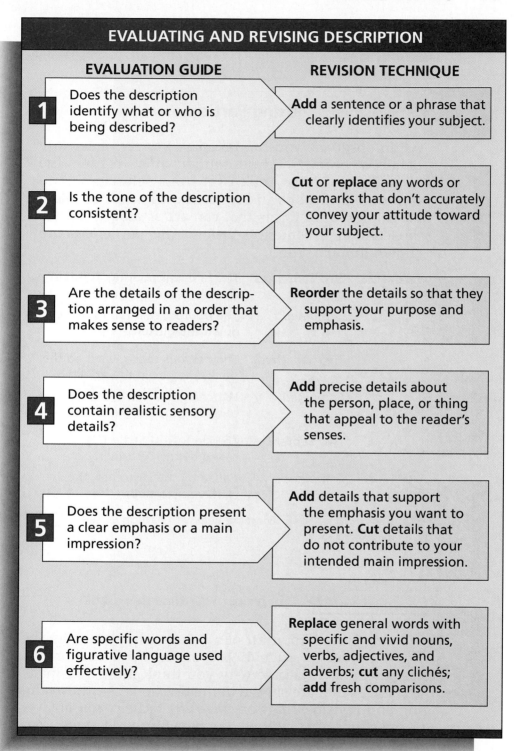

EVALUATING AND REVISING DESCRIPTION

EVALUATION GUIDE | **REVISION TECHNIQUE**

1 Does the description identify what or who is being described?

> **Add** a sentence or a phrase that clearly identifies your subject.

2 Is the tone of the description consistent?

> **Cut** or **replace** any words or remarks that don't accurately convey your attitude toward your subject.

3 Are the details of the description arranged in an order that makes sense to readers?

> **Reorder** the details so that they support your purpose and emphasis.

4 Does the description contain realistic sensory details?

> **Add** precise details about the person, place, or thing that appeal to the reader's senses.

5 Does the description present a clear emphasis or a main impression?

> **Add** details that support the emphasis you want to present. **Cut** details that do not contribute to your intended main impression.

6 Are specific words and figurative language used effectively?

> **Replace** general words with specific and vivid nouns, verbs, adjectives, and adverbs; **cut** any clichés; **add** fresh comparisons.

GRAMMAR HINT

Using Participles

As an observer, you can take in a variety of sensory details at once. Good description offers readers the same opportunity. Look over your sentences. You can combine actions and concentrate images by using participles, verb forms that can act as adjectives. (In the combined sentences below, the participles are shown in italic type.)

EXAMPLES

Two Sentences	The rain was pouring. It ran in rivulets down the gutter.
Combined	The *pouring* rain ran in rivulets down the gutter.
Two Sentences	The nervous coach watched the clock. She paced the sidelines.
Combined	*Watching* the clock, the nervous coach paced the sidelines.
Two Sentences	The clerk was startled. He was called by the customer.
Combined	*Called* by the customer, the clerk was startled.

👉 REFERENCE NOTE: For more help with participles, see pages 579–580.

E X E R C I S E 5 ▶ **Analyzing a Writer's Revisions**

Following is the first draft of a paragraph taken from the writer's model on page 199. Working with one or two classmates, try to decide why you think the writer made the changes that are shown in the revision. Use the evaluating and revising chart on page 201 to help you answer the questions that follow the paragraph. Discuss your responses with your classmates.

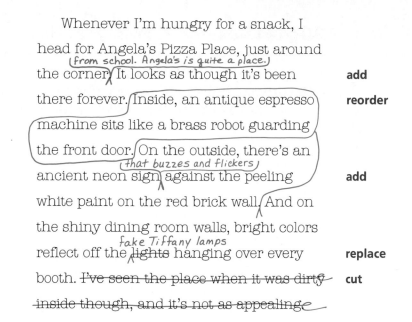

Whenever I'm hungry for a snack, I head for Angela's Pizza Place, just around the corner. (from school. Angela's is quite a place.) It looks as though it's been **add**

there forever. Inside, an antique espresso **reorder** machine sits like a brass robot guarding the front door. On the outside, there's an ancient neon sign (that buzzes and flickers) against the peeling **add**

white paint on the red brick wall. And on the shiny dining room walls, bright colors reflect off the fake Tiffany lamps ~~lights~~ hanging over every **replace**

booth. ~~I've seen the place when it was dirty~~ **cut**
~~inside though, and it's not as appealing.~~

1. Why did the writer add the words *from school* to the first sentence?
2. Why did the writer rearrange the order of the third and fourth sentences? What type of order does the paragraph now have?
3. Why did the writer add the words *that buzzes and flickers* to the description of the neon sign?
4. Why did the writer replace the word *lights* with *fake Tiffany lamps* in the next-to-last sentence?
5. Why did the writer cut the last sentence? [Hint: Review page 187].

WRITING ASSIGNMENT

PART 5:

Evaluating and Revising Your Description

Now try evaluating and revising your own description. Exchange descriptions with a classmate and evaluate each other's work. Next, go over your own paper, using the chart on page 201 as a guide. Think carefully about your classmate's suggestions and your own evaluation. Then, make any changes that will improve your description.

Proofreading and Publishing

Proofreading.   Polish your description by proofreading carefully so that your readers "see" your subject rather than any distracting errors.

Publishing.   When your polished description is ready for a wider audience, try these two suggestions to reach some readers.

- If your classmates are familiar with your subject, read your description aloud to them without naming your subject. Then ask classmates to identify your subject. If they guess correctly, ask them which details were most helpful in uncovering its identify.
- Submit your description to the school newspaper or literary magazine.

| **WRITING** |
| ASSIGNMENT |

PART 6:
Proofreading and Publishing

Let your readers "see" your subject by proofreading your description carefully, one line at a time, and correcting any errors. Then use one of the suggestions you've just read or one of your own to share your work with an audience.

Reflecting on Your Writing

To add your description to your **portfolio,** date your paper, and attach a brief written reflection prompted by these questions:

- What method helped you collect descriptive details for this assignment?
- Which part of the essay do you think is most vivid, and why?
- What main impression does your description make? Is that impression the one you intended to convey?

A STUDENT MODEL

In talking about her description, Alissa Bird says what she found hardest to do was "to get all the grammar correct" and "to write in a certain form." Nevertheless, Alissa—a student at Crestwood High School in Roswell, Georgia—vividly describes a person and a place important to her.

The Wise Lady
by Alissa Bird

I saw my great-grandmother for the first time when I was about seven years old. She was sitting in her blue quilted armchair with a copy of Reader's Digest in her small, soft, wrinkly hands. Blue veins protruded from her transparent skin. When she heard the banging of the screen door, she got up and scooped me up into her arms and planted a big kiss on my cheek.

The one thing that sticks out in my mind is her pink bathroom where everything was always spotless. The entire bathroom was pink: the towels, the carpet, the walls, the bathtub, and even the bottle of bubble bath on the rim. I also remember the mysterious winding stairs that went up to the unknown rooms. When I got the chance to explore the upstairs, I remember how the stairs creaked like a haunted house.

I can still hear the chirp of the birds in the backyard by the huge vegetable garden she always kept weedless. The sound of an oven buzzer reminds me of the times when I was at her house and her buzzer would go off. When she opened the oven door, the delicious aroma of chocolate chip cookies would fill the air.

I will forever remember the long summers I spent with that wise old lady. I will always remember how we took walks around the town and to the grocery store just about every day I was there. My great-grandmother taught me about real life and that life is what you make it. She has been a real inspiration to me, and I hope that when I have grandchildren of my own I can inspire them just as much.

WRITING WORKSHOP

A Free Verse Poem

A good description captures and expresses an image, feeling, or idea by using specific sensory detail. Free verse poetry also does this—but in a condensed way. When you write free verse poetry, you usually don't have a regular pattern of rhythm and rhyme. Instead, you arrange words in each line according to your natural speech patterns. And, as in a good subjective description, you use sensory details and figurative language.

The following free verse poem is about a plant that grows in the American West. Its name comes from the way the plant breaks off near the ground and tumbles over and over as the wind blows it.

Tumbleweed
by David Wagoner

Here comes another, bumping over the sage
Among the greasewood, wobbling diagonally
Downhill, then skimming a moment on its edge,
Tilting lopsided, bouncing end over end
And springing from the puffs of its own dust
To catch at the barbed wire
And hang there, shaking, like a riddled prisoner.

Half the sharp seeds have fallen from this tumbler,
Knocked out for good by head-stands and pratfalls
Between here and wherever it grew up.
I carry it in the wind across the road
To the other fence. It jerks in my hands,
Butts backwards, corkscrews, lunges and swivels,
Then yaws away as soon as it's let go,
Hopping the scrub uphill like a kicked maverick.
The air goes hard and straight through the wires and weeds.
Here comes another, flopping among the sage.

1. What sensory words does the poet use to show the actions or behaviors of the tumbleweeds?
2. What two similes does the poet use? How do they affect your feelings about the tumbleweeds?
3. Read the poem once as it is written, recognizing the line breaks. Then, read it again as though it were a paragraph, pausing for punctuation but ignoring the line breaks. What is the effect of the change?
4. If you read this poem on a symbolic level, what kinds of people might the tumbleweed represent?

Writing a Free Verse Poem

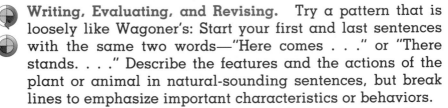

Prewriting. Many plants and animals have characteristics that remind us of people in general or of particular people. Brainstorm or freewrite to think of a plant or animal that has some interesting similarities to human beings. Then, use these questions to gather details for your poem:

- What are the most obvious characteristics, behaviors, or actions of the plant or animal you have identified?
- What features of the plant or animal could be compared to someone you know or to people in general?
- What sensory details could you include to highlight those features? visual details? details of sound?
- What similes would give your subject human qualities?

Writing, Evaluating, and Revising. Try a pattern that is loosely like Wagoner's: Start your first and last sentences with the same two words—"Here comes . . ." or "There stands. . . ." Describe the features and the actions of the plant or animal in natural-sounding sentences, but break lines to emphasize important characteristics or behaviors.

Read your poem aloud and see if your ideas are clear. Then, ask someone else to read your poem. Use your evaluation and your reader's feedback to revise your poem.

Proofreading and Publishing. Check the final copy of your poem. Are you satisfied with its presentation on the page? If your school has a literary magazine, consider submitting your poem. Or plan a poetry reading with classmates. Date your poem, and attach to it a brief reflection about the difference between prose and poetic description. Include both papers in your **portfolio.**

MAKING CONNECTIONS

COMBINING DESCRIPTION WITH NARRATION

Description is narrative's comfortable companion. In a narrative, the story's actions come alive through the descriptions of the people, places, objects, and feelings they involve.

Many people think Ernie Pyle was America's best war correspondent during World War II. Notice how he combines narration with description in the following dispatch from the front lines of Africa in 1943.

from Ernie's War: The Best of Ernie Pyle's World War II Dispatches
by Ernie Pyle

"A narrow path comes like a ribbon over a hill miles away, down a long slope, across a creek, up a slope and over another hill.

"All along the length of this ribbon there is now a thin line of men. For four days and nights they have fought hard, eaten little, washed none, and slept hardly at all. Their nights have been violent with attack, fright, butchery, and their days sleepless and miserable with the crash of artillery.

"The men are walking. They are 50 feet apart, for dispersal. Their walk is slow, for they are dead weary, as you can tell even when looking at them from behind. Every line and sag of their bodies speaks their inhuman exhaustion.

"On their shoulders and backs they carry heavy steel tripods, machine-gun barrels, leaden boxes of ammunition. Their feet seem to sink into the ground from the overload they are bearing.

"They don't slouch. It is the terrible deliberation of each step that spells out their appalling tiredness. Their faces are black and unshaven. They are young men, but the grime and whiskers and exhaustion make them look middle-aged.

"In their eyes as they pass is not hatred, not excitement, not despair, not the tonic of their victory—there is just the simple expression of being here as though they had been here doing this forever, and nothing else.

"The line moves on, but it never ends. All afternoon men keep coming round the hill and vanishing eventually over the horizon. It is one long tired line of antlike men."

Pyle reported events as he saw them, but his descriptive details help you to "see" them too. What figure of speech does Pyle use when he describes the line of moving men? What is Pyle's overall emphasis in his description of the soldiers? What details in his writing support this impression?

Until he was killed by a sniper's bullet in 1945, Pyle filed six newspaper columns a week for his thirteen million readers. He rarely reported the war's events on a "grand scale." Instead, Pyle's subjects were usually individual soldiers and their stories. Some of his best columns are collected in books, including *Ernie's War: The Best of Ernie Pyle's World War II Dispatches.* You might like to find one of these books and read about the very human face of war. Then share your reading in an oral report to your classmates.

DESCRIPTION ACROSS THE CURRICULUM

Objective Description in Science

Description in the sciences informs its readers about exact observations. Notice the realistic, factual details and specific words in the following description of a crocodile.

A crocodile is an aquatic, meat-eating reptile that has lived in the warmer parts of this earth for about 135 million years. It is often called a "living fossil" because scientists believe that it looks pretty much the same now as it originally did. It has thick, tough, dark green skin stretched over an armor of bony plates. A crocodile's long triangular snout contains forty to sixty razor-sharp teeth set in sockets in each jawbone. When the snout is closed, these teeth interlock, with two very large ones sticking out from the lower jaw. With eyes and nostrils on top of its head, the crocodile can see, breathe, and smell, while hiding most of its body under the often cloudy swamp water.

Is this an objective or subjective description? How can you tell? Reread the subjective description of the dog described on pages 184–185. Keeping the same subject, write a paragraph of objective description, as though you were describing the dog for a science report. (Remember that scientists take pride in using accurate, realistic details.)

6 CREATIVE WRITING: NARRATION

Imagining Other Worlds

Think about what life would be like without **imagination**—how boring it would be. Imagination takes us where we can never go in real life. It propels us into **other worlds** where things are whatever we want them to be.

Writing and You. Using their imaginations, writers write stories we never tire of reading and hearing—novels, mysteries, science fiction, children's stories. Some writers write about things that never were and never will be, yet they seem real because they play on our imaginations. Other writers start with real events and use their imaginations—and ours—to make them into something entirely new. How much do you use your imagination?

As You Read. In the following story, Marta Salinas writes about an event that seems believable to anyone who has faced unfairness. How is her story real? How is it fiction?

Julian Baum, *Ships of the Long Range Pioneer Fleet* (1985). Mixed media, 12" × 16". Science Photo Library/ Photo Researchers, Inc.

The small Texas school that I attended carried out a tradition every year during the eighth-grade graduation; a beautiful gold and green jacket, the school colors, was awarded to the class valedictorian, the student who had maintained the highest grades for eight years. The scholarship jacket had a big gold S on the left front side, and the winner's name was written in gold letters on the pocket.

My oldest sister Rosie had won the jacket a few years back and I fully expected to win also. I was fourteen and in the eighth grade. I had been a straight-A student since the first grade, and the last year I had looked forward to owning that jacket. My father was a farm laborer who couldn't earn enough money to feed eight children, so when I was six I was given to my grandparents to raise. We couldn't participate in sports at school because there were registration fees, uniform costs, and trips out of town;

THE
SCHOLARSHIP
JACKET

by Marta Salinas

so even though we were quite agile and athletic, there would never be a sports school jacket for us. This one, the scholarship jacket, was our only chance.

In May, close to graduation, spring fever struck, and no one paid any attention in class; instead we stared out the windows and at each other, wanting to speed up the last few weeks of school. I despaired every time I looked in the mirror. Pencil thin, not a curve anywhere, I was called "Beanpole" and "String Bean" and I knew that's what I looked like. A flat chest, no hips, and a brain, that's what I had. That really isn't much for a fourteen-year-old to work with, I thought, as I absent-mindedly wandered from my history class to the gym. Another hour of sweating in basketball and displaying my toothpick legs was coming up. Then I remembered my P.E. shorts were still in a bag under my desk where I'd forgotten them. I had to walk all the way back and get them. Coach Thompson was a real bear if anyone wasn't dressed for P.E. She had said I was a good forward and once she even tried to talk Grandma into letting me join the team. Grandma, of course, said no.

I was almost back at my classroom's door when I heard angry voices and arguing. I stopped. I didn't mean to eavesdrop; I just hesitated, not knowing what to do. I needed those shorts and I was going to be late, but I didn't want to interrupt an argument between my teachers. I recognized the voices: Mr. Schmidt, my history teacher, and Mr. Boone, my math teacher. They seemed to be arguing about me. I couldn't believe it. I still remember the shock that rooted me flat against the wall as if I were trying to blend in with the graffiti written there.

"I refuse to do it! I don't care who her father is, her grades don't even begin to compare to Martha's. I won't lie or falsify records. Martha has a straight-A-plus average and you know it." That was Mr. Schmidt and he sounded very angry. Mr. Boone's voice sounded calm and quiet.

"Look, Joann's father is not only on the Board, he owns the only store in town; we could say it was a close tie and—"

The pounding in my ears drowned out the rest of the words; only a word here and there filtered through. ". . . Martha is Mexican. . . . resign. . . . won't do it. . . ." Mr. Schmidt came rushing out, and luckily for me went down the opposite way toward the auditorium, so he didn't see me. Shaking, I waited

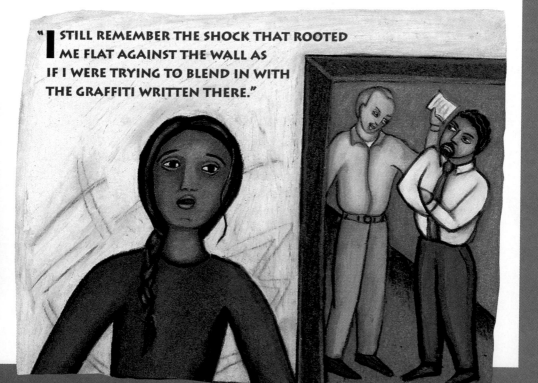

"I STILL REMEMBER THE SHOCK THAT ROOTED ME FLAT AGAINST THE WALL AS IF I WERE TRYING TO BLEND IN WITH THE GRAFFITI WRITTEN THERE."

a few minutes and then went in and grabbed my bag and fled from the room. Mr. Boone looked up when I came in but didn't say anything. To this day I don't remember if I got in trouble in P.E. for being late or how I made it through the rest of the afternoon. I went home very sad and cried into my pillow that night so Grandmother wouldn't hear me. It seemed a cruel coincidence that I had overheard that conversation.

The next day when the principal called me into his office, I knew what it would be about. He looked uncomfortable and unhappy. I decided I wasn't going to make it any easier for him, so I looked him straight in the eye. He looked away and fidgeted with the papers on his desk.

"Martha," he said, "there's been a change in policy this year regarding the scholarship jacket. As you know, it has always been free." He cleared his throat and continued. "This year the Board decided to charge fifteen dollars—which still won't cover the complete cost of the jacket."

"...IF YOU PAY FOR IT, MARTA, IT'S NOT A SCHOLARSHIP JACKET...."

I stared at him in shock and a small sound of dismay escaped my throat. I hadn't expected this. He still avoided looking in my eyes.

"So if you are unable to pay the fifteen dollars for the jacket, it will be given to the next one in line."

Standing with all the dignity I could muster, I said, "I'll speak to my grandfather about it, sir, and let you know tomorrow." I cried on the walk home from the bus stop. The dirt road was a quarter of a mile from the highway, so by the time I got home, my eyes were red and puffy.

"Where's Grandpa?" I asked Grandma, looking down at the floor so she wouldn't ask me why I'd been crying. She was sewing on a quilt and didn't look up.

"I think he's out back working in the bean field."

I went outside and looked out at the fields. There he was. I could see him walking between the rows, his body bent over the little plants, hoe in hand. I walked slowly out to him, trying to think how I could best ask him for the money. There was a cool breeze blowing and a sweet smell of mesquite in the air, but I didn't appreciate it. I kicked at a dirt clod. I wanted that jacket so much. It was more than just being a valedictorian and giving a little thank-you speech for the jacket on graduation night. It represented eight years of hard work and expectation. I knew I had to be honest with Grandpa; it was my only chance. He saw me and looked up.

He waited for me to speak. I cleared my throat nervously and clasped my hands behind my back so he wouldn't see them shaking. "Grandpa, I have a big favor to ask you," I said in Spanish, the only language he knew. He still waited silently. I tried again. "Grandpa, this year the principal said the scholarship jacket is not going to be free. It's going to cost fifteen dollars and I have to take the money in tomorrow, otherwise it'll be given to someone else." The last words came out in an eager rush. Grandpa straightened up tiredly and leaned his chin on the hoe handle. He looked out over the field that was filled with the tiny green bean plants. I waited, desperately hoping he'd say I could have the money.

He turned to me and asked quietly, "What does a scholarship jacket mean?"

I answered quickly; maybe there was a chance. "It means you've earned it by having the highest grades for eight years and that's why they're giving it to you." Too late I realized the significance of my words. Grandpa knew that I understood it was not a matter of money. It wasn't that. He went back to hoeing the weeds that sprang up between the delicate little bean plants. It was a time-consuming job; sometimes the small shoots were right next to each other. Finally he spoke again.

"Then if you pay for it, Marta, it's not a scholarship jacket, is it? Tell your principal I will not pay the fifteen dollars."

I walked back to the house and locked myself in the bathroom for a long time. I was angry with Grandfather even though I knew he was right, and I was angry with the Board, whoever they were. Why did they have to change the rules just when it was my turn to win the jacket?

It was a very sad and withdrawn girl who dragged into the principal's office the next day. This time he did look me in the eyes.

"What did your grandfather say?"

I sat very straight in my chair.

"He said to tell you he won't pay the fifteen dollars."

The principal muttered something I couldn't understand under his breath, and walked over to the window. He stood looking at something outside. He looked bigger than usual when he stood up; he was a tall, gaunt man with gray hair, and I watched the back of his head while I waited for him to speak.

"Why?" he finally asked. "Your grandfather has the money. Doesn't he own a small bean farm?"

I looked at him, forcing my eyes to stay dry. "He said if I had to pay for it, then it wouldn't be a scholarship jacket," I said and stood up to leave. "I guess you'll just have to give it to Joann." I hadn't meant to say that; it had just slipped out. I was almost to the door when he stopped me.

"Martha—wait."

I turned and looked at him, waiting. What did he want now? I could feel my heart pounding. Something bitter and vile tasting was coming up in my mouth; I was afraid I was going to be sick. I didn't need any sympathy speeches. He sighed loudly and went back to his big desk. He looked at me, biting his lip, as if thinking.

"Okay, damn it. We'll make an exception in your case. I'll tell the Board; you'll get your jacket."

I could hardly believe it. I spoke in a trembling rush. "Oh, thank you, sir!" Suddenly I felt great. I didn't know about adrenaline in those days, but I knew something was pumping through me, making me feel as tall as the sky. I wanted to yell, jump, run the mile, do something. I ran out so I could cry in the hall where there was no one to see me. At the end of the day, Mr. Schmidt winked at me and said, "I hear you're getting a scholarship jacket this year."

His face looked as happy and innocent as a baby's, but I knew better. Without answering, I gave him a quick hug and ran to the bus. I cried on the walk home again, but this time because I was so happy. I couldn't wait to tell Grandpa and ran straight to the field. I joined him in the row where he was working and without saying anything I crouched down and started pulling up the weeds with my hands. Grandpa worked alongside me for a few minutes, but he didn't ask what had happened. After I had a little pile of weeds between the rows, I stood up and faced him.

"The principal said he's making an exception for me, Grandpa, and I'm getting the jacket after all. That's after I told him what you said."

Grandpa didn't say anything, he just gave me a pat on the shoulder and a smile. He pulled out the crumpled red handkerchief that he always carried in his back pocket and wiped the sweat off his forehead.

"Better go see if your grandmother needs any help with supper."

I gave him a big grin. He didn't fool me. I skipped and ran back to the house whistling some silly tune.

READER'S RESPONSE

1. A good fiction story, though not true or factual, seems real. Does this story seem real to you? Is it easy to believe that the events in the story actually happened to a young girl? Explain.
2. Is there another way this story could have ended? Might the principal have been more honest? Could the girl have reacted differently to him? Use your imagination and write a new ending for the story.

WRITER'S CRAFT

3. The author uses dialogue and the narrator's thoughts to bring her characters to life. What do you know about the narrator? What do you know about the principal?
4. Every story has some kind of conflict or problem. What is the conflict in this story?

Ways to Write Creatively

A story, like the one you just read and the one you'll write in this chapter, is one way to write creatively. When people write creatively, they produce literature—stories, poems, songs and ballads, plays, and movie and television scripts. The key elements of creative writing are the use of imagination and the use of language in special and unique ways. Here are some ways in which writers develop creative writing.

- in a story, telling about a girl who witnesses events of the American Revolution
- in a movie script, telling the story of a Texas Ranger's life in a frontier settlement
- in a science fiction story, describing the interior of a space station
- in a poem about a festival, describing the smells of the food and the sounds of the games and music
- in a novel that takes place in London and Paris, comparing and contrasting the two cities
- in a poem about a fish, comparing its glistening scales to a kaleidoscope of silver, pink, and green
- in a play, showing how power can corrupt a person who becomes king
- in a story, creating a parody (an amusing imitation) of the fairly tale "Little Red Riding Hood"

LOOKING AHEAD

In the main assignment in this chapter, you'll use narration to write a story. As you work through the chapter, keep in mind that a short story

- has a plot involving a problem or conflict
- may contain characters, settings, plots, and details based on real life
- is developed mostly through the author's own imagination

Writing a Short Story

Prewriting

Exploring Story Ideas

Ideas for stories are everywhere. One way to find an idea is to ask yourself "What if?" questions, much as these writers may have.

- What if a ferocious shark terrorized a beach in the summer?
- What if a selfish Southern belle had to struggle through the Civil War and Reconstruction?
- What if a French nobleman escaped an unjust imprisonment, discovered a fabulous treasure, and sought revenge against his accusers?

Each of these questions inspired a book and then a movie. That's all you need to get started—a spark of an idea that your imagination can nurture and transform into a story.

Where can you find ideas? First, look around you. Notice people, events, places that intrigue you. Recall vivid experiences, crazy dreams, interesting conversations. Anything that interests, horrifies, tickles, or angers you might be an idea just waiting to become a story.

Reminder

To find story ideas, think about

- a journal entry about your first date, touchdown, or A+
- an early memory about a special family holiday
- a picture of your favorite place
- a top-ten list of your worst fears, biggest pet peeves, most embarrassing moments

WRITING ASSIGNMENT

PART 1:
Developing a Story Idea

Ignite your imagination to find a story idea. You might mull over your experiences, flip through photo albums, watch people, or talk to friends. "What if?" questions can jump-start your imagination if you're having a hard time getting started. Keep at it until you find an idea you'd like to develop into a story.

> "What I am trying to achieve is a voice sitting by a fireplace telling you a story on a winter's evening."
>
> Truman Capote

Prewriting

Planning Your Story

With just the spark of an idea, you're ready to start planning your story. Planning involves thinking about purpose, audience, and tone. You'll also be looking at point of view, characters, setting, and plot.

Thinking About Purpose, Audience, and Tone

Your main *purpose* in story writing is to be creative. And since you're the author, you have many opportunities to do so. Your characters, settings, and problems can be whatever you alone decide they should be. But another purpose in story writing is to entertain your *audience*—your readers. So you'll want to keep their interests and knowledge in mind as you plan. What will keep them entertained? Classmates, for example, might enjoy a detailed description of a teenage character's dress. Still another purpose might be to share an idea—about friendship or love, for example. Such an underlying idea is called a *theme.*

Writing stories also gives you flexibility in your tone. *Tone* is the attitude you take towards your characters and the events in your story. And you communicate that tone through the details and words you choose. The tone in your story can be serious, humorous, mysterious, or sarcastic. There are many other tones you can adopt as well.

CRITICAL THINKING

Analyzing Point of View

Point of view means who's telling the story. A story is always told by a narrator (who is not the author). Sometimes the narrator is a character in the story, and sometimes the narrator remains outside the story. You can use the following questions to analyze the point of view.

1. Is the narrator a character in the story? Does the narrator use first-person pronouns like *I* and *me*? Does the narrator express his or her own thoughts and feelings, but not those of other characters? If so, the story has a *first-person point of view.*
2. Is the narrator outside the story and not a character in the story? Does the narrator use third-person pronouns like *he* and *she*? If so, the story has a *third-person narrator.*
3. Does the third-person narrator look at the story through the eyes of *one character only*? This type of narrator can't tell what other characters are thinking or feeling. This is called a *limited narrator.*
4. Can the third-person narrator tell what *everyone* is thinking and feeling? This is called an *omniscient (all-knowing) narrator.*

CRITICAL THINKING EXERCISE:
Analyzing Point of View

What goes through a soldier's mind as he's facing battle? In this excerpt, the narrator describes the feelings of one soldier. The passage is written in the third-person point of view. You're Private Berlin. Working with some classmates, rewrite the passage from the first-person point of view. Use the pronouns *I* and *me*. Make up details if you wish. You might imagine, for example, what it is that Private Berlin is pretending about his camping trip.

> At the rear of the column, Private First Class Paul Berlin lay quietly with his forehead resting on the black plastic stock of his rifle, his eyes closed. He was pretending he was not in the war, pretending he had not watched Billy Boy Watkins die of a heart attack that afternoon. He was pretending he was a boy again, camping with his father in the midnight summer along the Des Moines River. In the dark, with his eyes pinched shut, he pretended.
>
> Tim O'Brien, "Where Have You Gone, Charming Billy?"

Thinking About Characters and Setting

Characters.   Who will be the people in your story? And what will they be like? You can create a completely made-up character, maybe using traits from all different kinds of people. Perhaps you'll create a character who has the humor of Bill Cosby, the looks of Kevin Costner, and the brains of Albert Einstein. Or you might take a person you know and change a few details to fit the character your story needs. Just keep developing details about your characters until you feel you know them well.

Setting.   Stories are always set in a particular time and place. The time and place might be as unusual as nine hundred years ago in a medieval castle in Scotland. Or they can be as ordinary as your back yard last week. When the time and place aren't central to the story, the details of setting may not be very important. But if you want to create a mood—or feeling, such as mystery or suspense—setting can be very important. That's why a ghost story set in an overgrown graveyard on a dark and stormy night is scary. The setting helps the reader feel the mood of mystery and heightens the suspense.

Reminder

Ask yourself the following questions to get ideas for your characters and setting.

Characters:
- How do the characters look, walk, and talk?
- How do they dress?
- How do they stand, move, and sit?
- What do they think about?
- What kind of personality do they have? Are they absent-minded? shy? anxious? bubbly?
- What do other characters in the story think about them?

Setting:
- What's the time and place of the story?
- What kind of houses do people live in at this time?
- What kind of work do they do?
- How important is the time and place to the story?
- Do I want the setting to create a mood, or feeling? What sights, sounds, and smells should I describe?

WRITING ASSIGNMENT

PART 2:
Developing Your Characters and Setting

Can you see your characters in your mind? Do you feel the setting? Write a short paragraph describing your main character with as much detail as you can. Then write another paragraph about your setting. Share your paragraphs with a couple of classmates. Ask them if your character seems real. Can they imagine your setting? What mood does it suggest?

Developing the Plot

What will happen in your story? Does boy meet girl? Does boy lose girl? What happens in a story is called the *plot.* Most plots open with a *conflict,* or problem, that can be either *external* or *internal.*

TYPES OF CONFLICT	
EXTERNAL CONFLICT	**EXAMPLES**
A character faces a conflict with another character or group.	John argues with his father over his curfew.
A character faces a conflict with nature.	As he is on his way home to make his curfew, a heavy rain causes Julio's car motor to die.
INTERNAL CONFLICT	**EXAMPLE**
A character struggles with opposite thoughts and feelings within himself or herself.	Sue wants to stay longer at the party—but she knows she'll be grounded if she breaks her curfew.

After the opening conflict, the plot unfolds in a series of events that build on and cause each other. Will Sally's speeding ticket cause her parents to take away the car? Will she lose her part-time job if she can't drive? *Suspense* builds when readers wonder about what will happen next. Event builds upon event until the main conflict is resolved at the end.

As you develop your plot, think about the order of events. Listing events in the order they happen (chronological order) can help you develop a quick plot outline. You'll also be able to see if the events lead logically to the ending. Maybe your ending is a surprise, but it should still flow naturally from the story's events and characters.

WRITING ASSIGNMENT

PART 3:
Gathering Plot Details

What will happen in your story? What conflict will set the chain of events in motion? What will be the order of events? How will the story end? Jot down your ideas, creating a chain of events that outlines your plot.

Making a Story Map.   As you plot your story's course, you may find it helpful to create a story map. Then you can see how all your story elements fit together. Here's how one writer developed a story map.

POINT OF VIEW:	*Third-person*
CHARACTERS:	*Marie Silvano, 16, only child; excited about getting her driver's license* *Marie's mother, a widow; protective of Marie; afraid for Marie to drive* *Carol, Marie's friend*
SETTING:	*Marie's town, after school, modern times*

PLOT:	<u>*Conflict.*</u> *Marie wants her driver's license so she can drive alone. Marie's mother is afraid of her having an accident and losing Marie. She's told Marie she won't let her drive alone.*
	
	<u>*Events.*</u>
	  (1) Marie's mother arrives late to take Marie to get her license.
	  (2) Marie and her mother argue as they drive to the test.
	  (3) Marie takes the test and passes.
	  (4) Mrs. Silvano won't let her drive home.
	  (5) Mrs. Silvano remembers when her parents didn't trust her.
	
	<u>*Outcome.*</u> *Mrs. Silvano decides she has to trust Marie and lets her take the car.*

WRITING ASSIGNMENT

PART 4:
Developing a Story Map

With the main landmarks for your story almost in place, you're ready to develop a story map. Using all the ideas you've developed so far, create a map for your story. Keep your plan handy as you write your story.

Writing Your First Draft

The Basic Elements of Stories

If you've read many stories, you know they vary widely. Most stories, however, center on effective characters—people who seem so real they almost leap off the pages—and their dialogue.

Writing stories gives you total creative control. You create characters, choose their hair color, decide their fate. While you're being creative, just remember that your readers want a good, suspenseful story. Effective characters and dialogue are sure to keep them reading.

Characters. Think of the people in your story as real. How can your readers get to know them? The answer is simple: the same way they get to know people in real life! Writers can reveal characters by

- telling readers directly what the character is like
- describing how the character looks and dresses
- having the character speak
- revealing the character's thoughts and feelings
- showing how others respond to the character
- showing the character's actions

Dialogue. The dialogue, or talk, of the characters does two important things. First, it shows what kind of people the characters are. Second, it moves the plot along in a natural, interesting way. Following are some questions to ask yourself as you write dialogue.

- Do the words and sentences fit the characters? Do the children talk like children and the adults talk like adults?
- Do the characters sound natural? Do they use phrases, contractions, and slang?
- Does the dialogue show what characters are like and/or move the story along?
- Do the dialogue tags—phrases like "they said," "he groaned," or "she screamed"—identify the speaker and add interest?

COMPUTER NOTE: Some computer programs help you format screenplays and keep track of characters in a story.

EXERCISE 1 ▶ **Speaking and Listening: Evaluating Dialogue**

Here's part of a story about two brothers who manage to argue about everything. The writer hasn't used much dialogue. Get together with three or four of your classmates. See if you can liven up the paragraph by writing convincing dialogue for the characters. Then take turns letting each group read its dialogue aloud. Listen to the different versions, and evaluate the dialogue. Make specific suggestions for improving the dialogue, using the questions on the previous page and above as a guide.

> World War III was just erupting when I walked into the kitchen. Jesse asked Tom if Tom was planning to ignore the full trash can. Tom said it wasn't his turn. After a few heated exchanges, Mom intervened. Then they tried to blame her for the argument. She silenced them both by banishing them to their rooms and taking away their car keys. Mom always was the world's greatest peacemaker.

Looking at a Short Story

The following excerpt is from the story "Spring," by professional writer Italo Calvino. It has a simple plot about a worker who discovers wild mushrooms growing in the city. The main conflict is not directly presented. To discover it, think about what the mushrooms represent to Marcovaldo. [Hint: Remember that one type of conflict can be nature versus man or woman.]

A SHORT STORY

Mushrooms in the city
by Italo Calvino

BEGINNING
Attention grabber

The wind, coming to the city from far away, brings it unusual gifts, noticed by only a few sensitive souls, such as hay-fever victims, who sneeze at the pollen from flowers of other lands.

Setting

One day, to the narrow strip of ground flanking a city avenue came a gust of spores from God knows where; and some mush-

Introduction of main character

rooms germinated. Nobody noticed them except Marcovaldo, the worker who caught his tram just there every morning.

This Marcovaldo possessed an eye ill-suited to city life: billboards, traffic-lights, shop-windows, neon signs, posters, no matter how carefully devised to catch the attention, never arrested his gaze, which might have been running over the desert sands. Instead,

Character development

he would never miss a leaf yellowing on a branch, a feather trapped by a roof-tile; there was no horsefly on a horse's back, no worm-hole in a plank, or fig-peel squashed on the sidewalk that Marcovaldo didn't remark and ponder over, discovering the changes of season, the yearnings of his heart, and the woes of his existence.

MIDDLE

Thus, one morning, as he was waiting for the tram that would take him to Sbav and Co., where he was employed as an unskilled laborer, he noticed something unusual near the stop, in the sterile, encrusted strip of earth beneath the avenue's line of trees; at certain points, near the tree trunks, some bumps seemed to rise and, here and there, they had opened, allowing roundish subterranean bodies to peep out.

Character development/ thoughts

Bending to tie his shoes, he took a better look: they were mushrooms, real mushrooms, sprouting right in the heart of the city! To Marcovaldo the gray and wretched world surrounding him seemed suddenly generous with hidden riches; something could still be expected of life, beyond the hourly wage of his stipulated salary, with inflation index, family grant, and cost-of-living allowance.

On the job he was more absent-minded than usual; he kept thinking that while he was there unloading cases and boxes, in the darkness of the earth the slow, silent mushrooms, known only to him, were ripening their porous flesh, were assimilating underground humors, breaking the crust of clods. "One night's rain would be enough," he said to him-

Suspense

self, "then they would be ready to pick." And he couldn't wait to share his discovery with his wife and his six children.

Character development/ dialogue

"I'm telling you!" he announced during their scant supper. "In a week's time we'll be eating mushrooms! A great fry! That's a promise!"

And to the smaller children, who did not know what mushrooms were, he explained ecstatically the beauty of the numerous species, the delicacy of their flavor, the way they should be cooked; and so he also drew

into the discussion his wife, Domitilla, who until then had appeared rather incredulous and abstracted.

"Where are these mushrooms?" the children asked. "Tell us where they grow!"

Conflict

At this question Marcovaldo's enthusiasm was curbed by a suspicious thought: Now if I tell them the place, they'll go and hunt for them with the usual gang of kids, word will spread through the neighborhood, and the mushrooms will end up in somebody else's

Character development/ thoughts

pan! And so that discovery, which had promptly filled his heart with universal love, now made him wildly possessive, surrounded him with jealous and distrusting fear.

Dialogue— suspense

"I know where the mushrooms are, and I'm the only one who knows," he said to his children, "and God help you if you breathe a word to anybody."

Suspense

The next morning, as he approached the tram stop, Marcovaldo was filled with apprehension. He bent to look at the ground and, to his relief, saw that the mushrooms had grown a little, but not much, and were still almost completely hidden by the earth.

He was bent in this position when he realized there was someone behind him. He straightened up at once and tried to act indifferent. It was the street-cleaner, leaning on his broom and looking at him.

Character development/ description

This street-cleaner, whose jurisdiction included the place where the mushrooms grew, was a lanky youth with eyeglasses. His name was Amadigi, and Marcovaldo had long harbored a dislike of him, perhaps because of those eyeglasses that examined the pavement of the streets, seeking any trace of nature, to be eradicated by his broom.

Conflict

It was Saturday; and Marcovaldo spent his free half-day circling the bed of dirt with an absent air, keeping an eye on the street-cleaner in the distance and on the mushrooms, and calculating how much time they needed to ripen.

That night it rained: like peasants who, after months of drought, wake up and leap with joy at the sound of the first drops, so Marcovaldo, alone in all the city, sat up in bed and called to his family: "It's raining! It's raining!" and breathed in the smell of moistened dust and fresh mold that came from outside.

At dawn — it was Sunday — with the children and a borrowed basket, he ran immediately to the patch. There were the mushrooms, erect on their stems, their caps high over the still-soaked earth. "Hurrah!" — and they fell to gathering them.

Conflict

"Papà! Look how many that man over there has found," Michelino said, and his father, raising his eyes, saw Amadigi standing beside them, also with a basket full of mushrooms under his arm.

Dialogue— suspense

"Ah, you're gathering them, too?" the street-cleaner said. "Then they're edible? I picked a few, but I wasn't sure . . . Farther down the avenue some others have sprouted, even bigger ones . . . Well, now that I know, I'll tell my relatives; they're down there arguing whether it's a good idea to pick them or not . . ." And he walked off in a hurry.

Marcovaldo was speechless: even bigger mushrooms, which he hadn't noticed, an unhoped-for harvest, being taken from him like this, before his very eyes. For a moment he was almost frozen with anger, fury, then —

Character development

as sometimes happens — the collapse of individual passion led to a generous impulse. At that hour, many people were waiting for the tram, umbrellas over their arms, because the weather was still damp and uncertain. "Hey, you! Do you want to eat fried mushrooms tonight?" Marcovaldo shouted to the crowd of

Dialogue— suspense

people at the stop. "Mushrooms are growing here by the street! Come along! There's plenty for all!" And he walked off after Amadigi, with a string of people behind him.

They all found plenty of mushrooms, and lacking baskets, they used their open umbrellas. Somebody said: "It would be nice to have a big feast, all of us together!" But, instead, each took his own share and went home.

OUTCOME

They saw one another again soon, however; that very evening, in fact, in the same ward of the hospital, after the stomach-pump had saved them all from poisoning. It was not serious, because the number of mushrooms eaten by each person was quite small.

Marcovaldo and Amadigi had adjacent beds; they glared at each other.

translated by William Weaver

WRITING NOTE

In this story, the writer doesn't present the conflict immediately. Instead, he begins with descriptions of the setting and of the main character, Marcovaldo. As you read the story, you realized that these descriptions are important to understanding the main conflict. It arises both from the city setting, where mushrooms are seldom found, and Marcovaldo's love of nature.

| E X E R C I S E 2 ▶ | **Analyzing the Organization of a Short Story** |

Meet with a small group of classmates to discuss the answers to the following questions about "Mushrooms in the City."

1. What is the main conflict in the story? What are some minor conflicts?
2. Marcovaldo might seem a little odd to you. How does Calvino make him seem real, despite his quirks? Point to specific examples in the story to explain your answer.
3. How important is the setting? Could the story have happened anywhere else?
4. Were you surprised by the ending? What clues in the story prepare you for the surprise ending?

A Basic Framework for a Story

"Mushrooms in the City" shows how a master of story-telling combines plot, characters, and setting to create several levels of meaning. The following story, which you might want to use as a model for your own, gives you a less complicated model to follow. The conflict in this story is revealed more through events and dialogue.

| A WRITER'S MODEL |

Licensed to Drive

BEGINNING
Event 1
Character development and conflict

"Where is she?" Marie sighed, checking her watch again. "It'd be just like her to forget--on purpose. You know she doesn't want me to do this."

"Calm down," Carol said. "Isn't that your mother's car?" She pointed to the old, blue car making a wide turn into the school parking lot, slowly heading toward the girls.

Dialogue

"Finally. Let me drive," Marie said as her mother pulled up. Marie drove slowly out of the parking lot as Carol gave her the thumbs up sign.

Event 2

Character development/ dialogue Conflict

Background

Event 3

Event 4 Suspense MIDDLE

Character development/ thoughts

Dialogue

Event 5 Character development/ dialogue

"You're fifteen minutes late, Mom," complained Marie.

"I couldn't get out of work earlier," Mrs. Silvano said. "This is too early, if you ask me. You just turned 16! I hope you don't pass. And even if you do, I'm not sure I'll let you drive alone."

Marie shook her head and bit her tongue to keep from speaking back to her mother. She knew this speech; she'd heard it a million times. Her father had been killed by a reckless teenage driver just three years before. Her mother couldn't stand the thought of Marie driving alone and had made that clear.

"I'd be more careful," Marie promised, as she turned into the test site. "You know you can trust me."

Marie was excited when she passed the test so easily, but her mother didn't say a word. When Marie asked to drive home, Mrs. Silvano snapped, "No, it's almost dark."

The ride home was silent and tense. Marie wanted desperately to take the car out, to show Carol, to drive with the windows down and the radio tuned to her favorite rock station. But she knew better than to push her mother now. Mrs. Silvano would only dig her heels in. She tried to think of something to say.

"Carol's brother's getting married."

"Who, Paul?" Mrs. Silvano asked, perking up just a bit.

"Yeah, and Carol's parents are furious. Said he's too young, it won't last, he should wait." Marie sighed, thinking of parents who don't understand their kids.

"Well, he's 20, isn't he? And he finished school? I was young when I married your papa." She smiled, thinking of the memory. "My parents didn't like it one bit, not one bit. But I knew better and I was right, too. He was such a good man, always thoughtful to me, and a wonderful father. We were married and happy for a long time. Marriage lasted 22 years. We'd still be married if he was alive."

238

She choked up and fell silent. Even after three years she couldn't talk about her husband without crying.

Dialogue

"I know, Mom," Marie said. "But not all kids are bad drivers."

"Maybe," grunted Mrs. Silvano, clenching the steering wheel tighter.

Suspense

Marie sighed and closed her eyes. It's hopeless. I'll be the only kid in school with a license who can't drive, she thought.

OUTCOME

They arrived home and got out. As Mrs. Silvano unlocked the front door, she paused as if she had something to say. Then she suddenly jabbed the keys into Marie's hand.

"Don't you want to drive over to Carol's?" she said roughly.

Dialogue

"You mean it, Mom? Really?"

"Well, I guess I have to trust you sometime. Might as well be now. Hearing about Paul made me remember when my parents didn't trust me. But I want you to be careful. Night driving can be tricky. And be back in thirty minutes or no more driving."

Marie gave her a quick hug and jumped in the car. The headlights of the old car shone through the darkness as she drove away.

 PART 5:
Writing a Draft of Your Story

By now you should have a good idea of how your story will develop. Use your prewriting ideas and story map to make your characters, setting, and plot come to life.

Evaluating and Revising

You may want to read your story to others in a small group and then listen to their feedback. You can also use the chart below to help you analyze and improve each other's stories. Ask yourself each question in the left-hand column. If your answer is no, use the revision technique suggested in the right-hand column.

EVALUATING AND REVISING SHORT STORIES

EVALUATION GUIDE	REVISION TECHNIQUE
1 Does a conflict set a chain of events in motion? Is the order of events clear?	**Add** a conflict between characters or within a character. **Reorder** events in the order they happen.
2 Do the events create suspense? Do the actions lead to a logical ending?	**Cut** events that slow the story down. **Add** details that build suspense. **Add** details that prepare for the ending.
3 Are the characters interesting and real?	**Add** details about what the characters do, feel, say, and think. **Add** realistic dialogue.
4 Is the point of view consistent? Is it either first-person or third-person?	**Cut** details that make the point of view inconsistent. **Add** first-person or third-person details as necessary.
5 Does the setting help readers picture the action or establish a mood?	**Add** specific sensory details. **Cut** details that detract from the mood.

EXERCISE 3 ▶ **Analyzing a Writer's Revisions**

Study the writer's revision of the first three paragraphs of the story on pages 236–238. Then, answer the questions that follow the paragraph.

"It'd be just like her to forget--on purpose. You know she doesn't want me to do this." "Where is she?" Marie ~~said~~ *sighed,* checking her watch again.   **replace/ reorder**

"Calm down," Carol said. "Isn't that your mother's car?" She pointed to the *old, blue* car   **add** making a wide turn into the school parking lot, slowly heading toward the girls.

"Finally. Let me drive," ~~I~~ *Marie* said as ~~my~~ *her*   **replace** mother pulled up. Marie drove slowly out of the parking lot as Carol gave her an *the thumbs up sign.* ~~encouraging look.~~   **replace**

1. Why did the writer move the third sentence to the beginning of the paragraph?
2. In the third sentence, why did the writer replace *Marie said* with *Marie sighed*?
3. In the second paragraph, why did the writer add the words *old, blue* before the word *car*?
4. In the last paragraph, why did the writer change the word *I* to *Marie* and the word *my* to *her*?
5. In the last sentence, why did the writer replace *an encouraging look* with *the thumbs up sign*?

WRITING ASSIGNMENT

PART 6:

Evaluating and Revising Your Story

Use feedback from your classmates and the chart on page 239 to revise your story. Like a professional writer, make changes that will make readers want to keep reading.

Proofreading and Publishing

Your story is almost ready, but don't forget to proofread. Once your story is ready, use these ideas for sharing it.

- Publish your stories in a literary magazine.
- If the story involves friends or family members, consider giving or mailing it with a brief note.

MECHANICS HINT

Punctuating Dialogue

Remember these points when proofreading dialogue.

1. Begin a new paragraph when the speaker changes.
2. Use quotation marks around the speaker's words.
3. Separate dialogue tags from the rest of the sentence with a comma, a question mark, or an exclamation point. Begin a new sentence with a capital letter.
4. Do not capitalize the second half of a sentence that is separated by the dialogue tag.

EXAMPLES   "Watch out!" he screamed. "There's a car coming!"
"I'm trying to get out of the way," she shouted, "as safely as I can."

☞ REFERENCE NOTE: For more information on punctuating dialogue, see pages 834–838.

WRITING ASSIGNMENT

PART 7:
Proofreading and Publishing Your Story

You've worked hard on your story, so proofread it carefully. Then publish or share your story with others.

Reflecting on Your Writing

To include it in your **portfolio,** date your story, and attach a short reflection answering the following questions.

- How did you make your characters seem real?
- What details help build suspense in your story?
- How do you think your story will affect readers?

Peanuts reprinted by permission of United Feature Syndicate, In

A STUDENT MODEL

This excerpt of a story about a boy at basketball camp was written by Noah Kramer-Dover, a student in Alexandria, Virginia. Notice how Noah builds event upon event to create suspense.

<u>from</u> Memoirs of an Adolescent
by Noah Kramer-Dover

It was my turn. My stomach sank to the floor. I walked all the way to the other side of the gym, so as to get a long runway. I turned around to face the basket, my team, and the cheerleaders. Everyone was staring at me. I had never felt so small in my whole life. The court had never looked longer. I then stretched my arms and legs, blew into the palms of my hands, wiped the bottom of my shoes, and proceeded to waste as much time as I possibly could.

I was then interrupted by the laughter of my teammates. I looked over and saw they were all doing their own imitations of me. The cheerleaders smirked.

I guessed it was now or never. I started running. When I got to the foul line, I slowed down. I looked at the rim. My left foot hit the floor and I pushed away from the ground. I rose. I was higher than I had ever been before. I was above the rim. I knew I could do it. I cocked my arm back. I slammed the ball through the hoop. My hand grasped the rim and the basket shook. When I came down to the floor, the basket still shook.

I looked around to make sure the ball hadn't flown off the rim. I was on the ground, so my hand had not gotten stuck in the net. I heard some applause. I had dunked it.

The temperature in the gym became quite pleasant to me. The sun seemed to shine a little brighter. I looked to my teammates, who were at half-court. I walked back to them with a little bit of a strut. I then approached one of our guards, Jerome, and said, "I believe it's your turn."

First appeared in *Merlyn's Pen: The National Magazines of Student Writing*.

WRITING WORKSHOP

A News Story

Did you notice the headline in today's newspaper? Maybe it said "Firefighter Rescues Baby" or "Jury Finds Defendant Not Guilty." These headlines summarize real-life stories that unfold every day. A news story is similar to a fictional story in that it usually tells about a conflict or problem. But it's different because it must rely only on facts, not on a writer's imagination, to tell its story.

News stories are usually short and follow a very tight structure. The opening paragraph is called the *lead.* It summarizes the important facts of the story by answering the *5W-How?* questions—*Who? What? When? Where? Why?* and *How?* The rest of the story then fills in the details, with the most important details first. See how the news story below follows this format.

Tornadoes Damage School

MIAMI—Tornadoes smashed windows and doors in an elementary school, injuring a teacher, and ripped through a small airport, damaged homes and tore off a warehouse roof Tuesday.

The first twister touched down near Sylvania Heights Elementary School in West Miami, injuring a teacher caught outside.

"It was a miracle only one person got hurt," Principal Lucy Williams said.

About 30 children under the supervision of the physical education teacher were outside waiting for parents to pick them up at dismissal time when the instructor spotted the oncoming tornado, she said.

Teachers and administrators rushed the children into a corridor moments before the storm hit, but a teacher was caught outside.

"It picked her up and dropped her down, and when she came in she was all covered in mud and had a cut on her forehead," said Williams.

The storm broke out the school's front doors and smashed windows, she said, and tore the tin covering off the roof.

A second tornado ripped through the Pembroke Pines area. Planes at North Perry Airport were overturned and torn apart.

The Ledger, Lakeland, Florida

1. Which *5W-How?* questions does the writer answer in the lead paragraph?
2. What facts do the other paragraphs give you about the tornadoes?
3. Why does the writer quote the principal?
4. Compare the average length of paragraphs in "Mushrooms in the City" (pages 231–235) to the average length of paragraphs in this news story. What is the difference?

Writing a News Story

Prewriting. To start your news story, look for a story that's important to your school or local community. Dig out all the facts of your story by asking *Who? What? When? Where? Why?* and *How?* Keep digging for facts and interviewing people until you know everything you possibly can about your story.

Writing, Evaluating, and Revising. Start your news story with a vivid lead that summarizes the story's important facts. Notice how the story about the tornado uses active verbs like *smashed* and *ripped* in its lead to catch the reader's interest. Then, use short, concise paragraphs to report the story's main facts. Be sure your story portrays the events and people accurately. Whenever possible, use quotes from the people involved. When you evaluate and revise, check the accuracy of your facts and quotes.

Proofreading and Publishing. Proofread your news story carefully for mistakes in grammar and usage. To publish it, consider submitting it to your school or local newspaper. A local radio or TV station might also like the angle a student reporter can give. Date your news story, and attach a reflection to include in your **portfolio:** Is reporting still creative writing? How?

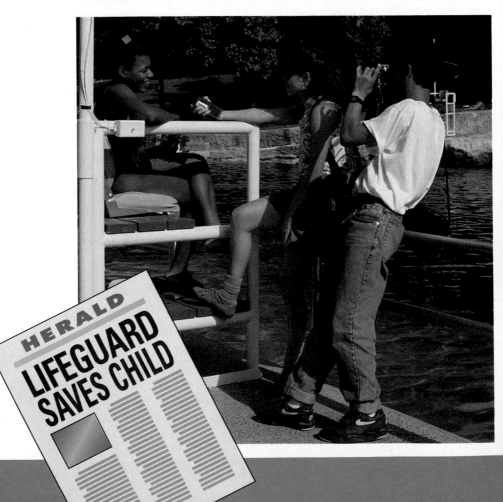

MAKING CONNECTIONS

SPEAKING AND LISTENING

Creating a Fable

Do you ever hear sayings like "A bird in the hand is worth two in the bush"? Many sayings started as the moral from a fable. A fable is a very short story that teaches a lesson about life. The characters in a fable are usually animals that speak and behave like humans.

To create your own fable, think of a proverb, motto, or saying that sums up an important truth about life. Then, make up a simple plot that contains just one or two incidents. Remember, the outcome of the conflict must teach the moral you've chosen. Think of animal characters and the human quality connected with each one. For example, foxes are often considered sly and crafty, while dogs are portrayed as loyal and friendly.

Read your first draft to a small group of your classmates. Ask them to guess the moral of your fable. Then, repeat the process as classmates read their fables to you.

SHORT-STORY WRITING ACROSS THE CURRICULUM

History

You're writing a biography or history book for young children. Choose an important event in history or in the life of a hero whose life you can research in an encyclopedia. Maybe you want to explain how Ponce de León arrived in what is now Florida or why Betsy Ross made a flag for the new nation. What will catch and keep your young readers' interest? Before you write, make a story map. Be sure that all the historical details are factual. Then, write a short story—geared toward small children—that explains this event.

7 WRITING TO INFORM: EXPOSITION

Seeing Patterns

Would you accept these challenges? Define *poetry* without saying the words *creative writing* or *literature*. Tell someone what the movie *Toy Story* is like without mentioning computer animation. Write a report on the Vietnam War without referring to any other U.S. war. No? No wonder. In life, nothing stands totally alone. **Seeing patterns and relationships** is one of the most natural ways to understand our world and to give information about it.

Writing and You.   You use this strategy in different ways. You define *poetry* by how it's like and unlike other literature. You discuss *Toy Story* within the category of animated film. You understand the Vietnam War by contrasting it with World War II. Look at whatever interests you: Are there patterns or relationships to explore?

As You Read.   In the following selection, Sidney Moncrief looks at patterns among three great basketball players. What does he see?

Leigh Behnke, *Still Life with Telephone and Flowers* (1983). Watercolor on paper, 40 1/2″ × 52 1/4″. Collection of Glenn C. Janss. Courtesy of Fischbach Gallery, N.Y.

from Moncrief: My Journey to the NBA

by Sidney Moncrief with Myra McLarey

My fear of being in the pros soon dissipated. It helped that I was never in awe of the talent of the big-name players—such as Larry Bird, Michael Jordan and Dr. J. I respected the stars and their talent, but I also knew I could compete.

Playing the best challenged me to be my best—to test my limits. It was also just plain fun to play against players with such skill. I found I could be playing very hard against a guy on another team and still be impressed with his play. If an opponent made a good shot or a great move or an impressive pass, in my mind I'd say, *What a play!* Sometimes I even complimented the player if I got the chance. I think you can play better if you allow yourself to respect your opponent.

I played against so many good players that it's impossible, really, to single out the best. Of course, Larry Bird would have to be high on anybody's list. He's intense, he works hard, he's versatile, and he's a real team player. With our difference in size I didn't guard Larry that much in the pros. I did go one-on-one with him the last game of my college career.

> **"Larry Bird [is]... intense, he works hard, he's versatile, and he's a real team player."**

No matter how great a college coach is, he doesn't have the time or the expertise to fully analyze an opponent. So when I played Bird in college, we didn't have any detailed tendency reports on him. When I guarded him the second half of the game, I had no idea of his specific moves. I had not seen him play before, and I was too busy the first half guarding someone else to watch him. I was simply playing defense the way I had always played it. His offensive skills were not nearly as refined as they are now, and he didn't have teammates who could get the ball to him like he does now, so my athletic ability allowed me to do a pretty good job on him. Sometimes I guarded Larry in the pros, but it was a different story then. I couldn't really play him in the pros—I'm too small.

If I were bigger and could play him, though, I'd push him to his right, because he likes to move to his left to shoot. I'd push him to his right, play him tight to force him to drive, and then I'd try to block him out on any shots. On post, I'd try to front him and not let him get the basketball.

What can I say about Magic Johnson except that he deserves his name? He controls the tempo of the game. He gets all the players involved and, like Bird, he plays an unselfish ball game. He's very right-handed, so he has a strong tendency to move to his right. Even though he's good enough to go left or right, you play him to go right. His outside shot is pretty good too, so you have to play him tight. If he's on the post, he's very difficult to guard because he's so big—he's 6'8"—and agile. You can't play behind him; if he gets the ball with his back to the basket, he's just going to hook it. You can't front him; he'll be able to catch a lob.

What you do with Magic is pick him up in the back court and make him turn. You don't want him coming at you face forward; you want him to come at you with his back turned and back you down the court. That way you can get help from your defense. Magic is not as difficult to keep from scoring as Jordan or Bird. But he's such a great all-around player, and like Bird, he can beat you so many different ways. If he can't beat you scoring, he'll beat you with his passing, and his play-making—he'll beat you by making things happen on the court.

"... he'll beat you by making things happen on the court."

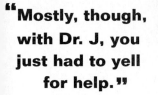

"Mostly, though, with Dr. J, you just had to yell for help."

Dr. J was extremely difficult to guard. He is big. And he is good. Doc is right-handed and he likes his right. But if he wanted to shoot a jump shot, he liked to move to his left, take one dribble, then pull up and bank it off the glass. With Doc, I tried to take away his right hand and force him to take the jumper. On the post, you couldn't front him, you couldn't play behind him—you had to play him in-between. I used a move Eddie Sutton had taught me in college (we called it half-mooning): face him from the side and get a hand in front of his face. You also had to try to keep Doc out of the open court—he was one of the best open-court players in the history of the sport—by picking him up early and not letting him get the basketball.

Mostly, though, with Dr. J, you just had to yell for help.

"Playing the best challenged me to be my best—to test my limits."

READER'S RESPONSE

1. Do you know anything about the three basketball players Moncrief is giving information about? Do you think it is interesting to see what one great athlete thinks about the skills of other great athletes? Why?

2. What sport or entertainment medium are you interested in—football? auto racing? rock music? movies? In your journal write about two or three of the big names in that field. How are they alike? How are they different?

WRITER'S CRAFT

3. Moncrief lets readers know all three athletes better by *comparing* and *contrasting* them. He starts out with the obvious similarities among the men; they are all great basketball players. How does he contrast them?

4. How is the information about the three players organized? How could Moncrief have organized the information to make the differences among the men more obvious? What is the advantage of the organization he used?

Ways to Inform

A quick glance at one general-interest magazine or a list of nonfiction best-sellers will show you that informative writing can be developed in many ways. Examining patterns and relationships is just one way to inform. Here are a few examples of ways to inform:

- in a travel essay, writing about your visit to the Taos Pueblo
- in a press release, writing a biographical sketch of a Nobel Prize winner
- in a paper for science class, describing the surface of Mars
- in an article for your school newspaper, describing the features of the new gymnasium
- in an essay for literature class, contrasting the hero and the villain of a short story
- in a presentation to new students, defining *advanced placement*
- on a World Wide Web page, listing nonprofit organizations that welcome teenage volunteers
- in a recipe, describing how to make tamales
- in a music review for the local paper, evaluating a new CD you think people would enjoy
- in a conversation with your supervisor, explaining why you think the store's merchandise should be rearranged

LOOKING AHEAD

In the main assignment in this chapter, you'll use comparison and contrast in an informative essay. You'll be using classification. As you work, keep in mind that a comparison/contrast essay

- looks at relationships or patterns
- focuses on two or more subjects
- discusses similarities, differences, or both

Writing a Comparison/Contrast Essay

Prewriting

Choosing Subjects

Sometimes a writing situation leads naturally to comparison/contrast subjects. For example, if you were interested in a new Civil War movie, you might naturally compare and contrast it with the classic film *Gone with the Wind*. In a newspaper article about a candidate for class president, you'd probably compare and contrast that candidate with others running for the same office.

When you write comparison/contrast essays, you have three choices:

1. You can write about the similarities only.
2. You can write about the differences only.
3. You can write about both similarities and differences.

If your teacher assigns a comparison/contrast essay, be sure to understand the assignment. Sometimes, *compare* is used as an "umbrella" term that means analyze *both* similarities and differences.

In choosing subjects for comparison and contrast, be sure of two things:

- the subjects have some basic similarities
- the subjects are different enough to be interesting

CRITICAL THINKING
Classifying Objects and Ideas

When you choose subjects to compare and contrast, you must understand (1) *if* they have anything in common, and (2) *what* it is they have in common. You're actually using the critical thinking skill of classifying: grouping objects or ideas into categories that show their similarities.

If you were playing a game that required you to identify categories, the questioner might ask you, "What is the category for algebra, history, physics?" One good answer, of course, would be "school courses"! After identifying the categories for "cars, buses, trains" (types of land transportation) and for "moon, sun, comet" (celestial bodies), you win!

CRITICAL THINKING EXERCISE:
Classifying Objects and Ideas

Now make your own game. Work with a partner to figure out the category that tells what each of the following groups has in common. Be as specific as you can in stating the category. [Hint: One group can't be classified because the items have nothing in common.]

EXAMPLE   **1.** honesty, kindness, courage, dependability
        1. *Category: desirable character traits*

1. Classical period, Middle Ages, Renaissance
2. lions, tigers, elephants, gorillas
3. mumps, chickenpox, German measles
4. football, baseball, soccer
5. oxygen, television, spaghetti
6. Washington, D.C.; Paris, France; Tokyo, Japan; London, England
7. Himalayas, Alps, Rockies
8. a poem, a painting, an opera
9. democracy, monarchy, dictatorship
10. a sunset, a ballgame, a movie

 *Prewriting*

Thinking About Purpose and Audience

Purpose. Your *purpose* in exploring subjects with comparison/contrast may be any one of the four basic purposes for writing: to inform, to persuade, to express yourself, or to be creative. In this chapter, however, you'll focus on informing. And within that basic purpose, you'll have a more narrow one. You may

- Show similarities between subjects

    EXAMPLE Show how competitive in-line skating and ice skating are alike

- Show differences between subjects

    EXAMPLE Show how factories in the United States and Japan are different

- Show both similarities and differences between the subjects

    EXAMPLE Show how two types of weight-training equipment available for home use have both similar and different features

Audience. When you inform, you have to think about what your *audience* knows and doesn't know so that you can define unfamiliar terms and give background information. It's also important to think about what will interest your readers—remember that you want to hold your readers' attention while you inform them! This can mean a subject that will be new to many of them, as high-tech Japanese factories might be. But it can also mean your approach to your subject. Perhaps your audience knows something about weight-training equipment but would really like to know how two systems compare for developing certain muscles. Perhaps your readers would like to know how two systems compare in possible modifications as the user's ability increases. Try to make your comparison/contrast one that will bring a new subject to light or shed new light on a familiar one.

WRITING NOTE As with other types of writing, remember to narrow your subjects. It's hard to write an interesting, detailed essay comparing the Middle Ages with today or even comparing New York with Miami. However, you could compare and contrast transportation in the Middle Ages with transportation today, or the architecture of New York and Miami.

WRITING ASSIGNMENT

PART 1:
Choosing Subjects for Comparison/Contrast

After digging around in your mind, select two subjects that interest you for your comparison/contrast essay. Test your subjects to make sure that they meet these two requirements: (1) they have some basic similarities, and (2) they have enough differences to make the comparison/contrast significant. Remember to consider the purpose and audience for your essay.

Prewriting

Gathering and Arranging Information

After you've chosen subjects and thought about your purpose and audience, you need to figure out the *relevant features* you'll compare and contrast. Then you can gather and organize information about these relevant features.

Gathering Information

On TV courtroom dramas, you'll hear lawyers saying things like, "That's not relevant, your honor." *Relevant* means "related to the main point." When you're exploring a subject by comparison/contrast, you look at the **relevant features** of both items. These are the features that will inform readers about your main idea.

Suppose your purpose is to inform readers about the TV programs *Home Improvement* and *The Cosby Show*. You think that both programs show families as they are in real life. That's the basic thing they have in common, and it's also your main idea. How can you inform readers of this main idea? What details will you use to support it? You might compare and contrast the settings (time and place), the ages of the main characters, and typical situations in the shows. These would be the relevant features, about which you'd gather information for your paper. What is relevant may differ depending on your audience, however. For example, a teenage audience might be interested in the typical situations, while another audience might be more interested in the settings.

If you're familiar with your subjects (two television programs, for example), you can probably recall or observe all of the information you'll need for your paper. But if your subjects are unfamiliar (two historical periods or two places you've never been), you'll need to do some research to gather information.

The following chart shows how you could gather information about two famous artists: Michelangelo and Leonardo da Vinci. Notice that most of the relevant features are similarities.

Relevant Features		
	Subject 1: Michelangelo	*Subject 2:* Leonardo da Vinci
Feature 1: accomplishments	sculptor, painter, architect, writer of sonnets	painter, sculptor, architect, engineer, scientist
Feature 2: commitment	dedicated to art; often went days without sleeping or eating	dedicated to art; often went days without sleeping or eating
Feature 3: innovations	master of perspective; pioneered un-painted statuary	master of perspective; inventor of classic style of painting during Renaissance
Feature 4: most famous work	murals of Sistine Chapel	*The Last Supper* and *Mona Lisa*
Feature 5: new information	restoration of Sistine Chapel shows use of brilliant, not dark, colors	restoration of *The Last Supper* shows use of brilliant, not dark, colors
Feature 6: fame	famous in his life-time and through-out history	famous in his life-time and through-out history

WRITING ASSIGNMENT

PART 2:
Gathering Information

Now it's your turn to gather information for your essay. As an aid in gathering information, make a chart like the one above for the two subjects you have chosen to compare and contrast. Decide what relevant features you will use, and write them in the chart. Don't forget your audience. What features do they care about? (You may need to do some research first.) As you gather information, you may need to revise the chart.

© Grimmy Inc. Reprinted with permission of Tribune Media Services.

Arranging Information

You need to make an important decision before you begin writing: how to organize your paper. There are two helpful ways to organize comparison/contrast writing: the *block method* and the *point-by-point method.*

With the **block method,** you discuss all the features of one subject and then all the features of the second subject. When you use this method, you discuss the same features for the second subject as you do for the first. With the **point-by-point method,** you discuss one feature of the first subject and the same feature of the second subject. Then you move to the second feature, and so on.

For example, in an essay about Leonardo da Vinci and Michelangelo, you might group information by discussing Leonardo first (his achievements, innovations, and major works.) Then you might discuss Michelangelo (his achievements, innovations, and major works). That's the block method.

Or you might start with the idea that both Michelangelo and Leonardo were geniuses in many fields. Then you could go on to the next features: their dedication, new contributions, most famous works, and fame in their lifetimes. This is the point-by-point method.

Remember to treat the relevant features in the same order for both subjects. The order of the relevant features is often most to least or least to most important.

The following chart on two African American writers from the colonial period to the Civil War illustrates the two methods of arranging information in a comparison/contrast essay.

HERE'S HOW

BLOCK METHOD	POINT-BY-POINT METHOD

<u>Subject 1: Phillis Wheatley</u> (1753?–1784)
   Feature 1: born a slave
   Feature 2: 1st black woman to publish volume of poetry in U.S.
   Feature 3: well read in the Bible and Latin classics
   Feature 4: dedicated her life to poetry
	<u>Feature 1: status at birth</u>
	   Subject 1: Phillis Wheatley born a slave
	   Subject 2: Jarena Lee born a free woman
	<u>Feature 2: accomplishment in writing</u>
	   Subject 1: Phillis Wheatley 1st black woman to publish volume of poetry in U.S.
	   Subject 2: Jarena Lee 1st black woman to write autobiography in U.S.

<u>Subject 2: Jarena Lee</u> (1783–?)
   Feature 1: born a free woman
   Feature 2: 1st black woman to write her autobiography in U.S.
   Feature 3: well read in the Bible; wanted to become female preacher
   Feature 4: dedicated her life to evangelizing
	<u>Feature 3: knowledge</u>
	   Subject 1: Phillis Wheatley well read in the Bible and Latin classics
	   Subject 2: Jarena Lee well read in Bible; wanted to become a female preacher
	<u>Feature 4: purpose in life</u>
	   Subject 1: Phillis Wheatley dedicated her life to poetry
	   Subject 2: Jarena Lee dedicated her life to evangelizing

The Granger Collection, New York.

Jarena Lee

Phillis Wheatley

Reminder

To gather and arrange information

- decide on the relevant features of the subjects
- make a chart showing similarities and/or differences
- choose the point-by-point method or the block method

WRITING ASSIGNMENT

PART 3:
Arranging Information

You've done most of the hard work by gathering information. Now you need to decide on how to arrange that information. It's your decision. Choose the organization that you think you'll be more comfortable with. Using the block method or the point-by-point method, make a chart like the one shown on page 263.

Prewriting

Developing a Thesis Statement

The thesis statement of a comparison/contrast paper should state your subjects and your approach. It must

- identify what people, things, or ideas you are comparing or contrasting
- identify whether you will emphasize comparisons, emphasize contrasts, or balance the two

Here is a thesis statement that will emphasize contrasts. First the writer identifies the two things she's going to write about—the American and the French revolutions. Then she shows that she'll concentrate on contrasts by saying that the two events had only one similarity.

> The American Revolution and the French Revolution both started out to give power to the common people, but the similarities stopped there.

👉 REFERENCE NOTE: For more information on writing thesis statements, see pages 113–114.

WRITING NOTE Very often in an essay that explores differences, you begin with the one or two similarities the subjects have in common and then explore the differences. In the same way, to explore similarities, you may begin with the one or two differences between the subjects and then devote most of your paper to exploring similarities.

WRITING ASSIGNMENT

PART 4:
Developing a Thesis Statement

Are you going to compare your subjects? Contrast them? Or compare and contrast them? Write a thesis statement that announces to your reader what you plan to do in your paper. Use your prewriting chart from page 261 for ideas.

Writing Your First Draft

You've completed much of the important work on your paper. All that's left to do is to put the information in your prewriting chart into sentences and paragraphs. You'll also have to think about an introduction, body, and conclusion.

The Elements of a Comparison/Contrast Essay

Introduction.   As in any essay, the introductory paragraph should capture your reader's attention. You might begin the introduction of a paper about two Renaissance artists by saying "Leonardo and Michelangelo are not just names for Ninja Turtles; they were real people with real gifts." The introduction should also include the thesis statement, usually placed at the end.

Body.   The body is the place to use the block method or the point-by-point method to present details about your subjects. Use transitions to connect and clarify ideas. Words and phrases like *also, similarly, both, in the same way,* and *just as* signal a comparison. *By contrast, however, unlike,* and *on the other hand* signal a contrast.

☞ REFERENCE NOTE: For more information about transitions, see pages 89–90.

In the body, you develop ideas with specific details, facts and examples, and quotations. In the paper about the two Renaissance artists, for example, you might discuss details about the artists' paintings: "Both Michelangelo and Leonardo recorded their ties to the church. Michelangelo painted the ceiling of the Sistine Chapel, and Leonardo painted a religious scene in *The Last Supper* on the wall of a monastery dining hall."

Conclusion.   The ending of any essay must make the reader feel satisfied. A good, safe way to end is to summarize the information in the body and show how it supports the thesis. Another way to end your essay is with an evaluation, a final comment that judges the relative worth of the two subjects. To end an essay comparing two sports cars, for example, you might say, "The Hawk and the Tornado are fairly evenly matched in terms of quality; but if you want to have fun, drive a Hawk."

Looking at a Comparison/Contrast Essay

The article that follows explains the similarities and differences (mostly the differences) between baseball in the United States and a Finnish sport called *pesapallo*. Notice how the writer inserts a reference to the comedy routine of Abbott and Costello, as well as background information on the game of *pesapallo*, to keep the reader interested.

A NEWSPAPER ARTICLE

Time out! Is baseball Finnished?
by Bob Secter

INTRODUCTION

Attention grabber

HANCOCK, Mich.—There were lots of reasons why Jimmy Piersall was known as a flake back when he played major league baseball; but one of the best came the day he hit a home run as a New York Met and ran the bases backward.

All of which has little to do with the subject of this story, except to illustrate the maxim that what may seem like buffoonery in one setting could make perfect sense in another. Had Piersall been playing in, say, Helsinki rather than New York, he might have fit right in.

Yes. Baseball has been Finlandized.

Background

The Finns call the game *pesapallo* and are so crazy about it that it is considered their national pastime. Of course they do it a little differently. They don't actually backpedal their way from base to base a la Piersall, but, looking at it from a chauvinist American perspective, they do take a backward route around the base paths.

Difference— Factual support

First base is where third base ought to be, second is sort of around where first should be and third is somewhere out in left field.

Difference— Factual support

That's right, Abbott. Who isn't on first. I Don't Know is. Sort of.

Background

Anyway, Finnish emigres have spread the game to Scandinavia, Canada and even Australia. And over the weekend, they took their first crack at the toughest market of all—the United States, the guarantor of all that is pure and noble about baseball.

Background

Here in Michigan's rugged upper peninsula, the heart of Finnish America, two Canadian *pesapallo* teams squared off Saturday in a demonstration game before thousands of slightly befuddled spectators at an ethnic festival. In a real slugfest, the Toronto Sisu eked out a 16–15 win over the archrival Thunder Bay Repais.

Organizers of the annual FinnFest say that they hope to field enough domestic talent to stage home-grown *pesapallo* matches at future gatherings. Already, the Hancock High School baseball coach is talking about teaching the Finnish version to his team.

**Difference—
Factual support**

The main selling point of *pesapallo,* devotees say, is action. There are no long pauses between pitches, the ball is almost constantly in play and both fielders and runners are forever scampering all over the place.

**Difference—
Quotation**

"In American baseball, a runner on second is in scoring position but in our game, he's just tired," winked Jari Lemonen, who plays for the Repais. "Usually when we get out there, we pack a lunch."

**Background—
History**

The Abner Doubleday of Finland was Lauri Pihkala, a professor who apparently was mesmerized by baseball during early 20th century study tours in the United States. He combined the American game with some native ball-playing sports and *pesapallo* was born.

**Similarities—
Factual support/
Statistics**

Both baseball and *pesapallo* feature four bases, three outs an inning, nine innings, nine players on a side, a hard ball, mitts and a bat—although the Louisville Slugger of Finland is called a "Jarvinen Kanuuna."

**Difference—
Factual support**

That's where the similarities end. The *pesapallo* pitcher, for instance, stands next to the plate and tosses the ball up in the air, varying his delivery not with curves or sliders but by the height the ball goes.

**Difference—
Factual support**

Instead of waiting in a dugout, teammates of the batter stand around what is roughly equivalent to the batter's box and scream out advice whether to swing or not at a pitch. The batter can hit as many as three fair balls before he has to run. And the route around the basepaths sort of zigzags first to the left, then the right, then the left again.

**Difference—
Factual support/
Statistics**

Confused? Try this. A three-base hit is a *kunnari,* or home run. The batter scores, even though he is allowed to stay on third and score again if somebody knocks him in. But getting a *kunnari* is not easy because a ball that's knocked out of the park—about 300 feet from home to the farthest point of the *pesapallo* outfield—is considered a *laiton* (foul).

Difference

When an outfielder catches a fly ball, that doesn't necessarily mean the batter is out. He might just be *haava* (wounded), a sort of purgatory state for sluggers that requires them to forfeit the turn at bat but doesn't exactly count toward ending the inning. And when someone does make an out, he's not just out, he's *pallo* (killed). This is no game for wimps, that's for sure.

**CONCLUSION
Difference—
Quotation**

There's one other important difference. At the end of the game, American ballplayers hit the showers. "When we're done," said Thunder Bay shortstop Pavli Kaki, "we go off to the sauna."

The Miami Herald

E X E R C I S E 1 ▶ **Analyzing the Organization of a
Comparison/Contrast Article**

Now it's your turn to analyze the professional's work. Meet with two or three classmates to answer the following questions about the *pesapallo* article.

1. Why do you think the writer doesn't give equal space to discussing the rules and history of baseball?
2. Besides discussing *pesapallo* rules, what background information does the article provide?
3. At the midpoint of the article (paragraph 13), the writer summarizes several similarities between baseball and *pesapallo*. Then he goes on to discuss another five features that apply only to *pesapallo*. Why is he able to do this without explaining each contrasting feature in baseball? [Hint: What does the audience know?]

A Basic Framework for a Comparison/ Contrast Essay

The professional model on *pesapallo* does not use a simple block or point-by-point method of organization—it doesn't give the two subjects equal time. (It's also written by a professional who earns his living by writing.) But using a simple block or point-by-point method may help you write and organize your essay more effectively. The following writer's model illustrates the block method of organization. Notice that the writer discusses all of the features (equipment, training, and dangers) for snorkeling, and then deals with all the same features for scuba diving.

A WRITER'S MODEL

Snorkeling and Scuba Diving

INTRODUCTION   If you're out on the water and see a red and white flag on a boat or pole, beware of creatures beneath the sea. The flag signals that human beings are underwater. They may be snorkeling or scuba diving. Both sports let people glimpse the amazing underwater plants and animals, but snorkeling and scuba diving are worlds apart.

Attention grabber

Thesis statement

BODY
Subject 1:
Snorkeling

Snorkeling is easy. It doesn't take any special training and requires minimum equipment. You need a mask to keep the water out of your eyes and nose, and a snorkel, a short breathing tube that fits in your mouth and has an opening at the surface. The snorkel lets you keep your head underwater and breathe air at the same time. Many snorkelers use fins, but they're optional. Snorkelers can dive below the surface of the water for as long as they can hold their breath--probably about ten feet. The only real danger that snorkelers face is being run over by a boat; that's the point of the diving flag.

Feature 1:
Training

Feature 2:
Equipment

Feature 3:
Time
underwater

Feature 4:
Dangers

Subject 2:
Scuba diving

Scuba diving is a much more elaborate sport with far greater rewards. If snorkelers get a peek at underwater life, scuba divers get a long and leisurely look. You must take classes (three to five weeks' worth in a classroom, pool, and natural body of water) to become a certified diver. Besides the mask and fins that snorkelers wear, scuba divers also need a tank of air, a weight belt, a regulator, a buoyancy compensator, and a watch. The air that you carry lets you stay under for forty-five minutes or an hour at a depth of thirty feet. Scuba divers also need one other

Feature 1:
Training

Feature 2:
Equipment

Feature 3:
Time
underwater

essential thing: a buddy. Scuba diving can be dangerous; divers are told not to dive alone. The dangers that scuba divers face include overexpansion of the lungs, air embolism to the brain, the bends, running out of air, disorientation, and nitrogen narcosis. You should be in good physical condition. But it's a safe sport if you know what you're doing. According to scuba divers, what you experience near a reef is like nothing else.

Feature 4: Dangers

CONCLUSION   So if you're willing to spend more money (you need access to a boat) and get special training, scuba diving lets you get a better, close-up, longer look at underwater life. But snorkeling is an inexpensive substitute, and it still gives you a breathtaking view of life in another medium. It's like visiting another planet.

Evaluation

Final comment

PART 5:
Writing a First Draft

Now is the time to use the information you developed in previous parts of your writing assignment to write a rough draft of your paper. Try to state your ideas as clearly as possible. Remember to give evidence in the form of facts, examples, and quotations to support each feature.

Evaluating and Revising

Cast a cold eye over your first draft as you look for ways to improve it. Use the following guidelines for both self-evaluation and peer evaluation (see pages 47–48). First, ask yourself the questions in the left-hand column of the chart on the next page. If you identify a weakness, use the revision technique suggested in the right-hand column.

COMPUTER NOTE: If the computers at your school are arranged in a network, you may be able to use them to do collaborative evaluation of writing assignments. Peer editors can use highlighting techniques such as italics or color-coding to mark words or phrases; then, they may type comments in brackets next to the highlighted text.

"In baseball you only get three strikes and you're out. In rewriting, you get almost as many swings as you want and you know, sooner or later, you'll hit the ball."

Neil Simon

EVALUATING AND REVISING COMPARISON/CONTRAST ESSAYS

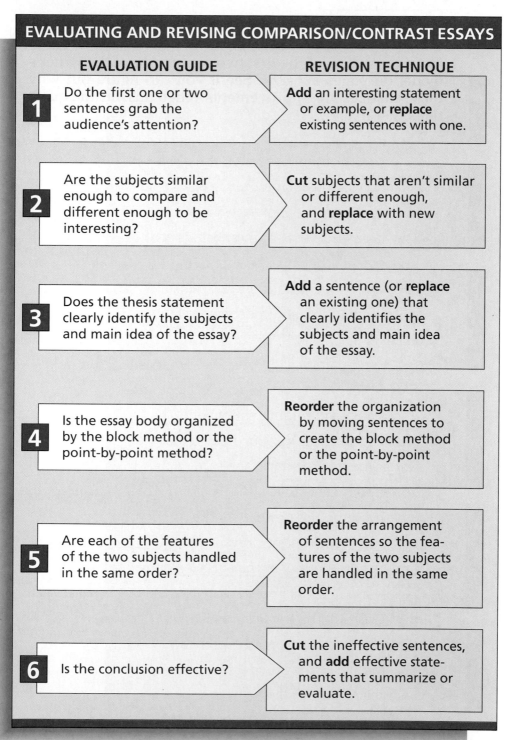

EVALUATION GUIDE	REVISION TECHNIQUE
1 Do the first one or two sentences grab the audience's attention?	**Add** an interesting statement or example, or **replace** existing sentences with one.
2 Are the subjects similar enough to compare and different enough to be interesting?	**Cut** subjects that aren't similar or different enough, and **replace** with new subjects.
3 Does the thesis statement clearly identify the subjects and main idea of the essay?	**Add** a sentence (or **replace** an existing one) that clearly identifies the subjects and main idea of the essay.
4 Is the essay body organized by the block method or the point-by-point method?	**Reorder** the organization by moving sentences to create the block method or the point-by-point method.
5 Are each of the features of the two subjects handled in the same order?	**Reorder** the arrangement of sentences so the features of the two subjects are handled in the same order.
6 Is the conclusion effective?	**Cut** the ineffective sentences, and **add** effective statements that summarize or evaluate.

> **EXERCISE 2** ▶   **Analyzing a Writer's Revisions**

Here's a revision of the first two paragraphs of the writer's model on pages 271–273. See if you can figure out why these changes are improvements. Then answer the questions that follow.

If you're out on the water and see a
red and white flag on a boat or pole,
beware of creatures beneath the sea.
The flag signals that human beings are
underwater. They may be snorkeling
or scuba diving. Both sports let people
glimpse the amazing underwater plants
and animals, *but snorkeling and scuba diving are worlds apart.*   **add**

Snorkeling is easy, but scuba diving is   **cut**
harder. It doesn't take any special training
and requires minimum equipment. The
snorkel lets you keep your head underwater and breathe air at the same time.
You need a mask to keep the water out of   **reorder**
your eyes and nose, and a snorkel, a short
breathing tube that fits in your mouth
and has an opening at the surface. Many
snorkelers *but they're optional.*
people use fins, Snorkelers can dive below   **replace/add**
the surface of the water for as long as
they can hold their breath--probably
about ten feet. The only real danger that
snorkelers face is being run over by a
boat; that's the point of the diving flag.

1. Why did the writer add the clause *but snorkeling and scuba diving are worlds apart* to the end of the first paragraph? [Hint: What is the thesis statement? Does the paper compare or contrast the two sports?]
2. In the first sentence of the second paragraph, why did the writer cut the clause *but scuba diving is harder*? [Hint: Is this paper developed by the block method or the point-by-point method?]
3. Why did the writer move the fourth sentence of the second paragraph?
4. In the fifth sentence of the second paragraph, why did the writer replace the word *people* with *snorkelers* and add the clause *but they're optional*?

PART 6:
Evaluating and Revising Your Comparison/Contrast Paper

It's hard to evaluate objectively the way your own hair looks before you leave for school in the morning. It's even harder to cast a cold, objective eye on your own writing. Use the questions from the chart on page 275 to evaluate your paper. Then exchange papers with a partner, and use the questions to evaluate each other's papers. Use your partner's comments and your own evaluations to revise your essay. Remember to be helpful in giving specific suggestions to your partner for improvements.

Proofreading and Publishing

Proofreading. Put the finishing touches on your paper by checking the revised draft for mistakes in spelling, capitalization, punctuation, and usage. (See page 56 for Guidelines for Proofreading.) Try peer proofreading, too. Your classmates may be able to spot mistakes you've missed.

Publishing. Then try these ideas for publishing your finished paper.

- Your comparison/contrast paper may be of interest to the teacher and students in another course in your school. For example, a physical education teacher might distribute your comparisons of two sports. A history teacher might share your paper on two American presidents.
- Post your opinions. You can post papers that compare/contrast subjects of interest (books, movies, TV shows, restaurants, cars) on a bulletin board where everyone in the class can read them.

GRAMMAR HINT

Using the Degrees of Comparison

What's wrong with these statements?
a. *Pesapallo* is most exciting than baseball.
b. Of all the kinds of swimming, I like scuba diving better.

When you use adjectives and adverbs in a comparison/contrast paper, you need to be aware of the degrees of comparison. Most adjectives and adverbs have three degrees of comparison:

POSITIVE	COMPARATIVE	SUPERLATIVE
cold	colder	coldest
bad	worse	worst
ridiculous	more ridiculous	most ridiculous

1. When comparing two items, use the comparative degree.

    Pesapallo is **more exciting** than baseball.

2. When comparing three or more items, use the superlative degree.

    Many people consider *pesapallo*, soccer, and lacrosse the **most exciting** sports of all.

☞ REFERENCE NOTE: For more help with degrees of comparison, see pages 719–722.

WRITING ASSIGNMENT

PART 7:
Proofreading and Publishing Your Essay

It's time to be picky. Proofread your essay carefully to correct all errors. Write your final version, and proofread it. Then decide how you will publish your essay or share it with others.

📁 Reflecting on Your Writing

Date your paper, and attach a brief reflection answering the following questions. Include both in your **portfolio.**

- What was the hardest part of selecting your topic?
- How did you decide on the order of your points?
- Which of your revisions were most effective? Why?

A STUDENT MODEL

Things to compare and contrast are all around you, as Chris Chavis shows in the following essay. Chris, a student at Central Mid High School in Norman, Oklahoma, effectively compares two all-American pastimes—playing football and playing a video game. As you read, see if you agree with his ideas.

Football and Cyberball
by Chris Chavis

The smell of hot popcorn and hot dogs drifts through the stadium. On the field, the home team scores a touchdown and the crowd ignites into a wild cheer. This is another typical afternoon watching one of America's favorite pastimes, but now, thanks to modern technology, you can play football in the comfort of your own home, or anywhere else for that matter. Today, instead of sitting in the hot sun watching football, you can actually participate in electronic Cyberball, one of the best arcade football games ever made. Football and Cyberball have many similarities, but, as usual, the shift from old technology to new creates many changes--some better and some worse.

Cyberball is easier to play than football. Cyberball requires the machine, the program, and, if you're playing at the arcade, several quarters. Cyberball also requires a significant amount of physical coordination. Manual dexterity is not necessarily a must, but if you expect to do well, you'll have to possess some hand-eye coordination.

Football requires a considerable amount of equipment. In order to play, you have to have enough people to form two teams, protective gear for each team--padding and helmets, and a football. Generally, football is played in a field or a vacant lot outdoors somewhere. And, in order for your team to be successful, you need to have several players with extra-ordinary physical skill.

Cyberball develops several important, fundamental skills. By having to control your futuristic, robotic players by ma-nipulating a joystick, you develop extraordinary hand-eye coordination. The computer's quick moves when it is on offense also demand that you develop even faster reflexes in order to dominate. You must learn problem-solving skills and develop your intellect.

Football also develops many important, though more physical, skills. Football builds many muscles and can greatly enhance your physical fitness. You can also develop stamina and quicker reflexes by running and dodging the opposing team. However, one of the greatest skills developed from football is strong leadership, which many football players keep the rest of their lives.

Football and Cyberball have several obvious similarities, and, in fact, Cyberball is strongly based on football. They are different in many ways, however. I believe that Cyberball has many advantages over football and is what I prefer to play.

WRITING WORKSHOP

An Extended Definition

Comparison/contrast is one way to use the strategy of *classification*. Definition is another. When you define, you reverse the process you use to compare and contrast. To compare and contrast, you start with a large group or class (artists or sports) and pull out individual members to examine. To **define,** you group individual things together in a common group or class. A **dictionary definition** is a brief explanation of a word's meaning. When the word being defined is a noun (an object, place, person, or idea), the definition does two things:

- names the general class or category to which the word belongs
- gives the characteristics that distinguish the word from all other words in its general class

In the following dictionary definition, the general class is underlined. The rest of the definition tells how the word differs from other members of its class.

> *Pesapallo* is a <u>sport</u> resembling baseball, generally played in Finland, having bases run in an order backward to U.S. baseball.

You can also write an extended definition that is anywhere from one paragraph to several pages long. Here are some ways to extend a definition.

- Give an example.
- Tell how it works.
- Describe its properties.
- Tell other facts about it.
- Use a quotation from an authority.

The following model gives an extended definition of an Athabascan Indian concept. As you read, think how the writer extends the definition.

Instead of "goodbye," Athabascans say "Tlaa" when they leave each other. <u>Tlaa</u> means something like "See you" or "Until we meet again." An Athabascan would be puzzled by our idea of "goodbye." To say goodbye is so final. An Athabascan would say that people cannot really leave each other because they are always in each other's mind and heart. People cannot really be away from each other when each one is a part of the other. If the daughter goes away to school, the mother says "Tlaa." The mother thinks the daughter is coming back home. And, if she doesn't come home, then they will see each other at another place. The Athabascan language has no word for goodbye.

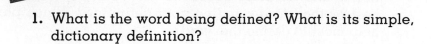

1. What is the word being defined? What is its simple, dictionary definition?
2. What examples or concepts does the author use to extend the definition?

Writing an Extended Definition

Prewriting. Choose as your subject an object or idea that interests you. Make sure that your subject is complex enough so that there's more to say about it than one sentence.

EXAMPLES

School:	a slang term, summer vacation, a hard class
Sports:	an athlete, a coach, a free agent
Society:	a shopping mall, a great car, a strict parent
Philosophy:	duty, freedom, wisdom

Think of examples, descriptive details, or facts, or find appropriate quotations to extend the definition. To get some ideas, consult several dictionaries or encyclopedias. Who is your audience? Make sure you include any necessary background information.

Writing, Evaluating, and Revising. To write a one- or two-paragraph definition, begin with a one-sentence definition similar to what a dictionary might give. (Don't copy a dictionary's definition. Reword it so that it is distinctly your own.) Then, extend your definition by adding an example, descriptive details, facts, or quotations. Use peer editing for suggestions on improving your definition. Consider these questions: Does the paragraph begin with a precisely worded one-sentence definition? Does the extended definition include an attention-getting example, descriptive details, or a quotation from an author?

Proofreading and Publishing. Proofread your definition to be sure it's free of careless errors before you give it to someone else to read. You could read your definition to a small group of classmates or to the whole class (withhold the word you are defining), and see if they can guess the subject.

Don't forget to date your paper. If you choose to include your definition in your **portfolio,** attach a brief written reflection to answer these questions: How did you decide on the best method for extending your definition? Which phrases help most to define the word?

MAKING CONNECTIONS

TEST TAKING

Writing for an Essay Test Question

In school, especially in civics and history classes, you'll often be faced with test questions that require comparison/contrast answers. You need to look carefully at each comparison/contrast question to decide whether to balance comparison and contrast, to emphasize comparison, or to emphasize contrast.

Here's some information on two women rulers you might study in a world history class. If your teacher gave you a test with an essay question asking you to compare and/or contrast them, what would you do? Do the two monarchs have more similarities or more differences? Would you base your paragraph on comparison or contrast? Write a paragraph about the two women in which you emphasize either their similarities or their differences.

WOMEN MONARCHS		
	ELIZABETH I	CATHERINE II
Position	absolute monarch	absolute monarch
Power	absolute	absolute
Title	Queen of England and Ireland	Empress of Russia
Birth-Death	1533–1603	1729–1796
Time of reign	1558–1603	1762–1796
Marital status	single	widow
Nickname	Good Queen Bess	Catherine the Great

(continued)

WOMEN MONARCHS *(continued)*		
	ELIZABETH I	CATHERINE II
Occurrences during reign	encouraged trade and commerce court as artistic center influenced by Renaissance encouraged rise of serious drama (Shakespeare) commissioned portraits by famous painters established large naval force, defeated Spanish Armada planned governmental reforms established Church of England	encouraged trade and commerce court as artistic center influenced by Enlightenment permitted private printing presses and relaxed the censorship of literature commissioned portraits by famous painters established large naval force increased landowners' control of serfs and stifled peasant rebellion granted freedom of worship

ELIZABETH I

CATHERINE II

Portraits courtesy of The Granger Collection, New York.

COMPARISON ACROSS THE CURRICULUM

Literature

A *metaphor* is a figure of speech that makes a direct comparison between two basically unlike things without using the words *like* or *as*. The poet Anne Sexton, for example, creates a metaphor when she says "each spring will be a sword you'll sharpen. . . ." What is compared in the following poem about a fan? Can you find the metaphors?

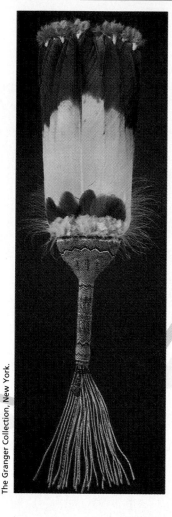

The Granger Collection, New York.

The Eagle-Feather Fan
by N. Scott Momaday

The eagle is my power,
And my fan is an eagle.
It is strong and beautiful
In my hand. And it is real.
My fingers hold upon it
As if the beaded handle
Were the twist of bristlecone.
The bones of my hand are fine
And hollow; the fan bears them.
My hand veers in the thin air
Of the summits. All morning
It scuds on the cold currents;
All afternoon it circles
To the singing, to the drums.

Bring a poem (you may write your own) to class that has a metaphor comparing two unlike things. Read the poem aloud, and ask everyone to listen carefully to find the metaphor. Have them tell what two things are being compared and how they are alike.

If you write your own poem, think about comparing two things that are not generally considered alike. Remember that a poem is not always rhymed and that it can be about many subjects—baseball, concrete mixers, and even giraffes. (See pages 207–208 on writing poems.)

Making Things Clear

"How's it going?" your friends ask when you're looking for a part-time job. Your younger brother asks the same question when you're fixing his bike. And your track coach asks it when you're training for a meet. People are naturally curious about other people's activities, and looking for explanations that **make things clear** is something we all do.

Writing and You. You look for explanations, too. You look to a newspaper's weather page for the status of a hurricane, to a magazine for in-depth coverage of a space shuttle mission, to a technical manual for information about your CD player. What activities of your own would you like to make clear to others?

As You Read. The following excerpt describes the moment when the narrator, Christy Brown, first tries to write. Brown was born with cerebral palsy, a disorder of the nervous system that results in lack of muscle control.

Mark Hayden, *The Master of Lowell's* (1991). Pastel, 20 × 24". Courtesy of the artist.

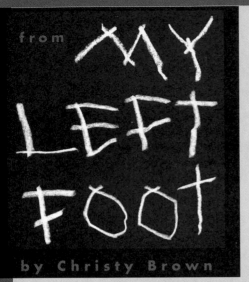

from MY LEFT FOOT

by Christy Brown

It happened so quickly, so simply after all the years of waiting and uncertainty that I can see and feel the whole scene as if it had happened last week. . . .

In a corner Mona and Paddy were sitting huddled together, a few torn school primers before them. They were writing down little sums on to an old chipped slate, using a bright piece of yellow chalk. I was close to them, propped up by a few pillows against the wall, watching.

It was the chalk that attracted me so much. It was a long, slender stick of vivid yellow. I had never seen anything like it before, and it showed up so well against the black surface of the slate that I was fascinated by it as much as if it had been a stick of gold.

Suddenly I wanted desperately to do what my sister was doing. Then—without thinking or knowing exactly what I was doing, I reached out and took the stick of chalk out of my sister's hand—*with my left foot.*

I do not know why I used my left foot to do this. It is a puzzle to many people as well as to myself, for, although I had displayed a curious interest in my toes at an early age, I had never attempted before this to use either of my feet in any way. They could have been as useless to me as were my hands. That day, however, my left foot, apparently on its own volition, reached out and very impolitely took the chalk out of my sister's hand.

I held it tightly between my toes, and, acting on an impulse, made a wild sort of scribble with it on the slate. Next moment I stopped, a bit dazed, surprised, looking down at the stick of yellow chalk stuck between my toes, not knowing what to do with it next, hardly knowing how it got there. Then I looked up and became aware that everyone had stopped talking and were staring at me silently. Nobody stirred. Mona, her black curls framing her chubby little face, stared at me with great big eyes and open mouth. Across the open hearth, his face lit by flames, sat my father, leaning forward, hands outspread on his knees, his shoulders tense. I felt the sweat break out on my forehead.

My mother came in from the pantry with a steaming pot in her hand. She stopped midway between the table and the fire, feeling the tension flowing through the room. She followed their stare and saw me, in the corner. Her eyes looked from my face down to my foot, with the chalk gripped between my toes. She put down the pot.

Then she crossed over to me and knelt down beside me, as she had done so many times before.

"I'll show you what to do with it, Chris," she said, very slowly and in a queer, jerky way, her face flushed as if with some inner excitement.

Taking another piece of chalk from Mona, she hesitated, then very deliberately drew, on the floor in front of me, *the single letter 'A.'*

"Copy that," she said, looking steadily at me. "Copy it, Christy."

I couldn't.

I looked about me, looked around at the faces that were turned towards me, tense, excited faces that were at that moment frozen, immobile, eager, waiting for a miracle in their midst. . . .

I tried again. I put out my foot and made a wild jerking stab with the chalk which produced a very crooked line and nothing more. Mother held the slate steady for me.

"Try again, Chris," she whispered in my ear. "Again."

Christy (Hugh O'Conor) makes his first successful attempt to communicate in the movie version of *My Left Foot* (1989).

"Try again, Chris. . . . Again."

I did. I stiffened my body and put my left foot out again, for the third time. I drew one side of the letter. I drew half the other side. Then the stick of chalk broke and I was left with a stump. I wanted to fling it away and give up. Then I felt my mother's hand on my shoulder. I tried once more. Out went my foot. I shook, I sweated and strained every muscle. My hands were so tightly clenched that my fingernails bit into the flesh. I set my teeth so hard that I nearly pierced my lower lip. Everything in the room swam till the faces around me were mere patches of white. But—I drew it— *the letter 'A.'* There it was on the floor before me. Shaky, with awkward, wobbly sides and a very uneven center line. But it *was* the letter 'A.' I looked up. I saw my mother's face for a moment, tears on her cheeks. Then my father stooped down and hoisted me on to his shoulder.

> "I had done it!
> It had started...."

I had done it! It had started—the thing that was to give my mind its chance of expressing itself. True, I couldn't speak with my lips, but now I would speak through something more lasting than spoken words—written words.

READER'S RESPONSE

1. Christy Brown mentions the tension in the room as he makes his first attempt to write. What was your response as you read?
2. Can you think of a moment when you or someone you know took a huge step forward or experienced a breakthrough? What were your feelings at the time?

WRITER'S CRAFT

3. Brown describes in great detail the few moments in which he struggles to write a letter. What is the sequence of events?
4. What, according to the narrator, is the significance of his accomplishment?

Ways to Explain

Christy Brown explains his breakthrough using *narration.* Narration presents events that happen over time; it shows change. Narration is just one of several ways you can write when your purpose is to explain. Here are some other examples.

- in an essay for history class, narrating the events leading to U.S. involvement in World War I
- in a letter to your cousin, telling about the effects of baking soda on electrical fires
- in a progress report, relating what tasks have been accomplished in a house-painting project
- in a field observation report for science class, explaining the environmental importance of wetlands
- in a student council report to the school board, proposing and giving evidence that a dance class should be classified as a physical education course
- in a business report, evaluating a computer printer by pointing out its various typefaces, its speed, and its controls
- on a Web site, reviewing the lyrics, melodies, and musical performances on a new CD

LOOKING AHEAD

In the main assignment in this chapter, you'll use narration to write a progress report. Your purpose in writing will be to explain. As you work through each writing assignment in this chapter, keep in mind that a progress report

- focuses on a particular project or activity
- explains the writer's accomplishments, findings, or results, and includes appropriate supporting information
- describes any unexpected problems the writer has encountered
- provides an overall view of the project's current standing

Writing a Progress Report

Prewriting

Showing Progress

When we want to demonstrate to someone—including ourselves—that we're making progress on a project, we can write a progress report. A progress report gives an account of the work done on an ongoing project over a specific time period. "Work done" can refer either to tasks accomplished on a project or to the results or findings of that project. In the workplace, progress reports are written for people who need to be kept informed about a project. They enable decision makers to decide whether the project should be continued as is, modified, or ended. Since progress reports are generally written at fixed intervals—every week, month, or few months—they also serve as a record of the project after it is completed.

Choosing a Subject

Progress reports written in the workplace have a set subject: the project or projects the employee is working on. Even as a student, your subject for a progress report may be decided for you. For example, your chemistry teacher may ask you to submit regular reports explaining the results of a series of lab experiments. The teacher may even give you forms to fill out, or describe the precise format you're expected to follow.

When you're free to choose your own subject, ideas can come from almost any area of your life. For school, you may be preparing a display for the history fair, learning to play the trombone, or designing sets for a play. At home, you may be working on a merit badge in photography for the Scouts, tutoring a neighbor's sixth-grader in math, or saving money to buy a used car. In the community, you may be circulating a petition for a new teen center, spearheading a neighborhood cleanup project, or training to become a tour guide at the zoo. Any of these activities—in fact, any ongoing activity (one you've begun but haven't completed yet)—is a suitable subject for a progress report, as long as it's one that leads toward a goal.

WRITING NOTE Remember that you're writing a short report, not a book. Choose a limited topic that you can explain clearly in a brief report.

TOO BROAD   Birdwatching
LIMITED   Creating a backyard habitat for birds

Thinking About Purpose, Audience, and Tone

Remember that the *purpose* of your progress report is to explain. You want to communicate to your readers what you've accomplished and the nature of any problems that have arisen.

Since you want your report to be useful, you'll want to ask yourself several questions about your readers. First, who is your *audience,* and what do they already know about your project? For example, your audience might be your teacher or your classmates; or it might be your supervisor, or colleagues working on different parts of the same project. It could even be people who don't know anything about your project. In each case, you'll want to adjust the information you provide to suit your audience. Second, what do your readers *need* to know—either as background or in order to carry on with or adjust their own activities? Finally, how much and what kind of information will make your readers confident that your report is sound and reliable?

Unless you haven't made any progress at all, aim for a *tone* that's confident and optimistic. You don't want to promise more than you can deliver, but you do want to reassure your readers that you're on top of the situation. If you've run into problems, explain them in a straightforward way. You can put a positive spin on setbacks by telling how you plan to overcome them.

Notice the difference in tone between these two approaches:

NEGATIVE   The plastic gauze I need for my 3-D sculpture is out of stock at the art-supply store.

POSITIVE   I ordered the plastic gauze I need from a mail-order house, which has promised delivery in five days.

You'll be discussing your own efforts, so plan to use the *first-person point of view:* Use pronouns such as *I, me,* and *my.*

EXERCISE 1 ▶ **Exploring Possible Subjects**

What are you trying to accomplish? Think of some ongoing projects or activities that you could explain in a progress report. Working with a small group, brainstorm several suitable subjects, including some about home and community projects as well as ones that focus on school activities.

WRITING ASSIGNMENT

PART 1:
Choosing a Subject

One benefit of writing a progress report is gaining an overall perspective on your project. In fact, charting your progress by writing about it may help you work through any difficulties you're having on your project. Consider these advantages as you choose a subject to write about— either one your group identified in Exercise 1 above or another ongoing project or activity.

Prewriting

Gathering and Organizing Information

Your goal is to give readers an overview of your project. In order to do so, you will need to provide relevant information that is organized so that readers can easily identify your accomplishments.

Gathering Information

What information—and how much of it—should you include in a progress report? Certainly, vague statements such as "Everything's coming along fine" aren't convincing, yet too much detail can make your report hard to read.

In most cases, you can gather information by mentally reviewing your activities since your last report. Take notes as you review your accomplishments. If you develop a habit of jotting down notes as you work on your project, you'll find them a useful tool when drafting your report.

Now that you have notes describing what you've done on your project, how do you select what information to include in your report? Remember that your primary purpose is to present a clear picture of your progress. You also want to convince readers that your report accurately reflects reality. With these goals in mind, you can use the following two rules of thumb in choosing information to include in your report.

First, select information that will be useful to your reader. For typical progress reports, useful information includes

- identification of the project and its purpose
- time period covered by the report, and a list of specific tasks accomplished in that period
- data, results, or findings that would be of immediate interest to your readers
- any unforeseen problems that have arisen and how you are dealing with them
- what the plans are for the immediate future
- any additional resources needed
- any changes to the project schedule

Avoid the temptation to talk about every detail that you've learned or every small obstacle you encountered: Readers of progress reports appreciate a narrative that sticks to essential information.

As a second guideline in selecting information to include, bear in mind that too little information is as ineffective as too much. Generalizations in progress reports are neither informative nor confidence-inspiring. For example, if your project is creating a video of your school, you can't simply state that things are going well and expect readers to take your word for it. They'll want evidence—perhaps details about what you've videotaped, how much of the soundtrack you've recorded, and whether you're on schedule to meet your original deadline. In other words, be as specific as you can when you list your accomplishments, without overwhelming your reader with details. Where appropriate, include "hard" evidence such as facts, statistics, or examples. In the case of the videotaping project, hard evidence could be a proposed title and the amount of footage (in minutes or hours) that has been videotaped or recorded.

CRITICAL THINKING

Analyzing Accomplishments

Sometimes your accomplishments on a project are obvious, especially when they're tangible ones—ones you can see or touch. For example, it's easy to see your progress when you're building a model of Shakespeare's Globe Theater—you can identify the parts you've constructed and explain the order in which you assembled them. But sometimes accomplishments are not so apparent; perhaps your project is still in the planning stage, or maybe you've spent a lot of time solving a problem. In cases like this, you'll need to analyze the specific tasks you've completed so that in your report you can point to concrete accomplishments.

For example, suppose you are working on an antilittering campaign for your school. If you haven't yet established a campaign, you may think there's nothing to report. But you may actually have done a great deal of work. To show your progress, you could break down the work you've done into the specific tasks involved.

Topic: Organizing a schoolwide antilittering campaign

Accomplishment: Established need for campaign

Task 1. Walked around school grounds every day for two weeks to monitor amount of litter on ground; on average, filled one 5-gallon garbage bag per day

Task 2. Counted number of trash cans on school grounds, calculated percentage overflowing by noon, and determined number of times they're emptied each day

Task 3. Conducted opinion poll among students and teachers about the problem; results overwhelmingly support need for a campaign

CRITICAL THINKING EXERCISE:
Analyzing Accomplishments

You've made progress—but how did you do it? With a partner, choose one of the following accomplishments, and break it down into each of the smaller tasks that had to be completed first.

- settled on a subject for a mixed-media collage for an art exhibit
- found a used car to buy
- submitted a proposal for starting a Spanish Club at school
- held a car wash to raise money for a local theater group
- was hired for a part-time job

Using Graphics to Present Information. If you have a lot of data to include, consider using graphics—tables, charts, or graphs in your report. You can introduce each visual with a sentence or two summarizing the findings it presents. If you have a number of graphics, put them in an appendix at the end of your report—that way, they will not interrupt your report. You can summarize the data in the body of your report and refer your readers to the actual table, chart, or graph. (See page 320 for more about using graphics.)

Addressing Problems. If you've run into problems with your project—or if you foresee problems in the time remaining—your best course is to bring them to your readers' attention and explain the causes. (Doing so helps inspire your readers' confidence in what you're reporting.) Then, you can either explain how you plan to resolve the problems or, if necessary, ask for help. For example, if a scheduled interview fell through because the person had to be out of town that day, you can explain that you've rescheduled (or plan to reschedule) the meeting. If the person has moved away, though, you might need to ask for help in identifying someone else to interview.

PART 2:

Gathering Information

Begin pulling your material together by making a list or chart itemizing your accomplishments; also, include any problems you've encountered. For each accomplishment or result, jot down at least one supporting fact, statistic, or example; for each problem, see if you can list one step you've taken to resolve it. Then, cross out details that would not be useful to your readers. If you have useful information that could be presented visually, decide what kind of graphic (chart, table, graph, and so on) would be most appropriate.

Organizing Information

"Hey! Where's my science project?"

© 1996; reprinted courtesy of Bunny Hoest and *Parade Magazine.*

Now that you've gathered information for your progress report, you need to decide how to organize it. Usually, writers of progress reports use *chronological* (time) *order:* They explain the tasks they've accomplished since the project began (or since the last report) in the order in which they performed them. But some projects require you to carry out several different tasks at the same time. In such cases, using *logical order*—organizing the material by tasks or findings instead of by time—would be much clearer.

The chart on page 302 shows how a writer arranged information about two different projects. For her first project—a plant biology experiment—the writer chose to organize topically because she was working with several groups of plants, each at a different stage of development. For her second project—a course in learning how to swim—she chose to organize her information chronologically because she learned a skill each week.

LOGICAL ORDER	CHRONOLOGICAL ORDER
Plant biology experiment	Swimming lessons
Task 1: Germinating (sprouting) seeds. Germinated three dozen bean plants and two dozen corn plants	Week 1: practiced survival bobbing
	Week 2: learned flutter and breaststroke kicks
Task 2: Planting seeds. Planted twenty bean seedlings one week after germination; watered them every second day	Week 3: learned crawl and backstroke arm techniques
	Week 4: learned breast-stroke arm technique
Task 3: Monitoring seed growth. Took daily measurements of corn seedlings after they'd been planted six weeks; noted an average weekly growth of 1 1/2 inches	Week 5: practiced synchro-nizing flutter kick and crawl arm technique
	Week 6: practiced flutter kick with backstroke arm technique
	Week 7: practiced breast-stroke arm technique with breaststroke kick

COMPUTER NOTE: Create tables within your word-processing program, and use them to record tasks as you accomplish them. That way, you will have notes to work from when you draft your progress report.

PART 3:
Organizing Information

Now's the time to decide whether you'll use chronological or logical order in your progress report. Arrange the information you selected in Writing Assignment, Part 2 (page 301) by numbering your accomplishments, and any problems, in the order you'll present them.

Writing Your First Draft

As you draft your report, try to make it as complete as possible without burdening it with excessive detail. Also, strive for accuracy and clarity; use the simplest terminology you can, and opt for concrete language whenever possible.

Writing the Introduction. Establish a context for your readers by identifying the project or activity you're reporting on and the time period covered. If necessary, refresh their memory by briefly stating the purpose of the report—exactly what it is you're trying to accomplish. For an example of an effective introduction, study the first paragraph of the Writer's Model on pages 307–308.

Writing the Body. Recall what your audience knows and what they need to know. Include any necessary background information, and define unfamiliar terms at the beginning of the body. Then, draft a separate paragraph for each significant accomplishment, finding, or result, using your information list or chart as a guide. Be sure to back up your statements with specific information from your list or chart (facts, examples, statistics). Depending on your situation, you may either explain any problems as you go along or deal with the problems in a separate section, as the Writer's Model on pages 307–308 does.

Writing the Conclusion. Use the conclusion of your report to give readers an overall view of your progress. You may also want to confirm—or revise—the time you originally estimated it would take to complete the project.

WRITING NOTE Progress reports may be written as memos, as letters, or as formal reports with title pages, summaries, tables of contents, and appendixes. For the assignment in this chapter, you may simply write your report as a narrative (see the Writer's Model on pages 307–308 for an example).

Looking at a Progress Report

The following report discusses a geography test administered by the National Assessment of Educational Progress (NAEP) and taken by students throughout the nation.

A PROGRESS REPORT

---

from the *NAEP 1994 Geography Report Card*

INTRODUCTION
Background information/ Purpose of overall project

For more than 25 years, the National Assessment of Educational Progress (NAEP) has probed students' abilities in a variety of subject areas, reporting both on what students know and can do and on the relationships between instructional, institutional, and background variables and differing levels of educational achievement. As the nation's foremost ongoing education survey, the national assessment data track trends in student performance and allow concerned readers to evaluate whether America's students have the skills and knowledge necessary to participate in today's economic and political worlds.

Project being reported on; time period

In 1994, NAEP conducted national assessments in reading, geography, and United States history at grades 4, 8, and 12. The geography results included in this *Report Card* describe students' achievement at each grade and within subgroups of the general population. This information will give educators a context for evaluating the geography achievement of students and data that may be used to guide reform efforts.

BODY

Student performance on the NAEP 1994 geography assessment is summarized on the NAEP geography scale, which ranges from 0 to 500. The geography scale allows for the discussion of what students *know and can do* in terms of the geography content covered by the assessment.

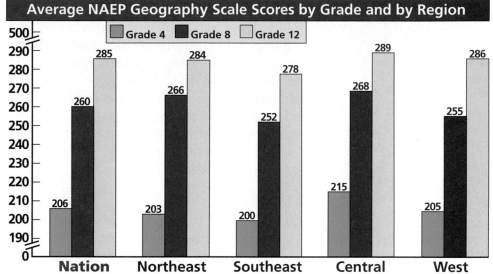

Average NAEP Geography Scale Scores by Grade and by Region

Grade 4 Grade 8 Grade 12

	Nation	Northeast	Southeast	Central	West
Grade 4	206	203	200	215	205
Grade 8	260	266	252	268	255
Grade 12	285	284	278	289	286

SOURCE: National Center for Education Statistics, National Assessment of Educational Progress (NAEP), 1994 Geography Assessment.

For each grade, three levels were set— *Basic, Proficient,* and *Advanced.* These are based on judgments, made by broadly representative panels, about what students *should know and should be able to do* in geography.

The *Proficient* achievement level represents solid academic performance that demonstrates competency over challenging subject matter for each grade assessed. The *Basic* achievement level denotes partial mastery of prerequisite knowledge and skills that are fundamental for proficient work. The *Advanced* achievement level signifies superior performance.

Major Findings for the Nation

Finding 1

■ The *Proficient* achievement level was reached by 22 percent of fourth-graders, 28 percent of eighth-graders, and 27 percent of twelfth-graders.

Finding 2

Finding 3

Finding 4

- At each grade, roughly 70 percent of students were at or above the *Basic* level.
- As students' geography scores increased, the complexity and sophistication of the geographic knowledge and skills they exhibited increased.
- Generally, students across grades in the higher percentiles exhibited greater abilities to work with a range of geographic tools, create maps based on tabular or narrative data, grasp processes and relationships, bring outside knowledge to bear on answering questions, and analyze data.

Summary

CONCLUSION
Summary and future prospects

While the NAEP results presented in this report cannot be used to draw causal inferences, they do point out interesting characteristics and patterns of student performance. Future research and other projects and analyses can use NAEP data to shed more light on relationships between performance and background data, which in turn can be used by policymakers, educators, and citizens to bring change to the United States educational system.

EXERCISE 2 ▶ **Analyzing a Progress Report**

After reading the NAEP report, meet with two or three classmates to discuss the following questions.

1. What is the purpose of the project, and over what time period was it conducted?
2. How do the writers organize this information, topically or chronologically? Why do you think they chose this method of organization?
3. In your own words, summarize the NAEP findings.
4. If you were a consultant to the NAEP, what follow-up projects would you recommend the organization pursue?

A Writer's Model for You

Because the NAEP report describes a completed project, you could think of it as a final progress report. Your own progress report, however, will cover an ongoing project, like the one discussed in the report below. Notice what kinds of evidence the writer uses to support her statements.

A WRITER'S MODEL

INTRODUCTION
Project, purpose, and time period

This is a report on the progress I have made on my history fair project during the last two weeks. My project is a display illustrating the major events in the life of Elizabeth Blackwell, the first woman in the United States to receive a medical degree.

BODY
Accomplishment 1
Evidence

During this period, I completed a diorama of Blackwell's office at the New York Infirmary for Women and Children. The diorama includes miniatures of many of the items pictured in a photograph that I found in a biography of the doctor. I included an examining table, a doctor's scale, and a stethoscope.

Accomplishment 2
Evidence

I also completed a combination map/time line showing the sequence of important events in Blackwell's life. For this section of the display, I used different-colored pushpins to show the location of the events, and I color-coded the time line to match.

Problem—
Discussion

The only item I'm still waiting for is a copy of Blackwell's diploma from the Geneva (N.Y.) Medical College. I called the New York State Historical Society yesterday and spoke with Mr. Roy Lassiter, who explained that he was on vacation when my letter of request arrived. He assured me that he will ship the copy by the end of this week. Since I've already purchased a frame for it, once it arrives I can simply mount it.

CONCLUSION
Overall standing
of project

Although I'm a few days behind the schedule I originally set for myself, overall the project is going well. I'm confident that I will have the finished display ready for judging by the deadline, February 22.

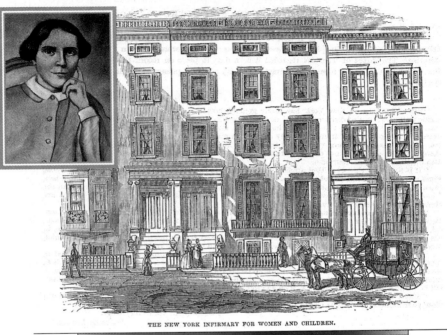

THE NEW YORK INFIRMARY FOR WOMEN AND CHILDREN.

If you organize your report by tasks, you can follow the pattern of the Writer's Model, illustrated in the following chart.

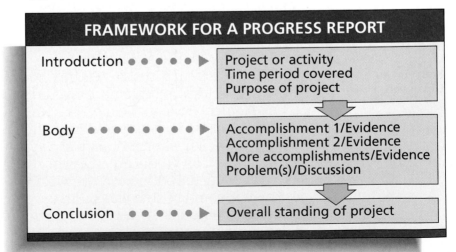

FRAMEWORK FOR A PROGRESS REPORT

Introduction ● ● ● ● ● ▶	Project or activity Time period covered Purpose of project
Body ● ● ● ● ● ● ● ● ▶	Accomplishment 1/Evidence Accomplishment 2/Evidence More accomplishments/Evidence Problem(s)/Discussion
Conclusion ● ● ● ● ● ▶	Overall standing of project

A progress report organized chronologically will follow a slightly different pattern: It would list accomplishments in the order they were completed. Other differences may grow out of the needs of your readers or out of the topic itself. If you haven't encountered any problems, for example, you won't need to devote a section to explaining and proposing solutions to them.

As you draft your paper, remember that a progress report should

- clearly answer these questions: *What have you accomplished so far? What problems have you encountered?*
- include evidence to support findings or results
- present information in an effective order
- have a confident, optimistic tone

WRITING ASSIGNMENT	PART 4: **Writing a First Draft**

Your notes from Writing Assignment, Part 3, page 302, are all you need to write your first draft. These reminders will help you get started:

1. Write a sentence or two identifying your project, the time period your report covers, and the purpose of the project.
2. Write the body—limiting one accomplishment (or finding or result) to a paragraph. Be sure to develop each paragraph with facts, examples, and so on. Discuss any problems—their causes and what you've done (or plan to do) to resolve them—as you go along or in a separate section.
3. Write a conclusion that explains the overall standing of the project.
4. As you write your report, keep in mind your purpose and audience. Remember to keep your tone confident and optimistic.

Evaluating and Revising

With a first draft in hand, you're ready to evaluate and revise your description. Remember that the goal of progress reports is to inform other people of the work you've accomplished on a project. It's important to make sure that your report includes all the information your readers need. One way to do this is to put your draft aside for a day or two; then read it carefully to make sure it presents a clear record of your progress. Are there any accomplishments or findings you neglected to include? If so, add them along with supporting details.

To evaluate other aspects of your draft, use the chart on page 311 to help you make changes. Begin by asking yourself a question in the left-hand column of the chart. If you identify a particular weakness, use the revision technique suggested in the right-hand column.

BOOTH

Drawing by Booth; © 1974 The New Yorker Magazine, Inc.

"It seems some days like I make a little progress, then other days it seems like I'm not getting anywhere at all."

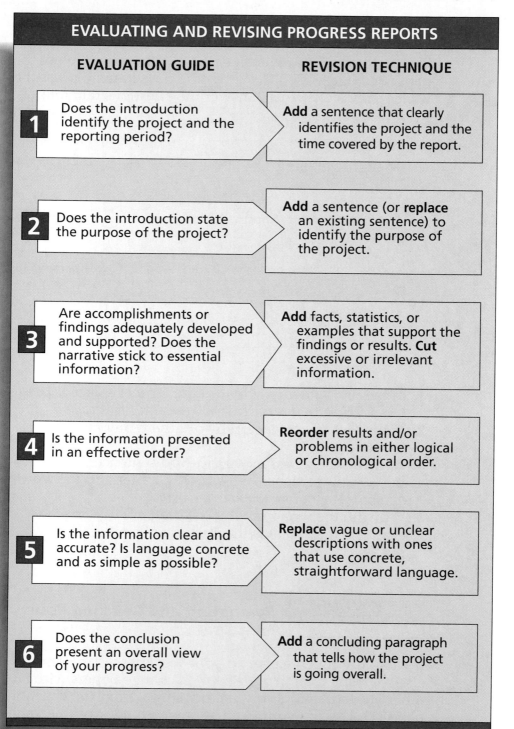

EVALUATING AND REVISING PROGRESS REPORTS

EVALUATION GUIDE	REVISION TECHNIQUE

1 Does the introduction identify the project and the reporting period?

Add a sentence that clearly identifies the project and the time covered by the report.

2 Does the introduction state the purpose of the project?

Add a sentence (or **replace** an existing sentence) to identify the purpose of the project.

3 Are accomplishments or findings adequately developed and supported? Does the narrative stick to essential information?

Add facts, statistics, or examples that support the findings or results. **Cut** excessive or irrelevant information.

4 Is the information presented in an effective order?

Reorder results and/or problems in either logical or chronological order.

5 Is the information clear and accurate? Is language concrete and as simple as possible?

Replace vague or unclear descriptions with ones that use concrete, straightforward language.

6 Does the conclusion present an overall view of your progress?

Add a concluding paragraph that tells how the project is going overall.

E X E R C I S E **3** ▶ **Analyzing a Writer's Revisions**

Here is the writer's revision of the second paragraph of the paper on pages 307–308. With some classmates, discuss the writer's revisions. Then, answer the questions that follow.

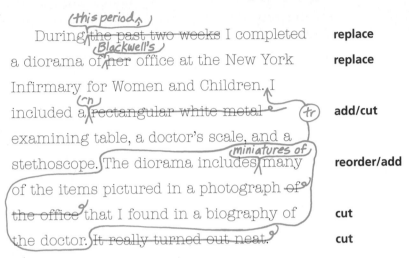

During ~~the past two weeks~~ (this period.) I completed

a diorama of ~~her~~ (Blackwell's) office at the New York

Infirmary for Women and Children. I

included a ~~rectangular white metal~~ (*n*) (*tr*)

examining table, a doctor's scale, and a

stethoscope. The diorama includes (miniatures of) many

of the items pictured in a photograph ~~of~~

~~the office~~ that I found in a biography of

the doctor. ~~It really turned out neat.~~

replace
replace
add/cut
reorder/add
cut
cut

1. In the first sentence, why did the writer replace *the past two weeks* with *this period* and *her* with *Blackwell's*?
2. In the second sentence, why did the writer cut *rectangular white metal*?
3. Why did the writer move the third sentence?
4. In the same sentence, why did the writer add the words *miniatures of* before *many of the items*?
5. Why did the writer cut the last sentence of this paragraph? (Hint: What is the purpose of a progress report?)

WRITING ASSIGNMENT	PART 5: **Evaluating and Revising Your** **First Draft**

It's usually much easier to spot weaknesses in someone else's writing than in your own. Exchange papers with another student, and apply the questions from the chart on page 311. Discuss your evaluations with your partner, and make changes to improve your paper.

Proofreading and Publishing

Proofreading. You've worked hard on your progress report. Now, give it the final touches. If you have even the slightest doubt about the spelling of a word, the placement of a comma, or the form of a verb, consult a dictionary or the Handbook that begins on page 510.

USAGE HINT

Verb Tenses

When you're explaining change over time, you may need to use different tenses to show the sequence of events. When you do so, make sure you've used verb tenses correctly so that your readers understand the relationship between the events.

CONFUSING   After I finished the frame, I **have cut** out the plywood for the side walls.

CLEAR   After I finished the frame, I **cut** out the plywood for the side walls.

☞ REFERENCE NOTE: For more information about clear tense sequence, see pages 684–692.

Publishing. Remember that the purpose of your report is to explain your progress to one or more readers. Here are some suggestions for sharing your progress report:

- Give a copy to the person who assigned the project or to someone who has encouraged your efforts.
- With a group of classmates, prepare a panel presentation of your progress reports.
- Working with classmates whose reports fall into the same general category as yours (for example, art projects), compile your reports into a "progress anthology."

WRITING
ASSIGNMENT

PART 6:
Proofreading and Publishing Your Paper

Proofread your progress report carefully, and correct all errors. When you've made your corrections, share your essay with an audience.

Reflecting on Your Writing

To add your progress report to your **portfolio,** date it and answer these questions in a brief reflection:

- How did you decide on a subject for your report?
- Did writing the report help you gain an overall perspective on your project? Did it help you work through any difficulties you faced?

A STUDENT MODEL

This final progress report was written by Chad Stoloff, a student in Carson City, Nevada. His advice about writing a progress report is to have all your facts together before you start to write. This, says Chad, will make the writing go more smoothly.

Progress Report: A Holiday Gift Drive
by Chad Stoloff

Over Christmas our English class decided to collect holiday food and other gifts for needy people because I came up with the idea from a previous project and mentioned it to my teacher. We decided to have a competition between Mrs. Anderson's English classes. Our goal was to contribute enough food for some needy families so they could have good meals over the Christmas holidays. The winning class of the competition would win a pizza party, and so both classes tried very hard to win.

A point system was set up for the food collected. We gave certain foods more points than others. For example, turkeys and hams were top on the list for points, while canned foods were at the bottom of the list with the least number of points.

Starting the competition two weeks before they let us out of school for Christmas vacation gave us a good amount of time to get our items together. Along with many kinds of food, our class contributed bikes, clothes, and toys to the families that needed them. Several class members sold suckers after school; the money from that was used to buy much needed clothes for the families.

The fund-raiser was for a good cause, and helping people out gave us a great feeling inside. Our class provided a large amount, while the other class contributed a lesser amount, but their effort was still very important to the needy. Every person in each class provided time and effort, and many also contributed money or items to help people out. The whole experience brought my classmates and me closer together.

WRITING WORKSHOP

Writing a Cause-and-Effect Essay

In the course of writing your progress report, you may have found yourself explaining the origins and results of a problem you encountered. If your aim was to help your readers understand a situation by explaining its causes, effects, or both, you were writing a *cause-and-effect explanation.*

If you can ask and answer one or both of these questions about a topic, the topic is suitable for a cause-and-effect essay:

1. *Why did it happen?* [CAUSE]
2. *What is the result?* [EFFECT]

Cause-and-effect writing has two other main characteristics.

- It focuses on a particular situation or event.
- It gives evidence that the explanation is sound.

A sound explanation avoids two common thinking errors, or *fallacies,* in cause-and-effect explanations: **false cause and effect,** in which the writer incorrectly assumes that an effect is the direct result of a cause, and **oversimplifying,** in which the writer identifies a major cause but ignores other causes.

The following excerpt is from a magazine article about the benefits of regular workouts. What does the writer say are the effects of exercise?

> Sarah Cain loves to run. Most days after work she makes her way along the trails that cut through the redwood forest near her home, leaping over roots that snake across the tree-lined path. And when winter's failing light darkens the forest, she pounds the streets of the small towns that edge California's Monterey Bay. Forty-five miles each week, more than 2,000 miles a year. Year in and year out.

The 35-year-old agricultural research technician likes what exercise does for her body. It keeps her fit, muscular, and slim. But she *loves* what it does for her mind. "It keeps me from being depressed and calms me down," she says. "I get a warm, glowing feeling after I run. It takes the edge off."

Although many people are lured to exercise for its well-known cardiovascular benefits or because it makes them look good, a growing number are working up a sweat for the psychological benefits. Exercise can't transform an aggressive, type A personality into a calm type B, but scientists now know that even moderate activity—say, a brisk walk at lunchtime—can lift spirits or dispel tension. And therapists are increasingly prescribing exercise to help their patients cope with more long-term psychological ailments such as anxiety and clinical depression.

Susan Chollar, "The Psychological Benefits of Exercise"

1. List the benefits, or the effects, of exercise mentioned in the article.
2. What information does the writer present as evidence for the benefits of exercise?
3. Does the article present any false causes and effects, attributing benefits to exercise that may be caused by another source? Explain.
4. Consider that this article was printed in *American Health* magazine. Do you think the writer's purpose is just to explain, or is she also trying to persuade? Why?

Writing a Cause-and-Effect Essay

 Prewriting. Choose a limited topic that you can discuss thoroughly in a brief essay. Remember: If you can answer one or both of these questions—*Why did it happen? What is the result?*—your topic is a suitable one. Also, remember to choose a topic that will interest your audience: your classmates. In your essay, you will be helping them understand a situation by explaining its causes, effects, or both. Your essay might analyze one of the following:

1. The causes of a situation or event (for example, why the African elephant is endangered)
2. The effects of a situation or event (for example, the results of a high school's change to block scheduling)
3. Both causes and effects of a situation or event (for example, why someone begins practicing vegetarianism and what happens as a result)

When you've chosen a topic, brainstorm the causes, effects, or both by asking *Why did it happen?* or *What is the result?* and listing your answers. Arrange your information in one of these ways: *order of importance, chronological order,* or *most familiar to least familiar.* Be sure you have evidence to back up your statements.

Writing, Evaluating, and Revising. First, draft an introduction that entices your reader with a question, a brief story, or a striking example. Your introduction should also include a thesis statement. For the body of your essay, draft a separate paragraph for each cause or effect, including information to back up your statements. Conclude by summarizing your main points. Ask two classmates to read your first draft and tell you if anything confuses them. Then, revise your essay for clarity and completeness.

Proofreading and Publishing. Proofread your revised version carefully (see the guidelines for proofreading on page 56). To share your writing, read your essay aloud to your class; or, if your essay covers a timely topic, convert it to a letter to the editor, and send it to your local newspaper. If you include this paper in your **portfolio,** date it and write a brief reflection explaining how you chose a topic to explore.

MAKING CONNECTIONS

PROCESS EXPLANATIONS

Cause-and-effect explanations are very closely related to another kind of explanation—the *process explanation.* Both explanations are narrative; they explain events over the course of time. Cause-and-effect explanations focus on *why* something happens, and process explanations focus on *how* something happens, for example: How does a forward slam-dunk a basketball? How does a compact disc player work? How does a tadpole become a frog?

There are two basic types of process explanations.

1. **How to perform a process.** In this type of essay, you explain a process you know well or one you'd like to learn, for example: how to make spinach lasagna, how to play a guitar, how to handpaint a T-shirt, or how to snorkel. By following your step-by-step directions, readers should be able to do the process.

2. **How something works or happens.** This type of essay explains a process that's more abstract or technical, one that readers can't "do" themselves. For example, you may explain how a computer files information, how an automatic teller machine works, or how fluorocarbons destroy the ozone layer of the atmosphere.

Both types of process essays have three requirements: completeness, order, and tone.

- **Completeness.** Mention every step in the process; don't leave anything out. Depending on your audience, you may need to explain necessary materials and define unfamiliar terms.
- **Order.** In process essays, order is crucial. Discuss each step in chronological order, the order in which each step must be done.
- **Tone.** Use simple, straightforward language. An ideal process essay is not only clear but also lively and interesting.

Graphics (diagrams, drawings, charts) can make a complicated process or a set of directions much easier to understand. What complicated process does the following graphic explain?

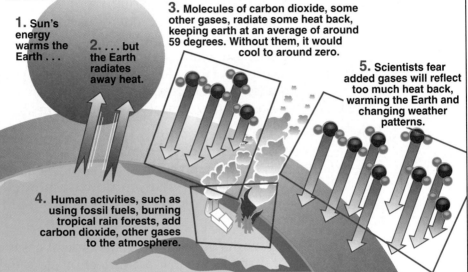

How 'greenhouse effect' works

This year has been the USA's third-warmest on record, putting new focus on the debate about the "greenhouse effect." The current amount of greenhouse warming makes the Earth livable, but more could cause trouble.

1. Sun's energy warms the Earth . . .

2. . . . but the Earth radiates away heat.

3. Molecules of carbon dioxide, some other gases, radiate some heat back, keeping earth at an average of around 59 degrees. Without them, it would cool to around zero.

5. Scientists fear added gases will reflect too much heat back, warming the Earth and changing weather patterns.

4. Human activities, such as using fossil fuels, burning tropical rain forests, add carbon dioxide, other gases to the atmosphere.

USA Today, December 4, 1990. © 1990, *USA Today.* Reprinted with permission.

Think of a process you can explain or a set of directions you can give to other students in your class. (For example, you might explain how a pearl is formed in an oyster shell or how to change the oil in a car.) Create a visual that illustrates the steps or directions you are describing. Then, prepare an oral presentation for the class.

CAUSE AND EFFECT IN LITERATURE

Folktales

Just as we do today, our ancestors wondered why the world is the way it is: why animals are the way they are and why people have certain characteristics. To make connections between the causes and effects they saw and to explain the world of human and animal behavior, our ancestors told folktales. As you read the following Nigerian folktale, ask yourself what it is trying to explain about beauty and character.

Why No One Lends His Beauty
by Harold Courlander with Ezekiel A. Eshugbayi

BEFORE, before, in the beginning of things, people wore their beauty as they wore clothes. It is said that there was a girl named Shoye who possessed beauty that was the pride of her village. Wherever she went, people said: "When before has anyone seen such beauty?"

There was another girl in the village named Tinuke. She did not have such beauty to wear. She envied Shoye. She went to her one day and said: "I must go on a journey for my family. I have no beauty. Lend me your good looks until I return." Shoye did not hesitate. She gave her good looks to Tinuke. Tinuke took the beauty. Her face shone with it. She walked gracefully. She left the village and went on her journey.

People who saw her said: "Whenever has such a beautiful girl been seen?" She went to the town where a chief lived. His friends told him: "There is a girl in the town. She comes from another place. She has great beauty." The chief sent for Tinuke. He saw her beauty. He took her as a wife. She did not return to her own village.

Shoye waited. She was very ugly. When she went to the market, people said: "When before has anyone seen such ugliness?"

Tinuke did not return. Shoye's friends said: "Tinuke has surely stolen your beauty. You must find her." So Shoye went in search of Tinuke. She came to the town of the chief.

People said: "What ugliness! She has a hideous face! It will bring bad luck on us. Send her away!" But Shoye would not go away. She heard that Tinuke now lived in the house of the chief. She went there. She asked for Tinuke. Tinuke would not come. She hid behind the walls of the chief's compound.

When the chief passed through his gate, he saw Shoye there. He said: "Who is the girl with the ugly face crouching before my estate?"

His guards said: "She asks for Tinuke. Tinuke will not see her."

The chief spoke to Shoye. He said: "Why do you wait here?"

Shoye answered: "I have a friend in my village. She borrowed my beauty. She came here. She now lives in your house. She does not return to her village. She does not return what she borrowed."

The chief said: "You mean that beautiful girl that I have taken as my wife? How could such beauty not belong to the one who wears it?" He sent for Tinuke. She came. She saw Shoye. She was ashamed. She gave Shoye's beauty back to her. Shoye took it. Her face shone. She walked gracefully. Tinuke was now ugly.

People said: "Whenever has a chief had so ugly a wife?"

The chief said: "Beauty and good character are not the same thing. Because a woman wears beauty does not mean that she behaves well. This girl Tinuke came to me wearing beauty, but her character was faulty. Shoye, who was ugly because someone else borrowed her beauty, her behavior was good. One may borrow beauty but not good character. Thus, beauty deceives. And, therefore, I order that henceforth one may not lend his beauty to another. Each person shall wear what is his own."

Thereafter, it was this way. One could neither lend nor borrow beauty. Each person wore what was his own. And there came to be a saying:

"Beauty is only worn; it is not the same as character."

Get together with two or three classmates, and complete the following activities. You might want to divide up the questions among you and do some library research.

1. How is the problem between Tinuke and Shoye resolved? How does this folktale explain the expression "Beauty is only skin-deep"? What false cause and effect is described in this tale?

2. Many cultures (groups of people) have myths or folk-tales that attempt to explain some aspect of human behavior. Find another folktale or myth, and share it with your class. (For example, in the story of Daedalus and Icarus, the Greeks explained the dangers of being over-confident.)

3. Try writing a folktale, myth, or other narrative that explains a human trait or characteristic.

"WHEN THE CHARACTER'S RIGHT, LOOKS ARE A GREATER DELIGHT."

OVID

9 WRITING TO PERSUADE

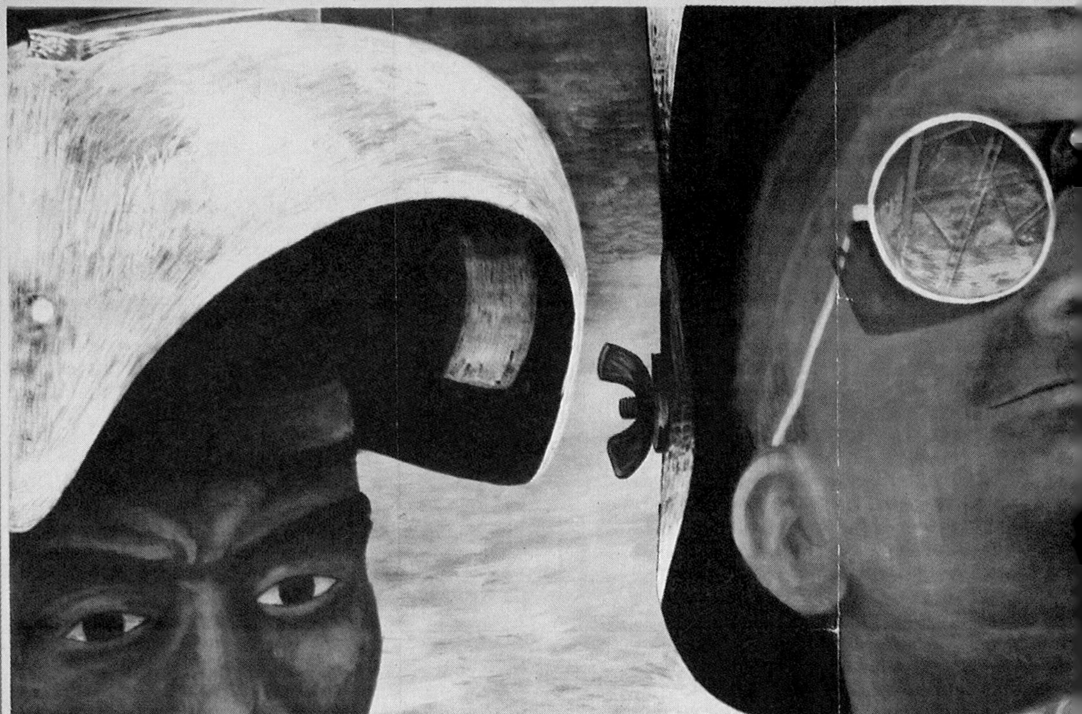
for full employment after th
REGISTER

Taking a Stand

Persuasion is the world of beliefs and opinions—the world where people **take a stand** and try to convince others to join them.

Writing and You. Like the artist whose work appears on these pages, we all take a stand at some time. Sometimes we use logical reasons to persuade others, but most of the time we use both logical reasons and emotional appeals. Politicians, for example, try to convince you to vote for them. Advertisers try to get you to buy their products. And you try to convince your parents to let you borrow the car on Saturday night. When was the last time you took a stand on something?

As You Read. Following is a letter written by Leonardo da Vinci in the fifteenth century. As you read, notice how he tries to persuade an Italian nobleman to give him a job.

A Letter to the
Duke of Milan

by Leonardo da Vinci

Having, most illustrious lord, seen and considered the experiments of all those who pose as masters in the art of inventing instruments of war, and finding that their inventions differ in no way from those in common use, I am emboldened, without prejudice to anyone, to solicit an appointment of acquainting your Excellency with certain of my secrets.

I I can construct bridges which are very light and strong and very portable, with which to pursue and defeat the enemy; and others more solid, which resist fire or assault, yet are easily removed and placed in position; and I can also burn and destroy those of the enemy.

II In case of a siege I can cut off water from the trenches and make pontoons and scaling ladders and other similar contrivances.

III If by reason of the elevation or the strength of its position a place cannot be bombarded, I can demolish every fortress if its foundations have not been set on stone.

IV I can also make a kind of cannon which is light and easy of transport, with which to hurl small stones like hail, and of which the smoke causes great terror to the enemy, so that they suffer heavy loss and confusion.

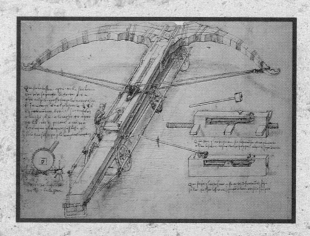

V I can noiselessly construct to any prescribed point subterranean passages either straight or winding, passing if necessary underneath trenches or a river.

VI I can make armored wagons carrying artillery, which shall break through the most serried ranks of the enemy, and so open a safe passage for his infantry.

VII If occasion should arise, I can construct cannon and mortars and light ordnance in shape both ornamental and useful and different from those in common use.

VIII When it is impossible to use cannon I can supply in their stead catapults, mangonels, *trabocchi*, and other instruments of admirable efficiency not in general use—In short, as the occasion requires I can supply infinite means of attack and defense.

IX And if the fight should take place upon the sea I can construct many engines most suitable either for attack or defense and ships which can resist the fire of the heaviest cannon, and powders or weapons.

X In time of peace, I believe that I can give you as complete satisfaction as anyone else in the construction of buildings both public and private, and in conducting water from one place to another.

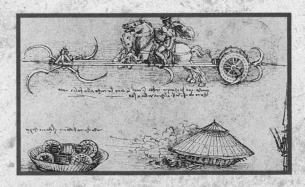

I can further execute sculpture in marble, bronze or clay, also in painting I can do as much as anyone else, whoever he may be.

Moreover, I would undertake the commission of the bronze horse, which shall endue with immortal glory and eternal honour the auspicious memory of your father and of the illustrious house of Sforza.——

And if any of the aforesaid things should seem to anyone impossible or impracticable, I offer myself as ready to make trial of them in your park or in whatever place shall please your Excellency, to whom I commend myself with all possible humility.

READER'S RESPONSE

1. Does this letter seem convincing to you? If you were the duke, would you hire Leonardo? Why?
2. Like Leonardo, have you ever tried to persuade someone to give you a job? What about the opposite—to persuade someone (probably a parent or a teacher) *not* to give you a job? In your journal, write a paragraph or two about your experience. Were you convincing?

WRITER'S CRAFT

3. What examples does Leonardo use to convince the duke that his inventions are different? Why does he include so many?
4. In the last paragraph, Leonardo uses a technique advertisers often use to persuade you to try something. What does he offer to do?
5. What picture of the writer comes through by the end of the letter?

Ways to Persuade

Writers trying to persuade are like Leonardo—they want to get their readers to accept their opinion or move their readers to action.

Persuasive writing appears in many different forms and places—as newspaper editorials, as magazine articles, as speeches, and even as business memos. In each case, you as a writer or speaker are trying to convince others to accept your opinion. Here are some examples of the ways you can develop a persuasive message.

- in a speech to convince people not to litter our lakes and rivers, telling a story about a duck you found with a plastic ring around its neck
- in a memorandum, explaining to your supervisor that a traffic incident caused you to be late
- in a flyer, describing your bicycle to interested potential buyers
- in a postcard, describing a beach to convince your friends to join you there next summer
- in an editorial, defining the word *freedom* to convince people that they should register to vote
- in a conversation, describing two shopping centers to convince your best friend that one is a better place to go
- in a review, explaining a book you just read and recommending it to other readers
- in a letter to the editor of the local newspaper, stating your opinion about the importance of seat belts and making a recommendation about them to readers

Council should approve environmental package

BUDGET CUTS WARRANT CLOSER LOOK

Education bill deserves speedy approval

LOOKING AHEAD

In the main assignment in this chapter, you'll develop a persuasive essay. As you work through the writing assignments in the chapter, keep in mind that an effective piece of persuasive writing

- states the writer's opinion, or point of view, about the topic
- provides convincing support for the writer's opinion
- may use reasons and evidence as well as emotional appeals

This is Earth.

This is Earth without the ozone layer.

Writing a Persuasive Essay

Prewriting

Choosing a Topic

You have opinions on many different questions. For example, do you believe it's right or wrong to kill animals so that people can wear fur? Do you think that the government should ban the use of chemicals that may be changing the earth's climate? Or should the government wait for more evidence to come in?

Those particular questions may not matter much to you, but you may feel strongly about other issues that would be good topics for a persuasive essay. Before you choose a topic, think about these questions.

1. Is the topic important to you?
2. Do you have an opinion on the topic?
3. Do people have different opinions about the topic?
4. Is there an audience for you to convince?

An Important Topic.   You may write about a topic of local interest, such as the need for a traffic signal at an intersection in your town. Or you may choose a topic of national interest, such as whether U.S. companies should sell advanced weapon systems to other countries.

Whatever topic you choose should matter to you, and it should be important enough to argue about. You won't change your readers' minds about a question of personal taste. For example, you can't persuade a cat owner that dogs are better pets than cats. Don't even try. But you might want to argue for or against clearing the streets of all stray dogs and cats.

An Opinion, Not a Fact. Remember the difference between an opinion and a fact. An *opinion* is a belief or a point of view. People can have different opinions about the same subject. For example, some people think that all teenagers are excellent drivers, but others believe that all teenagers are terrible drivers. You can't prove that either opinion is true—or untrue.

A *fact,* on the other hand, is a statement that can be checked—in reference works, for example. It's a fact, for instance, that insurance companies charge teenagers a higher premium than older drivers.

Opposing Opinions. The saying "There are two sides to every question" applies especially to choosing a topic for a persuasive essay. A good topic has at least two conflicting sides. For instance, some people believe that students in public high schools should be required to wear uniforms. Others believe that such uniforms violate students' freedoms. And both sides offer sound arguments to support their opinion.

Finding Your Audience. As you consider different topics, you need to think about who your audience will be. What group of people will most strongly object to what you have to say? And what are their reasons? As part of your essay, you'll have to refute (argue against) their reasons.

An Opinion Statement

Stating your opinion on the topic in one clear sentence will help you focus your thinking. Because this statement tells where you stand (your "position" on the topic), it's also called a position statement or proposition. Here are some examples.

> Our school should offer courses in an Asian language.
> Baseball stars deserve the high salaries they receive.
> Two years of community or military service should be
>   required after graduation from high school.

Reminder

When choosing a topic for a persuasive essay

- find a topic that's important to you by looking through magazines and newspapers, listening to television and radio, and brainstorming (see pages 27 and 32–33)
- know the opinions that conflict with yours on the issue
- identify the part of your audience that disagrees with you, the people that you want to convince
- write an opinion statement, a sentence that clearly states the topic and your opinion on it

---

E X E R C I S E   1 ▶   Distinguishing Fact from Opinion

In an argument, you can't let anyone pass off an opinion as if it were a fact. How good are you at telling them apart? Work with a partner or small group to decide whether each of the following statements is an *opinion* or a *fact*. Remember that an opinion is a point of view or a belief. A fact is a statement that can be checked or proved.

1. Earth is the most important planet in the solar system.
2. In 1609 Galileo aimed a telescope at the stars and discovered four of Jupiter's moons.
3. When it re-enters the earth's atmosphere, the space shuttle orbiter is traveling more than 16,000 miles per hour.
4. We know that there must be other intelligent beings in the universe.
5. The Hubble space telescope cost 1.5 billion dollars.

WRITING ASSIGNMENT

PART 1:

Choosing a Topic

Now you're ready to decide on a topic for your persuasive essay. Choose a topic that's important to you. For example, if you think that your community needs a youth center, who do you think should pay for it? When you have your topic clearly in mind, write an opinion statement.

Prewriting

Thinking About Purpose, Audience, and Tone

Your *purpose* in writing persuasion is to convince your readers (1) to follow the course of action you suggest or (2) to think differently about an issue.

To win your *audience* to your point of view, you must find out as much as you can about them. What do they already know about the issue? What concerns do they share with you? Why is their opinion different from yours? What's the strongest argument that they can come up with? For example, if you think that the food in the high school cafeteria should be improved, you may have to persuade several different groups. To analyze their concerns, you might make a chart like this one.

HERE'S HOW

AUDIENCE	CONCERNS
Your classmates	More ethnic food; more variety; food that tastes better
Parents	Nutritious food that students will eat
Principal and teachers	Reasonable cost; no junk food
Cafeteria manager	Staying within budget; serving food that's easy to prepare, keep warm, and clean up

The *tone* of your essay is important because it reveals your attitude toward both your topic and your audience. (Remember that your attitude is conveyed by the language you use to write about your topic.) Describing the cafeteria food in a sarcastic tone may entertain your classmates, but it might turn off the people you most need to convince. A little humor might be effective, but your overall tone should be serious and formal.

EXERCISE 2 ▶	**Speaking and Listening: Identifying Opposing Arguments**

A good debater can argue either side of an issue. This exercise gives you practice in looking at issues from opposing points of view. Work in a small group to focus on these two questions:

a. *What group might strongly disagree with this opinion?*
b. *What might their reasons be for disagreeing?*

For each opinion statement, let one person identify an audience that might strongly disagree. Then have other group members pretend to be that opposing audience, thinking of their reasons for disagreeing with the opinion statement.

> EXAMPLE OPINION: Motorcyclists should be required to wear safety helmets.
>
> *What group might strongly disagree?* some motorcyclists
> *What reasons might they give for disagreeing?*
> **1.** A helmet takes away much of the pleasure we get from riding a motorcycle. We like to feel the wind in our hair.
> **2.** It's our right to make decisions about our own safety.

1. The school year should be extended year-round to twelve months.
2. Our community must create bicycle lanes on all major roads.
3. Commercials should be banned on children's television programs.
4. Physical education classes are unnecessary for high school students.
5. High school athletes should be required to have a 3.0 grade-point average to participate in school sports.

© 1990 Los Angeles Times Syndicate

Bad Debater!

Wow. You gotta point there.

hickerson

The Quigmans, copyright, 1990. Distributed by Los Angeles Times Syndicate. Reprinted with permission.

Prewriting

Supporting Your Opinion

Experience may have already taught you that most people won't change just because you tell them they should change. To persuade others, you have to present your reasons logically and back up each reason with evidence. Sometimes it helps to appeal to their emotions, too.

No matter what you write, you may be unable to persuade people who strongly oppose your opinion. But your essay will be successful if you can at least make them understand and respect your point of view.

Logical Appeals

Two kinds of logical appeals—*reasons* and *evidence*—are aimed at your audience's ability to think.

Reasons. *Reasons* tell why readers should accept an opinion. For example:

Opinion: A drivers' training course should be a requirement for high school graduation.

Reasons: 1. Teenagers who take drivers' training courses are better drivers.
2. Good driving is an essential skill for nearly every adult.

But reasons alone will persuade few readers. Most readers want proof that your reasons make sense.

Evidence. *Evidence* supplies proof for your reasons. There are two kinds of evidence:

■ *facts*—statements that can be checked by testing, personal observation, or reading a reliable reference source.

　a. Of the students who took drivers' training at our school last year, 93 percent passed the state licensing examination on the first try.
　b. Because teenagers who take drivers' training have fewer accidents, insurance companies charge them lower rates.

■ *expert opinion*—statements by a recognized authority on the subject.

Alida Shumway, state highway commissioner, has said, "Teenagers who have completed a driver training course are safe drivers. There's no substitute for quality instruction from professionals in a school setting."

Finding Reasons and Evidence. For some opinions, you'll be able to use reasons and evidence that come from common knowledge and your own observations. For other issues, such as those having to do with national policy or science, for example, you may depend heavily on expert opinions and current information from reliable sources. You may also want to use nonprint sources—such as documentary and instructional videotapes and audiotapes—to gather support for your opinion. As you collect ideas and information, be sure to take notes. Don't try to sort out the stronger reasons and pieces of evidence from the weak ones until you've finished your research.

Reminder

To find reasons and evidence to support your opinion

■ brainstorm, cluster, or freewrite to find out what you already know (see pages 26–29)
■ read books, magazine articles, or newspapers for information on your topic
■ talk with experts and others interested in the topic

Emotional Appeals

Which do you think are more powerful—appeals to logic or appeals to emotion (feelings)? Don't underestimate emotions. Advertisers rely almost entirely on emotional appeals to persuade you to buy their products. Emotional appeals can be convincing in a persuasive essay, too.

Think about how you want your audience to feel about your topic. Then tell about a personal experience or include an example that appeals to that emotion. For example, if you want to convince your audience to volunteer to read at a nursing home, you might use examples that awaken feelings of compassion. You could describe your visit with a stroke patient, a former teacher who helped many children learn to read, but can no longer read on her own.

Emotional appeals alone won't persuade people who strongly disagree with you. In fact, they are likely to become angry at this tactic. Use emotional appeals only when you think they might convince the audience.

WRITING NOTE As you know, words have both denotative and connotative meanings. The *denotative* meaning is the dictionary definition. *Connotative* meanings are the feelings or attitudes that a word suggests. Words like *predator, slaughter, victim, home, family,* and *freedom* are just a few of the many words that are loaded with emotional meanings. Recognize the power of emotional words, and choose them carefully in an essay that emphasizes logical reasons and evidence.

Peanuts reprinted by permission of United Feature Syndicate, Inc.

CRITICAL THINKING

Evaluating Your Reasoning

Your persuasive essay should be based on sound reasons and factual evidence. Here are five kinds of statements that look like reasons but really aren't because they're not logical. Study these five kinds of tricky statements carefully. When you're the person who's being persuaded, you should read and listen critically and be able to say, "Hey, wait a minute. *That's* not logical at all."

Statements Disguised as Reasons

1. **Attacking the Person.** Called "negative campaigning" in politics, this technique is also known as "name-calling." It weakens an argument because it doesn't deal with the real issues.

Attacking the Person	People who vote "no" on the school referendum don't care about children.
Facing the Issue	We need to hire more teachers. If we don't pass the school referendum, classes will have 35–40 students next year.

2. **False Cause and Effect.** Don't assume that one event caused the event that happened next. One event can follow another without having anything to do with the first event. What's wrong with the reasoning in this example?

First Event	A pharmaceutical company built a plant near the river this spring.
Second Event	Tests this summer show that the river is polluted.
False Cause-Effect	This plant is causing the river's pollution.

3. **Hasty Generalization.** Don't base a conclusion on inadequate evidence.

Inadequate Evidence	The first time I played baseball, I hit a home run.
Hasty Generalization	Baseball is an easy game that I can play well without having to practice.

4. **Circular Reasoning.** When you restate your opinion in different words, don't try to pass off the restatement as a reason. In this example, both sentences say the same thing.

Statement of Opinion   Anna is the best choice for tenth-grade student council representative.

Circular Reasoning   She's the person who can do the finest job as tenth-grade student council representative.

5. **Either-Or.** The either-or thinker describes a situation in terms of two extreme alternatives and suggests that there is only one correct choice. Usually there are several choices between the two extremes.

Either-Or Reasoning   If you don't call me every night, you don't love me.

There may be several other reasons why someone doesn't call every night.

CRITICAL THINKING EXERCISE:
Evaluating Reasons

Can you detect illogical statements disguised as reasons? Read the opinion and the statements that support it. Tell whether each statement is (a) attacking the person, (b) false cause and effect, (c) hasty generalization, (d) circular reasoning, or (e) either-or reasoning.

Opinion: Offering advanced placement (AP) classes is a waste of school time and money.

Supporting Statements:
1. Some AP students score poorly on the AP exam, which proves that AP classes don't get results.
2. Anyone who thinks that AP classes should be kept must be completely out of touch with reality.
3. We must cut the AP classes, or we won't be able to give an adequate education to our average students.

4. AP classes are the courses that are most easily dispensed with. Therefore, these are the courses that should be cut from the curriculum.
5. Before we had AP classes, our overall dropout rate at the high school was 10 percent. Now our overall dropout rate is 18 percent. It's obvious that our concentration of time and money on AP classes has increased the number of dropouts.

WRITING ASSIGNMENT

PART 2:
Supporting Your Opinion

Build your argument on a solid foundation of reasons and evidence to support your opinion. To organize your ideas, you can use a chart like the following one. As you list your reasons and evidence, decide what order you'll put them in. If you need more reasons, facts, and expert opinions, find them by reading and talking about your topic. Try to include an emotional appeal unless your teacher asks you to use only logical appeals.

HERE'S HOW

OPINION

AUDIENCE

REASONS	EVIDENCE
1.	1.
2.	2.
3.	3.

Writing Your First Draft

The Basic Elements of Persuasive Essays

You've gathered your ideas for a persuasive essay. Now it's time to organize them into a composition that will convince your audience.

Keep in mind that a persuasive essay

- takes a stand on a topic that people disagree on
- tries to persuade an audience to think and perhaps act as the writer suggests
- uses reasons and evidence
- sometimes appeals to the audience's emotions

Professional writers combine these basic elements in different ways. As you read the following editorial, notice how the writer uses these basic elements to convince you.

A MAGAZINE EDITORIAL

Opinion

Attention grabber

Background

Emotional appeal

Opposing opinion

Emotional appeal

Opinion

Can Bicycles Save the World?
by Jane Bosveld

"**G**reat Britain isn't as advanced as we are," wrote an American student in 1967. "Probably half the people still ride bicycles." The student was wrong about bicycle ridership in Britain—only about one in four Brits owns a bike, and most ride for leisure, not as alternative transport. But the American student's observation reflects the prevailing attitude in industrial nations that bicycles are somehow second-class vehicles, dwarfed by the power and convenience of automobiles. A bike, of course, won't win any contests of speed or long-distance commuting, but in an age when the implications of pollution threaten the health of the world, human power is looking better and better.

Emotional appeals

Opinion

Reasons

Bicycle lovers have longed for the day when their machines would regain the respectability lost after horseless carriages took over the streets. They have proselytized about the joys of bike riding: the closeness one feels to nature when pedaling through the countryside; the exhilaration one feels at making it up a long hill or skillfully maneuvering through a busy intersection. Biking, they contend, is the one exercise suitable for just about everyone. When you ride a bike, the bike bears the weight of your body, allowing you to exercise your muscles without taxing your joints. Many an individual suffering from arthritis or knee trouble has turned to the bicycle for relief.

Background

Emotional appeal

Bicycle activists have mobilized in most North American and European cities, lobbying transportation departments for bike lanes and trying to rustle up support from nonbicycle riders. Despite these efforts, however, transportation planners have remained notoriously unsympathetic to the needs of bikers. It is a stance we may all come to regret. Consider these facts published in a recent article by the Worldwatch Institute, a major think tank for environmental conservation:

Evidence/Facts

- Gasoline and diesel fuel emissions are major contributors to acid rain and the depletion of the ozone layer. They are also linked to about 30,000 deaths each year in the United States alone. Interestingly, the worst pollution comes from short car trips, because a cold engine is particularly inefficient, releasing a high percentage of unburned hydrocarbons into the atmosphere. Many of these short trips could easily be done on a bike.

Evidence/Facts

- If just 10 percent of the Americans who commute to work by car rode their bikes to work or to a train or bus that would take them to work, more than $1.3 billion could be cut from the U.S. oil import bill. Oil imports account for nearly a quarter of the country's $171 billion trade deficit. . . .

Expert opinion

"In their enthusiasm for engine power," writes Marcia D. Lowe, author of the Worldwatch article, "transit planners have overlooked the value of human power. With congestion, pollution, and debt threatening both the industrial and developing worlds, the vehicle of the future clearly rides on two wheels. . . ."

Call to action

But what would happen if we began to use bicycles more frequently? If, say, we hopped on a bike to go get a gallon of milk or to visit friends on the other side of town? What if we saved the car for big hauls and long trips? Before this can happen, of course, much must be done to make bicycle riding

Summary of reasons

Emotional appeal

safe and pleasurable. Biking may be wonderful exercise and environmentally sound, but few individuals will be willing to pedal down roads where cars and trucks zoom past them with inches to spare, leaving the biker to wobble in a blast of air. Until roads are built

Call to action

with bike lanes or at least wide shoulders, few people are likely to get in the habit of biking. Even with those improvements, it will

take a shifting of attitudes to get most people to take up two-wheel travel. People will need to believe that even one less trip in the car adds up to something, that riding a bicycle is, like recycling paper or conserving electricity, an endeavor worth pursuing. Deciding to ride a bike is taking on responsibility. Not everyone will choose to do so, but for everyone who does, the world, rest assured, will be at least a little better off.

Omni

Emotional appeal

Call to action

Emotional appeal

EXERCISE 3 ▶ Analyzing a Persuasive Essay

Meet with two or three classmates to discuss the following questions.

1. What opinion statement do you think Jane Bosveld might have started with? Does she convince you?
2. What does the essay's title have to do with the writer's opinion? How do you like her title?
3. Which reason for her opinion does Bosveld emphasize? Why do you think she supplies so much evidence for this reason? What other reason(s) does she give?
4. Find some words that have strong connotative meanings. What would you say is the tone of this essay?

Professional writers' persuasive essays aren't all alike. For instance, the statement of opinion may come right at the beginning of the essay, or it may appear much later. It may be stated directly in a sentence or two, or indirectly in a question or title. The number of reasons varies, and so does the order in which they're given. (The most important reason can be first or saved for last.) Some writers stick to logical appeals alone, but most include emotional appeals. A call to action—telling readers what action to take—may be present or left out entirely.

A Simple Framework for a Persuasive Essay

The essay "Can Bicycles Save the World?" shows you how one professional writer put together a persuasive essay. The following essay illustrates a framework or basic structure that you can use for your own essay.

A WRITER'S MODEL

Something Good for the Earth

INTRODUCTION   Garbage! It smells bad and looks disgusting. Most people prefer not to think about trash more than once a day when they "take it out." We in the United States get rid of a great deal of garbage. In fact, we throw away 40 percent of all the garbage in the world.

BODY   What's in that garbage that we toss out? Of the 200 million tons of garbage that U.S. citizens produce yearly, approximately 42 percent is paper (made from trees), 8 percent is glass, 9 percent is metal (from ore, a natural resource), 7 percent is plastic (from petroleum, a natural resource), 8 percent is rubber (from rain forests), 8 percent is food waste, and 18 percent is yard waste.

Attention grabber

Background

Facts and statistics

Government officials estimate that 60 percent of our nation's trash could be recycled. Environmentalists suggest a much higher figure—as much as 70 to 90 percent.

Statistics

You can help do something good for the earth by recycling. Perhaps the most important reason for recycling is that it saves precious natural resources. Every week, for example, 50,000 trees are sacrificed to produce Sunday newspapers in the United States. Just by recycling newspapers, you can help to save a forest.

Statement of opinion

Reason

In addition to the direct savings of natural resources, recycling saves water and energy. Recycling paper instead of making paper from trees reduces water use by 60 percent and energy use by 70 percent. Aluminum cans show the biggest saving from recycling. It takes 95 percent less energy to produce a can from recycled aluminum than from ore.

Reason

Explanation

Evidence/ Facts

The third reason for recycling is that it reduces the mountains of garbage we produce. Garbage, unfortunately, doesn't disappear like magic after it's hauled away. For many years garbage was dumped into landfills, which also created

Reason

Explanation

monumental pollution problems. In older
landfills, toxins leached into the soil and
ground water, finding their way eventually into the food chain. And now we're
running out of places that will accept
garbage for landfill. The Environmental
Protection Agency estimates that in the
next ten years 10 percent of our cities will
run out of landfill space.

**Evidence/
Facts**

**Evidence/
Expert
opinion**

     People object to recycling projects for
two reasons. Recycling costs too much,
they complain, adding to already over-
burdened budgets. But most taxpayers
also approve recycling fees, and recycling
actually saves money because there's
less solid waste disposal. Their second
objection is that people are too lazy to
separate trash and wash out cans and
bottles. But that's not true. Across the
nation, officials have been amazed at
how willing residents pitch in and
recycle.

**Opposing
argument**

**Facts
against**

**Opposing
argument**

**Facts
against**

CONCLUSION   Recycling is something each of us can
do to help the earth. Trash makes our
home, this planet, less livable for the
children of today and tomorrow. We
caused the problem, and we can solve it.
Will you help?

**Restatement
of opinion**

**Emotional
appeal**

**Call to
action**

You may find it helpful to model your own persuasive essay after the one on recycling. It follows the framework given below. The number of reasons and amount of evidence you use will depend on your topic and your audience.

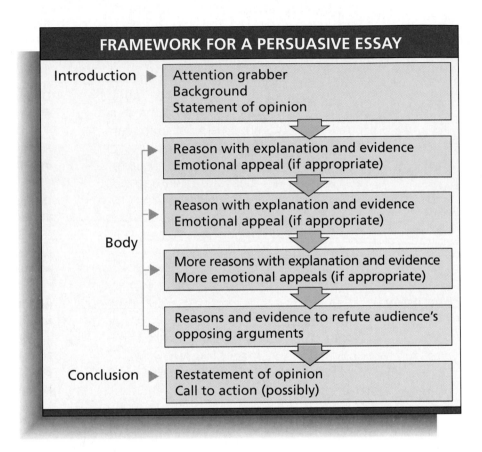

FRAMEWORK FOR A PERSUASIVE ESSAY

Introduction ▶ Attention grabber
Background
Statement of opinion

Body

Reason with explanation and evidence
Emotional appeal (if appropriate)

Reason with explanation and evidence
Emotional appeal (if appropriate)

More reasons with explanation and evidence
More emotional appeals (if appropriate)

Reasons and evidence to refute audience's opposing arguments

Conclusion ▶ Restatement of opinion
Call to action (possibly)

WRITING ASSIGNMENT

PART 3:
Writing a Draft of Your Persuasive Essay

You have everything you need to start writing. Using the basic framework as a model, write a first draft of your persuasive essay. Keep your audience in mind as you write. Think of the strongest objection opponents might have to your opinion. What reasons and evidence can you use to convince them to change their thinking?

Evaluating and Revising

You have what looks like a whole essay, but you're not really finished yet. Now you need to decide what changes would make it better. Most professional writers treat evaluating and revising as essential parts of the writing process. Ellen Goodman is a Pulitzer Prize winner and a nationally syndicated columnist—and here's what she has to say about making that extra effort in her writing.

© 1998, The Boston Globe Newspaper Co./Washington Post Writers Group. Reprinted with permission.

> What makes me happy is rewriting. In the first draft, you get your ideas and your theme clear. If you're using some kind of metaphor you get that established, and certainly you have to know where you're coming out. But the next time through, it's like cleaning house, getting rid of all the junk, getting things in the right order, tightening things up. I like the process of making writing neat. When I read my column in the paper and I find I've used the same word twice close together or if I've got something dangling, I can't stand it.
>
> Ellen Goodman, from *On Being a Writer*

 COMPUTER NOTE: Your word-processing program's Find command can help you look for overused words. Use the online thesaurus to replace them with synonyms.

Use the chart on the next page to improve your first draft. Ask yourself each of the questions in the left-hand column. When you discover a weakness in your essay, use the revision technique suggested in the right-hand column.

EVALUATING AND REVISING PERSUASIVE ESSAYS

EVALUATION GUIDE	REVISION TECHNIQUE
1 Do the first one or two sentences grab the reader's attention?	**Add** an interesting example, fact, or observation, or **replace** existing sentences with one.
2 Does a clear statement of the writer's opinion appear early in the essay?	**Add** a sentence (or **replace** one) that clearly states the topic and your opinion.
3 Is background information given to help explain the topic?	**Add** examples or facts that will help your audience understand the topic.
4 Are there enough reasons and evidence to convince readers?	Research and **add** more reasons, facts, or expert opinions to your essay.
5 Are all of the reasons strong?	**Cut** statements that aren't real reasons at all (see pages 340–341). **Add** sound reasons that will make sense to your readers.
6 Does the essay respond to opposing arguments?	**Add** (or **replace**) reasons, explanations, and evidence to refute your opponents' strongest arguments.
7 If appropriate, does the essay contain emotional appeals?	**Add** sentences (or **replace** existing sentences) that clearly appeal to the emotions of your audience.
8 Is the conclusion effective?	Rewrite the conclusion. **Add** a sentence that uses different words but restates your opinion. **Add** a call to action.

EXERCISE 4 ▶   **Analyzing a Writer's Revisions**

Study the changes the writer made in her first draft of the second paragraph on page 348. Figure out why each change is an improvement by answering the questions.

You can help *^do something good for the earth* by recycling. Perhaps   **add**

the most important reason for recycling is

that it saves precious natural resources.

~~And the earth's natural resources are~~   **cut**

~~too precious to waste.~~ Every week, for

example, ~~many~~ *^50,000* trees are ~~used~~ *^sacrificed* to produce   **replace**

Sunday newspapers in the United States.

Just by recycling *^(newspapers)* you can help *^to save a forest.*   **add**

1. Why did the writer change the first sentence? (Hint: Do the changes appeal to logic or feelings?)
2. Why did the writer cut the third sentence?
3. Which is more persuasive: *many trees* or *50,000 trees*? Why?
4. In the fourth sentence, what kind of appeal did the writer add by changing the word *used* to *sacrificed*?
5. Why did the writer add the word *newspapers* in the last sentence? What kind of appeal does the phrase "to save a forest" have?

EXERCISE 5 ▶   **Evaluating a Persuasive Essay**

Following is the first part of a brief essay. Work with others in a small group to decide what changes might improve this first draft. Be sure to refer to the evaluating and revising chart on page 352.

I guess pretty much everyone already has an opinion on this issue, but I want to tell you how I feel. First of all I think that nobody in this town should pay for swimming lessons. Swimming is a skill that everybody needs because it's important to everyone. There are some poor families here who can't afford even a small fee. If kids from these families drown, we'll have nobody to blame but ourselves for being stingy.

GRAMMAR HINT

Changing Sentence Length for Emphasis

To persuade others to your point of view, you need to be forceful. A short sentence gains force or emphasis if it's a change of pace from mostly longer sentences.

EXAMPLES   *Not emphatic*   There's a great deal of disunity on this issue, but we must work together.

Emphatic   There's a great deal of disunity on this issue. We must work together.

☞ REFERENCE NOTE: For more information on sentence variety, see page 481.

WRITING
ASSIGNMENT

PART 4:

Evaluating and Revising Your Persuasive Essay

Two heads are better than one, the saying goes. Borrow another head by exchanging essays with a classmate. Evaluate each other's essay by using the questions on page 352. After reading your partner's comments, evaluate your own essay, and revise any weaknesses you find.

Proofreading and Publishing

Proofreading and Publishing. Proofread to correct errors in punctuation, spelling, usage, and capitalization. Then, think about publishing your essay.

- Send your essay to the school board or to a local or national official. Be sure you include your name and address.
- With your classmates, choose the strongest essays in the class to send to your newspaper and to radio or television stations.

WRITING ASSIGNMENT

PART 5:
Proofreading and Publishing Your Essay

Proofread your essay carefully, and correct any errors you find. To find spelling errors, try reading one line at a time. Recopy your essay and share it with others.

Reflecting on Your Writing

To include it in your **portfolio,** date your paper and attach a brief reflection addressing the following questions.

- How did you grab the reader's attention?
- How did you make the paper convincing?
- Which reasons do you think were strongest? Why?

A STUDENT MODEL

Controversial issues touch everyone's life. Katie Baker, who attends Holmes High School in Covington, Kentucky, supports the opinion that public school students should wear uniforms. Does Katie's essay convince you to make the switch to a school uniform?

Uniforms Reduce Problems
by Katie Baker

Students enrolled in a public high school should be required to wear a school uniform. Many studies show improvement in both attitude and school work. Wearing uniforms
would also reduce clothing costs and many problems
related to competition in dress.

Mrs. Chung, a principal at a high school, conducted research on the results of wearing uniforms. She said, "In the
past two or three years, several schools in the nation have
begun to require a school uniform. All of these schools are
reporting improved student grades and improved student
behavior."

Uniforms are also less expensive than regular clothing.
An outfit for a student can easily cost sixty dollars. A uniform
would cost fifty-four dollars or less and would save money.
This would be especially helpful to families on a low budget.

Last, uniforms would reduce the competition in dress
among students. Students who don't have as much money as
others wouldn't have to be embarrassed about their parents'
income.

Uniforms wouldn't cause a threat to a student's individual
freedom because there are lots of other things that make you
"you" besides clothing. Wearing uniforms would reduce many
problems and would improve grades and behavior. Therefore,
students enrolled in a public high school should be required
to wear a school uniform.

WRITING WORKSHOP

A Letter to the Editor

Like a persuasive essay, a persuasive letter states an opinion, supports the opinion with reasons and evidence, and
suggests a course of action. When you write a letter to persuade a friend to stay with your family during the summer,
you expect an answer.

One way to get people to respond to your ideas is to
write a letter to the editor of a magazine or newspaper. Such
letters reach not only the editor, but also a specific audience
of readers concerned about the topic.

The following letter to the editor responds to an article
in a previous issue of the magazine. As you read, decide
whether you agree or disagree with the writer's opinion.

To the Editor,

Your attempt to help the "older generation" understand adolescents by packaging them into neat little
bundles like "Malljammers" or "House Hoppers". . .
unwittingly touched upon what is perhaps the greatest
problem in high schools today: stereotyping. Rather
than letting their own identities come out, many teens
are assigning themselves to one of these groups and
adopting a prescribed personality. Your promotion of
these cliques as a means of expression for teens who
need to feel accepted does nothing to encourage them
to seek their own selves. I am about to enter my senior
year in high school, and it appalls me to see people
erect invisible barriers between themselves and other
groups. In the future, please try to remind us all of the
merits of individualism.

Emily R. Alling
Ledyard, Conn.
Newsweek

1. What caused Emily Alling to write this letter?
2. What topic concerns the writer? What is her opinion?

3. In addition to the editor, what audience might the writer be trying to reach? What strong opposing argument does she mention? How does she try to refute it?

4. What logical and emotional appeals does the writer use to persuade her readers? Does she convince you?

Writing a Letter to the Editor

 Prewriting. Think of a current topic you really care about. Have you heard some name-calling at school that makes you angry? Do you feel strongly that no child in the United States should go to bed hungry? Look through your favorite magazine or newspaper for topic ideas. Once you've found a topic, write a sentence that states your opinion. Then, list the reasons and evidence you'll use to support your opinion. If you need more support, do some reading or talk to someone who knows something about your topic.

"Letters are expectation packaged in an envelope." Shana Alexander

Writing, Evaluating, and Revising. Before you begin writing, read some published letters to the editor. Notice that these letters are short and to the point. They immediately catch the reader's attention, often by stating the writer's opinion in an interesting way. After you've written a rough draft of your letter, ask a friend to read and evaluate it. Then, revise your draft to make it more convincing.

Proofreading and Publishing. Proofread your letter carefully, and then send it to a newspaper or magazine whose readers will be interested in the topic. For example, if you're writing about teenagers and dating, you might send your letter to *Seventeen* magazine. Remember: Editors receive many more letters than they can print, so they choose only those that make the best impression.

When you are ready to put your paper in your **portfolio,** attach a short, written reflection explaining why your letter should effectively persuade your readers.

MAKING CONNECTIONS

PERSUASION ACROSS THE CURRICULUM

Advertising and Persuasion

Advertisers use a wide array of techniques to persuade people to buy products. In addition to logical reasoning, they rely heavily on these emotional appeals:

- *Loaded words* are words that carry strongly positive or negative connotations. (See page 505.) Advertisers appeal to your emotions by using words that suggest positive feelings. Who can resist a breakfast food, for instance, that's *delicious* and *crunchy*?
- *Snob appeal* uses words and pictures that appeal to your dreams of being rich and carefree. Ads that sell perfume and watches, for example, may show a woman driving an expensive car.
- *Testimonials* bring praise for the product from famous or wealthy people (not experts). Advertisers hope you'll transfer your admiration for the movie star to the cat food she recommends.

Study the following 1931 advertisement (page 360) for a Pierce-Arrow car. Analyze the ad to see what kinds of appeals it uses. Then find and bring to school a full-page car ad from a recent newspaper or magazine. Compare the modern ad to the 1931 ad. What similar and different techniques can you find? What emotional appeals do you notice? Are they convincing? You and your classmates might enjoy sharing your observations.

After you analyze the Pierce-Arrow ad, try this activity by yourself or with a partner. Write and design an ad for the car of the future, perhaps the year 2500. Be sure that the words and the picture work together to sell the product. Use emotional appeals to help convince your audience.

SPEAKING AND LISTENING

Public Speaking and Persuasion

Dr. Martin Luther King, Jr., one of the great speakers of the twentieth century, was awarded the Nobel Peace Prize in 1964. The following excerpt is from a persuasive speech given by Dr. King's wife, Coretta Scott King, on April 8, 1968, shortly after Dr. King was killed. This excerpt does not include Mrs. King's opinion statement for the whole speech. What do you think her opinion statement might be? Notice how Mrs. King skillfully combines logical and emotional appeals.

from My Life with Martin Luther King, Jr.
by Coretta Scott King

We must carry on because this is the way he would have wanted it to have been. We are not going to get bogged down.

I hope in this moment we are going to go forward; we are going to continue his work to make all people truly free and to make every person feel that he is a human being. His campaign for the poor must go on. . . .

We are concerned about not only the Negro poor, but the poor all over America and all over the world. Every man deserves a right to a job or an income so that he can pursue liberty, life, and happiness. Our great nation, as he often said, has the resources, but his question was: Do we have the will? Somehow I hope . . . the will will be created within the hearts, and minds, and the souls, and the spirits of those who have the power to make these changes come about. . . .

He often said, unearned suffering is redemptive, and if you give your life to a cause in which you believe, and which is right and just — and it is — and if your life comes to an end as a result of this, then your life could not have been lived in a more redemptive way. And I think that this is what my husband has done.

But then I ask the question: How many men must die before we can really have a free and true and peaceful society? How long will it take? If we can catch the spirit, and the true meaning of this experience, I believe that this nation can be transformed into a society of love, of justice, peace, and brotherhood where all men can really be brothers.

Think of someone whose actions you admire. Your hero may be an important historical figure such as Abraham Lincoln or Joan of Arc. Or it may be someone you know personally. Write and present a brief speech that you might give in tribute to this person. Try to persuade your audience to admire your hero.

Reading and Responding

We're all critics at heart. We **read** a book or see a movie, then **respond** by saying, "That was great!" or "That was awful!" Responding to what we read, see, or hear is a big part of our everyday lives.

Writing and You. Writers also respond to what they read, see, and hear. Professional critics write about the latest books or movies. In literature class, you write about the story you've just read. These written responses are more than casual reactions. The writer looks closely at plot and characters to see what makes a book or movie work. Do you ever read a review before you see a movie?

As You Read. Following is a review of the movie *Frankenstein*. As you read it, notice how the writer responds to all the various elements of the movie.

John Frederick Peto, *Books on a Table* (1900). Oil on canvas. The Nelson-Atkins Museum of Art, Kansas City, Missouri. (Purchase: Nelson Trust through the exchange of a Gift of the Friends of Art.)

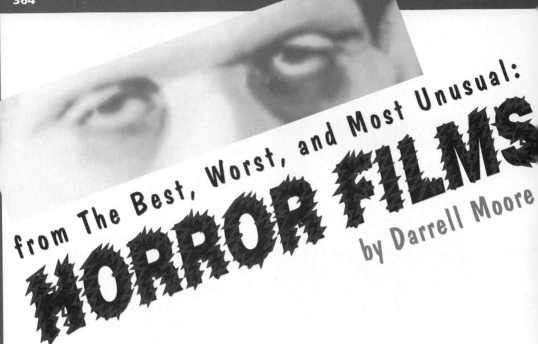

from The Best, Worst, and Most Unusual: HORROR FILMS
by Darrell Moore

FRANKENSTEIN (1931) is a cultural phenomenon, the most famous horror film of all time. It was made by a great director, James Whale, and it featured a great actor, Boris Karloff. But there's more working here than the proper combination of great cinematic talents. The idea of the film, the portrayal of the film, the image and look of the film—even the timing of its release— are inseparable from its success.

This is, of course, the story of the scientist who created a monster from graverobbed parts. It is significant that Dr. Frankenstein is not mad. He is merely a brilliant scientist who wants to develop and test some equally brilliant theories. The basic plot is structured around the creation of the monster and the impact that creation has on a parochial and superstitious society. And while the story plays out as tragedy—with the monster trapped and burned by the townspeople at the end— the film encourages the viewer to speculate: What would have happened if Dr. Frankenstein's assistant Fritz had procured a healthy, instead of a criminal, brain? Is the film tragic because the doctor dared too much, or simply because his experiment failed?

"The horror of the creature is matched only by our desire that such a creature exist."

The movie takes a stand on the question: The doctor dared too much. That stand is made evident once the creature breathes life and the doctor must imbue that life with meaning. The doctor—or any mortal man—is fundamentally unable to give meaning to the creature's existence. Man is an insufficient God. This is the real tragedy of the film, and what sets it apart from an inspired mad-scientist film like *The Island of Lost Souls*.

This theme is sounded without being spoken. But great films are not sermons; *Frankenstein* is exciting and physical. Through a scientific magic show (that we don't believe for a minute) of scrap iron and pure energy, Dr. Frankenstein (Colin Clive) gives life to a body made up of dead

graverobbed parts. Suddenly, there is a living creature on the slab. The horror of the creature is matched only by our desire that such a creature exist. Fifty years of familiarity take away the shock—but not the marvel—of the creature's appearance.

The credit for the creature's enduring look goes to Universal make-up man Jack Pierce—who took five hours a day to build up Karloff's face. It was an image so striking that Universal was able to copyright it. But it was not created on a whim. Pierce had discovered—after research in several areas, including surgery, criminology, and electrodynamics—that there are "six ways a surgeon can cut the skull." Pierce went on to say that: "I figured Dr. Frankenstein, who was not a practicing surgeon, would take the easiest. That is, he would cut the top of the skull off, straight across like a pot lid, hinge it, pop the brain in, and clamp it tight. That's the reason I decided to make the Monster's head square and flat like a box, and dig that big scar across his forehead, and have metal clamps hold it together."

Karloff was further fitted with a five-pound steel spine, eighteen-pound asphalt spreader's boots, and steel struts on his legs. The make-up of the monster was so critical to the success of the horror film that Karloff was led to and from the set with his head under a cloth (much like the Elephant Man in the steamboat scene) to conceal his appearance during production. He ate alone, and was totally isolated from everyone not connected with the film.

Ironically, Bela Lugosi was originally offered the role of the creature in Universal's *Frankenstein*. He refused the role, apparently because of the lack of a speaking part. The role went, of course, to Boris Karloff, who became more of a cultural icon as Frankenstein's monster than Lugosi did as Dracula.

READER'S RESPONSE

1. Does the author convince you that *Frankenstein* is a great film? Why or why not?
2. How would your feelings about the film have been different if Dr. Frankenstein had succeeded in his experiment?

WRITER'S CRAFT

3. In this review of *Frankenstein*, the writer focuses attention on plot and make up. What might a music review stress? a review of a novel?
4. Why do you think the author gives such a thorough description of Boris Karloff's makeup and costume?
5. The author's evaluation—judgment—of *Frankenstein* is that it is "exciting and physical." What evidence does he give to support this evaluation?

Purposes for Writing About Literature

The writer of the *Frankenstein* review had a specific purpose: to evaluate the movie and make a recommendation to readers. You might write about literature for the same reason, in book reviews and in some book reports. But there are other reasons to write about literature. Your purpose may be just to jot down a few notes that only you will ever see. Or your purpose may be to analyze the work in great detail and to share what you've learned with your readers. Here are some specific examples of the many purposes for writing about literature.

- in a journal, writing about a book you read that made you feel especially good about yourself
- in a letter to a friend, saying that you think Tolkien's hobbits are the greatest characters ever created
- in a book review, urging your readers to borrow or buy a book you think is worthwhile
- in a letter to the editor, asking parents to read a particular story to their children
- in a critical analysis for a literature course, explaining the similarities between the characters in two novels
- in a presentation for a book club, giving a summary of the novel that members will be discussing
- in an original poem, imitating the style of another poem
- in a short story, creating a sequel to a story you've read

LOOKING AHEAD

In the main assignment in this chapter, you'll write a critical analysis. Your basic purpose will be to inform your readers of the results of your analysis. Keep in mind that an effective literary analysis

- has a thesis statement that presents at least one literary element and a main idea about it
- includes details from the work being analyzed
- is organized so it makes sense to the reader

Writing a Critical Analysis

Prewriting

Reading and Responding to Stories

When you read a story, all sorts of thoughts and feelings buzz around in your head, thoughts like *Don't trust her—she's lying!* or *Boy, all this talking is boring.* Shouldn't serious readers shut off this mental activity? Absolutely not!

Responding to Stories as an Active Reader

The thoughts and feelings you have while you're reading mean you're reading actively—just like a lively conversation between you and the story. And the more you put into it, the more you'll get out of it. So tune in your inner thoughts, and use the following tips to expand them. (In parentheses you'll see active-reading thoughts about "An Astrologer's Day," a story you'll read on pages 370–375.)

- **Always respond personally** to what you read. (*I sort of like this phony stargazer and his funny sales lines.*)
- **Use your own experience and knowledge** to understand a character, action, or situation. (*This Town Hall Park sounds more like our flea market.*)
- **Question** anything that confuses, puzzles, or provokes you. (*"Honest" work? Should I buy this?*)
- **Predict** what will happen. If you're wrong (which is okay), figure out why you are. (*Something shadowy in this guy's past is going to haunt him.*)
- **React to the whole story,** and be definite about what you do and don't like. (Sorry, you'll have to supply your own example for that last hint.)

Looking at a Story

Following is a story about appearances. As you read, try to decide what kind of man the astrologer is. As always, "listen" to yourself read—pay attention to your own response.

A SHORT STORY

An Astrologer's Day
by R. K. Narayan

Punctually at midday he opened his bag and spread out his professional equipment, which consisted of a dozen cowrie shells, a square piece of cloth with obscure mystic charts on it, a notebook, and a bundle of palmyra writing. His forehead was resplendent with sacred ash and vermilion, and his eyes sparkled with a sharp abnormal gleam which was really an outcome of a continual searching look for customers, but which his simple clients took to be a prophetic light and felt comforted. The power of his eyes was considerably enhanced by their position—placed as they were between the painted forehead and the dark whiskers which streamed down his cheeks: even a half-wit's eyes would sparkle in such a setting. To crown the effect he wound a saffron-colored turban around his head. This color scheme never failed. People were attracted to him as bees are attracted to cosmos or dahlia stalks. He sat under the boughs of a spreading tamarind tree which flanked a path running through the Town Hall Park. It was a remarkable place in many ways: a surging crowd was always moving up and down this narrow road morning till night. A variety of trades and occupations was represented all along its way: medicine sellers, sellers of stolen hardware and junk, magicians, and, above all, an auctioneer of cheap cloth, who created enough din all day to attract the whole town. Next to him in vociferousness came a vendor of fried groundnut, who gave his ware a fancy name each day, calling it "Bombay Ice Cream" one day, and on the next "Delhi Almond," and on the third "Raja's Delicacy," and so on and so forth, and people flocked to him. A considerable portion of this crowd dallied before the astrologer too. The astrologer transacted his business by the light of a flare which crackled and smoked up above the groundnut heap nearby. Half the enchantment of the place was due to the fact that it did not have the benefit of municipal lighting. The place was lit up by shop lights. One or two had hissing gaslights, some had naked flares stuck on poles, some were lit up by old cycle lamps, and one or two, like the astrologer's, managed without lights of their own. It was a bewildering crisscross of light rays and moving shadows. This suited the astrologer very well, for the simple reason that he had not in the least intended to be an astrologer when he began life; and he knew no more of what was going to happen to others than he knew what was going to happen to himself next minute. He was as much a stranger to the stars as were his innocent customers. Yet he said things which pleased and astonished everyone: that was more a matter of study, practice, and shrewd guesswork. All the same, it was as much an honest man's labor as any other, and he deserved the wages he carried home at the end of a day.

He had left his village without any previous thought or plan. If he had continued there he would have carried on the work of his forefathers—namely, tilling the land, living, marrying, and ripening in his cornfield and ancestral home. But that was not to be. He had to leave home without telling anyone, and he could not rest till he left it behind a couple of hundred miles. To a villager it is a great deal, as if an ocean flowed between.

He had a working analysis of mankind's troubles: marriage, money, and the tangles of human ties. Long practice had sharpened his perception. Within five minutes he understood what was wrong. He charged three pies per question, never opened his mouth till the other had spoken for at least ten minutes, which provided him enough stuff for a dozen answers and advices.

When he told the person before him, gazing at his palm, "In many ways you are not getting the fullest results for your efforts," nine out of ten were disposed to agree with him. Or he questioned: "Is there any woman in your family, maybe even a distant relative, who is not well disposed toward you?" Or he gave an analysis of character: "Most of your troubles are due to your nature. How can you be otherwise with Saturn where he is? You have an impetuous nature and a rough exterior." This endeared him to their hearts immediately, for even the mildest of us loves to think that he has a forbidding exterior.

The nuts vendor blew out his flare and rose to go home. This was a signal for the astrologer to bundle up too, since it left him in darkness except for a little shaft of green light which strayed in from somewhere and touched the ground before him. He picked up his cowrie shells and paraphernalia and was putting them back into his bag when the green shaft of light was blotted out; he looked up and saw a man standing before him. He sensed a possible client and said: "You look so careworn. It will do you good to sit down for a while and chat with me." The other grumbled some reply vaguely. The astrologer pressed his invitation; whereupon the other thrust his palm under his nose, saying: "You call yourself an astrologer?" The astrologer felt challenged and said, tilting the other's palm toward the green shaft of light: "Yours is a nature . . ." "Oh, stop that," the other said. "Tell me something worthwhile. . . ."

Our friend felt piqued. "I charge only three pies per question, and what you get ought to be good enough for your money. . . ."

At this the other withdrew his arm, took out an anna, and flung it out to him, saying: "I have some questions to ask. If I prove you are bluffing, you must return that anna to me with interest."

"If you find my answers satisfactory, will you give me five rupees?"

"No."

"Or will you give me eight annas?"

"All right, provided you give me twice as much if you are wrong," said the stranger. This pact was accepted after a little further argument. The astrologer sent up a prayer to heaven as the other lit a cheroot. The astrologer caught a glimpse of his face by the matchlight. There was a pause as cars hooted on the road, *jutka* drivers swore at their horses, and the babble of the crowd agitated the semidarkness of the park. The other sat down, sucking his cheroot, puffing out, sat there ruthlessly. The astrologer felt very uncomfortable. "Here, take your anna back. I am not used to such challenges. It is late for me today. . . ." He made preparations to bundle up. The other held his wrist and said: "You can't get out of it now. You dragged me in while I was passing." The astrologer shivered in his grip; and his voice shook and became faint. "Leave me today. I will speak to you tomorrow." The other thrust his palm in his face and said: "Challenge is challenge. Go on." The astrologer proceeded with his throat drying up: "There is a woman . . ."

"Stop," said the other. "I don't want all that. Shall I succeed in my present search or not? Answer this and go. Otherwise I will not let you go till you disgorge all your coins." The astrologer muttered a few incantations and replied: "All right. I will speak. But will you give me a rupee if what I say is convincing? Otherwise I will not open my mouth, and you may do what you like." After a good deal of haggling the other agreed. The astrologer said: "You were left for dead. Am I right?"

"Ah, tell me more."

"A knife has passed through you once?" said the astrologer.

"Good fellow!" He bared his chest to show the scar. "What else?"

"And then you were pushed into a well nearby in the field. You were left for dead."

"I should have been dead if some passerby had not chanced to peep into the well," exclaimed the other, overwhelmed by enthusiasm.

"When shall I get at him?" he asked, clenching his fist.

"In the next world," answered the astrologer. "He died four months ago in a far-off town. You will never see any more of him." The other groaned on hearing it. The astrologer proceeded:

"Guru Nayak—"

"You know my name!" the other said, taken aback.

"As I know all other things. Guru Nayak, listen carefully to what I have to say. Your village is two days' journey due north of this town. Take the next train and be gone. I see once again great danger to your life if you go from home." He took out a pinch of sacred ash and held it to him. "Rub it on your forehead and go home. Never travel southward again, and you will live to be a hundred."

"Why should I leave home again?" the other said reflectively. "I was only going away now and then to look for him and to choke out his life if I met him." He shook his head regretfully. "He has escaped my hands. I hope at least he died as he deserved." "Yes," said the astrologer. "He was crushed under a lorry." The other looked gratified to hear it.

The place was deserted by the time the astrologer picked up his articles and put them into his bag. The green shaft was also gone, leaving the place in darkness and silence. The stranger had gone off into the night, after giving the astrologer a handful of coins.

It was nearly midnight when the astrologer reached home. His wife was waiting for him at the door and demanded an explanation. He flung the coins at her and said: "Count them. One man gave all that."

"Twelve and a half annas," she said, counting. She was overjoyed. "I can buy some jaggery and coconut tomorrow. The child has been asking for sweets for so many days now. I will prepare some nice stuff for her."

"The swine has cheated me! He promised me a rupee," said the astrologer. She looked up at him. "You look worried. What is wrong?"

"Nothing."

After dinner, sitting on the *pyol,* he told her: "Do you know a great load is gone from me today? I thought I had the blood of a man on my hands all these years. That was the reason why I ran away from home, settled here, and married you. He is alive."

She gasped. "You tried to kill!"

"Yes, in our village, when I was a silly youngster. We drank, gambled, and quarreled badly one day—why think of it now? Time to sleep," he said, yawning, and stretched himself on the *pyol.*

EXERCISE 1 ▶ **Speaking and Listening: Responding and Reading Actively**

Did you ever wish you could talk to an author or a character? After reading "An Astrologer's Day," freewrite a response for one minute, *as if you're speaking directly to the writer or a character.* Here are some questions to get you started: Did you like the way the story ended? Or did you feel tricked? How do you feel about the astrologer? Then act out your freewriting response with a partner, following these pointers:

1. Look your partner in the eye; then read your response.
2. Your partner—taking the place of author or character—will listen carefully and "answer" you.
3. Keep the back-and-forth active responses going as long as you can.
4. Change places. Become the author or character, and answer your partner's freewriting response.

Understanding and Using Literary Elements

Already you've been responding to some basic elements of a short story, perhaps the main character or the plot of "An Astrologer's Day." To write about a story, you need a good understanding—a working knowledge—of literary elements, and you need to keep them clearly in mind as you read.

You'll find that the elements below make your reading and writing more specific and sharp. They let you look *inside* a story—at its parts and the writer's techniques—and talk about it in clear, precise terms.

Plot. *Plot* is the story's "action," or series of events. Look closely, and you'll see that *conflict*—the problems the characters face—keeps the plot moving. Conflicts can be external (struggles with people, nature, or society) or internal (struggles with the character's own feelings or beliefs). The *climax* of a plot is the tense or exciting scene that settles the story's main conflict—that determines how things turn out.

Setting. *Setting* is the story's time and place; it may include weather, clothes, landscape, buildings, cars, rickshaws—many physical and social details. Setting provides important background for understanding people and events, and it may also create conflict (imagine a destructive avalanche, for example) or set an emotional mood, or atmosphere (imagine a festive carnival).

Character. Characters are the individuals in a story (animals or aliens, as well as people), and *characterization* is the way the writer reveals their qualities and traits. Writers can describe personality directly, but they can also show it indirectly through the characters' speech, appearance, thoughts, actions, and effects on others (what people say and feel about them). To understand a character, you may need to consider the motivation for actions and decide whether the character changes in the story.

Point of View. *Point of view* is the angle from which a story is told: who tells it, how close this narrator is to the action, what *is* told, and what *isn't*.

In *first-person point of view,* the narrator is a character in the story and speaks as *I.* This narrator can only tell us what he or she sees and hears, is told, or *believes.* Maybe the character is reliable, but maybe not: Readers must decide.

In *third-person point of view,* the narrator is outside the story—not a character—and doesn't use the words *I, me,* and *mine,* but does use *he, her,* and *them* (third-person pronouns). A *third-person omniscient* narrator can tell the thoughts of any character (*omniscient* means "all-knowing"), relate any event, and even speak right to the reader or skip around in time.

In *third-person limited point of view,* the outside narrator reveals the thoughts of just one character. The story's events are filtered through the mind of one person.

Foreshadowing. *Foreshadowing* is a hint or suggestion of coming events—a clue, in a way, that heightens our interest or prepares us for significant actions. Sometimes we recognize foreshadowing immediately: A jeweled bracelet shines "coldly" in its "padded coffin of a case," and we're instantly on alert for danger. But sometimes foreshadowing is less obvious: A character sees two dogs fight to exhaustion over a bone, but we don't learn until later that he will battle his brother—for a girl who loves neither one.

Irony.   *Irony* is basically a contrast between appearance or expectation and reality. Writers use surprising, ironic twists to make us laugh but also to make us thoughtful or sad: Life and people don't always behave as we want. Writers use three kinds of irony. (All three examples come from a famous ironic story, Edgar Allan Poe's "The Cask of Amontillado." Read it if you haven't!)

- *verbal irony:* one thing is said but another is meant: A man who plans to kill his unsuspecting friend offers the toast "To your health!"
- *situational irony:* what is expected is not what happens: The friend attends a carnival expecting fun but instead meets his death.
- *dramatic irony:* the reader (or playgoer or moviegoer) knows something that a character does not: Readers know the man plans murder, but his friend does not.

Theme.   *Theme* is an important idea about life or human nature revealed in a story. It isn't just a subject (like "war"), but an insight ("War wounds are not just physical; they are carried inside forever"). Writers often don't state their themes directly, and you have to draw your own conclusions from characters, events, description, and dialogue. (Sometimes the title or the conflict may be clues.) You may find more than one theme in a story.

Reminder

When you read a short story (or any other literary work)

- respond freely, by letting your thoughts and feelings flow naturally
- read actively, by responding personally, applying your own experience, questioning, predicting, and reacting to the whole
- think about the work's literary elements and how the writer uses them to get you to respond as you do

EXERCISE 2 ▸ **Exploring Stories and Literary Elements**

What hooks you in a story? A shocking twist (heavy on the irony)? Weird settings in the future? Believable characters? Find out for yourself. Choose two stories (favorite or unknown ones), and respond to them actively, in writing, as you did in Exercise 1. This time, though, focus specifically on literary elements, using what you've just learned. Write out your comments to share with your classmates: "What I Like or Don't Like in Stories—and Why."

CRITICAL THINKING

Analyzing a Short Story

Analyzing means examining in detail: looking closely at the parts of a whole and their relationships. You're doing this naturally whenever you respond to different parts of stories—funny dialogue, a tragic ending—and you simply do it in a deeper, systematic way when you write a critical analysis.

Here are some questions that can help you analyze any short story. But remember: Literature is not a statement of scientific fact, but a creation in words of experience. Its readers vary, and so will its interpretations. In discussions, you'll naturally compare your answers with those of your classmates, but don't look for right or wrong answers.

1. What important conflicts or problems, external and internal, does the main character(s) face?
2. What is the story's climax, the outcome of the central conflict?
3. Where and when does the story take place?
4. Does the setting help explain characters and events, cause a conflict, or set a mood? (More than one may apply.) Explain.
5. What is the story's main character(s) like? (Use appearance, speech, thoughts, actions, and reactions of others.)

6. What motivates the main character(s) to act? Does the character(s) change in the story? If so, how?
7. Is the point of view first-person, omniscient, or third-person limited? Does the point of view affect what *you* know and feel? How?
8. Does foreshadowing help prepare for later events or situations? If so, give examples that you found effective.
9. Is irony—verbal, situational, or dramatic—at work in this story? Give examples, and discuss its effect.
10. What important idea about life or people do you find in this story?

CRITICAL THINKING EXERCISE:
Analyzing a Short Story

Working with a partner or a small group, analyze "An Astrologer's Day" by asking the questions above and on page 379. Your group might enjoy exchanging interpretations with another group—and remember that it's okay for your viewpoints to differ. (In fact, discussing with your group *why* your individual interpretations are different can also be interesting.)

PART 1:
Choosing a Story and Analyzing Its Elements

It's time to settle on a story that you'd like to think more about, feel and understand better, analyze closely, and tell others about in writing. Choose a story from your literature textbook or a favorite story of your own. Then use the questions above and on page 379 to analyze it.

Prewriting

Planning a Critical Analysis

Now it's time to turn your ideas about your short story into the raw material you'll use to write your essay.

Thinking About Purpose and Audience

You can write about literature for many purposes, but this chapter focuses on *critical analysis*. In your essay, you're taking on the role of "literary investigator": a close reader who knows, and can tell an audience, something about the literary elements in a short story.

For a critical analysis, you assume that your audience has read the story, which means that you don't need to retell the plot. Think of your audience as interested readers who want to know more.

Finding a Focus and Developing a Main Idea

In a short essay, you'll usually write about one story element or two or three that fit together somehow. Your choice depends on two things: (1) your interest (What drew you to the story? A crazy character? A great historical setting?) and (2) the story itself (What did your analysis uncover? For what parts or aspects of the story do you have many notes or probing questions?). Write about something that attracts you and seems important in the story.

With a topic (element) in mind, your next step is to develop a main idea. What do you want to say *about* the element and the story? Write a sentence—a thesis statement—that connects your topic and main idea.

Following are some thesis statements you might write about "An Astrologer's Day":

Nayak's violent character is shown through his actions and speech.

The setting of "An Astrologer's Day" gives us a good picture of what life is like for the city's people.

The setting of "An Astrologer's Day" creates a "bewildering" mood and also brings about the plot's main conflict.

In "An Astrologer's Day," verbal, dramatic, and situational irony are used to make us doubt the astrologer, to build suspense, and to develop theme.

Notice that the examples show you basic *kinds* of ideas used in literary analysis. You can write about an element's

- function (how it works in the story)
- effect (what you feel or understand because of it)
- development (how the writer builds or creates it)

The sample thesis statements also show how much flexibility you have in writing about elements. For example, you can write about one function of setting or two; you can write about one type of irony or about all three types plus theme. As long as you match the topic to the length of the assignment, the focus is yours.

**WRITING
ASSIGNMENT**

PART 2:
Writing a Thesis Statement

You may already have a writing focus in mind once you've analyzed your story. What made you choose this story? What did you discover about it? Pinpoint your focus and the main idea you want to convey. Write your thesis statement in one sentence.

Collecting Support and Organizing Your Ideas

Collecting Support. A critical analysis of literature, like persuasive writing, requires evidence to support your ideas. The "evidence" in this case, though, comes from the literature. In other words, you don't just tell readers that Nayak has a violent character; you *show* them. Evidence may take the form of quotations, paraphrases, summaries, or specific details.

 REFERENCE NOTE: For more information on using sources to support your ideas, see pages 414–415.

Organizing Your Ideas. With your main points listed and supporting details recorded, you can produce an early plan by arranging the information. Often your topic and ideas will suggest a natural way to do this.

For example, if you're analyzing a character and showing how he or she changes, chronological order (the plot order) makes sense. If a setting both sets a mood and causes a major plot problem, you'll probably want to begin with mood (which is background) and end with conflict. And you can also order ideas and supporting details by importance (most-to-least, least-to-most). Look for an arrangement that readers can easily follow.

"*Once upon a time, they lived happily ever after.*"

Drawing by H. Martin, © 1991 by the New Yorker Magazine, Inc.

WRITING ASSIGNMENT	PART 3: **Collecting Support and Organizing Your Ideas**

Remember: You want to *show* your readers, not just *tell* them. Now is the time to make notes of story details that led you to your ideas in the first place. (And you may also discover new evidence.) After collecting support, arrange both ideas and details, and create either a rough or a formal outline.

 COMPUTER NOTE: Use the multiple-window feature of your word-processing program to view your prewriting notes and your outline at the same time.

Writing Your First Draft

Now that you've collected support and organized your ideas, you're ready to write your first draft. The ***introduction*** to your critical essay must include (1) the title and author of the short story and (2) your thesis statement. It can be simple, but it has the goal of all introductions: to interest readers. Why were you attracted to the story? Set down your own interest, and you'll catch the reader's.

The essay's ***body*** develops your main points, using the support you've gathered. Incorporating this support smoothly into your sentences is a special element of critical writing. You can paraphrase, quote, or summarize, but all references to the story must fit grammatically into your writing, as the following examples show.

HERE'S HOW

> Because the narrator tells us that the astrologer doesn't know the future, calling his work "an honest man's labor" is irony with a sharp bite.
>
> Just as ironically, Nayak might have passed on by, but the astrologer was insistent.

paraphrase

quotation

summary

The ***conclusion*** of an analysis is often a restatement of the thesis or summary of points. Other essay techniques are possible, such as echoing the introduction's ideas and details or ending with a larger observation about the story. Remember that the conclusion shouldn't be mechanical: "Now I will summarize my main points. . . ." It should be a satisfying finish for your readers.

The following Writer's Model shows you these basic essay parts for a critical analysis.

A WRITER'S MODEL

An Analysis of Irony in
"An Astrologer's Day"

INTRODUCTION
Title and author

"An Astrologer's Day," by R. K. Narayan, is ironic through and through. Almost nothing is what it seems to be, and one unexpected event follows another--for both readers and characters.

Thesis statement

This is a comic but thought-provoking story in which irony is used for several purposes: to make us doubt the astrologer, to build suspense, and to develop theme.

BODY
Support: Quotation and details

From the first sentence, Narayan uses irony to make us doubt the astrologer. His "professional" equipment (the shells, the cloth with mysterious writing, and so on) is only for show. Ordinary listening skills, not the stars, help him astonish his "simple clients" with "shrewd guesswork."

Paraphrase and quotation

Because the narrator tells us that the astrologer doesn't know the future, calling his work "an honest man's labor" is irony with a sharp bite. The narrator's comments expose the astrologer as a greedy fake.

Support: Summary/ Details

The narrator also uses irony to build suspense during the fortunetelling scene. From previous clues, we realize that the astrologer is the one who knifed and left Nayak--but Nayak doesn't know it. Will the astrologer pull off his risky trick? What will happen if he doesn't? The irony of knowing something Nayak doesn't makes the scene fascinating and tense.

Support: Summary/ Details and quotation

The story's strongest irony, however, runs all through the plot and helps create theme. One important irony is that the astrologer has tried to escape his past but ends up, in a way, bringing it to himself. He's become an astrologer to get away from his crime, but his victim is attracted to an astrologer. As Nayak says, " 'I have some questions to ask.' " Just as ironically, Nayak might have passed on by, but the astrologer was insistent.

**Summary/
Details**

But the story gets still more ironic: When the astrologer recognizes Nayak, he uses the truth to deceive him! For once, the astrologer really does know facts about a customer, and he uses them to save his own life. In the end, posing as an astrologer is an advantage.

**Support:
Interpretation
of theme**

Every situation in this story takes an unexpected twist, and we are left with the message that life never turns out as expected and that even good and bad aren't what they seem. For example, it is awful that the astrologer can say

Quotation

" 'why think of it now?' " about leaving a man for dead, but we certainly didn't want Nayak to shed more blood to punish him. It is dishonest to take money for fake prophecies, but the astrologer's

**Quotations
Summary/
Details**

customers are "comforted" and "pleased." It is the astrologer who is guilty of a violent crime, but Nayak was probably violent too--and still is.

CONCLUSION

The irony is so strong in "An Astrologer's Day" that good, bad, guilt, and punishment aren't clear-cut. What should we think? Obviously, R. K.

**Return to
introduction**

Narayan doesn't want us to take this tale too seriously. Because no real harm is done, we can laugh at this upside-down world, not be shocked by it. We can simply enjoy all of the author's ironies.

PART 4:

Writing a First Draft of Your Critical Analysis

The writer's model you just read was a final draft. Don't panic: A polished, finished paper isn't expected of you now. Just let the model rest in your mind as you use your rough outline to get a first draft on paper. (But if the model gave you concrete ideas for your essay, use them!) Remember: Your goal is to support your thesis with evidence from the story so that your readers will understand your interpretation.

Evaluating and Revising

The following checklist will help you to correct your paper's weaknesses. Ask yourself each question in the left-hand column. Then use the technique in the right-hand column to correct any problems.

EVALUATING AND REVISING A LITERARY ANALYSIS

EVALUATION GUIDE	REVISION TECHNIQUE
1 Does the introduction include the title and the author?	**Add** the missing title or author.
2 Does the introduction identify the thesis, or focus, of the analysis?	**Add** a sentence or two (or replace an existing one) identifying a literary element and your main idea about it.
3 Is there enough support from the story for your ideas?	**Add** quotations, plot events, or other details.
4 Is support smoothly incorporated into the sentences?	**Add** or **replace** words and punctuation so that quotations and paraphrases are grammatically complete.
5 Have purpose and audience been considered in writing the critical analysis?	**Cut** informal expressions. **Cut** plot details that the audience may know or that are not related to your purpose.
6 Does the conclusion bring the essay to a definite close?	**Add** a sentence or two (or **replace** existing ones) that restate your main idea or summarize existing points.

EXERCISE 3 ▶   Analyzing a Writer's Revisions

Study the writer's revisions of the first two paragraphs of the model analysis on page 385. Then answer the questions that follow the paragraphs.

("An Astrologer's Day," by R. K. Narayan's)

~~This~~ story is ironic through and   **replace**
through. Almost nothing is what it seems
to be, and one unexpected event follows
another--for both readers and characters.

This is a comic but thought-provoking
                        in which irony is used for several purposes:
story~~, In it, an astrologer meets the man~~   **replace**
            to make us doubt the astrologer, to build suspense,
~~he once wounded with a knife, pushed in~~
            and to develop theme.
~~a well, and left for dead.~~

   Because the narrator tells us that the
astrologer doesn't know the future, calling
            "an honest man's labor")
his work ~~honest~~ is irony with a sharp bite.   **replace**

From the first sentence, Narayan uses   **reorder**
irony to make us doubt the astrologer. His
"professional" equipment (the shells, the
cloth with mysterious writing, and so on)
is only for show. Ordinary listening skills,
not the stars, help him astonish his
"simple clients" with "shrewd guesswork."

The narrator's comments expose the
            as a greedy fake.
astrologer.   **add**

1. Why did the writer add the title and author of the story to the first line?
2. Why did the writer make such extensive changes in the last sentence of the first paragraph? [Hint: What is the thesis statement of the critical analysis?]

3. In the first sentence of the second paragraph, why did the writer replace the word *honest* with the quote *"an honest man's labor"*?
4. Why did the writer move the second, third, and fourth sentences of the second paragraph?
5. Why did the writer add the words *as a greedy fake* to the last sentence of the second paragraph?

WRITING NOTE As you evaluate and revise your paper, remember that not all your support should be direct quotations. Too many quotations can have a choppy, unoriginal, and even irritating effect (do *you* like to read strung-together quotations?). Use quotations when the author's exact wording is especially striking, important to your point, or more precise than a paraphrase. The rest of the time you can paraphrase or summarize ideas and details from the literary work.

WRITING ASSIGNMENT

PART 5:
Evaluating and Revising Your Critical Analysis

Exchange papers with another student, and use the questions from the evaluating and revising chart on page 387 to evaluate each other's papers. Be prepared to explain to your partner where changes are needed to improve his or her essay. Then use your partner's comments and your own evaluation to revise your critical analysis.

"The answers you get from literature depend upon the questions you pose."

Margaret Atwood

Proofreading and Publishing

Proofreading.   Use your usual method of proofreading, but then proofread again another way (perhaps backward). For this essay, also pay special attention to

- quotation marks (Do you have opening *and* closing marks?)
- punctuation used with quotation marks (See pages 834–836.)
- the story title (Is it enclosed in quotation marks?)

> ## MECHANICS HINT

Denoting Titles

When you write about literature or other art forms, you need to know how to indicate the title of the work. Sometimes you use quotation marks, and sometimes you use underlining. (The italic type produced on a computer serves the same purpose as underlining.)

1. Use quotation marks to enclose the titles of stories, poems, songs, book chapters, and articles.

   > One of Elizabeth Bishop's poems is called "The Fish."
   > Alice Walker's short story "Everyday Use" is told in the first-person point of view.

2. Underline the titles of books, paintings, television programs, plays, and movies.

   > The setting of Stephen Crane's novel *The Red Badge of Courage* is a battlefield during the Civil War.
   > The movie *Sense and Sensibility* won an Oscar.

   ☞ REFERENCE NOTE: See pages 831–840 for more information about quotation marks and underlining.

Publishing.   With your teacher's help, you might use the following ideas to share your paper with others.

■ Get together with other students who wrote on the same general topic: character, conflict, point of view, and so on. Read each other's papers, and talk about what attracted you to the story and literary element you wrote about.

■ Make a class file of essays as a reference tool for future assignments. Make an index that will let students look up essays by topic, story title, or story author.

WRITING
ASSIGNMENT

PART 6:
Proofreading and Publishing Your Critical Analysis

Proofread your paper (remember to try a new method as a double-check). Then, use the suggestions above, take your essay home to your family, or surprise a former teacher by offering it (name removed, if you like) for his or her files.

Reflecting on Your Writing

Write a brief reflection answering the following questions. Date it, and include it with your paper in your **portfolio.**

■ How did you choose support for your thesis?
■ What was hardest about writing this paper? Why?
■ What skills did you learn from this assignment?

A STUDENT MODEL

Matt Sanders, a student at East Mecklenburg High School in Charlotte, North Carolina, discusses Thomas Mann's "The Infant Prodigy." Matt has this advice for you: "It is very important to know the work of literature thoroughly and to understand it. Prewriting and planning are very important in getting your thoughts analyzed and your ideas organized. Once a suitable thesis is concocted, the paper should write itself."

The Big Picture
by Matt Sanders

A full portrait of a character cannot be created by revealing just his or her thoughts. The thoughts of others about that character play a crucial role in telling the complete story. By using the omniscient point of view, Thomas Mann creates a full portrait of Bibi, the main character in "The Infant Prodigy."

Many different pictures of Bibi are painted. One picture shows Bibi as an innocent, prodigious child who is full of talent. One character, the old man, sees Bibi's talent as being a gift from God. The businessman, while analyzing the monetary aspects of the performance, says " 'Really he does not play so badly.' " The young girl sees Bibi as an innocent child with a talent of expressing passion. The critic also sees the innocence and talent in Bibi. " 'As an individual he still has to develop, but as a type he is already quite complete, the artist par excellence.' "

Another picture created by the omniscient narrator shows Bibi and his performance as a hoax used to play up to the audience. It sees through Bibi's dazzling performance. The piano teacher criticizes his performance as being unoriginal. Of his form she thinks, " 'And his hand position is entirely amateur. One must be able to lay a coin on the back of his hand--I would use a ruler on him.' " The critic also sees through Bibi's performance. He sees every move as a publicity stunt. The impresario's kiss is a " 'good old gag.' "

The third and final picture painted by the omniscient narrator is painted by Bibi himself. This is a picture of contempt for the audience. Bibi, on the outside, is a talented performer who loves pleasing the audience. However, through his thoughts, the true Bibi is seen. He thinks that the audience is unaware of true musical talent: "Now I will play the fantasy, it is a lot better than Le Hibou, of course, especially the C-sharp passage. But you idiots dote on the Hibou, though it is the first and silliest thing I wrote." When the princess talks to him about his music, he thinks, " 'Oh, what a stupid old princess!' "

By using the omniscient point of view, the author can tell the complete story. By combining the thoughts of Bibi and the other characters in the story, Thomas Mann paints a full portrait of Bibi.

WRITING WORKSHOP

A Critical Review

Everyone is a movie and television reviewer once in a while. "Don't bother spending money on *Killer Cows III*," you tell a friend. "Even the cows are bored, not scary." Your reviews for friends are casual, but they have the same final purpose as published reviews: to judge whether the movie or program is worth watching.

Reviews (whether for films, television, or books) combine critical analysis of a work's elements with evaluation, or judgment. How good or effective is the movie—in its elements and as a whole? Judgments like this are opinions, but they're opinions based on standards (for example, the standard that a horror movie like *Killer Cows* should be scary). A reviewer who conveys only the message that "This was the stupidest excuse for a movie I've ever seen" without telling *why* won't convince anyone (or keep many readers).

Of course, reviews must tell you something of the work's subject, plot, or theme. Yet they have to strike a careful balance: enough information for understanding but not enough to spoil enjoyment. A special kind of review is the mini-review that newspapers and magazines often publish of movies they have reviewed at greater length in previous issues. The mini-review must combine information about the film for the reader who hasn't yet seen it and the reviewer's evaluation of it—the acting, directing, production values, and so on in a very short space. Following is a mini-review of the film *Driving Miss Daisy*. What do you learn about the content of the film itself? What is the reviewer's opinion of the film?

Alfred Uhry's adaptation of his much honored play is still full of manipulative bits—it's virtually all manipulative bits—but the director, Bruce Beresford, understands how to work them while cutting down on their obviousness. Set in Atlanta, starting in 1948, the movie is the story of the companionship that develops between stubborn, suspicious Miss Daisy (Jessica Tandy), a wealthy Jewish widow of seventy-two, and her resilient chauffeur, Hoke (Morgan Freeman), a widower about a decade younger than she is. Essentially, it's about how he changes her. He's made upright, considerate, humane—he's made perfect—so that nothing will disturb our appreciation of the gentle, bittersweet reverie we're watching. But it's acted (and directed) eloquently. Tandy and Freeman achieve a beautiful equilibrium. And Dan Aykroyd comes through with a fine performance as Miss Daisy's good-old-boy son.

Pauline Kael, *The New Yorker*

Writing a Mini-Review of a Movie or Television Program

Prewriting. Choose a movie or television show to review. Before anything else, think clearly about your standards: the elements, and qualities you'll be looking for. If possible, work with a group to identify the most important story elements, like characterization and plot, acting, and photography. Remember that a mini-review is condensed; you won't have much space.

As you watch the movie or program, make notes of specific details and your reactions. Then, review your notes to focus your ideas. You can use a simple focusing tool like *The good things about the movie (program) are ____. The things that don't work well are ____.*

Writing, Evaluating, and Revising. Remember that the reader is looking to you for basic information in a very short space: title, director and writer (if possible), actors, and a one- or two-sentence plot summary. In the body of your short review, use as many details as possible so readers can picture what you mean. When you have a draft, ask a partner to answer these questions: Is there enough plot information for people who haven't seen the movie? Are specific elements of the movie praised or criticized? Does the review bring the movie or show to life? Use your partner's evaluation as you revise. Try to keep your review as short as Pauline Kael's review of *Driving Miss Daisy*.

Proofreading and Publishing. Proofread your revised review, ask your partner to check it, and correct all errors. (Titles of films and television programs are underlined or italicized.) Then, go on the air with your review: Stage it for your classmates in pairs as though you were Roger Ebert and Gene Siskel (above), or another pair of film reviewers.

Include your review in your **portfolio** with a reflection: How did this paper affect the way you look at movies? Why?

MAKING CONNECTIONS

RESPONDING TO LITERATURE

Many times in life, "Don't take it personally" is good advice—but not when you're reading literature. As you saw in this chapter, even for a formal critical essay the starting point is your individual reaction. Personal involvement is one of the pleasures and powers of art in any form: to feel that what you're reading, seeing, or hearing makes a direct connection.

Here's a poem you may have read and then one reader's response to it. As you read, think of your own thoughts and feelings about the poem. Does it remind you of anyone? What does it make you think of? What do you think of the poem?

The Bean Eaters
by Gwendolyn Brooks

They eat beans mostly, this old yellow pair.
Dinner is a casual affair.
Plain chipware on a plain and creaking wood,
Tin flatware.

Two who are Mostly Good.
Two who have lived their day,
But keep on putting on their clothes
and putting things away.

And remembering . . .
Remembering, with twinklings and twinges,
As they lean over the beans in their rented back room that
    is full of beads and receipts and dolls and cloths,
    tobacco crumbs, vases and fringes.

Response

I guess at first I just felt sort of sorry for these older
people. What I thought was really sad was that they
seemed to be good people, but they just didn't have
anything—they must be very lonely. Then I thought
about this "remembering" and the things their room
seems to be full of. And I thought about all the times I
felt down and would get out my old scrapbook full of
stupid, little things like drawings and postcards from
friends and ribbons I won six years ago. And I would feel
sad that those times were past, but glad that I had
them to remember. And then I thought these people still
have their memories—their "twinklings." And I didn't feel
so sad about them anymore.

Now write your own response to the poem—or to any
poem, story, or play that you want to choose. Write it as if
you're talking to someone you feel comfortable with—
perhaps your best friend.

CRITICAL ANALYSIS ACROSS THE CURRICULUM

In critical analysis, you use a knowledge of elements (component parts) to analyze something in detail. You can apply this skill not only to short stories but also to cars, snow skis, scientific equipment—to anything whose parts and features you know well. Following is an analysis of CD changers.

from CD & VIDEODISC PLAYERS

Remember jukeboxes? Today's CD equivalents can hold and play as many as 100 discs at a time . . . and sell for as little as $400. Here you select which discs you want to play by flipping through a three-ring binder that holds the small booklets that come with the CDs, and you enter the numbers of the desired discs via a remote control.

The more-common and less-costly three- to six-disc changers generally come in two varieties: the carousel, which rotates discs on a round platter, and changers that store discs in a small cartridge called a "magazine" and slide them out one at a time for playback. Our tests indicate that the carousel-type CD changers tend to be more reliable than those that use magazine cartridges to hold the discs.

Note that not all carousel players are created equal; some, for example, allow changing one or more CDs while another is playing. The 100-disc megachangers are a little slow and clunky in operation, but they make up for it with convenience and capacity.

. . . Most experts agree that the audible differences between players of any kind are actually quite small, though not all CD players perform equally well in all areas. It's generally believed that dual D/A (digital-to-analog) converters offer the best design, at least from a theoretical point of view . . . , but experts advise that the type of D/A converter often isn't as important as how well the CD player is designed in the first place.

Consumers Digest

What are you interested in and fairly expert in (if you do say so yourself): maps? athletic equipment? telescopes? clarinets? Choose something that you would enjoy explaining clearly—either in writing or in an informal talk.

You can analyze, as in the example above, a certain *type* or *category* of your subject area. For example, if your subject area is "bicycles," you could analyze the recent "hybrid bikes." Or you can analyze a *particular example*, such as a specific new model of hybrid bicycle, whose features you'd like to scrutinize.

If you're writing your analysis, imagine that it's going to be published in a magazine specifically for lovers of your subject (and give the magazine a name: *Map Maniacs*, say, or *Clarinet Freaks*). If you're outlining and delivering a talk, imagine that it's for a club (like the Grand Order of Off-road Vehicle Owners).

Calvin & Hobbes copyright 1987 Watterson. Distributed by Universal Press Syndicate. Reprinted with permission. All rights reserved.

11 WRITING A RESEARCH PAPER: EXPOSITION

Exploring Your World

Research is a way of **exploring your world.** It's how we learn about the past and the present, and how we make decisions about the future.

Writing and You. Reports of research are everywhere—in books, magazines, and newspapers. Science writers report the latest findings on the environment, health, and astronomy. Historians and biographers dig up new information or give old information a new twist. Reporters turn their research into news stories. What other kinds of writers write research reports?

As You Read. Researchers have discovered that the ancient Incan and Mayan people knew a great deal about astronomy. As you read the following report, see if you can tell which information is factual and which is yet to be proved.

Billy Morrow Jackson, detail of *Cosmic Blink* (1988–89). Oil on panel. Entire painting is 48 × 96". Collection of Parkland College, Champaign, Ill.

FROM

AMERICA'S ANCIENT SKYWATCHERS

by Robert B. Carlson

For many pre-Columbian Americans, whether Inca, Maya, Anasazi—or indeed many among their living descendants—astronomy was not a science as we who are schooled in the Western tradition tend to think of it. Rather, the movements of sun and moon were the journeys of gods personified. In Mesoamerica the stars and the bright planets in their intricate wanderings were often conceived of as gods moving through the night sky en route to rebirth each sunup. They wove an enormous celestial tapestry mirrored in the warp and weft of the lives of the people themselves.

To observe and predict the recurrent paths of divine lights was to know the fates of kings and empires, to discern the proper day for rituals, to forecast animal migrations, the season of the life-giving rain, and the time for planting. The power to foretell required that observers, probably specially trained shamans or priests, make accurate records and preserve them. The information must have been accumulated over generations and generations, the observers using naked-eye sighting techniques to discover the patterns of movement in the universe. Their knowledge reached a level comparable to that of ancient cultures of the Old World.

> "...the movements of sun and moon were the journeys of gods personified."

Their records were preserved in calendars made of wood, string, and stone or, in Mesoamerica, written in accordion-fold books of animal hide or plaster-coated bark paper. Heavenly comings and goings were also recorded in the alignment of buildings and in city plans. These provided sight lines to mark significant risings and settings of celestial bodies. Such constructions often approached our own scientific astronomy in accuracy, but they had a sacred purpose. We might compare this combination of technical knowledge and religious motive to a church window so placed that sunlight passing through it will illuminate a saint's statue on the saint's day.

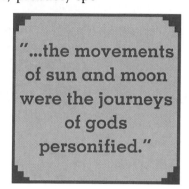

Stone Calendar

Earth too was invested with divinity. Many pre-Columbian American groups believed that their ancestors emerged from the underworld by way of a cave—the mouth of the earth. The earth's surface they divided into four quarters, often endowed

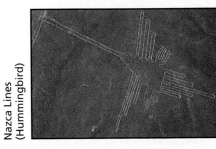

Nazca Lines (Hummingbird)

with distinctive trees, animals, deities, periods of time, and colors. Just as they marked the sky, so they set down paths of pilgrimage on the sacred landscape.

The most notable—and controversial—of these routes may be the ground drawings made on the bone-dry desert of southern Peru. The geometric figures of animals and plants; the spirals, zigzags, trapezoids, triangles; and the straight lines that stretch as far as the eye can see—all these are called Nazca Lines for the culture that established itself in that forbidding terrain 2,000 years ago.

Many speculations, some reasonable, some fanciful, have been made about the significance of the lines. One explanation suggests that the straight lines were aligned to astronomical risings and settings. Another that at least some of the effigy figures represented constellations. Still

another idea, recently investigated in depth by astronomer-anthropologist Anthony Aveni and anthropologists Gary Urton and Persis Clarkson, maintains that the long, straight

Nazca Lines (Bird)

lines connected sacred sites and marked ritual pathways walked by celebrants to make offerings at the far ends. These hypotheses are not mutually exclusive; all may have an element of truth.

Nazca Lines (Spider)

READER'S RESPONSE

1. When the ancient Americans looked up at the night sky, they saw more than just stars and planets—they saw stories in the sky. As a child (or even now), you may have done the same thing, perhaps at a summer camp-out. In a brief journal entry, tell about your own skywatching stories or experiences.
2. Like the ancient skywatchers, people who believe in astrology depend on the stars to plan their daily lives. What's your opinion of astrology?

WRITER'S CRAFT

3. What's the difference between a *fact* and a *theory*? Give two examples of facts in this report. Where does Carlson give some theories?
4. Writers of research reports must support their main ideas with specific examples and details. Give three details that Carlson uses to support his idea that Mesoamericans believed the movements of the sun and moon were related to the activities of their gods.
5. Carlson identifies some sources for some of the information he is sharing. What are those sources?

Ways to Develop Research

You live at a time when you can find out more than you want to know about almost anything. Newspapers, magazines, and journals give the latest information about research results. Universities, libraries, businesses, and others post regularly updated information on the Internet.

Some of these research papers are informal, and some are formal. Robert Carlson's paper on ancient skywatchers is *informal* because it doesn't give a detailed list of sources. A *formal* report, on the other hand, like the ones in journals (periodicals that publish scientific reports) and the ones you write for school, always has a detailed list of sources. Readers of formal reports demand to know, "Where does this information come from?" Reports can be developed in various ways. Here are some examples:

- in a biographical report, describing the role your favorite athlete played in an important game
- in a world history report, recounting political changes in Africa during the twentieth century
- in an art report, describing a Navajo sand painting
- in a science report, describing a space-shuttle liftoff
- in a report for a biology class, classifying the functions of different parts of the human brain
- in a workplace report, evaluating your job duties and describing your short- and long-term career goals
- in a report for a chemistry class, evaluating the claims made in TV commercials for beauty products

LOOKING AHEAD

In the main assignment in this chapter, you'll write a formal research paper. Before you write the actual report, you'll need to collect and organize information on your topic. Keep in mind that a research paper

- presents factual information about the topic
- presents information from several sources
- tells readers the source of the information

Writing a Research Paper

Prewriting

Finding and Limiting a Subject

You've probably heard the expression "starting off on the right foot." In writing a research paper, the "right foot" is an interesting subject that you can develop into a suitable topic.

Choosing a Subject

A good research subject is one that's interesting to both you and your readers. To be interesting, however, your subject does not have to be exotic or far away. In looking for a subject, don't neglect what's available right in "your own back yard." After all, you may not be able to travel to the ruins in Peru, but you can discover the origins of your town or village just by visiting your library or historical society. Remember that some research captures our attention and imagination merely by shedding new light on familiar subjects.

Reminder

To find possible research subjects, you can

- browse the World Wide Web using a directory that organizes Web sites into subject categories
- look through the materials in your library's vertical file
- browse through the nonfiction shelves in the library or along the documentary shelves in a videotape store
- skim articles of local and national interest in current newspapers and magazines
- watch television programs, such as *NOVA,* on scientific or historical topics
- talk with adult relatives or friends who have unusual or interesting jobs or backgrounds
- visit local museums and historical societies

Limiting Your Subject to a Specific Topic

You may already know that the key to good writing is using specific details. Even if your research paper were twenty pages long, you still wouldn't have space to discuss a broad subject in any detail. Suppose, for example, you chose the subject "the civil rights movement." You'd be faced with the impossible task of trying to cover dozens of subtopics, including "voting rights," "sit-ins," and "Montgomery bus boycott."

Maybe you chose the subject "the civil rights movement" because you vaguely remember an interesting magazine article about it. But at this point you have no specific information. Start by getting some general knowledge, an overview, of your subject. That will help you identify some smaller parts of the broad subject. Here are some ways to go about getting an overview.

- Read two or three general articles in reference books like encyclopedias. Notice headings and subheadings in the articles.
- Search the World Wide Web for pages or sites containing keywords related to your subject.
- Look up your subject in the *Readers' Guide to Periodical Literature* or in the library's card catalog or online catalog. Note the topics that are listed under the subject headings.
- Discuss your subject with someone (a teacher, neighbor, parent, and so on) who has expert knowledge about it.

Selecting a Suitable Topic

After getting an overview of your subject, you will probably have several possible topics in mind. But they may not all work well as topics for a research paper. To choose the best possible topic, ask yourself the following questions:

1. *Are there a variety of sources for this topic?* A highly personal topic such as "my experience on opening night of the class play" would not be a good choice because it has only one source: *you*. On the other hand, "favorite opening night experiences of three leading ladies" might have real possibilities. You

could read the autobiographies of several famous stage actresses and perhaps interview the "star" of a local theater group.

2. *Are sources of information readily available?* You may have trouble finding the information you need if a topic is too recent or too technical, or if the source material isn't available locally. For example, information about "legal precedents for *Brown v. Board of Education of Topeka*" would be too technical to appear in most popular publications.

EXERCISE 1 ▶ Evaluating Topics for Research

Which of the following topics could you use for a five-page research report? Some topics are too personal or technical, and some would be difficult to find information about. Which topics are too general to be covered in detail in a short paper? For each topic that seems unsuitable, first identify the problem, and then suggest a more limited or workable topic.

1. Chinese immigration to America
2. two successful experiments in a recent U.S. space mission
3. detailed analysis of evidence of microbial life in a Mars meteorite
4. ancient art of Egyptian hieroglyphics
5. my favorite grade-B horror movies

 **WRITING ASSIGNMENT**

PART 1:
Developing a Specific Topic

Get off on the right foot by thinking about your own choice of a subject. Choose one subject that interests you, and use the techniques listed on page 408 to get an overview. Next, identify three or four possible topics related to your subject. After making certain that there are sources of information available, choose one of these topics for your report.

This chapter takes you step-by-step through the process of writing a research paper, but you'll find that you often move through the steps differently from your classmates. For example, if you are already very familiar with your subject, you may jump ahead to limiting your topic right away. Or, you may move "backward" if you realize that your topic isn't a good choice. If you do repeat a step, don't get discouraged. You'll make up for lost time and produce a much better report by changing direction when you need to.

Thinking About Purpose, Audience, and Tone

Purpose. The basic purpose of a research paper is to inform. As you conduct your research, you will gather information and develop your own ideas about your topic. When you write your report, you'll inform readers about what you've learned.

Audience. People who read a research report are looking for information. They want to come away from the report with a better understanding of the topic. As you explore your topic and write your report, consider your audience's interest level and information level.

- *Interest level.* Look for an unusual approach to the topic or surprising details about it.
- *Information level.* Take your readers beyond what they already know. But don't get so technical or complex that your readers will have difficulty understanding your report.

Tone. TV documentaries, such as the Public Broadcasting System's *NOVA* or the National Geographic specials, often have a narrator who explains the images that you see on the screen. The narrator's tone of voice—usually calm, serious, and formal—lends authority to the information you're getting. If you use a serious, relatively formal tone in your report, your readers will be more likely to take it seriously.

EXERCISE 2▶ **Analyzing Purpose, Audience, and Tone**

What do you know about how secret codes work? Read the following paragraph from a report on secret codes. Then get together with a small group of classmates to discuss the questions that follow on page 412.

A typical code takes ideas in the message—words or even whole phrases—and changes them into something else, usually groups of numbers taken out of a codebook resembling a small dictionary. To compose a coded message, the sender first writes what he intends to say ("Attack is imminent") and then looks up the words in his codebook. "Attack" is 1140, and "imminent" is 4539. And that's his message: 1140 4539. To further confound the enemy, the sender might scramble the signal by using a special key to encipher those numbers, by switching around the order, or both. The receiver must have an identical codebook and know anything extra the sender has done to scramble the number groups.

James R. Chiles, "To Break the Unbreakable Codes"

1. The writer's purpose is to inform readers about secret codes. How might the paragraph have been different if the subject stayed the same but the writer's purpose were to entertain readers?
2. How can you tell the writer assumed that most readers had never seen a codebook? What does the writer do to make the explanation of how a secret code works clear to readers?
3. How would you describe the tone of this paragraph?

EXERCISE 3 ▶ **Speaking and Listening: Analyzing the Audience for Your Report**

To help you get a better feeling for your audience, interview one or more of the classmates who will be the readers of your report. Start by telling your classmate briefly what you've learned about your topic and what you plan to find out. Then ask your classmate these questions.

1. How much do you already know about the topic? Have you ever read any articles or books about it? Do any television shows or tapes discuss it?
2. What seems interesting to you about the topic? What would you like to know about it?
3. Is anything about the topic confusing to you? What would help you understand the topic better?

Developing Research Questions

Your research will be much easier if you're searching for the answers to specific questions. Rely on your natural curiosity. Think about what you want to know about your topic, and jot down some questions to research. Here are some general questions that will help you think of specific questions about your topic.

- What is the topic? How can you define it?
- What groups, or classes, make up the topic?
- What are the topic's parts, and how do they work together?
- How has the topic changed over time?
- How is the topic similar to or different from related topics?
- What are the topic's advantages or disadvantages?

Reminder

To find a topic and begin your research

- use resource materials to find a general subject
- limit the general subject to a suitable topic
- stop to think about your purpose, audience, and tone
- develop a list of research questions about your topic

WRITING ASSIGNMENT

PART 2:
Beginning Your Research

Use your natural curiosity and what you already know about the topic to begin your research. Start by thinking about your purpose and audience. Then make a list of three or four research questions about your topic.

 *Prewriting*

Finding and Evaluating Sources of Information

We're bombarded daily with so much information that this has been called "the age of information." You may not even realize how many sources of information surround you. Here are some library and community sources you can use for your research.

LIBRARY RESOURCES	
RESOURCE	**SOURCE OR INFORMATION**
Card catalog or online catalog	Books listed by title, author, and subject (most libraries also list audiovisual materials)
Readers' Guide to Periodical Literature or *National Newspaper Index*	Subject and author index to magazine and journal articles, index to major newspapers
Microfilm or microfiche	Indexes to major newspapers such as *The New York Times* and *The Washington Post*, back issues of newspapers and magazines
General reference books or CD-ROMs	Encyclopedias, encyclopedia yearbooks, dictionaries
Specialized reference books or CD-ROMs	Biographical reference sources, encyclopedias of special subjects (sports, art, etc.), atlases, almanacs (See pages 955–957 for more about reference sources.)
Videotapes and audiotapes	Movies, documentaries, filmstrips, videotapes, audiotapes of books
Vertical file	Pamphlets listed by subject, clippings
The librarian	Help in finding and using sources

☞ **REFERENCE NOTE:** For more information on using the library, including online catalogs, online databases, and the Internet, see pages 952–957.

COMMUNITY RESOURCES	
RESOURCE	**SOURCE OR INFORMATION**
World Wide Web and online services	Articles, interviews, bibliographies, pictures, videos, sound recordings
Local government offices	Facts and statistics, information on local government policies, experts on local government
Local offices of state and federal officials	Voting records of government officials, recent or pending legislation, experts on state and federal government
Museums and historical societies	Special exhibits, libraries and bookstores, experts on various subjects
Schools and colleges	Libraries, experts on various subjects
Local newspaper offices	Clippings, files on local events and history

Evaluating Sources of Information

Some sources are more useful than others. Before you use a source, make sure that the 4 *R*'s apply.

1. *Relevant.* Does the source have information directly related to your topic? For a book, check the table of contents and the index. For a nonprint source, read a review or summary of the work.
2. *Reliable.* Can you trust your source to be accurate and objective? Well-respected magazines and newspapers such as *Smithsonian* or the *Christian Science Monitor* are usually reliable sources.
3. *Recent.* How up-to-date is the information? What is the copyright date? Even a historical topic, such as "women artists in the Middle Ages," should have some recent sources. New information is continually being researched and published.
4. *Representative.* If your topic is controversial, you need to find sources with opinions and information on both sides of the issue. For example, if some scientists say exercise adds to life span and others say it doesn't, you must report both theories.

Preparing Source Cards

You have this great quotation you want to use in your report, but you can't remember where you found it. If you've ever had anything like that happen, you know it's important to keep a record of your sources. That's where source cards come into the picture.

For each of your sources, record the author, title, and publication information on an index card or sheet of notebook paper, or in a computer file. (Source cards are sometimes called *bibliography cards*.) Give each source a number. With good source information, you won't need to run back again and again to the card catalog or *Readers' Guide*. These source cards will also make it easier to prepare the final list of sources, or *Works Cited*, that accompanies your report.

The following guidelines tell you how to record the necessary information for different types of sources. As you fill out your cards, refer to these guidelines, and note the special uses of punctuation.

GUIDELINES FOR RECORDING SOURCE INFORMATION

1. **Book with One Author.** Write the author's or editor's name, last name first (follow the names of editors with a comma and the abbreviation *ed.*); the title of the book; the place of publication; the publishing company's name; and the year of publication. (To make it easier to locate a book later, put its call number in the upper right-hand part of the index card, paper, or computer file.)

   EXAMPLE Piña Chan, Román. The Olmec: Mother Culture of Mesoamerica. New York: Rizzoli, 1989.

2. **Source with More Than One Author.** For the first listed author, write the last name first. For all other authors, write the first name first.

   EXAMPLE Rust, William F., and Robert J. Sharer. . . .

(continued)

GUIDELINES FOR RECORDING
SOURCE INFORMATION *(continued)*

3. Magazine or Newspaper Article. Write the author's name (if given), last name first; the title of the article; the name of the magazine or newspaper; the day (if given), month, and year of publication; and page numbers on which the article begins and ends. For an article in a newspaper that has different editions or multiple sections, specify the edition (use *ed.*) and/or section before the page number.

EXAMPLE   Stuart, George E. "New Light on the Olmec." National Geographic Nov. 1993: 88-114.

EXAMPLE   Mack, Tara. "The 9 1/2-ton Head of State." Washington Post 6 June 1996, early ed.: C1.

4. Encyclopedia Article. Write the author's name (if given), last name first; the title of the article; the name of the encyclopedia; the edition (if given); and the year of publication. (Use the abbreviation *ed.* for *edition.*)

EXAMPLE   "Pre-Columbian Civilizations." The New Encyclopaedia Britannica: Macropaedia. 15th ed. 1988.

5. Radio or Television Program. Write the program title; the name of the network; the call letters and city of the local station (if any); and the broadcast date.

EXAMPLE   NBC Nightly News. NBC. WNBC, New York. 8 July 1997.

6. Movie or Video Recording. Write the title of the work and the director or producer's name; for movies, write the original distributor's name (for movies not available on video) and year of release; for video recordings, write the word *Videocassette* or *Videodisc,* the distributor's name, and the year the video recording was released. (Use *Dir.* for *Director* and *Prod.* for *Producer.*)

EXAMPLE   Maya: Lords of the Jungle. Dir. John Angier. Videocassette. PBS Home Video, 1981.

(continued)

GUIDELINES FOR RECORDING SOURCE INFORMATION *(continued)*

7. **Interview.** Write the interviewee's name, last name first; the type of interview (Personal or Telephone); and the day, month, and year of the interview.

   EXAMPLE   Sutphin, Andrea. Telephone interview. 17 Apr. 1997.

8. **Electronic Materials.** Write the author's name (if given), last name first; title (include print publisher, date, and page numbers if material was first in a print source); posting date (online); title of CD-ROM or database (if any, for online sources); type of source (*CD-ROM* or *Online*); location of source (*Internet,* online service, or city, if given, for CD-ROMs); distributor (CD-ROMs); date of publication (CD-ROMs) or date of access; and Internet address (if any), preceded by the word *Available.*

   EXAMPLE   Follensbee, Billie. Olmec Heads: A Product of the Americas. 30 Apr. 1996. Online. Internet. 12 Dec. 1997. Available http://copan.bioz .unibas.ch/meso/olmec.html.

☞ **REFERENCE NOTE:** For help with capitalizing and punctuating titles, see pages 777–778, 831–832, and 840.

Reminder

As you prepare your source cards, be sure to

- follow a specific format for recording source information
- record all information accurately, double-checking authors' names, titles, and page numbers
- use quotation marks to indicate when you are quoting an author's exact words
- follow the rules for punctuating and capitalizing titles (pages 777–778, 831–832, and 840) and for using quotation marks to give an author's exact words (pages 834–836)

WRITING NOTE The format for identifying sources in this chapter is that of the Modern Language Association of America (MLA). You'll use it for preparing source cards, taking notes, and preparing your final list of sources. Your teacher may instead ask you to use a different format, such as that of the American Psychological Association (APA).

EXERCISE 4▶ **Using Library and Community Resources**

With a small group, brainstorm some sources for answering the two practical, everyday questions that follow. For each question, try to think of two library sources and two community sources. Check the 4 *R*'s: Are your sources relevant, reliable, recent, and representative?

1. What percentage of eligible people voted in the last election? are registered? How can we get more 18-year-olds to register and vote?
2. What approaches are your community and the nation taking to decrease the dropout rate?

WRITING ASSIGNMENT PART 3: **Collecting and Evaluating Sources**

Explore your library and community sources to see what you can find out about your topic. (Find five or six sources of information.) Then evaluate each source by checking its 4 *R*'s (see page 415). You and a classmate might exchange your lists and evaluate each other's sources.

WRITING ASSIGNMENT PART 4: **Preparing Source Cards**

Prepare a source card for each source you've decided to use. Use the guidelines and examples on pages 416–418.

 *Prewriting*

Planning, Recording, and Organizing Information

You've identified some sources that look promising. Now you need to collect information and find some way of organizing it.

Drafting an Early Plan

Faced with a stack of books or an interview date, you may be uncertain about where to begin. After all, you can't take notes or ask questions about *everything* concerning your topic. One way to get some idea about where to start is to make an *early plan*—a list of points that you plan to research. For example, suppose you read some new information about the Olmecs' form of government and learned that the Olmecs developed a calendar and a form of writing. Here's the way you could use this information in an early plan.

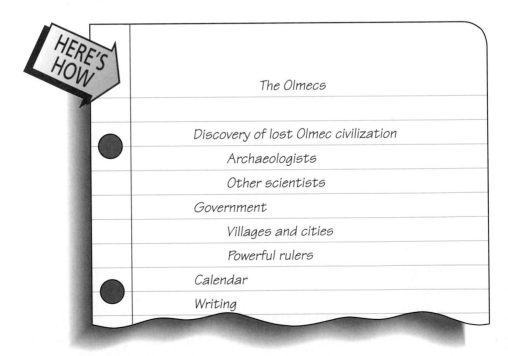

HERE'S HOW

The Olmecs

• Discovery of lost Olmec civilization
    Archaeologists
    Other scientists
Government
    Villages and cities
    Powerful rulers
• Calendar
Writing

Refer to your early plan as you take notes, and use its headings in deciding what information to record. But remember that your early plan can be changed. If you discover new information related to your topic, add a heading to your early plan. Or, if you decide not to develop a point in your early plan, delete the heading.

Taking Notes

As you take notes from a source, you can either quote, summarize, or paraphrase the material. Notice how these three techniques are used to take notes on Billie Follensbee's *Olmec Heads: A Product of the Americas.*

TECHNIQUE	EXAMPLE
Quote only when the author's exact words, as well as ideas, are important. To quote, copy the source material word for word, and put quotation marks around it.	"There is . . . overwhelming archaeological evidence that the Olmec Colossal Heads were made by and for Native Americans." "In short, those who have claimed the Olmec Colossal Heads to be of foreign origin have only noticed some superficial physical similarities with groups of people on the other side of the ocean, and without any concrete evidence for support, they have given credit for these works to far-away foreign cultures."
Summarize when you need to remember only the main idea. Read or listen to the material first. Then, write your notes in your own words.	Follensbee says that the Olmec colossal heads were created by Native Americans. She says that others have claimed, without support, that they were created by people from a foreign culture.
Paraphrase when you need to remember more detailed information. Restate the material by using your own vocabulary and sentence structure.	Follensbee says that the creators of the Olmec great stone heads clearly were Native Americans. Though people see a likeness between the physical features of the statues and those of other groups, Follensbee says there is no clear evidence to suggest that the creators came from a culture in a distant part of the world.

Whichever method you use, always check your notes against the original to be certain that you have quoted, summarized, or paraphrased accurately.

Unless you attack note taking in an orderly way, you'll be faced with trying to untangle a jumble of notes. Experienced note-takers give this advice:

- If you take notes on 4" × 6" note cards, use a separate card for each item of information and each source. If you use paper or computer files, use a separate sheet or file for each source.
- In the upper left corner, write a keyword or key phrase (perhaps a heading from your early plan) so you can tell at a glance what the note is about.
- In the upper right-hand corner, write the source card number (see page 416). End each note with the page number where you found the information.

| importance | 6 |

"The Olmec culture is generally considered to have given rise to all the other great civilizations that developed in Central America, including the Mayan and, much later, the Aztec."

p. 76

WRITING NOTE

Unless you're quoting a source directly, *always* take notes in your own words. Change the sentence structure, too. When you use someone else's words or ideas without giving proper credit, you're *plagiarizing.* No matter how you ultimately use your source (direct quotation, paraphrase, or summary), you must give credit for other people's ideas as well as their words.

PART 5:
Planning and Note Taking

Use what you've already learned about your topic to identify points you'd like to explore further. Make these the headings as you draft your early plan. Then, start taking notes from your sources. You can't, of course, take notes about *everything*. Use the headings in your early plan to decide what information to record.

Developing a Thesis Statement

Your *thesis statement* is a signpost to guide both you and your reader. It expresses the main idea of your report and indicates what you plan to cover. Think about the ideas and conclusions you've drawn from your research so far, and write a preliminary thesis statement. (You can always revise it later.) Right now it will help focus your note taking, and later it will help you organize your report.

 REFERENCE NOTE: See pages 113–114 for more help with writing thesis statements.

CRITICAL THINKING

Analyzing Your Topic

When you *analyze* a topic, you break it down into its smaller parts and think about how the parts are related. For any topic it's possible to take several different approaches. Analyzing the possible approaches is an important first step in writing your thesis statement.

For example, following are four possible approaches and sample thesis statements for the topic "the role of women in the American military services." Notice that each approach emphasizes a different aspect of this topic.

- **Exploring new information**

    EXAMPLE   In the 1990s, women in the American military services have many varied roles.

■ **Examining how the topic has changed over time**

EXAMPLE   Women's roles in the American military services have changed drastically since women were first admitted to the armed services.

■ **Demonstrating a cause-and-effect relationship**

EXAMPLE   Past successes of American women in the military have resulted in their broader roles in the 1990s.

■ **Demonstrating a comparison/contrast relationship**

EXAMPLE   Roles for American women in the military services are much more limited than those for women in the armed services of many other countries.

 CRITICAL THINKING EXERCISE:
Analyzing a Topic

Suppose you're planning to write a research report about some aspect of space exploration. You've done some research, and you're ready to develop a preliminary thesis statement. How will you approach your topic? Write four thesis statements to illustrate these different approaches: (1) exploring new information, (2) examining how the topic has changed over time, (3) demonstrating a cause/effect relationship, and (4) demonstrating a comparison/contrast relationship. To get some ideas, look back at the example thesis statements on women in the armed forces. Make up whatever details you need for your thesis statements.

Preparing an Outline

Your early plan helped you organize your research. Now that you've found information, you'll need to do more organizing. You may not know exactly how you will organize your report until you have written and revised your first draft, but it helps to make a plan before you start writing. One good way to do this is to create an outline.

To create an outline, group your note cards into sets, using the headings in your early plan. Then, create sub-headings and divide your sets into smaller sets, or group several small, related sets together under a single heading.

COMPUTER NOTE: Use a stand-alone outlining program or your word-processing program's outline feature to organize your prewriting notes into an outline for your first draft.

Here's an outline a writer created after doing research on the Olmecs. A *formal* outline like this, with Roman numerals and capital letters, can also be made after a report is written. It then serves as a table of contents for the report.

👉 **REFERENCE NOTE:** For help with writing a formal outline, see page 118.

HERE'S HOW

The Olmecs: New Light on a Dark Past

I. Early research on the Olmecs
  A. Work of archaeologist Melgar
  B. Theory about relics and unknown culture
  C. Excavations and scientific study
II. Olmec society and government
  A. Villages and cities
  B. Powerful rulers
    1. Colossal heads
    2. Stones moved by sledge, raft
    3. Earthen mounds
III. Olmecs as advanced civilization
  A. Sophisticated calendar
  B. Hieroglyphic writing
IV. Speculation about Olmec origins
V. Importance of Olmecs

WRITING ASSIGNMENT

PART 6:
Preparing an Outline

Organize your notes and create an outline. Use it as a guide as you write, but feel free to revise it as needed.

Writing Your First Draft

All your careful preparations will finally pay off. Now that you've collected and organized your information, the actual writing will be easy.

Combining the Basic Elements of a Research Report

Keep these two goals in mind as you begin writing. You want to interest your readers and help them understand your topic. You also need to pull together, or synthesize, ideas and information from a variety of sources and state them in your own words. Like any informative composition, your research report should include all of these elements:

- an interesting opening that captures your reader's attention
- a thesis statement that presents your main idea
- a series of body paragraphs that develop and support the thesis statement
- a clear order for your ideas and information
- a conclusion that restates your main points

☞ **REFERENCE NOTE:** To review the basic elements of a composition, see pages 122–134.

As you write the first draft of your body paragraphs, be guided by your final outline. You'll develop each main heading into one or two paragraphs.

"I believe more in the scissors than I do in the pencil."

Truman Capote

MECHANICS HINT

Using Quotations

To give your paper credibility, sprinkle it lightly with direct quotations, following these guidelines:

1. **Place a directly quoted phrase or clause into your own sentence, and enclose it in quotation marks.**

   Researcher Michael D. Coe says experts are almost unanimous in their belief that "the Olmec civilization is older than any other in Mesoamerica" (183).

2. **Run a short quotation (four lines or fewer) into your text. Introduce it in your own words, and enclose it in quotation marks.**

   According to Coe, "There is now little or no dissent from the proposition that the Olmec civilization is older than any other in Mesoamerica, including the Classic Maya" (183).

3. **Set off a longer quotation by indenting each line ten spaces from the left margin. Introduce the quotation in your own words, usually followed by a colon, but do not use quotation marks.**

   Archaeologists have solved the mystery of when the Olmecs flourished:

   > There is now little or no dissent from the proposition that the Olmec civilization is older than any other in Mesoamerica, including the Classic Maya. Recent excavations in both lowland and highland Mexico have proved this beyond all doubt (Coe 183).

   (**Source:** Coe, Michael D. "Olmec and Maya: A Study in Relationships." The Origins of Maya Civilization. Ed. Richard E. W. Adams. Albuquerque: U of New Mexico P, 1977. 183-195.)

Giving Credit to Your Sources

In your report you'll document your sources throughout the paper itself and in a separate list at the end, labeled *Works Cited*.

Giving Credit Within the Body of Your Report.

Every researcher-writer faces two problems: (1) when to give credit, and (2) how to give credit.

1. *How do you decide when to give credit?* As a rule, it's not necessary to acknowledge general information you already know or can easily find in general reference sources. (*In Chinatown in San Francisco, signs are written in both Chinese and English.*) You also don't have to acknowledge general information from public sources like newspapers or TV. (*Smoking may cause cancer and heart disease.*)

2. *How do you show the credit?* There are several styles for giving credit. In this chapter, documentation follows the format recommended by the Modern Language Association of America (MLA), which uses parenthetical citations. Some teachers prefer footnotes, placed at the bottom of the page and corresponding to numbers in the text. Here's one example; but if you need to use footnotes, you'll have to follow another style guide.

[1] Román Piña Chan, The Olmec: Mother Culture of Mesoamerica (New York: Rizzoli, 1989) 25.

GUIDELINES FOR GIVING CREDIT WITHIN THE REPORT

Place the information in parentheses at the end of the sentence in which you've used someone else's words or ideas.

1. **Source with One Author.** Author's last name followed by the page number(s). (Piña Chan 83)

2. **Sources by Authors with the Same Last Name.** First and last names of each author followed by the page number(s). (Mary Smith 21) (John Smith 102)

3. **Source with More Than One Author.** All authors' last names, followed by the page number(s). (Rust and Sharer 102)

GUIDELINES FOR GIVING CREDIT WITHIN THE REPORT *(continued)*

4. **Source with No Author Given.** Title, or a shortened form, and the page number(s). ("New Information" 34)

5. **One-page Source, Unpaginated Source, CD-ROM or Online Source, or Article from an Encyclopedia or Other Work Arranged Alphabetically.** Author's name only. If no author's name is given, title only. (Follensbee)

6. **More Than One Source by the Same Author.** Author's last name and the title or a shortened form of it, followed by the page number(s). (Nissen, "Olmec Legacy" 21) (Nissen, "New Discoveries" 45)

7. **Author's Name Given in Paragraph.** Page number only. (76)

Preparing the List of Sources. The citations in the body of your report refer to a detailed list, the *Works Cited* page at the end of your report. (If you've used print sources only, you can call this a *Bibliography*.) Readers who want to know complete publication information can refer to this page as they read your paper.

GUIDELINES FOR PREPARING THE LIST OF WORKS CITED

1. On a separate sheet, center the words *Works Cited* (or the word *Bibliography*) one inch from the top.
2. For each entry on the list, follow the format you used for your source cards (pages 416–419).
3. List your sources by the author's last name. If no author is given, alphabetize by the first important word in the title. If you use two or more sources by the same author, write the author's name in the first entry only. For all other entries, write three hyphens where the author's name should be, followed by a period. Then give the title, publication information, and page number(s).
4. Begin each listing at the left margin. If a listing is longer than one line, indent all the following lines five spaces.

Now, read the following research report about the Olmecs. Notice how the report combines basic composition form with documentation of sources.

A WRITER'S MODEL

The Olmecs: New Light on a Dark Past

**INTRODUCTION
Interest
grabber**

In an old movie, a dashing adventurer hacks his way through tangled jungle vines, searching for a lost civilization. Suddenly he stumbles upon a dark pit hidden by the dense undergrowth. At the bottom, he finds a huge stone monument covered with strange carvings. He smiles because he realizes right away that he has chanced upon the remains of an unknown civilization that existed thousands of years ago.

**Background
information**

More than three thousand years ago, in the jungles near the Gulf of Mexico, the people now known as the Olmecs developed a complex civilization that lasted for at least eight hundred years before mysteriously disappearing (Autry). Today, thanks to the work of many scholars and

archaeologists, people from around the world can learn about the Olmecs and see the artifacts they left behind. There was no solo adventurer who, after stumbling upon Olmec monuments, immediately realized their significance. Instead, researchers have gradually pieced together the story of the Olmecs after years of puzzling finds, careful excavation, and cooperative research.

Thesis statement

Field research related to the Olmecs began around 1860 in Tres Zapotes, Mexico. Villagers there unearthed a five-foot-high stone head in a field a workman had been clearing (Stuart 95). In 1862, the scholar José Melgar saw the head and went on to publish an article about it in 1869 (Piña Chan 25). Over the years, other archaeologists wrote about discoveries of similar stone heads, old monuments, and smaller relics which did not seem to have been created by any of the early cultures that were already documented. Archaeologists gradually started to theorize that the objects must have come from a previously unknown ancient culture, one they began to call "Olmec," because it seemed to have been centered in Olman, the ancient Aztec "Rubber Country" (Fagan 97).

BODY
Rediscovery of Olmecs

Source with one author

Summary

Since full-scale excavations of the Olmec areas began in 1938, archaeologists have used many scientific methods to locate the Olmec ruins and learn about Olmec culture. Some of

Topic sentence— introduces paragraph

Specific examples

the ruins, for example, were discovered or mapped by aerial photography or, more recently, by satellites. Scientists used radioactive carbon dating to establish the age of bones and relics found at the sites. Specialists studied the fossil remains of plants and animals (Grove 27).

Olmec society

Using these methods, researchers have learned much about how the Olmecs lived. From the excavations, experts learned that the Olmec society consisted of farming villages grouped around large centers or "cities." At first scholars believed that the Olmecs used these centers only for religious ceremonies (Piña Chan 83). However, excavations in 1986 convinced many archaeologists that the Olmecs also lived in the centers, not

One-page source

just in the outlying villages (Bower).

Early Olmecs probably struggled to grow enough food to eat. Gradually, though, as they developed irrigation and improved farming methods, they were able to grow a surplus of food. This surplus probably became controlled by a class of strong leaders, allowing some Olmecs to become specialized artisans instead of farmers. The leaders built the centers discovered during excavations and commissioned artisans to create monuments to their power (Piña Chan 83).

Olmec rulers

Two different sources

Two pages from the same source

Fifteen more heads like the one Melgar wrote about have been found over the years. These stone heads, which may preserve the features of actual Olmec rulers, are from five to eleven feet high, and weigh as much as thirty-six thousand pounds (Stuart 104; Autry). The stone used to create them is not native to many of the areas where they have been found; it came from mountains nearby. Experts believe the Olmecs may have moved the huge stones first on sledges or rolling logs, and then down rivers on large rafts (Stuart 95, 102). Along with the heads, the Olmecs built large earthen mounds. Scholars surmise that only powerful rulers would have had the means to plan such colossal projects and to command the many people needed to create them (Stuart 104).

Advanced civilization

Calendar

Evidence indicates that the Olmec civilization was highly advanced. Dates carved on some Olmec artifacts suggest that the Olmecs may have used one of the world's first carefully constructed calendars, even before the Mayas. It was a ritual calendar, based on a 260-day cycle. Since the average term of a human pregnancy is about 266 days, and the planting-and-harvesting cycle in the Olmec area lasts about the same number of days, some writers have suggested that the Olmecs might have associated the calendar with fertility (Fagan 120).

Writing

Background information/ definition

Many archaeologists also believe that the Olmecs were the first to use hieroglyphic writing within Mesoamerica. (In hieroglyphic writing, a picture represents a word, syllable, or sound.) Evidence for this includes an Olmec sculpture carved with the figure of a man who seems to be walking. Behind him is a carving of a human foot, which experts believe is the hieroglyphic symbol for "walking" or "marching." Other sculptures have carvings of stars and clouds which appear to be hieroglyphic symbols (Piña Chan 184). Olmec hieroglyphics, along with the quality of Olmec art, hint at the sophistication and learning of the culture that produced them.

Speculation

Olmec art has also inspired speculation about Olmec origins. To some writers, the features of the stone heads and other artifacts suggest that the Olmecs had contact with people from Africa and Europe, and that the Olmec rulers originally came from distant lands. Olmec archaeology specialist Billie Follensbee responds:

Longer direct quotation

> Those who have claimed the Olmec Colossal Heads to be of foreign origin have only noticed some superficial physical similarities with groups of people on the other side of the ocean, and without any concrete evidence for support, they have given the credit for these works to far-away foreign cultures. This is both academically irresponsible and unfair to the cultures that truly produced them.

Online source— author's name mentioned in paragraph

Follensbee, along with many others, concludes that there is "overwhelming archaeological evidence that the Olmec Colossal Heads were made by and for Native Americans."

Encyclopedia article

About twenty-four hundred years ago, the last great Olmec cultural center was violently destroyed ("Pre-Columbian Civilizations"). Archaeologists disagree about the cause. Some believe the Olmec peasants revolted against their rulers, bringing down the civilization in the process. Others believe that invaders from nearby may have been responsible (Piña Chan 208).

Importance

Most archaeologists, however, agree that the Olmecs played an important and influential role in the early history of the region. One writer summarizes the opinion of many scholars in the field when he writes that the Olmecs "created Mesoamerica's first civilization 3,000 years ago-- and left a rich cultural heritage to later groups, from the Maya to the Aztec" (Stuart 88). For many years, not much was known about this important civilization. Today, however, thanks to years of research and analysis, scientists are bringing light to a dark past.

Direct quotation

CONCLUSION
Summary statement

Works Cited

Autry, William O. "Olmec Indians." World Book
    Multimedia Encyclopedia. 1995 ed.
    CD-ROM. World Book, 1995.
Bower, B. "Domesticating an Ancient 'Temple
    Town.'" Science News 15 Oct. 1988: 246.
Fagan, Brian M. Kingdoms of Gold, Kingdoms of
    Jade. London: Thames and Hudson, 1991.
Follensbee, Billie. Olmec Heads: A Product of the
    Americas. 30 Apr. 1996. Online. Internet.
    12 Dec. 1997. Available http://copan.bioz
    .unibas.ch/meso/olmec.html.
Grove, David C. Chalcatzingo: Excavations on the
    Olmec Frontier. New York: Thames and
    Hudson, 1984.
Piña Chan, Román. The Olmec: Mother Culture
    of Mesoamerica. New York: Rizzoli, 1989.
"Pre-Columbian Civilizations." The New
    Encyclopaedia Britannica: Macropaedia.
    15th ed. 1988.
Stuart, George E. "New Light on the Olmec."
    National Geographic Nov. 1993: 88-114.

WRITING ASSIGNMENT	PART 7: **Writing Your First Draft**

Now you're ready to write! Using your final outline and note cards as a guide, write the first draft of your report. Give credit to your sources by using parenthetical citations following the MLA format in this chapter. Then prepare your Works Cited list. Be sure to list only the sources you actually used in your report.

Evaluating and Revising

Use the chart on page 438 to evaluate and revise your report. Ask yourself the questions on the left. Then, use the revision techniques on the right to fix any problems.

EXERCISE 5 ▶ **Analyzing a Writer's Revisions**

Below are the revisions that were made to a first draft of the ninth paragraph of the Writer's Model (page 433). Study the revisions, and answer the questions that follow.

Olmec hieroglyphics, along with the quality of Olmec art, hint at the sophistication and learning of the culture that produced them. Many archaeologists also believe that ~~these people~~ *the Olmecs* were the first to use hieroglyphic writing within Meso-	**reorder** **replace**

(In hieroglyphic writing, a picture represents a word, syllable, or sound.)

america. Evidence for this includes an **add**
Olmec sculpture carved with the figure of
a man who seems to be walking. Behind
him is a carving of a human foot, which
experts believe is the hieroglyphic symbol
for "walking" or "marching." Other sculptures have carvings of stars and clouds
which appear to be hieroglyphic symbols
(Piña Chan, 184). ~~Of course, the Egyptians~~ **cut/cut**
~~also had a calendar and used hieroglyphic~~
~~symbols for similar purposes, but the Egyp~~
~~tian hieroglyphics were very different from~~
~~the ones that the Olmecs and Mayans used.~~

1. Notice that the writer moved the first sentence from the beginning to the end of the paragraph. Why do you think this change was made?
2. Why did the writer replace the phrase *these people* with the phrase *the Olmecs*?
3. Why was a new sentence added after the second sentence of the paragraph?
4. For what reason did the writer delete the sentence that begins *Of course, the Egyptians . . .*?
5. Why did the writer delete the comma from the citation in the fifth sentence of the paragraph?

WRITING ASSIGNMENT

PART 8:

Evaluating and Revising Your Report

Get some help by exchanging your report with a classmate. Use the evaluating and revising guidelines in the chart on page 438 to give each other friendly advice. Apply the guidelines to your own report also, and make changes to improve your first draft.

Calvin & Hobbes copyright 1989 Watterson. Distributed by Universal Press Syndicate. Reprinted with permission. All rights reserved.

EVALUATING AND REVISING RESEARCH REPORTS

EVALUATION GUIDE	REVISION TECHNIQUE
1 Does a thesis statement appear early in the report?	**Add** a thesis statement to the first or second paragraph of your report.
2 Is the report suitable for its audience? Is it interesting, informative, and clear?	**Add** interesting, unusual, or surprising details. **Add** necessary definitions, background information, and explanations.
3 Is the tone of the report appropriate?	**Replace** words or phrases that give your report a casual or informal tone.
4 Are sources relevant, reliable, recent, and representative?	**Cut** information that is irrelevant or out-of-date. **Replace** with information from better sources.
5 Are ideas and information pulled together (synthesized) and stated in the writer's own words?	Check that each topic sentence expresses your ideas in your own words. **Add** or **replace** topic sentences as necessary.
6 Are ideas developed and supported with adequate information? Will readers find the information complete?	**Add** facts and figures, theories, and expert opinions about your topic where necessary.
7 Does all the information relate directly to the topic and approach?	**Cut** unnecessary information.
8 Is proper credit given for each source of information?	**Add** documentation for any information that isn't common knowledge. Check format guidelines.
9 Does documentation follow the format recommended by your teacher?	**Replace** as necessary to follow the MLA format or other format recommended by your teacher.

Proofreading and Publishing

So far, you've focused on the content of your paper. Now it's time to work on its appearance. Take another look at your report, and clean up all grammar, mechanics, and usage errors. Make a final check of your documentation as well. To share what you've learned, try one of the ideas below, or come up with a publishing idea of your own.

- If you're applying for a part-time job or for a special award or honor, submit your report as an example of your ability to plan and carry out a long-term project.
- Plan a bulletin board that features research as a theme. Select one in a location where all students can stop and look—maybe the front hall of your school. Post examples of research reports from your English class as well as from history and science classes.

WRITING ASSIGNMENT

PART 9:
Proofreading and Publishing Your Report

Proofread your report carefully and correct any errors. Be extra careful to get your documentation (citations and *Works Cited* page) just right. Publish or share your report with others.

Reflecting on Your Writing

If you plan to add your report to your **portfolio,** make sure to date the report and to include written responses to each of the following questions.

- How did you narrow your subject down to a topic?
- What kinds of research materials did you find most useful? Which were not so useful? Explain.
- How did your notes or outline help you when you began to write your report?

A STUDENT MODEL

The following paragraphs were excerpted from a report by Lam Votran, a student in Walnut Creek, California. Lam advises other student writers to "always make an outline" before starting a draft of a report.

A Moving Tune
by Lam Votran

Music has extraordinary power. It can inspire, it can irritate, and it can provide deep states of mental relaxation. Sometimes you can't say what it is about a particular piece of music that touches you, but the attraction is so strong that you can't resist it.

Therapists have found that music and singing can be effective in the treatment of children with emotional and mental problems. In their book *Music Therapy in Special Education*, Paul Nordoff and Clive Robbins write about their experiences of using songs to educate children about their emotions. They say that every song has "an emotional content that it can impart to the children who sing it. . . . Songs can arouse children to excitement, gladden them with pleasure, calm them to thoughtfulness" (32).

Even violent criminals can be touched by certain kinds of music. In a letter published in the *Canadian Medical Association Journal*, the medical director of a psychiatric prison hospital in British Columbia writes that classical music seemed to have a calming effect on the inmates he worked with-- men who had been convicted of violent offenses like murder and assault.

The inmates were given a chance to voluntarily take part in music-listening sessions. They chose the music selections themselves, and they were asked to participate in discussions afterward. Although the inmates sometimes became disruptive while listening to rock music, the medical director says that they listened to classical music "intently," without any disruptions. Tchaikovsky and Debussy, he says, were the two most popular listening choices (Roy 1170).

WRITING WORKSHOP

A Book Report That Evaluates

You evaluate movies by judging them against criteria, or guidelines. For example, you may like movies that are filled with action. You can also use criteria to evaluate a book. Below are guidelines for evaluating an autobiography.

GUIDELINES FOR EVALUATING AUTOBIOGRAPHY

1. Is the author honest? Does he or she write about details that make the author's life seem less than perfect?
2. Does the author present details of places, people, and events that we otherwise wouldn't have known about?
3. Does the author use fresh and natural-sounding language?
4. Does the author write about his or her thoughts and feelings, as well as events?

Here is the opening of a report on an autobiography. See if you think the writer evaluates it using the criteria above.

Golden Lilies by Kwei-li is a series of letters by a Chinese woman who was born in 1867. In the first half of the book, eighteen-year-old Kwei-li writes letters to her husband. He has been appointed to a distant political post, and has left his young wife in the home of her mother-in-law. Twenty-five years later, in the book's second half, Kwei-li writes letters to her mother-in-law. She now lives in Kiang-su with her politically powerful husband. Throughout this superior autobiography, the voice of a real woman shines through.

In her letters Kwei-li writes of both her joys and her sorrows. Early in the book she speaks of her love for her husband: "Few women have the joy I feel when I look into my loved one's face and know that I am his and he is mine, and that our lives are twined together for all the days to come" (34-35). She writes also of her great joy at the birth of her first son and her almost unbearable sorrow at his death even before his father has seen him. In the second half, she mourns the passing of the old Chinese ways: Her daughter wants to be a doctor; and her son is accused of treason.

Kwei-li's details help the reader to understand the old and new China. We see the endless labor of peasants doomed to spend the rest of their lives grinding herbs. They are "harnessed to great stones" and go "round and round all day, like buffalo at the waterwheel" (40). Throughout the book, Kwei-li paints in words China's great beauty. She watches "the mists cling lovingly to the hilltops, while leaves from giant banyan trees sway idly in the morning wind . . ." (171).

1. In the first paragraph, the writer provides some background information. Why is this information important?
2. In the second paragraph, why do you think the writer quoted some of Kwei-li's words from the book?
3. The third paragraph evaluates Kwei-li's use of details. What do you think is the writer's evaluation on this point?
4. Based on this portion of the book report, do you think the writer's evaluation is positive or negative? Why?

Writing a Book Report

 Prewriting. Read an autobiography by someone you admire. Insert slips of paper between pages with information you want to refer to later. Jot down notes.

 Writing, Evaluating, and Revising. Your first paragraph should end with a statement of your overall evaluation. Each body paragraph should discuss one of the criteria in the guidelines on page 441. Your report should end with a summary of your evaluation.

 Proofreading and Publishing. Check carefully for errors in spelling, punctuation, and usage. Ask your school librarian whether you could put your report in the library along with a copy of the autobiography.

If you decide to include your book report in your **portfolio,** date the report and attach a note responding to these questions: How did the guidelines on page 441 help you to write your report? What other criteria did you consider?

MAKING CONNECTIONS

RESEARCH ACROSS THE CURRICULUM

The Visual Arts

Research is playing an important role in the preservation of two of the world's greatest art masterpieces which might otherwise be someday lost forever. Leonardo da Vinci's *Last Supper*, painted on a wall of a monastery in Milan, Italy, and Michelangelo's frescoes, painted on the ceiling of the Sistine Chapel in Rome, are about five hundred years old. Over the years, heat, humidity, dirt, pollution, and wars have badly damaged both works. Previous attempts at restoration damaged them even further when layers of paint, glue, and varnish were added to the originals.

During the 1970s restorers began extensive projects to clean, preserve, and restore both works as nearly as possible to their original condition. Research has been an important part of both projects. Restorers need to know as much as possible about how da Vinci and Michelangelo actually painted—what kinds of brush strokes they used and how they mixed their colors, for example. In earlier restorations, painters often added new layers of colors and even beards or clothes to the figures. Understanding the techniques of da Vinci and Michelangelo helps restorers decide what is original and what was added later.

A *NOVA* episode, available on videotape, documents the restoration of the Sistine Chapel. Popular magazines, such as *Time, Newsweek,* and *National Geographic,* gave the restorations extensive coverage including photographs. You might want to view the videotape (it's available at many video stores). Or use the *Readers' Guide* to find articles about both restoration projects. Bring the articles to class to share with your classmates. As you view the videotape or read the articles, look for ways that research has played a role in the restorations.

SPEAKING AND LISTENING

Creating Research Sources: Public Opinion Polls

You've probably been met in shopping malls by people conducting public opinion polls about your shopping habits and product preferences. The results of these polls are used to help businesses increase their sales.

Consider taking some public opinion polls in your own school. If you want the poll to represent the opinions of all students, you need to poll students from all grade levels. Or, you might restrict the poll to your own grade level. Try to poll ten percent of the population. If there are three hundred students in your grade, for instance, talk to thirty of them. Also try to select students who represent the entire group. You might, for example, select every tenth person from an alphabetical listing of the class.

Write some objective questions with answers that you can easily tally. For example, if you want to find out about favorite and least favorite lunchroom foods, have students rank five foods from 1 to 5 (with 5 being the favorite). To find out students' opinions on an issue, give them a neutral statement and then ask whether they agree or disagree. Such a statement might be "A constitutional amendment should be passed prohibiting the burning of the American flag."

Try one of the ideas on the following list, and conduct a public opinion poll in your school. (You may also have ideas about different topics.)

- Favorite/least favorite foods served in the lunchroom
- Favorite/least favorite musicians, actors, television shows, movies, and so on
- Ideas to improve education in your community
- Opinions on national/foreign policy issues

When you finish your poll, tally your findings and present the results to your class. Consider using the results in an article for your school newspaper or a letter to the editor of your local newspaper.

12 WRITING COMPLETE SENTENCES

LOOKING AHEAD

Sentences are the building blocks of your writing. That's why it's important to check your sentences for clarity and completeness. As you work through this chapter, you will learn how to

- identify and correct sentence fragments
- identify and correct run-on sentences

Sentence Fragments

A *sentence fragment* is a group of words that is only a part of a sentence. Since a fragment of something is not the whole thing, it won't be as useful to you as it could be. Just as a fragment of a bowl can't hold much food, a fragment of a sentence may not communicate what you want to say. To communicate clearly, whether at school or in the workplace, you must write complete sentences.

To be complete, a sentence must (1) have a subject, (2) have a verb, and (3) express a complete thought. If any of these pieces are missing, the group of words is a fragment rather than a complete sentence.

FRAGMENT	Is one of the largest snakes. [The subject is missing. *What* is one of the largest snakes?]
SENTENCE	The anaconda is one of the largest snakes.
FRAGMENT	Anacondas to a length of thirty feet. [The verb is missing. *What* do they do to a length of thirty feet?]
SENTENCE	Anacondas can grow to a length of thirty feet.
FRAGMENT	Although these snakes aren't poisonous. [The word group has a subject and a verb, but it doesn't express a complete thought.]
SENTENCE	Although these snakes aren't poisonous, their teeth can inflict deep wounds.

Fragments usually occur when you're writing in a hurry or are a little careless. For example, you might create a fragment by leaving out an important word or two. Or you might chop off part of a sentence by putting in a period too soon.

To find out if what you've written is a fragment, you can use this simple three-part test:

1. Does the group of words have a subject?
2. Does it have a verb?
3. Does it express a complete thought?

If even one of your answers is "no," then you have a fragment.

 COMPUTER NOTE: Some word-processing programs have a tool to check grammatical construction. This tool can find sentence fragments and run-on sentences for you to revise.

By itself, a sentence fragment doesn't express a complete thought. But a fragment can make sense in writing if it is clearly related to a sentence that comes before or after it.

Read the following groups of words from Maya Angelou's autobiography *I Know Why the Caged Bird Sings:*

> The birthday girl. The center.

By themselves, these fragments don't make sense because we don't know what they relate to. But now read them along with the sentence that the writer placed before them:

> In the Store I was the person of the moment.
> The birthday girl. The center.

As you can see, the sentence gives the fragments meaning. It fills in the missing parts.

Experienced writers like Maya Angelou sometimes use sentence fragments for effect. As a beginning writer, however, you should avoid using fragments. Eventually you'll feel comfortable enough to experiment, but it's important to master the basics first.

EXERCISE 1 ▶ **Identifying Sentence Fragments**

Try the three-part test on each of the following groups of words. In each case, identify what, if anything, is missing. If the group of words is missing a subject, write *S*. If it is missing a verb, write *V*. If the group of words has both a subject and a verb but doesn't express a complete thought, write *I*. Write *C* if the words form a complete sentence.

1. Vampire bats only in the tropics of Central and South America.
2. Most horror tales about vampire bats aren't true.
3. Vampire bats very small mammals.
4. Although they do bite other animals.
5. Don't drain their victims of blood.

6. Their small teeth are as sharp as needles.
7. While animals are sleeping.
8. But can be dangerous.
9. The greatest danger to victims is infection.
10. Vampire bats carriers of rabies.

"What was it like back in the days when people talked and wrote in complete sentences?"

Berry's World reprinted by permission of Newspaper Enterprise Association, Inc.

Phrase Fragments

A *phrase* is a group of words that does not contain a subject and a verb. Because it doesn't have all the basic parts of a sentence, a phrase by itself is a fragment. Three kinds of phrases are often mistaken for sentences: *verbal phrases, appositive phrases,* and *prepositional phrases.*

Verbal Phrases

A *verbal* is a word that is formed from a verb but is used as another part of speech. Because verbs and verbals are look-alikes, it is sometimes hard to tell the difference between them. That's why *verbal phrases*—phrases that contain verbals—are easily mistaken for sentences. They can appear to have verbs in them when they really don't.

Watch for verbals in phrases. Some verbals have endings such as *–ing, –d,* or *–ed* and may have helping verbs (like *is, were,* or *have*). Another kind of verbal has the word *to* in front of it (*to run, to look*). A verbal phrase alone doesn't express a complete thought.

FRAGMENT   To see Devils Tower National Monument.
SENTENCE   We stopped in northeastern Wyoming to see Devils
           Tower National Monument.

FRAGMENT   Established in 1906.
SENTENCE   Established in 1906, Devils Tower was the first
           national monument in the United States.

FRAGMENT   Seeing the movie *Close Encounters of the Third Kind.*
SENTENCE   Seeing the movie *Close Encounters of the Third Kind*
           made me interested in Devils Tower.

Appositive Phrases

An *appositive* is a word that identifies or explains a
nearby word in the sentence. An *appositive phrase* is
an appositive and its modifiers. Because an appositive
phrase does not have a verb and does not express a
complete thought, it cannot stand alone as a complete
sentence.

FRAGMENT   A strange rock formation.
SENTENCE   Devils Tower, a strange rock formation, has special
           significance in the movie.

Prepositional Phrases

A *prepositional phrase* is a group of words that begins
with a preposition and ends with a noun or pronoun.

FRAGMENT   Of volcanic rock.
SENTENCE   Devils Tower is an 865-foot-tall tower of volcanic
           rock.

WRITING NOTE When a verbal phrase modifies, or describes,
another word in the sentence, it's usually best to
place the phrase as close as possible to the word it
modifies. For instance, in the example at the top of this page, the
verbal phrase *established in 1906* needs to stay close to *Devils
Tower.* But some verbal phrases, such as the phrase *to see Devils
Tower National Monument,* make sense either at the beginning
or at the end of the sentence.

☞ REFERENCE NOTE: For more help with phrase placement in
sentences, see pages 465–466 and 728–730.

EXERCISE 2 ▶ **Revising Phrase Fragments**

Using the photograph to help spark your imagination, create a sentence from each of the following phrase fragments. You may (1) add the fragment to a complete sentence or (2) develop the fragment into a complete sentence by adding a subject, a verb, or both.

EXAMPLE   **1.** climbing up the cliff
   1. *Climbing up the cliff, I tried not to look down.*
   or
   I was climbing up the cliff.

   1. in the jungle
   2. watching for wild animals
   3. to swing on huge vines
   4. on the way
   5. scratched and bruised
   6. the fearless explorer
   7. led by experienced guides
   8. at the top of the cliff
   9. surprised by a loud noise
   10. to write about the experience

Subordinate Clause Fragments

A *clause* is a group of words that has a subject and a verb. One kind of clause, an *independent clause,* expresses a complete thought and can stand alone as a sentence. For example, the independent clause *I missed the bus* is a complete sentence. But another kind of clause, a *subordinate clause,* doesn't express a complete thought and can't stand alone as a sentence. A subordinate clause fragment is easy to identify because it suggests a question that it doesn't answer.

FRAGMENT   Because the weather often changed several times a day. [*What* was the result of the weather changing?]

SENTENCE   Because the weather often changed several times a day, filming *White Fang* in Alaska was very difficult.

FRAGMENT   Who directed *White Fang.* [Note that this group of words would be a complete sentence if it ended with a question mark. But as a statement, it doesn't express a complete thought. It doesn't tell *who* directed the movie.]

SENTENCE   Randal Kleiser, who directed *White Fang,* thought it was worth the trouble to film the movie in Alaska.

FRAGMENT   That needed constant care. [*What* needed constant care?]

SENTENCE   The cast of *White Fang* included many animals that needed constant care.

👉 **REFERENCE NOTE:** For more about independent and subordinate clauses, see pages 597–611.

WRITING NOTE   A subordinate clause telling *why, where, when,* or *how* (an adverb clause) may be placed before or after the independent clause. When you combine sentences by inserting an adverb clause, try the clause in both positions to see which sounds best to you.

EXAMPLES   Because the setting added to the beauty of the film, everyone was glad *White Fang* had been filmed in Alaska.

or

Everyone was glad *White Fang* had been filmed in Alaska because the setting added to the beauty of the film.

When the subordinate clause comes first, remember to separate it from the independent clause with a comma.

EXERCISE 3 ▶ Revising Subordinate Clause Fragments

Use what you've learned about subordinate clause fragments to correct the following paragraph. First, find the clause fragments. Then, revise the paragraph, combining the subordinate clauses with independent clauses. (There may be more than one way to do this.) Change the punctuation and capitalization as necessary.

Before and during the Civil War, the Underground Railroad helped hundreds of slaves to escape to the North. The Underground Railroad was a system of travel. That moved the slaves from one house to another. Until they reached the North and freedom. "Conductors" on the Underground Railroad would plan the slaves' journey to the next "station." One conductor on the Underground Railroad was Harriet Tubman. Who was born a slave in 1821. She escaped from the South in 1849. Which was a very dangerous thing for a female slave to do alone. Because of Harriet Tubman. More than three hundred people were able to reach freedom.

The Granger Collection, New York.

> **EXERCISE 4** ▶ **Using Subordinate Clauses in Sentences**

You've had some practice at revising subordinate clause fragments. Now use your skills and your imagination to make a complete sentence from each of the following subordinate clauses. To make a complete sentence, add an independent clause at the beginning or at the end of the subordinate clause. Add capitalization and punctuation wherever you need to.

EXAMPLE   **1.** because her family came from Mexico
           1. *Because her family came from Mexico, Linda Ronstadt heard many Mexican folk songs while she was growing up.*

1. who is a popular singer
2. when you played your new record album
3. because the concert is next Friday
4. if the tickets aren't sold out
5. which is my favorite song

WRITING NOTE   You've seen that it's easy to mistake phrases and subordinate clauses for complete sentences. It's also easy to mistake a series of items for a complete sentence. In the following example, the series of items in dark type is a fragment. It may make sense along with the sentence that comes before it, but it can't stand on its own because it doesn't express a complete thought.

FRAGMENT   I tried out for different positions on the team. **Pitcher, shortstop, and catcher.**

To correct the series fragment, you can
■ make it into a complete sentence
■ link it to the previous sentence with a colon

SENTENCE   I tried out for different positions on the team. **I tried out for** pitcher, shortstop, and catcher.

or

I tried out for different positions on the team: pitcher, shortstop, and catcher.

EXERCISE 5 ▶	**Identifying and Revising Fragments**

The writer of the following paragraph wants to describe the high point of her summer—a white-water rafting trip. But the sentence fragments in the paragraph make the meaning unclear. Help make the paragraph clearer by finding and revising the fragments. To correct each fragment, you can (1) link it to an independent clause or (2) develop it into a complete sentence.

Whenever I look at photographs of white-water rafting, I remember what a great time I had on my first raft trip. The first mile or so of the raft trip was easy. As we paddled slowly in the moving current. The guide pointed out the strange rock formations along the banks of the river. Once we got used to paddling, we were ready for adventure. Wanted to experience the thrill of the white water. The guide helped us navigate "the eye of the needle." Which was a difficult stretch of the rapids. Paddling through the rapids, I almost hit a rock. Lost my balance and almost fell overboard. The white water was scary. But was exhilarating too. I hope I can take another raft trip next summer!

Run-on Sentences

A *run-on sentence* is two or more complete sentences that are written as one sentence. Because run-on sentences don't show where one idea ends and another begins, they are confusing to the reader. There are two kinds of run-on sentences: the *fused sentence* and the *comma splice.*

In a *fused sentence,* the writer has joined two or more sentences with no punctuation between them.

RUN-ON   Measurements originally were related to the sizes of people's hands, arms, and feet an inch was the width of a thumb.

CORRECT   Measurements originally were related to the sizes of people's hands, arms, and feet. An inch was the width of a thumb.

In a *comma splice,* the writer has joined two or more sentences with only a comma to separate them.

RUN-ON   A foot was the length of a person's foot, a yard was the distance from a man's nose to the end of his thumb when his arm was outstretched.

CORRECT   A foot was the length of a person's foot. A yard was the distance from a man's nose to the end of his thumb when his arm was outstretched.

WRITING NOTE   To identify run-on sentences, try reading your writing aloud. A natural, distinct pause in your voice usually means that you've come to the end of a thought. If your voice pauses but your sentence keeps going, you may have a run-on.

Another way to spot run-ons is to look for subjects and verbs. This will help you see where one complete thought ends and another one begins.

Revising Run-on Sentences

There are several ways to revise a run-on sentence. As shown in the examples on this page, you can always make two separate sentences. But you can also make a compound sentence if the independent clauses in the run-on are closely related.

1. You can make a compound sentence by adding a comma and a coordinating conjunction (*and, but, or, yet,* or *nor*).

RUN-ON   Spanish is the official language of Guatemala many Guatemalans speak Maya Indian languages.

REVISED   Spanish is the official language of Guatemala**, but** many Guatemalans speak Maya Indian languages.

2. You can make a compound sentence by adding a semicolon.

RUN-ON   About half the people in Guatemala are descended from Maya Indians about half have mixed Spanish and Indian ancestry.

REVISED   About half the people in Guatemala are descended from Maya Indians**;** about half have mixed Spanish and Indian ancestry.

3. You can make a compound sentence by adding a semicolon and a *conjunctive adverb*—a word such as *therefore, instead, meanwhile, still, also, nevertheless,* or *however*. A conjunctive adverb needs to be followed by a comma.

RUN-ON   Guatemala's rich soil is its greatest natural resource, agriculture is one of the country's main industries.

REVISED   Guatemala's rich soil is its greatest natural resource**;** **therefore,** agriculture is one of the country's main industries.

☞ REFERENCE NOTE: For more information about how to form compound sentences, see pages 467–469 and 610–611.

E X E R C I S E 6 ▶   **Revising by Correcting Run-ons**

The following items are confusing because they're run-on sentences. Clear up the confusion by correcting them. To correct each run-on, use the method of revision that is given in parentheses.

1. Knights in the Middle Ages were bound by a code of honor it was called the code of chivalry. (two sentences)
2. Knights were supposed to be brave and loyal they were supposed to protect defenseless people. (comma and coordinating conjunction)
3. Some knights were true to the code of chivalry, many fell short of the ideal. (semicolon and conjunctive adverb)
4. A knight could be punished for showing cowardice his sword would be broken in half to show his disgrace. (semicolon)
5. A knight depended on his horse for transportation and in battle, his horse was very valuable to him. (semicolon and conjunctive adverb)
6. Many knights belonged to strict religious orders they were monks who fought as soldiers. (two sentences)
7. Originally, knighthood wasn't a mark of distinction the first knights were ordinary mounted soldiers. (semicolon)
8. Eventually knighthood became a sign of nobility the knights were considered part of the upper class. (comma and coordinating conjunction)
9. Orders of knighthood still exist in Great Britain knighthood doesn't have the same meaning that it did in the Middle Ages. (comma and coordinating conjunction)
10. Knighthood is now an honorary order it is bestowed on people to recognize great achievements. (semicolon)

| R E V I E W ▶ | **Revising Fragments and Run-on Sentences** |

When you read the following paragraphs, you'll notice several sentence fragments and run-on sentences. First identify each fragment and run-on. Then rewrite the passage correctly. Change the punctuation and capitalization wherever necessary.

Today, the pyramids of Egypt are fascinating to tourists, archaeologists, and historians. Who travel to Africa to see them. The pyramids symbolize a great ancient civilization, Egypt was a powerful influence. For thousands of years in the ancient world.

The main purpose of the pyramids. Was to entomb the pharaohs. Sometimes a pharaoh's wife was buried with him in the pyramid. All his worldly possessions also buried, food, clothing, and water were provided for the journey. To the other world.

Although many pyramids have been emptied of their treasures. The pyramids themselves continue to interest people they are the only one of the Seven Wonders of the Ancient World. That is still standing.

MAKING CONNECTIONS

Fill in the Missing Pieces

You've learned that sentence fragments are confusing because they are missing some important parts. Here's a chance to see just how confusing fragments can be.

First, team up with one of your classmates. Working together, write a paragraph in response to the photograph that follows. Use complete sentences, and make your paragraph as clear as possible.

Next, write a second version of the paragraph, leaving out several subjects and verbs and creating phrase and clause fragments. Then, trade your second version with that of another team. Try to fill in the missing pieces of each other's paragraphs to reconstruct the original, complete sentences.

Compare your final versions to the original paragraphs. How well did you do in supplying the missing parts? How has the meaning of each paragraph changed?

13 WRITING EFFECTIVE SENTENCES

LOOKING AHEAD

You've heard that "variety is the spice of life." In this chapter, you will learn how to add spice, or variety, to your sentences by

- using sentence-combining techniques
- improving your sentence style

Combining Sentences

Whether you are writing a school or workplace assignment or a personal letter, your goal is to communicate your ideas. Therefore, you want your writing to be clear, effective, and interesting. Short sentences can be effective, but too many of them make writing sound choppy. For example, notice how the many short sentences in the following paragraph make it boring to read.

Penguins have black backs. Penguins have white fronts. These colors act as camouflage. Some of a penguin's enemies fly. Some of a penguin's enemies swim. From above, a penguin's black back doesn't show in the water. From below, its white front just looks like sunlight on the water.

Sentence combining is a way to improve choppy writing. See how the paragraph about penguins can be improved by combining the short sentences into longer, smoother sentences.

Notice that even though the sentences are longer, the revised paragraph is shorter and more precise. That's because sentence combining has helped to eliminate repeated words and ideas.

Penguins have black backs and white fronts that act as camouflage. Some of a penguin's enemies fly and some swim. From above, a penguin's black back doesn't show in the water, and from below, its white front just looks like sunlight on the water.

Inserting Words

You can combine short sentences by taking a key word from one sentence and inserting it into another sentence. When you do this, you may need to delete one or more words. You may also need to change the form of the word you insert.

USING THE SAME FORM	
ORIGINAL	James Thurber wrote many short stories. His stories are amusing.
COMBINED	James Thurber wrote many **amusing** short stories.
CHANGING THE FORM	
ORIGINAL	Thurber's illustrated stories are especially fun to read. The illustrations are humorous.
REVISED	Thurber's **humorously** illustrated stories are especially fun to read.

WRITING NOTE When you change the form of a word before inserting it into a sentence, you often add an ending that makes the word an adjective or an adverb. The endings you'll use most frequently are *–ed, –ful, –ing,* and *–ly.*

EXERCISE 1 ▶ **Combining Sentences by Inserting Words**

Here are five sets of sentences about the many uses of common plants. Combine each set into one sentence by inserting the italicized word(s) into the first sentence. The directions in parentheses will tell you how to change the form of a word if it is necessary to do so.

EXAMPLE **1.** You can find books that describe the uses of herbs. These books describe the *many* uses that herbs have.
1. *You can find books that describe the many uses of herbs.*

1. Plants have always been valued for their properties. These properties are *medicinal.*
2. Digitalis, a medicine for heart failure, is extracted from the foxglove plant. Digitalis is an *effective* medicine.
3. The recipes for many old-fashioned herbal remedies have been lost. The loss of these recipes is *unfortunate.* (Add an *–ly.*)

4. Some herbal remedies have been passed down through many generations of families. The families *trust* these remedies. (Add an *–ed*.)
5. Plants are still used to make products such as shampoos and hair dyes. These products are *beauty* products.

EXERCISE 2 ▶ **Combining Sentences by Inserting Words**

In Exercise 1, the key words were italicized for you. Now it's up to you to decide which words to insert. There may be more than one way to combine each set of sentences; choose the combination you think is best. Change the forms of words wherever you need to.

1. Isak Dinesen's book *Out of Africa* tells about her experiences on a plantation in Africa. It was a coffee plantation.
2. Dinesen managed the plantation for ten years. She managed it single-handedly.
3. One year, a swarm of grasshoppers descended on her farm. The swarm was huge.
4. Dinesen's descriptions paint a vivid picture of her life in Africa. Her descriptions have a lot of detail.
5. *Out of Africa* was made into a movie. The movie was a success.

Inserting Phrases

You also can combine closely related sentences by reducing one sentence to a phrase and inserting it into the other sentence. When it is inserted, the phrase gives additional information about an idea expressed in the sentence.

Prepositional Phrases

A *prepositional phrase* contains a preposition and its object. Usually, you can insert a prepositional phrase into another sentence without changing it in any way.

ORIGINAL   My sister loaned me a copy of *The Martian Chronicles.* It is by Ray Bradbury.
REVISED   My sister loaned me a copy of *The Martian Chronicles* **by Ray Bradbury.**

Participial Phrases

A *participle* is a word that is formed from a verb but is used as an adjective. A participle usually ends in *–ing* or *–ed*. A *participial phrase* contains a participle and words related to it. The whole participial phrase acts as an adjective in a sentence.

Sometimes you can combine sentences by reducing one sentence to a participial phrase. When you insert the participial phrase into the other sentence, place it close to the noun or pronoun it modifies. Otherwise you may confuse your reader.

ORIGINAL   Juanita Platero describes the conflict between old and new ideas. She does this as she writes about Navajo culture.
REVISED   **Writing about Navajo culture,** Juanita Platero describes the conflict between old and new ideas.

Appositive Phrases

An *appositive phrase* is made up of an appositive and its modifiers. It identifies or explains a noun or pronoun in a sentence. Sometimes you can change one sentence into an appositive phrase and insert it into another sentence. Like a participial phrase, an appositive phrase needs to be placed directly before or after the noun or pronoun it modifies. The phrase should be separated from the rest of the sentence by a comma (or two commas if you place the phrase in the middle of the sentence).

ORIGINAL   Ray Bradbury is best known for his science fiction stories. Ray Bradbury is an American writer.

REVISED   Ray Bradbury**, an American writer,** is best known for his science fiction stories.

 REFERENCE NOTE: For more information about the different kinds of phrases, see pages 573–591.

EXERCISE 3 ▶   **Combining Sentences by Inserting Phrases**

Insert phrases to combine each of the following sets of sentences into one sentence. (There may be more than one way to combine each set.) For each sentence set, the hints in parentheses will tell you when to change the forms of words and when to add commas. To help you get started, the words you need to insert are italicized in the first five sentence sets.

EXAMPLE   **1.** Migrant farm workers move from region to region. They follow the seasonal crop harvests. (Change *follow* to *following*.)

1. *Following the seasonal crop harvests, migrant farm workers move from region to region.*

1. Migrant laborers move constantly. They *search for work.* (Change *search* to *searching*, and add a comma.)
2. Many live in extreme poverty. They live *without adequate food, shelter, and medical care.*

3. Many migrant laborers are unable to find other kinds of work. They *lack education.* (Change *lack* to *lacking,* and add a comma.)

4. César Chávez championed the rights of migrant farm workers. He was *a labor union organizer.* (Add two commas.)

5. Chávez was born in Arizona. He was born *on a farm.*

6. His family became migrant workers. They became migrant workers after losing their farm.

7. Chávez helped make the voices of farm workers heard. He organized grape pickers in the 1960s. (Change *organized* to *organizing,* and add a comma.)

8. He established a union. It was called the National Farm Workers Association. (Add a comma.)

9. Chávez organized strikes and boycotts. He was committed to nonviolent protest. (Add a comma.)

10. He helped to improve working conditions for migrant laborers. He did this through his organizing efforts.

Using Compound Subjects and Verbs

You can also combine sentences by using compound subjects and verbs. Just look for sentences that have the same subject or the same verb. Then use coordinating conjunctions (such as *and, but, or, nor, for,* and *yet*) to make a compound subject, a compound verb, or both.

ORIGINAL   Jaguars are large, spotted cats. Leopards are large, spotted cats.

REVISED   **Jaguars and leopards** are large, spotted cats.
[compound subject with the same verb]

ORIGINAL   Jaguars live in the Americas. Jaguars hunt in the Americas.

REVISED   Jaguars **live and hunt** in the Americas.
[compound verb with same subject]

ORIGINAL   Jaguars hunt and attack other animals. Leopards hunt and attack other animals. These cats rarely attack humans.

REVISED   **Jaguars and leopards hunt and attack** other animals **but rarely attack** humans. [compound subject and compound verb]

GRAMMAR HINT

Checking for Subject–Verb Agreement

When you combine sentences by using compound subjects and compound verbs, check to make sure your subjects and verbs agree in number.

ORIGINAL Asia is home to the leopard. Africa is home to the leopard.

REVISED Asia and Africa **are** home to the leopard.

☞ **REFERENCE NOTE:** For more information on agreement of subjects and verbs, see pages 619–634.

EXERCISE 4 ▶ **Combining Sentences by Using Compound Subjects and Verbs**

Here are five sets of short, choppy sentences. Combine each set into one sentence by using a compound subject, a compound verb, or both.

1. Glaciers shape landforms. Volcanoes also shape landforms.
2. Antarctica is mostly covered by glaciers. Greenland is mostly covered by glaciers.
3. Glaciers move slowly. Glaciers shape the land as they flow across it.
4. A volcano begins as molten rock beneath the earth's surface. It gradually rises upward.
5. Volcanoes can create land area. Glaciers can also create land area. They both can destroy land area.

Creating a Compound Sentence

If the thoughts in two sentences are related to one another and are equal in importance, you can combine the sentences to form a *compound sentence*. A compound sentence is two or more simple sentences joined by

- ■ a comma and a coordinating conjunction
  or
- ■ a semicolon
  or
- ■ a semicolon and a conjunctive adverb

ORIGINAL Lions and tigers are the largest cats.
Cheetahs are the fastest.

REVISED Lions and tigers are the largest cats, **but** cheetahs are the fastest. [comma and coordinating conjunction]
or

Lions and tigers are the largest cats; cheetahs are the fastest. [semicolon]
or

Lions and tigers are the largest cats; **however,** cheetahs are the fastest. [semicolon and conjunctive adverb]

☞ **REFERENCE NOTE:** For more information about how to create compound sentences, see pages 610–611.

WRITING NOTE You can use the coordinating conjunctions *and, but, or, nor, for, so,* and *yet* to form compound sentences. However, because *so* is often overworked in writing, you should think twice before using it.

EXERCISE 5 ▶ **Combining Sentences into Compound Sentences**

The following sentences are fine by themselves, but together they would make a choppy paragraph. Using the three methods you've learned, combine each pair of sentences into a compound sentence. Try to use each method at least once. Add commas as necessary.

1. Amy Tan grew up in the United States. Her parents were born in China.
2. She began her writing career as a business writer. She eventually turned to fiction.
3. Her first novel was published in 1989. It became a best-seller almost immediately.

4. Tan's Chinese heritage is important to her. Much of her writing focuses on relationships in Chinese American families.

5. Her fiction often explores the positive aspects of being a second-generation American. It also explores the difficulties.

Book Signing
Thursday, 2:30
Amy Tan, author of
The Joy Luck Club

Creating a Complex Sentence

If two sentences are unequal in importance, you can combine them by forming a *complex sentence.* Just turn the less-important idea into a subordinate clause and attach it to the other sentence (the independent clause).

☞ **REFERENCE NOTE:** For information about independent and subordinate clauses, see pages 597–606.

Adjective Clauses

You can make a sentence into an adjective clause by replacing its subject with *who, which,* or *that.* Then you can use the adjective clause to give information about a noun or pronoun in another sentence.

ORIGINAL   The Sargasso Sea is a strange, still area. It is part of the Atlantic Ocean.

REVISED   The Sargasso Sea is a strange, still area **that is part of the Atlantic Ocean.**

ORIGINAL   Christopher Columbus noted the unusual quantity of floating seaweed. He crossed the Sargasso Sea.

REVISED   Christopher Columbus, **who crossed the Sargasso Sea,** noted the unusual quantity of floating seaweed.

MECHANICS HINT

Punctuating Adjective Clauses

If an adjective clause is not essential to the meaning of the sentence, set it off with commas. If it is essential to the meaning, no commas are necessary.

NONESSENTIAL   That poster, **which was a birthday present,** is one of my favorites.

ESSENTIAL   The poster **that I got for my birthday** is hanging on the wall.

☞ REFERENCE NOTE: For more about essential and nonessential clauses, see pages 797–799.

Adverb Clauses

You can also combine sentences by turning one sentence into an adverb clause. The adverb clause modifies a verb, an adjective, or another adverb in the sentence you attach it to.

To make a sentence into an adverb clause, add a subordinating conjunction *(although, after, because, if, when, while)* at the beginning. The conjunction shows the relationship between the ideas in the adverb clause and the independent clause. If the adverb clause comes first, set it off from the independent clause with a comma.

☞ REFERENCE NOTE: For a complete list of subordinating conjunctions, see page 604.

ORIGINAL   Sailing ships were sometimes trapped in the Sargasso Sea. There wasn't enough current to sail by.

REVISED   Sailing ships were sometimes trapped in the Sargasso Sea **when there wasn't enough current to sail by.**

ORIGINAL   Sailors used to fear the Sargasso Sea. They heard strange tales about it.

REVISED   **Because they heard strange tales about it,** sailors used to fear the Sargasso Sea.

Noun Clauses

You can make a sentence into a noun clause by adding a word like *that, how, what, whatever, who,* or *whoever.* Then you can insert it into another sentence just like an ordinary noun. When you combine the sentences, you may need to change or delete some words.

ORIGINAL   Someone ate my lunch. That person had better confess.
 REVISED   **Whoever ate my lunch** had better confess.

ORIGINAL   Jerome hasn't heard. Hockey practice is canceled.
 REVISED   Jerome hasn't heard **that hockey practice is canceled.**

EXERCISE 6 ▶   **Combining Sentences into a Complex Sentence**

Here are ten pairs of sentences about Greek mythology. Combine each pair by turning the second sentence into a subordinate clause and inserting it into the first sentence. For the first six pairs, you are given hints about how to create the subordinate clauses. For the last four, you'll need to use your own judgment. You may have to add or delete some words in the sentences. Add commas where necessary. [Hint: Before you begin, review the words that can be used to introduce subordinate clauses. These words are included in the explanations on pages 600–604.]

1. Hercules was a brave hero of Greek mythology. He was given twelve difficult tasks. (Use *who.*)
2. The Parthenon was once a temple for the goddess Athena. The Parthenon is located in Athens. (Use *which.*)
3. Perseus was able to kill the Gorgon Medusa. The god Hermes and the goddess Athena helped him. (Use *because.*)
4. Cassandra had the power to predict the future. No one believed her prophecies, though. (Use *although.*)
5. Helios lived on the Greek island of Rhodes. Helios was the sun god of the Greeks. (Use *who.*)
6. The Greeks believed something about Hestia. Hestia protected the homes of faithful worshipers. (Use *that.*)
7. Hercules accidentally killed Linus. At the time, Linus was trying to teach him how to play the lyre.
8. Scylla was a dangerous sea monster. She lived in a cave.
9. Odysseus had many adventures. He was trying to get home to his wife and son.
10. King Midas wanted everything he touched to turn to gold. He was greedy.

| R E V I E W A ▶ | **Revising a Paragraph by Combining Sentences** |

Using all the sentence-combining skills you have learned, revise and rewrite the following paragraph. Use your judgment about which sentences to combine and how to combine them. Try for smooth, varied sentences that are easy to understand, but don't change the original meaning of the paragraph.

People have always been fascinated by dreams. No one knows for certain why we dream. Scientists have found out something about when we dream. Scientists try to find out about dreaming. Scientists do this by studying people as they sleep. They've learned that dreaming takes place during a particular phase of sleep. The phase is called REM sleep. REM stands for something. It stands for "rapid eye movement." REM sleep occurs each night. It lasts for about ninety minutes.

Improving Sentence Style

In the first part of this chapter, you learned how to reduce choppiness in your writing by combining sentences. Now you'll learn several more ways to polish your sentence style and make your writing more effective.

Using Parallel Structure

When you join several equal or related ideas in a sentence, it's important that you express these ideas in a similar way. You do this by balancing the structure of your sentence parts. For example, you balance an adjective with an adjective, a phrase with a phrase, and a clause with a clause. This kind of balance in writing is called *parallel structure.* Begin to look for parallel structure in sentences when you combine words, phrases, and clauses by using the coordinating conjunction *and.*

NOT PARALLEL A successful athlete is three things: healthy, alert, and showing consideration. [two adjectives and a phrase]

PARALLEL A successful athlete is three things: **healthy, alert, and considerate.** [three adjectives]

NOT PARALLEL It takes a careful use of time to play a sport, to keep up with schoolwork, and social life. [two phrases and a noun]

PARALLEL It takes a careful use of time **to play a sport, to keep up with schoolwork,** and **to have a social life.** [three phrases]

NOT PARALLEL I promised that I would spend more time studying and to help out more around the house. [a clause and a phrase]

PARALLEL I promised **that I would spend more time studying** and **that I would help out more around the house.** [two clauses]

 **E X E R C I S E 7**   **Revising Sentences to Create Parallelism**

Some of the following sentences are out of balance. Bring balance to them by putting the ideas in parallel form. You may need to delete or add some words. If a sentence is already correct, write C.

1. Athens, the capital of Greece, is known for its ancient ruins, busy lifestyle, and enjoying fine Greek food.
2. Because it is nearly three thousand years old and having a rich history, Athens attracts many visitors.
3. Athens attracts artists and historians and is attractive to tourists.
4. People drive very fast in Athens and scare the pedestrians.
5. Athens is fun to visit if you watch out for traffic and to learn to jump out of the way of cars.

Revising Stringy Sentences

What's a *stringy sentence*? Read this one.

> I woke up early so that I could get ready to catch the school bus, and I was going to the state band championships, and I hoped I would play well, and I pretended I wasn't excited, but I could barely eat my breakfast.

You've learned to combine sentences, but someone overdid this one! A **stringy sentence** has too many independent clauses strung together with coordinating conjunctions like *and* or *but*. Because the ideas are all treated equally, it's difficult to see how they are related to one another.

To fix a stringy sentence, you can

- break the sentence into two or more shorter sentences
- turn some of the independent clauses into subordinate clauses or phrases

Now read the following sentences aloud and hear the difference. Notice how the writer has broken up the stringy sentence into three shorter sentences and turned an independent clause into a subordinate clause.

> I woke up early so that I could get ready to catch the school bus. I was going to the state band championships, and I hoped I would play well. Although I pretended I wasn't excited, I could barely eat my breakfast.

There are usually several ways to revise a stringy sentence. The important thing is to make the meaning clear for your reader.

EXERCISE 8 ▶ **Revising Stringy Sentences**

Revise each of the following stringy sentences to make the meaning clear. For some items, you can just break the stringy sentence into two or more shorter sentences. For others, you'll need to turn an independent clause into a subordinate clause or a phrase to show the relationship between the ideas. Change the punctuation wherever necessary.

1. Music is used for entertainment, relaxation, and self-expression, and it is used in every culture, and it is an important part of our lives.
2. Music is an ancient art, and people learned to make flutes around 10,000 B.C., and they began to write music around 2500 B.C.
3. Today, much popular music is electronically produced, and many musicians play electric guitars and synthesizers, and some even play electric violins.
4. Different countries have different kinds of music, but some kinds of music are internationally popular, and those kinds include rock music.

5. Rock music first became popular in the 1950s, and it was inspired by blues and jazz music, but its sound was different from anything people had heard.

Revising Wordy Sentences

When you read sentences like the following one, you probably wonder what language the writer is using: "Anticipating that tomorrow's forthcoming examination may be perplexing, I have made the astute conclusion that we should diligently scrutinize our scholarly tomes at the decline of day." How much easier and clearer to say "The test tomorrow may be hard, so let's study tonight."

BLOOM COUNTY

PLEASE PASS ME THAT TOME, THERE.

"TOME"?! YOU MEAN "BOOK," DON'T YOU?! WHY SAY "TOME" WHEN "BOOK" WILL DO NICELY?! WHY COMPLICATE LIFE?! WHATEVER HAPPENED TO COMMON SIMPLENESS!?

OO! THIS SORTA THING ALWAYS BURNS ME UP!

HERE'S THE **BOOK.**   MY, IT CERTAINLY IS ELEPHANTINE...

Bloom County © 1984 Berkeley Breathed. Used by permission.

Here are three tips for creating sentences that aren't too wordy.

- Don't use more words than you need to.
- Don't use fancy, difficult words where plain, simple ones will do.
- Don't repeat words or ideas unless it's absolutely necessary.

WORDY	My brother's room has a lot of mess in it.
IMPROVED	My brother's room is messy.
WORDY	The reason I am undertaking the pursuit of ballet study is that I want to be a professional dancer someday.
IMPROVED	I am taking ballet lessons because I want to be a professional dancer someday.
WORDY	Makana has trained as a singer for years and is a well-trained, talented singer.
IMPROVED	Makana is a well-trained, talented singer.

EXERCISE 9 ▶   **Revising Wordy Sentences**

Some of the following sentences are wordy and need improving. For each sentence, ask: Does it have any unnecessary words? Does it have any fancy words that can be replaced with simple ones? Does it repeat any ideas? If you answer "yes" to any of these questions, revise the sentence to reduce the wordiness. If a sentence doesn't need improving, write *C.*

1. Caves are dark, damp areas that don't have any light.
2. Many caves have beautiful, icicle-like mineral formations called speleothems.
3. Luray Caverns, which is a cave system situated in the area of northern Virginia, is famous for its colorful speleothems.
4. Lascaux Cave, a famous cave in southwestern France, has many ancient, prehistoric wall paintings.
5. Cavefish are small, cave-dwelling fish that are not equipped with optical organs.

Varying Sentence Beginnings

You would probably get bored if you ate the same food at every meal. Variety is as important in your writing as it is in your diet. The basic subject-verb sentence pattern is fine sometimes, but if it's all you ever use, your writing will be monotonous.

Read the following paragraph. Notice that, while the paragraph is correct, it is boring because every sentence follows the same subject-verb pattern.

> The pool was nearly empty on an early weekend morning. Dedicated swimmers swam multiple laps. A few sunbathers and parents with small children sat on the grass at the edge of the pool and watched. The day grew hotter, and the sun rose higher. The pool became more crowded. The pool was soon filled with young people. They laughed as they played games and splashed each other.

Now read a revised version of the paragraph. Notice how the varied sentence beginnings break the monotony of the subject-verb pattern.

> On an early weekend morning, the pool was nearly empty. Dedicated swimmers swam multiple laps. A few sunbathers and parents with small children sat on the grass at the edge of the pool and watched. As the day grew hotter and the sun rose higher, the pool became more crowded. Soon the pool was filled with young people. Laughing, they played games and splashed each other.

Instead of starting all your sentences with subjects, try opening sentences in a variety of ways. Begin with single-word modifiers, with phrases, and with subordinate clauses. Remember to add commas as necessary after introductory words, phrases, or clauses.

VARYING SENTENCE BEGINNINGS
SINGLE-WORD MODIFIERS
Grotesquely, Dr. Frankenstein's monster began to rise from the table. [adverb]   **Frightened,** Dr. Frankenstein jumped back. [participle]   **Cackling,** Igor ran from the room. [participle]
PHRASES
With little hope Sam entered the writing contest. [prepositional phrase]   **Excited that he won,** Sam accepted the award. [participial phrase]
SUBORDINATE CLAUSES
Because Manuel was tall, people expected him to play basketball.   **Although Manuel wasn't interested in playing basketball,** he always went to the games.

E X E R C I S E **10** ▶ **Varying Sentence Beginnings**

Using what you've learned about varying sentence beginnings, revise each of the following sentences. The hint in parentheses will tell you whether to begin with a phrase, a clause, or a single-word modifier.

EXAMPLE   **1.** The United Nations is a worldwide organization, and it includes delegates from many nations. (phrase)

           1. *Including delegates from many nations, the United Nations is a worldwide organization.*

1. The United Nations was established in 1945, and it was designed to promote world peace and human rights. (phrase)
2. Fifty nations joined the United Nations when the organization was founded. (clause)
3. Over 150 nations belong to the United Nations today. (single-word modifier)
4. The United Nations tried to keep peace after World War II by getting countries to discuss their problems. (phrase)
5. The United Nations is not always successful in its efforts, but it has helped many nations to resolve their conflicts peacefully. (clause)
6. The headquarters of the United Nations are located in New York City and include several large buildings. (phrase)
7. The United Nations helps many refugees by providing food, shelter, and legal protection. (phrase)
8. The World Food Council is an important part of the United Nations' relief efforts because it supplies food to famine-stricken countries. (clause)
9. The United Nations Children's Fund (UNICEF) initially provided aid for children who were victims of World War II. (single-word modifier)
10. UNICEF was awarded the Nobel Peace Prize in 1965. (phrase)

Varying Sentence Structure

You've learned to create different kinds of sentences by combining and rearranging ideas. Now you can use this skill to create a better writing style. For varied, interesting paragraphs, it sometimes isn't enough just to create sentences of different lengths. You also need to use a variety of sentence structures. That means using a mix of simple, compound, complex (and sometimes even compound-complex) sentences in your writing.

☞ REFERENCE NOTE: For a discussion of how simple, compound, complex, and compound-complex sentences differ, see pages 610–611.

Read the following short paragraph, which is made up of only simple sentences.

> I visited a friend on her grandparents' farm. I was about ten years old at the time. There wasn't much room in the farmhouse. My friend and I begged hard. We got to sleep in the hayloft in the barn. It was wonderful. We lay awake at night. We counted shooting stars. We told each other our dreams and our hopes for the future.

Now read the revised version of the paragraph. The writer has included a variety of sentence structures to break the monotony of the first version.

> When I was about ten years old, I visited a friend on her grandparents' farm. Because there wasn't much room in the farmhouse and because we begged hard, my friend and I got to sleep in the hayloft in the barn. It was wonderful. We counted shooting stars as we lay awake at night, and we told each other our dreams and our hopes for the future.

In particular, notice how the use of subordinate clauses improved some sentences and made the paragraph clearer. Besides adding variety to your sentences, subordinate clauses help show how the ideas in a sentence are related.

☞ REFERENCE NOTE: For more information about using subordinate clauses in sentences, see pages 470 and 598–611.

Using what you've learned about combining sentences and varying structure, revise the following paragraph to make it smoother and more varied. A combination of different kinds of sentences will make the paragraph much more fun to read.

> My friends and I had lunch. We ate at a food court on the second floor of a mall. The food court has food from different countries. About twenty restaurants are there. Lin had soup and salad. I had a burrito. It was delicious. Joe and Debbie split a pizza. Then we walked around and looked at the people. We all thought they looked pretty funny. There was a fashion show on the main floor. Debbie and I admired the clothes. Lin and Joe liked watching the models. We looked at a display of new cars. We talked about the kinds of cars we'd like to have.

REVIEW B **Writing a Composition Using a Variety of Sentence Structures**

It's Academy Award time, and your school newspaper is publishing students' nominations for the awards. Write a paragraph nominating your favorite movie, actor, or actress. If you want your reader to be convinced that your choice is the best one, you'll need to make your paragraph lively and clear. Capture your reader's attention by using a variety of interesting sentence structures. Avoid wordy and stringy sentences, and be sure to check for parallel structure as you revise.

MAKING CONNECTIONS

Enter a Contest

You know there are many contests that give awards for good writing. But did you know that there are also contests for *bad* writing? The most famous of these is the Bulwer-Lytton Contest, which awards prizes for the worst first sentence of an imaginary novel. The first year the contest was held, over 10,000 people entered their worst sentences.

Have your own classwide sentence contest. The rules are given here. Be creative and think of a good name for the contest.

Part I

1. Each contestant submits the most awkward, boring, and confusing sentence he or she can develop. (Reviewing the examples of stringy and wordy sentences on pages 475–477 will help you get started.)
2. After all entries are submitted, the class votes on which entry should be awarded the prize for worst sentence.

Part II

1. Each contestant now revises the winning worst sentence, making it clear, straightforward, and interesting.
2. The class votes on the second set of entries, selecting the entry that has turned the worst sentence into the best sentence.

COMPUTER NOTE: Use your word-processing program's Cut and Paste commands to move words, phrases, paragraphs, or blocks of text within a document. If you change your mind, you can always move the text again.

---

14 ENGLISH: ORIGINS AND USES

LOOKING AHEAD

In this chapter, you will take a close look at the English language. You will learn

- where English comes from
- how English continues to grow and change
- how to choose among the many varieties of English when you speak and write

Where English Comes From

Have you ever wanted to trace your ancestry through the centuries—to discover your roots? You would find that your family tree goes back farther than recorded history. Its roots may even be in a land you never heard of.

The English language also has a family tree. It is one of dozens of languages that branched off from a single source, an original parent language. We call this original language ***Proto-Indo-European.*** Proto-Indo-European was spoken so long ago that we have no records of its beginnings. But we do know that it was being spoken in Eastern Europe about five thousand years ago.

The people who spoke Proto-Indo-European were wanderers. Gradually, they split up into tribes and migrated all across Europe and as far east as India. As the tribes branched off in different directions, so did their language. Each tribe developed its own *dialect,* or separate version, of Proto-Indo-European. Soon the dialects developed into distinct languages.

English, French, German, Spanish, and Italian are just a few of the languages that began as offshoots of Proto-Indo-European. These languages still bear a family resemblance. For example, notice how similar the words for *north* are in several Indo-European languages.

ENGLISH	FRENCH	GERMAN	SPANISH	ITALIAN
north	**nord**	**norden**	**norte**	**nord**

Old English (450–1100)

The first speakers of English were tribes known as the Angles and Saxons. In about A.D. 450, the Angles and Saxons migrated to the pleasant, fertile island of Britain, which was already inhabited by a Celtic tribe known as the Britons. The island looked like a good place to call home, and the Anglo-Saxons settled down—after killing or driving off many of the Britons. The Anglo-Saxons named their new home "land of the Angles," or *Englalond*—which eventually became *England*. We call their language *Old English.*

Old English was similar to Modern English in many ways. In fact, the Anglo-Saxons used many of the same words we do, in somewhat different forms.

OLD ENGLISH	etan	drincan	dæg	niht
MODERN ENGLISH	eat	drink	day	night

However, Old English had a very different structure from Modern English. While Modern English mostly uses word order to show the roles of words in a sentence, Old English used many different word endings to show gender, number, case, and person. For example, the noun *hund* (*hound*) had to be written *hund, hundes, hunde, hundas, hunda,* or *hundum* depending on its use in a sentence.

EXERCISE 1 ▶ **Matching Old English and Present-Day English Words**

See if you can match each present-day English word in the first column with its Old English ancestor in the second column. [Hint: Use the process of elimination.]

1. calf	**a.** fot
2. cow	**b.** eage
3. foot	**c.** cealf
4. snow	**d.** geong
5. nose	**e.** snaw
6. eye	**f.** sealt
7. heart	**g.** heorte
8. young	**h.** niwe
9. new	**i.** nosu
10. salt	**j.** cu

Old English Gains New Words

In about A.D. 600, missionaries began a vigorous conversion of the English to Christianity. The missionaries introduced a new language as well as a new religion. Educated English people began to learn Latin, the language of the Church. They borrowed many Latin words and made them part of English. For example, the words *school, altar, candle,* and *paper* are all **loanwords,** or borrowed words, from Latin.

The English also learned new words from another—at first unwelcome—source. Around 790, Vikings from Scandinavia began to raid Britain, launching savage attacks over the next several centuries. Many Vikings ended up settling in England. Eventually, about nine hundred loanwords from their language, Old Norse, entered Old English. Many of the English words that come from Old Norse begin with *sc* or *sk.*

OLD NORSE	skalpr	skrap	skith	sky
MODERN ENGLISH	scalp	scrap	ski	sky

"Egad! Vikings! And they mean business!"

Middle English (1100–1500)

In 1066, England was attacked again—this time by the Normans from France. The army led by William of Normandy defeated the English at the Battle of Hastings and took control of the country. For the next 150 years, a few thousand French-speaking people governed English life. French became the language of government, law, business, and literature. Latin remained the language of religion. The few English people who received schooling were educated in these languages. Not surprisingly, many English words that are linked to wealth and power were borrowed from French after the Norman Conquest.

OLD FRENCH	jurer	leisir	taxer
MODERN ENGLISH	jury	leisure	tax

LOOKING AT Language

A Feast of Loanwords

Some of our everyday words give clues to what English life was like after the Norman Conquest. For example, the words *hog, calf,* and *sheep* came to us from Old English; but the words *bacon, veal,* and *mutton* were borrowed from French before the fifteenth century. These word origins reflect the social structure of the times. The English peasants raised the livestock, while the French nobles got to *feast* (another French word!) on the meats.

French, the language of the educated, was used for almost all written communication. But English didn't die. It was still the spoken language of the common people— the farmers, herders, servants, and craftspeople. As these people spoke it, however, the language changed into a form we call *Middle English.* English grammar became more regular. For example, as shown on page 486, the Old English word *hund* originally had six different forms. Speakers of Middle English kept only two forms—*hund* and *hundes.*

English Triumphs

For a few hundred years, it seemed that French might prevail as the national language of England. But several factors weighed in favor of English. For one thing, the English-speaking people outnumbered the French rulers. For another, the Normans in England gradually lost contact with France.

By the mid-1300s, educated people were again using English for writing as well as for speaking. As you can see from the following passage by the fourteenth-century poet Geoffrey Chaucer, Middle English wasn't far removed from the English we use.

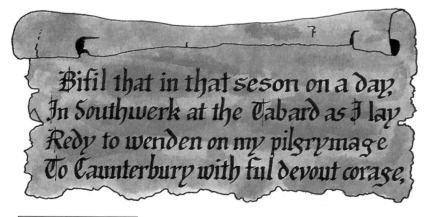

Bifil that in that seson on a day,
In Southwerk at the Tabard as I lay
Redy to wenden on my pilgrymage
To Caunterbury with ful devout corage,

EXERCISE 2 ▶ **Researching the Hundred Years' War**

The fate of English hung in the balance after the French conquered England. However, several factors, including the Hundred Years' War, helped English survive. Read about the Hundred Years' War in an encyclopedia or another reference source. How did the war affect English people's attitude toward the French? Why do you think the French language lost popularity in England as a result of the war?

Major Sources of Loan Words through 1500

Greek

Latin

Latin

Old English

Middle English

Early Modern English

Scandinavian

French

Modern English (1500–Present)

Several different things happened to English as it moved into the modern period. It underwent changes in pronunciation, grammar, and spelling; it became standardized; and it expanded into an international language.

The Great Vowel Shift

Middle English sounded very different from the English we speak. For example, in Chaucer's time, *care* would have sounded like *car*, *meek* like *make*, and *bite* like *beet*. The changes in pronunciation happened gradually. By the late 1400s, they were just about complete. We call this shift in pronunciation the *Great Vowel Shift.*

LOOKING AT
Language

Is't Modern English?

If you've ever read *Romeo and Juliet* or another of Shakespeare's plays, you know that you have to get used to Shakespeare's English. For example, he used words like *sooth* ("truth") and *thence* ("from there") that we hardly ever hear in present-day English. He also used unfamiliar contractions such as *ne'er* ("never") and *is't* ("is it").

However, Shakespeare's writing looks much more familiar to us than Chaucer's does. That's because Shakespeare used an early form of Modern English.

| EXERCISE 3 ▶ | **Evaluating Contributions to Early Modern English** |

Listed below are five very ordinary words in our language. These words—along with many others— were added to the language during early Modern English times. Try to write the thought expressed by the word without using the word. How important to the language are these contributions to the Modern English vocabulary?

1. leapfrog
2. lonely
3. dislocate

4. laughable
5. critical

London Sets the Standard

By 1500, almost everyone in England spoke English. But for a long time there was no standard version of the language, and different regions used completely different dialects. Scribes wrote in the dialects of their areas and spelled words whatever way they chose. However, the dialect of London eventually became the most widely used dialect, since London was the center of English culture, business, and trade.

When William Caxton brought the first printing press to England around 1475, he set up his print shop in London and began printing books in the London dialect. Printed books—which could be made faster and more cheaply than hand-copied ones—began to spread across England. As the spellings of many words were "fixed" in print, the London dialect became a national standard.

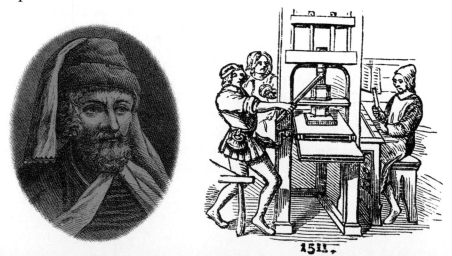

1511.

Soon handbooks of "proper" English usage, spelling, and pronunciation appeared on the market. People also compiled lists of "hard words" and their definitions. Some of the lists grew long enough to be called dictionaries.

English had become standardized, but it didn't stop changing. Even as the first printers were setting up shop, the Renaissance was sweeping England, sparking a renewed interest in the classical languages. As a result, thousands of Greek and Latin loanwords entered English.

English Travels Abroad

In about 1600, English merchants and adventurers began to seek out riches in foreign lands across the sea. As they explored, traded with, and colonized other places, they helped to make English an international language. They also enriched English with a rich crop of loanwords from other languages. Here are just a few examples.

NATIVE AMERICAN	moccasin, raccoon
AFRICAN	chigger, marimba
HINDI	jungle, bandanna

LOOKING AT *Language*

Loanwords from English

Words are like people: when they move to a foreign country, they often take on the accent of the native speakers. For example, Japanese speakers adopted the English term *personal computer* but shortened it to *paso-kon*. The Polish word *ajskrym* is a respelling of *ice cream*. And the Italian word *schiacchenze* is actually *shake hands* spelled as Italian speakers pronounce it.

Sometimes English loanwords become the basis for new words. For instance, after borrowing the English word *teens*, people in Germany went a step further and coined the word *twens*. German people also use the term *steadyseller* for a book that isn't quite a "best-seller."

Every time someone uses English in a new way, the language becomes richer and more complex. How do you think English loanwords will affect the growth of other languages?

| EXERCISE 4 ▶ | **Identifying the Origins of Loanwords** |

Each of the following English words was borrowed from another language. Look up each word in a dictionary that gives etymologies (word histories). What language was it borrowed from? What word was it derived from?

1. geology
2. geyser
3. cigar
4. studio
5. psychology

6. violin
7. complex
8. desperado
9. boom
10. machine

American English

American English was born when English colonists brought the English language to the Western Hemisphere. They borrowed words from Native American languages, invented new words of their own, and changed the pronunciations and uses of some old words. At the same time, they kept some older pronunciations and grammatical uses that the British back in England began to change. By 1776, the American dialect was distinct enough to be called American English.

Native Americans, Africans who came as slaves, and immigrants from most countries around the world have left their mark on American English. Following are just a few of the loanwords that took an American route into English.

NATIVE AMERICAN	coyote, toboggan
GERMAN	kindergarten, frankfurter
AFRICAN	gumbo, okra
CHINESE	yen, chop suey
SPANISH	canyon, patio

Just as America has emerged as a world power, American English has quickly become the standard for English in the twentieth century. American television, radio, movies, books, and newspapers have spread American English to even the most remote corners of the globe.

English Around the World

English has come a long way from its humble beginnings. From a dialect spoken by a few Anglo-Saxons, it has become the most widely used language in the world. About one third of the world's population speaks English, and as of 1995 it was an official language in eighty-seven nations and territories. This graph shows how the number of speakers of English has grown since the beginning of the Modern English period.

Speakers of English (in millions)

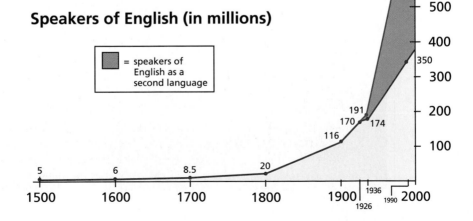

In many fields, English is the common language that allows people from different cultures to communicate. It is the world language of

- commerce
- science
- teaching
- computers
- air traffic control

A Changing Language

The history of English is a history of growth and change. Today, English is growing and changing at an even faster rate than ever.

One source of growth is English-speaking people's constant interaction with the world's many cultures and languages. This interaction brings a steady flow of new words—and new uses of old words—into the language.

Another major source of growth is the vocabulary of science and technology. At last count, over 500,000 scientific and technical terms had become part of the English language. That's about equal to the number of words in our general vocabulary!

Will English ever stop changing? The answer is probably not. Four hundred years from now, English may have changed so much that our descendants will need a translator to decode our language. Twentieth-century English will probably look as strange to them as Old English looks to us.

EXERCISE 5 ▶ **Identifying New Words in English**

Spend a week watching and listening for words that you think are new to English (invented within the past year). Pay attention to new slang words and technical terms that you read in magazines, that you hear on television, and that you and your friends invent. Jot down any that you find. Then look up each in a current dictionary to see if it is a new word or an old word that has been given a new meaning.

How English Is Used

How many ways can you think of to say "hello" to someone? If you made a list of these words, you would have just a glimpse of the choices you make when you use English. There are many different ways of saying the same thing, and each word or expression has its appropriate use.

The words you use fall into two basic categories. They depend on

- background—where you come from and what your cultural heritage is
- circumstances—the person to whom you are talking or writing, your purpose, and the situation

Becoming familiar with the different forms, uses, and meanings of English will help you become a better writer. The more you know about your language, the more precise and effective your word choices will be.

Dialects of American English

English is spoken in many different places by many different groups of people. Because each group of English-speakers is unique, it's natural that each would develop its own special form of the language. These special forms are called *dialects.*

It's important to know that the words "right" and "wrong" don't apply to varieties of English. Different varieties can be correct for different groups of people. For people in Great Britain, British English is the correct form of English; for people in the United States, American English is the accepted form. They are simply different versions of the language.

Regional Dialects

If you live in Texas, you may think people from New York talk "funny." They may think you talk "funny" as well. Your English sounds different from theirs because you and they speak different *regional dialects.*

There are four major regional dialects in the United States: *New England, Northern, Midland,* and *Southern.* People in one region often pronounce words differently from people in another region. Some Northerners tend to drop the *r* from a word, so that *barn* sounds like "bahn." Some Midlanders and Southerners tend to add an *r* sound, so that *wash* sounds like "warsh."

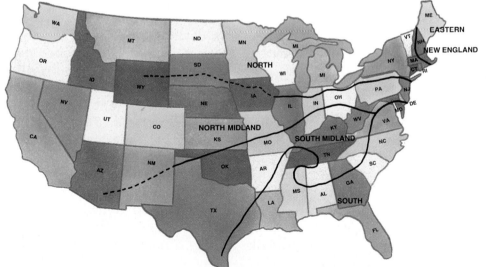

Regional dialects also differ from one another in vocabulary and grammar. For example, someone from New England might call a soft drink *tonic,* while people in other parts of the country might call it *soda* or *pop.* Someone from the South might say "sick *at* my stomach," while someone from the North might say "sick *to* my stomach."

Ethnic Dialects

An *ethnic dialect* is a dialect used by people who share the same cultural heritage. Because the United States is made up of many cultures, American English is also made up of many ethnic dialects. These dialects include the Irish English brought by Irish immigrants, the Yiddish English spoken by many Jews, and the Spanish-influenced English of people from Cuba, Mexico, and Puerto Rico. Black English, one of the largest ethnic dialects, has elements of African languages as well as of Southern dialect.

EXERCISE 6 ▶ Identifying Features of a Dialect

The following passage is told from the point of view of a young African American girl. The writer has written the narrative in a special way to capture the sounds of the narrator's language. Is the narrator's way of talking different from yours? How would you express the same thoughts in your own words?

> "Well. No. I love dancin', that's all. If somebody knows somethin' that's gonna make me dance more and better, I wanna know what that is. And yeah, I guess I do wanna be as close to perfect as I can be, but I want as many people to dance as want to. I want the whole world to dance, but dancers are a strange breed, Cypress—don'tchu know that. We are compulsive-obsessive, I think that's the phrase. We dance all day, move round dancers, in our spare time go see other dancers and for fun we go dancin'. There's no way to make us less intense, unless we fall in love . . . but not with another dancer."
>
> Ntozake Shange, *Sassafrass, Cypress & Indigo*

Standard American English

Every variety of English has its own set of rules and guidelines. No variety is the best or the most correct. However, one kind of English is more widely used and accepted than others in the United States. This variety is called *standard American English.*

Standard American English is the one variety that belongs to all of us. Because it's commonly understood, it allows people from many different regions and cultures to communicate with one another clearly. It is the variety of English you read and hear most often in books and magazines, on radio and television. It is the kind of English that people are expected to use in most school and business situations.

The **Handbook** in this textbook gives you some of the rules and guidelines for using standard American English. To identify the differences between standard American English and other varieties of English, the **Handbook** uses the labels *standard* and *nonstandard*. *Nonstandard* doesn't mean wrong language. It means language that is inappropriate in situations where standard English is expected.

☞ REFERENCE NOTE: For more about standard English, see page 738.

| EXERCISE 7 ▶ | Revising Nonstandard English |

The following paragraph is a speech that the writer plans to give to the members of a drama club. The writer has a worthwhile message, but the inappropriate use of nonstandard English is likely to distract his audience. First, identify the nonstandard features in the paragraph. Then, revise the paragraph to make it standard throughout.

This here club isn't going to get nowhere unless we members cooperate. For one thing, we gotta start getting more enthusiastic about coming to the meetings. There's been too many absences, with too many excuses like "I would of come, but I had to feed my dog." Everybody knows about the meetings ahead of time, so you don't have no excuse for not showing up. Another thing is that the members should all take equal responsibility for the club. The same people hadn't ought to always take care of refreshments, plan the program, and books the meeting room. I'm not saying that you're all lazy, but we got a long way to go toward getting this club organized good.

Standard English—Formal to Informal

The flexibility of English lets you adapt your language to almost any situation. The kinds of language that you use in different situations are called *levels of usage.* The levels of usage in standard English reach from the very formal to the very informal, with a wide range in between. No level of usage is "higher" or better than another; each has its appropriate use.

The following chart lists some of the uses of formal and informal English.

USES OF FORMAL AND INFORMAL ENGLISH		
	FORMAL	INFORMAL
SPEAKING	formal, dignified occasions, such as banquets and dedication ceremonies	everyday conversation at home, school, work, and recreation
WRITING	serious papers and reports	personal letters, journal entries, and many newspaper and magazine articles

Formal and informal English differ from one another in several ways. The main differences between them are in sentence structure, word choice, and tone.

FEATURES OF FORMAL AND INFORMAL ENGLISH		
	FORMAL	INFORMAL
SENTENCE STRUCTURE	long and complex	short and simple
WORD CHOICE	precise; often technical or scientific	simple and ordinary; often including contractions, colloquialisms, and slang
TONE	serious and dignified	conversational

Uses of Informal English

In using language, people constantly make up new words and attach new meanings to old ones. Some of the most colorful and inventive uses of English occur in informal speaking and writing. The informal words and expressions that we use fall into two categories: *colloquialisms* and *slang*.

Colloquialisms

The word *colloquial* comes from a Latin word that means "conversation." *Colloquialisms* are the colorful expressions of conversational language. They add a friendly, informal tone to speaking and writing.

EXAMPLES   Carlota was **on top of the world** after she **aced** her
            history exam.
            The teacher knew you were trying to **put one over on**
            her when you said the dog ate your homework.
            What's the matter? You look **down in the mouth.**

Many colloquialisms are also idioms. An ***idiom*** is a word or phrase that means something different from the literal meanings of the words. For example, *to put one over on* somebody has the colloquial meaning "to deceive or trick" somebody. But the literal meaning of the phrase is something quite different.

EXERCISE 8 ▶	**Explaining the Meanings of Colloquialisms**

A pen pal from another country wants to learn some American colloquialisms. She has asked you to explain the following expressions, which are confusing to her because they can't be taken literally. Explain the meaning of each expression in simple, straightforward language. Use a dictionary to find the meanings of any expressions you can't explain.

1. clue me in
2. (I don't) get it
3. hang in there
4. play it by ear
5. slip one over on (someone)

Slang

Slang is highly informal English. It consists of made-up words or of old words used in new ways. Slang is usually clever and colorful, and it can make the user seem up-to-date. The following words are all considered slang when used with the given meanings.

> *bad:* good, excellent
> *dude:* man or boy
> *humongous:* huge, enormous
> *make like:* imitate
> *scarf down:* eat greedily

Slang words are often a special vocabulary for close-knit groups, such as students, musicians, sailors, and surfers. For example, in the 1980s the word *tubular* was surfers' slang for "pleasing, fine." Like *tubular*, most slang words live a short life.

EXERCISE 9 ▶	**Identifying Slang Words**

What slang words do you and your classmates use to mean "disgusting" and "amazing"? List as many as you can think of. Which ones do you think will become a lasting part of the language? Which will likely live a short life?

How to Say What You Mean

A word can have many lay-
ers of meaning. It can also
have different meanings
depending on where and
how it is used. To use words
well, you need to understand
some of the meanings and
associations they may have.
You want to be sure that
your words will say what
you want them to say.

© 1991 Jim Unger/Distributed by Universal Press Syndicate

"It states quite clearly . . . 'evening dress.'"

Synonyms

Using *synonyms*—different words that have similar
meanings—is a way to bring variety to your writing. But
it's important to remember that no two words are exactly
alike. Each word has its own shade of meaning, and some
words have more precise meanings than others. For
example, read the following sentences:

> The child on the bus **looked** at me.
> The child on the bus **stared** at me.

Look and *stare* are synonyms, but they can suggest quite
different things. *Look* is a very general word; *stare* is a
specific word that describes a particular way of looking at
something. Since the first synonym that occurs to you
might not be the best one, use a thesaurus (a book of synonyms) along with a dictionary to find just the right word.

EXERCISE 10▶ **Choosing Appropriate Synonyms**

For each sentence, decide which of the words in parentheses is the better replacement for the italicized word. Keep
in mind the overall meaning of the sentence. Use a dictionary to check any words you're not sure about.

1. She wrinkled her nose slightly at the *unpleasant* smell
of burned oatmeal. (*revolting, distasteful*)

2. Marcia was furious at Carl for *telling* her most guarded secret. (*uttering, divulging*)
3. *Laughing* happily, the two children showered each other with crisp fall leaves. (*giggling, snickering*)
4. Each *symmetrical* snowflake glistened as it melted. (*equal-sided, well-balanced*)
5. Emphasizing the importance of the upcoming election, the senator *urged* everyone to vote. (*nagged, pressed*)

Denotation and Connotation

Compare the meanings of the following sentences:

Nan's persistence surprised everyone.
Nan's stubbornness surprised everyone.

The two sentences mean basically the same thing. *Stubbornness* is another word for *persistence*, "the quality of not giving up easily." This is the **denotation** of the words. But the effect of the words on the reader or listener can be quite different. *Stubbornness* suggests that Nan is unreasonable, narrow-minded, and unwilling to listen to others. This is the **connotation** of the word *stubborn*.

It is especially important to consider the connotations of words when you are choosing synonyms. Otherwise, you may replace a word with one that has an unintended effect on your reader.

EXERCISE 11▶   **Responding to the Connotations of Words**

Which of the following words have favorable connotations for you? Which have unpleasant connotations? Which don't stir any feeling at all? Compare your reactions with those of your classmates. Note which words have the same effect on everyone and which bring different responses from different people.

1. duty
2. propaganda
3. proud
4. fake
5. puppy
6. creeping
7. smile
8. serious
9. laughter
10. rain

Loaded Words

A word that has very strong connotations, either positive or negative, is said to be *loaded.* Loaded words appeal to our emotions. They can bias us for or against something because of the feelings they arouse.

EXAMPLES   The local diner serves cheap, greasy chicken.
The local diner serves inexpensive, home-fried food.

The mob of protesters shouted their demands.
The group of protesters made their voices heard.

A writer or speaker who wants to influence your opinion may use loaded words. For example, politicians, advertisers, and writers of editorials tend to use loaded language.

Euphemisms

Sometimes a word or phrase may be considered offensive because it is too direct. You may choose to replace it with a *euphemism*—an agreeable term that stands for a more direct, less pleasing one.

EUPHEMISM	MORE DIRECT TERM
dentures	false teeth
memorial park	cemetery
substandard housing	slum
washroom	toilet

Sometimes euphemisms are used to misrepresent facts or to cover up the truth. For example, a salesperson may tell you a car is "experienced" when it is actually used. And a politician may say he "misspoke" when he actually lied.

STYLE NOTE   Keep in mind the emotional effect your words are likely to have. Loaded words and euphemisms can be effective in writing, but you need to choose them carefully. Avoid words that may mislead your readers.

EXERCISE 12▶   **Analyzing Loaded Words and Euphemisms**

Look through a popular magazine, and pick an ad or an article that you find especially convincing. What makes the writing effective? What loaded words or euphemisms does the advertiser use, and how do the words influence your emotions?

Jargon

Jargon can refer to language that has a special meaning for a particular group of people, such as people who share the same profession, occupation, or hobby. For example, publishers and printers use the word *bleed* as jargon for "run an illustration off the edge of a page." This kind of jargon can be practical because it reduces many words to just one or two.

The second kind of jargon, also called *gobbledygook*, is wordy, puffed-up language. Users of gobbledygook choose big words over short ones, difficult words over simple ones. They confuse their readers with vague, pretentious language. For example, in the following cartoon, the senator uses puffed-up language to make his statement sound impressive. See how his "translator" sums up the unimpressive truth.

Shoe reprinted by permission: Tribune Media Services.

EXERCISE 13▶   **Revising Jargon**

The following passage is confusing because it is written in jargon. First, figure out what the writer was trying to say. Then, rewrite the passage in clear language, using only as many words as you need.

In spite of the fact that government aviation agencies were not in agreement with respect to the question of the cause of the accident at Hartsfield Airport, the court has decided that one of the factors contributing to the crash was a motor mount that had been structurally weakened.

Handle with Care

Some words can get in the way of your meaning. They can confuse your audience or make your topic seem dull. There are three kinds of expressions you should handle with care: *mixed figures of speech, tired words,* and *clichés.*

Mixed Figures of Speech

A *figure of speech* describes one thing by comparing it to another thing. A figure of speech is not meant to be taken literally. For example, if your sister calls your room a *pig-pen,* she doesn't mean that you keep pigs there. She means that your room looks rather dirty, like a pigpen.

It's important to use figures of speech in a consistent way. If you begin with one comparison and switch to another, you create a *mixed figure of speech.*

MIXED   Great waves of embarrassment broke over her, all but drying up the little confidence she had. [*Great waves* suggest water, which would hardly *dry up* anything.]

BETTER   Great waves of embarrassment broke over her, all but **washing away** the little confidence she had.

Tired Words

A *tired word* is a word that was once clear and forceful. But it has been used so often and so carelessly that it has become vague and weak. For example, overuse has watered down the original, clear meaning of *wonderful,* "causing wonder and amazement." Similar tired words are *good, nice, fine,* and *great.* These words may be acceptable in conversation, but they are too vague to be effective in writing.

Clichés

A tired expression is called a *cliché.* Like tired words, many clichés were once fresh and original. For example, *butterflies in my stomach* was probably a striking turn of phrase the first time it was used to describe stage fright. But it has become stale through constant use. Some clichés are overused figures of speech: *blanket of snow, busy as a bee, white as a sheet.* Others are overused phrases such as *easier said than done, fair and square, last but not least.*

EXERCISE 14▶   **Revising Sentences by Replacing Clichés**

The clichés in each of the following sentences are italicized. Rewrite each sentence, substituting simple, straightforward language for the clichés.

1. After *a meal fit for a king,* we agreed that *a good time had been had by all.*
2. *In this day and age,* political figures who remain *on the fence* when *burning questions* are argued will be *doomed to disappointment* when election day comes.
3. Although warned not to *bite off more than I could chew,* I signed up for six courses.
4. *To make a long story short,* I failed two courses, and *to add insult to injury,* I had to go to summer school.
5. The novel's main character wandered from *the straight and narrow path* and was eventually *embraced by the long arm of the law.*

 COMPUTER NOTE: When you revise the drafts of your papers, use bold, italic, or underline formatting to highlight words or phrases you plan to change. The thesaurus tool can help you find substitutes for jargon, tired words, or clichés.

MAKING CONNECTIONS

Writing a Travel Ad

A beach resort has decided to advertise in a travel magazine to attract more customers. You've been hired to create their new ad. As the ad writer, your job is to convince people that the resort is a beautiful, fun, exciting place to spend their vacation. You've decided to use this collage of photographs to catch your reader's eye, but you also need to write some convincing copy.

Write an ad that will convince readers to send off for more information about the resort. Remember that ad writers don't have much space to work with. You'll need to make every word count.

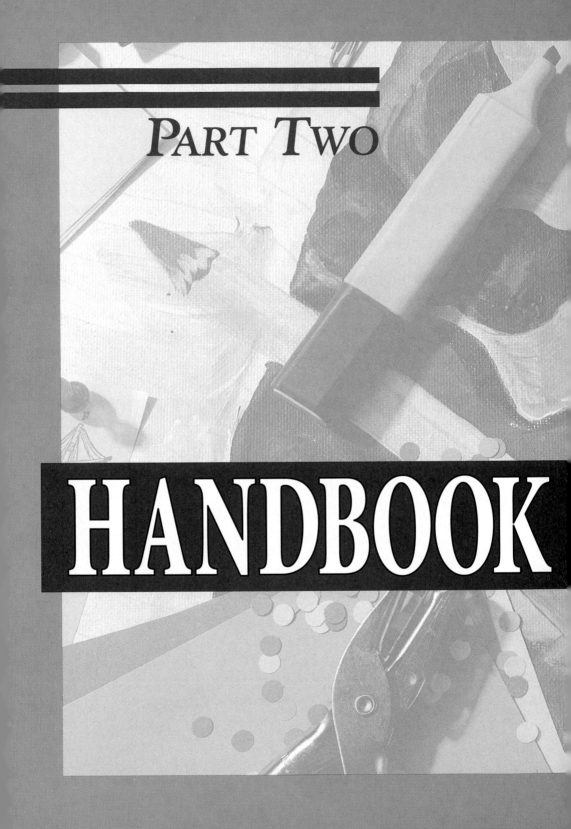

PART TWO

HANDBOOK

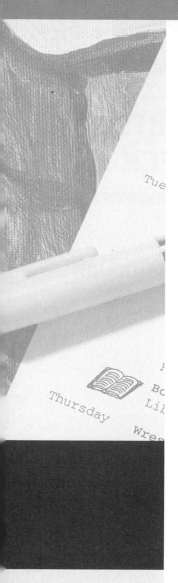

GRAMMAR

15 The Parts of Speech

16 The Sentence

17 The Phrase

18 The Clause

USAGE

19 Agreement

20 Using Pronouns Correctly

21 Using Verbs Correctly

22 Using Modifiers Correctly

23 A Glossary of Usage

MECHANICS

24 Capitalization

25 End Marks and Commas

26 Semicolons and Colons

27 Italics and Quotation Marks

28 Apostrophes, Hyphens, Dashes,
    Parentheses

29 Spelling

30 Correcting Common Errors

15 THE PARTS OF SPEECH

Their Identification and Function

Diagnostic Test

A. Identifying the Parts of Speech in Sentences

Identify the part of speech of each italicized word in the following sentences.

EXAMPLE **1.** In the nineteenth century, many men *worked* as cowboys on *cattle* drives.
     1. *worked—verb; cattle—adjective*

1. When the drive was *over*, the cattle were shipped to northern cities to meet the *need* for hides, meat, and tallow.
2. There *were few* comforts on the trail.
3. Some *improvement* came after *Charles Goodnight* put together the first chuck wagon.
4. A hinged lid swung *down* from the wagon to reveal a simple *but* complete kitchen.

5. The *first* chuck wagons were pulled *by* oxen.
6. *These* were later replaced by mules *or* horses.
7. *Most* of the cowhands who took part in the historic cattle drives remain *nameless.*
8. Cowboys were *instrumental* in opening trails used by the men and women who *settled* the frontier.
9. *Railroads soon* began to crisscross the country; the cowboy was no longer needed to drive cattle.
10. *Hey!* Did you know that ranchers still hire *cowboys* to brand and herd cattle, repair fences, and do many other jobs?

B. Identifying the Parts of Speech in a Paragraph

Identify the part of speech of the italicized word or words in each sentence in the following paragraph.

EXAMPLE   [1] *Neither* the cowboys *nor* the cattle had an *easy* life on the trail.
       1. *Neither-nor—conjunction; easy—adjective*

[11] In the *thirty* years following the Civil War, millions of longhorn cattle were driven *over* long trails from ranches in Texas to railroads in Kansas. [12] During this *period*, the cowboy *became* an American hero. [13] Novels *and* magazine articles *glorified* life on the range. [14] The men *who* rode this rugged land, however, had to endure *many* hardships. [15] Cowboys spent most of their *time* in the saddle, rounding up strays and moving the herd *along*. [16] Caring for sick animals, repairing fences, and, *well*, doing what needed to be done were *all* part of a normal working day. [17] At the end of such a day, each cowboy *not only* had to look after his horse *but also* had to cook dinner for *himself* and do a host of other chores. [18] The quiet *evenings* gave cowboys a chance to relax by telling stories and singing *campfire* songs. [19] Such details of trail life are *realistically* portrayed in the *popular* paintings of Charles M. Russell. [20] *Because of* these images and our need for a *truly* American hero, cowboys have become a colorful part of our history.

GRAMMAR

> ## THE EIGHT PARTS OF SPEECH
>
> | | | |
> |---|---|---|
> | noun | pronoun | adjective |
> | verb | adverb | preposition |
> | conjunction | interjection | |

Nouns

15a. A *noun* is a word used to name a person, place, thing, or idea.

Your name is a noun, and so is the name of your state. *Tree* is a noun. The names of things that you cannot see or touch are nouns: *sympathy, fairness, generosity, truth.* These words name qualities or ideas.

▶ EXERCISE 1 **Identifying Nouns in Sentences**

Identify the twenty-five nouns that appear in the following paragraph. Treat as single nouns all capitalized names containing more than one word. Do not include years, such as *1815.*

EXAMPLE [1] Elizabeth Cady Stanton was born in Johnstown, New York, in 1815.
1. *Elizabeth Cady Stanton, Johnstown, New York*

[1] As a young woman, Elizabeth Cady Stanton studied the classics and mathematics both at home and at Troy Female Seminary, from which she graduated in 1832. [2] Beginning at an early age, she recognized the injustices suffered by women, especially in education and politics. [3] In 1840 she married Henry Stanton, a prominent abolitionist. [4] At an antislavery convention in London, Mrs. Stanton was outraged at the treatment of the female delegates. [5] She later helped to organize the first meeting addressed to women's rights. [6] At that convention, she read her "Declaration of Sentiments," outlining the inferior status of women and calling for reforms.

Proper Nouns and Common Nouns

A *proper noun* names a *particular* person, place, thing, or idea. A *common noun* names a *class* of persons, places, things, or ideas.

PROPER NOUNS	COMMON NOUNS
Atlanta, Nantucket, Mount McKinley	city, island, mountain
Louisa May Alcott, General Powell	novelist, general
Museum of Fine Arts, World Trade Center	museum, building
Queen Elizabeth 2, Spirit of St. Louis	ship, airplane

NOTE: Compound nouns are two or more words put together to form a single noun. Some compound nouns are written as one word, some as two or more words, and some with hyphens.

ONE WORD	TWO OR MORE WORDS	HYPHENATED WORD
basketball newspaper	car pool Arts and Crafts Club	passer-by sister-in-law

EXERCISE 2 **Replacing Common Nouns with Proper Nouns**

For each of the following common nouns, give a proper noun.

EXAMPLE **1.** river
1. *Mississippi River*

1. play	**3.** street	**5.** president	**7.** ocean	**9.** poem
2. state	**4.** song	**6.** newspaper	**8.** writer	**10.** car

Concrete Nouns and Abstract Nouns

Concrete nouns name objects that can be perceived by the senses. *Abstract nouns* name a quality or an idea.

CONCRETE NOUNS   dog, sunset, thunder, silk, apple
ABSTRACT NOUNS   liberty, beauty, kindness, success

▶ REVIEW A   **Classifying Nouns**

Identify each of the italicized nouns in the following paragraph as *proper* or *common*, and *concrete* or *abstract*. Also, tell if a noun is compound.

[1] *Cajuns* are descended from French settlers who were expelled from Acadia (Nova Scotia) by the British in 1755. When some of these displaced people settled in the [2] *Atchafalaya Basin* in southeastern Louisiana, they had to invent [3] *ways* to use local foods in their traditional French recipes. If you've never tried Cajun food, the [4] *crawfish* and gumbo in these pictures may be unfamiliar to you. In addition to the plentiful crawfish, shrimp, oysters, and other [5] *seafood*, freshwater fish, alligator meat, rice, and many [6] *spices* find their way into Cajun cooking. Gumbos, like this one, are soups flavored with [7] *filé*, which is powdered sassafras leaves. [8] *Gumbos* often contain okra and a meat such as sausage, chicken, or seafood. The [9] *popularity* of these and other Cajun dishes has spread throughout the [10] *United States* in recent years.

Pronouns

15b.   A *pronoun* is a word used in place of one or more nouns or pronouns.

EXAMPLE   Susan watched the monkey make faces at her little brother and sister. **She** laughed at **it** more than **they** did. [*She* is used in place of *Susan*, *it* in place of *monkey*, and *they* in place of *brother and sister*.]

Personal Pronouns

	SINGULAR	PLURAL
FIRST PERSON	I, my, mine, me	we, our, ours, us
SECOND PERSON	you, your, yours	you, your, yours
THIRD PERSON	he, his, him she, her, hers it, its	they, their, theirs, them

Other Commonly Used Pronouns

RELATIVE PRONOUNS *(used to introduce adjective and noun clauses)*

who	whom	whose	which	that

INTERROGATIVE PRONOUNS *(used to begin questions)*

Who . . . ?	Whose . . . ?	What . . . ?
Whom . . . ?	Which . . . ?	

DEMONSTRATIVE PRONOUNS *(used to point out a specific person, place, thing, or idea)*

this	that	these	those

INDEFINITE PRONOUNS *(used to refer to an indefinite person, place, thing, or idea)*

all	each	more	one
another	either	most	other
any	everybody	much	several
anybody	everyone	neither	some
anyone	everything	nobody	somebody
anything	few	none	someone
both	many	no one	such

REFLEXIVE AND INTENSIVE PRONOUNS *(used to refer to or to intensify a personal pronoun)*

myself	ourselves
yourself	yourselves
himself, herself, itself	themselves

GRAMMAR

GRAMMAR

The words *my, your, his, her, ours,* and *their* are considered possessive pronouns in this book, rather than adjectives. Follow your teacher's instructions in referring to such words.

▶ EXERCISE 3   **Identifying Pronouns in Sentences**

Identify the pronouns in each sentence in the following paragraph. If a pronoun is used more than once, note it each time it appears. [Note: The paragraph contains a total of twenty-five pronouns.]

[1] Everybody in my family likes to go camping, but few enjoy the outdoors more than I do. [2] Last summer several of my cousins and I stayed at a rustic camp in the Rocky Mountains, which are not far from our hometown. [3] At camp we learned how to build a campfire and how to keep it going. [4] A group of us even went beyond that—we learned to cook food over an open fire. [5] One of our counselors showed those who were interested how to cook simple meals. [6] Each of his recipes was easy to follow, and everyone ate everything in sight. [7] All of us enjoy eating anything cooked over an open fire.

Adjectives

15c.   An *adjective* is a word used to modify a noun or pronoun.

Adjectives make the meaning of a noun or a pronoun more definite. Words used in this way are called *modifiers.*

An adjective may modify a noun or pronoun by telling *what kind, which one,* or *how many (how much).*

WHAT KIND?	WHICH ONE?	HOW MANY?
blue ink	**this** park	**twenty** miles
old friends	**these** papers	**less** time
strong winds	**that** house	**several** apples
Italian food	**Monday** morning	**one-half** inch

An adjective may be separated from the word it modifies by other words.

EXAMPLES   She is **clever.**
The sky, which had been clear all day, became **cloudy.**

Articles

The most frequently used adjectives are *a, an,* and *the.*
These words are usually called *articles.*

A and *an* are *indefinite articles.* They indicate that a
noun refers to one of a general group. *A* is used before
words beginning with a consonant sound; *an* is used
before words beginning with a vowel sound. *An* is also
used before words beginning with the consonant *h* when
the *h* is not pronounced.

EXAMPLES   **A** ranger helped us.
They planted **an** acre with corn.
We kept watch for **an** hour.

The is the *definite article.* It indicates that a noun refers
to someone or something in particular.

EXAMPLES   **The** ranger helped us.
The hour dragged by.
They planted **the** acre with corn.

▶ EXERCISE 4   Identifying the Words That Adjectives Modify

For each italicized adjective in the following sentences,
identify the word the adjective modifies.

[1] By the 1890s, an *extraordinary* craze for bicycling had
swept the United States. [2] Though bicycles had been
available for years, the *early* versions made for an *awkward*
ride. [3] *Ungainly* cycles like the ones shown on the next
page had a very *large* wheel in the front and a *small* wheel
in the back. [4] In 1885, however, a more *sensible* model
was introduced, one that resembled the *modern* cycle.
[5] *Energetic* people everywhere took to *this* kind of bicycle.
[6] Bicycling quickly became a *national* sport. [7] Cyclists
joined *special* clubs, which took *vigorous* tours through the
countryside. [8] A *typical* ride might cover *twenty* miles,

with a *welcome* stop along the way for refreshments. [9] Races were also *popular* with *enthusiastic* spectators, who often outnumbered those at ball games. [10] The fans enjoyed watching *these* tests of endurance, which sometimes lasted *six* days.

Pronoun or Adjective?

Some words may be used either as adjectives or as pronouns. To tell them apart, keep in mind what they do.

Adjectives *modify* nouns; pronouns *take the place of* nouns.

ADJECTIVE **Those** fans are excited.
PRONOUN **Those** are excited fans.

ADJECTIVE He is taller than **most** other players.
PRONOUN He is taller than **most** of the other players.

NOTE: Many pronouns, such as *my, your,* and *their,* may also be classified as adjectives. Follow your teacher's directions in labeling these words.

EXERCISE 5 **Identifying Words as Adjectives or Pronouns**

Identify each italicized word in the following paragraph as a *pronoun* or an *adjective.* For each adjective, give the word it modifies.

Although ants are related to wasps, [1] *these* two kinds of insects differ greatly from [2] *each* other. [3] *All* ants are social insects. They live together in colonies, [4] *each* made up of three castes: a queen, males, and workers.

Unlike ants, [5] *most* wasps are solitary insects. Of [6] *these*, [7] *many* are hunting wasps [8] *that* make individual nests in soil or in decaying wood. However, not all wasps are antisocial; [9] *some* behave more like their cousins the ants. [10] *These* wasps live in permanent colonies of adults and young.

Nouns Used as Adjectives

When a noun is used as an adjective, call it an adjective.

EXAMPLES   **salad** bowl   **chicken** dinner
               grocery store   **gold** chain

NOTE: Sometimes pairs of nouns are used together so often that the first noun is no longer considered an adjective and the pair becomes a compound noun. When you are not sure about the form of a compound noun, look it up in a dictionary.

     EXAMPLES   city hall   sun deck   Brazil nut

WRITING APPLICATION

Using Adjectives to Describe an Imagined Self

When you use adjectives to describe a person or thing, you help your readers to understand something about the nature of that person or thing. Adjectives describe by telling *what kind, which one,* or *how many.*

WITHOUT ADJECTIVES   I sang at the wedding.
   WITH ADJECTIVES   **Happy** but **nervous,** I sang at the **large, formal** wedding.

The sentence without adjectives tells you nothing about the nature of "I" or "the wedding." Substitute different adjectives, and you'll see how the natures of both change.

▶ WRITING ACTIVITY

Some outstanding writers have imagined themselves as an object or an animal. In the story "Metamorphosis," Franz

Kafka writes about a man who becomes an insect! Imagine that you are changed into an animal or an object. Using at least ten carefully chosen adjectives, write a paragraph or a poem describing yourself.

 Prewriting Select an object or an animal that you think you would like to be. Next, freewrite descriptive words about the object or animal. You may want to consult an article in an encyclopedia for additional details or pictures of your chosen topic.

 Writing As you write your first draft, concentrate on using the most vivid adjectives that you have listed.

Evaluating and Revising Read through your first draft and underline each adjective. For each one, ask yourself whether any other word more precisely describes your topic. Be sure that you have used at least ten different adjectives. Remember to count nouns used as adjectives.

Proofreading Check your paragraph or poem to be sure that all words are spelled correctly, especially any adjectives that you use infrequently in writing.

▶ REVIEW B **Identifying Nouns, Pronouns, and Adjectives**

Identify the nouns, pronouns, and adjectives used in the following sentences. For each adjective, give the word that it modifies. (Do not include the articles *a, an,* and *the.*)

1. Our teacher, Mr. López, identified the various trees along the nature trail.
2. The bird feeder in the elm tree in my yard attracts cardinals and chickadees.
3. The flag over the hotel was a welcome sight to the two travelers.
4. The antique doll was dressed in a sailor hat and a blue suit.
5. A large cake sat in the center of the kitchen table.

6. Along miles of the Hudson River, autumn leaves colored the highway with bright splashes of orange and red.
7. Someone has filled the fruit bowl with dates and walnuts.
8. As a young girl, Susan B. Anthony was taught the religious tenets of the Quakers, which include the belief in the equality of all people.
9. Many people are working to clean up polluted rivers and streams to make them livable environments for wildlife again.
10. The dust jacket of that anthology has certainly seen better days.

▶ REVIEW C   **Identifying Nouns, Pronouns, and Adjectives**

Identify each numbered, italicized word in the following paragraph as a *noun*, a *pronoun*, or an *adjective*.

EXAMPLE   The Spanish built the first *ranchos,* or ranches, in the
[1] *United States.*
1. *noun*

The [1] *man* in this picture is a *vaquero,* but it's okay if you call [2] *him* a cowboy—he is. *Vaqueros* got their name from the [3] *Spanish* word *vaca,* which means "cow." In fact, cowboys were at [4] *home* on the range in Mexico long

Hugo Wilhelm Arthur Nahl (1833–1889), *Californians Catching Wild Horses with Riata.* Collection of The Oakland Museum, The Oakland Museum Kahn Collection.

before they gained [5] *legendary* status in the United States. Notice that this *vaquero* wears [6] *leather* chaps (*chaparejos*) to protect his legs and uses a [7] *lariat* (*la reata*) to rope the steer. [8] *Many* other words that we associate with cowboys came into the English language from [9] *Spanish.* [10] *These* include *rodeo, stampede,* and *bronco.*

Verbs

15d. A *verb* is a word that expresses action or a state of being.

Action Verbs

Words such as *bring, say, shout,* and *jump* are **action verbs.** Some action verbs express actions that cannot be seen—for example, *ponder, trust, evaluate,* and *review.*

Transitive Verbs

A *transitive verb* expresses an action directed toward a person or a thing named in the sentence. The action passes from the doer—the subject—to the receiver of the action, called the *object.*

EXAMPLES   She **trusts** her friend. [The action of the verb *trusts* is directed toward *friend.*]
Zora Neale Hurston **wrote** novels. [The action of the verb *wrote* is directed toward *novels.*]

Intransitive Verbs

An *intransitive verb* expresses action or a state of being without reference to an object.

EXAMPLES   The audience **applauded.**
The train **stops** here.

The same verb may be transitive in one sentence and intransitive in another. An intransitive verb is often used when the emphasis is on the action rather than on the person or thing affected by it.

EXAMPLES   Elsa **swam** the channel. [transitive]
Elsa **swam** for many hours. [intransitive]

Miss Castillo **weeds** the garden every day. [transitive]
Miss Castillo **weeds** every day. [intransitive]

"I MISS THE GOOD OLD DAYS WHEN ALL WE HAD TO WORRY ABOUT WAS NOUNS AND VERBS.

© 1984 by Sidney Harris—Punch.

EXERCISE 6   Identifying Verbs as Transitive or Intransitive

Identify the verb in each of the following sentences, and tell whether it is *transitive* or *intransitive*.

1. The strong winds died down.
2. We quickly packed lunch for a trip to the seashore.
3. The whitecaps on the ocean disappeared.
4. The sunlight sparkled on the splashing surf.
5. At low tide, Rosita suddenly spotted a starfish.
6. She noticed its five purplish arms.
7. She touched a soft, brown sponge floating nearby.
8. She added it to her collection of seashells, dried seaweed, and driftwood.
9. Her collection includes several conch shells.
10. Three horseshoe crabs swam in the tidal pool.

Linking Verbs

Linking verbs (also called *state-of-being verbs*) help to make a statement by serving as a link between two words.

The most commonly used linking verbs are forms of the verb *be*.

GRAMMAR

Commonly Used Forms of *Be*			
be	were	shall have been	should be
being	shall be	will have been	would be
am	will be	can be	could be
is	has been	may be	should have been
are	have been	might be	would have been
was	had been	must be	could have been

Other Commonly Used Linking Verbs					
appear	feel	look	seem	sound	taste
become	grow	remain	smell	stay	turn

In the following sentences, each noun or adjective that follows the linking verb refers to the subject of the verb.

> *Kelp* **is** the scientific name for seaweed. [*Kelp* = name]
> Kelp **tastes** good in a salad. [good kelp]
> As it ages, kelp **becomes** brown. [brown kelp]
> Kelp **can be** a basic source of iodine. [Kelp = source]

Many linking verbs can be used as action (nonlinking) verbs as well.

EXAMPLES Emilia **felt** calm at the seashore. [linking verb: calm Emilia]
Emilia **felt** the waving strands of kelp. [action verb]

Some kelps **grow** long. [linking verb: long kelps]
Some kelps **grow** large bulbs. [action verb]

Even *be* is not always a linking verb. It may be followed by only an adverb. In the sentence *They are here,* the word *here* is an adverb. It does not refer to the subject, *They.* To be a linking verb, the verb must be followed by a noun, a pronoun, or an adjective that refers to the subject.

EXERCISE 7 **Writing Sentences Using Verbs as Both Linking and Action Verbs**

For each of the following verbs, write two sentences. In the first sentence, use the verb as a linking verb; in the second sentence, use it as an action verb.

1. appear   **2.** sound   **3.** smell   **4.** grow   **5.** look

The Verb Phrase

A *verb phrase* consists of the main verb and its *helping verbs* (also called *auxiliary verbs*).

Commonly Used Helping Verbs				
have	do	may	can	could
has	does	might	will	would
had	did	must	shall	should

The forms of the verb *be* are also helping verbs.

EXAMPLES   **Did** she **paint** the house?
You **might** even **have seen** this movie before.
Sally **will be launching** the canoe.
This year's budget **has** not **been approved.**

NOTE: The word *not* in a phrase such as *could not go* is not a helping verb. Both *not* and the contraction *–n't* are adverbs.

 REFERENCE NOTE: For more about helping verbs, see page 548.

EXERCISE 8   **Identifying Verbs as Action Verbs or Linking Verbs**

Identify each italicized verb in the numbered sentences in the following paragraph as an *action verb* or a *linking verb.*

[1] Situated on the banks of the Nile River in Egypt, these ruins at Karnak *are* some of the most impressive sights in the world. [2] The largest structure there *is* the

Great Temple of Amon-Re. [3] As you can see, its immense size *dwarfs* people who come to view this architectural marvel. [4] When visitors follow the avenue of sphinxes that leads to the entrance, they *are amazed* at the 42-meter-high gateway. [5] The ceiling of the temple *rests* more than 23 meters above the floor. [6] Of course, the central columns that support the stone roof *are* enormous. [7] The surfaces of these huge columns *are decorated* with carvings. [8] Even an amateur engineer or artist *can appreciate* the tremendous efforts that must have gone into the completion of this temple. [9] We now *know* that inclined planes, combined with levers and blocking, enabled the ancient Egyptians to raise the large stones. [10] A remarkable technical achievement, the Great Temple of Amon *remains* a monument to the ancient builders' skills.

▶ EXERCISE 9　**Identifying Verbs and Verb Phrases**

Identify the verbs and verb phrases in each numbered sentence in the following paragraph. Be sure to include all helping verbs.

[1] Because of the cold weather, the members of the marching band were worried about their first performance. [2] Marcia and the other saxophone players were clapping their hands vigorously so that their fingers wouldn't become even number in the raw, icy air. [3] They imagined what would happen if their fingers froze to the keys of their instruments. [4] Instead of music, harsh noise would blare out and likely startle the spectators. [5] The other band members would likely skip a beat, and chaos would soon spread across the field. [6] Out of step, the flute players might stumble into the clarinet players, collide with the trombone players, or even trip over the drummers. [7] When half time was called, Marcia and her friends rolled their eyes and laughed about the dreadful scene they had just pictured. [8] Such a disaster couldn't possibly happen, could it? [9] As the band marched onto the field, large, white snowflakes swirled in the air and settled on the brand-new uniforms and shiny instruments. [10] People were already leaving the stands when the principal announced over the loudspeaker: "Ladies and gentlemen, the band will now play 'Jingle Bells.'"

Adverbs

15e. An *adverb* is a word used to modify a verb, an adjective, or another adverb.

Adverbs modify by telling *how, when, where,* or *to what extent.*

Adverbs Modifying Verbs

Just as adjectives modify nouns and pronouns, adverbs modify verbs. An adverb makes the meaning of the verb clearer and more definite.

EXAMPLES The bird was chirping **outside.** [*where*]
The bird chirped **today.** [*when*]
The bird chirped **loudly.** [*how*]
The bird chirped **constantly.** [*to what extent*]

 EXERCISE 10 **Identifying Adverbs and the Verbs They Modify**

Identify the adverbs in each numbered sentence in the following paragraph. For each adverb, give the verb that it modifies.

[1] The first balloonists floated gently above Paris in a hot-air balloon that had been cleverly designed by the Montgolfier brothers. [2] Although their earlier attempts

had failed, the Montgolfiers kept trying and finally settled on a balloon made of paper and linen. [3] Early balloons differed significantly from modern balloons like those on the previous page, which are sturdily constructed of coated nylon. [4] Despite their ingenuity, the Montgolfiers originally thought that smoke, rather than hot air, would effectively push a balloon skyward. [5] Consequently, in their experiments they initially produced hot smoke by burning straw and wool.

Adverbs Modifying Adjectives

EXAMPLES   It was a **fiercely** competitive game. [The adverb *fiercely* modifies the adjective *competitive*.]
The **exceptionally** brave police officer was given an award. [The adverb *exceptionally* modifies the adjective *brave*.]

NOTE: Some of the most frequently used adverbs are *too, very*, and *so*. Try to avoid these overused words in your writing. Instead, think of more precise adverbs to make your meaning clearer.

EXERCISE 11   **Identifying Adverbs and the Adjectives They Modify**

In each of the following sentences, an adverb modifies an adjective. Identify the adverb and the adjective it modifies.

1. An immensely long wagon train started out from Denver, Colorado.
2. Both oxen and mules were used to pull unusually large wagons.
3. Even in good weather, the trail through the mountains was fairly hazardous.
4. A moderately hard rain could turn the trail into a swamp.
5. When the trail was too muddy, the heavier wagons became mired.
6. Wagons that were extremely heavy then had to be unloaded before they could be moved.
7. Stopping for the night along the trail was a consistently welcome experience.

8. It offered relief to thoroughly tired bones and muscles.
9. Nights in the mountains could be quite cold.
10. On terribly cold nights, the travelers would roll in blankets and sleep close to their campfires.

Adverbs Modifying Other Adverbs

EXAMPLES   The guide spoke **extremely** slowly. [The adverb *extremely* modifies the adverb *slowly*, telling *how* slowly.]

We will go **later** today. [The adverb *later* modifies the adverb *today*, telling *when* today.]

NOTE: Many adverbs end in *–ly*. However, not all words ending in *–ly* are adverbs. For instance, the following words are adjectives: *homely, kindly, lovely, deadly.* To determine a word's part of speech, look at how the word is used in the sentence. Do not rely on spelling alone.

EXERCISE 12   **Identifying Adverbs and the Words They Modify**

The following paragraphs contain twenty adverbs. Identify the adverb or adverbs in each sentence. After each adverb, give the word it modifies and the part of speech of that word.

[1] A couple of months ago, my sister Juana and I finally decided to buy a houseplant. [2] The large ones we saw were too expensive for us. [3] In addition, they are almost always raised in hothouses, and, as a result, they do not adjust easily to living in cold climates. [4] Suddenly Juana had a brainstorm. [5] "Let's buy some seeds and grow them indoors. [6] That way, the seedlings will automatically adapt themselves to the climate in our house."

[7] At the seed store, the owner, Mrs. Miller, greeted us cheerfully. [8] We explained that we wanted to grow a large plant but that our room hardly ever gets bright sunlight and in the winter it can be especially chilly and dark. [9] We also mentioned that we wanted seeds for a plant seldom sold in local shops. [10] "I know what you need," Mrs. Miller promptly replied. [11] "These are seeds of the

bo tree, an unusually hardy member of the fig family native to India. [12] There this tree is sacred to Buddhists because it is said that the Buddha received enlightenment under a bo tree." [13] When we got back to our house, we planted the seeds. [14] In a short time, they sprouted, and we now have an unusual houseplant that is suited to our cold environment.

PICTURE THIS

You are directing this production of Shakespeare's play *Romeo and Juliet*. The actors are in position and are waiting for your instructions on how to play the famous balcony scene in which the young lovers proclaim their feelings for each other. Shakespeare provided little direction, so it's up to you. Write five sentences of stage directions that you think would be appropriate for the scene. In each sentence, use at least one adverb to tell the actors how, when, where, or to what extent to do something.

Subject: stage directions for *Romeo and Juliet*
Audience: actors playing Romeo and Juliet
Purpose: to instruct actors how to play a scene

▶ EXERCISE 13 **Using Words as Adjectives and Adverbs**

Write a pair of sentences for each word. In the first sentence, use the word as an *adjective;* in the second, use it as an *adverb.*

EXAMPLE **1.** kindly
1. *She had a kindly manner—adjective.*
She spoke kindly—adverb.

1. daily   **2.** fast   **3.** late   **4.** more   **5.** far

▶ REVIEW D **Identifying Parts of Speech**

Identify the part of speech of each italicized word in the following paragraphs. If the word is an adjective or an adverb, be able to tell what it modifies.

With a [1] *thunderous* roar, a mighty avalanche [2] *crashes* [3] *headlong* down a mountainside. [4] *Some* of these slides travel at speeds of more than 200 miles an hour and pose a [5] *deadly* threat to skiers, mountain climbers, and the people [6] *who* live and work in the mountains.

One [7] *common* suggestion for surviving an avalanche is to make swimming motions to remain on top of the snow. However, people caught in avalanches [8] *rarely* can save [9] *themselves.* They are [10] *usually* immobilized, and the slide [11] *forces* snow into their nose and mouth.

Avalanche workers in the [12] *United States* and abroad have [13] *long* realized the [14] *potential* [15] *destructiveness* of selected slide paths. They [16] *have concluded* that an avalanche can be [17] *greatly* reduced if [18] *explosives* [19] *are used* to trigger a [20] *series* of [21] *smaller* slides before [22] *one* large mass of snow can build up. [23] *Today,* the detonation of explosives has become a standard [24] *practice* for controlling avalanches in [25] *this* country.

▶ EXERCISE 14 **Using Parts of Speech to Write a Description**

In the painting on the next page, folk artist Mattie Lou O'Kelley recorded her impressions of a circus parade that came through her town when she was growing up in the early 1900s. Imagine that you were with O'Kelley, watching the parade, and write ten sentences giving your impressions of that day. Use action verbs and vivid adjectives and adverbs to capture the excitement of this spectacle. Be prepared to identify the nouns, pronouns, adjectives, verbs, and adverbs in your sentences.

EXAMPLE   **1. *The acrobat skips lightly on the elephant's back.***

Mattie Lou O'Kelley, *The Circus Parade.* Photograph courtesy of the Museum of American Folk Art, N.Y. From FROM THE HILLS OF GEORGIA by Mattie Lou O'Kelley. © 1983 by Mattie Lou O'Kelley. By permission of Little, Brown and Company.

Prepositions

15f. A *preposition* is a word that shows the relationship of a noun or a pronoun to some other word in the sentence.

Notice in the following examples how the prepositions show six different relationships between *village* and *rode.*

> I rode **past** the village.   I rode **near** the village.
> I rode **through** the village.   I rode **around** the village.
> I rode **toward** the village.   I rode **beyond** the village.

A *prepositional phrase* includes a preposition, a noun or pronoun called the *object of a preposition,* and any modifiers of the object. In the examples above, the object of each preposition is *village.*

 REFERENCE NOTE: For more about prepositional phrases, see pages 574–576.

Commonly Used Prepositions

aboard	below	for	past
about	beneath	from	since
above	beside	in	through
across	besides	inside	to
after	between	into	toward
against	beyond	like	under
along	but (meaning	near	underneath
amid	*except*)	of	until
among	by	off	up
around	concerning	on	upon
at	down	onto	with
before	during	outside	within
behind	except	over	without

Compound Prepositions

according to	in addition to	instead of
because of	in front of	on account of
by means of	in spite of	prior to

NOTE: The same word may be either an adverb or a preposition, depending on its use in a sentence.

EXAMPLES   Marge climbed **down.** [adverb]
Marge climbed **down** the ladder. [preposition]

Above, buzzards circled lazily. [adverb]
Above the dry riverbed, buzzards circled lazily. [preposition]

▶ EXERCISE 15   **Writing Sentences Using Words as Prepositions and as Adverbs**

For each of the following words, write two sentences. In the first sentence, use the word as a preposition and underline the prepositional phrase. In the second sentence, use the word as an adverb. Be able to tell which word the adverb modifies.

EXAMPLE   **1.** In
1. *We are going in the house now.*
We are going in now.

1. around   3. inside   5. up
2. behind   4. on

Conjunctions

15g. A *conjunction* is a word used to join words or groups of words.

Conjunctions join parts of a sentence that function in the same way. The parts that are joined may be words, phrases, or clauses.

☞ REFERENCE NOTE: For a discussion on using conjunctions in sentence combining, see pages 467–470. For the rules governing the use of punctuation with conjunctions, see pages 467–468, 794–796, and 816–819.

Coordinating Conjunctions

Conjunctions that join equal parts of a sentence are called *coordinating conjunctions.*

and	for	but	so
or	yet	nor	

EXAMPLES   The orchestra played one waltz **and** two polkas.
We can walk to the mall **or** take a bus.
I looked for Hal, **but** he had already left.

Correlative Conjunctions

Conjunctions that are used in pairs are called *correlative conjunctions.* Like coordinating conjunctions, correlative conjunctions join equal parts of a sentence.

both . . . and	neither . . . nor
not only . . . but also	whether . . . or
either . . . or	

EXAMPLES   **Neither** the baseball team **nor** the soccer team has practice today.
Both the track team **and** the volleyball team enjoyed a winning season.
Their victories sparked the enthusiasm **not only** of students **but also** of teachers and townspeople.

☞ REFERENCE NOTE: **Subordinating conjunctions** are discussed with subordinate clauses on pages 603–604.

▶ EXERCISE 16   **Identifying Coordinating and Correlative Conjunctions**

Identify the coordinating and correlative conjunctions in the sentences in the following paragraph.

[1] Once Nantucket and New Bedford, Massachusetts, were home ports of huge whaling fleets. [2] Whaling brought tremendous profits into these ports, but the golden days of whaling ended about the time of the American Civil War. [3] Even when it was successful, a whaling trip was no pleasure cruise for either the captain or the crew. [4] Maintaining order was no easy task on a long voyage because the food and living conditions were often dreadful. [5] Inevitably, the sailors had time on their hands, for they didn't encounter a whale every day. [6] To relieve the monotony and resulting boredom, whaling ships often would exchange visits. [7] Not only the captain but also the whole crew looked forward to such visits. [8] Everyone enjoyed the chance to chat and exchange news. [9] The decline of whaling and of the whaling industry was signaled by the development of a new fuel. [10] By 1860, our country no longer needed large quantities of whale oil because kerosene, a cheaper and better fuel, had replaced it.

Interjections

15h.   An *interjection* is a word that expresses emotion and has no grammatical relation to other words in the sentence.

EXAMPLES   **Ouch!   Ugh!   Wow!   Oops!   Aha!**

These words are usually followed by an exclamation mark. An interjection that shows only mild emotion is set off from the sentence by a comma or commas.

EXAMPLES   **Well,** I'm just not sure.
When I'm having a bad week, **oh,** I can hardly wait for the weekend.

▶ EXERCISE 17   **Using Interjections**

You just took your driver's license test. Wanting to share your feelings about the test and your results, you call your best friend. Write your conversation, using at least five interjections. You may choose interjections from the list below or use ones of your own. Be sure to use the words as interjections and not as adjectives or adverbs. Check to see that you have punctuated your interjections with exclamation points or commas as needed.

ah	cool	hey	wow	ugh
aw	great	no	yes	excellent

Determining Parts of Speech

15i.   What part of speech a word is depends on how the word is used.

EXAMPLES   Rich heard the **light** patter of raindrops. [adjective]
The room was filled with **light**. [noun]
Let's **light** some candles this evening. [verb]

▶ EXERCISE 18   **Determining the Parts of Speech of Words**

Determine the part of speech of the italicized word in each of the following sentences. Be prepared to explain your answers.

1. They decided that the hedge needed a *trim*.
2. Their hedges always look *trim* and neat.
3. We usually *trim* the tree with homemade ornaments.
4. Mom always *shears* a couple of inches off the top of the tree.
5. Later, she uses *shears* to cut straggling branches.
6. My brother *spices* peach preserves with nutmeg and allspice.
7. These *spices* are available in most stores.
8. Sage adds a tangy *flavor* to stew.
9. Many chefs also *flavor* stew with basil.
10. In their family, a *cross* word is rarely spoken.

▶ REVIEW E   **Writing Sentences Using Words as Different Parts of Speech**

Write three sentences for each of the following words, using the word as a different part of speech in each sentence. At the end of the sentence, write what part of speech the word is in that sentence.

1. long   **2.** cut   **3.** back   **4.** fast   **5.** iron

▶ REVIEW F   **Determining the Parts of Speech of Words**

Identify the part of speech of each italicized word or expression in the following paragraph.

[1] *Early* farmers on the [2] *Great Plains* eked out a rough existence, [3] *for* there were few towns, stores, or other hallmarks of civilization. [4] *Many* farm homes were constructed with sod bricks, [5] *which* were cut [6] *out of* the prairie. Trees were in short supply on these wind-swept lands, but the resourceful settler might find a few [7] *cottonwoods* growing [8] *along* a stream. [9] *These* [10] *could be used* to build a frame for the roof, which was then covered [11] *lightly* with grassy earth. Grass, both [12] *on* the roof [13] *and* in the sod, helped to hold the house together. Some of [14] *these* rugged homes had a door made of timber, but [15] *usually* a cowhide [16] *was draped* across the entrance. [17] *Inside* was a dirt floor covered with a bearskin [18] *or* a buffalo hide. As more settlers moved [19] *west* bringing furnishings and [20] *building* materials, farmers eventually abandoned these first, primitive dwellings and built more conventional homes.

▶ EXERCISE 19   **Using Words as Different Parts of Speech**

Your friend has just returned from a vacation in Europe. During her trip, she made the collage shown on the following page, picturing different types of transportation she used while traveling. After flying from the United States, she rode a bike in France, a train through the Swiss Alps, and a bus in Italy. She also went by ship to a Greek island, where she rode a donkey. Write your comments and questions about her travels, using the following words as the parts of speech indicated. Each word will be used as two different parts of speech.

bike [noun, verb]
up [preposition, adverb]
cool [adjective, interjection]
for [conjunction, preposition]
that [pronoun, adjective]

Review: Posttest 1

Determining the Parts of Speech of Words

Identify the part of speech of each italicized word in the following paragraphs.

Since the [1] *condition* of the roads prevented [2] *extensive* use of wheeled vehicles, the most reliable means of transportation in colonial times was the [3] *saddle horse*. Some

[4] *exceptionally* wealthy people kept carriages, but [5] *these* were usually heavy vehicles [6] *that* were pulled by two or more horses. Such carriages were [7] *satisfactory* for short trips, [8] *but* they were not practical for long journeys.

Stagecoaches were introduced in [9] *America* about 1750. By this time, roads ran [10] *between* such major cities as New York and Boston. Although these roads [11] *were* little more than muddy tracks, [12] *most* were wide enough for a four-wheeled coach. [13] *Three* or four pairs of horses [14] *were harnessed* to a coach. However, the vehicles were so heavy that [15] *coach* horses tired [16] *quite* [17] *rapidly* [18] *and* either had to be rested frequently [19] *or* changed at post houses along the route. The design of horse-drawn vehicles soon improved, and until the early years of the twentieth century, buggies and wagons remained a common [20] *form* of transportation.

Review: Posttest 2

Writing Sentences with Words Used as Different Parts of Speech

Use each of the following words or groups of words in a sentence. Then indicate what part of speech the word or word group is.

EXAMPLE   **1.** gold
        1. *Tamisha bought a gold bracelet. (adjective)*

1. novel	**11.** hiked
2. Park Avenue	**12.** appeared
3. this	**13.** tasted
4. are laughing	**14.** quietly
5. yesterday	**15.** often
6. tomorrow	**16.** inside
7. or	**17.** underneath
8. but	**18.** oh
9. both . . . and	**19.** whew
10. silver	**20.** in

GRAMMAR

SUMMARY OF PARTS OF SPEECH

Rule	Part of Speech	Use	Examples
15a	noun	names	**Larry** picks **grapefruit.**
15b	pronoun	takes the place of a noun	**Who** said **that these** are the **ones we** need?
15c	adjective	modifies a noun or a pronoun	That was a **happy** sight. They were very **noisy.**
15d	verb	shows action or a state of being	He **jumps** and **spins.** She **is** the winner.
15e	adverb	modifies a verb, an adjective, or another adverb	He learns **quickly.** She is **always** right. It flies **quite** high.
15f	preposition	relates a noun or a pronoun to another word	The cat was **by** itself **under** the oak tree **next to** the garage.
15g	conjunction	joins words or groups of words	Kyoko **and** Sheila passed the test. We can **either** go hiking **or** go swimming.
15h	interjection	expresses emotion	**My goodness!** **Hey,** stop that!

16 THE SENTENCE

Subjects, Predicates, Complements

Diagnostic Test

A. Identifying Subjects, Verbs, and Complements

Identify the italicized word or word group in each of the following sentences as a *subject,* a *verb,* a *predicate adjective,* a *predicate nominative,* a *direct object,* or an *indirect object.*

1. Native *cactuses* in the Southwest are in trouble.
2. Some species are already *vulnerable* to extinction.
3. Cactuses *are being threatened* by landscapers, tourists, and collectors.
4. Many people illegally harvest these wild *plants.*
5. There are many unique *species* in Arizona.
6. Arizona is, therefore, an active *battlefield* in the war against the removal of endangered cactuses.
7. "Cactus cops" *patrol* the streets of Phoenix on the lookout for places with illegally acquired cactuses.
8. Authorized dealers must give *purchasers* permit tags as proof of legal sale.

9. First violations are *punishable* by a minimum fine of five hundred dollars.
10. Illegally owned cactuses *may be confiscated* by the police.
11. What a thorny problem cactus *rustling* has become!
12. Why are illegal harvesters so *hard* to keep track of?
13. Many work at night and sometimes use permit *tags* over and over.
14. Always *examine* a large cactus for bruises.
15. Legally harvested cacti *should* not *show* any damage.

B. Classifying Sentences as Declarative, Interrogative, Imperative, or Exclamatory

Classify each of the following sentences as *declarative, interrogative, imperative,* or *exclamatory*. Then give the proper end punctuation.

16. Read this article about imperiled cactuses
17. The author describes a trip into the desert with a legal hauler
18. Can you imagine a saguaro worth three hundred dollars
19. A crested saguaro is even rarer and can sell for thousands of dollars
20. No wonder illegal harvesting is booming

Sentences and Sentence Fragments

In conversation, you may leave out part of a sentence without confusing your listeners. In writing, though, it's better to use complete sentences because readers rely on them for help in understanding your meaning.

 A *sentence* is a group of words that contains a subject and a verb and expresses a complete thought.

To express a complete thought, a sentence must say something that makes sense by itself. A group of words that does not express a complete thought is a *fragment,* or a piece of a sentence; it is not a sentence itself.

SENTENCE	Cara won the essay contest sponsored by the magazine.
FRAGMENT	the essay contest sponsored by the magazine
SENTENCE	Her essay was chosen as the best one from over two thousand entries.
FRAGMENT	was chosen as the best one from over two thousand entries
SENTENCE	When the judges announced the winner, everyone applauded.
FRAGMENT	when the judges announced the winner

☞ **REFERENCE NOTE:** Fragments can be confusing when they are written as sentences, beginning with a capital letter and ending with an end mark of punctuation. See pages 446–447 for information on how to correct sentence fragments.

▶ EXERCISE 1 **Identifying Sentences and Fragments**

Identify each of the following word groups as a *sentence* or a *fragment.*

1. Willa Cather was born in Back Creek Valley in northern Virginia.
2. In 1883, when she was nine years old.
3. Her family moved to the treeless prairie of Nebraska.
4. Fascinated by the wild and rolling plains.
5. She tracked buffalo and collected prairie flowers.
6. Listening to the stories of neighboring settlers.
7. They told memorable tales about the harsh struggles of the homesteaders.
8. After she graduated from high school in the village of Red Cloud, Nebraska.
9. The picture of Red Cloud on the next page shows shops and people that would have been familiar to Willa Cather.
10. And the Opera House at the end of the street where Cather and her class graduated in 1890.

▶ EXERCISE 2   **Identifying Sentences and Fragments**

Identify each of the numbered word groups in the following paragraph as either a *sentence* or a *fragment*. Be prepared to explain your answers.

[1] In college, Willa Cather discovered her talent for writing. [2] Contributing stories and reviews to local newspapers in Lincoln, Nebraska. [3] At first, her writing failed to reach a wider audience outside her region. [4] After some years as a schoolteacher and a magazine editor in New York City. [5] She succeeded in establishing herself as a writer. [6] Although Cather enjoyed living in New York. [7] She never lost touch with the sights and sounds of her childhood. [8] In her first novel, *O Pioneers!* [9] She describes how farmers turned the unruly plains into orderly fields of wheat and corn. [10] In a later novel, *My Ántonia*, the immigrant neighbors of her childhood play prominent roles.

Subject and Predicate

16b.   A sentence consists of two parts: the *subject* and the *predicate.*

The *subject* names the person, place, thing, or idea spoken about in the rest of the sentence. The *predicate* says something about the subject.

The subject may come at the beginning, the end, or even the middle of a sentence.

EXAMPLES

SUBJECT	PREDICATE
Some residents of the desert	can survive a long drought.

PREDICATE	SUBJECT
Noteworthy is	the Australian frog.

PREDICATE	SUBJECT	PREDICATE
For up to three years	these frogs	can live without rainfall.

PREDICATE	SUBJECT	PREDICATE
How do	animals	survive that long?

In these examples, the words labeled *subject* make up the **complete subject.** The words labeled *predicate* make up the **complete predicate.** Notice in the third and fourth examples that parts of the complete predicate can come before and after the subject.

▶ EXERCISE 3 **Identifying Subjects and Predicates**

Identify the complete subject and the complete predicate in each of the following sentences. Keep in mind that the subject may come after the predicate.

1. The discovery of platinum has been credited to people from a variety of countries.
2. Spanish explorers in search of gold supposedly discovered this precious metal in the rivers of South America.
3. However, they considered it a worthless, inferior form of silver.
4. Their name for platinum was *platina,* meaning "little silver."
5. Back into the river went the little balls of platinum!
6. The platinum might then become gold, according to one theory.
7. Europeans later mixed platinum with gold.
8. This mixture encouraged the production of counterfeit gold bars and coins.
9. Platinum commands a high price today because of its resistance to corrosion.
10. Such diverse products as jet planes and jewelry require platinum in some form.

The Simple Subject

16c. The *simple subject* is the main word or group of words in the complete subject.

EXAMPLES A dog with this pedigree is usually nervous.
Complete subject   A dog with this pedigree
Simple subject   dog

The Taj Mahal in India is one of the most beautiful buildings in the world.
Complete subject   The Taj Mahal in India
Simple subject   Taj Mahal

☞ REFERENCE NOTE: Compound nouns, such as *Taj Mahal,* are considered one noun. For more about compound nouns, see page 515.

NOTE: In this book, the term *subject* refers to the simple subject unless otherwise indicated.

The Simple Predicate

16d. The *simple predicate,* or *verb,* is the main word or group of words in the complete predicate.

EXAMPLE Spiders snare their prey in intricate webs.
Complete predicate   snare their prey in intricate webs
Simple predicate   snare

The simple predicate may be a single verb or a *verb phrase* (a verb and one or more helping verbs).

EXAMPLES walks   has been walking   might have walked

When you identify the simple predicate, be sure to find all parts of a verb phrase.

EXAMPLES Did Rosa find you?
Complete predicate   did find you
Simple predicate   did find

She has been looking for you all morning.
Complete predicate   has been looking for you all morning
Simple predicate   has been looking

NOTE: In this book, the term *verb* refers to the simple predicate unless otherwise indicated.

▶ EXERCISE 4　**Identifying Verbs and Verb Phrases in Sentences**

Identify the verb in each sentence in the following paragraph. Be sure to include all parts of a verb phrase.

[1] Scientists throughout the world have expressed concern about the fate of the giant panda of China. [2] In recent years, this animal's natural habitat has slowly become smaller. [3] Many forests of bamboo, the panda's favorite food, have died. [4] A panda like the one pictured here may devour as much as forty pounds of bamboo daily. [5] However, each tender green shoot of bamboo contains only a small amount of nutrients. [6] In addition, the large but sluggish panda is not known as a successful hunter. [7] In their concern for the panda's survival, scientists are now studying the habits of this animal. [8] A captured panda is held in a log trap for several hours. [9] During this time, scientists attach a radio to the panda's neck. [10] The radio sends the scientists valuable information about the freed animal's behavior.

How to Find the Subject of a Sentence

Finding the subject of a sentence is easier if you pick out the verb first. Then ask "Who?" or "What?" followed by the verb.

EXAMPLES   My cousin from Finland will arrive this afternoon.
[The verb is *will arrive.* Who will arrive? *My cousin*
will arrive; therefore, *cousin* is the subject.]
On the other side of the brook stands a cabin. [The
verb is *stands.* What stands? *A cabin* stands; *cabin* is
the subject.]

▶ EXERCISE 5   **Identifying Subjects and Verbs**

Identify the subject and the verb in each sentence in the
following paragraph.

[1] Despite their fragile appearance, butterflies have a
lot of stamina. [2] They often fly more than one thousand
miles during migration. [3] The painted lady butterfly, for
example, has been seen in the middle of the Atlantic
Ocean. [4] In fact, this species was once spotted over the
Arctic Circle. [5] During the spring, millions of these
insects flutter across North America. [6] Huge flocks of
these colorful butterflies fly from their winter home in
New Mexico to places as far north as Newfoundland,
Canada. [7] Another long-distance traveler, the brilliant
orange-and-black monarch butterfly, flies south each September from Canada toward Florida, Texas, and California. [8] The migratory flight of the monarch may cover a
distance of close to two thousand miles. [9] Every winter
for the past several decades, monarchs have gathered in a
small forest not far from San Francisco. [10] The thick clus-
ters of their blazing orange wings make this forest very
popular with tourists.

16e.   The subject is never in a prepositional phrase.

A *prepositional phrase* is a group of words that begins
with a preposition and ends with a noun or pronoun.

EXAMPLES   through the years   of mine   on the team

☞ REFERENCE NOTE: For more about prepositional phrases, see
pages 574–576.

The noun or pronoun that ends a prepositional phrase
cannot be the subject of a sentence.

EXAMPLES **One of my cousins has visited Ghana.** [Who has visited? *One* has visited, not *cousins,* which is part of the prepositional phrase *of my cousins.*]
On top of the building is an observatory. [What is? *Observatory* is, not *top* or *building,* which are parts of prepositional phrases.]

In many sentences you can easily isolate the subject and verb simply by crossing out all prepositional phrases.

EXAMPLE The team ~~with the best record~~ will play ~~in the state tournament.~~
Subject   team
Verb   will play

▶ EXERCISE 6   **Identifying Subjects and Verbs**

Identify the subject and the verb of each sentence in the following paragraph. Remember that the subject won't be in a prepositional phrase.

[1] The people in this picture are celebrating an ancient Chinese tradition—heralding the arrival of the New Year. [2] These festivities, however, are occurring in the United States. [3] The Chinese New Year celebration, with its dragon parades and colorful decorations, has added another dimension to American culture. [4] In the 1850s, the earliest Chinese immigrants came to the United States for jobs in the gold mines and on the railroads. [5] At first, only men were allowed to immigrate. [6] Not until much

later were they able to send home to China for their wives and sweethearts. [7] As a result, not until the 1920s did the close-knit society of America's Chinatowns develop. [8] Do you want to know more about the Chinese experience in America? [9] I recommend the book *Longtime Californ': A Documentary Study of an American Chinatown.* [10] In this book, Victor G. Nee and Brett de Bary Nee trace the history of Chinese immigration to the United States and the development of the Chinese American community in San Francisco.

▶ EXERCISE 7 **Completing Sentences by Supplying Predicates**

Complete each of the following sentences by adding a predicate to the complete subject. Then, underline the subject once and the verb twice.

EXAMPLE   **1.** One of the horses ____.
               1. *One of the horses has escaped from the corral.*

1. Last month ____.
2. A white fence ____.
3. The surf ____.
4. The road by my house ____.
5. The students in our school ____.

▶ REVIEW A **Identifying Complete Subjects and Complete Predicates**

Identify the complete subject and the complete predicate in each sentence in the following paragraph. Then underline the subject once and the verb twice.

[1] Benjamin Banneker (1731–1806) was born near Baltimore, Maryland, of a free mother and an enslaved father. [2] Considered free, Banneker was able to attend an integrated private school. [3] There he began his lifelong study of science and math. [4] Despite having only an eighth-grade education, this young man became a noteworthy American astronomer and mathematician. [5] His astronomical research led to his acclaimed prediction of the solar eclipse of 1789. [6] A few years later, the first of his almanacs was published. [7] Banneker's almanacs contained tide tables and data on future eclipses. [8] Some

bits of practical advice, as well as famous sayings, were also included. [9] These popular almanacs came out every year for more than a decade. [10] In addition to his scientific discoveries, Banneker is known for his work as a surveyor during the planning of Washington, D.C.

Sentences Beginning with *There* or *Here*

The word *there* or *here* may begin a sentence, but it is usually not the subject.

EXAMPLE   There are two **apples** left. [What are left? *Apples.* Therefore, *apples* is the subject.]

NOTE: In this use, *there* is an **expletive,** a word that fills out the structure of a sentence but doesn't add to the meaning.

There and *here* may be used as adverbs telling where.

EXAMPLES   There are your **gloves.** [What are there? *Gloves.*]
Here is my **idea.** [What is here? *Idea.*]

Sentences That Ask Questions

Questions usually begin with a verb, a helping verb, or a word such as *what, when, where, how,* or *why.* In most cases, the subject follows the verb or helping verb.

EXAMPLES   Did **you** make the team?
Why is **he** running?

In a question that begins with a helping verb, the subject always comes between the helping verb and the main verb. One way to find the subject in any question is to turn the question into a statement and find the verb. Then ask "Who?" or "What?" in front of the verb.

EXAMPLES   Were your friends early?
becomes
Your friends were early.
[Who were early? *Friends* were.]

Where did the horses cross the river?
becomes
The horses did cross the river where.
[What did cross the river? *Horses* did.]

▶ EXERCISE 8 **Identifying Subjects and Verbs**

Identify the verb and the subject in each of the following sentences. Select the verb first.

1. There were three questions on the final exam.
2. Here is my topic for the term paper.
3. What did you choose for a topic?
4. Will everyone be ready on time?
5. There will be a study-group meeting tomorrow.
6. When should we go to the library?
7. There were very few books on the subject.
8. Are there many magazine articles about Nelson Mandela?
9. Where will our conference be held?
10. Have you begun the next chapter?

The Understood Subject

In requests and commands, the subject is usually not stated. In such sentences, *you* is the understood subject.

REQUEST   (You) Please rake the yard.
COMMAND   (You) Pick up the fallen branches.

When a request or command includes a person's name, the name is not the subject. The name is called a *noun of direct address.* *You* is still the understood subject.

EXAMPLE   (You) Wash the dishes, Jason.

Compound Subjects and Verbs

16f. A *compound subject* consists of two or more subjects that are joined by a conjunction and have the same verb. The conjunctions most often used to link the parts of a compound subject are *and* and *or.*

EXAMPLES   **Mr. Olivero** and his **daughter** planted the garden. [Who planted the garden? *Mr. Olivero, daughter.*]
Either Mr. Olivero or his **daughter** planted the garden. [Again, the two parts of the compound subject are *Mr. Olivero* and *daughter.*]

GRAMMAR

16g. A *compound verb* consists of two or more verbs that are joined by a conjunction and have the same subject.

EXAMPLES At the street festival, we **danced** the rumba and **sampled** the meat pies.
I **have written** the letter but **have** not **addressed** the envelope.

NOTE: If the helping verb is the same for the two verbs in a compound verb, it may or may not be repeated. Both the subject and the verb may be compound.

EXAMPLE My **aunt** and her **children will arrive** tomorrow and **stay** with us for the holidays.

 EXERCISE 9 **Identifying Subjects and Verbs**

Identify the subject and the verb in each of the following sentences. If the subject is understood, write *(You)*.

1. Jackets and ties are required in that restaurant.
2. Are there any bears or wildcats living in these woods?
3. On our math test, Ann and Mark scored the highest.
4. Bring both a pencil and a pen to the history exam.
5. Miguel neither sings nor plays an instrument.
6. Where do you and Liz buy your cassettes?
7. The front and back tires are low and need air.
8. Play ball!
9. Humor and wisdom are often used in folk sayings.
10. Either Bill or Jan may stay and help us.

EXERCISE 10 **Using Subjects and Verbs**

In preparing a report on the history of the typewriter, you've gathered the following notes and the pictures shown on the next page. Using information from these sources, write a paragraph about the development of typewriters. Underline the subject of each sentence once and the verb twice.

First typewriter designed by C. L. Sholes, 1867.
Had only capital letters—keys hard to press down.
Typed onto underside of paper, so typist couldn't see what was being typed.

Odd arrangement of letters on first typewriter still used today.

1878—typewriter had shift key and lowercase letters.

1904—Royal was first modern typewriter, keys easier to press.

First portable typewriter—early 1900s.

Electric typewriters come into use—1920s.

Modern typewriters have computer features.

Beautiful Work in 1799.

THE YOST

TYPEWRITER

is noted not alone for its Beautiful Work, but for the way it continues to produce it during years of constant use.

Send for Art Catalogue.
YOST WRITING MACHINE CO
New York   London

REVIEW B   **Identifying Subjects and Verbs**

Identify the subject and the verb in each of the following sentences. If the subject is understood, write *(You)*. Then underline the subject once and the verb twice.

1. Bats, most birds, and many insects can fly.
2. Other animals can move through the air without flying.
3. The flying fish swims fast and then leaps out of the water.
4. How does the flying squirrel glide from tree to tree?
5. There are flaps of skin between its legs.
6. How do birds fly?
7. Their wings lift and push them through the air.
8. Look carefully at an insect's wings.
9. Most have two sets of wings.
10. The pair in front covers the pair in back.

GRAMMAR

PICTURE THIS

While on a tour at the Delphi Museum in Greece, you enter a large room and see this life-size bronze statue of a young charioteer. A museum guide tells you that this statue, created in about 475 B.C., was originally part of a larger work that included a bronze chariot and four bronze horses. Write a postcard to a friend back home telling him or her about this statue and your reactions to it. Begin one sentence with *there* or *here,* include one question, and have at least one sentence in which the subject is understood.

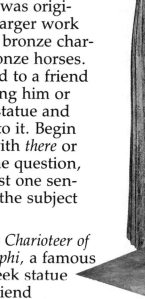

Subject: *The Charioteer of Delphi,* a famous Greek statue

Audience: a friend

Purpose: to comment on a work of art

Complements

16h. A *complement* is a word or group of words that completes the meaning of a predicate.

A group of words may have a subject and a verb and still not express a complete thought. Notice how the boldfaced words complete the meanings of the following sentences.

$$\overset{\text{S}}{\text{That}} \; \overset{\text{V}}{\text{book is}} \; \overset{\text{C}}{\text{an \textbf{autobiography.}}}$$

That book is an **autobiography.**

S   S V   C
Both Eric and Bob felt **confident.**

S   V   C   C
Sandra Cisneros writes **poetry** and **fiction.**

As you can see in the last example above, a complement may be a compound.

NOTE: Every sentence has a basic framework called a *base.* In a sentence with no complement, the base is simply the subject and verb. In a sentence with a complement, the base includes the complement.

Complements can be found in both independent clauses and dependent clauses.

EXAMPLES
                 S   V   C
Although he appeared **sluggish** at the start,

      S   V   C
Ricardo won the **race.**

      S V   C   S   V
Josie is an **engineer** who designs computer

      C
hardware.

☞ REFERENCE NOTE: For a discussion of independent and dependent clauses, see Chapter 18.

NOTE: Complements are never in prepositional phrases.

    EXAMPLES   Li Hua quoted the **poem.** [*Poem* is the complement.]
                        Li Hua quoted from the **poem.** [*Poem* is part of the prepositional phrase *from the poem.*]

An adverb modifying a verb is not a complement. Only nouns, pronouns, and adjectives serve as complements.

EXAMPLES
    Lucy plays **hard.** [*Hard* is an adverb, not a complement.]
    These pears are **hard.** [*Hard,* an adjective, is a complement.]

▶ EXERCISE 11   **Writing Sentences with Subjects, Verbs, and Complements**

Construct five sentences from the following sentence parts. Try to add more than only a word or two.

SUBJECT	VERB	COMPLEMENT
cyclists	planned	trip
musicians	performed	duet
speaker	looked	enthusiastic
dancer	tapped	rhythm
novel	is	suspenseful

EXERCISE 12 Identifying Subjects, Verbs, and Complements

Identify the subject(s) and the verb(s) in each sentence in the following paragraph. Then identify the complement if there is one.

[1] A hurricane is a powerful storm that can measure two or three hundred miles in diameter. [2] Such storms are notorious for causing death and destruction. [3] To be classified as a hurricane, a storm must have winds of at least seventy-four miles per hour. [4] These winds swirl around the *eye*, an area of calm in the center of the storm. [5] *Wall clouds* surround the eye of a hurricane. [6] Within these clouds the strongest winds and heaviest rain of the storm occur. [7] The winds and rain, along with the force of the sea, often produce enormous waves, called a *storm surge*. [8] In a surge, tides rise several feet above normal. [9] Huge waves produce floods that destroy life and property. [10] In fact, 90 percent of hurricane-related deaths result from drowning in floods.

United States of America

Gulf of Mexico

Cuba

Hispaniola

Puerto Rico

Yucatan Peninsula

The Subject Complement

16i. A *subject complement* is a noun, a pronoun, or an adjective that follows a linking verb. A subject complement identifies or describes the subject.

EXAMPLES   Lani is a soccer **player.** [*Player* identifies *Lani.*]
This could be **it.** [*It* identifies *This.*]
Roscoe seems **worried.** [*Worried* describes *Roscoe.*]

☞ REFERENCE NOTE: For more information about linking verbs, see pages 525–526.

Remember that subject complements can appear in dependent clauses.

EXAMPLES   Although the watch is an **antique,** my aunt says that it is always **accurate.** [*Antique* identifies *watch* in the introductory adverb clause. *Accurate* describes *it* in the noun clause beginning with *that.*]

(1) A *predicate nominative* is a noun or a pronoun in the predicate that identifies or renames the subject of a sentence or a clause.

EXAMPLES   Some caterpillars become **butterflies.**
The winners should have been **they.**

(2) A *predicate adjective* is an adjective in the predicate that describes the subject of a sentence or a clause.

EXAMPLES   You look **happy.**
Norma appeared **calm.**

Subject complements may be compound.

EXAMPLES   Our cats' names are **Wimpy** and **Henry.** [compound predicate nominative]
The yogurt tasted **sweet** and **creamy.** [compound predicate adjective]

NOTE: The subject complement may come before the subject of a sentence or a clause.

EXAMPLES   How **silly** that commercial is! [*Silly* is a predicate adjective describing *commercial.*]
Now we know what a fine **speaker** you are. [*Speaker* is a predicate nominative identifying *you.*]

▶ EXERCISE 13　**Identifying Predicate Nominatives and Predicate Adjectives**

Identify the subject complements in the following sentences. Then, tell whether the complement is a predicate nominative or a predicate adjective. [Note: A sentence may have more than one subject complement.]

1. The last scene of the play is very intense.
2. Those two small birds are finches.
3. The music sounded lively.
4. It is difficult to choose a winner when each contestant's costume looks so elegant.
5. My goldfish Alonzo grows larger every day.
6. Andrea's report on digital recording is a highly detailed and technical one.
7. The setting of the story is a Spanish castle that looks old and deserted.
8. Your solution to this algebra problem is clever.
9. We felt full after we had eaten Thanksgiving dinner.
10. When did Uncas become a chief of the Mohegans?

▶ EXERCISE 14　**Identifying Subjects, Verbs, and Subject Complements**

Each sentence in the following paragraph contains at least one subject complement. Identify each subject, verb, and subject complement. Make a chart like the following one, and fill in the correct words.

EXAMPLE　[1] **Although jazz is now popular all over the world, it was originally the music of African Americans.**

SUBJECT	VERB	SUBJECT COMPLEMENT
1. *jazz*	*is*	*popular*
it	*was*	*music*

[1] A typically American musical form, jazz was the sound of Louis Armstrong, "Count" Basie, Scott Joplin, and Ella Fitzgerald. [2] Created in the early twentieth century, jazz is a blend of elements from African and European music, but its irregular, or syncopated, rhythms are strictly African. [3] Early jazz was a combination of the cakewalk, a dance that was popular with many African Americans in the 1800s, and ragtime, which was mainly

instrumental music. [4] After 1917, the future of jazz appeared bright when jazz phonograph records became popular. [5] People remain fascinated by jazz, perhaps because it sounds new each time it's played.

Objects

Objects are complements that do not refer to the subject. They follow action verbs rather than linking verbs.

EXAMPLES   The cat was chasing a **moth.**
             Jeff's mother gave **him** some **grapes.**

☞ **REFERENCE NOTE:** For more information about action verbs, see pages 524–525.

Like subject complements, objects can be found in dependent clauses.

EXAMPLE   After we read the **story,** the teacher said that she would give **us** a **quiz** on it.

16j.   A *direct object* is a noun or pronoun that directly receives the action of a verb or shows the result of the action. A direct object answers the question "What?" or "Whom?" after an action verb.

EXAMPLES   The mechanic fixed their **car.** [Fixed what? *Car.*]
             She asked **them** to wait in the lobby. [Asked whom? *Them.*]

Verbs that express mental action, such as *study, dream,* and *understand,* are just as much action verbs as are verbs that express physical action, such as *push, leap,* and *stumble.*

EXAMPLE   Paco still **remembers** his first day of school. [Remembers what? *Day.*]

NOTE: Direct objects are never found in prepositional phrases.

       EXAMPLES   Mom and I painted the **porch.** [*Porch* is the direct object.]
                    Mom and I painted on the **porch.** [*Porch* is part of the prepositional phrase *on the porch.*]

▶ EXERCISE 15   **Identifying Verbs and Their Direct Objects**

Identify the verbs and the direct objects in the following sentences.

1. I borrowed my parents' new camera recently.
2. First I loaded the film into the camera.
3. Then I set the shutter speed.
4. I focused the camera on a distant object.
5. I could read the shutter speed in the viewfinder.
6. A flashing red light signals an incorrect setting.
7. Slowly and carefully, I pressed the button.
8. I then moved the film forward for the next shot.
9. By the end of the day, I had snapped more than thirty-six pictures.
10. Unfortunately, the film processor lost my roll of film.

16k.   An *indirect object* is a noun or pronoun that precedes the direct object and tells *to whom* or *for whom* (or *to what* or *for what*) the action of the verb is done.

DIRECT OBJECT	Meli read her **report**. [Read what? *Report.*]
INDIRECT OBJECT	Meli read **us** her report. [Read to whom? *Us.*]

If the word *to* or *for* is used in the sentence, the noun or pronoun following it is part of a prepositional phrase, not an indirect object.

EXAMPLES   Jeff wrote **me** a note. [*Me* is the indirect object.]
Jeff wrote a note to **me**. [*Me* is part of the prepositional phrase *to me.*]

Both direct and indirect objects may be compound.

EXAMPLES   Our family recycles **glass** and **aluminum**. [compound direct object]
The ski trip had given **Lucia** and **me** a wonderful vacation. [compound indirect object]

NOTE: Don't confuse adverbs in the predicate with complements.

EXAMPLES   They turned **right**. [*Right* is an adverb telling where.]
You have the **right** to remain silent. [*Right* is a noun used as a direct object.]

▶ EXERCISE 16   **Identifying Direct and Indirect Objects**

Identify the direct objects and indirect objects in the sentences in the following paragraph. Not all sentences contain both kinds of objects.

[1] Last summer, Leroy told us his plans for the future. [2] He wants a place on the U.S. swim team in the next Olympic Games. [3] Of course, this goal demands hours of hard practice. [4] Every day, Leroy swims one hundred laps in the college pool and works out with weights for an hour. [5] Such intense training could have cost him his social life. [6] With his rigorous schedule, Leroy doesn't have much time to spend with friends. [7] However, all of us understand and give him encouragement and support. [8] But we can't teach him the fine points of competitive swimming. [9] His coach does that. [10] Working together, they've already improved Leroy's best time.

▶ EXERCISE 17   **Using Direct and Indirect Objects**

It's your first day working at a restaurant, and you've just taken this family's order. Because you want to be sure to get the order right, you take a minute in the kitchen to go over what each person wanted. Write five sentences that you might say to yourself to remember who should get what. In your sentences, use five direct objects and at least two indirect objects. For indirect objects, you could use pronouns or general terms such as *man* or *children*, or imagine that you know the people and use their names.

EXAMPLE   **1.** *Give Margot the squid and spinach appetizer.*

▶ REVIEW C | **Identifying Sentences and Fragments; Identifying Complements**

Identify each of the following word groups as a *sentence* or a *fragment*. If a word group is a complete sentence, identify its subject and verb. If a sentence has a complement, label it as a *predicate adjective,* a *predicate nominative,* a *direct object,* or an *indirect object.*

1. Has the planning committee announced the date of the school carnival?
2. Perhaps next week.
3. Linda gave us a summary of her science project.
4. It was long and interesting.
5. Although it was well written.
6. Books and papers covered the desk and spilled onto the floor.
7. One of those dogs is not very well trained.
8. Ming Chin gave the children a handful of oatmeal cookies.
9. Kim, Juan, and Tracey were winners at the track meet last Saturday.
10. How happy they were!

Sentences Classified by Purpose

16l. Sentences may be classified as *declarative, imperative, interrogative,* or *exclamatory.*

(1) A ***declarative sentence*** makes a statement. All declarative sentences are followed by periods.

EXAMPLES Gwendolyn Brooks is the poet laureate of Illinois.
Although we were tired after working all day, we still wanted to go dancing.

(2) An ***imperative sentence*** gives a command or makes a request. Imperative sentences usually end with periods, but strong commands may end with exclamation points

EXAMPLES Pass the salt, please.
Speak softly.
Wait!

(3) An ***interrogative sentence*** asks a question. Interrogative sentences are followed by question marks.

EXAMPLES   Can you speak Spanish**?**
What did you say**?**

(4) An ***exclamatory sentence*** expresses strong feeling. Exclamatory sentences are followed by exclamation points.

EXAMPLES   What a beautiful day this is**!**
How I enjoy autumn**!**

NOTE: Any sentence may be spoken in such a way that it is exclamatory. In this case, it should be followed by an exclamation point.

EXAMPLES   This is inexcusable**!** [Declarative becomes exclamatory.]
Stop the car**!** [Imperative becomes exclamatory.]
How could you say that**!** [Interrogative becomes exclamatory.]

☞ REFERENCE NOTE: For a discussion of how sentences are classified by structure, see pages 610–611. For more on end marks of punctuation, see pages 789–792.

▶ EXERCISE 18   **Classifying Sentences as Declarative, Imperative, Interrogative, or Exclamatory**

Classify each of the following sentences as *declarative, imperative, interrogative,* or *exclamatory.*

1. The loudspeakers in our living room are small yet powerful.
2. Turn down the sound!
3. Is that music or noise, Ramona?
4. Listening to loud music every day can damage a person's hearing.
5. How many watts does your amplifier produce?
6. Sound levels are measured in units called decibels.
7. Do you know that an increase of ten decibels represents a doubling in the sound level?
8. Do not blast your sound system.
9. Keep it quiet!
10. Music played softly is relaxing.

▶ EXERCISE 19 **Using the Four Kinds of Sentences**

These colorful Tlingit totem poles stand in Saxman Indian Village in Ketchikan, Alaska. The Tlingits, who have lived in Alaska for hundreds of years, are well known for their carving skills, as well as their sense of humor. Yes, that's a short-legged Abraham Lincoln atop one of the poles! Write five sentences expressing your reactions to these poles. Use at least one of each kind of sentence: *declarative*, *imperative*, *interrogative*, and *exclamatory*.

EXAMPLE **1.** *What a surprise to see Abraham Lincoln on a totem pole!*

GRAMMAR

WRITING APPLICATION

Catching a Reader's Interest with Appropriately Varied Sentences

In fishing, you need the right bait to catch the kind of fish you want. In writing, you need the right bait to catch your reader's interest. Your opening sentence is this bait.

OPENER 1:   I think we should have a party.
OPENER 2:   Shouldn't we have a party?
OPENER 3:   Let's party!

These opening sentences contain similar information. Which of them would interest you to read further? Why?

GRAMMAR

▶ WRITING ACTIVITY

Your neighborhood Residents' Council would like to sponsor a dance for the teenagers on your block. However, the council is not sure what kind of dances teens would like. You've decided to write a short letter to the council to give your opinion. Write some different opening sentences for your letter. Select the one that is the best "bait" for your audience, and then write a short letter.

Prewriting   Decide how you feel about this issue. Then, jot down a few notes about why having the dance would or would not be a good idea. Next, write some different opening sentences. Choose the opener that you think will be the most interesting and effective.

Writing   As you write your letter, be sure to refer often to your prewriting notes.

Evaluating and Revising   Ask an adult you know to listen to your letter. Does he or she think your opening sentence is interesting? Does he or she find your letter persuasive? Revise any sentences or sections that aren't clear.

Proofreading   Imagine that you are a council member, and read through your letter. Are there any grammar, punctuation, or spelling errors? Does the letter follow the proper business letter form? (See pages 973–979 for the correct forms of business letters.) Make all needed corrections, and then write a clean, final copy of your letter.

▶ REVIEW D   **Understanding the Parts of a Sentence**

In your own words, define each of the following terms, and give an example to illustrate it.

1. a sentence
2. a complete subject
3. a verb (simple predicate)
4. a verb phrase
5. a complete predicate
6. a simple subject
7. a subject complement
8. a direct object
9. an understood subject
10. an indirect object

REVIEW E ### Identifying Subjects, Verbs, and Complements

Identify each of the italicized words in the following passage as a *subject*, a *verb*, a *predicate adjective*, a *predicate nominative*, a *direct object*, or an *indirect object*.

The Great Pyramid of Khufu (Cheops) is [1] *one* of the wonders of the ancient world. [2] *It* was once encased with blocks of polished limestone. However, [3] *weather and thievery* [4] *have combined* to destroy the original structure. As you [5] *can see*, the pyramid [6] *looks* [7] *weather-beaten*. Still, it is an impressive [8] *sight*.

Hundreds of years ago, one invading Arab [9] *ruler* decided to rob the tomb of Khufu. With many workers at his disposal, he gave the [10] *men* his [11] *instructions*. The workers [12] *hacked* through the incredibly hard solid blocks of granite. Unexpectedly, [13] *they* broke into a tunnel. Imagine their [14] *excitement*! All too soon, however, they [15] *discovered* an enormous [16] *plug* of granite blocking their way. They cut around the plug and finally reached the inner [17] *chamber*.

Strangely enough, there was no [18] *gold*. No vast treasures [19] *sparkled* under the light of the torches. The tomb [20] *had* probably *been robbed* many centuries earlier by Egyptians familiar with its secret entrances.

Review: Posttest 1

A. Identifying Subjects, Verbs, and Complements

Identify each of the italicized words in the following sentences as a *subject*, a *verb*, a *predicate adjective*, a *predicate nominative*, a *direct object*, or an *indirect object*.

1. Have *you* ever met a robot?
2. In the field of robotics, scientists have built vastly complex *robots*.
3. Today these machines *are put* to work in factories, laboratories, and outer space.
4. How were these complex *machines* first used?
5. There are a *number* of interesting early examples of robots at work.
6. One of the first robots was a mechanical *figure* in a clock tower.
7. It raised a hammer and struck a *bell* every hour.
8. At the 1939 New York World's Fair, Elektro and Sparko were popular *attractions*.
9. Elektro was *tall*, more than seven feet high.
10. Electric motors gave *Elektro* power for a variety of amazing tricks.
11. Sparko was Elektro's *dog*.
12. Sparko *could bark* and even *wag* his tail.
13. Today, *some* of the simplest robots are drones in research laboratories.
14. Basically, drones are *extensions* of the human arm.
15. They can be *useful* in many different ways.

B. Classifying Sentences as Declarative, Interrogative, Imperative, or Exclamatory

Classify each of the following sentences as *declarative*, *interrogative*, *imperative*, or *exclamatory*. Then give the proper end punctuation.

16. Can you picture a robot twenty-five feet tall
17. Step up and say hello to Beetle

18. Perhaps you have already heard of CAM, an even more advanced robot
19. It can travel on long legs across rough terrain as rapidly as thirty-five miles per hour
20. How much it looks like a science fiction creature

Review: Posttest 2

Writing Sentences

Write sentences according to the following guidelines. Underline the subject once and the verb twice in each sentence. If the subject is understood, write *(You)*.

EXAMPLE   **1.** a sentence with a direct object
　　　　　1. *(You) Have another glass of milk.*

1. a declarative sentence with a verb phrase
2. a sentence beginning with *There*
3. an interrogative sentence
4. an exclamatory sentence
5. an imperative sentence
6. a sentence with a compound subject
7. a sentence with a predicate nominative
8. a sentence with a compound direct object and an indirect object
9. a sentence with a predicate adjective
10. a sentence with a compound verb

17 THE PHRASE

Prepositional, Verbal, and Appositive Phrases

Diagnostic Test

A. Identifying Phrases in Sentences

Identify each italicized phrase in the following sentences as *prepositional, participial, gerund, infinitive,* or *appositive.*

1. The sundial was one of the first instruments used for *telling time.*
2. *Regarded chiefly as garden ornaments,* sundials are still used in some areas *to tell time.*
3. The shadow-casting object *on a sundial* is called a gnomon.
4. Forerunners of the sundial include poles or upright stones *used as gnomons by early humans.*
5. *To improve the accuracy of the sundial,* the gnomon was set directly parallel to the earth's axis.
6. The development of trigonometry permitted more precise calculations *in the construction* of sundials.
7. For everyday use, *owning a watch* has obvious advantages over *using a sundial.*

8. *In the past,* sundials were used *to set and check the accuracy of watches.*

9. The heliochronometer, *a sundial of great precision,* was used until 1900 *to set the watches of French railway workers.*

10. The difference *between solar time and clock time* is correlated by the use of tables *showing daily variations in sun time.*

B. Identifying Phrases in a Paragraph

Identify each italicized phrase in the following paragraph as *prepositional, participial, gerund, infinitive,* or *appositive.*

[11] A sundial is not difficult *to make with simple materials.* [12] First, find a stick *to use as a gnomon.* [13] At high noon, put the stick in the ground, *tilting it slightly northward.* [14] *To mark the first hour,* place a pebble at the tip of the shadow made by the stick. [15] An hour later, put another pebble at the tip *of the shadow.* [16] Continue this process *throughout the afternoon.* [17] *Starting the next morning,* repeat the hourly process. [18] Be sure *to place the last pebble at high noon.* [19] Observing the completed sundial, you will note that the hour markers, *the pebbles,* are not equidistant. [20] *The uneven spacing of the markers* demonstrates that shadows move faster in the morning and the evening than during the middle of the day.

17a. A *phrase* is a group of related words that is used as a single part of speech and does not contain both a verb and its subject.

EXAMPLES   should have waited [verb phrase; no subject]
            for you and her [prepositional phrase; no subject or verb]

A group of words that has both a subject and a verb is not a phrase.

EXAMPLES   They will be here soon. [*They* is the subject of *will be.*]
            after she leaves [*She* is the subject of *leaves.*]

REFERENCE NOTE: A group of words that has both a subject and a verb is called a *clause.* Clauses are discussed in Chapter 18.

Prepositional Phrases

17b. A *prepositional phrase* includes a preposition, a noun or a pronoun, and any modifiers of that noun or pronoun.

EXAMPLES   The woman **with the helmet** is a motorcyclist.
The cashier gave the change **to me.**

NOTE: Don't confuse the common preposition *to* with the *to* that is the sign of the infinitive form of a verb: *to watch, to learn, to drive.* For more on infinitives, see pages 586–588.

17c. The noun or pronoun that ends a prepositional phrase is the *object of the preposition* that begins the phrase.

PREPOSITIONAL PHRASE	PREPOSITION	OBJECT
before the second stoplight	before	stoplight
along the highway	along	highway
according to him	according to	him

 REFERENCE NOTE: For a list of commonly used prepositions, see page 535.

A preposition may have a compound object.

EXAMPLES   near **forests** and **rivers**
despite the **rain, snow,** and **ice**

Adjective Phrases

17d. A prepositional phrase that modifies a noun or a pronoun is an *adjective phrase.*

EXAMPLES   The cottages **by the lake** are quite picturesque. [The adjective phrase *by the lake* modifies the noun *cottages.*]

No one **in the class** has seen the movie yet. [The adjective phrase *in the class* modifies the pronoun *no one.*]

Two or more adjective phrases may modify the same noun or pronoun.

EXAMPLE   The picture **of their candidate in today's newspaper** is not at all flattering. [The two adjective phrases *of their candidate* and *in today's newspaper* both modify the same noun, *picture.*]

An adjective phrase may also modify the object of another prepositional phrase.

EXAMPLE   The coconut palms in the park **near the bay** were planted a long time ago. [*Near the bay* modifies *park,* the object of the preposition *in.*]

NOTE: Unlike single-word adjectives, adjective phrases always follow the noun or pronoun they modify.

EXERCISE 1   **Identifying Adjective Phrases**

Identify the adjective phrases in each of the following sentences. After each phrase, give the word that the phrase modifies.

EXAMPLE   **1.** Julius Caesar was one of the most successful generals in ancient Rome.
1. *of the most successful generals—one*
in ancient Rome—generals

1. Roman roads were one reason for Caesar's military successes.
2. The roads of ancient Rome linked the far corners of the empire.
3. Large blocks of hard stone provided a sound foundation for most major routes.
4. Caesar's interest in military roads showed his understanding of the importance of communication.
5. Close communication among the empire's provinces strengthened the power of the Roman rulers.

Adverb Phrases

17e. A prepositional phrase that modifies a verb, an adjective, or another adverb is an *adverb phrase.*

EXAMPLES   The mole burrowed **under the lawn.** [The adverb phrase *under the lawn* modifies the verb *burrowed.*]

Althea Gibson was graceful **on the tennis court.** [The adverb phrase *on the tennis court* modifies the adjective *graceful.*]

The baby speaks quite clearly **for a two-year-old.** [The adverb phrase *for a two-year-old* modifies the adverb *clearly.*]

Adverb phrases tell *when, where, why, how,* or *to what extent.*

EXAMPLES   The town grew quiet **after the storm.** [*when*]
He glanced **out the window.** [*where*]
Most street musicians play **for tips.** [*why*]
This summer we're going **by car.** [*how*]
She won the game **by two points.** [*to what extent*]

Adverb phrases may come before or after the words they modify, and more than one adverb phrase may modify the same word.

EXAMPLE   **In the first inning** she pitched **with great control.** [*In the first inning* tells *when* she pitched, and *with great control* tells *how* she pitched.]

EXERCISE 2   Identifying Adverb Phrases

Identify each adverb phrase in the following sentences. Then give the word it modifies and the part of speech of that word.

[1] On Friday, Dad and I were alarmed by eerie sounds that came from the abandoned house next door. [2] We searched inside the house from the attic to the basement. [3] In the basement we found two stray kittens. [4] They were crying for food. [5] The noises we'd heard had been made by them. [6] I found an empty box in the corner and gently placed the kittens in it. [7] They seemed happy

with their temporary home. [8] Then we took the kittens back to our house. [9] We lined the box with an old towel and set it in the kitchen. [10] Now the eerie sounds come from our house at all hours of the night and day.

REVIEW A   **Completing Sentences by Inserting Prepositional Phrases**

Provide a prepositional phrase for the blank in each sentence. After the sentence, identify each phrase as an *adjective phrase* or an *adverb phrase*.

EXAMPLE   **1.** ___ Mrs. Bowen reads the newspaper.
    1. *In the evening Mrs. Bowen reads the newspaper.—adverb phrase*

1. ___ the children played hopscotch.
2. I saw a spider ___.
3. We planned a drive ___.
4. Her team played ___.
5. The sky divers jumped fearlessly ___.
6. Hundreds ___ stared.
7. ___ the cyclists unpacked their lunch.
8. There ___ winds a narrow road.
9. This movie will be playing ___.
10. ___ the dancers swayed with the music.

EXERCISE 3   **Using Prepositional Phrases**

You are the guest director for an episode of *The Cosby Show*. It's your chance to tell Bill Cosby and the other actors in his television family what to do. Write five sentences giving directions for what should happen next in the scene on the previous page. If you are unfamiliar with *The Cosby Show,* imagine that these actors are characters in one of your favorite TV shows. Make up names and roles for them. In your sentences, use at least two adjective phrases and three adverb phrases, and underline each of these phrases.

EXAMPLE   **1.** *Theo should run into the kitchen and start stacking the dishes in the sink.*

WRITING APPLICATION

Using Prepositional Phrases to Write Clear Directions

It's useful to be able to explain how to do something. By giving readers a detailed and accurate explanation, you help them duplicate your method and results. Information given in prepositional phrases can make your instructions clearer and more helpful.

HELPFUL   To set the dye, rinse your new red shirt thoroughly.

MORE HELPFUL   To set the dye, rinse your new red shirt thoroughly in a basin of cool water with one quarter cup vinegar.

▶ WRITING ACTIVITY

A friend has asked you to explain how to perform a useful task that you are good at. Write a paragraph explaining exactly how to accomplish the task. Use at least five prepositional phrases in explaining the process.

Prewriting   First, think of something that you know how to do and can explain. Examples are how to change a tire, how to make gift-wrapping paper, and how to serve a tennis ball. When you have chosen a topic, make a simple outline of the necessary steps in the process.

Writing Remember to refer frequently to your outline as you write your first draft.

Evaluating and Revising Read your directions to a classmate to find out if the information is clear and detailed enough. Revise any steps that your listener finds confusing. Be sure that you have used a combination of adverb and adjective phrases in your directions.

Proofreading and Publishing Read your directions carefully, step by step. Pay special attention to the correct placement of prepositional phrases and to the clear use of verb tenses to show when each step should occur. Members of your class may want to share their knowledge and abilities by putting together a how-to book to share with other students in your school.

Verbals and Verbal Phrases

Verbals are forms of verbs that are used as adjectives, nouns, or adverbs. They may be modified by adverbs and adjectives and may have complements.

The three kinds of verbals are *participles*, *gerunds*, and *infinitives*.

 REFERENCE NOTE: For a discussion of verbal phrases as sentence fragments, see pages 449–450. For more on verbals as dangling modifiers, see page 728.

The Participle

17f. A *participle* is a verb form that can be used as an adjective.

EXAMPLES   The **simmering** soup smelled delicious. [*Simmering,* formed from the verb *simmer,* modifies the noun *soup.*]

A **chipped** fingernail can be annoying. [*Chipped,* formed from the verb *chip,* modifies the noun *fingernail.*]

There are two kinds of participles: *present participles* and *past participles.*

(1) *Present participles* end in *–ing.*

EXAMPLES   The **smiling** graduates posed for the photographer. [The present participle *smiling* modifies the noun *graduates.*]
Checking the weather forecast, the captain changed course. [The present participle *checking* modifies the noun *captain.*]

A present participle can't be used alone as a verb, but it can be combined with a helping verb to form a verb phrase.

EXAMPLES   The graduates **were smiling.**
The captain **is checking** the weather forecast.

When a present participle is used in a verb phrase, it is part of the verb and is not a verbal used as an adjective.

(2) Most *past participles* end in *–d* or *–ed.* A few are formed irregularly.

EXAMPLES   **Discovered** by the guard, the **startled** burglar was led away. [The past participles *discovered* and *startled* modify the noun *burglar.*]
Hidden under the front porch, the toy truck was safely out of the rain. [The past participle *hidden* modifies the noun *truck.*]

Like a present participle, a past participle can be part of a verb phrase. When used in a verb phrase, a past participle is part of the verb and is not a verbal used as an adjective.

EXAMPLES   The burglar **was startled** when he **was discovered** by the guard.
Why **has** Jonathan **hidden** his toy truck under the front porch?

☞ REFERENCE NOTE: For more on verb phrases, see pages 527 and 548.

▶ EXERCISE 4   **Identifying Participles**

Identify the present participles and past participles used as adjectives in the following sentences. (Some sentences contain more than one participle.) Give the noun or pronoun each participle modifies. Remember not to confuse participles used as verbals with participles used as part of a verb phrase.

EXAMPLE   **1. We have been studying one of the most feared animals in the sea—the killer whale.**
            1. *feared—animals*

1. Killer whales, long known as wolves of the sea, are not nearly as vicious as many people have thought.
2. Seeking to test the supposedly ferocious nature of the killer whale, scientists studied the whales' behavior.
3. After extensive study, scientists discovered that there is no proven case of an attack on a human by a killer whale.
4. In fact, scientists working with killer whales have confirmed that their charges are intelligent and can be quite gentle.
5. Gathered together in Johnstone Strait, a narrow channel between Vancouver Island and British Columbia in Canada, killer whales spend the summer and fall in large family groups.
6. Choosing this spot to observe the mammals, researchers were able to identify more than one hundred whales.
7. The team of scientists, noting the unique shape of each whale's dorsal fin, named each whale in order to keep more accurate records.
8. Impressed by the long life span of killer whales, scientists have estimated that males may live fifty years and females may survive a century.
9. Cruising in groups called pods, killer whales are highly social animals.
10. During the summer and fall in Johnstone Strait, many pods gather, splashing and playing in "superpods."

▶ EXERCISE 5   **Revising Sentences by Adding Participles**

Each of the following sentences has a participle in parentheses after it. Revise each sentence by inserting the participle next to the noun it best modifies.

EXAMPLE   1. We collected funds for the restoration of the building. (*damaged*)
1. *We collected funds for the restoration of the damaged building.*

1. The space shuttle was greeted with loud cheers. (*returning*)
2. The committee selected three television shows for their educational value. (*nominating*)
3. My sister was in the kitchen and did not hear the doorbell. (*ringing*)
4. The carpenter is supposed to show us how to fix this chair. (*broken*)
5. In 1949, Luis Muñoz Marín became Puerto Rico's first governor. (*elected*)
6. The stream crosses the farmer's land at three places. (*winding*)
7. We handed the envelope to the mail carrier. (*crumpled*)
8. This book includes many interesting facts about dinosaurs. (*illustrated*)
9. The Douglas fir behind our house has become a haven for several small creatures. (*fallen*)
10. The plane narrowly missed a radio antenna. (*circling*)

The Participial Phrase

17g.   A *participial phrase* consists of a participle and any complements or modifiers it may have. The entire participial phrase acts as an adjective.

In each of the following sentences, an arrow connects the participial phrase with the noun or pronoun the phrase modifies.

EXAMPLES **Climbing the tree,** the monkey disappeared into the branches. [participle *climbing* with object *tree*]

I heard him **whispering to his friend.** [participle *whispering* with prepositional phrase modifier *to his friend*]

We watched the storm **blowing eastward.** [participle *blowing* with adverb modifier *eastward*]

Voted back into office, the mayor thanked her supporters. [participle *Voted* with adverb modifier *back* and prepositional phrase modifier *into office*]

The concert **scheduled for tomorrow at the park** has been postponed until next week. [participle *scheduled* with two prepositional phrase modifiers: *for tomorrow* and *at the park*]

👉 **REFERENCE NOTE:** For information on the correct placement of participial phrases near the words they modify, see pages 465 and 728–730. See pages 797–800 for the punctuation of participial phrases.

▶ EXERCISE 6 **Identifying Participial Phrases**

Identify each participial phrase in the following sentences. Then give the noun or pronoun modified by the phrase.

[1] Hoping to be the first to reach the South Pole, the British explorer Robert Scott (back row, center, in the photograph) took these four men with him on his final dash to

the pole in November 1911. [2] Leading Scott by sixty miles, however, a Norwegian expedition, commanded by Roald Amundsen, was moving swiftly. [3] Having learned about Amundsen, Scott realized a race to the pole was on. [4] Plagued by bad weather and bad luck, Scott fell farther behind Amundsen. [5] Reaching the pole on January 17, the British found that the Norwegians had already been there. [6] Weakened by scurvy, frostbite, and exhaustion, as is evident in the photograph, the five explorers set out on the eight-hundred-mile journey back to their base ship. [7] One member of the party, overcome by exhaustion and injuries, died before half the journey had been completed. [8] On March 15, another member, leaving the camp at night, walked deliberately to his death in a violent blizzard. [9] Eight months later, a rescue mission, sent to find out what had happened, found the bodies of Scott and his companions. [10] Today, the ill-fated Scott expedition, acclaimed for its heroism, is better known than the successful Amundsen expedition.

The Gerund

17h. A *gerund* is a verb form ending in *–ing* that is used as a noun.

Like nouns, gerunds can be subjects, predicate nominatives, direct objects, or objects of prepositions.

EXAMPLES **Reading** will increase your vocabulary. [subject]
One popular winter sport is **tobogganing**. [predicate nominative]
I enjoyed **seeing** you again. [direct object]
She cleared a path by **shoveling** the snow. [object of a preposition]

▶ EXERCISE 7 **Identifying Gerunds and Participles**

Identify the verbal in each of the following sentences and tell whether it is a gerund or a participle. If the verbal is a gerund, tell how it is used: as *subject, predicate nominative, direct object,* or *object of a preposition.* If the verbal is a participle, tell what word it modifies.

EXAMPLES **1.** Sleeping on the job is foolish.
           1. *Sleeping, gerund—subject*
           2. Let sleeping dogs lie.
           2. *sleeping, participle—dogs*

GRAMMAR

1. Their giggling annoyed the other viewers.
2. Virginia looks forward to fishing.
3. After studying, how do you relax?
4. I am reading a fascinating mystery novel.
5. Making friends in a new school can be difficult.
6. The highlight of the season was watching our team win the regional tournament.
7. Spinning one full turn, she performed a pirouette.
8. Carlota makes money by walking dogs.
9. My grandmother and I enjoy digging for clams.
10. Sensing the danger nearby, he shouted for help.

The Gerund Phrase

17i. A *gerund phrase* consists of a gerund and any modifiers and complements it may have. The entire gerund phrase acts as a noun.

Because gerunds act as nouns, they may be modified by adjectives and adjective phrases.

EXAMPLE **The sudden shattering of glass** broke the silence. [The article *the,* the adjective *sudden,* and the adjective phrase *of glass* modify the gerund *shattering.* The gerund *shattering* is the subject of the sentence.]

Because gerunds are verb forms, they may also be modified by adverbs and adverb phrases.

EXAMPLE She enjoys **hiking in the mountains occasionally.** [The adverb phrase *in the mountains* and the adverb *occasionally* modify the gerund *hiking.* The gerund *hiking* is the direct object of the verb *enjoys.*]

NOTE: When a noun or pronoun comes before a gerund, it should be in the possessive form.

      EXAMPLES **Eli's** dancing won him first prize in the contest.
                   His dancing has greatly improved since last year.

EXERCISE 8   **Writing Sentences with Gerund Phrases**

Have you ever played Build a Story? The first player writes the story opener, and then the next player adds another sentence. The players take turns adding sentences to make up a story. With a friend or classmate, try your hand at building a story. A special requirement for this version of the game is that each sentence must contain a gerund. Use gerunds as subjects, objects of the verb, predicate nominatives, or objects of prepositions. Be able to tell how each gerund is used. [Note: Make sure that each player goes five rounds.]

EXAMPLES   Player 1: *At first we enjoyed walking in the forest. (direct object)*
Player 2: *Seeing the grizzly bear, however, gave us a scare. (subject)*

The Infinitive

17j.   An *infinitive* is a verb form, usually preceded by *to,* that can be used as a noun, an adjective, or an adverb.

INFINITIVES	
USED AS	**EXAMPLES**
Nouns	**To err** is human. [*To err* is the subject.] His dream is **to travel.** [*To travel* is the predicate nominative.] Betty wants **to act.** [*To act* is the direct object of the verb *wants*.]
Adjectives	The candidate **to believe** is Villegas. [*To believe* modifies the noun *candidate.*] She is the one **to ask.** [*To ask* modifies the pronoun *one.*]
Adverbs	Grandmother has come **to stay.** [*To stay* modifies the verb *has come.*] The favored team was slow **to score.** [*To score* modifies the adjective *slow.*]

NOTE: The word *to* plus a noun or a pronoun (*to bed, to the movies, to her*) is a prepositional phrase, not an infinitive.

▶ EXERCISE 9   **Identifying and Classifying Infinitives**

Identify the infinitives in the following sentences and tell how each is used: as *subject, predicate nominative, direct object, adjective,* or *adverb.*

1. Do you want to meet at the corner?
2. We are eager to go.
3. One way to relax is to listen to classical music.
4. I am ready to leave.
5. We are waiting to talk with the principal.
6. The soup is still too hot to eat.
7. To excel, one must practice.
8. This summer she hopes to travel in the West.
9. To hike through the woods is fun.
10. To forgive is sometimes difficult.

The Infinitive Phrase

17k. An *infinitive phrase* consists of an infinitive together with its modifiers and complements. The entire infinitive phrase can be used as a noun, an adjective, or an adverb.

EXAMPLES   **To hit a curve ball solidly is very difficult.** [The infinitive phrase, used as a noun, is the subject of the sentence. The infinitive *to hit* has an object, *ball,* and is modified by the adverb *solidly.*]

She wants **to be a truck driver.** [The infinitive phrase, used as a noun, is the direct object of the verb *wants.* The infinitive *to be* is followed by the predicate nominative *truck driver.*]

It is sometimes difficult **to listen attentively.** [The infinitive phrase, used as an adverb, modifies the adjective *difficult.* The infinitive *to listen* is modified by the adverb *attentively.*]

NOTE: An infinitive may have a subject.

EXAMPLE   I asked **him to come** to my party. [*Him* is the subject of the infinitive *to come.*]

The infinitive, together with its subject, complements, and modifiers, is sometimes called an **infinitive clause.**

GRAMMAR

The Infinitive Without *to*

Sometimes the *to* that is the sign of the infinitive is omitted in a sentence.

EXAMPLES   Did you watch her (to) **play** volleyball?
He will help us (to) **paddle** the canoe.
We don't dare (to) **go** outside during the storm.

▶ EXERCISE 10   **Identifying and Classifying Infinitive Phrases**

Identify the infinitive phrases in the following sentences and tell how each is used: as *subject, predicate nominative, direct object, adjective,* or *adverb.*

1. Our assignment was to read *I Know Why the Caged Bird Sings.*
2. We were asked to examine Maya Angelou's descriptions of her childhood.
3. To grow up in Stamps, Arkansas, in the 1930s was to know great hardship.
4. Maya Angelou tried to show the everyday lives of African Americans during the Great Depression.
5. To accomplish this purpose meant including many descriptions; one such passage told about the process for curing pork sausage.
6. Angelou has an extraordinary ability to capture vivid details in her writing.
7. She helps us see her grandmother's store through the eyes of a fascinated child.
8. Angelou was eager to experience life beyond her hometown.
9. Her talents and ambition enabled her to gain success as a writer, a dancer, and an actress.
10. To dramatize her African American heritage was a dream she realized by writing a television series.

▶ REVIEW B   **Identifying Types of Verbals and Verbal Phrases**

Identify the ten verbals or verbal phrases in the following paragraph. Then tell whether each verbal or verbal phrase is a *participle,* a *gerund,* or an *infinitive.*

EXAMPLE   [1] Looking at these control panels in the flight deck of a jumbo passenger jet, most of us feel completely lost.

1. *Looking at these control panels in the flight deck of a jumbo passenger jet—participle*

[1] Fortunately, there are trained people in the flight deck who know how to use these controls and instruments. [2] Sitting in front of identical control panels, both the captain and the first officer can fly the plane. [3] The captain, who uses the left-hand panel, operates a lever called a yoke, which controls the wing flaps and helps in steering the plane. [4] Operating the brake panels is another one of the captain's jobs. [5] To the captain's right is the first officer, whose job is to help the captain. [6] The throttle, which governs the engines' ability to move the plane forward, is located between the captain and the first officer. [7] Some of the bewildering instruments that you see are parts of the plane's navigation, autopilot, and communication systems. [8] At another station in the flight deck, the flight engineer monitors gauges and operates switches to control the plane's generators and the pressure and temperature in the cabin.

▶ REVIEW C   **Identifying Verbal Phrases**

Identify the twenty verbal phrases in the following paragraph. Then, tell what kind each phrase is: *participial, gerund,* or *infinitive.*

[1] Finding a summer job can be a difficult task. [2] The first step is to scan the classified ads listed in your local newspaper. [3] After discovering available opportunities, you can embark on the second step, which is matching your skills with the requirements of a specific job. [4] In most cases you can then contact a prospective employer by making a phone call or by writing a letter requesting an interview. [5] If you are asked to interview for a job, be sure to take care in preparing for the interview. [6] To make a good impression, be sure to arrive on time, to dress neatly, and to speak courteously. [7] Remember to avoid such nervous habits as constantly checking your watch or shuffling your feet. [8] By presenting yourself as calm, confident, and courteous, you may hear the magic words "We'd like you to work for us."

Appositives and Appositive Phrases

17l. An *appositive* is a noun or pronoun placed beside another noun or pronoun to identify or explain it.

EXAMPLES   My cousin **Bryan** is my best friend. [The noun *Bryan* is an appositive that identifies the noun *cousin.*]
My cousin **Bryan** is my best friend. [The noun *Bryan* is an appositive that identifies the noun *cousin.*]
Soledad, an excellent **driver,** has never had an accident. [The noun *driver* is an appositive that explains the noun *Soledad.*]

17m. An *appositive phrase* is made up of an appositive and its modifiers.

EXAMPLES   We saw three birds, **two robins and a cardinal.**
His grandparents, **the Vescuzos,** live on Miller Road, **a wide street lined with beech trees.**

An appositive or appositive phrase usually follows the noun or pronoun it refers to. Sometimes, though, it comes before the noun or pronoun.

EXAMPLE   **A diligent and quick-witted student,** Mark always gets good grades.

Appositives and appositive phrases are usually set off by commas unless the appositive is a single word closely related to the preceding noun or pronoun. Commas are always used with appositives that refer to proper nouns.

EXAMPLES   My sister **Karen** is a tennis player.
Dr. Rosen, **our family dentist,** is a marathon runner.

EXERCISE 11   **Identifying Appositives and Appositive Phrases**

Identify the appositives and appositive phrases in each of the following sentences. Be prepared to tell which word each one identifies or explains.

1. Soccer, my favorite sport, is very popular in South America and Europe.
2. The internationally famous soccer star Pelé is from Brazil.
3. Hausa, a Sudanese language, is widely used in western Africa.
4. Have you met my teacher Mr. Zolo?
5. My youngest sister, Susan, speaks fluent Spanish.

PICTURE THIS

You are looking at some real winners. As a reporter for the local newspaper, you just saw these contestants win

at the annual dog show. Now you have to write a short news article on the show. Tell about the winners—their names, their breeds, their owners, their personalities. Describe how the winners were chosen, and tell why each winner was judged to be the best in its class. You may also want to describe other features of the show, such as the setting, the size and enthusiasm of the crowd, or the owners' preshow grooming of the contestants. In your article, use at least five appositives and appositive phrases. Newspaper articles usually present the most important information first, so be sure to include the *who, what, when,* and *where* of the dog show in the beginning of your article.

Subject: a dog show
Audience: local newspaper readers
Purpose: to inform

REVIEW D   ### Identifying Verbal and Appositive Phrases

The following paragraph contains ten phrases. Identify each phrase as a *participial phrase,* a *gerund phrase,* an *infinitive phrase,* or an *appositive phrase.*

[1] The Brooklyn Bridge, a remarkable feat of design, spans the East River in New York City. [2] Linking the boroughs of Brooklyn and Manhattan, it was once the longest suspension bridge in the world. [3] Most of the pedestrians who cross the bridge are impressed by the grandeur of its graceful cables—a sensation the postcard on the next page cannot fully evoke. [4] To support the twin towers on the bridge, the brilliant John A. Roebling, its engineer, designed airtight caissons filled with concrete. [5] Working underwater on the caissons was painstakingly slow and extremely dangerous. [6] The workers also faced great danger when they had to spin the cables from one side of the river to the other. [7] Because of these hazards, the bridge is remembered not only for being a masterpiece of engineering but also for having cost the lives of many of its builders.

Review: Posttest 1

Identifying Prepositional, Verbal, and Appositive Phrases

Identify each italicized phrase in the following paragraphs as a *prepositional phrase*, a *participial phrase*, a *gerund phrase*, an *infinitive phrase*, or an *appositive phrase*.

EXAMPLE   An interesting profession [1] *to consider as a career* is
           [2] *practicing law.*
           1. *to consider as a career—inf.*
           2. *practicing law—ger.*

Susana, [1] *our next-door neighbor,* wanted [2] *to become an attorney.* After she earned a degree [3] *from a four-year college,* she took the Law School Admissions Test [4] *to gain acceptance at an approved law school.* [5] *Having completed three full years of law school,* Susana was then awarded a J.D. degree. Before [6] *practicing law,* however, she took an exam [7] *required by the state board of bar examiners.* Only after [8] *passing this exam* was she ready [9] *to be admitted to the bar* and [10] *to practice law.*

[11] *Working as an attorney,* Susana provides service and advice [12] *relating to legal rights.* Although some attorneys try hard [13] *to keep cases out of court,* Susana enjoys the challenge [14] *of presenting cases to a jury.* [15] *Representing a*

client in court, however, is only part [16] *of Susana's job.* She devotes hours to [17] *gathering enough evidence* [18] *to defend a client.* She also spends time [19] *on research* and is required [20] *to write numerous reports.*

Review: Posttest 2

Writing Sentences with Phrases

Write ten sentences, following the directions below for each sentence. Underline the phrase in each sentence.

EXAMPLE   **1.** Use *to get there from here* as an infinitive phrase acting as an adjective.
         1. *What is the fastest way* <u>*to get there from here*</u>?

1. Use *in the garage* as an adjective phrase.
2. Use *for our English class* as an adverb phrase.
3. Use *from an encyclopedia* as an adverb phrase.
4. Use *by train* as an adverb phrase.
5. Use *walking by the lake* as a participial phrase.
6. Use *playing the piano* as a gerund phrase that is the subject of the sentence.
7. Use *to hit a home run* as an infinitive phrase that is the direct object of the verb.
8. Use *to find the answer to that question* as an infinitive phrase acting as an adverb.
9. Use *the new student in our class* as an appositive phrase.
10. Use *my favorite writer* as an appositive phrase.

18 THE CLAUSE

Independent and Subordinate Clauses

Diagnostic Test

A. Identifying and Classifying Clauses

Identify the italicized clause in each of the following sentences as an *independent clause* or a *subordinate clause.* Also, identify each subordinate clause as an *adjective clause,* an *adverb clause,* or a *noun clause.*

EXAMPLES   **1.** A soccer field measures 100–130 yards by 50–100 yards, and *the netted goals at each end of the field are 8 yards wide by 8 feet high.*
      1. *independent clause*

      2. Soccer, *which is the national sport of many European and Latin American countries,* has enjoyed only limited success in the United States.
      2. *subordinate clause—adjective clause*

1. During a career *that spanned twenty years,* Pelé was probably the most popular athlete in the world.
2. He was named Edson Arantes do Nascimento, but *hardly anyone recognizes that name.*
3. Soccer fans the world over, however, knew Pelé, *who was considered the world's best soccer player.*
4. *While he was still a teenager,* he led his Brazilian team-mates to the first of their three World Cup titles.
5. *Whenever he played,* his skill and agility awed fans.
6. Once, he juggled the ball on his foot for fifty yards, eluding four opponents *who were trying to take the ball away from him.*
7. *That he soon became a superstar* is not surprising.
8. *Even though soccer has never become as popular as baseball or football in the United States,* Pelé managed to spark considerable interest in the game.
9. After he signed with the New York Cosmos, *people flocked to the stands to watch him play.*
10. They soon recognized *that Pelé was an entertainer as well as an athlete.*

B. Classifying Sentences According to Structure

Classify each sentence in the following paragraph as *simple, compound, complex,* or *compound-complex.*

[11] Because tennis is so physically demanding, it's a sport in which strong young players can really shine. [12] Steffi Graf of Germany began playing tennis profession-ally at the age of thirteen. [13] Graf was still a teenager when she won the four Grand Slam tennis championships and an Olympic gold medal in 1988. [14] Another Olympic winner, Zina Garrison-Jackson, began playing tennis at the age of ten, and at seventeen, she won the junior sin-gles titles at Wimbledon and the U.S. Open. [15] The Ger-man tennis star Boris Becker won his first tournament competitions at the age of nine, but he didn't become a professional player until he graduated from high school. [16] Jennifer Capriati, who was born on Long Island, New York, won many national and international tennis compe-titions and had earned nearly eighty thousand dollars by the age of fourteen. [17] Another American player, Andre

GRAMMAR

Agassi, started serving on a tennis court at the age of two, and he, too, excelled at an early age. **[18]** Agassi won six major tournaments when he was only eighteen. **[19]** Tracy Austin and Chris Evert also started young; in fact, Tracy Austin was only sixteen years old when she made headlines by winning the women's title at the U.S. Open. **[20]** In tennis, young players really can become big winners.

Kinds of Clauses

18a. A *clause* is a group of words that contains a verb and its subject and is used as part of a sentence.

Every clause has a subject and a verb, but not all clauses express a complete thought. Those that do are called *independent clauses.* Those that do not make complete sense by themselves are called *subordinate clauses.*

Independent Clauses

18b. An *independent* (or *main*) *clause* expresses a complete thought and can stand by itself as a sentence.

EXAMPLES   The outfielders were missing easy fly balls.
          The infielders were throwing wildly.

Independent clauses that express related ideas can be joined together in a single sentence. Often, the clauses are linked by one of the coordinating conjunctions (*and, but, or, nor, for, so, yet*).

EXAMPLE   The outfielders were missing easy fly balls, **and** the infielders were throwing wildly.

Independent clauses can also be joined by a semicolon.

EXAMPLE   The outfielders were missing easy fly balls; the infielders were throwing wildly.

A conjunctive adverb can be used after the semicolon to express the relationship between the independent clauses.

EXAMPLE   The outfielders were missing easy fly balls; **moreover,** the infielders were throwing wildly.

☞ **REFERENCE NOTE:** See pages 816–819 for more information on using semicolons between independent clauses.

Subordinate Clauses

18c.   A *subordinate* (or *dependent*) *clause* does not express a complete thought and cannot stand alone.

Subordinate means "less important." Words such as *who, that, because, if, when, although,* and *since* signal that the clause they introduce is subordinate and must be joined to an independent clause to make a complete sentence.

SUBORDINATE   who spoke to our class yesterday
CLAUSES   that many students are eligible for scholarships
         because no students have applied for them

SENTENCES   The woman **who spoke to our class yesterday** told us about sources of financial aid for college applicants.
         She said **that many students are eligible for scholarships.**
         Some scholarships are still available **because no students have applied for them.**

▶ EXERCISE 1   **Identifying Independent and Subordinate Clauses**

For each sentence in the following paragraph, identify the italicized clause as *independent* or *subordinate.*

[1] *Whenever I think of Barbara Jordan,* I remember her as she looks in this picture, delivering the commencement address at my sister's graduation in 1986. [2] In front of a huge audience, *Jordan spoke eloquently about the importance of values in our society.* [3] *Of course, her choice of subject matter*

surprised no one since Jordan had long been known as an important ethical force in American politics. [4] *When Jordan began her public service career in 1966,* she became the first African American woman to serve in the Texas Legislature. [5] In 1972, she won a seat in the U.S. House of Representatives, *where only one other black woman— Shirley Chisholm—had ever been a member.* [6] However, Jordan was still not widely recognized *until she gave the*

 *keynote speech at the 1976 Democratic National Convention.* [7] Seen on television by millions of people, *Jordan immediately gained national attention.* [8] Two years later, Jordan decided *that she would retire from national politics.* [9] *After she returned to Texas in 1978,* Jordan taught at the University of Texas at Austin. [10] From 1991 until her death in 1996, she served on various government committees and used *what she had learned in her many years of public service* to fight corruption in politics.

Complements and Modifiers in Subordinate Clauses

A subordinate clause may contain complements and modifiers.

EXAMPLES   Since she told **us** the **truth** . . . [*Us* is the indirect object of *told; truth* is the direct object of *told.*]
When I am **busy** . . . [*Busy* is a predicate adjective modifying *I.*]
After he had cooked **for us** . . . [*For us* is an adverb phrase modifying *had cooked.*]
The portrait **that** he painted . . . [*That* is the direct object of *painted.*]
We couldn't tell **who** they were. [*Who* is a predicate nominative: They were *who.*]

 EXERCISE 2 **Identifying Subjects, Verbs, and Complements in Subordinate Clauses**

Identify the subject and the verb in each italicized subordinate clause in the following sentences. Then identify any complements in the clause as *direct object, predicate nominative,* or *indirect object.*

EXAMPLE **1.** *After he shows us his new boat,* we will go swimming.
1. *he—subject; shows—verb; us—indirect object; boat—direct object*

1. We couldn't see *who had won the race.*
2. They couldn't tell *who the winner was.*
3. She is the celebrity *whom we saw at the restaurant.*
4. Look for the mouse *that you heard last night.*
5. He spotted a horse *that galloped away.*
6. *After we passed the test,* we celebrated.
7. Do you know *which country she is from?*
8. *Because you had not given us the right address,* we missed the party.
9. The package will arrive on time *if you ship it today.*
10. *Until Mike lent me this book,* I had never heard of John Steinbeck.

The Uses of Subordinate Clauses

Subordinate clauses can be used in sentences as either adjectives, adverbs, or nouns.

The Adjective Clause

18d. An *adjective clause* is a subordinate clause that modifies a noun or a pronoun.

An adjective clause always follows the word it modifies. If the clause is necessary, or *essential,* to the meaning of the sentence, it is not set off with commas. If the clause simply adds information and is *nonessential* to the meaning of the sentence, commas are used to set it off.

EXAMPLES   The novel **that I'm reading now** is about the Irish
revolt of 1798. [The clause is necessary to identify the
novel, so it is not set off by commas.]
Our town's civic center, **which was renovated last
year,** has been declared a landmark. [The clause adds
nonessential information, so it is set off by commas.]

☞ REFERENCE NOTE: See pages 797–799, rule 25i, for help in
deciding whether a clause is essential or nonessential.

Relative Pronouns

Adjective clauses are usually introduced by *relative
pronouns.*

Relative Pronouns				
who	whom	whose	which	that

These pronouns are called *relative pronouns* because they
relate an adjective clause to the word the clause modifies—
the antecedent of the relative pronoun. Each relative pronoun also has a function within the adjective clause.

EXAMPLES   Isabella Baumfree was an abolitionist **who is better
known as Sojourner Truth.** [The relative pronoun
who relates the adjective clause to *abolitionist. Who*
also is the subject of the adjective clause.]

She is the person **whom I trust most.** [*Whom* relates
the adjective clause to *person. Whom* is also the
direct object of the verb *trust* in the adjective clause.]

The topic **about *which* he is writing** is controversial.
[*Which* relates the adjective clause to *topic* and is the
object of the preposition *about* in the adjective
clause.]

Do you know the name of the group **whose
recording is number one on the charts?** [*Whose*
relates the adjective clause to *group. Whose* is also a
possessive pronoun modifying *recording* in the
adjective clause.]

Sometimes the relative pronoun is left out of a sentence. In such cases, the pronoun is understood, and it
still has a function in the adjective clause.

EXAMPLE **Ms. Chung is the legislator** *[that* or *whom]* **we met.**
[The relative pronoun *that* or *whom* is understood. It
relates the adjective clause to *legislator* and is the
direct object of the verb *met* in the adjective clause.]

The relative adverbs *where* and *when* are sometimes
used to introduce adjective clauses.

EXAMPLES **Here is the spot *where* we will have lunch.**
This is the season *when* it rains almost every day.

▶ EXERCISE 3 **Identifying Adjective Clauses**

Identify each adjective clause in the following sentences,
and underline the relative pronoun or relative adverb in
the clause. Then, tell what word the relative pronoun or
relative adverb refers to.

EXAMPLE **1. The topic that Melissa chose for her paper was a
difficult one.**
1. *that Melissa chose for her paper—topic*

1. A speech community is a group of people who
speak the same language.
2. There are speech communities that contain millions
of people and some that have only a few.
3. The first language that you learn is called your
native language.
4. People who master another language are bilingual.
5. People who conduct business internationally often
need to know more than one language.
6. English, French, and Spanish, which many
diplomats can speak, are among the six official
languages of the United Nations.
7. Russian, Chinese, and Arabic are the other three
languages that are used officially at the UN.
8. People for whom language study is important
include telephone operators, hotel managers, and
police officers.
9. Many tourists each year find themselves in parts of
the world where they would benefit from knowing
the language spoken locally.
10. French, for example, is a language that is widely
understood in parts of Europe, Africa, and
Southeast Asia.

The Adverb Clause

18e. An *adverb clause* is a subordinate clause that modifies a verb, an adjective, or an adverb.

An adverb clause tells

how	when
where	why
to what extent	under what condition

An adverb clause may modify the action of the *main verb* (the verb in the sentence's independent clause).

EXAMPLES   Donna sounds **as if she has caught a cold.** [*As if she has caught a cold* tells how Donna sounds.]
Before we left, we turned off the lights. [*Before we left* tells when we turned off the lights.]
You will see our house **where the road turns right.** [*Where the road turns right* tells where you will see our house.]
As long as he starts early, he will arrive on time. [*As long as he starts early* tells under what condition he will arrive on time.]
Will you move over **so that I can see?** [*So that I can see* tells why I want you to move over.]

☞ **REFERENCE NOTE:** Introductory adverb clauses are usually set off with commas. See page 801.

An adverb clause may also modify an adjective or an adverb in the independent clause.

EXAMPLES   Your stereo is louder **than it should be.** [The adverb clause modifies the adjective *louder,* telling to what extent the stereo is louder.]
The skates cost less **because we got them on sale.** [The adverb clause modifies the adverb *less,* telling under what condition the skates cost less.]

Subordinating Conjunctions

Adverb clauses are introduced by *subordinating conjunctions.* Unlike relative pronouns, which introduce adjective clauses, subordinating conjunctions do not serve a function in the clause they introduce.

GRAMMAR

Common Subordinating Conjunctions

after	before	unless
although	even though	until
as	if	when
as if	in order that	whenever
as long as	since	where
as soon as	so that	wherever
as though	than	whether
because	though	while

NOTE: Many of the words in this list can be used as other parts of speech, such as adverbs and prepositions.

EXERCISE 4 Identifying Adverb Clauses and Subordinating Conjunctions

Identify the adverb clause in each sentence of the following paragraph, and circle the subordinating conjunction.

[1] Because the house had been vacant for so long, we had to clean up the lawn and gardens. [2] The grass looked as if it hadn't been cut in months. [3] Ruth began mowing the lawn while Lou and I weeded the flower beds. [4] We had to borrow some tools because the weeds were so thick. [5] We hadn't been able to cut through the heavy undergrowth until we started using a machete. [6] Before we pulled out the weeds, we couldn't even see the roses. [7] We stacked the debris in a mound so that it could be hauled away later. [8] After Ruth had mowed the lawn, she was exhausted. [9] We all stretched out in the shade when we stopped for a rest. [10] Long hours in the sun had made us feel as though the day would never end.

EXERCISE 5 Writing Sentences with Adverb Clauses

Have you written any good songs lately? What? You say you don't write songs! Then here's your chance to give it a try. You don't have to write the whole song. Instead, think of ten song titles and a first line for each song. In each first line, use a different subordinating conjunction from the list given at the top of this page.

EXAMPLE   Title: *Baby Sitters' Blues*
First Line: *If only you'd eat your carrots, I'd let you watch TV.*

▶ REVIEW A   **Identifying Adjective and Adverb Clauses**

Identify the subordinate clauses in the following paragraph. Then, tell whether each is an *adjective clause* or an *adverb clause*.

[1] In 1978, the aeronauts Ben Abruzzo, Max Anderson, and Larry Newman, whose home was Albuquerque, New Mexico, became the first people to pilot a balloon across the Atlantic Ocean. [2] Although Abruzzo and Anderson had been forced to land in the ocean in an earlier attempt in *Double Eagle*, they didn't give up. [3] Instead, they acquired a new balloon, which they named *Double Eagle II.* [4] Newman joined them because experience had shown the need for a third crew member. [5] On its journey from Maine to France, *Double Eagle II* was airborne for 137 hours, which is a little less than six days. [6] The aeronauts stressed the fact that *Double Eagle II* didn't just drift across the Atlantic; they flew it across. [7] Abruzzo, Anderson, and Newman had to understand meteorology so that they could take advantage of favorable winds. [8] They also had to regulate their altitude constantly by adjusting their supply of helium and by losing ballast, as the balloonists shown here are doing. [9] When the balloon gained too much altitude, the crew lowered it by releasing some of the gas. [10] If the balloon lost altitude, the crew raised it by discarding ballast.

GRAMMAR

The Noun Clause

18f. A *noun clause* is a subordinate clause used as a noun.

A noun clause may be used as a subject, a predicate nominative, a direct object, an indirect object, or the object of a preposition.

SUBJECT	**What I need** is my own room.
DIRECT OBJECT	She believes **that lost time is never found again.**
INDIRECT OBJECT	The store owner will give **whoever wins the contest** a valuable prize.
OBJECT OF PREPOSITION	She has written an article about **how she was elected to the Senate.**
PREDICATE NOMINATIVE	The happiest time in my life was **when we went to Colombia for the summer.**

Noun clauses are usually introduced by

that	where	whoever	whose
what	whether	whom	why
when	who	whomever	how

☞ REFERENCE NOTE: Many of these words can be used to introduce adjective clauses. See page 601.

Sometimes the introductory word has a function in the clause and sometimes it doesn't.

EXAMPLES Do you know **what the problem is?** [The introductory word *what* is a predicate nominative—*the problem is what.*]

I know **that she is worried.** [The introductory word *that* has no function in the clause.]

In some sentences, the word that introduces a noun clause can be omitted.

EXAMPLE He told us **attendance is improving.** [The introductory word *that* is understood.]

She is the judge **we interviewed.** [The introductory word *whom* is understood.]

▶ EXERCISE 6 — **Identifying and Classifying Noun Clauses**

Identify the noun clauses in the following sentences. Then, tell how each clause is used: as *subject, predicate nominative, direct object, indirect object,* or *object of a preposition.* [Note: A sentence may have more than one noun clause.]

1. Mr. Perkins, the band director, announced that we would play at half time this week.
2. We can never predict whether he will choose a march or a show tune.
3. He always gives whoever will play each selection a chance to express an opinion of it.
4. He is genuinely interested in what we think of his choices.
5. A drummer once told Mr. Perkins she did not like most show tunes.
6. How she could say that was a mystery to me.
7. Mr. Perkins told us we would play a medley of marches.
8. What everyone wanted to know was who would play the solos.
9. He understands why that was our first question.
10. The crowd always applauds enthusiastically for whoever plays a solo.

▶ REVIEW B — **Identifying Adjective, Adverb, and Noun Clauses**

Each sentence in the following paragraph has at least one subordinate clause. Identify each subordinate clause, and tell whether it is an *adjective clause, adverb clause,* or *noun clause.*

[1] What's so special about the Blue Grotto, or *Grotta Azzurra,* as the Italians say? [2] In the painting on the next page, you can see that the color and the hidden location of the Blue Grotto have made it famous. [3] The grotto is a cavern that can be entered only from the sea. [4] It is located on the west side of the Italian island of Capri, which lies at the entrance to the Bay of Naples. [5] Since the only opening to the cavern is approximately three feet high, visitors must lie down in a rowboat to enter it. [6] The

sapphire blue of the water inside the spacious, oval-shaped cavern is caused by light that is refracted through the deep pool. [7] Although the calm, blue water looks inviting, the grotto is no longer a swimming hole. [8] In the past, however, people who lived in the area greatly enjoyed swimming there. [9] Tour guides tell whoever goes there that centuries ago Tiberius, the Roman emperor, used the Blue Grotto as his private swimming pool. [10] Seeing it today, you would agree that it's a pool fit for an emperor.

Sandro Chia, *Grotta azzurra* (1980). Oil on canvas, 147 cm × 208 cm. Courtesy Galerie Bruno Bischofberger, Zürich, Switzerland. © 1998 Sandro Chia/Licensed by VAGA, New York, NY.

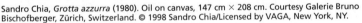

WRITING APPLICATION

Using Subordination to Reflect Your Thoughts

When you were a child, you probably used short, choppy sentences to express your thoughts. Almost all children do. But as you got older, your thoughts became more complex, and so did your sentences.

IMMATURE   Mary Cassatt was an American painter. I enjoy her works. She was an Impressionist.

GRAMMAR

MATURE   I enjoy the works of Mary Cassatt, who was an American impressionist painter.

How was subordination used to make the second example sound more mature than the first?

▶ WRITING ACTIVITY

The student council has decided to decorate your school with prints of popular artworks. To decide which prints to get, the council has asked for recommendations, along with brief descriptions, for artworks that students would like to see. Write two paragraphs about two works (one paragraph on each work) that you would like to recommend. Use specific details and include at least five subordinate clauses.

Prewriting   Think of two paintings or prints that are your favorites. If you do not know their titles, try looking in books or asking a librarian or art teacher to find out what they are titled. Think about why you particularly like these works, and jot down your reasons.

Writing   As you write, you may think of additional details and reasons. If you do, pause for a moment and consider how they fit in with the rest of your notes. Add to your rough draft any of this new information that fits in smoothly.

Evaluating and Revising   Read through your paragraphs to be sure they each have a topic sentence supported by your reasons for recommending a specific artwork. Check to see that you have used a total of at least five subordinate clauses in the two paragraphs. If you have not, try combining sentences by creating adjective, adverb, or noun clauses.

Proofreading   Put your paragraphs aside for a while, and then read them again, looking for errors in grammar, punctuation, and spelling. Pay special attention to the proper use of the relative pronouns *which, that, who,* and *whom.* (See pages 751 and 661–662). Also, be sure that you have punctuated all subordinate clauses correctly (see pages 797–801).

Sentences Classified According to Structure

The *structure* of a sentence is determined by the number and types of clauses it has.

18g. Sentences are classified according to their structure as *simple, compound, complex,* or *compound-complex.*

(1) A *simple sentence* has one independent clause and no subordinate clauses. It may have a compound subject, a compound verb, and any number of phrases.

EXAMPLES
          S   S   V
Cora and **Kareem bought** party supplies at the mall.

                S   V   V
Later, **they drove** to school and **decorated** the cafeteria for the Latin Club's annual banquet.

(2) A *compound sentence* has two or more independent clauses but no subordinate clauses.

A compound sentence is actually two or more simple sentences joined together either by a comma and a coordinating conjunction, by a semicolon, or by a semicolon and a conjunctive adverb such as *therefore, however,* or *consequently.*

EXAMPLES
          S   V
Cora hung colorful streamers from the ceiling, and

      S   V
Kareem set party favors on the tables.

                     S   V   S
After an hour, **they took** a short break; then **they**

V
went back to work.

      S   V
They agreed not to take any more breaks; otherwise,

      S   V
they would be late getting home.

☞ REFERENCE NOTE: See pages 796 and 816–819 for more information on punctuating compound sentences.

NOTE: Don't confuse a compound predicate in a simple sentence with the two subjects and two predicates in a compound sentence.

COMPOUND
PREDICATE
$$\overset{\text{S}}{}\quad\overset{\text{V}}{}$$
To pass the time, **they talked** about school

$$\overset{\text{V}}{}$$
and **told** stories about their families.

COMPOUND
SENTENCE
$$\overset{\text{S}}{}\quad\overset{\text{V}}{}$$
To pass the time, **they talked** about school,

$$\overset{\text{S}}{}\quad\overset{\text{V}}{}$$
and **they told** stories about their families.

(3) A *complex sentence* has one independent clause and *at least* one subordinate clause.

EXAMPLE
$$\qquad\quad\overset{\text{S}}{}\quad\overset{\text{V}}{}\qquad\qquad\qquad\overset{\text{S}}{}$$
When **they had finished** their work, **they**

$$\overset{\text{V}}{}$$
complimented each other on the results.

(4) A *compound-complex sentence* has two or more independent clauses and *at least* one subordinate clause.

EXAMPLE
$$\quad\overset{\text{S}}{}\quad\overset{\text{V}}{}$$
Cora waited for just the right moment to ask

$$\qquad\qquad\qquad\qquad\qquad\qquad\overset{\text{S}}{}$$
Kareem to go to the banquet with her, and **he**

$$\quad\overset{\text{V}}{}$$
promptly **accepted** her invitation, adding that

$$\overset{\text{S}}{}\qquad\overset{\text{V}}{}$$
he had been planning to ask her the same thing.

REFERENCE NOTE: For information on how sentences are classified according to purpose, see pages 565–566.

EXERCISE 7   **Classifying Sentences According to Structure**

Classify each of the sentences in the following paragraph as *simple, compound, complex,* or *compound-complex.*

[1] Our club, the Key Club, sponsored a rummage sale and requested donations from everyone at school. [2] We accepted whatever was donated, but we welcomed housewares most. [3] The principal donated a vacuum cleaner; the coach contributed a set of dishes; and several of the teachers provided towels and sheets. [4] We sold

almost everything that had been donated, and we celebrated our success with pitchers of lemonade. [5] Afterward, we gave all the profits that we had made from the
sale to the city's homeless shelter.

EXERCISE 8 **Using the Four Kinds of Sentences**

You and your family won a vacation to Hawaii. While you
were there, you attended this luau. *Luau* is a Hawaiian
word meaning "feast," and that's exactly what it was!
There were different kinds of meats and fruits to eat, and,
for entertainment, hula dancers and fire jugglers performed. Write five sentences describing the luau. If you
have ever eaten any of the foods that are shown, give
your impressions of them. Use at least one of each of the
four kinds of sentences—simple, compound, complex,
and compound-complex. Be prepared to identify the
kinds of sentences that you use.

EXAMPLE   **1.** *The fresh pineapple at the luau wasn't as sweet as
pineapple that comes in a can. (complex)*

PICTURE THIS

You are an adventurer in a strange land and have just
wandered into the mysterious place shown on the next
page. Before going one step farther, you decide to make
some notes about what you see. Write down your impressions of this scene. Think of reasons for the distinctive
mood of the place, and theorize about who may live here.

What should you explore first? Why? In your journal entries, include at least one simple sentence, one compound sentence, one complex sentence, and two compound-complex sentences.

Subject: thoughts at *The Rose Tower*
Audience: you and whoever may read your journal in the future
Purpose: to help you decide what to do next

Giorgio de Chirico, *The Rose Tower*. Peggy Guggenheim Collection.
© 1998 Giorgio de Chirico Foundation/Licensed by VAGA, New York, NY.

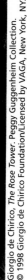

Review: Posttest 1

A. Identifying Independent and Subordinate Clauses; Classifying Subordinate Clauses

Identify each italicized clause in the following sentences as an *independent clause* or a *subordinate clause*. Then, classify each italicized subordinate clause as an *adjective clause*, an *adverb clause*, or a *noun clause*.

EXAMPLE   **1.** The Brooklyn Bridge, *which was built in the latter half of the nineteenth century,* was the world's first steel-wire suspension bridge.
          1. *subordinate clause—adjective clause*

1. The Brooklyn Bridge, *which spans the East River between Brooklyn and Manhattan in New York City,* is one of the engineering wonders of the world.
2. Massive granite towers *that are supported by concrete-filled shafts* are among its remarkable features.
3. *The bridge was designed and built by John and Washington Roebling, a father-and-son engineering team* who were pioneers in the use of steel-wire cables.
4. The steel-wire cables give the bridge a graceful appearance *that resembles a spider's web.*
5. *That the bridge combines strength with beauty* remains a tribute to the Roebling family.
6. The Roeblings discovered *that construction work could be both slow and dangerous.*
7. *Although she was not an engineer,* Nora Roebling assisted in the efforts to complete the bridge.
8. *Because they were required at times to work underwater in airtight chambers called caissons,* many workers, including Washington Roebling, suffered from caisson disease, or decompression sickness.
9. Sailors, *who were used to working at great heights,* were hired to string the miles of cable.
10. *John Roebling injured his foot at the work site,* and as a result, he died of tetanus shortly after construction was begun.

B. Classifying Sentences According to Structure

Classify each of the following sentences as *simple, compound, complex,* or *compound-complex.*

[11] After succeeding his father on the project, Washington Roebling was stricken by caisson disease; therefore, he was confined to bed. [12] The Roeblings lived in a house that was near the construction site, and Washington supervised the work through a telescope. [13] He dictated instructions to Nora, and she relayed them to the work crew. [14] Whether the work on the bridge could

have continued without her assistance is doubtful. [15] When the bridge was finally completed in 1883, President Chester A. Arthur attended the dedication ceremonies. [16] Because of his illness, Washington Roebling was unable to attend the ceremonies. [17] Instead, the president visited Roebling's home to honor the man who had struggled so valiantly to complete the bridge. [18] The bridge took fourteen years to build. [19] At the time of its completion, it was the world's longest suspension bridge. [20] The bridge is now more than a century old, and it still stands as a monument to the artistry, sacrifice, and determination of all the people who planned and built it.

Review: Posttest 2

Writing Sentences with Varied Structures

Write your own sentences according to the following guidelines.

EXAMPLE   **1.** a simple sentence with a compound subject
          1. *My aunt and uncle live nearby.*

1. a simple sentence with a compound verb
2. a compound sentence with two independent clauses joined by the conjunction *but*
3. a compound sentence with two independent clauses joined by a semicolon and a conjunctive adverb
4. a complex sentence with an adjective clause
5. a complex sentence beginning with an adverb clause
6. a complex sentence ending with an adverb clause
7. a complex sentence with a noun clause used as a direct object
8. a complex sentence with a noun clause used as the subject
9. a complex sentence with a noun clause used as the object of a preposition
10. a compound-complex sentence

19 AGREEMENT

Subject and Verb, Pronoun and Antecedent

Diagnostic Test

A. Selecting Verbs That Agree with Their Subjects

For each sentence, choose the verb in parentheses that agrees with the subject.

EXAMPLE   **1.** Both coats *(is, are)* on sale this week.
1. *are*

1. The jury (*has, have*) been paying close attention to the evidence in this case.
2. There (*is, are*) four herbs that almost any gardener can grow: basil, thyme, marjoram, and oregano.
3. All of these old letters (*was, were*) tied with ribbon and stored in a trunk in the attic.
4. Each of them (*is, are*) penned in bold, flowing handwriting, embellished with many flourishes.
5. Both Alicia and Isabel (*thinks, think*) that the former owner of the house put the letters in the attic.

6. Neither of them (*knows, know*) for sure who wrote that message.
7. The two songs we played in the Martin Luther King Day concert (*was, were*) written by Keneisha Watson.
8. Did you know that *archy & mehitabel* (*is, are*) a series of poems supposedly written by a cockroach that lives in a newspaper office with his friend, a cat?
9. Here (*is, are*) the latest scores of today's basketball games.
10. Neither potatoes nor peanuts (*is, are*) grown on this farm anymore.

B. Identifying Verbs That Agree with Their Subjects and Pronouns That Agree with Their Antecedents

In many of the following sentences, either a verb does not agree with its subject, or a pronoun does not agree with its antecedent. Identify each incorrect verb or pronoun, and give the correct form. If a sentence is correct, write *C*.

EXAMPLES
1. The flock of birds, almost blackening the sky, were an awe-inspiring sight.
1. *were—was*

2. Only a decade ago their number was declining.
2. *C*

11. The meeting got out of hand when the discussion period began since everyone tried to express their opinion at the same time.
12. There on the corner of your desk is the books that I returned and that you claimed you never received.
13. Two students from each class is going to the state capital to attend a special conference on education.
14. Each of them are expected to bring back a report on the conference so that classmates can get firsthand information.
15. Since they will be on vacation next month, neither Miguel nor his sister are going to enter the mixed-doubles tennis tournament.
16. The audience expressed their admiration for the dancer's grace and skill by applauding wildly.

17. After the senator had read the proposed amendment, anyone who disagreed with the ruling was allowed to state their reason.
18. This collection of old African American folk tales demonstrate the wisdom, humor, and creativity of my ancestors.
19. She is one of those competitive people who perform best under pressure.
20. Since neither of you have ever tasted fried plantains, my mother would like you to eat a Cuban meal at our house tonight.

Number

19a. When a word refers to one person or thing, it is *singular* in number. When a word refers to more than one, it is *plural* in number.

SINGULAR	video	child	I	thief	herself
PLURAL	videos	children	we	thieves	themselves

In general, nouns ending in *–s* are plural (*aunts, uncles, towns, crimes*); verbs ending in *–s* are singular (*gives, takes, does, has, is*).

 REFERENCE NOTE: For more information on the plural forms of nouns, see pages 877–880.

EXERCISE 1 **Identifying Words as Singular or Plural in Number**

Identify each of the words listed below as either *plural* or *singular*.

1. stories
2. one
3. several
4. applies
5. people
6. mouse
7. genius
8. civics
9. ability
10. says
11. data
12. has
13. both
14. mumps
15. woman
16. some
17. donates
18. donation
19. mathematics
20. many

Agreement of Subject and Verb

19b. A verb should agree with its subject in number.

(1) Singular subjects take singular verbs.

EXAMPLES   Earline **attends** college. [The singular verb *attends* agrees with the singular subject *Earline.*]
That boy **delivers** newspapers. [The singular verb *delivers* agrees with the singular subject *boy.*]

(2) Plural subjects take plural verbs.

EXAMPLES   They **attend** college. [The plural verb *attend* agrees with the plural subject *they.*]
Those boys **deliver** newspapers. [The plural verb *deliver* agrees with the plural subject *boys.*]

Verb phrases also agree in number with their subjects. In a verb phrase, only the first auxiliary (helping) verb changes form to agree with the subject.

EXAMPLES   Earline **is attending** college.
They **are attending** college.
A boy in my class **has been delivering** newspapers.
Two boys in my class **have been delivering** newspapers.

The form *were* is plural except when used with the singular *you* and in sentences that are contrary to fact.

EXAMPLES   **You were** right. [*You* used as subject]
If I were in charge, I would make some changes. [contrary to fact]

USAGE

▶ EXERCISE 2   **Selecting Verbs That Agree with Their Subjects**

Choose the verb in parentheses that agrees with the subject given.

1. people (*walks, walk*)
2. you (*is, are*)
3. cattle (*runs, run*)
4. we (*talks, talk*)
5. Joan (*was, were*)
6. house (*stands, stand*)
7. result (*is, are*)
8. they (*believes, believe*)
9. crews (*sails, sail*)
10. women (*seems, seem*)

Intervening Phrases

19c. The number of the subject is not changed by a phrase following the subject.

The subject is never part of a prepositional phrase.

EXAMPLES   The **woman** on the stairs **is** Senator Reyes. [*woman is*]
The **women** in the front row **are** Cabinet officers.
[*women are*]

Remember that prepositional phrases may begin with compound prepositions such as *together with, in addition to, as well as,* and *along with.* These phrases do not affect the number of the verb.

EXAMPLES   **Tammy,** along with her mother and aunt, **is** going to
the concert. [*Tammy is going.*]
The **wind,** together with the rain and fog, **was**
making navigation difficult. [*wind was making*]
Jack's **imagination,** as well as his sense of humor, **was**
delightful. [*imagination was*]

A negative construction following the subject does not change the number of the subject.

EXAMPLE   **Carl,** not Juan and I, **is** doing the artwork.

EXERCISE 3   **Selecting Verbs That Agree with Their Subjects**

Identify the subject of each of the following sentences. Then, choose the verb in parentheses that agrees in number with the subject.

EXAMPLE   **1.** The price of haircuts (*has, have*) gone up.
1. *price—has*

1. A heaping basket of turnip greens (*was, were*) sitting on the counter.
2. Displaying disregard for the rights and comforts of others (*is, are*) rude.
3. The community college course on collecting stamps (*attracts, attract*) many people.
4. The members of the Pak family (*meets, meet*) for a reunion every year.

5. The carpeting in the upstairs and downstairs rooms (*is, are*) getting worn.
6. The turquoise stones in this Navajo ring certainly (*is, are*) pretty.
7. One friend of my brothers (*says, say*) that I look like Whitney Houston.
8. The package of radio parts (*was, were*) smashed in the mail.
9. The cost of two new snow tires (*was, were*) more than I expected.
10. Burt, not Anne and Laura, (*has, have*) borrowed the bicycle pump.

REVIEW A **Completing Sentences That Demonstrate Agreement**

Anna Mary Robertson Moses (1860–1961), better known as "Grandma Moses," became famous in old age for her paintings of rural America. Add words to the word groups on the following page to complete ten sentences about this Grandma Moses painting, titled *The Barn Dance*. Make sure that all verbs agree with their subjects and all pronouns agree with their antecedents. Be prepared to identify the subject of each sentence.

EXAMPLE **1.** barn are
1. *The doors of the barn are wide open.*

Grandma Moses (1860–1961), *The Barn Dance*. Copyright © 1989 Grandma Moses Properties Co., New York.

USAGE

1. clouds look
2. musician is playing
3. horses pulls
4. barn dance are enjoying
5. buildings in the distance is
6. green wagon are waving
7. along with laughter and conversation, fills
8. guests have noticed the cloudy
9. I were at this barn dance
10. horse is drinking

Indefinite Pronouns

19d. The following indefinite pronouns are singular: *each, either, neither, one, everyone, everybody, no one, nobody, anyone, anybody, someone, somebody.*

Indefinite pronouns are pronouns that do not refer to a specific person or thing.

EXAMPLES **No one leaves** early.
One of the guitar strings **was** broken. [One was broken.]
Neither of them **knew** the answer.
Someone who likes apple juice **raids** the refrigerator at night.

Notice that a phrase or a clause following one of these pronouns does not affect the verb.

EXAMPLES **Everybody likes** my uncle.
Everybody in my neighborhood **likes** my uncle.
Everybody who meets my uncle **likes** him.

19e. The following indefinite pronouns are plural: *several, few, both, many.*

EXAMPLES **Several** of the women **are** pilots.
A **few** in the crowd **were** rowdy.
Have both tried harder?
Many of the students **write** and **edit** on word processors.

USAGE

19f. The indefinite pronouns *some, all, any, most,* and *none* may be either singular or plural, depending on the word they refer to.

These pronouns are singular when they refer to a singular word and plural when they refer to a plural word.

SINGULAR **Most** of the day **was** gone. [*Most* refers to singular *day.*]

PLURAL **Most** of the steers **were** grazing. [*Most* refers to plural *steers.*]

SINGULAR **Has any** of the shipment arrived? [*Any* refers to singular *shipment.*]

PLURAL **Are any** of the coins new? [*Any* refers to plural *coins.*]

SINGULAR **None** of the damage **was** serious. [*None* refers to singular *damage.*]

PLURAL **None** of the students **have** finished. [*None* refers to plural *students.*]

In each of the examples above, the prepositional phrase following the subject provides a clue to the number of the pronoun. When these pronouns are used alone, their number depends on the number of the item the speaker or writer has in mind.

EXAMPLES **Most were** interesting. [a number of books, photographs, ideas, etc.]

Most was interesting. [a portion of a book, movie, conversation, etc.]

ORAL PRACTICE 1 **Using Verbs That Agree with Indefinite Pronouns**

Read the following sentences aloud, stressing the italicized words.

1. *One* of those cups *is* broken.
2. *Either* of the bikes *is* ready to go.
3. A *few* of the girls *are* experienced riders.
4. *Each* of the mariachi bands *has* performed one number.
5. *Some* of the mice *were* eating the cheese.
6. *Most* of the milk *is* gone.
7. *Neither* of the cars *has* a radio.
8. *None* of the apples *were* ripe.

USAGE

EXERCISE 4 **Writing Sentences with Verbs That Agree with Their Subjects**

Rewrite each of the following sentences according to the directions in parentheses. If necessary, change the number of the verb to agree with the new subject.

1. Everyone easily understands the rules of this game. (Change *everyone* to *most people*.)
2. Neither of the actresses was nominated. (Change *neither* to *both*.)
3. Has each of your cousins had a turn? (Change *each* to *both*.)
4. Some of the trees were destroyed. (Change *trees* to *crop*.)
5. Have any of the apples been harvested? (Change *apples* to *wheat*.)
6. Nobody visits that haunted house. (Change *nobody* to *many of our neighbors*.)
7. Each is well trained. (Change *each* to *several*.)
8. One of the tires needs air. (Change *one* to *all*.)
9. All of the fruit was eaten. (Change *fruit* to *pears*.)
10. There is baked chicken for everybody. (Change *chicken* to *potatoes*.)

EXERCISE 5 **Identifying Subject-Verb Agreement in Sentences**

The subjects and verbs in some of the following sentences do not agree. If a sentence is incorrect, write the correct form of the verb. If the sentence is correct, write *C*.

1. Several of the crew was commended by the captain.
2. Neither of the coaches were happy with the decision.
3. Each of us are going to make a large poster for the upcoming election.
4. Some of the frozen yogurt has started to melt.
5. Does both of those games require special gear?
6. Either of the assistants usually gets the mail.
7. None of the buildings were damaged by the hail.
8. None of the food has been frozen.
9. Neither of the book reports were finished on time.
10. Anyone who wants to can help me make gefilte fish for the Passover feast.

Selecting Verbs That Agree with Their Subjects

For each of the following sentences, choose the verb in parentheses that agrees with the subject.

1. (*Has, Have*) any of you ever wondered how meals are served to space-shuttle astronauts?
2. Each item for the day's menu (*come, comes*) sealed in its own container.
3. To help reduce weight on the spacecraft, many of the foods (*is, are*) dehydrated.
4. At mealtime, someone in the crew (*add, adds*) water to the scrambled eggs, vegetables, and puddings.
5. All of the water mixed with these foods (*is, are*) a byproduct of the fuel cells that provide the space-craft's electricity.
6. Of course, not one of the beverages (*is, are*) pour-able because there is no gravity.
7. As you can see, uncovered liquid (*bounce, bounces*) into the air like a ball if its container is accidentally jolted.
8. Much of the food (*is, are*) covered in sauce so that surface tension will help to keep the food in dishes.
9. Amazingly, most of the foods (*taste, tastes*) delicious.
10. The menu for the astronauts even (*includes, include*) steaks and strawberries.

USAGE

PICTURE THIS

You are the captain of the first spacecraft sent from the planet Zan Dor to explore Earth. As your invisible ship skims above the edge of a landmass, you look down and see this strange assembly of alien beings near a large body of water. You order your crew to cruise slowly above this scene while you try to figure out what the aliens are doing. Write a brief entry in the spacecraft's daily log, recording what you see below and speculating on what it means. As you write your log entry, use at least five of the following words as subjects: *aliens, everybody, inhabitants, we, many, most, all, none, any, some.* Be sure your subjects and verbs agree.

Subject: earthling behavior
Audience: you and future space travelers
Purpose: to inform

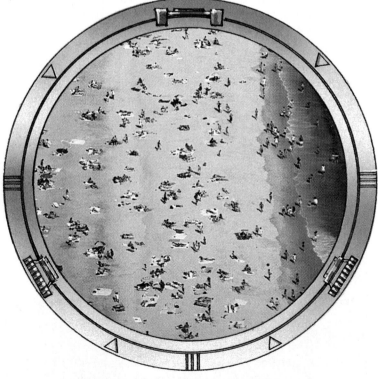

Compound Subjects

A *compound subject* consists of two or more nouns or pronouns that are joined by a conjunction and have the same
verb.

19g. Subjects joined by *and* usually take a plural
verb.

EXAMPLES   **Ramón** and **she like** hiking.
Her **brother,** her **uncle,** and her **cousin are** teachers.

NOTE: Subjects joined by *and* that name only one person or thing take
a singular verb.

EXAMPLES   Pork and beans **goes** well with barbecued chicken.
[One dish goes.]
Rock-and-roll **is** here to stay. [One kind of music is.]

19h. Singular subjects joined by *or* or *nor* take a
singular verb.

EXAMPLES   Marcelo or Donya **knows** the address.
Does either Dad or Mom have the key?
Neither our phone nor our doorbell **was** working.

NOTE: Singular subjects that are joined by the correlative conjunction
both . . . and take a plural verb.

EXAMPLE   Both the scout and the counselor **were** helpful
guides.

19i. When a singular subject and a plural subject are
joined by *or* or *nor,* the verb agrees with the
subject nearer the verb.

EXAMPLES   Either Harry or his **aunts are** planning the activities
for the beach party.
Neither the potatoes nor the **roast is** done.

You can usually avoid such awkward constructions by
rewording the sentence so that each subject has its own
verb.

EXAMPLES   Either **Harry is** planning the activities for the beach
party, or his **aunts are.**
The **potatoes are** not done, and neither **is** the **roast.**

USAGE

> ORAL
> PRACTICE 2

Using Verbs That Agree with Compound Subjects

Read the following sentences aloud, stressing the italicized words.

1. Every *one* of the kittens *has* been given away.
2. A *few* of us *are* going to Chicago.
3. *Each* of the photographs *was* in black and white.
4. *Neither* Sam *nor* Miguel *likes* sports.
5. *Either* Judy *or* Claudia *does* the dishes tonight.
6. Not *one* of the stations *is* coming in clearly.
7. *Several* of the plates *were* cracked.
8. *Both* Marilyn *and* Marge *have* summer jobs.

> EXERCISE 6

Selecting Verbs That Agree with Their Subjects

For each of the following sentences, choose the verb in parentheses that agrees with the subject of the sentence.

1. Neither my brother nor I (*has, have*) a car.
2. Marlon and she (*is, are*) the dance champions.
3. Our relatives and theirs (*is, are*) having a barbecue together.
4. Both Michael Chang and Zina Garrison-Jackson (*plays, play*) a good game of tennis.
5. Either the director or the actors (*is, are*) going to have to compromise.
6. Neither the grapes nor the cantaloupe (*was, were*) ripe enough to eat.
7. Both Hakeem Olajuwon and Michael Jordan (*is, are*) popular with fans.
8. Our class or theirs (*is, are*) going to sponsor the dance.
9. Either the faucet or the shower head (*leaks, leak*).
10. Either a transistor or a capacitor (*has, have*) burned out in this receiver.

Other Problems in Agreement

19j. Collective nouns may be either singular or plural.

A *collective noun* is singular in form, but it names a *group* of persons or things.

Collective Nouns			
army	club	group	series
assembly	committee	herd	squad
audience	crowd	jury	staff
band	faculty	majority	swarm
choir	family	number	team
class	flock	public	troop

Use a singular verb with a collective noun when you mean the group as a unit. Use a plural verb when you mean the members of the group as individuals.

EXAMPLES   The class **has met** its substitute teacher. [the class as a unit]

The class **were disagreeing** with one another about the answers. [the class as individuals]

The team **is** on the field. [the team as a unit]
The team **are working** together. [the team as individuals]

NOTE: A pronoun that refers to the collective noun should agree in number with the noun, as in the examples above.

EXERCISE 7   **Using Collective Nouns in Sentences**

You are at the soccer game shown on the following page. During the game, you see many different groups of people on the field, in the bleachers, and on the bench. You notice that sometimes the members of a group act separately and sometimes a group acts together as a whole. Think of five collective nouns that name the groups you see. (See the top of this page for a list of collective nouns.) Use each noun as the subject in two sentences. After each sentence, identify the collective noun as *singular* or *plural* in that sentence.

EXAMPLE   **1.** crowd
        1. *The crowd seem to be enjoying themselves.—plural*
          The crowd has nearly filled the bleachers.—singular

USAGE

EXERCISE 8   **Writing Sentences with Verbs That Agree with Their Subjects**

Rewrite the following sentences according to the instructions in parentheses, changing the number of the verb if necessary.

1. Both of the records are in the Top Forty. (Change *both* to *neither.*)
2. The Boys Choir of Harlem has been rehearsing with the conductor. (Change *with the conductor* to *in small groups.*)
3. Either my cousins or Adrienne is bringing the pizza. (Reverse the order of the subjects.)
4. Neither Carrie nor Jana is in the Pep Club. (Change *neither . . . nor* to *both . . . and.*)
5. Gabriel García Márquez and Octavio Paz have won prizes in literature. (Change *and* to *or.*)
6. All of your papers were graded. (Change *all* to *each.*)
7. Some of the wood burns. (Change *wood* to *logs.*)
8. The delighted team was waving and grinning widely. (Change *waving and grinning widely* to *assembling to accept their medals.*)
9. Everybody in the chorus is trying out for the play. (Change *everybody* to *no one.*)
10. Macaroni and cheese always tastes good. (Change *and* to *or.*)

19k. A verb agrees with its subject, not with its predicate nominative.

EXAMPLES
The main **ingredient** in my hot sauce
is jalapeño **peppers.**

Jalapeño **peppers are** the main **ingredient** in my hot sauce.

When such a construction seems awkward to you, revise the sentence to avoid using a predicate nominative.

EXAMPLE
I use jalapeño **peppers** as the main ingredient in my hot sauce.

19l. When the subject follows the verb, make sure that the verb agrees with it.

In sentences beginning with *here* or *there* and in questions, the subject follows the verb.

EXAMPLES
Here **is** a **set** of keys.
Here **are** the **keys.**
Where **is** my **jacket**? Where **is** my **scarf**?
Where **are** my **jacket** and my **scarf**?

NOTE: Remember that contractions such as *here's, how's, what's,* and *where's* include the singular verb *is.* Use one of these contractions only if a singular subject follows it.

INCORRECT   There's several photos of the oil spill in an article in this month's *Smithsonian.*
CORRECT   There **are** several **photos** of the oil spill in an article in this month's *Smithsonian.*
CORRECT   In this month's *Smithsonian,* there**'s** an **article** with several photos of the oil spill.

▶ EXERCISE 9   **Identifying Sentences with Subject-Verb Agreement**

For each of the following sentences, if the verb agrees with the subject, write *C.* If the subject and verb do not agree, write the correct form of the verb. Be ready to explain your correction.

USAGE

1. Soap and water is the best cleanser for my face.
2. There's the boats I told you about.
3. Both my father and sister wants to see the Dodgers game on Saturday.
4. Either the twins or Jamie are playing a practical joke.
5. How was the swimming and sailing at the beach?
6. Each of these old photos show your Uncle Ahmad wearing a colorful, flowing dashiki.
7. Neither the windows nor the door is locked.
8. Contemporary rock-and-roll are rooted in the ancient rhythms of African music.
9. There's always a number of football games on television on New Year's Day.
10. Where's my socks?

19m. Words stating an amount are usually singular.

When a weight, a measurement, or an amount of time or money is thought of as a unit, it takes a singular verb.

EXAMPLES   Two years **is** a long time.
Fifteen dollars **was** the price.
Ninety percent of the student body **is** present.

When the amount is thought of as individual pieces or parts, a plural verb is used.

EXAMPLES   **Two** of the years **were** especially rainy.
Fifteen of the dollars **were** torn.
Ninety percent of the students **are** present today.

NOTE: The expression *the number* takes a singular verb. The expression *a number* takes a plural verb.

EXAMPLES   **The number** of female athletes **is** growing.
A number of girls **like** strenuous sports.

19n. The verb in a clause following *one of those* should be plural.

EXAMPLE   Melba is one of those **students** who always **try** their best.

19o. *Every* or *many a* before a subject takes a singular verb.

EXAMPLES   **Every** mother, father, and grandparent **is** looking on
proudly.
Many a hopeful performer **has** gone to Broadway in
search of fame.

19p.   The title of a work of art, literature, or music,
even when plural in form, takes a singular verb.

EXAMPLES   Paul Laurence Dunbar's *Majors and Minors* **is** a
collection of his poetry. [one book]
Jean-François Millet's *The Gleaners* **is** a famous
nineteenth-century painting. [one work of art]
Four Saints in Three Acts, with music by Virgil Thomson
and words by Gertrude Stein, **was** first produced in
1934, with an African American cast. [one musical
work]

19q.   *Don't* and *doesn't* must agree with their
subjects.

Use *don't* (the contraction for *do not*) with the subjects *I*
and *you* and with plural subjects.

EXAMPLES   **I don't** have any paper.
You don't need special permission.
The **players don't** seem nervous.

Use *doesn't* with singular subjects.

EXAMPLES   **It [he, she] doesn't** show up in this picture.
The **tire doesn't** have enough air.

19r.   Some nouns, although plural in form, take
singular verbs.

EXAMPLES   **Linguistics is** the science of language.
News of the concert's cancellation **was** disappointing
to the band members.

A few nouns ending in *–ics* may be singular or plural.

EXAMPLES   **Acoustics deals** with the transmission of sound.
The **acoustics** in the new auditorium **are** excellent.

Does politics interest you?
Your **politics are** distasteful to me.

USAGE

> **NOTE:** Check a dictionary when you're not sure whether to use a singular verb or a plural verb with a noun that ends in *–ics*.

Some nouns that end in *–s* always take a plural verb even though they name a single item.

EXAMPLES **Are** the **scissors** sharp enough?
Your gray **slacks are** in the laundry.
The **pliers seem** to be missing.

▶ EXERCISE 10 **Using *Don't* and *Doesn't* Correctly in Sentences**

Choose the correct form (*don't* or *doesn't*) for each of the following sentences.

1. The calf ___ look very strong.
2. It ___ matter if the weather is bad.
3. She ___ play racquetball.
4. ___ these piñatas look colorful?
5. I ___ mind helping out.
6. You ___ have to watch the program.
7. Loretta ___ enjoy cleaning house.
8. A few of the contests ___ award cash prizes.
9. ___ it arrive soon?
10. ___ he tinker with cars?

▶ EXERCISE 11 **Selecting Verbs That Agree with Their Subjects**

Choose the correct form of the verb given in parentheses in each of the following sentences.

1. Nguyen, along with her family, (*have, has*) invited me to the Vietnamese National Day celebration in the park.
2. They (*wasn't, weren't*) interested in learning how to play the accordion.
3. Carlos, not Martha or Jan, (*was, were*) answering all the letters.
4. Many of them (*has, have*) already read the novel.
5. *The Birds* (*was, were*) one of Alfred Hitchcock's great movies.
6. (*Doesn't, Don't*) Chuck intend to join the air force when he graduates?

7. Caroline, like most of her classmates, (*wishes, wish*) vacation could last forever.
8. There (*is, are*) some good programs on educational television.
9. Neither of those books by Naguib Mahfouz (*is, are*) on our reading list.
10. It (*doesn't, don't*) look good for our baseball league this season.

EXERCISE 12 **Selecting Verbs That Agree with Their Subjects**

For each of the sentences following the picture below, choose the correct form of the verb in parentheses.

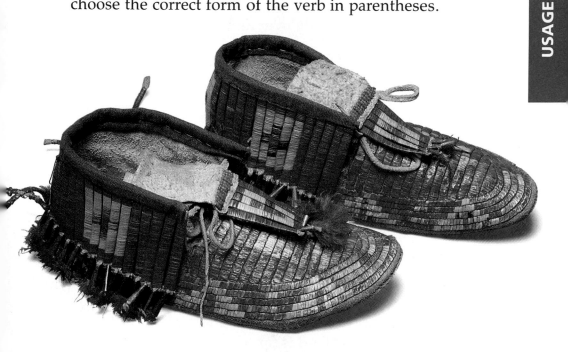

1. (*Doesn't, Don't*) these quilled moccasins look as if they are beaded?
2. Quillwork, one of the traditional Plains Indians handicrafts, (*is, are*) an ancient and sophisticated art form.
3. The number of quills that grow on one porcupine (*is, are*) higher than you might think—about thirty thousand!

USAGE

4. Five inches (*is, are*) the maximum length of these tubular spines.
5. Before being used in quillwork, every porcupine quill (*is, are*) dyed a bright color, softened in water, and flattened in an unusual way.
6. The quillworker, usually a woman, (*squeezes, squeeze*) each quill flat by pulling it between her teeth.
7. Among the Sioux, worn teeth were considered a badge of great honor because items decorated with colorful quillwork (*was, were*) so important in tribal life.
8. Working the quills into complex geometric patterns (*require, requires*) great skill and coordination.
9. In quill weaving, each of the ribbonlike quills (*is, are*) passed tightly over and under threads of fiber or leather.
10. The finished quillwork (*is, are*) sewn onto clothing, saddlebags, or cradleboards as a decoration.

▶ REVIEW C   **Making Verbs Agree with Their Subjects**

For each of the following sentences, if the verb and subject agree, write C. If the verb and the subject do not agree, supply the correct form of the verb.

1. There are one strain of measles that lasts only three days.
2. Few objections, besides the one about chartering the bus, was raised.
3. *Six Characters in Search of an Author* is a modern play that raises many interesting questions about art and reality.
4. Some of this land is far too hilly to farm.
5. In Maine, there's many miles of rocky coastline.
6. Four minutes were his record time in that race.
7. Performing in front of a thousand people don't seem to bother the cellist Yo-Yo Ma.
8. Two thirds of a cup of milk is needed for this recipe.
9. Every three years my family visit Sierra Leone, the land our ancestors came from.
10. Every student, teacher, and administrator are contributing to the fund-raising drive.

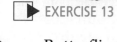

▶ EXERCISE 13   **Using Subject-Verb Agreement in Sentences**

Butterflies come in many shapes and sizes—and in every color of the rainbow! Make up ten sentences about the butterflies shown here. Use one of the words listed below as the subject of each sentence. Do not use the same word as the subject of more than one sentence. Be sure that each verb you use agrees with its subject.

a few	each	neither	one
all	either	none	several
both	everyone	not one	some

EXAMPLE   **1.** *All of these butterflies look like flying flowers!*

USAGE

Agreement of Pronoun and Antecedent

The word that a pronoun refers to is called its *antecedent*.

19s.   A pronoun should agree with its antecedent in gender and number.

Most personal pronouns can refer to antecedents that are masculine or feminine or both or neither.

EXAMPLES   **I** am **your** coach.
You are **my** friend.
We are with **them**.
They are **our** cousins.

Only the third-person singular pronouns indicate the gender of their antecedents. Masculine pronouns refer to males, feminine pronouns to females, and neuter pronouns to things and, often, animals.

MASCULINE	he	him	his
FEMININE	she	her	hers
NEUTER	it	it	its

EXAMPLES   Does **Margaret** like **her** dance class?
Arturo is doing **his** homework.
Because the **car** wouldn't start, **it** had to be towed.

When the antecedent of a personal pronoun is another kind of pronoun, determine the gender to use by looking in a phrase following the antecedent.

EXAMPLES   **Neither** of the **girls** brought **her** own lunch.
One of the **men** lost **his** keys.

When the antecedent could be either masculine or feminine, use both the masculine and feminine forms.

EXAMPLES   **One** of the students left **his or her** pen behind.
Everybody in the club has paid **his or her** dues.

NOTE: You can often avoid the *his or her* construction by revising the sentence and using the plural form of the pronoun.

EXAMPLE   **All** of the club members have paid **their** dues.

In conversation, plural personal pronouns are often used to refer to singular antecedents that could be either masculine or feminine. This form is being used more often in writing, too, and it may eventually be considered acceptable in written standard English.

EXAMPLES   **Nobody** rode **their** bikes.
Everybody brought **their** fishing rods.

(1) Use a singular pronoun to refer to *each, either, neither, one, everyone, everybody, no one, nobody, anyone, anybody, someone,* or *somebody.* The use of a phrase or a clause after the antecedent does not change the number of the antecedent.

USAGE

EXAMPLES   **Each** of the teams had **its** mascot at the game.
One of the boys left **his** pen behind.
Everybody in the women's league has paid **her** dues.

NOTE: When the meaning of *everyone* or *everybody* is *clearly* plural, use the plural pronoun or, better, revise the sentence.

CONFUSING   When **everybody** has arrived, explain the situation to **him.**

CLEAR   When **everybody** has arrived, explain the situation to **them.**

BETTER   When **all** the people have arrived, explain the situation to **them.**

(2) Use a singular pronoun to refer to two or more singular antecedents joined by *or* or *nor.*

EXAMPLE   Neither Heidi nor Beth took **her** umbrella with **her.**

(3) Use a plural pronoun to refer to two or more antecedents joined by *and.*

EXAMPLE   The guide and the ranger wrapped **their** rain ponchos in **their** saddle rolls.

NOTE: The number of a relative pronoun (*who, which,* and *that*) is determined by the number of the word to which it refers—its antecedent.

EXAMPLES   Jessica is one **person who** has faith in **herself.** [*Who* is singular because it refers to *person.* Therefore, the singular forms *has* and *herself* are used to agree with *who.*]

All **who want** to volunteer should raise **their** hands. [*Who* is plural because *all* is plural. Therefore, the plural forms *want* and *their* are used to agree with *who.*]

▶ EXERCISE 14   **Selecting Pronouns That Agree with Their Antecedents**

For each blank in the following sentences, select a pronoun that will agree with its antecedent.

1. Each of the players had ____ own odd superstition.
2. Someone on the boy's swimming team has parked ____ car in my space.
3. Neither of the sweaters had ____ price tag removed.

USAGE

4. Did everybody at the press conference change ____ mind as soon as Mayor Bradley stated the facts?
5. Many of the crew got ____ first case of seasickness in the storm.
6. One of the houses had ____ windows broken by the hail last night.
7. All of the art students buy ____ own paper.
8. Anyone who needs a pencil should raise ____ hand.
9. Either Stu or Mike will lend me ____ fishing gear.
10. Each of the characters in Chinese calligraphy has ____ own beauty, mystery, and grace.

▶ EXERCISE 15 **Making Pronouns Agree with Their Antecedents**

Most of the following sentences contain pronouns that do not agree with their antecedents. If all of the pronouns in a sentence agree with their antecedents, write *C*. If any pronoun does not agree with its antecedent, supply the correct pronoun.

1. All of these students at the Royal School of Dance in College Park, Florida, are learning traditional dances that come from her African heritage.
2. Some of the African and Caribbean dances have its roots in African folk tales.
3. At performances, the audience are often seen clapping its hands and swaying along with the music.

4. Before the last dance recital, I noticed either Carla or Shana practicing their steps.
5. Carla is one of those students who always know their steps ahead of time.
6. Angelique and Pamela waved her arms gracefully during the first dance.
7. Every authentic costume adds their color and movement to the dramatic spectacle.
8. Everyone in the class brings their own personal style to the dances.
9. Many of the dancers and singers give a great deal of credit to the traditional sources of their art form.
10. Both their hip-hop dancing and their clothing style have its origins in ancient African culture.

 REVIEW D

Identifying Subject-Verb Agreement and Pronoun-Antecedent Agreement in Sentences

In some of the following sentences, either a verb does not agree with its subject or a pronoun does not agree with its antecedent. If a verb or pronoun is wrong, correct it. If the sentence is correct, write C.

1. Both Sid and Nikki like their new neighborhood and their new apartment.
2. Are either of you a member of the African American Cultural Society?
3. Anthony, in addition to the other contestants, were ready for the competition to start.
4. One of the local police officers was the top scorer on the rifle range.
5. Neither Fernando nor Bruce has brought all of their camping gear.
6. *The Three Little Pigs* are my young nephews' all-time favorite animated feature.
7. Which pair of these Navajo earrings were made by Narciso?
8. Where is the Athletics Department?
9. Just before the parade started, each of the eight men inside the gigantic dragon costume got their final instructions from Mr. Yee.

10. A few of the crowd was murmuring impatiently.
11. Is there any of those peanuts left?
12. Either Chi Chi Rodriguez or Nancy Lopez is my golf hero.
13. Every one of those stray cattle are going to have to be rounded up.
14. An additional feature of these models is the built-in stereo speakers.
15. Somebody has gone off and left their car running.
16. If anybody calls, tell them I'll be back by six o'clock this evening.
17. Each team has its own colors and symbol.
18. One of the goats were nibbling on a discarded popcorn box.
19. Here's the pair of gloves that you forgot.
20. Are there no end to these questions?

▶ REVIEW E

Selecting Verbs That Agree with Their Subjects and Pronouns That Agree with Their Antecedents

In each sentence, choose the correct one of the two forms given in parentheses.

1. Neither the manager nor the two salespeople (*was, were*) prepared for the number of customers.
2. Neither of the sets of barbells (*was, were*) easy to lift.
3. Where (*is, are*) the box of nails that came with this bookshelf kit?
4. A few of our classmates (*was, were*) invited.
5. The Harlem Globetrotters (*is, are*) surely one of the best-loved basketball teams in the world.
6. There (*is, are*) leftover macaroni and cheese in the refrigerator.
7. If anybody likes a spectacle, (*he or she, they*) will love seeing a drum corps competition.
8. Several of the audience (*was, were*) waving wildly, hoping that Martin Yan would wave back.
9. Where (*has, have*) the sports section of today's newspaper gone?
10. Anyone who wants to get (*his or her, their*) program autographed by Edward James Olmos had better hurry.

▶ EXERCISE 16   **Using Subject-Verb Agreement Correctly in Sentences**

The same thought can almost always be expressed in more than one way. Read each of the following sentences, and then express the same thought in two more sentences. For each new sentence, use one of the two subjects given in parentheses. Be sure that your subjects and verbs agree.

EXAMPLE   **1.** The boys desperately want to go to the circus. *(Both, Each)*

1. *Both of the boys desperately want to go to the circus.*
Each of the boys desperately wants to go to the circus.

1. Their father, as well as their mother, has agreed to the idea. *(Both of their parents, One of their parents)*
2. Not one of the townspeople wants to miss tonight's performance. *(Nobody, None)*
3. Each person has earned a lighthearted evening of watching clowns, horses, and elephants like those shown in these posters. *(Everybody, All)*
4. But because the Great Depression has begun, not all of the families in town have money for tickets. *(not every one, a few)*
5. Forty-nine of the fifty free tickets to the circus have been spoken for. *(All but one, Only one)*

USAGE

USAGE

WRITING APPLICATION

Using Agreement to Make Meaning Clear

If you want your reader to know exactly what you mean, your pronouns must clearly refer to their antecedents and agree with them. Suppose you are telling a friend about what happened at the movies last night. You say, "Melba said that Jo Ann ate all of the popcorn Bill bought for her." Whose popcorn did Jo Ann eat? The sentence should be revised to make the meaning clear.

CLEAR   Melba said that Bill bought popcorn for her, but Jo Ann ate all of it.

CLEAR   Melba said that Bill bought popcorn for Jo Ann, who ate all of it.

▶ WRITING ACTIVITY

Your best friend moved away two months ago. You have just received a postcard from him or her, asking what's been happening recently in the old neighborhood. You answer the postcard by writing a short letter that brings your friend up to date. In your letter, include at least five pronouns that agree with their antecedents.

 Prewriting   Make a list of several interesting things to tell your friend. You may write about your real neighborhood or about one you have made up. Decide on the order in which you will tell about the items on your list. You may want to use time order (telling when things happened) or spatial order (telling where things happened).

 Writing   As you write, think about how to make your letter interesting to your friend. Use details that will help him or her picture the neighborhood and its people.

Evaluating and Revising   Ask a classmate to read your letter. Are the events you tell about interesting? Is it absolutely clear who did what and what belongs to whom? Use your helper's suggestions to revise your letter so that nothing in it is confusing.

Proofreading Check over the grammar, punctuation, and form of your letter. Use a dictionary to look up the spelling of any word you are not sure of. Be sure each pronoun agrees with its antecedent and each verb agrees with its subject.

Review: Posttest

A. Selecting Verbs That Agree with Their Subjects and Pronouns That Agree with Their Antecedents

In the following sentences, write the correct form of each incorrect verb or pronoun. If a sentence is correct, write C.

EXAMPLES
  1. Each leaf, flower, and seedpod were glimmering with frost.
  1. *was*

  2. Were any tickets left at the box office for me?
  2. *C*

  1. There was women, as well as men, who set out on the perilous journey into new territory.
  2. The test results showed that about 80 percent of the class was in the average group.
  3. A hostile crowd gathered outside the courtroom to show their disapproval of the verdict.
  4. *Bronzeville Boys and Girls* are a collection of poems by Gwendolyn Brooks.
  5. Neither of the candidates has prepared their speech.
  6. Mr. Ortega, along with other members of his firm, have established a scholarship fund for art students.
  7. To apply for the scholarship, a student must submit at least four samples of their work.
  8. Chester or Nina, I think, have the best chance of winning.
  9. Senator Hayakawa's committee was preparing their speeches for the meeting.
  10. All of the bread are on the table.

B. Selecting Verbs That Agree with Their Subjects and Pronouns That Agree with Their Antecedents

For each sentence in the following paragraph, write the correct form of each incorrect verb or pronoun. A sentence may contain more than one error. If a sentence is correct, write C.

[11] Neither my brothers nor my dad were surprised to hear that Aunt Bonnie is going to Africa next month as a Peace Corps volunteer. [12] First, she and the other members of the Kenya group gathers in Philadelphia for a few days of orientation. [13] Their focus at this point are to meet one another and get acquainted. [14] Then the whole group travels together to Nairobi, Kenya, where everyone will have their last chance for months to enjoy hot running water! [15] After one night in Nairobi, half of them leaves for the town of Naivasha for eleven weeks of cultural sensitivity training. [16] Each of the volunteers get to live with a Kenyan family during this period of training. [17] The close daily contact will help them learn to converse in Swahili, one of the languages that is spoken in Kenya. [18] Bonnie don't know yet where exactly in Kenya she is going to be posted. [19] She, as well as the other members of her group, expects to be assigned to the area of greatest need. [20] No one in the group has been told their specific job assignment, but Bonnie say she will probably be helping Kenyans develop small businesses.

20 USING PRONOUNS CORRECTLY

Nominative and Objective Case

Diagnostic Test

A. Using Pronouns Correctly in Sentences

Choose the correct word in parentheses in the following sentences.

EXAMPLE **1.** Was it (*he, him*) driving the car when the accident occurred?

1. *he*

1. Francis said that in a few years he would give his stamp collection to his brother and (*I, me*).
2. Everyone was waiting impatiently to find out (*who, whom*) the new cheerleader would be.
3. My little sister is a much better basketball player than (*I, me*).
4. Rep. Ben Nighthorse Campbell is one congressman (*who, whom*) thinks Native Americans should be consulted more often about legislation that concerns them.

5. We found that it was (*she, her*) who called twice while we were out of town.
6. The teacher said that (*whoever, whomever*) was ready could give a speech first.
7. Speaking of Ken Griffey, Jr., (*he, him*) and his dad are the first father and son ever to play professional baseball together on the same team.
8. Seeing a car with an out-of-state license plate in my driveway, I ran inside, and (*who, whom*) do you think was there?
9. Mrs. Martin and (*she, her*) have been friends since childhood.
10. As you swim, you use nearly all of your major muscles, which makes (*it, swimming*) one of the best forms of exercise.

B. Identifying Correct Pronoun Forms in a Paragraph

In each sentence in the following paragraph, choose the correct form from each pair of words in parentheses.

I recently read that anyone **[11]** (*who, whom*) comes from a large family grows up with a desire to be surrounded by people all the time. Well, just between you and **[12]** (*I, me*), that isn't always true! There aren't many teenagers who enjoy their privacy as much as **[13]** (*I, me*). Because I'm the oldest child, I've spent years settling squabbles between my brothers and sisters, helping with homework, and feeding **[14]** (*whoever, whomever*) was hungry. When my brothers got into trouble, I always smoothed things over between **[15]** (*they, them*) and Dad. And when **[16]** (*he, him*) and Mom were busy in the evening, I read to **[17]** (*whoever, whomever*) had an earlier bedtime than **[18]** (*I, me*). Even now that we're all older, the laughing, yelling, bickering, and commotion always let you know exactly **[19]** (*who, whom*) is home at any moment. You'd better believe that **[20]** (*this, this hectic upbringing*) has given me a deep craving for privacy, not for company!

Case Forms of Personal Pronouns

Case is the form of a noun or pronoun that shows how it is used in a sentence. In English, there are three cases: *nominative, objective,* and *possessive.* Nouns have the same form in both the nominative and the objective case. They usually add an apostrophe and an *s* to form the possessive case.

☞ REFERENCE NOTE: See pages 848–849 and 851 for information on forming the possessives of nouns.

Personal pronouns change form in the different cases.

USAGE

CASE FORMS OF PERSONAL PRONOUNS		
SINGULAR		
NOMINATIVE CASE	OBJECTIVE CASE	POSSESSIVE CASE
First Person I	me	my, mine
Second Person you	you	your, yours
Third Person he, she, it	him, her, it	his, her, hers, its
PLURAL		
NOMINATIVE CASE	OBJECTIVE CASE	POSSESSIVE CASE
First Person we	us	our, ours
Second Person you	you	your, yours
Third Person they	them	their, theirs

Notice that only *you* and *it* have the same form in the nominative and the objective case.

☞ REFERENCE NOTE: For more information on possessive personal pronouns, see page 850.

▶ EXERCISE 1   **Identifying Personal Pronouns in a Paragraph**

Each sentence in the following paragraph contains at least one pronoun. Identify each pronoun. Then, give its person, number, and case; also give its gender if applicable.

EXAMPLE [1] Jeffrey and I were chatting in front of his locker before the Art Club meeting.
1. *I—first person singular, nominative case; his—third person singular, possessive case, masculine*

[1] Jeffrey mentioned your interest in African art and Francine's interest in modern art. [2] Did you and she know that African tribal masks like the one below in the middle influenced the development of the Modernist movement in art? [3] I've learned that African carvings inspired such twentieth-century artists as Pablo Picasso, who created the painting on the left. [4] The year 1905 was probably when he and his friends first saw African masks exhibited in Paris. [5] Amedeo Modigliani was especially affected by the stark masks, and he and Picasso created many works based on them. [6] Notice that the eyes in Modigliani's carving on the right are very close together and that they and the lips look much like small knobs. [7] I used to think that Modigliani made his faces too long by mistake, but the error was mine. [8] Ms. Keller told me that he was copying the exaggerated shapes of Ivory Coast masks. [9] Picasso and Modigliani were only two of many European artists who got their inspiration from African art. [10] Obviously, we students weren't giving credit where credit was due!

[left] ©1998 Estate of Pablo Picasso/Artist Rights Society (ARS), New York.

USAGE

The Nominative Case

20a. The subject of a verb is in the nominative case.

EXAMPLES **I** solved the problem. [*I* is the subject of *solved.*]
Al and **she** cleaned the house. [*Al* and *she* is the compound subject of *cleaned.*]
They know that **we** are going. [*They* is the subject of *know,* and *we* is the subject of *are going.*]

When both parts of a compound subject are pronouns, you may not be sure which form to use.

EXAMPLE (*She, Her*) and (*I, me*) studied for the test.

To choose the correct form, try each pronoun separately with the verb.

SEPARATELY *She* studied for the test. *I* studied for the test. [*Her studied for the test* and *me studied for the test* sound strange.]

TOGETHER **She** and **I** studied for the test.

Using *we* and *they* as the parts of a compound subject may sound awkward to you, even though doing so is correct. If so, revise the sentence.

ORIGINAL **We** and **they** will go to the movie.
REVISED **We** will go to the movie with **them.**

 ORAL
PRACTICE 1   **Using Pronouns as Subjects**

Read each of the following sentences aloud, stressing the italicized words.

1. *She* and *I* gave the dog a bath.
2. Terry and *he* plan to try out for the soccer team.
3. *We* sophomores organized the drive.
4. James Earl Jones and *she* are excellent role models for young actors.
5. Are *you* and *he* doing the report?
6. Either *we* or *they* may go to the championship finals.
7. The drill team and *we* band members took the bus.
8. The twins and *they* go everywhere together.

USAGE

▶ EXERCISE 2

Using Personal Pronouns in the Nominative Case to Complete Sentences

Supply a personal pronoun for each blank in the following sentences. Vary your pronouns. Do not use *you* or *it*.

1. The judge and ____ studied the evidence.
2. Ted and ____ took the wrong train.
3. Linda and ____ are planning a party.
4. ____ students are having a science fair.
5. Either Julius or ____ will give you a ride.
6. ____ and ____ have been rivals for years.
7. I'm sure ____ knew about the meeting.
8. Soon ____ and ____ will be graduating.
9. Did you know that ____ and ____ saw Chita Rivera in a Broadway production of *West Side Story*?
10. ____ and ____ love those little Chinese dumplings served at dim sum restaurants.

▶ EXERCISE 3

Writing Sentences with Pronouns in the Nominative Case

Use the following subjects in sentences of your own.

1. we teenagers
2. the other shoppers and I
3. he and his friends
4. Liz, Michelle, and she
5. they and their classmates

▶ EXERCISE 4

Writing Sentences Using Personal Pronouns

Your cousin was too young to understand what happened during Operation Desert Storm, but now that she is older, she is curious. You show her the map and pictures appearing on the next page and explain as well as you can what happened before, during, and after the Persian Gulf Conflict. Write at least five sentences that include ten personal pronouns in the nominative case. Underline the nominative case pronouns you use.

EXAMPLE   **1.** *When I saw the photos in a magazine, they made me very sad and very proud.*

20b. A predicate nominative is in the nominative case.

USAGE

A **predicate nominative** is a noun or pronoun that follows a linking verb and explains or identifies the subject of the sentence. A pronoun used as a predicate nominative always follows a form of the verb *be* or a verb phrase ending in *be* or *been*.

☞ REFERENCE NOTE: See page 560 for more information on predicate nominatives.

COMMON FORMS OF *BE*		PREDICATE NOMINATIVE
am is, are was, were may be, can be, will be, etc. has been, have been, had been, may have been, etc. should be, could be, would be	are followed by	I he she we you they

EXAMPLES   It was **I** who took the message.
The winner might be **he.**
Could the caller have been **she**?

NOTE: In casual conversation, expressions such as *It's me* and *That's her*, are acceptable. Avoid them in more formal speaking situations such as job interviews. In your written work, don't use them unless you're creating casual conversation in dialogue.

EXERCISE 5 **Using Predicate Nominatives in Sentences**

Complete each of the following sentences by supplying the personal pronoun called for in parentheses.

1. Do you think it was ____? (*third person singular, masculine*)
2. It must have been ____. (*third person singular, feminine*)
3. Good friends are ____. (*third person plural*)
4. The pranksters were ____. (*first person plural*)
5. It was ____ at the door. (*third person plural*)

▶ REVIEW A **Using Pronouns in the Nominative Case Correctly in Sentences**

Supply a personal pronoun for each blank in the following sentences. Use as many different pronouns as you can. Do not use *you* or *it*. Be ready to explain the reasons for your choice.

1. When I saw Dame Kiri Te Kanawa in front of Lincoln Center, I couldn't believe it was ____.
2. Everyone applauded when Patty and ____ took a bow.
3. Where did Barry and ____ go after school?
4. Jimmy and ____ caught the runaway piglets.
5. It is ____ that you need to see.
6. Skip argued that it was Lana and ____ who made the error.
7. Was it Teresa or ____ who hit the home run?
8. Either David or ____ might be able to do it.
9. My sister and ____ love the South African musical group Ladysmith Black Mambazo.
10. I believe that the Masked Marvel has to be ____.

▶ REVIEW B **Using Pronouns in the Nominative Case Correctly in a Paragraph**

For each numbered blank in the following paragraph, supply an appropriate personal pronoun. Do not use *you* or *it*.

[1] ____ tenth-grade students are determined to win this year's "Save the Earth" trophy at our school. The two

most enthusiastic people in our class are probably Pilar and [2] _____. I guess that's why Mrs. Nakamura asked if [3] _____ and [4] _____ would organize the paper drive by ourselves. Pilar explained to the class that if [5] _____ Americans recycled only our Sunday newspapers, half a million trees would be saved every Sunday! To illustrate her point, she showed this photo. That's [6] _____ standing next to 580 pounds of paper—the amount an average American uses in one year. [7] _____ have gathered some other facts to inspire our classmates to recycle. Our friend Ben said that [8] _____ and his mother heard on the radio that the average American uses 1,500 aluminum drink cans every year. [9] _____ were amazed to learn that the energy saved from recycling just one aluminum can could keep a TV set running for three hours! No matter who wins the trophy, it will definitely be [10] _____ who share the prize of a cleaner, healthier planet.

The Objective Case

Pronouns in the objective case are used as direct objects, indirect objects, and objects of prepositions.

 REFERENCE NOTE: See pages 562–563 and 574 for more information about the three kinds of objects.

20c. Direct objects and indirect objects are in the objective case.

A *direct object* is a noun or pronoun that receives the action of the verb or shows the result of the action.

EXAMPLES   Coach Johnson has been training **us.**
The coach has turned **them** into the best team in the
state.

An *indirect object* is a noun or pronoun that tells *to whom* or *for whom* the action of the verb is done.

EXAMPLES   Serena paid **him** a compliment.
Carlos saved **me** a seat in the first row.

When a direct object or an indirect object is compound, try each pronoun separately with the verb. For the sentence to be correct, all parts of the compound must be correct.

EXAMPLE: The news surprised them and we.
The news surprised them is correct.
The news surprised we is incorrect.
ANSWER: The news surprised **them** and **us.**

EXAMPLE: Bao showed her and I pictures of Vietnam.
Bao showed her pictures of Vietnam is correct.
Bao showed I pictures of Vietnam is incorrect.
ANSWER: Bao showed **her** and **me** pictures of Vietnam.

▶ EXERCISE 6   **Using Pronouns in the Objective Case to Complete Sentences**

Supply a personal pronoun for each blank in the following sentences. Use a variety of pronouns. Do not use *you* or *it.*

1. The old sailor warned ＿＿ about the danger.
2. The city awarded ＿＿ its highest honor for their bravery in rescuing earthquake victims.
3. You could ask Deborah or ＿＿.
4. The crowd cheered ＿＿ heartily.
5. Make sure that you ask ＿＿ what her Social Security number is.
6. The shark in that movie didn't scare ＿＿ at all.
7. How can I recognize ＿＿?
8. We saw Norman and ＿＿ in their horse costume at the party.
9. Did you give Paula and ＿＿ their assignments?
10. I bought my father and ＿＿ identical birthday presents this year.

REVIEW C   **Using Pronouns in the Nominative and Objective Cases in Sentences**

The cheerleading squad is learning a new pyramid routine. To help get everyone organized, the coach has assigned each cheerleader a number. In each of the following sentences, replace the cheerleader's number with a correct personal pronoun. If *Number 1* is specified, use *I, we, me,* or *us.*

EXAMPLES   **1.** Coach Welber told Cara and *Number 5* where to position themselves.
   1. *her*

   2. I asked if *Number 8 and Number 1* could be in the pyramid next time.
   2. *we*

1. The three people forming the base of the pyramid were Harley, Michael, and *Number 5.*
2. Kimiko is the smallest, so it was *Number 6* who got to be at the top first.
3. The coach asked *Number 8 and Number 1* to give *Number 6* a boost.
4. After *Number 4* and Emilio had been in the middle row awhile, Rosie and *Number 1* asked for a turn.
5. Please tell Luisa and *Number 6 and Number 3* to stop laughing and pay attention.
6. Give Rosie or *Number 1* a signal when you want to jump down, Kimiko.

7. Next time, the ones in the middle row will be Harley and *Number 8.*
8. If anyone can support the person on top well, it's *Number 3.*
9. The winners of the next cheerleading meet will surely be *Numbers 1 through 8.*
10. Come here and I'll tell you and *Number 4* about the next new formation.

| **20d.** | The object of a preposition is in the objective case. |

A prepositional phrase begins with a preposition and ends with a noun or pronoun called the *object of the preposition.*

EXAMPLES   to **them**   for **her** and **us**   with **him**

When the object of a preposition is compound, try each pronoun separately in the prepositional phrase.

NONSTANDARD   Gwen wrote to her and I. [*Gwen wrote to her* is correct. *Gwen wrote to I* is incorrect.]
STANDARD   Gwen wrote to **her** and **me.**

NOTE: Using incorrect pronoun forms after the prepositions *between* and *for* is a common error. The pronouns should be in the objective case.

INCORRECT   between *you* and *I*, for *she* and *they*
CORRECT   between you and **me**, for **her** and **them**

ORAL PRACTICE 2   **Using Pronouns as Objects of Prepositions**

Read each of the following sentences aloud, stressing the italicized words.

1. There were calls *for* Walker and *us.*
2. This message is *from* Dolores and *her.*
3. We sat *with* Arnie and *them.*
4. Margo looked *toward* Francine and *me.*
5. They gave copies *to him* and *me.*
6. This drawing is *by* either Hector or *him.*
7. Don't hold this *against* Cho and *her.*
8. I walked *between* Vince and *him.*

▶ EXERCISE 7   **Identifying the Correct Pronoun Forms for Objects of Prepositions**

Identify the correct pronoun in parentheses in the following sentences.

1. The referee called fouls on (*he, him*) and (*I, me*).
2. Maggie is off fishing with Grandpa and (*he, him*).
3. We didn't want to leave without you and (*she, her*).
4. They assigned the same lab equipment to (*they, them*) and (*we, us*).
5. The duke directed a haughty sneer at the jester and (*he, him*).
6. After Carmen rolled the corn husks around the tamales, she handed them to Arturo and (*I, me*).
7. Everyone but Kevin and (*she, her*) thinks Ed Bradley is the best news commentator on television.
8. The player tried to dodge between Sherrie and (*I, me*).
9. The wary skunk circled around (*she, her*) and (*I, me*).
10. Uncle Vic will get the details from you and (*she, her*).

▶ EXERCISE 8   **Writing Sentences Using Pronouns as Objects of Prepositions**

Write sentences of your own, using each of the following prepositions with a compound object. Use a personal pronoun for at least one of the objects in each sentence.

1. against   **2.** for   **3.** except   **4.** without   **5.** by

PICTURE THIS

You are a helper at a day-care center. The teacher wants you to entertain the group of children shown on the next page and, at the same time, teach them something about getting along with people who look different. She asks you to write a short fable with animal characters and read it to the children. In your fable, use at least ten personal pronouns. Use some of them as compound subjects, some as compound direct or indirect objects, and some as compound objects of prepositions. Be sure to use the correct case for your pronouns. However, in the animals' dialogue, you may include such informal expressions as "It's me."

Subject: a fable about getting along well together
Audience: a group of four- to six-year-olds
Purpose: to entertain and to teach

▶ REVIEW D   **Identifying Correct Forms of Pronouns**

Choose the correct pronoun in parentheses in each numbered sentence in the following paragraph.

[1] Last fall, Tina talked Susan and (*I, me*) into going on a canoe trip with the Wilderness Club. [2] She warned (*we, us*) that we might get a good dunking before we were through. [3] When we set out, Susan and (*I, me*) could barely steer our canoe. [4] We watched another canoeist and saw how (*she, her*) and her partner maneuvered their craft. [5] They and (*we, us*) both did well until we hit the rapids or, rather, the rapids hit (*we, us*). [6] Susan grabbed for our sleeping bags, and (*she, her*) and (*I, me*) both scrambled for our food cooler. [7] All of (*we, us*) would-be

campers were drenched, but no quitters were (*we*, *us*). [8] Tina's warning haunted all of (*we*, *us*) as (*we*, *us*) hungry adventurers contemplated waterlogged sandwiches, soggy salads, and banana muffins with tadpoles in them. [9] Later, Susan and (*I*, *me*) discovered that our bedrolls had become portable water beds. [10] After a cold, squishy night, (*I*, *me*) concluded that wise are (*they*, *them*) who heed the voice of experience.

Special Problems in Pronoun Usage

Who and *Whom*

NOMINATIVE CASE	who, whoever
OBJECTIVE CASE	whom, whomever

NOTE: In spoken English, the use of *whom* is gradually dying out. Nowadays, it's acceptable to begin any spoken question with *who* regardless of whether the nominative or objective form is grammatically correct. In writing, though, it's still important to distinguish between *who* and *whom*.

20e. The use of *who* and *whom* in a subordinate clause depends on how the pronoun functions in the clause.

REFERENCE NOTE: See pages 598–606 for information on subordinate clauses.

Follow these steps to decide whether to use *who* or *whom* in a subordinate clause.

STEP 1: Find the subordinate clause.
STEP 2: Decide how the pronoun is used in the clause—as subject, predicate nominative, direct object, indirect object, or object of a preposition.
STEP 3: Determine the case of the pronoun according to the rules of standard English.
STEP 4: Select the correct form of the pronoun.

EXAMPLE: Roscoe is the only student *(who, whom)* got a perfect score.

STEP 1: The subordinate clause is *(who, whom) got a perfect score.*

STEP 2: In this clause, the pronoun is the subject of the verb *got*.

STEP 3: As a subject, the pronoun should be in the nominative case.

STEP 4: The nominative form is *who.*

ANSWER: Roscoe is the only student **who** got a perfect score.

EXAMPLE: Do you know *(who, whom)* she is?

STEP 1: The subordinate clause is *(who, whom) she is.*

STEP 2: In this clause, the pronoun *(who, whom)* is the predicate nominative: *she is (who, whom).*

STEP 3: A pronoun used as a predicate nominative should be in the nominative case.

STEP 4: The nominative form is *who.*

ANSWER: Do you know **who** she is?

EXAMPLE: I saw Sabrina, *(who, whom)* I know from school.

STEP 1: The subordinate clause is *(who, whom) I know from school.*

STEP 2: In this clause, the pronoun is the direct object of the verb *know: I know (who, whom).*

STEP 3: As a direct object, the pronoun should be in the objective case.

STEP 4: The objective form is *whom.*

ANSWER: I saw Sabrina, **whom** I know from school.

Remember that no words outside the subordinate clause affect the case of the pronoun. In the second example above, the whole clause *who she is* is the direct object of the verb in the independent clause, *do know.* In the subordinate clause, though, *who* is used as a predicate nominative, which takes the nominative case.

NOTE: *Whom* is often left out of a subordinate clause, but its function is understood.

EXAMPLES The actor (whom) I wrote to sent these photos. [*Whom* is understood to be the object of the preposition *to.*]

The man (whom) we saw on the elevator looked familiar. [*Whom* is understood to be the direct object of *saw.*]

Peanuts reprinted by permission of United Feature Syndicate, Inc.

EXERCISE 9   ### Determining the Use of *Who* and *Whom* in Subordinate Clauses

Identify the subordinate clause containing *who* or *whom* in each of the following sentences. Then, tell how the relative pronoun (*who* or *whom*) is used in its own clause—as *subject, predicate nominative, direct object,* or *object of a preposition.*

EXAMPLE   **1.** She is someone whom we all admire.
  1. *whom we all admire—direct object*

1. The people who are born in Puerto Rico live in a commonwealth, with its own Senate, Supreme Court, and governor's Cabinet.
2. In 1969, the governor needed a secretary of labor on whom he could depend.
3. The person whom he appointed would occupy the most difficult and sensitive position in the Cabinet.
4. Do you know who the choice was?
5. The choice fell to Mrs. Julia Rivera De Vincenti, who became the first woman to occupy a Cabinet post in Puerto Rico.
6. De Vincenti, who had completed the requirements for a Ph.D. degree in management and collective bargaining at Cornell University, was a good choice.
7. De Vincenti, who was later appointed to the U.S. Mission to the United Nations, was the first Puerto Rican to serve in that capacity.
8. She addressed the General Assembly and showed that she was a person who knew her job well.
9. She praised her compatriots, from whom new advances in agriculture had recently come.
10. And De Vincenti made history again, for she was the first woman who ever wore a pantsuit to address the General Assembly!

USAGE

Appositives

20f. Pronouns used as appositives should be in the same case as the word they refer to.

An *appositive* is a noun or pronoun given with another noun or pronoun to identify or explain it.

EXAMPLES   The late arrivals, **she, he,** and **I,** missed the first act. [The pronouns are in the nominative case because they are in apposition with the subject *arrivals.*]

The co-captains should be the best bowlers, **he** and **she.** [The pronouns are in the nominative case because they are in apposition with the predicate nominative *bowlers.*]

The article mentions the winners, **her** and **me.** [The pronouns are in the objective case because they are in apposition with the direct object *winners.*]

Ms. Lee gave the debaters, **them** and **us,** name tags. [The pronouns are in the objective case because they are in apposition with the indirect object *debaters.*]

The finalists were narrowed to two, **him** and **her.** [The pronouns are in the objective case because they are in apposition with the object of the preposition *two.*]

The pronouns *we* and *us* are sometimes used with noun appositives.

EXAMPLES   **We** sophomores raised the most money for charity. [The pronoun is in the nominative case because it is the subject of the sentence.]

The judges awarded **us** members of the jazz band a superior rating. [The pronoun is in the objective case because it is the indirect object of the verb *awarded.*]

To decide which form is correct for a pronoun used as an appositive or with an appositive, read the sentence with only the pronoun.

EXAMPLES   Coach Karas congratulated the two starting forwards, Angela and (*I, me*). [Omit the direct object *forwards*: Coach Karas congratulated Angela and **me.**]

(*We, Us*) girls made the playoffs! [Omit the appositive *girls*: **We** made the playoffs!]

REFERENCE NOTE: See pages 590–591 for more information on appositives.

▶ REVIEW E **Selecting Pronouns to Complete Sentences Correctly**

Choose the correct pronoun in parentheses in each of the following sentences. Then, tell whether each is used as a *subject*, a *predicate nominative*, a *direct object*, an *indirect object*, an *object of a preposition*, or an *appositive*.

1. The two winners, Sean and (*she, her*), received huge green ribbons decorated with shamrocks.
2. Will Meg and (*she, her*) run the concession stand?
3. The coach asked you and (*I, me*) for help with the equipment.
4. Becky and (*she, her*) rode their bikes to the meeting.
5. The lighting crew for the play was Manuel and (*I, me*).
6. They treat (*whoever, whomever*) they hire very well.
7. I think it was Denzel Washington and (*he, him*) who starred in *Glory*.
8. They met Jennie and (*she, her*) at the airport.
9. Joe Leaphorn and Jim Chee are the Navajo detectives (*who, whom*) Tony Hillerman writes about in his crime stories.
10. I think that the people who were costumed as pirates are (*they, them*).

▶ REVIEW F **Proofreading a Paragraph for Correct Pronoun Forms**

Some of the sentences in the following paragraph contain one or more pronouns that are used incorrectly. If a pronoun is incorrect, write the correct form. If the sentence is correct, write *C*.

[1] Us cousins were getting so confused at the family reunion that Rochelle, Darla, and me made the Family Relationship Chart shown on the next page. [2] Before long, the busiest people at the picnic were they and me! [3] Aunts and uncles consulted us to find out who they were related to and just how they were related. [4] It all started when Jules wanted to know the connection

USAGE

between him and Vicky. [5] We figured out that Vicky is the great-granddaughter of Jules's grandmother's brother, so her and Jules are second cousins once removed. [6] Looking at our chart, we could see that Vicky and Jules are in different generations, even though him and her are the same age. [7] All afternoon, curious relatives besieged Rochelle, Darla, and I with questions. [8] We helped whomever asked us. [9] Grandmother said she didn't know who to be prouder of, we or our cousins who made the refreshments. [10] Everyone learned something new about our family ties that day and gave the two other girls and I a big round of applause.

Family Relationship Chart

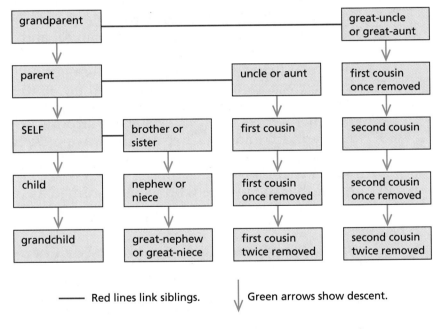

——— Red lines link siblings.   ↓ Green arrows show descent.

REVIEW G   **Determining the Proper Case of Pronouns in Sentences**

For each of the following sentences, write *C* if the pronouns are all in the proper case. If a pronoun is incorrect, write the correct form.

1. Be careful who you tell.
2. May Marie and I cut a few pictures out of this old copy of *Ebony*?

3. My family goes to the dentist who Ms. Calhoun recommended.
4. Coretta said there would be other flag bearers in addition to Hugh and I.
5. At the head of the parade were us Girl Scouts.
6. The treaty gave them and the Ojibwa people the right to harvest wild rice there.
7. Nobody except Josh and him finished the marathon.
8. We wish we had neighbors like Sylvia and him.
9. Did your father and them reach an agreement about the boundary dispute?
10. Joanne and us found a great beach.

USAGE

▶ EXERCISE 10   **Composing Sentences Using Pronouns**

Last month you joined the Climbing Club, and today you have just completed your first full day's climb. The club's advisor, Mr. Kraslow, has asked you to prepare a short report sharing your impressions of your first big climb. Use these pictures you took to help you write ten sentences for your report. Include one of the following phrases in each sentence. Be prepared to tell how each phrase is used.

1. Mr. Kraslow and us
2. Thomas and her
3. him and us
4. whoever
5. we newer climbers
6. they and Mr. Kraslow
7. he and they
8. Terri and me
9. Thomas and them
10. he and the Climbing Club

Pronouns in Incomplete Constructions

20g. After *than* or *as* introducing an incomplete construction, use the pronoun form that would be used if the construction were completed.

> I know Mac better than **he** (knows Mac).
> I know Mac better than (I know) **him.**
> Do you visit Aunt Bessie as often as **we** (visit Aunt Bessie)?
> Do you visit Aunt Bessie as often as (you visit) **us**?

 EXERCISE 11   **Selecting Pronouns to Complete Incomplete Constructions in Sentences**

For each of the following sentences, choose the correct form of the pronoun in parentheses. Also supply in parentheses the missing part of the incomplete construction. Then, give the use of the pronoun in its clause. If a sentence may be completed in two different ways, provide both completions.

EXAMPLE   **1.** I like Arsenio Hall better than (*she, her*).
    1. *she* (*likes Arsenio Hall*)—*subject;* (*I like*) *her*—*direct object*

1. We played defense better than (*they, them*).
2. When Michael Chang won the men's singles title at the French Open, nobody was as pleased as (*I, me*).
3. Nobody tried harder than (*she, her*).
4. You are a month younger than (*he, him*).
5. I know Millie better than (*she, her*).
6. Did you get as far in that book as (*I, me*)?
7. Richard wanted more tickets than (*we, us*).
8. Bianca lives farther away than (*we, us*).
9. She visited Lisa more often than (*I, me*).
10. Carlos plays classical guitar in the style of Andrés Segovia but, of course, not as well as (*he, him*).

Inexact Pronoun Reference

20h. A pronoun should always refer clearly to its antecedent.

(1) Avoid an ambiguous reference.

In an ***ambiguous reference,*** a pronoun can refer to either of two antecedents.

AMBIGUOUS   Marissa called Yolanda while she was at the library.
[Who was at the library, Marissa or Yolanda?]

CLEAR   While **Marissa** was at the library, **she** called Yolanda.

or

CLEAR   While **Yolanda** was at the library, Marissa called **her.**

AMBIGUOUS   After viewing Roy's paintings and Elton's sculpture, the judges awarded his work the blue ribbon.
[Whose work won the blue ribbon?]

CLEAR   The judges awarded **Elton** the blue ribbon after viewing **his** sculpture and Roy's paintings.

or

CLEAR   The judges awarded **Roy** the blue ribbon after viewing **his** paintings and Elton's sculpture.

(2) Be sure that each pronoun you use has a specific, stated antecedent.

The pronouns *it, this, that, which,* and *such* are often used to refer to a general idea rather than to a specific noun. Using these pronouns in this way can lead to ***general reference*** errors.

GENERAL   Paul has a job interview after school today. That explains why Paul is all dressed up. [no specific antecedent for *That*]

CLEAR   Paul is all dressed up because he has a job interview after school today.

or

CLEAR   The reason that Paul is all dressed up is that he has a job interview after school today.

GENERAL   My biology class is going on a field trip to the coast this week, which should be fun. [no specific antecedent for *which*]

CLEAR   My biology class is going on a field trip to the coast this week. The trip should be fun.

or

CLEAR   Going on a field trip to the coast with my biology class this week should be fun.

USAGE

Sometimes a writer will suggest a particular word or idea without stating it. A pronoun that refers to this unstated word or idea is said to have a *weak reference* to the antecedent.

WEAK   When I listen in the car, I turn it up loud. [*It* may refer to a radio, tape player, or CD player. The writer suggests one of these devices but does not state which one.]

CLEAR   When I listen to the **radio** in the car, I turn **it** up loud.

WEAK   Royale writes stories, and she hopes to make it her career. [*It* most likely refers to the unstated noun *writing;* consequently, the writer has not made the pronoun-antecedent relationship clear.]

CLEAR   Royale writes stories, and she hopes to make **writing** her career.

In conversation, people often use the pronouns *it, they,* and *you* unnecessarily. In writing, be sure to avoid such *indefinite reference* errors.

INDEFINITE   In the newspaper, it reported that the robbers had been caught. [The pronoun *it* is not necessary to the meaning of the sentence. Revise the sentence to eliminate the wordiness caused by the indefinite reference.]

CLEAR   The newspaper reported that the robbers had been caught.

INDEFINITE   In the article, they include a toll-free number to call for more information. [The pronoun *they* is not necessary to the meaning of the sentence.]

CLEAR   The article includes a toll-free number to call for more information.

NOTE: Familiar expressions such as *it is raining, it's early,* and *it seems like* are correct even though they contain inexact pronoun references. The antecedents to these pronouns are commonly understood to be the weather, time, and so forth.

► EXERCISE 12   **Correcting Inexact Pronoun References**

Revise each sentence in the following paragraph, correcting the inexact pronoun reference. If a sentence is correct, write *C*.

EXAMPLE   [1] In a brochure recently published by the Environmental Protection Agency (EPA), it promotes recycling to reduce waste.

1. *A brochure recently published by the Environmental Protection Agency (EPA) promotes recycling to reduce waste.*

[1] The newest twist in recycling is *precycling*—cutting it off at its source. [2] Last month, after reading the EPA's brochure, my family decided to put its ideas into practice. [3] We now choose products that have less packaging; we carry groceries home in cloth bags instead of paper or plastic ones; and we buy containers that can be refilled, which is easy. [4] We even wrote to the Mail Preference Service, Direct Marketing Association, and asked that our names not be sold to mailing-list companies. [5] That greatly reduced the amount of junk mail we get. [6] When we do have waste products, inventing new ways to use them becomes a challenge in creative thinking; one of them was mine. [7] Now, we pack fragile objects in bits of plastic foam and other nonrecyclable materials so that they don't get broken in shipping. [8] We use plastic produce bags as sandwich wrappers or as liners for small trash cans, and it works just fine. [9] We also convert cottage cheese cartons and margarine tubs into food-storage containers, and we plan to make a habit of it. [10] In just a few short weeks, we've learned that in the 1990s, you recycle by remembering the three *r*'s: *r*educe, *r*euse, and *r*ecycle.

WRITING APPLICATION

Using Pronouns Correctly in a Letter

When you are writing about a complex event involving several people doing and saying things, your meaning can be lost if an antecedent is unclear.

UNCLEAR   Howard slipped, and Kiley recovered the ball and made a basket. **This** caused pandemonium among the fans. [What is the *this* that caused the pandemonium?]

CLEAR   **The quick recovery** caused pandemonium among the fans.

How else could you revise the unclear sentence to make its meaning clear?

▶ WRITING ACTIVITY

Your favorite musical group isn't happy with the director of their latest video. As a result, they are sponsoring a "Be a Music Video Director" contest. To enter, you have to write a letter explaining your idea for a different video of the same song. Tell which singers, dancers, and musicians you would cast in your video. Include at least ten pronouns in your sentences. Be sure that no pronoun has an unclear antecedent.

Prewriting   Start by choosing the song you want to create a video for. Then, list some ideas for three or four scenes in your video. Next to each scene idea, list the performers you would use in that scene and describe the action. In addition to actual people, you may want to have cartoon characters or other animated figures in your video.

Writing   As you write sentences about your music video, make the sequence of events clear. Make the spatial relationships clear, too, telling where the cast members are located.

Evaluating and Revising   Check your rough draft to be sure that your explanation is clear. If you have included too many performers or too many details, eliminate the least interesting ones now. Have a classmate read your letter, looking for inexact uses of the pronouns *it, this, that,* and *which.* If he or she is confused by any sentences with inexact pronoun references, revise those sentences.

Proofreading   Carefully read your letter again to be sure that all pronouns are in the correct case.

> **REVIEW H**   **Selecting Pronouns to Complete Sentences**

Choose the correct pronoun in parentheses in each of the following sentences. Be prepared to give reasons for your answers.

1. Heather and (*he, him*) live on a blueberry farm.
2. Did the teacher give that assignment to (*whoever, whomever*) was absent yesterday?
3. We wondered (*who, whom*) started the rumor.
4. Do you intercept passes as well as (*she, her*)?
5. The supporting players were Dina, Janelle, and (*she, her*).
6. I was standing in line behind Dave and (*he, him*).
7. You and (*I, me*) could write biographical sketches about General Colin L. Powell, who was chairman of the Joint Chiefs of Staff under President Bush.
8. The skit was written by Cy and (*he, him*).
9. The electrician warned (*he, him*) and (*I, me*) about the frayed wires.
10. Amy Tan, (*who, whom*) the critics had praised, autographed a copy of her novel *The Joy Luck Club* for me.

> **REVIEW I**   **Using Pronouns Correctly in Original Sentences**

Outdoor murals like the one on the next page give artists a chance to express themselves on a grand scale! The owners of an enormous warehouse have made one long wall available to your class. Each team of students can paint whatever they wish on a thirty-foot section. The artwork can be serious or humorous, or it can just be a colorful design. Write ten sentences about the teams and their paintings. In each sentence, use a different pronoun or phrase from the following list. Be sure all pronouns are used in the way indicated in the exercise.

Francisco and I	me and my team	he
Matthew, Talbot, and us	Trenice and she	whoever
her and them	who	them and you
they and Luann	whom	whomever

EXAMPLE **1.** predicate nominative
1. *The painters outlining the black unicorn are Trenice and she.*

1. object of a preposition
2. subject of a clause
3. indirect object
4. subject appositive
5. subject of the sentence
6. predicate nominative
7. direct object
8. object appositive
9. subject of an incomplete construction
10. direct object of an incomplete construction

Review: Posttest

A. Determining the Proper Case of Pronouns in Sentences

If a pronoun is used incorrectly in the following sentences, write the correct form of the pronoun. If a sentence is correct, write C.

1. Del can't do math any better than her.
2. There was some misunderstanding between him and his brother.
3. To who was the letter addressed?
4. I showed the negatives to Cecilia and she.
5. It can't be them; that's not their car.

6. Ben and you can come with them and me.
7. Leontyne Price's accomplishments were familiar to everyone in the class except him and I.
8. Us band members have to be at school early to practice marching.
9. He's the sportscaster who irritates me with his pretentious talk.
10. In front of the school stood two drenched children, Charlene and he.

B. Proofreading Sentences for the Correct Use of Pronouns

Most of the following sentences contain one or more incorrect pronouns. Identify each incorrect pronoun, and write the correct form. If all of the pronouns in a sentence are correct, write C.

11. There's nothing like an action-packed all-star basketball game to give Dad and I a thrill!
12. Our team was only two points behind the opposing team when Barkley's shot bounced off the rim, and Barkley and Robinson rushed for it.
13. As gravity pulled him and Robinson toward the floor, Barkley managed to tip the ball to Thomas.
14. Thomas saw Stockton coming and dribbled behind his back to elude he and Olajuwon.
15. When Stockton and Olajuwon collided, nobody was more surprised than them.
16. "If we make this, the score will be tied," thought Thomas.
17. Thomas looked for Jordan and realized that the blur streaking upcourt on the left was him.
18. "Five seconds to go—I have to pass to whomever is open, and Bird's the one."
19. Bird took a shot and missed; four players struggled for the ball and it went in, which meant that Thomas and his teammates had won.
20. In the whirlwind action during the last couple of seconds, the frantic referee couldn't see whom had fouled who.

USAGE

21 USING VERBS CORRECTLY

Principal Parts, Tense, Voice

Diagnostic Test

A. Writing the Past or Past Participle Form of Verbs

Write the correct past or past participle form of the verb given before each of the following sentences.

EXAMPLE **1.** *do* Because he ___ his work so well, he got a raise.
1. *did*

1. *write* Although Emily Dickinson ___ poetry most of her life, very little of her work was published until after her death.

2. *drink* When he saw that the animals had ___ all the water, he gave them more.

3. *throw* Regarding weeds as unwanted intruders, she pulled them from the ground and ___ them over the fence.

4. *swim* The water was cold and daylight was fading, so he ___ only a short distance before turning back to shore.

5. *freeze*   The dew ___ during the night, covering each twig and blade of grass with a crisp, silvery coating.

6. *give*   After my brother had ___ his new puppy a bath, he seemed to be wetter than the dog.

7. *speak*   She ___ in such a low, hushed voice that the people in the audience had to strain to hear her remarks.

8. *run*   Frightened by the traffic, the deer ___ back into the forest.

9. *ride*   Leading the parade was an officer who ___ a prancing black horse.

10. *ring*   When the church bell ___ on Tuesday evening, the villagers became alarmed.

USAGE

B. Revising Verb Tense or Voice

Revise the following paragraph, correcting verbs that are in the wrong tense or that use an awkward passive voice. If a sentence is correct, write *C.*

[11] Katherine Davalos Ortega is born in 1934 in Tularosa, New Mexico, and worked in her family's restaurant and other businesses since she has been a small child. [12] Early in life a teaching career was chosen by her, but she was told that being Hispanic might prevent her from getting a teaching position. [13] As a result, she decided to pursue a business career instead, and by 1975, she has become the first woman president of a California bank. [14] In recognition of her professional abilities, Ms. Ortega was nominated by President Reagan to be Treasurer of the United States and was sworn in on October 3, 1983. [15] Her signature may be familiar to you, because it is appearing on more than twenty billion dollar bills and other types of U.S. currency.

C. Determining Correct Use of *Lie* and *Lay, Sit* and *Set,* and *Rise* and *Raise* in Sentences

Most of the following sentences contain at least one error in the use of *lie* or *lay, sit* or *set,* or *rise* or *raise.* Identify each incorrect verb, and give the correct verb. If a sentence is correct, write *C*.

16. We left our lawn furniture setting on the patio.
17. They lain the bricks next to where we sat the wood.
18. When the dough has risen for fifteen minutes, turn it out onto the floured board.
19. When we are rising from bed in the morning, the Chinese are laying down to sleep.
20. The escaping slaves laid quietly in the undergrowth.

The Principal Parts of Verbs

Every verb has four basic forms called *principal parts.* All of a verb's other forms come from its principal parts.

21a. The principal parts of a verb are the **base form,** the **present participle,** the **past,** and the **past participle.**

PRINCIPAL PARTS OF *WALK* AND *DO*			
BASE FORM	PRESENT PARTICIPLE	PAST	PAST PARTICIPLE
walk	(is) walking	walked	(have) walked
do	(is) doing	did	(have) done

The words *is* and *have* are included to remind you that when the present participle and past participle are used to form verb tenses, they're preceded by forms of these two helping verbs.

EXAMPLES   I **am doing** my homework now.
I **have done** all my homework already.

 REFERENCE NOTE: See page 527 for more information on using helping verbs with present participles and past participles.

NOTE: Some teachers refer to the base form as the infinitive. Follow your teacher's directions in labeling these words.

Regular Verbs

21b. A *regular verb* is one that forms its past and past participle by adding –*d* or –*ed* to the base form.

BASE FORM	PRESENT PARTICIPLE	PAST	PAST PARTICIPLE
work	(is) working	worked	(have) worked
receive	(is) receiving	received	(have) received

 REFERENCE NOTE: For guidelines on spelling verbs when adding –*ed* or –*ing*, see pages 874–875.

A few regular verbs have an alternate past and past participle form ending in –*t*.

BASE FORM	PRESENT PARTICIPLE	PAST	PAST PARTICIPLE
burn	(is) burning	burned or burnt	(have) burned or burnt
leap	(is) leaping	leaped or leapt	(have) leaped or leapt

NOTE: The regular verbs *deal* and *mean* always form the past and past participle by adding –*t: dealt, (have) dealt; meant, (have) meant.*

Irregular Verbs

21c. An *irregular verb* is one that forms its past and past participle in some way other than by adding –*d* or –*ed* to the base form.

An irregular verb forms its past and past participle in one of the following ways:

- changing vowels *or* consonants
- changing vowels *and* consonants
- making no change

EXAMPLES

BASE FORM	PAST	PAST PARTICIPLE
fly	flew	(have) flown
bend	bent	(have) bent
sell	sold	(have) sold
beat	beat	(have) beaten
let	let	(have) let

NOTE: When you're not sure whether a verb is regular or irregular, check a dictionary that lists the principal parts of irregular verbs.

PRINCIPAL PARTS OF COMMON IRREGULAR VERBS

BASE FORM	PRESENT PARTICIPLE	PAST	PAST PARTICIPLE
begin	(is) beginning	began	(have) begun
blow	(is) blowing	blew	(have) blown
break	(is) breaking	broke	(have) broken
bring	(is) bringing	brought	(have) brought
burst	(is) bursting	burst	(have) burst
choose	(is) choosing	chose	(have) chosen
come	(is) coming	came	(have) come
dive	(is) diving	dove (*or* dived)	(have) dived
do	(is) doing	did	(have) done
draw	(is) drawing	drew	(have) drawn
drink	(is) drinking	drank	(have) drunk
drive	(is) driving	drove	(have) driven
eat	(is) eating	ate	(have) eaten
fall	(is) falling	fell	(have) fallen
freeze	(is) freezing	froze	(have) frozen
give	(is) giving	gave	(have) given
go	(is) going	went	(have) gone
hear	(is) hearing	heard	(have) heard
know	(is) knowing	knew	(have) known
leave	(is) leaving	left	(have) left
ride	(is) riding	rode	(have) ridden
ring	(is) ringing	rang	(have) rung
run	(is) running	ran	(have) run

(continued)

USAGE

	PRINCIPAL PARTS OF COMMON IRREGULAR VERBS (*continued*)		
BASE FORM	**PRESENT PARTICIPLE**	**PAST**	**PAST PARTICIPLE**
see	(is) seeing	saw	(have) seen
sing	(is) singing	sang (*or* sung)	(have) sung
sleep	(is) sleeping	slept	(have) slept
speak	(is) speaking	spoke	(have) spoken
steal	(is) stealing	stole	(have) stolen
swim	(is) swimming	swam	(have) swum
take	(is) taking	took	(have) taken
teach	(is) teaching	taught	(have) taught
think	(is) thinking	thought	(have) thought
throw	(is) throwing	threw	(have) thrown
write	(is) writing	wrote	(have) written

USAGE

▶ ORAL PRACTICE 1   **Using Regular and Irregular Verbs**

Read each sentence aloud, stressing each italicized verb.

1. Keisha *is braiding* Tiffany's hair in cornrows.
2. Bob *read* the want ads today, just as he *has read* them each day this week.
3. Mom, I *am bringing* you breakfast in bed, but I *have burned* your toast!
4. Warren *designed* the posters for the fall program.
5. Paloma Picasso, the jewelry designer, *has chosen* an artistic career different from her famous father's.
6. Carrie *went* to Penn State; Hector *is going* to Boston College.
7. Someone *ate* all the leftover spaghetti, but nobody *has touched* the baked beans.
8. If you *have* never *seen* a meteor shower, *run* outside right now!

▶ EXERCISE 1   **Writing the Past or Past Participle Form of Irregular Verbs to Complete Sentences**

Give the correct past or past participle form of the verb given before each of the following sentences.

1. *sing*   The first drops of rain began to fall just after we had ___ the national anthem.
2. *begin*   I had already ___ my homework.
3. *freeze* The sub-zero winds nearly ___ the Pawnee hunters as they tracked the herd of bison.
4. *fly*   Last summer we ___ in a lighter-than-air balloon.
5. *see*   During our visit to Hawaii, we ___ a group of performers do a traditional hula dance.
6. *take*   My sister has ___ that course.
7. *fall*   By the time Rolando finished carving the little figure of a saint, hundreds of tiny wood shavings had ___ to the floor.
8. *throw*   The horse had ___ its shoe.
9. *break*   We hoped we hadn't ___ the machine.
10. *speak* Harley's grandmother ___ to our class about her parents' life as sharecroppers in the early 1900s.

EXERCISE 2   **Using the Correct Past or Past Participle Form of Verbs**

Give the correct form of each italicized verb in the following paragraph.

We recently [1] (*see*) paintings by the African American artist Henry Ossawa Tanner. Tanner had [2] (*choose*) his lifelong career in art by the time he was thirteen years old. While walking in a park one day with his father, they had [3] (*come*) upon a landscape artist at work. Years later, Tanner [4] (*write*), "It was this simple event that . . . set me on fire." Young Henry [5] (*bring*) such eagerness to his work that, before long, he [6] (*teach*) himself to draw well enough to be admitted to one of the finest art schools in the country. His paintings were beautiful but did not sell well, so Tanner [7] (*go*) abroad. He [8] (*fall*) in love with the city of Paris, and lived and worked there for the rest of his life, winning many important painting awards. Shown on the next page is his best-known work, *The Banjo Lesson*, which he painted in Paris from sketches he had [9] (*draw*) years earlier in North Carolina. In 1969, long after Tanner's death, a touring exhibit finally [10] (*give*) Americans a look at the work of this gifted artist.

Henry Ossawa Tanner, *The Banjo Lesson* (1893). Hampton University Museum, Hampton, Va.

▶ EXERCISE 3   **Selecting the Past or Past Participle Form of Verbs**

Choose the correct form of the verb in parentheses.

1. We (*did, done*) everything we could to help him.
2. Who has (*drank, drunk*) the rest of the orange juice?
3. Someone has already (*tore, torn*) out the coupon.
4. I wish you had (*spoke, spoken*) to me about it sooner.
5. I dived off the high board and (*swam, swum*) the length of the pool.
6. You must have (*rang, rung*) the doorbell while I was out.
7. Nancy had never (*ate, eaten*) a tamale before.
8. Lois (*blowed, blew*) up the balloon.
9. Suddenly the balloon (*burst, bursted*).
10. We were (*drove, driven*) to the train station in a taxi.

▶ EXERCISE 4   **Using the Past and Past Participle Forms of Verbs**

You have just joined a traveling circus, and you are in an acrobatic troupe with the performers shown on the next page. You work hard—not only perfecting your act but also helping with daily chores. Animals must be cared for, tents set up and taken down, and costumes made ready. You must also attend classes with a tutor! However, there's still time for fun. Write a short letter to your family, telling about your circus adventure. Use at least five past and five past participle forms of the irregular verbs listed on pages 680–681, and underline each one.

Tense

21d. Learn the names of the six tenses and how each tense is formed.

Verbs change form to show the time of the action or the idea they express. The time indicated by the form of a verb is called its *tense.* In English, every verb has six tenses:

present	present perfect
past	past perfect
future	future perfect

The following charts show all six tenses of a regular verb (*talk*) and of an irregular verb (*throw*). Listing the verb forms in this way is called *conjugating* the verb.

CONJUGATION OF THE VERB *TALK*

Present infinitive: *to talk*   Perfect infinitive: *to have talked*

PRINCIPAL PARTS OF *TALK*

BASE FORM	PRESENT PARTICIPLE	PAST	PAST PARTICIPLE
talk	(is) talking	talked	(have) talked

PRESENT TENSE

SINGULAR	PLURAL
I talk	we talk
you talk	you talk
he, she, it talks	they talk

PAST TENSE

SINGULAR	PLURAL
I talked	we talked
you talked	you talked
he, she, it talked	they talked

FUTURE TENSE
(*will* or *shall* + the base form)

SINGULAR	PLURAL
I will (shall) talk	we will (shall) talk
you will talk	you will talk
he, she, it will talk	they will talk

PRESENT PERFECT TENSE
(*have* or *has* + the past participle)

SINGULAR	PLURAL
I have talked	we have talked
you have talked	you have talked
he, she, it has talked	they have talked

PAST PERFECT TENSE
(*had* + the past participle)

SINGULAR	PLURAL
I had talked	we had talked
you had talked	you had talked
he, she, it had talked	they had talked

(continued)

USAGE

CONJUGATION OF THE VERB *TALK* (*continued*)	
FUTURE PERFECT TENSE (*will have* or *shall have* + the past participle)	
SINGULAR I will (shall) have talked you will have talked he, she, it will have talked	**PLURAL** we will (shall) have talked you will have talked they will have talked

☞ **REFERENCE NOTE:** For the conjugation of a verb in the passive voice, see pages 694–695.

In each tense another form, called the *progressive form,* may be used to show continuing action. The progressive form is made up of a form of *be* plus the verb's present participle.

Present Progressive	am, are, is talking
Past Progressive	was, were talking
Future Progressive	will (shall) be talking
Present Perfect Progressive	has, have been talking
Past Perfect Progressive	had been talking
Future Perfect Progressive	will (shall) have been talking

CONJUGATION OF THE VERB *THROW*			
Present infinitive: *to throw* Perfect infinitive: *to have thrown*			
PRINCIPAL PARTS OF *THROW*			
BASE FORM	**PRESENT PARTICIPLE**	**PAST**	**PAST PARTICIPLE**
throw	(is) throwing	threw	(have) thrown

SINGULAR	**PLURAL**
I throw	we throw
you throw	you throw
he, she, it throws	they throw
Present progressive: *am, are, is throwing*	

(continued)

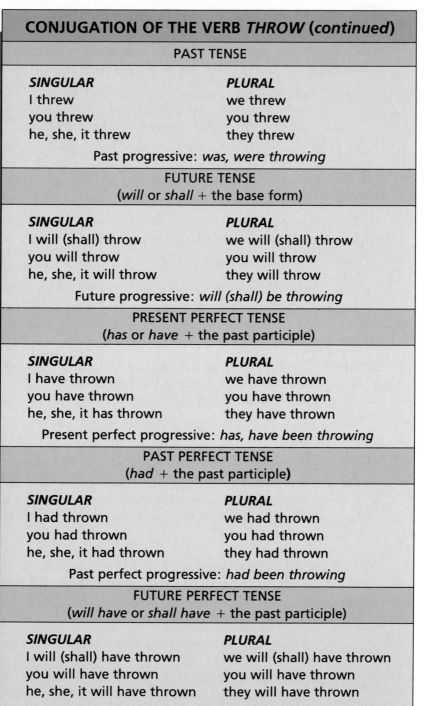

CONJUGATION OF THE VERB *THROW* (*continued*)

PAST TENSE

SINGULAR	PLURAL
I threw	we threw
you threw	you threw
he, she, it threw	they threw

Past progressive: *was, were throwing*

FUTURE TENSE
(*will* or *shall* + the base form)

SINGULAR	PLURAL
I will (shall) throw	we will (shall) throw
you will throw	you will throw
he, she, it will throw	they will throw

Future progressive: *will (shall) be throwing*

PRESENT PERFECT TENSE
(*has* or *have* + the past participle)

SINGULAR	PLURAL
I have thrown	we have thrown
you have thrown	you have thrown
he, she, it has thrown	they have thrown

Present perfect progressive: *has, have been throwing*

PAST PERFECT TENSE
(*had* + the past participle)

SINGULAR	PLURAL
I had thrown	we had thrown
you had thrown	you had thrown
he, she, it had thrown	they had thrown

Past perfect progressive: *had been throwing*

FUTURE PERFECT TENSE
(*will have* or *shall have* + the past participle)

SINGULAR	PLURAL
I will (shall) have thrown	we will (shall) have thrown
you will have thrown	you will have thrown
he, she, it will have thrown	they will have thrown

Future perfect progressive: *will (shall) have been throwing*

USAGE

21e. Learn the uses of the six tenses.

(1) The *present tense* is used to express an action or a state of being occurring now, at the present time.

EXAMPLES Sonja **owns** a calculator.
Larry **is** in the Chess Club.
We **are rehearsing** the play. [progressive form]

The present tense may be used to indicate habitual action.

EXAMPLE He **runs** two miles a day.

The present tense is also used to express a general truth—something that is true at all times.

EXAMPLE Haste **makes** waste.

The present tense is often used in discussing literary works, particularly in summarizing the plot or subject of a work. This use of the present tense is called the *literary present.*

EXAMPLES In Act III of *Julius Caesar,* the conspirators **gather** around Caesar. Casca **is** the first to stab him; then the others **plunge** their knives into Caesar.

Sometimes the present tense is used to relate past events in order to make them seem vivid. This use is called the *historical present.*

EXAMPLES During the unstable years following the 1910 Mexican Revolution, Emiliano Zapata **commands** a large army of revolutionaries and **occupies** Mexico City three different times.

(2) The *past tense* is used to express an action or a state of being that occurred in the past but did not continue into the present.

EXAMPLES I **ran** toward the door.
I **was running** toward the door. [progressive form]

(3) The *future tense* is used to express an action or a state of being that will occur. The future tense is formed with *will* or *shall.*

EXAMPLES   I **will leave** this week.
I **will be leaving** this week. [progressive form]

There are several other ways to indicate future time.

EXAMPLES   I **am going to leave** this week.
I **leave later** this week. [present tense with a word or phrase clearly indicating future time]

(4) The ***present perfect tense*** is used to express an action or a state of being that occurred at some indefinite time in the past. The present perfect tense is formed with *have* or *has.*

EXAMPLE   She **has visited** Chicago.

The present perfect tense is also used to express an action (or a state of being) that occurred in the past and continues into the present.

EXAMPLES   She **has worked** there several years.
I **have been playing** guitar for nearly six months. [progressive form]

(5) The ***past perfect tense*** is used to express an action or a state of being that was completed before some other past action or event took place. The past perfect tense is formed with *had.*

EXAMPLES   After she **had revised** her essay, she handed it in. [The action of revising was completed before the action of handing in.]
When he **had washed** the dishes, he sat down to rest. [The action of washing was completed before the action of resting.]

(6) The ***future perfect tense*** is used to express an action or a state of being that will be completed before some other future occurrence. The future perfect tense is formed with *shall have* or *will have.*

EXAMPLES   By the time I leave, I **will have packed** all my clothes. [The action of packing will be completed before the action of leaving.]
At the end of next year, I **will have been attending** school for eleven years. [progressive form]

USAGE

USAGE

▶ EXERCISE 5   **Explaining the Uses of the Tenses of Verbs in Sentences**

Explain the difference in meaning between the sentences in the following pairs. Both sentences in each pair are correct. Identify the tense of the verb in each sentence.

1. I will start working by this afternoon.
   I will have started working by this afternoon.
2. What happened at the game?
   What has been happening at the game?
3. She lived in Cleveland for four years.
   She has lived in Cleveland for four years.
4. Before next year I will get a driver's license.
   Before next year I will have gotten a driver's license.
5. Some Green Berets were practicing tae kwon do during their lunch break.
   Some Green Berets have been practicing tae kwon do during their lunch break.

▶ EXERCISE 6   **Using the Different Tenses of Verbs in Sentences**

Change the tense of the verb in each of the following sentences, according to the directions given after the sentence.

1. Otto lived here for a year. (Change to past perfect.)
2. When the alarm goes off, I will get up. (Change *will get* to future perfect.)
3. Have you read Thomas Sowell's excellent how-to book *Choosing a College*? (Change *have read* to present perfect progressive.)
4. When I get back, will you go? (Change *will go* to future perfect.)
5. Were they at the party? (Change to past perfect.)
6. Were you invited? (Change to present perfect.)
7. The soloist sings well. (Change to present perfect.)
8. The bus arrives on time. (Change to future.)
9. By the time you get here, Cammi will find out. (Change *will find* to future perfect.)
10. At ten o'clock, the klezmer band will play for an hour without a break. (Change to future perfect progressive.)

PICTURE THIS

Recently, you visited your cousins who live on this ranch. While you were there, heavy rains caused a nearby river to flood. You and your aunt and uncle and cousins managed to save their home from the rising water by quickly building a dike. After returning home, you decide you want your future children and grandchildren to know what your experience was like. You write a short account of what you did and how you felt as the waters rose and you and your family fought to hold them back. Use at least five different verb tenses in your journal entry. Be prepared to tell the tense of each verb you use.

Subject: your experiences during a flood
Audience: your descendants
Purpose: to inform

USAGE

Consistency of Tense

21f. Do not change needlessly from one tense to another.

NONSTANDARD Roy **raised** his binoculars and **sees** a large bear as it **raced** back to the woods. [All the verbs refer to actions that happened at approximately the same time. However, the verbs are a mixture of past and present tenses.]

STANDARD Roy **raised** his binoculars and **saw** a large bear as it **raced** back to the woods. [The verbs are all in the past tense.]

STANDARD Roy **raises** his binoculars and **sees** a large bear as it **races** back to the woods. [The verbs are all in the present tense.]

NOTE: Sometimes, to show a sequence of events, you will need to mix verb tenses.

EXAMPLE Before we **had gone** five miles, the car **started** making funny noises, and now it **won't run** at all.

▶ EXERCISE 7 **Proofreading Paragraphs for Correct Verb Forms**

Some of the sentences in the following passage have at least one incorrect verb form. If a verb form is incorrect, write the correct form. If a sentence is correct, write *C*.

[1] The painting on the next page depicts the outcome of one of the most important battles of the Revolutionary War, a battle that took place in September and October 1777 at Saratoga, New York. [2] The leader of the British troops, General John Burgoyne, had set up camp near Saratoga and is planning to march south to Albany. [3] Burgoyne's army has been weakened by a recent attack from an American militia, which had ambushed some of his troops at Bennington, Vermont. [4] Although the march to Albany is dangerous, Burgoyne decided to take the risk because he feels bound by orders from London. [5] Meanwhile, also near Saratoga, the American troops under General Horatio Gates gather reinforcements and supplies. [6] The American forces outnumbered their British enemies by a margin of nearly two to one. [7] The

Americans are much better equipped than the British, whose provisions are badly depleted.

[8] In spite of these disadvantages, the British launch an attack on the Americans on September 19, 1777. [9] After four hours of fierce fighting, the Americans, led by General Gates or General Benedict Arnold (who later became an infamous traitor to the American cause), withdraw. [10] The British, however, have suffered serious losses, including many officers. [11] Burgoyne urgently sends messages to the British command in New York and asked for new orders. [12] He never received a response, possibly because the messages are intercepted. [13] Burgoyne's tactics became desperate. [14] He boldly leads a fresh attack against the Americans on October 7. [15] This time, however, his troops endure even worse casualties, and the next day Burgoyne prepares to retreat.

[16] The Americans surround Burgoyne's army before it could leave Saratoga. [17] As the painting shows, Burgoyne had surrendered to Benedict Arnold. [18] The Convention of Saratoga, by which Burgoyne gave up his entire force of six thousand troops, is signed on October 17. [19] Saratoga becomes a turning point in the Revolutionary War. [20] Six years later, in 1783, the British signed a peace treaty with the Americans, and the Revolutionary War ended.

Active Voice and Passive Voice

21g. A verb in the *active voice* expresses an action performed *by* its subject. A verb in the *passive voice* expresses an action done *to* its subject.

ACTIVE VOICE   The blazing fire **destroyed** the outside walls. [The subject (*fire*) performs the action.]

PASSIVE VOICE   The outside walls **were destroyed** by the blazing fire. [The subject (*walls*) receives the action.]

Notice that the object of the active sentence becomes the subject of the passive sentence. The subject of the active sentence is now given in a prepositional phrase, which could even be omitted in the passive sentence.

PASSIVE VOICE   The outside walls were destroyed.

Notice, too, that the verb has been changed from *destroyed* to the verb phrase *were destroyed.* In a passive sentence, the verb phrase always includes a form of *be* (*is, was,* etc.) plus the past participle. Other helping verbs may also be included, depending on the tense.

ACTIVE VOICE   She **grows** corn on her farm.

PASSIVE VOICE   Corn **is grown** on her farm.

ACTIVE VOICE   She **will plant** the corn in two weeks.

PASSIVE VOICE   The corn **will be planted** in two weeks.

CONJUGATION OF THE VERB *PAY* IN THE PASSIVE VOICE

PRESENT TENSE

SINGULAR	PLURAL
I am paid	we are paid
you are paid	you are paid
he, she, it is paid	they are paid

Present progressive: *am, are, is being paid*

(continued)

USAGE

CONJUGATION OF THE VERB *PAY* IN THE PASSIVE VOICE (*continued*)

PAST TENSE

SINGULAR	PLURAL
I was paid	we were paid
you were paid	you were paid
he, she, it was paid	they were paid

Past progressive: *was, were being paid*

FUTURE TENSE

SINGULAR	PLURAL
I will (shall) be paid	we will (shall) be paid
you will be paid	you will be paid
he, she, it will be paid	they will be paid

Future progressive: *will (shall) be being paid*

PRESENT PERFECT TENSE

SINGULAR	PLURAL
I have been paid	we have been paid
you have been paid	you have been paid
he, she, it has been paid	they have been paid

Present perfect progressive: *has, have been being paid*

PAST PERFECT TENSE

SINGULAR	PLURAL
I had been paid	we had been paid
you had been paid	you had been paid
he, she, it had been paid	they had been paid

Past perfect progressive: *had been being paid*

FUTURE PERFECT TENSE

SINGULAR	PLURAL
I will (shall) have been paid	we will (shall) have been paid
you will have been paid	you will have been paid
he, she, it will have been paid	they will have been paid

Future perfect progressive: *will (shall) have been being paid*

NOTE: Because the use of *be* or *been* with *being* is awkward, the progressive form is usually used only in the present tense and past tense.

USAGE

Using the Passive Voice

The passive voice emphasizes the person or thing receiving the action rather than the one performing the action. The passive voice is useful

- when the performer is difficult to specify
- when you don't know who performed an action
- when you don't want to give away the performer's identity

EXAMPLES   The mayor **was reelected** by a landslide. [performer difficult to specify]

My brother's bicycle **was stolen** yesterday. [performer unknown]

Vicious rumors **have been spread** about him. [performer deliberately concealed]

In general, though, it's a good idea to avoid the passive voice. The active voice makes your writing much more direct and forceful.

> **EXERCISE 8** **Identifying Sentences in the Active or Passive Voice**

Label the verb in each of the following sentences as *active* or *passive*. Then rewrite each passive voice sentence in the active voice.

1. The art of Lucia Wilcox was admired by many artists around the world.
2. Her blindness during her last years made her final works particularly interesting.
3. She was befriended and taught by Raoul Dufy, Fernand Léger, Robert Motherwell, and Jackson Pollock.
4. Exhibits of her paintings were shown in art galleries all over the world.
5. Her blindness occurred suddenly, though not unexpectedly.
6. It was caused by a tumor near the optic nerve.
7. After becoming blind, she claimed she had better sight than anyone else.
8. Her vision and her mind were described by her as "free of static" and "distractions."

9. Because of her blindness, her style was altered from energetic silhouettes to larger canvases in lush colors.
10. This style was imitated by many well-known artists.

USAGE

Six Troublesome Verbs

Lie and *Lay*

The verb *lie* means "to rest" or "to recline." It never takes an object.

The verb *lay* means "to put" or "to place" (something). It usually takes an object.

PRINCIPAL PARTS OF *LIE* AND *LAY*			
BASE FORM	**PRESENT PARTICIPLE**	**PAST**	**PAST PARTICIPLE**
lie (rest)	(is) lying	lay	(have) lain
lay (put)	(is) laying	laid	(have) laid

EXAMPLES   The cat often **lies** on the porch, sunning itself.
It is **lying** there now.
A thick fog **lay** over the city.
The old papers **had lain** on the desk for months.

Lay your packages here.
I am **laying** your packages here.
The mason **laid** the bricks.
He **had laid** his keys on the ledge.

To decide whether to use *lie* or *lay,* ask yourself two questions:

QUESTION 1:   What do I mean? (Is the meaning "to be in a lying position," or is it "to put something down"?)
QUESTION 2:   What time does the verb express, and which principal part accurately shows this time?

EXAMPLE: Feeling drowsy, I (lay, laid) on the couch.
QUESTION 1:   *Meaning*? Here the meaning is "to rest." Therefore, the verb should be *lie.*
QUESTION 2:   *Principal part*? The time is past. Therefore, the principal part should be *lay.*
ANSWER: Feeling drowsy, I **lay** on the couch.

EXAMPLE: The teacher (lay, laid) the cards on the desk.
QUESTION 1:   *Meaning*? Here the meaning is "to put." Therefore, the verb should be *lay.*
QUESTION 2:   *Principal part*? The time is past. Therefore, the principal part should be *laid.*
ANSWER: The teacher **laid** the cards on the desk.

ORAL PRACTICE 2   **Stressing the Correct Forms of *Lie* and *Lay* in Sentences**

Read each of the following sentences aloud, stressing the italicized verbs.

1. The ketchup bottle should *lie* on its side.
2. A light haze *lay* over the hills.
3. The cat *laid* its toy on the doorsill.
4. Someone's books are *lying* in the hall.
5. She had *lain* down for a nap.
6. Where could I have *laid* the recipe?
7. *Lay* the material on the counter.
8. You could *lie* down and relax.

▶ EXERCISE 9 ## Selecting the Correct Form of *Lie* and *Lay* to Complete Sentences

In each of the following sentences, choose the correct verb in parentheses.

1. He (*lay*, *laid*) out the silverware.
2. Eduardo (*laid*, *lay*) the strips of grilled meat on the tortilla.
3. The pasture (*lies*, *lays*) in the valley.
4. A sheet (*lay*, *laid*) over the rug to catch the paint.
5. The clothing had (*lain*, *laid*) on the floor all week.
6. Kitty (*lay*, *laid*) the book down.
7. Mrs. Nakamoto was (*lying*, *laying*) out everything necessary for the tea ceremony.
8. The theories developed by Albert Einstein (*lay*, *laid*) the groundwork for many later scientific discoveries.
9. The cat has been (*lying*, *laying*) on my coat.
10. (*Lying*, *Laying*) the tip by my plate, I rose to leave the restaurant.

▶ EXERCISE 10 ## Determining the Correct Use of *Lie* and *Lay* in Sentences

For each of the following sentences, write *C* if the verb is correct. If the verb is incorrect, write the correct form.

1. The towels laying in the corner all need to be washed.
2. After I had tripped, I sat there feeling embarrassed, my groceries lying all around me.
3. Jackie Joyner-Kersee crossed the finish line and, exhausted, laid down in the grass.
4. The fox was lying hidden in the thicket.

5. Yesterday, all we did was lie around and play CDs.
6. He was lying under the car, tinkering with the muffler.
7. The workers had lain down their tools and gone to lunch.
8. My gym bag was laying right where I had left it.
9. In his speech, César Chávez lay the responsibility for social change on the shoulders of all citizens.
10. She sighed and lay down the phone receiver.

▶ EXERCISE 11　**Proofreading a Paragraph for the Correct Use of *Lie* and *Lay***

In each sentence of the following paragraph, a form of *lie* or *lay* is used. If the wrong form is used, write the correct form. If a sentence is correct, write *C*.

[1] Brent had planned to spend all day Saturday laying new tile in the kitchen. [2] Before he started, he lay out all his materials and read the directions on the can of adhesive carefully. [3] At first, he made good progress and had lain sixteen rows of tile by lunchtime. [4] Then he ate a sandwich and laid down on the sofa for a few minutes. [5] When he returned to the kitchen, Brent found that his dog, Stanley, was laying where the next row of tiles was supposed to go. [6] Brent had forgotten that Stanley liked to lay in that particular place on the kitchen floor. [7] Unfortunately, Stanley weighed almost as much as Brent, and laying down the law to the dog had never worked. [8] Brent got a juicy meat scrap out of the refrigerator and laid it on the floor just beyond Stanley's snoring nose. [9] But the wily Stanley had been laying in wait and, in a flash, grabbed the meat. [10] To Brent's dismay, Stanley resumed his nap with a satisfied sigh, and Brent learned that the worker isn't the only one who can lay down on the job!

Sit and *Set*

The verb *sit* means "to rest in a seated position." It almost never takes an object.

The verb *set* means "to put," "to place" (something). It usually takes an object. Notice that *set* does not change form in the past or the past participle.

NOTE: In a few uses, *set* does not mean "to put" or "to place."

EXAMPLES   the sun sets, setting hens, set your watch, set a record, set out to accomplish something

PRINCIPAL PARTS OF *SIT* AND *SET*			
BASE FORM	**PRESENT PARTICIPLE**	**PAST**	**PAST PARTICIPLE**
sit (rest)	(is) sitting	sat	(have) sat
set (put)	(is) setting	set	(have) set

EXAMPLES   **You may sit.**   The car **sat** in the driveway.
　　　　　　　Set your books here.   We **set** the books there.

USAGE

ORAL PRACTICE 3   **Stressing the Correct Forms of *Sit* and *Set* in Sentences**

Read each of the following sentences aloud, stressing the italicized verb.

1. *Set* the groceries on the counter.
2. *Sit* down anywhere you like.
3. Would you please *set* the lawn chairs under the tree in the front yard?
4. The bird *sat* on the wire.
5. During Hanukkah, we always *set* the menorah in a place of honor.
6. We had *sat* in the lobby for an hour.
7. They have been *sitting* on the porch.
8. Rosa Parks made history when she chose to *sit* rather than to give up her seat to a white passenger.

EXERCISE 12   **Selecting the Correct Form of *Sit* and *Set* to Complete Sentences**

In each of the following sentences, choose the correct verb in parentheses.

1. A few of us were (*sitting, setting*) at our desks.
2. He (*sat, set*) in the rocker, reading.
3. He (*sat, set*) the package on the doorstep.
4. Ida was (*sitting, setting*) out the chips and dip for the guests.
5. We had been (*sitting, setting*) on a freshly painted bench.
6. They (*set, sat*) the seedlings in the window boxes.
7. She (*sits, sets*) in front of me.
8. (*Set, Sit*) this Pueblo pottery in the display case.
9. I could (*sit, set*) and watch the sunset every evening.
10. Bowls of Cuban black bean soup were (*sat, set*) in front of the hungry travelers.

▶ EXERCISE 13   **Writing the Forms of *Sit* and *Set***

For each numbered blank in the following paragraph, write the correct form of *sit* or *set*.

To gain a view of the surrounding land, Lewis and Clark's group climbed to an outcropping of gray rocks that [1] ____ atop the bluff. It was late afternoon, and the Shoshone guide Sacagawea [2] ____ her pack down beside the rocks and [3] ____ down in their shade to rest. Meriwether Lewis saw her from where he was [4] ____ nearby and approached with a friendly "May I [5] ____ here with

USAGE

you?" Several other members of the expedition saw them [6] ____ together and wondered what they were discussing. In fact, Lewis was asking her in what direction she thought the party should [7] ____ out in the morning. Gazing westward from the bluff, Sacagawea saw that she was in familiar territory and soon [8] ____ her mind on heading down the mountainside toward the northwest. By the time the sun had [9] ____, Lewis agreed that the route she had chosen would be the easiest to follow. A wise leader, he realized that he had never [10] ____ foot in these lands, while she had passed this way before.

▶ REVIEW A

Selecting the Correct Form of *Lie* and *Lay* and *Sit* and *Set* to Complete Sentences

In each of the following sentences, choose the correct verb in parentheses.

1. (*Sitting, Setting*) on the table was a pair of scissors.
2. Please (*sit, set*) the carton down carefully.
3. Sakura folded her kimono and (*lay, laid*) down on the soft, padded futon to sleep.
4. (*Sit, Set*) all the way back in your seat.
5. The dirty dishes had (*lain, laid*) in the sink for hours.
6. Yesterday Tom (*lay, laid*) the blame for his lateness on his alarm clock.
7. The cat always (*sits, sets*) on the couch.
8. If only we could have (*lain, laid*) our hands on that buried treasure!
9. The tickets to the Wynton Marsalis concert were (*sitting, setting*) right where I left them.
10. King Tut's tomb (*lay, laid*) undisturbed for centuries.
11. Have you ever (*sat, set*) around with nothing to do?
12. She (*sat, set*) down at her desk with her checkbook and calculator in front of her.
13. Santa Anna, (*sitting, setting*) on his horse, ordered his troops to attack the Alamo.
14. The beached rowboat (*lay, laid*) on its side.
15. She (*sat, set*) looking toward the horizon.
16. Laura had just (*sat, set*) down when the phone rang.
17. Julie (*lay, laid*) her handbag on the counter.

18. Pieces of the jigsaw puzzle were (*laying, lying*) on the floor.
19. Jack was (*sitting, setting*) outside on the top step.
20. Were you (*laying, lying*) down for a while before dinner?

Rise and *Raise*

The verb *rise* means "to go upward." It never takes an object.

The verb *raise* means "to move (something) upward" or "to bring up." It usually takes an object.

PRINCIPAL PARTS OF *RISE* AND *RAISE*			
BASE FORM	PRESENT PARTICIPLE	PAST	PAST PARTICIPLE
rise (go upward)	(is) rising	rose	(have) risen
raise (move [something] upward)	(is) raising	raised	(have) raised

EXAMPLES   I usually **rise** at 6:00 A.M.
Prices **rose** rapidly in the early 1980s.

Raise your hand if you know the answer.
The coach **raised** the bar on the high jump.

ORAL PRACTICE 4   **Stressing the Correct Form of *Rise* and *Raise* in Sentences**

Read each of the following sentences aloud, stressing the italicized verb.

1. *Has* the moon *risen* yet?
2. The tower *rose* high into the darkening air.
3. The temperature *rose* as the sun climbed higher.
4. Listening to "I Have a Dream," a speech by Martin Luther King, Jr., always *raises* my spirits.
5. Trails of mist were *rising* from the lake.
6. How much did the river *rise* during the flood?
7. The butterfly *rose* from the leaf and flitted away.
8. The dough was *rising* in the bowl.

▶ EXERCISE 14 **Writing the Correct Form of *Rise* and *Raise* to Complete Sentences**

For each blank in the following sentences, write the correct form of *rise* or *raise*.

1. ____ the flags higher, please.
2. The gigantic Kodiak bear ____ on its hind legs and looked around.
3. The tide ____ and falls because of the moon.
4. Carlos and Pilar ____ the piñata above the heads of the children.
5. Up toward the clouds ____ the jet.
6. Many Native American peoples ____ corn as a staple food crop.
7. Prices have ____ in the last few years.
8. The traffic officer ____ his hand to signal us.
9. My sister and I ____ before the sun came up this morning.
10. César Chávez ____ to fame in the 1960s.

▶ REVIEW B **Determining Correct or Incorrect Use of *Lie* and *Lay*, *Sit* and *Set*, and *Rise* and *Raise* in Sentences**

If a sentence is correct, write C. If it is incorrect, revise the incorrect word or words.

1. Set the eggs down carefully.
2. The frog was setting on the lily pad and croaking loudly.
3. The judge studied the papers, then lay them beside her gavel.
4. The cattle were lying in the shade by the stream.
5. Do you think the temperature will raise much higher?
6. Wanda sat out the equipment for the experiment.
7. Why don't you lie those things down?
8. Instead of laying down, you should be getting some type of strenuous exercise.
9. Let's sit where we can get a good view of the Juneteenth parade.
10. Set down for a while and relax.

USAGE

WRITING APPLICATION

Using Verb Tense to Establish Time of Action

To show the precise order of events, a writer sometimes needs to use several different tenses in a paragraph—or even in the same sentence.

EXAMPLE   The Japanese students *had planned* a tea ceremony, but because another group *was using* the activity room, they *will reschedule* the ceremony.

Each verb in the preceding sentence is in a different tense. If the verbs were all in the same tense, a reader would be confused about the order of the events.

▶ WRITING ACTIVITY

It's Cultural Appreciation Week at your school. Your teacher has asked you to write a short essay about your own cultural or ethnic group. In your essay, you should explore several ways in which people from your heritage have enriched life in your community. Use correct verb tenses to describe some of the contributions these people have made in the past, some activities they are currently involved in, and what you think they might offer in the future. Use at least five different verb tenses in your essay.

Prewriting   Brainstorm a list of your ethnic or cultural group's outstanding leaders, scholars, athletes, and artists, as well as activities, events, clubs, and community service projects. Select three or four of the group's main contributions to mention in your essay. Many people can claim more than one ethnic or cultural heritage. If you can, you may want to write about the group you know the best or the one you are most interested in.

Writing   While you are writing your first draft, try to add details that show the uniqueness of your cultural heritage. Consider how you can control verb tenses to make the sequence of events in your essay clear.

Evaluating and Revising Read through your essay to be sure you have included at least one contribution from each different time period: the past, the present, and the future. Check to see that you have used at least five different tenses.

Proofreading and Publishing Using your textbook, make sure that you have formed all verbs correctly. Pay special attention when checking the forms of irregular verbs. With your classmates, you might create a bulletin board display of all the essays your class has written. Or your class may wish to prepare a cultural-appreciation presentation for another class or for the whole school.

REVIEW C   **Choosing the Correct Forms of Verbs to Complete Sentences**

In each of the following sentences, choose the correct verb or form of the verb given in parentheses.

1. Little Billy was (*lying, laying*) in wait for us.
2. He had accidentally (*thrown, throwed*) his homework away.
3. The spilled laundry (*lay, laid*) in a wet heap.
4. We ate until we almost (*burst, bursted*).
5. The kitten (*shrank, shrunk*) from the barking dog.
6. Haven't you ever (*swam, swum*) in a lake before?
7. When Chief Dan George walked to the podium, a cheer (*rang, rung*) out.
8. Have you ever (*rode, ridden*) a roller coaster?
9. I knew I should have (*brought, brung*) my camera.
10. Uh-oh, I think this phone is (*broke, broken*).

REVIEW D   **Choosing the Correct Forms of Irregular Verbs**

Supply the correct form of each italicized verb in the following paragraph.

Have you ever [1] (*see*) this fascinating picture of an impossible structure? It is called *Waterfall*, and it was [2] (*draw*) by the Dutch artist M. C. Escher. He [3] (*take*) the basic idea for this artwork from the optical illusion shown beside it. As you can see, a two-story waterfall has [4] (*set*) a miller's wheel in motion. Then, after the water has [5] (*leave*) the wheel, it zigzags through a channel until it [6] (*come*) to the top of the waterfall again. But wait—has the water [7] (*go*) uphill on its way back to the top of the waterfall? No, obviously the stream has [8] (*run*) away from the fall on the same level as the bottom of the fall. But then how can the water now be back at the top where it [9] (*begin*)? Escher never said, but he once wrote that if the miller simply [10] (*throw*) in a bucket of water now and then to replace water that had evaporated, he would have a "perpetual motion" machine!

1961 M. C. Escher/Cordon Art-Baarn-Holland.

© 1954 Roger Penrose.

![arrow] EXERCISE 15   ## Using Verbs to Express Time Relationships Clearly

The time line on the next page shows several key events from American history. Make up five sentences that establish time relationships between two or more of the events named. In each sentence, use more than one verb and make each verb a different tense. Vary your sentence structure. Be prepared to tell how the tenses you used help explain the sequence of events.

EXAMPLE   *As De Soto was finishing his exploration of the Southeast, Cabrillo started to investigate the Pacific coast.*

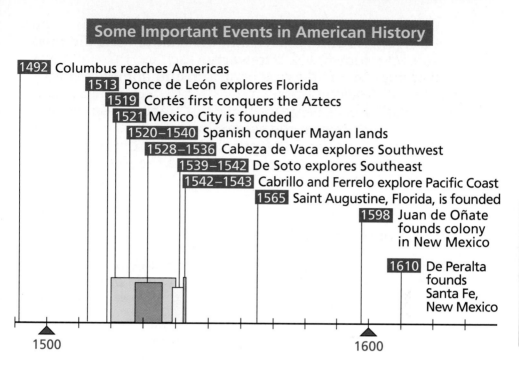

Some Important Events in American History

1492 Columbus reaches Americas
1513 Ponce de León explores Florida
1519 Cortés first conquers the Aztecs
1521 Mexico City is founded
1520–1540 Spanish conquer Mayan lands
1528–1536 Cabeza de Vaca explores Southwest
1539–1542 De Soto explores Southeast
1542–1543 Cabrillo and Ferrelo explore Pacific Coast
1565 Saint Augustine, Florida, is founded
1598 Juan de Oñate founds colony in New Mexico
1610 De Peralta founds Santa Fe, New Mexico

1500   1600

USAGE

Review: Posttest

A. Writing the Past or Past Participle Form of Verbs

For each of the following sentences, write the correct past or past participle of the verb given before the sentence.

1. *ride*   Jeffrey and Lee have ____ their bikes fifty miles today.
2. *write* I read the letters Grandpa ____ to Grandma in 1930.
3. *take*   Dad, I know that you've ____ us to two rap concerts this year, but please take us to just one more.
4. *fall*   All that winter day the snow ____, blanketing everything.
5. *see*   Rebecca soon ____ why the old house had sold so cheaply.

6. *drink* The gerbil has ____ most of its water.
7. *begin* As darkness fell and the children still did not return, I ____ to worry.
8. *bring* Margot has ____ popcorn and apples for the party.
9. *speak* Police Sergeant Liakos ____ about responsible driving at the assembly yesterday.
10. *give* The Nez Percé people had ____ the starving fur traders food and helped them repair their canoes.

B. Revising Verb Tense or Voice

Rewrite the following sentences, correcting verbs that are in the wrong tense or that use an awkward voice. If a sentence is correct, write *C*.

EXAMPLES 1. Genna gave her report on Captain James Cook and shows us some maps and pictures of the areas he explored.
1. *Genna gave her report on Captain James Cook and showed us some maps and pictures of the areas he explored.*

2. We were surprised to learn how many places were explored by him.
2. *We were surprised to learn how many places he explored.*

11. Captain Cook, one of the greatest explorers of all time, sailed large areas of the Pacific Ocean and makes accurate maps of the region.
12. Cook joins the navy as a seaman in 1755, and many promotions were received by him before he became the master of a ship in 1757.
13. Because of his knowledge of geography, astronomy, and mathematics, he is selected to lead a scientific expedition to the Pacific.
14. The purpose of Cook's expedition is to observe the passage of Venus between Earth and the sun, a very rare occurrence.
15. On the voyage, Cook wins a battle against scurvy, a serious disease caused by lack of vitamin C.

16. Raw cabbage, which was rich in vitamin C, was eaten by the sailors to prevent scurvy.
17. By the time the voyage is over, the ship traveled around Cape Horn to Tahiti in the Pacific Ocean.
18. After he observes the passage of Venus, Cook sails off to explore the east coast of New Zealand, which was claimed by him for England.
19. The Hawaiian Islands were later explored by Cook on his final voyage to the Pacific and were named the Sandwich Islands by him.
20. In a dispute over a canoe, Cook was killed by island inhabitants and in naval tradition was buried at sea in 1779.

C. Determining Correct Use of *Lie* and *Lay*, *Sit* and *Set*, and *Rise* and *Raise* in Sentences

If a verb in one of the following sentences is incorrect, write the correct form. If a sentence is correct, write *C*.

21. You can sit the wastebasket in the corner and then set up the chairs.
22. Everyone rose when the judge entered the courtroom and sat when she was seated.
23. The mysterious shape suddenly raised from the shadows.
24. I like to lay out under the stars and just think.
25. The servant had lain out the emperor's silken robes of yellow, the color that only members of Chinese royalty were permitted to wear.

USAGE

22 USING MODIFIERS CORRECTLY

USAGE

Forms, Comparison, and Placement

Diagnostic Test

A. Correcting Errors in the Use of the Comparative and Superlative Forms

Write the incorrect word or words from each sentence. Then write the correct form, adding or deleting words if necessary.

EXAMPLES   **1.** I was more hungrier than I had thought, so I ordered three sandwiches.
1. *more hungrier—hungrier*

2. This storm was even badder than the last one.
2. *badder—worse*

1. During the 1960s, Ralph Abernathy and Medgar Evers were among the most best-known civil rights activists.
2. He was the more able and intelligent of the three job applicants.
3. Is Pocahontas famouser than Sacagawea?

712

4. John, Richard's twin brother, was the oldest by three and a half minutes.
5. After Diego had started lifting weights, he bragged that he was stronger than anyone in town.
6. People who live along this road complain because it is the worstest in the entire township.
7. Floyd and his brother are landscape designers who are in demand throughout the state, but Floyd is the best known in this area.
8. After the band had practiced, their music sounded more better.
9. When I had a choice of strawberry or vanilla, I took vanilla because I like it best.
10. Looking across the water at sunset, you can see the beautifullest view you can imagine.

USAGE

B. Revising Sentences by Correcting Dangling and Misplaced Modifiers

Each of the following sentences contains either a dangling or a misplaced modifier. Revise each sentence, arranging the words so that the meaning is logical and clear. You may have to add or delete some words. Be sure to use commas where they are needed to set off introductory and interrupting modifiers.

EXAMPLE **1.** The class sent a get-well message to their teacher on a balloon.
   1. *The class sent their teacher a get-well message on a balloon.*

11. Yipping and running in circles, they saw that the dogs could herd the sheep into the pen.
12. The winners marched off the platform carrying ribbons and trophies.
13. A police officer warned students who drive too fast about accidents during the defensive-driving class.
14. After escaping from slavery, the importance of education was often stressed by Frederick Douglass.
15. We went to visit my grandmother, who used to be a history teacher at my school yesterday.
16. Mother found a package outside our house tied with ribbons.

17. Maria took a close-up photograph of a lion with a telephoto lens.
18. Sitting in a tree outside my window, I see a small bird, apparently building a nest on one of the limbs.
19. A young woman knocked on the door wearing a suit and a hat.
20. Walking in the sunshine, it felt warm to us.

Adjective and Adverb Forms

A *modifier* is a word or a group of words that makes the meaning of another word more definite. Two parts of speech are used as modifiers: *adjectives* and *adverbs.* Adjectives modify nouns and pronouns. Adverbs modify verbs, adjectives, and other adverbs.

ADJECTIVE   Lisa does **strenuous** exercise.
  ADVERB   Lisa exercises **strenuously.**

NOTE: Many adverbs end in *–ly,* but not all of them do. A few common adjectives also end in *–ly.*

> EXAMPLES   **costly** repairs   **daily** schedule
>   **lively** discussion   **lonely** scene

Some words have the same form whether they're used as adjectives or as adverbs. Therefore, you can't tell whether a word is an adjective or an adverb just by looking for the *–ly* ending. Instead, you have to determine how the word is being used.

ADJECTIVES	ADVERBS
We took an **early** flight.	We left **early** this morning.
She asked a **hard** question.	She tried **hard.**
They took the **first** step.	They went **first.**

22a. If a word in the predicate modifies the subject of the verb, use the adjective form. If it modifies the verb, use the adverb form.

ADJECTIVE   **The swimmer was careful.** [careful swimmer]
   ADVERB   **He swims carefully.** [swims carefully]

In many cases, linking verbs are followed by a predicate adjective.

Common Linking Verbs

appear	grow	smell
be (am, is, are, etc.)	look	sound
become	remain	stay
feel	seem	taste

Many linking verbs can also be used as action verbs. To tell whether a verb is a linking verb or an action verb, try a form of *seem* in its place.

LINKING   **She felt happy.** [*She seemed happy* makes sense. Therefore, *felt* is a linking verb in this sentence.]

ACTION   **She felt the fabric.** [*She seemed the fabric* doesn't make sense. Therefore, *felt* is an action verb in this sentence.]

LINKING   **The old car appeared abandoned.** [*The old car seemed abandoned* makes sense.]

ACTION   **The car appeared suddenly.** [*The car seemed suddenly* doesn't make sense.]

☞ **REFERENCE NOTE:** See pages 524–526 and 560–563 for more information on linking verbs and action verbs.

▶ EXERCISE 1   **Identifying Adjectives and Adverbs**

The following paragraph contains fifteen adjectives and ten adverbs. For each sentence, identify each adjective and adverb and give the word it modifies. [Note: Do not include the articles *a*, *an*, and *the*.]

EXAMPLE   [1] First get a craft knife and some stiff black paper.
   1. *First—adverb—get; craft—adjective—knife; some—adjective—paper; stiff—adjective—paper; black—adjective—paper*

[1] In many cultures, cutting paper to make pictures is a traditional art. [2] For example, Mexican artisans use a small, very sharp knife to cut designs in pieces of colored paper. [3] As the oddly shaped scraps fall away, an image

USAGE

USAGE

is slowly revealed. [4] Planning the work is a challenge because each part of the picture must connect somehow to the border or to another part of the design. [5] As you can see in these designs, the artist sometimes leaves a background pattern of stripes or lines to support the main subject. [6] The knife must not be even slightly dull, or the artist might accidentally tear one of the tiny paper bridges!

Three Troublesome Pairs

Bad and *Badly*

Bad is an adjective. In most uses, *badly* is an adverb.

EXAMPLES	**ADJECTIVES**	**ADVERBS**
	The dog was **bad**.	The dog behaved **badly**.
	The milk smelled **bad**.	The roof leaked **badly**.

Remember that a linking verb calls for an adjective form.

NONSTANDARD	The medicine tasted badly.
STANDARD	The medicine tasted **bad**.

☞ **REFERENCE NOTE:** See pages 498–499 for a discussion of standard and nonstandard English.

NOTE: In conversations, either *bad* or *badly* is acceptable after *feel*.

ACCEPTABLE IN CONVERSATION	He feels **bad** about the accident. He feels **badly** about the accident.

In writing, though, use *bad* after *feel*.

CORRECT IN WRITING	He feels **bad** about the accident.

Well and *Good*

Well may be used either as an adjective or as an adverb. As an adjective, *well* has two meanings:

(1) "in good health"

EXAMPLE   Fran is **well**.

(2) "satisfactory"

EXAMPLE   Everything is **well**.

As an adverb, *well* means "capably."

EXAMPLE   We did **well** on the test.

Good is always an adjective. It should not be used to modify a verb.

NONSTANDARD	She sings good.
STANDARD	She sings **well**.

NONSTANDARD	The car runs good.
STANDARD	The car runs **well**.

STANDARD	That color looks **good** on you. [adjective following linking verb]

NOTE: *Well* is also acceptable in sentences such as the last example above.

EXAMPLE   That color looks **well** on you.

☞ **REFERENCE NOTE:** For more discussion about *good* and *well*, see pages 743–744.

Slow and *Slowly*

Slow is used as both an adjective and an adverb.

EXAMPLES   We took a **slow** walk through the park. [*Slow* is an adjective modifying *walk*.]
Go **slow**. [*Slow* is an adverb modifying *go*.]

Slowly is always an adverb. In most adverb uses (other than *go slow* or *drive slow*), it is better to use *slowly*.

EXAMPLES   The tiger **slowly** crept forward.
Proceed **slowly** through each step.

USAGE

> EXERCISE 2 | **Selecting Adjectives or Adverbs to Complete Sentences**

Choose the correct word in parentheses in each of the following sentences.

1. I can't hear you (*well, good*) when the water is running.
2. The opening paragraph is written (*well, good*).
3. The situation looks (*bad, badly*).
4. Why does ketchup come out of the bottle so (*slow, slowly*)?
5. She certainly plays the marimba (*well, good*).
6. Can you dance as (*well, good*) as you sing?
7. These shoes don't fit (*bad, badly*) at all.
8. Our coach told us to do the exercise (*slow, slowly*).
9. Did you do (*well, good*) on the last algebra test?
10. The chef at the corner cafe cooks very (*bad, badly*).

> EXERCISE 3 | **Using Adjective and Adverb Forms Correctly in a Paragraph**

Each sentence in the following paragraph contains at least one italicized adjective or adverb. If an italicized word is incorrect, give the correct form. If the sentence is correct, write *C*.

[1] My brother opened Skipper's Skate City last April 1, and as the graph on the next page shows, the shop did not do *well* at first. [2] Skipper wondered whether business had started *slow* because he wasn't advertising enough or because his window wasn't drawing people in. [3] He'd see people walking *slow* past the shop and pointing at the gear on display, but hardly anyone came in. [4] By the end of May, Skipper even thought about giving up, because he was doing so *bad*. [5] He would have felt really *bad* about failing, especially because my dad had loaned him money to help get started. [6] Then school let out, and within days, business was going *good*. [7] In-line skates started selling like crazy, and all summer, Skipper did so *well* that he was able to pay Dad back. [8] When school started, skateboards kept selling *good*, but total sales fell somewhat. [9] Skipper's receipts looked pretty *badly* during the fall, but thanks to Christmas and Hanukkah, all went

good in December. [10] By then, Skipper was a veteran of seasonal business cycles, so it didn't faze him a bit when January's receipts weren't as *well* as expected.

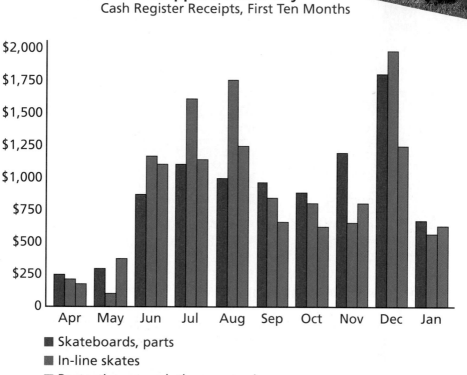

Skipper's Skate City
Cash Register Receipts, First Ten Months

- ■ Skateboards, parts
- ■ In-line skates
- ■ Protective gear, clothes, magazines

Comparison of Modifiers

Adjectives state qualities of nouns or pronouns.

EXAMPLES   **expensive** jacket   **fluffy** clouds
           shiny metal   **original** one

You can show the degree or extent to which a noun or pronoun has a quality by comparing it with another noun or pronoun that has the same quality.

EXAMPLES   This jacket is **larger** than that jacket.
           Does it look **better** than the other one?

Similarly, you can show degree or extent by using adverbs to make comparisons.

EXAMPLES   I ran well, but you ran **better.** [The adverb *better* modifies the verb *ran.*]
The other clerk will be better able to help you. [The adverb *better* modifies the adjective *able.*]

22b.   Modifiers change form to show comparison.

The three degrees of comparison are *positive, comparative,* and *superlative.*

POSITIVE	COMPARATIVE	SUPERLATIVE
low	lower	lowest
fearful	more fearful	most fearful
bad	worse	worst
good	better	best
promptly	more promptly	most promptly

Regular Comparison

Most modifiers follow these regular methods of forming their comparative and superlative degrees.

(1) One-syllable modifiers form their comparative and superlative degrees by adding *–er* and *–est.*

POSITIVE	COMPARATIVE	SUPERLATIVE
thin	thinner	thinnest
safe	safer	safest
dry	drier	driest

☞ **REFERENCE NOTE:** See pages 873–875 for guidelines on spelling words with suffixes.

(2) Some two-syllable modifiers form their comparative and superlative degrees by adding *–er* and *–est.* Other

two-syllable modifiers form their comparative and superlative degrees with *more* and *most.*

POSITIVE	COMPARATIVE	SUPERLATIVE
lovely	lovelier	loveliest
tricky	trickier	trickiest
awkward	more awkward	most awkward
quickly	more quickly	most quickly

NOTE: A few two-syllable modifiers may use either *–er, –est* or *more, most: able, abler, ablest,* or *able, more able, most able.*

When you're not sure about the comparative or superlative form of a two-syllable modifier, look up the positive form in an unabridged dictionary.

(3) Modifiers that have more than two syllables form their comparative and superlative degrees with *more* and *most.*

POSITIVE	COMPARATIVE	SUPERLATIVE
catastrophic	more catastrophic	most catastrophic
predictably	more predictably	most predictably

(4) Modifiers indicate less or least of a quality with the words *less* and *least.*

POSITIVE	COMPARATIVE	SUPERLATIVE
frequent	less frequent	least frequent
carefully	less carefully	least carefully

Irregular Comparison

Some adjectives and adverbs do not follow the regular methods of forming their comparative and superlative degrees.

POSITIVE	COMPARATIVE	SUPERLATIVE
bad	worse	worst
good well	better	best
little	less	least
many much	more	most

NOTE: Do not add *–er, –est* or *more, most* to irregularly compared forms: *worse,* not *worser* or *more worse.*

▶ EXERCISE 4 **Writing the Comparative and Superlative Forms of Modifiers**

Write the comparative and superlative forms of the following modifiers.

1. little
2. bad
3. humid
4. smart
5. silly
6. good
7. likely
8. well
9. fundamental
10. congenial

Use of Comparative and Superlative Forms

22c. Use the comparative degree when comparing two things. Use the superlative degree when comparing more than two.

COMPARATIVE   Omaha is **larger** than Lincoln.
Roberto is a **better** student than I am.
Which of these two shirts is **less** expensive?

SUPERLATIVE   Omaha is the **largest** city in Nebraska.
Roberto is the **best** student in the class.
Which of these four shirts is **least** expensive?

NOTE: In conversation, the superlative degree is commonly used to compare two things.

EXAMPLES   May the **best** team [of two] win.
Put your **best** foot forward.

In writing, however, the comparative degree should always be used when two things are being compared.

EXERCISE 5

Writing Sentences Using the Comparative and Superlative Forms of Modifiers

At the beginning of the twentieth century, teenagers thought a ride on an elaborate, hand-carved carousel was exciting. Today, as we approach the year 2000, young people are more likely to be interested in a wild roller-coaster ride! Write five sentences using adverbs and adjectives to compare the two rides shown below. Then write five sentences comparing three rides—the carousel, the roller coaster, and a ride you imagine will be a favorite at the turn of the twenty-second century. In your sentences, use ten or more modifiers from the boxes below. After you use at least two modifiers from each box, you may use any of the others that you wish.

bright	happy	good	intense	exciting
simple	high	many	colorful	stressful
young	pretty	little	expensive	thrilling
scary	fast	much	compelling	mature
safe	long	bad	enjoyable	romantic

A HOLIDAY

22d. Include the word *other* or *else* when comparing one thing with others in the same group.

NONSTANDARD	Stan is taller than anyone in his class. [Stan is a member of the class, and he cannot be taller than himself. The word *else* should be added.]
STANDARD	Stan is taller than anyone **else** in his class.
NONSTANDARD	Rhode Island is smaller than any state in the Union. [Rhode Island is a state, and it cannot be smaller than itself. The word *other* should be added.]
STANDARD	Rhode Island is smaller than any **other** state in the Union.

22e. Avoid double comparisons.

A *double comparison* is one that uses both *−er* and *more* (or *less*) or *−est* and *most* (or *least*).

NONSTANDARD	The second movie was more funnier than the first one.
STANDARD	The second movie was **funnier** than the first one.
NONSTANDARD	What is the most deadliest snake?
STANDARD	What is the **most deadly** [or **deadliest**] snake?

22f. Be sure your comparisons are clear.

In making comparisons, always state clearly what things are being compared.

UNCLEAR	The climate of Arizona is drier than South Carolina. [The sentence incorrectly compares a climate to a state.]
CLEAR	The climate of Arizona is drier than **the climate** of South Carolina.
CLEAR	The climate of Arizona is drier than **that** of South Carolina.
UNCLEAR	The Millers would rather grow their own vegetables than canned ones.
CLEAR	The Millers would rather grow their own vegetables than **buy** canned ones.

Use a complete comparison if there is any chance that an incomplete one could be misunderstood.

UNCLEAR	We know her better than Dena.
CLEAR	We know her better than **we know** Dena.
CLEAR	We know her better than Dena **does.**

EXERCISE 6   Using Modifiers Correctly in Sentences

In each of the following sentences, if a modifier is used incorrectly, write the correct form. If the sentence is correct, write C.

1. Laurie is more friendlier than she used to be.
2. Which of the four seasons do you like better?
3. I never saw a tribal leader more stronger than Chief Billie of the Seminoles.
4. Margaret Mead was one of the world's most famous anthropologists.
5. Of the two colleges that I am considering, Spelman College in Atlanta looks more interesting.
6. The cheetah is the most fastest running animal in the world.
7. Muscles in the leg are stronger than the arm.
8. Denver has a higher elevation than any major city in the United States.
9. I wrote to Sally more often than Carlos.
10. This year's drought was much worser than last year.

REVIEW A   Identifying and Correcting Errors in the Use of Modifiers

The following paragraph contains ten errors in the use of adjectives and adverbs. Find each error and supply the necessary correction.

[1] Among Pueblo potters of the Southwest, perhaps the famousest are the four women who made the coiled pots shown on the next page, using techniques handed down for more than 2,000 years. [2] Lucy Lewis's Acoma pottery is more delicate than any Southwest pottery. [3] She used the most whitest clay. [4] Because this clay is scarce, the walls of her pots are the most thin. [5] Maria Martinez' San Ildefonso pottery is more thicker and heavier than Lewis. [6] Of all the Southwest pottery styles, Martinez' black-on-black pottery may be the wellest known. [7] No color is used, but the background areas of

USAGE

the black pot are burnished slowly with a small smooth stone until they become quite a bit more shinier than the main design. [8] Many of Margaret Tafoya's Santa Clara pots are also solid black, but of these two kinds of black pottery, the Santa Clara pots are the heaviest. [9] The bold, colorful Hopi pots of Fannie Nampeyo may be the more impressive achievement of all, because Nampeyo's family had to re-create the technique by studying shards of ancient pots found in 1895.

LUCY
LEWIS

MARGARET
TAFOYA

MARIA
MARTINEZ

FANNIE
NAMPEYO

WRITING APPLICATION

Using Comparative and Superlative Degrees to Make Comparison Clear

Have you ever read a "buyer's guide" article before deciding which brand of a product to buy? People who write such articles must be especially precise in using comparatives and superlatives so that consumers can be sure which brand best suits their needs and budgets.

COMPARING TWO   Of these models, the Matsuo 2000 is less expensive.

COMPARING THREE
OR MORE   Of these models, the Matsuo 2000 is least expensive.

▶ WRITING ACTIVITY

You and your sister Charlotte plan to buy a piece of audio equipment together. You have found a magazine article comparing several brands and showing the information in a big table. However, because Charlotte is blind, the table can't help her decide. She asks you to narrow the choices to four brands, and then to write and tape on a cassette for her a short comparison of their prices and features so that the two of you can make a decision.

Find a magazine article at home or in the library that has a table comparing different brands of a piece of audio equipment that interests you. You might choose a CD player, speakers, or a portable cassette player. Choose three products that seem acceptable. Write a clear comparison that you would tape for Charlotte, giving the most important information listed in the table about these three products. As you write, include each of the degrees of comparison: positive, comparative, and superlative.

USAGE

Prewriting Study the table. List the features that you think would be most important to you and to Charlotte. Then, write down several comparisons you want to explain in your paragraph.

Writing As you write your first draft, carefully select comparative and superlative modifiers so that your explanation is not confusing. Tell why you would eliminate certain models from consideration. Remember, though, you are not deciding *for* Charlotte. You must present the information objectively to help her make her own decision.

Evaluating and Revising Exchange paragraphs, along with the magazine article you used, with a classmate. Ask him or her to evaluate the information you decided to include and the clarity of your presentation. Rephrase any confusing comparisons.

Proofreading and Publishing Using your textbook, check to be sure you have correctly used adjectives to modify nouns and pronouns and used adverbs to modify verbs, adjectives, and other adverbs. Pay special attention to the "troublesome pairs" section on pages 716–717 of this chapter. Your class may wish to collect all the paragraphs and bind them in a booklet titled *An Audio Equipment Consumer Guide.*

Dangling Modifiers

22g. A modifying word, phrase, or clause that does not clearly and sensibly modify a word in the same sentence is a *dangling modifier.*

When a sentence begins with a verbal phrase, the phrase is followed by a comma. The word that the phrase modifies should come immediately after that comma.

DANGLING   Hurrying, my books slipped out of my hands and fell down the stairs. [The participle seems to modify *books.*]

CORRECT   **As I was hurrying,** my books slipped out of my hands and fell down the stairs.

DANGLING   Looking back over my shoulder, the team went into a huddle. [The participial phrase seems to modify *team.*]

CORRECT   Looking back over my shoulder, **I** saw the team go into a huddle.

NOTE: When *you* is the understood subject of a sentence, an introductory verbal phrase is not dangling. The phrase modifies the understood subject.

EXAMPLE   To get to Amy's house, (you) go south on First Street.

Correcting Dangling Modifiers

You can correct a dangling modifier by adding words that make the meaning clear and logical.

DANGLING   Going to the store, my bicycle tire went flat.

CORRECT   Going to the store, I got a flat tire on my bicycle.

DANGLING   While filling the fuel tank, some of the gas spilled on the runway.

CORRECT   While filling the fuel tank, the mechanic spilled some of the gas on the runway.

CORRECT   While the mechanic was filling the fuel tank, some of the gas spilled on the runway.

DANGLING   To qualify for the Olympics, many trial heats must be won.

CORRECT   To qualify for the Olympics, a runner must win many trial heats.

CORRECT   Before a runner may qualify for the Olympics, he or she must win many trial heats.

> **EXERCISE 7** **Revising Sentences by Correcting Dangling Modifiers**

Revise each sentence so that the modifier *clearly* and *sensibly* modifies a word in the sentence. You will have to supply some words to fill out the sentence properly.

1. Caught in the net, escape was impossible.
2. Looking through the telescope, the moon seemed enormous.
3. While out running, his mouth got dry.
4. The ocean came into view going around the bend.
5. Doing a few tap-dance steps, the floor got scratched.
6. Built on a steep hillside overlooking the ocean, we found the view breathtaking.
7. To grow plants successfully, light, temperature, and humidity must be carefully controlled.
8. After finishing the housework, the room almost sparkled.
9. To make manicotti, pasta is stuffed with ricotta cheese.
10. Exhausted, the job had finally been finished!

USAGE

Misplaced Modifiers

22h. A modifying word, phrase, or clause that makes a sentence awkward or unclear because it seems to modify the wrong word or group of words is a *misplaced modifier.*

Modifying words, phrases, and clauses should be placed as near as possible to the words they modify. Notice how changing the placement of a modifier affects the meanings of the following sentences.

EXAMPLES **Only** on Saturdays, my brother and I watch cartoons on television for an hour.
On Saturdays, my **only** brother and I watch cartoons on television for an hour.
On Saturdays, my brother and I watch cartoons on television for **only** an hour.

Misplaced Phrase Modifiers

MISPLACED I'm lucky because I always feel that I can talk about my problems with my dad.
CORRECT I'm lucky because I always feel that I can talk with my dad about my problems.

MISPLACED Early Spanish explorers encountered hostile native peoples searching for gold in the Americas.
CORRECT Searching for gold in the Americas, early Spanish explorers encountered hostile native peoples.

▶ EXERCISE 8 **Revising Sentences by Correcting Misplaced Word and Phrase Modifiers**

In each of the following sentences, pick out the misplaced word or phrase and revise the sentence, placing the misplaced modifier near the word it should modify.

1. Rosa Parks calmly refused to move with quiet dignity to the back of the bus.
2. I found a huge boulder taking a shortcut through the woods.
3. Mr. Tate noticed some caterpillars pruning his fruit tree.

4. Our ancestors hunted deer, bison, and other large animals armed with weapons made of wood and stone.
5. Missie saw a heron driving over the bridge.
6. We noticed several signs riding down the highway.
7. We could see corn growing from our car window.
8. Barking wildly and straining at the chain, the letter carrier was forced to retreat from the dog.
9. The softball team almost practices every afternoon.
10. He recounted an incident about a nuclear chain reaction during his chemistry lecture.

▶ EXERCISE 9 **Using Modifiers Correctly**

Looking through a box of old photographs, you find this photo and several others of a treehouse that you and your best friend built years ago. The pictures remind you that you have not written to your friend in a long time. Taking this photo from the box, you decide to send it along with a letter to your friend. As you write your letter, include the five phrases listed below, or use five of your own. Be sure your phrases correctly modify the words you intend.

- armed with hammers and nails
- climbing up the ladder
- from the platform
- to hold our club meetings
- resting on several branches

Misplaced Clause Modifiers

MISPLACED   We saw a building in the city that was being demolished.

CORRECT   In the city we saw a building that was being demolished.

MISPLACED   The bowl fell on the floor which was full of gravy and broke.

CORRECT   The bowl, which was full of gravy, fell on the floor and broke.

MISPLACED   Lynn got a package from one of the stores we had visited that she hadn't ordered.

CORRECT   From one of the stores we had visited, Lynn got a package that she hadn't ordered.

☞ **REFERENCE NOTE:** See pages 797–801 and 805–806 for information on when to use commas to set off modifying phrases and clauses.

▶ EXERCISE 10   **Revising Sentences by Correcting Misplaced Clause Modifiers**

Revise each of the following sentences by placing the misplaced clause near the word it modifies. If you find a misplaced phrase, correct it also.

1. I gave four olives to my friend that I had stabbed with my fork.
2. The plane landed safely on the runway that had the engine trouble.
3. The picture was hanging on the wall that we bought in Canada.
4. They took the kitten to the manager's office that appeared to be lost.
5. Jan showed the rooms to her visitors that she had painted.

▶ REVIEW B   **Identifying and Correcting Errors in the Use of Modifiers**

Most of the sentences in the following paragraph contain at least one error in the use of modifiers. If a modifier is incorrect, write the sentence correctly. You may need to rearrange words or add words to make the meaning clear. If a sentence is correct, write *C*.

[1] Much about life in ancient Egypt before the 1800s was unknown because nobody could read Egyptian hieroglyphics. [2] Then this black stone found in the Nile delta gave Egyptology the most publicity than it had ever had before. [3] Found in 1799 near a village called Rosetta, archaeologists called the slab the Rosetta Stone. [4] The slab was inscribed with three bands across its polished surface of writing, each in a different language: hieroglyphics on the top, another unknown language in the middle, and Greek on the bottom. [5] Scholars could read the Greek writing, which stated that each of the three bands contained the same decree in honor of Ptolemy V. [6] Full of excitement, it was hoped by archaeologists that they could use the Greek part to figure out the hieroglyphics. [7] But progress in translating the individual hieroglyphics went very slow. [8] It had been thought that each of the symbols stood for a whole word until this time. [9] However, a French scholar working on the Rosetta Stone named Jean François Champollion wondered why it took more hieroglyphic symbols than Greek words to write the same message. [10] He correctly guessed that certain symbols stand for parts of words, and after working hard for twenty years, many of the signs were proved to stand for sounds.

USAGE

The Granger Collection, New York.

Review: Posttest

A. Revising Sentences by Correcting Errors in the Use of Modifiers

Most of the following sentences contain errors in the use of modifiers. Revise such sentences, correcting the faulty modifiers. If a sentence is correct, write C.

1. While building a fire in front of the hogan, Manaba's dog began to tug at the hem of her doeskin dress.
2. I bought these clothes with my birthday money that I'm wearing.
3. Adrianne knows more about chemistry than anybody in her class.
4. Hank worked rather hasty so he could catch up with Clay and Nina.
5. Although Marian felt bad about losing the game, she knew things could be worser.
6. Millie can sing as well as Scott, but of the two, he's the best dancer.
7. By playing carefully, the game was won.
8. Steady and confident, a keen sense of balance enables Mohawk ironworkers to help build tall bridges and buildings.
9. Because one carton of chemicals smelled badly, it was examined before being used in the laboratory.
10. Although Helen is the better actress, Wenona will probably get the leading part because she is more reliable.

B. Revising a Paragraph by Correcting Errors in the Use of Modifiers

Some sentences in the following paragraph contain errors in the use of modifiers. If you find an error, write the sentence correctly. You may need to add or rearrange words for clarity. If a sentence is correct, write C.

[11] Hailed by many critics as one of today's greatest male vocalists, my aunt Penny took me on my birthday to

see Bobby McFerrin. [12] Waiting for the concert to start, the auditorium was filled with eager fans. [13] Wondering where the band was, I kept my eyes on the empty stage. [14] When it was time for the show to start, a slender, barefoot man walked out from the wings, carrying a cordless microphone dressed only in blue jeans. [15] Assuming he was a stagehand, he began to sing, and then I realized that this was Bobby McFerrin! [16] Instantly, the complex rhythm of the music fascinated the audience that he made up as he went along. [17] I suddenly understood why one of his popularest albums is called *Spontaneous Inventions*! [18] Alone in the spotlight with only his voice and no band at all, two thousand people sat spellbound until he took his final bow. [19] All his life, Bobby McFerrin has enjoyed listening to and performing jazz, pop, rock, soul, African, and classical music. [20] Bobby's parents are both classical musicians, and he thanks them for giving him this rich musical environment on the back of every album he makes.

USAGE

23 A GLOSSARY OF USAGE

Common Usage Problems

Diagnostic Test

Revising Expressions by Correcting Errors in Usage

In each of the following sets of expressions, one expression contains an error in usage. Rewrite this expression correctly, using standard formal usage.

EXAMPLE **1. a.** She taught me to sing.
   b. fewer letters in the box
   c. Set down in the shade and rest.
   1. *c. Sit down in the shade and rest.*

1. **a.** anywheres you travel
   b. as fast as sound travels
   c. Learn French cooking from him.
2. **a.** affect the outcome
   b. candidate implied in his speech
   c. among his two opponents
3. **a.** made illusions to the Bible
   b. fewer participants in the contest
   c. What kind of car is that?

4. **a.** family emigrated from Germany
   b. should of gone yesterday
   c. discovered a new planet
5. **a.** Try and win the game.
   b. draw as well as her mother
   c. that kind of car
6. **a.** Let the dog out.
   b. an effect of cold weather
   c. books, pencils, papers, and etc.
7. **a.** ate everything accept the peas
   b. older than you
   c. Bring your records with you.
8. **a.** I heard nothing.
   b. can't hardly tell the difference
   c. Lay the book on the shelf.
9. **a.** picture fell off the wall
   b. What kind of a dog is that?
   c. larger than he
10. **a.** sitting beside the tree
    b. going a little ways
    c. not reality but illusion
11. **a.** coat doesn't fit well
    b. Fewer people learned how to read back then.
    c. inside of the cabinet
12. **a.** car looks like it had been wrecked
    b. chair that was blue
    c. water jug that burst
13. **a.** She effected an improvement.
    b. a problem that must be resolved
    c. Less students joined the club this year.
14. **a.** Take the package to the mailroom.
    b. Apples fell off of the tree.
    c. will scarcely be enough food for all of them
15. **a.** invented a better safety device
    b. No one beside my aunt knows.
    c. played well in the tournament
16. **a.** Funds were allotted among six counties.
    b. Where is my hammer at?
    c. This is as far as the fence extends.
17. **a.** going nowhere
    b. Doesn't he know the way?
    c. She finished reading; than she wrote her essay.

USAGE

18. **a.** We were gone for a hour.
    b. Try to learn this poem.
    c. Leave the green grapes on the vine.
19. **a.** Set the brake on the car.
    b. The fog will rise from the lake.
    c. One of them glasses broke.
20. **a.** It was an illusion caused by light on the surface.
    b. Their report implies a need for funds.
    c. That dog he limps.
21. **a.** no exception to this rule
    b. being that she is the oldest
    c. Bring your own tools with you.
22. **a.** Set that down there.
    b. looked like it had been burned
    c. They ought to study before the test.
23. **a.** The ice busted a pipe.
    b. He lay on the couch and rested.
    c. emigrate from their birthplace
24. **a.** Leave me have my turn.
    b. the mechanic that worked on our car
    c. somewhat cold for swimming
25. **a.** haven't only three days of vacation
    b. the effect of smoking on the lungs
    c. learned that the winner had been announced

This chapter contains a short glossary of common usage problems. You will notice that some examples are labeled *standard* and *nonstandard*. **Standard English** is the most widely accepted variety of English. It's used in most books, newspapers, and magazines. **Nonstandard English** is language that doesn't follow the rules and conventions of standard English.

☞ REFERENCE NOTE: For more information on the features of standard English and nonstandard English, see pages 498–499.

a, an These words, called *indefinite articles*, refer to one of the members of a general group.

> EXAMPLES   In ancient Greece and Rome, **a** person would go to see **an** oracle to consult the gods.
> The tourists searched for **a** hotel for more than **an** hour.

Use *a* before words beginning with a consonant sound; use *an* before words beginning with a vowel sound. In the second example, *a* is used before *hotel* because the *h* in *hotel* is pronounced. *An* is used before *hour* because the *h* in *hour* is not pronounced.

accept, except *Accept* is a verb that means "to receive." *Except* may be either a verb or a preposition. As a verb, it means "to leave out." As a preposition, *except* means "excluding."

> EXAMPLES   Gary could not **accept** defeat.
> Students who were absent last week will be **excepted** from today's test.
> Everybody **except** me knew the answer.

affect, effect *Affect* is usually a verb meaning "to influence." *Effect* used as a verb means "to accomplish" or "to bring about." Used as a noun, *effect* means "the result of some action."

> EXAMPLES   The heat did not seem to **affect** the team.
> Did the medicine **effect** a cure?
> The heat had no **effect** on the team.

all the farther, all the faster These expressions are used informally in some parts of the country to mean "as far as, as fast as."

> DIALECT   This is all the farther we can go.
> STANDARD   This is **as far as** we can go.

allusion, illusion An *allusion* is a reference to something. An *illusion* is a mistaken idea or a misleading appearance.

> EXAMPLES   The poem's title is an **allusion** to a Hopi folk tale.
> The documentary shattered viewers' **illusions** about migrant workers.
> The magician was a master of **illusion**.

among See **between, among.**

and etc. *Etc.* is an abbreviation of the Latin *et cetera*, which means "and other things." Thus, *etc.* already includes *and.*

> EXAMPLE   I earn money by baby-sitting, running errands, mowing lawns, **etc.** [not *and etc.*]

anywheres, everywheres, nowheres, somewheres Use these words without the *s* at the end.

EXAMPLE   **Anywhere** [not *anywheres*] you travel, you see the same hotel chains.

as See **like, as.**

as if See **like, as if.**

at Do not use *at* after *where.*

NONSTANDARD   Where did you see them at?
STANDARD   Where did you see them?

being as, being that Avoid using these expressions. Use *because* or *since* instead.

NONSTANDARD   Being as her grades were so good, she got a scholarship.
STANDARD   **Because** her grades were so good, she got a scholarship.

NONSTANDARD   Being that he was late, he had to stand.
STANDARD   **Since** he was late, he had to stand.

beside, besides *Beside* means "by the side of." *Besides* as a preposition means "in addition to." As an adverb, *besides* means "moreover."

EXAMPLES   He glanced at the person **beside** him.
Did anybody **besides** you see what happened?
I liked the sweater, and it didn't cost much; **besides,** I needed a new one.

between, among Use *between* when you are referring to two things at a time, even if they are part of a larger group.

EXAMPLES   A strong bond exists **between** the twins.
The survey reveals many differences **between** the New England states. [Although there are more than two New England states, each one is being compared with each of the others separately.]

Use *among* when referring to all members of a group rather than to separate individuals in the group.

EXAMPLES   We distributed the pamphlets **among** the crowd.
There was some disagreement **among** the editorial staff about the lead story.

bring, take *Bring* means "to come carrying something." *Take* means "to go away carrying something." Think of *bring* as related to *come* and *take* as related to *go*.

EXAMPLES **Bring** your radio when you come.
Don't forget to **take** your coat when you go.

bust, busted Avoid using these words as verbs. Instead, use a form of *break* or *burst*.

EXAMPLES I **broke** [not *busted*] the switch on the stereo.
The water main **burst**. [not *busted*]

▶ EXERCISE 1 **Identifying Correct Expressions**

For each sentence, choose the correct word from the pair given in parentheses.

1. The tasks were divided evenly (*among, between*) the two scouts.
2. The audience was deeply (*affected, effected*) by Simon Estes' powerful baritone voice.
3. We were afraid the bull had (*busted, broken*) loose.
4. No one (*accept, except*) the sophomores is supposed to attend.
5. Please (*bring, take*) these papers when you leave.
6. Penicillin has (*affected, effected*) some remarkable recoveries.
7. I couldn't find the cat (*anywhere, anywheres*).
8. The crosslike rays radiating from the moon were an (*allusion, illusion*) caused by the screen door.
9. (*Beside, Besides*) Julie, who else has signed up for Saturday's 10K walk?
10. In his remarks about Dr. King, the speaker made an (*allusion, illusion*) to Gandhi, whose nonviolent protests paved the way for the civil rights movement in the United States.

▶ EXERCISE 2 **Proofreading a Paragraph to Correct Usage Errors**

Correct all the usage errors you find in each sentence in the following paragraph. Give the incorrect usage, followed by the correct usage. If a sentence is correct, write *C*.

USAGE

[1] In 1903, this young Japanese artist, Frank Matsura, arrived in the backwoods settlement of Conconully, Washington. [2] This was all the farther he would go, for he lived in this rough frontier area for the remaining ten years of his life. [3] When he came to town, Matsura was wearing a elegant formal suit and was carrying bulky camera equipment he had taken with him. [4] Back in Seattle, Matsura had excepted a job in Conconully as a helper and laundryman at the Elliott Hotel. [5] Soon he was living in a tiny room behind the kitchen and bringing energy and cheer to his menial job. [6] When he was off duty, he carried his camera everywheres he went, photographing the area's people, scenery, events, and etc. [7] Later, he settled in nearby Okanogan and opened this small studio. [8] Being that Matsura was a warm, extroverted person, he made many friends between settlers and Native Americans alike. [9] Oddly, though, he never told anyone about his past. [10] To this day, nobody knows who he really was, where he was born at, or why he chose to live and die so far from his home.

can't hardly, can't scarcely See **The Double Negative** (page 756).

could of Do not use *of* with the helping verb *could*. Use *could have* instead. Also avoid *had of, ought to of, should of, would of, might of,* and *must of.*

EXAMPLE   Muriel could **have** [not *of*] gone with us.

discover, invent *Discover* means "to find, see, or learn about something that already exists." *Invent* means "to be the first to make or do something."

EXAMPLES   Luis W. Alvarez **discovered** many subatomic particles.
Sarah Boone **invented** the ironing board.

don't, doesn't *Don't* is the contraction of *do not. Doesn't* is the contraction of *does not.* Use *doesn't,* not *don't,* with *he, she, it, this, that,* and singular nouns.

EXAMPLES   It **doesn't** [not *don't*] matter to me.
The poem **doesn't** [not *don't*] rhyme.

effect See **affect, effect.**

emigrate, immigrate *Emigrate* means "to leave a country to settle elsewhere." *Immigrate* means "to come into a country to settle there."

EXAMPLES   My great-grandfather **emigrated** from Mexico.
Much of Australia's population is composed of people who **immigrated** there.

everywheres See **anywheres,** etc.

except See **accept, except.**

fewer, less *Fewer* is used with plural nouns. It tells "how many." *Less* is used with singular words. It tells "how much."

EXAMPLES   There are **fewer** whales than there once were.
We should have bought **less** meat [but: **fewer** eggs].

good, well *Good* is an adjective. Do not use it to modify a verb. Instead, use *well.*

NONSTANDARD   They skate **good.**
STANDARD   They skate **well.**

Although it is usually an adverb, *well* is used as an adjective to mean "healthy," "well dressed or well groomed," or "satisfactory."

EXAMPLES   I didn't feel **well.**
He looked **well** in his uniform.
All seems **well.**

USAGE

NOTE: *Feel good* and *feel well* mean different things. *Feel good* means "to feel happy or pleased." *Feel well* means "to feel healthy."

> EXAMPLES The victory made us feel **good**.
> If you don't feel **well,** lie down.

Using *good* as an adverb is acceptable in conversation but not in writing.

had of See **could of.**

had ought, hadn't ought Do not use *had* or *hadn't* with *ought.*

> NONSTANDARD You hadn't ought to say such things.
> STANDARD You **ought** not to say such things.
> *or*
> You **shouldn't** say such things.
>
> NONSTANDARD They had ought to have left earlier.
> STANDARD They **ought** to have left earlier.
> *or*
> They **should** have left earlier.

hardly See **The Double Negative** (page 756).

he, she, they Do not use unnecessary pronouns after nouns. This error is called the *double subject.*

> NONSTANDARD My father he works downtown.
> STANDARD My **father works** downtown.

illusion See **allusion, illusion.**

immigrate See **emigrate, immigrate.**

imply, infer *Imply* means "to suggest something." *Infer* means "to interpret" or "to get a certain meaning from a remark or an action."

> EXAMPLES In her speech, the candidate **implied** that she is for tax reform.
> From the candidate's speeches, I **inferred** that she is for tax reform.

invent See **discover, invent.**

▶ EXERCISE 3 **Identifying Correct Expressions**

For each sentence, choose the correct word from the pair given in parentheses.

1. Was it George Washington Carver or Thomas Edison who (*invented, discovered*) all those uses for peanuts?
2. From his letter I (*implied, inferred*) he would be away all summer.
3. He (*don't, doesn't*) always say what he means.
4. (*Emigration, Immigration*) to Alaska was spurred by the gold rush.
5. The heat has affected the growing season; we'll harvest (*fewer, less*) crops this year.
6. Many French Canadians (*emigrated, immigrated*) from Quebec to work in the industries of New England.
7. As beasts of burden, dogs served the Comanches (*good, well*), often pulling a travois laden with more than forty pounds of baggage.
8. Mary Beth Stearns (*discovered, invented*) a technique for studying electrons.
9. You could (*have, of*) borrowed some paper and a pencil from me.
10. Audrey must (*have, of*) taken my jacket by mistake.

USAGE

▶ EXERCISE 4   **Proofreading a Paragraph to Correct Usage Errors**

Correct all the usage errors you find in each sentence in the following paragraph. Give the incorrect usage, followed by the correct usage. If a sentence is correct, write *C*.

[1] The scientist/philosopher/writer Douglas R. Hofstadter he enjoys creating perfectly symmetrical designs from written words. [2] He and a friend discovered a new pastime; the resulting designs are called *ambigrams*. [3] Every word don't lend itself good to this method, but you'd be surprised how often a word can be made into an ambigram. [4] As you might of known already, a *palindrome* is a word or expression that has the same letters in the same sequence both forward and backward—for example, *toot* or *Madam, I'm Adam*. [5] I don't mean to infer, though, that an ambigram has to be a palindrome— an ambigram simply has to *look* symmetrical. [6] Usually, ambigrams can't hardly be formed unless you tinker with the letter shapes and connect them in new ways. [7] You had ought to start with a word that has six letters or less.

[8] For some good ideas, look below at the ambigrams for the words *Jamal, Steve, Chris, Felix, Wendy, Mexico,* and *dance.* [9] Don't forget that you can mix cursive, printed, capital, and lowercase letters to create affects like the ones in these ambigrams. [10] If you become stumped, you might find that you could of succeeded by adding some decorative flourishes.

Steve

Jamal

Chris

dance

Mexico

Wendy

Felix

kind, sort, type These words should always agree in number with the words *this* and *that* (singular) or *these* and *those* (plural).

EXAMPLE   I know more about **that kind** of music than about any of **those** other **kinds**.

kind of, sort of These expressions, widely used in conversation, mean "rather" or "somewhat." Avoid them in writing.

ACCEPTABLE IN   She seemed kind of bored.
CONVERSATION   The waves were sort of rough.

CORRECT IN   She seemed **rather** bored.
WRITING   The waves were **rather** [or *somewhat*] rough.

kind of a, sort of a The *a* (or *an*) is unnecessary. Omit it.

EXAMPLE   This bolt takes a special **kind of** [not *kind of a*] nut.

learn, teach *Learn* means "to acquire information." *Teach* means "to instruct" or "to show how."

EXAMPLES   She **learned** how to saddle a horse.
The stable owner **taught** her how.

leave, let *Leave* means "to go away." *Let* means "to allow" or "to permit."

NONSTANDARD   Leave them go first.
STANDARD   **Let** them go first.
STANDARD   We **let** [not *left*] the trapped bird go free.

less See **fewer, less.**

lie, lay See pages 697–698.

like, as *Like* is usually a preposition. In informal English, *like* is often used in place of the conjunction *as*. Formal English calls for *as* to introduce a subordinate clause.

EXAMPLES   The animal looked **like** a snake. [The preposition *like* introduces a prepositional phrase.]
It shed its skin **as** a snake does. [The conjunction *as* introduces a subordinate adverb clause.]

☞ REFERENCE NOTE: Phrases are discussed in Chapter 17, and clauses are covered in Chapter 18. For more on informal and formal English, see pages 500–501.

like, as if In informal speech, *like* is often used in place of the subordinating conjunction *as if* or *as though* to introduce a subordinate clause. When writing, avoid using *like* in place of these two conjunctions.

INFORMAL   This looks like it might be the right place.
FORMAL   This looks **as if** [or *as though*] it might be the right place.

might of, must of See **could of.**

no, none, nothing See **The Double Negative** (page 756).

nowheres See **anywheres,** etc.

of Do not use *of* with prepositions such as *inside, off,* and *outside.*

EXAMPLES   The diver jumped **off** [not *off of*] the board.
Outside [not *outside of*] the building was a patio.

☞ REFERENCE NOTE: For information on using *of* with helping verbs (*had of* and *must of,* for example), see the listing for **could of.** For information on using *of* in the expressions *kind of* and *sort of,* see the listings for **kind of, sort of** and **kind of a, sort of a.**

off of See **of.**

ought to of See **could of.**

USAGE

USAGE

▶ EXERCISE 5 **Identifying Correct Expressions**

For each sentence, choose the correct word or words from the choices given in parentheses.

1. The total length of the Great Wall of China is about 4,000 miles, if branches (*off, off of*) the main wall are included.
2. Carlos was (*nowhere, nowheres*) in sight.
3. We went to the hardware store for a special (*kind of, kind of a*) wrench.
4. Rachel Carson's books (*learned, taught*) me to care about ecology.
5. (*Leave, Let*) us listen without any interruptions.
6. We could (*of, have*) left earlier, I suppose.
7. Why did she feel (*like, as if*) she'd said something wrong?
8. T. J. (*ought, had ought*) to see this program.
9. Why didn't the U.S. government (*leave, let*) the Cherokee people stay in their Southeast homelands?
10. They didn't want to take the boat out because the waves looked (*kind of, rather*) choppy.

▶ EXERCISE 6 **Proofreading a Paragraph to Correct Usage Errors**

Correct all the usage errors you find in each sentence in the following paragraph. Give the incorrect usage, followed by the correct usage. If a sentence is correct, write *C*.

[1] Until recent times, young girls had to master fancy needlework. [2] Beginning when a girl was kind of young, her mother or another woman would learn her many embroidery stitches. [3] Then, at the age of eight or ten, the girl would be given the task of making a sampler like the one shown on the next page, using every kind of a stitch she knew. [4] Usually, the girl's parents wouldn't leave her be idle. [5] She had to work on the sampler every day like her life depended on it! [6] When the sampler was finished, it didn't lay inside of a drawer either. [7] Instead, it was displayed to prove that the girl was industrious and well educated in the homemaking skills. [8] Many people

think that samplers must of been popular in America and nowheres else. [9] However, these kind of needlework exercises have been practiced in Europe, Asia, and Africa for centuries. [10] Today, girls aren't judged by their stitchery like they once were, and some never learn anything about needlework.

Lucy Lathrop's Sampler. Cooper-Hewitt, National Museum of Design, Smithsonian Institution. Bequest of Marian Hague. Photo: Scott Hyde. Courtesy of Art Resource, NY.

rise, raise See page 704.

scarcely See **The Double Negative** (page 756).

she See **he, she, they.**

should of See **could of.**

sit, set See pages 700–701.

some, somewhat In writing, do not use *some* as an adverb in place of *somewhat*.

> EXAMPLE This medicine should help your cough **somewhat** [not *some*].

somewheres See **anywheres,** etc.

sort See **kind, sort, type.**

sort of See **kind of, sort of.**

take, bring See **bring, take.**

USAGE

teach See **learn, teach.**

than, then *Than* is a conjunction used in comparisons. *Then* is an adverb telling "when."

EXAMPLES   She is younger **than** you.

I swept the floor; **then** I emptied the trash.

that See **which, that, who.**

them Do not use *them* as an adjective. Use *those* instead.

EXAMPLE   It's one of **those** [not *them*] fancy show dogs.

they See **he, she, they.**

this here, that there *Here* and *there* are unnecessary after *this* and *that*.

EXAMPLE   Let's rent **this** [not *this here*] movie instead of **that** [not *that there*] one.

try and The correct expression is *try to.*

EXAMPLE   When you're at bat, you must **try to** [not *try and*] concentrate.

type See **kind, sort, type.**

unless See **without, unless.**

way, ways Use *way,* not *ways,* in referring to a distance.

EXAMPLE   She lives quite a **way** [not *ways*] from here.

well See **good, well.**

what Do not use *what* in place of *that* to introduce a subordinate clause.

EXAMPLE   This is the book **that** [not *what*] I told you about.

when, where Do not use *when* or *where* incorrectly in writing a definition.

NONSTANDARD   *S.R.O.* is when tickets for all the seats have been sold, leaving standing room only.

STANDARD   *S.R.O.* means that tickets for all the seats have been sold, leaving standing room only.

or

S.R.O. is the abbreviation for *standing room only,* meaning that tickets for all the seats have been sold.

where Do not use *where* for *that*.

> EXAMPLE I read **that** [not *where*] the word *bayou* comes from the Choctaw word *bayuk*, meaning "small stream."

where . . . at See **at**.

which, that, who *Which* refers only to things. *That* refers to either people or things. *Who* refers only to people.

> EXAMPLES These running shoes, **which** are on sale now, are the ones I want.
> This is the bulb **that** needs replacing.
> Is she the runner **that** won the medal?
> Is she the runner **who** won the medal?

who, whom See pages 661–662.

without, unless Do not use the preposition *without* in place of the conjunction *unless*.

> EXAMPLE I can't use the car **unless** [not *without*] I ask Mom.

would of See **could of**.

USAGE

▶ EXERCISE 7 **Correcting Errors in Usage**

Revise each sentence, correcting errors in usage.

1. A solar eclipse is when the moon comes between the earth and the sun.
2. The workers which put up that office building were certainly fast.
3. Ronald E. McNair was the only African American astronaut aboard the space shuttle what exploded in January 1986.
4. I really like them science fiction movies.
5. A run-on sentence is where two sentences are erroneously joined as one.
6. As soon as the rain lets up some, we'll leave.
7. Them mosquitoes can drive a person nearly crazy.
8. Jerry Rice carried the ball a long ways down the field before he was tackled.
9. I read in the paper where Amy Tan has a new novel coming out soon.
10. I'm tired of trying to cut the grass with this here old lawn mower that should be in an antique exhibit.

USAGE

WRITING APPLICATION

Using Standard English to Make a Good Impression

How you present yourself affects the way other people respond to you. When you appear to be intelligent and well-spoken, others usually have a higher regard for what you say. Like individuals, most businesses and organizations try hard to present themselves at their best. One of the ways they do so is by creating advertisements or public relations fliers. The use of correct standard English in such ads and fliers makes a good impression. Notice what different impressions you get from these two examples.

NONSTANDARD   Leave me tell you about some of the accomplishments of our association. You may of already heard about our very successful Thanksgiving food drive. Well, we also rose money for the new mobile clinic. This here clinic brings affordable, high-quality health care to people living in remote areas of our county.

STANDARD   Let me tell you about some of the accomplishments of our association. You may have already heard about our very successful Thanksgiving food drive. Well, we also raised money for the new mobile clinic. This clinic brings affordable, high-quality health care to people living in remote areas of our county.

Which of these statements would make a better impression on a potential volunteer or contributor?

▶ WRITING ACTIVITY

Create a flier for an organization that will soon be providing a public service in your community. The organization you choose might provide health, recreation, or housing services, or it might do something else. In a one-page flier, describe the organization's achievements and goals, and tell about some of the services it offers. Include at least five examples of the standard usage guidelines covered in this chapter, and underline each example.

Prewriting Begin by listing services that your community needs and noting what kinds of organizations supply these services. You may write about a real service group, such as the American Heart Association, or you may wish to write about a group that you make up. Also, list some of the positive effects the group will likely have on your community. Organize your notes so that you can present your information in several coherent paragraphs.

Writing As you write your first draft, you may think of points you'd like to add or changes you'd like to make in the presentation of your information. If so, look back over your prewriting notes, and figure out where your additions and changes will best fit.

Evaluating and Revising Exchange papers with a classmate, and as the two of you read each other's ads or fliers, ask the following questions:

- What does this group or organization do?
- Why should I trust this organization to provide the services it promises?
- How will these services benefit the people in my community?
- What other services could this organization provide that would be more useful to my community?
- What is my overall impression of this organization or group?

Use your partner's responses to these questions to help you revise your draft for clarity and audience appeal. You may also want to get pamphlets or fliers from some local public service groups to see how information is presented in these publications.

Proofreading Now that you've worked so hard on creating a good impression, don't spoil the effect with incorrect punctuation. See Chapters 25–28 for guidelines on using marks of punctuation. Read over your paper again, checking for errors in grammar, spelling, and usage. Be sure that you have included five correct expressions from this chapter.

▶ REVIEW A   **Identifying Correct Expressions**

For each sentence, choose the correct word or words from the choices given in parentheses.

1. Thanks to modern medicine, there are (*fewer, less*) cases of tetanus and diphtheria nowadays.
2. I tried to (*learn, teach*) my dog to do tricks, but he just sat and stared at me.
3. I see (*where, that*) pandas are an endangered species.
4. Cape Porpoise is (*somewhere, somewheres*) near Portsmouth.
5. Priscilla wrote a longer paper (*than, then*) Tammy did.
6. To make Native American fry bread, you need flour, baking powder, salt, (*and etc., etc.*)
7. We (*hadn't ought, ought not*) to decide until we know more facts.
8. It (*don't, doesn't*) make any difference when we finish.
9. Someone must (*of, have*) left the door unlocked.
10. Lewis Latimer (*discovered, invented*) and patented the first electric light bulb.

▶ REVIEW B   **Selecting Appropriate Expressions**

For each sentence, choose the correct word or words from the choices given in parentheses.

1. Stevie Wonder has written a number of hit songs since the 1960s, and it (*don't, doesn't*) look (*as if, like*) he's ever going to stop.
2. (*Inside, Inside of*) the box was (*a, an*) heap of glittering gems.
3. May I (*imply, infer*) from your yawns that you are bored?
4. My great-grandmother (*emigrated, immigrated*) from Italy when she was a young woman.
5. (*Beside, Besides*) speaking Spanish, Vera can speak a little Portuguese, and she reads both very (*good, well*).
6. Linda (*doesn't, don't*) enjoy doing (*them, those, that*) sort of exercise.
7. Ahead of us on the desert, a lake seemed to sparkle, but it was only an (*allusion, illusion*).
8. This water shortage will (*affect, effect*) the whole state (*accept, except*) for two counties.

9. I don't think my parents will (*leave, let*) me borrow the car in this kind of weather.
10. Because of the indiscriminate slaughter, each year there were (*fewer, less*) bison.

REVIEW C Proofreading a Paragraph to Correct Usage Errors

Correct each usage error you find in each sentence in the following paragraph. Give the incorrect usage, then the correct usage. If a sentence is correct, write C.

[1] Imagine single-handedly discovering a system for writing a language that had never before been written! [2] In about 1809, the Cherokee scholar Sequoyah became aware of "talking leaves," the written pages used by whites to communicate with one another. [3] Being that Sequoyah he felt that the ability to write had greatly helped whites, he decided he had ought to create a similar system for his people. [4] Instead of making up an alphabet like the one used in English, he chose to create this here *syllabary*. [5] Each character in Sequoyah's syllabary stands for one of the eighty-five syllables what are used in speaking Cherokee. [6] Sequoyah copied some letters from a English book, but in his system they have different meanings. [7] During the twelve years that it took Sequoyah to complete his writing system, he was ridiculed by many Cherokees who thought his efforts were kind of foolish. [8] But after the syllabary was finished and accepted by most Cherokees, they realized they should not of scoffed. [9] Within a few months' time, thousands learned

CHEROKEE SYLLABARY
Invented by SEQUOYAH

D a	R e	T i	Ꭹ o	Ꮕ u	i v
S ga Ꭶ ka	Ꮢ ge	Ꭹ gi	A go	J gu	E gv
Ꮤ ha	Ꭾ he	� hi	Ꮶ ho	� hu	Ꮛ hv
W la	Ꮯ le	Ꮒ li	G lo	M lu	Ꮭ lv
Ꮉ ma	Ꮊ me	H mi	Ꮉ mo	Ꮿ mu	
Ꮎ na Ꮏ hna Ꮐ nah Ꮑ ne	Ꮒ ni	Z no	Ꮎ nu	Ꮕ nv	
Ꮖ qua	Ꮗ que	Ꮖ qui	Ꮙ quo	Ꮚ quu	Ꮫ quv
Ꮜ sa Ꮝ s	Ꮞ se	Ꮟ si	Ꮠ so	Ꮡ su	R sv
Ꮃ da Ꮺ ta	Ꮪ de Ꮦ te	Ꮪ di Ꭲ ti	V do	S du	Ꮼ dv
Ꮬ dla Ꮝ tla	Ꮭ tle	C tli	Ꮬ tlo	Ꮯ tlu	P tlv
Ꮳ tsa	Ꮴ tse	Ꮵ tsi	K tso	Ꮷ tsu	Ꮳ tsv
Ꮹ wa	Ꮺ we	Ꮻ wi	Ꮼ wo	Ꮽ wu	Ꮾ wv
Ꮿ ya	Ᏸ ye	Ᏹ yi	Ᏺ yo	Ᏻ yu	Ᏼ yv

PRONUNCIATION GUIDE
(In words the pronunciation may be different)

a, as in ah   o, as in oh   g, as in go
e, as in they   u, as in true   ts, as j in joy
i, as in ski   v, as uh in huh

d, h, k, l, m, n, qu, s, t, w, y, as in English
NOTE: The character 'nah' is not in use.

Adapted from "Cherokee Alphabet" created by Harry A. Moneyhun, 1991.

how to read and write, and soon books and newspapers were being printed in Cherokee. [10] Sequoyah was honored by his people for learning them to read and write, and his writing method is still used today.

The Double Negative

A *double negative* is the use of two negative words when one is enough. Before the 1700s, two or more negatives were often used in the same sentence for emphasis. Today this usage is no longer considered correct, and a double negative is regarded as nonstandard. Avoid using double negatives in your writing and speaking.

hardly, scarcely Do not use the words *hardly* and *scarcely* with another negative word.

EXAMPLES You **can** [not *can't*] **hardly** see ten feet in this fog.
We **had** [not *hadn't*] **scarcely** enough time to finish the test.

no, none, nothing Do not use any of these negative words with another negative word.

NONSTANDARD There isn't no reason to be nervous.
STANDARD There **is no** reason to be nervous.
STANDARD There **isn't any** reason to be nervous.

NONSTANDARD We searched for clues but didn't find none.
STANDARD We searched for clues but **found none.**
STANDARD We searched for clues but **didn't find any.**

NONSTANDARD I didn't hear nothing.
STANDARD I **heard nothing.**
STANDARD I **didn't hear anything.**

EXERCISE 8   ## Revising Sentences That Contain Too Many Negative Words

Each of the following sentences contains too many negative words. Revise each sentence in two correct ways. Be careful not to change the intended meaning.

EXAMPLE   **1.** Before Sequoyah's syllabary, the Cherokee language hadn't never been written down.

1. *Before Sequoyah's syllabary, the Cherokee language had never been written down.*
Before Sequoyah's syllabary, the Cherokee language hadn't ever been written down.

1. As a young man, Sequoyah didn't have scarcely no contact with whites.
2. Before Sequoyah, not no person in history hadn't never single-handedly created no written language!
3. Some Cherokees didn't want no part of Sequoyah's system of writing.
4. It didn't take hardly no time at all for thousands of Cherokees to learn Sequoyah's symbols.
5. The Cherokees had a rich oral tradition, but they hadn't never been able to put none of it on paper.

REVIEW D   ## Revising Sentences by Correcting Errors in Usage

Rewrite each sentence, correcting its error or errors in usage. Practice saying aloud the corrected sentences.

1. They don't have hardly any chance to score before the buzzer sounds; the situation looks sort of hopeless to me.
2. You ought to have seen how beautiful Santa Fe was at Christmas, with nearly every house surrounded by flickering *farolitos*—paper-bag lanterns that have candles inside of them.
3. I might of gone to the concert if I'd of heard about it earlier.
4. Pam and her sister Stacey look so much alike that you can't hardly see much difference among them.
5. My cousins didn't hardly know how to swim, but they wouldn't of missed going to the lake.

USAGE

6. Them reference books in the library are kept in some kind of a special section.
7. This here is the car what I told you about.
8. Hadn't you ought to try and help them?
9. Many of the American Indian leaders which visited Washington, D.C., in the late 1800s proudly wore their traditional clothing rather than dress like their white hosts did.
10. I wonder where them fishing poles are at.
11. We don't live in that there neighborhood no more.
12. We might of gone on the tour, but we wouldn't of had no camera to take pictures.
13. A foot fault in tennis is when the server steps over the base line before hitting the ball.
14. Since there wasn't scarcely any rainfall last spring, there are less mosquitoes this summer.
15. When the play was over, the audience seemed sort of subdued.
16. Shing searched for *lomein* noodles in the grocery store, but didn't find none.
17. I saw on the news where manufacturers will start putting them air bags into all the new cars.
18. Miss Kim she likes to give those kind of surprise quizzes.
19. Let's try and finish early so we can relax some.
20. In the early 1500s, Ponce de León searched for the Fountain of Youth somewheres on the island of Bimini.

PICTURE THIS

You are a professional artist looking for a fresh medium in which to work. You've just seen an unusual exhibit of painted chifforobes—pieces of furniture that combine a wardrobe with a chest of drawers. The secondhand chifforobes were decorated, inside and out, by New Orleans high school students. You admire how these young artists have presented scenes from their lives to illustrate their dreams and fears. You have so many thoughts and impressions that you decide to write some notes to yourself to remind you of your reactions to the exhibit. Describe in detail one of the chifforobes shown here. (You can describe an imaginary one if none of these three interests you.) Tell whether you were inspired by the exhibit and how you might use the chifforobe art to enrich your own work. In your paragraph, use correctly at least five expressions covered in this chapter.

Subject: an exhibit of chifforobes painted by high school students
Audience: you, a professional painter
Purpose: to inform, to remind, to inspire

USAGE

Review: Posttest

A. Revising Expressions by Correcting Errors in Usage

In each set of expressions, one expression contains an error in usage. Write the expression correctly, using standard formal usage.

EXAMPLE **1. a.** Her speech implies that a change is needed.
    b. Leave me have some oranges, too.
        c. This house is somewhat larger than our old one.
    1. *b. Let me have some oranges, too.*

1. **a.** wasn't no reason
    b. words had no effect
    c. can hardly wait
2. **a.** families that emigrated to new lands
    b. sail as far as the channel marker
    c. made allusions to classical literature
3. **a.** being that he was alone
    b. The people accepted new ways.
    c. the woman who was elected
4. **a.** what kind of gloves
    b. There is overtime besides the regular work.
    c. an historic moment
5. **a.** saw on TV that our team had won
    b. Lee Haney proudly excepted his seventh straight Mr. Olympia trophy.
    c. the house beside the highway
6. **a.** those lockers beside the gym
    b. Leave him have his own way.
    c. Leave the door open when you go.
7. **a.** Teach your dog this trick.
    b. I'm feeling kind of ill.
    c. might have been too late
8. **a.** taller than her sister
    b. Dough will rise in a warm place.
    c. We read where the damage was extensive.
9. **a.** Try to be on time.
    b. They walked a long way.
    c. Them stairs are dangerous and need repairs.

10. **a.** The bag burst, spilling the rice.

  b. The Polynesian alphabet has twelve characters, fewer than half the letters in the English alphabet.

  c. Take those books off of that shelf.

B. Proofreading Paragraphs to Correct Usage Errors

Correct each usage error you find in each sentence in the following paragraphs. Give the incorrect usage, followed by the correct usage. [Note: A sentence may contain more than one error.]

[11] After the Civil War ended, Joseph E. Clarke decided that African Americans had ought to start a town of their own. [12] He wanted to build such a town, but no one would sell or donate land for this kind of an endeavor. [13] But Joe Clarke was a man who had great determination, and he wasn't hardly going to give up hope. [14] Finally in 1877, with money what was donated by a New York philanthropist and land offered by a Floridian named Josiah Eaton, Clarke obtained the first twelve acres of what would become Eatonville, Florida.

[15] Eatonville, located just besides Orlando, is recognized as the oldest incorporated African American town anywheres in the United States. [16] This here community has always been populated and governed entirely by blacks. [17] The African Americans which flocked to Eatonville built homes, churches, and schools, and they cultivated gardens and orange groves. [18] The residents didn't lose no time in establishing a library, a post office, and a newspaper. [19] Today, after more than a hundred years of self-government, the citizens of Eatonville continue to feel the affects of Joe Clarke's courage and vision. [20] With its light industry, new businesses, and booming real estate development, Eatonville enjoys economic growth just like the rest of Central Florida does.

USAGE

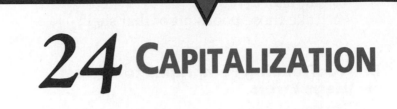

24 CAPITALIZATION

Standard Uses of Capitalization

Diagnostic Test

Correcting Sentences by Using Capitalization Correctly

For each of the following sentences, identify the word or words containing an error in capitalization. If a sentence is correct, write *C*.

EXAMPLE   **1.** In the Fall the trees along Main street are lovely.
      1. *fall; Street*

1. This year my easiest classes are geometry, spanish, and American history.
2. Mexico city is built on the site of tenochtitlán, the capital of the aztec empire.
3. We rent videotapes from the Grand Video company.
4. Colorado is located West of the Great Plains.
5. Lansing, Michigan, is in Ingham county.
6. She lives at 321 Maple boulevard, which is south of here.

7. My RCA Stereo is ten years old and still works well.
8. Carla entered her Saint Bernard in the Centerville Dog club's show.
9. They live half a block north of Twenty-First Street.
10. Our neighbors are alumni of Howard university in Washington, d.c.
11. Last Spring my step-sister Lisa joined the National Audubon society.
12. While we were in San Juan, puerto rico, we toured El Morro Castle.
13. The club members celebrated bastille day by having dinner at a French restaurant.
14. Has Ms. Davis written to the U.S. department of Agriculture for information on soybean cultivation in the Midwest?
15. Mars was the Roman God of war.
16. We're holding a carwash next Saturday to raise money for the junior Prom.
17. The Islands that make up the west indies separate the Atlantic ocean from the gulf of mexico and the Caribbean sea.
18. Would you like to be the first student to ride in a Space Shuttle that orbits the earth?
19. The post-Civil war period known as reconstruction officially ended in 1877, when federal troops were withdrawn from the south.
20. Erica wants to be Secretary of the Shutterbug club.

MECHANICS

In your reading, you'll notice that some writers do not always follow the rules presented in this chapter. However, you will see that most writers do follow these rules most of the time. In your own writing, following these rules will help you communicate clearly with the widest possible audience.

NOTE: Some modern writers, for reasons of style, do not follow the rules governing capitalization. When you quote from a writer's work, always use capital letters exactly as the writer uses them.

☞ REFERENCE NOTE: See pages 834–835 for more about using capital letters in quotations.

24a. Capitalize the first word in every sentence.

EXAMPLES   **The Second Seminole War lasted nearly eight years.**
After the war many Seminoles remained in the
Everglades and never officially made peace with
the U.S. government.
After studying reports on new cars, my mom said,
"The models with front-wheel drive have been
improved."

Traditionally, the first word in a line of poetry is capitalized.

EXAMPLES   **Storm, blow me from here**
With your fiercest wind
Let me float across the sky
'Till I can rest again.

Maya Angelou, "Woman Work"

24b. Capitalize the pronoun *I* and the interjection *O*.

The interjection *O*, usually used only for invocations, is followed by the name of the person or thing being addressed. Don't confuse *O* with the common interjection *oh*, which is capitalized only when it begins a sentence or is part of a title.

EXAMPLES   **The first line I read in the poem was "Hear us,**
O Zeus."
I finished the race, but oh, was I exhausted.

24c. Capitalize proper nouns and proper adjectives.

A *common noun* names one member of a group of people, places, or things. A *proper noun* names a particular person, place, or thing. *Proper adjectives* are formed from proper nouns.

☞ REFERENCE NOTE: See page 515 for more about common nouns and proper nouns.

Common nouns are not capitalized unless they

- begin a sentence
- begin a direct quotation
- are part of a title

COMMON NOUNS	PROPER NOUNS	PROPER ADJECTIVES
a **writer**	Shakespeare	Shakespearean sonnet
a **country**	France	French bread
a **queen**	Victoria	Victorian era
a **planet**	Venus	Venusian terrain

In proper nouns that have more than one word, all articles and short prepositions (those with fewer than five letters) are not capitalized.

EXAMPLES   Prince **of** Wales
National Association **for the** Advancement **of** Colored People

In a compound adjective, the proper noun or proper adjective is usually the only part capitalized.

EXAMPLES   **Spanish**-speaking countries   northern **Italian** cuisine

NOTE: Proper nouns and proper adjectives may lose their capitals after long use.

EXAMPLES   **diesel**   **bologna**   **braille**

When you're not sure whether to capitalize a word, check a dictionary to see in which uses (if any) it is capitalized.

(1) Capitalize the names of persons.

GIVEN NAMES	Matthew	Jennifer	Latrice	Nguyen
SURNAMES	Bowman	Cruz	Kantor	Ryan

NOTE: Some names contain more than one capital letter. Always verify the spelling with the person, or check it in a reference source.

EXAMPLES   **De La Cruz   La Porte   McEnroe   O'Shea**
Red Cloud   Wells-Barnett   St. John   Van Gogh

The abbreviations *Jr.* (*junior*) and *Sr.* (*senior*) should always be capitalized.

EXAMPLES   Jerome W. Wilson, **Jr.**   Simon L. Snyder, **Sr.**

MECHANICS

▶ EXERCISE 1   **Correcting Paragraphs by Using Capitalization**

If the capitalization of a sentence is correct, write *C*. If not, write the correct form of each incorrect word.

EXAMPLE   [1] These pictures capture only a few of the many sides of Gordon parks, renowned Photographer, film director, writer, and composer.
  1. *Parks; photographer*

[1] A Self-taught photographer, gordon Parks grew up in Fort Scott, Kansas. [2] after winning a rosenwald Fellowship for a series of pictures about life in Chicago's Slums, He got his first full-time photography job with the Farm Security Administration in Washington, D.C. [3] In 1949, he joined the staff of *Life* Magazine. [4] During his nearly twenty years with *Life,* Parks covered assignments ranging from Junior High School science conventions to Paris Fashion Shows. [5] He also wrote many of the essays that accompanied his photographs, as well as Two Volumes of autobiography, *A Choice of Weapons* and *Voices in the Mirror.*

Mary Ellen Mark Library.

MECHANICS

[6] Turning to a career in the movie industry in 1968, Parks moved to Hollywood, where his son Gordon Parks, jr., took this photograph of him preparing to direct a scene from the film version of *The Learning Tree*. [7] Parks also wrote the film's screenplay and, working at the grand piano in his Hollywood apartment, its musical score. [8] His success with the film led to other writing and directing projects, including *Shaft*, *Shaft's Big Score*, and *Leadbelly*, the story of blues musician Huddie ledbetter.

[9] In August 1988, in a White House Ceremony, parks was awarded the National Medal of Arts, and two years later he was inducted into the National Association of Black Journalists Hall of Fame. [10] His most recent projects have included an Autobiographical work, *Voices in The Mirror*, and the words and music for *Martin*, a classical Ballet honoring the late martin luther king, jr.

(2) Capitalize geographical names.

TYPE OF NAME	EXAMPLES	
Countries	Mexico Ghana	the United States of America
Towns, Cities	Chicago Berlin San Diego	Laredo Stratford-on-Avon St. Petersburg
Counties, Townships, Parishes	Orange County Franklin Township Manhattan	Caddo Parish Yorkshire Third Precinct
States	Oregon New York	Texas South Carolina
Regions	the South the West the Northeast	New England Yukon Sun Belt

MECHANICS

NOTE: Words such as *south*, *east*, and *northwest* are not capitalized when they indicate direction.

EXAMPLES   **west** of the bridge   heading **north**

TYPE OF NAME	EXAMPLES	
Continents	South America Asia	Europe Africa
Islands	Galveston Island the Lesser Antilles	the Isle of Wight Key West
Mountains	Allegheny Mountains Sierra Madre	Mount St. Helens Pikes Peak
Bodies of Water	Atlantic Ocean Red Sea Persian Gulf	Suwanee River Rio Grande Lake of the Ozarks
Parks	Redwood State Park Central Park	Stone Mountain Memorial Park
Roads, Highways, Streets	Route 41 Interstate 10 Sunshine State Parkway	Central Avenue South Fiftieth Street Pleasant Hill Road

The second word in a hyphenated number begins with a small letter: *Fifty-third Street.* Words such as *city, island, river, street,* and *park* are capitalized when they are part of a name. Otherwise, they are common nouns and are not capitalized.

PROPER NOUNS	COMMON NOUNS
traffic in Mexico City visiting Captiva Island bridging the Ohio River across Delancy Street	traffic in a large city visiting a barrier island bridging the river across a congested street

MECHANICS

▶ EXERCISE 2 **Correcting Phrases by Capitalizing Words**

If a phrase is correct, write *C.* If a word or words should be capitalized, write the entire phrase correctly.

EXAMPLE **1.** atop granite peak
1. *atop Granite Peak*

1. zion national park
2. gulf of tonkin
3. explored Mount ararat
4. the hiking trails in a nearby state park
5. at moon lake
6. a house on starve island
7. beside the ohio river
8. in lancaster county
9. the illinois oil fields
10. across baffin bay
11. ventura boulevard
12. the tides in the bay
13. new york skyline
14. forty-fifth street
15. near the isle of man
16. the west side of the river
17. the north
18. near dundee mountain
19. coffee from brazil
20. coast of australia

▶ EXERCISE 3 **Proofreading a Paragraph to Correct Capitalization**

Capitalize the words that should begin with a capital letter in each sentence in the following paragraph. Do not include the words already capitalized. If a sentence is correct, write *C*.

EXAMPLE [1] Until last year I'd never been farther from lawrenceburg, tennessee, than pulaski, which is only seventeen miles east.
  1. *Lawrenceburg, Tennessee, Pulaski*

[1] Naturally, I was excited when our choir decided to have an international arts and crafts fair to raise money for a trip to washington, d.c. [2] Colleen O'Roark suggested that the fair feature crafts and food from countries in europe, africa, and asia. [3] Juana Santiago, whose family is from venezuela, pointed out that we should also include items from central america and south america. [4] Julian Moore, who recently returned from visiting his aunt in Monrovia, said he'd bring a display of Liberian baskets. [5] Karen Cohen offered items from quebec, our neighbor to the north. [6] Erin McCall, whose family moved to lexington avenue from phoenix, arizona, volunteered to bring rocks from petrified forest national park. [7] Since Maxine Hirano was born in tokyo, japan, she promised to demonstrate paper-folding. [8] Some of us met later at Paula Bowen's house, on the northeast corner of columbus street and hickory lane, to choose items to represent the united states. [9] We selected Native American artifacts

MECHANICS

from the southwest, country crafts from the appalachian mountains, and shell gifts from the southern states along the gulf of mexico. [10] When the fair was over, we had raised enough money to include on our trip to the nation's capital a tour of mammoth cave national park in kentucky.

(3) Capitalize the names of organizations, teams, business firms, institutions, buildings, and government bodies.

TYPE OF NAME	EXAMPLES	
Organizations	American Medical Association National Honor Society Organization of American States	
Teams	New York Rangers Houston Oilers Eastside Jets	Harlem Globetrotters Portsmouth Chess Masters
Business Firms	Eastern Airlines International Business Machines	Xerox Corporation National Broadcasting Company
Institutions, Buildings	Stanford University Sears Tower Fox Theater	Good Samaritan Hospital Ridgemont High School
Government Bodies	the Senate Parliament Congress Tampa City Council	Department of the Interior the Nuclear Regulatory Commission

NOTE: Do not capitalize words such as *democratic, republican,* and *socialist* when they refer to principles or forms of government. Capitalize these words only when they refer to a specific political party.

EXAMPLES   Voting is part of the **d**emocratic process.
George Bush was the **R**epublican nominee.

The word *party* in the name of a political party may be capitalized or not; either way is correct.

EXAMPLE   Republican **party**
or
Republican **Party**

MECHANICS

👉 **REFERENCE NOTE:** Do not capitalize words such as *building, hotel, theater, college, high school, post office,* and *courthouse* unless they are part of a proper name. For more discussion about the differences between common and proper nouns, see pages 764–765 and 515.

(4) Capitalize the names of historical events and periods, special events, and holidays and other calendar items.

TYPE OF NAME	EXAMPLES	
Historical Events and Periods	the Dark Ages Great Depression Paleolithic Period Children's Crusade	the Battle of Gettysburg the Yalta Conference
Special Events	the Iowa State Fair the Boston Marathon	the All-Star Game the National Minority Job Expo
Holidays and Other Calendar Items	Friday March	Valentine's Day Earth Day

NOTE: Do not capitalize the name of a season unless the season is being personified or is part of a proper name.

EXAMPLES We looked forward to spring after the long winter.
Are you going to the **W**inter Wonderland Dance?

"And **W**inter slumbering in the open air,
Wears on his smiling face a dream of **S**pring!"
Samuel Taylor Coleridge, "Work Without Hope"

▶ EXERCISE 4 **Writing a Paragraph Using Capitalization Correctly**

Your family recently inherited the abandoned town shown on the next page. Write a paragraph explaining how you would go about revitalizing the town. What would you name the town? What names would you give to streets and avenues? What organizations, business firms, institutions, government offices, and special events would you set up? Include in your paragraph a combined total of at least twenty proper nouns and proper adjectives. Use a variety of names, not just your family name.

MECHANICS

EXAMPLE   *I'd name the town New Century City, and the first business I'd open would be a teenagers-only club called Syncopation.*

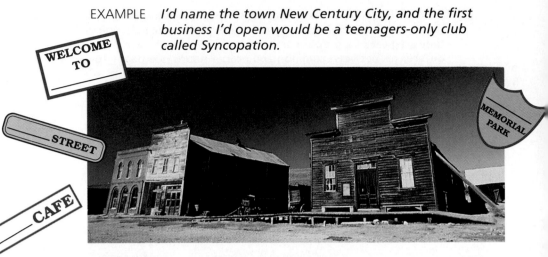

(5) Capitalize the names of nationalities, races, and peoples.

EXAMPLES   Italian, Canadian, Caucasian, Asian, Jewish, Hispanic, Navajo, Micronesian, Indo-Iranian

(6) Capitalize the brand names of business products.

EXAMPLES   Sealtest frozen yogurt, Kraft cheese, Kodak camera

Notice that the noun that often follows a brand name is not capitalized: an Apple computer.

(7) Capitalize the names of ships, monuments, awards, planets, and any other particular places, things, or events.

TYPE OF NAME	EXAMPLES	
Ships, Trains	the *Titanic*	the *Orient Express*
Aircraft, Spacecraft, Missiles	the *Spirit of St. Louis*	*Apollo* *Patriot*
Monuments, Memorials	Aztec Ruins National Monument Vietnam Veterans Memorial	
Awards	Nobel Prize Bronze Star Medal	Academy Award Stanley Cup
Planets, Stars, Constellations	Pluto Ursa Major	Betelgeuse Big Dipper

MECHANICS

NOTE: Do not capitalize the words *earth, moon,* and *sun* unless they are being used along with other astronomical names that are capitalized.

24d. Do *not* capitalize the names of school subjects, except for names of languages and course names followed by a number.

EXAMPLES   **English, Latin, German, geography, algebra, chemistry, music, Algebra II, Chemistry I**

NOTE: Do not capitalize the class names *senior, junior, sophomore,* and *freshman* unless they are part of a proper noun.

EXAMPLES   A number of sophomores attended the Junior Prom.
The Sophomore Singers performed for the freshmen.

REVIEW A   **Correcting Sentences by Capitalizing Words**

Identify the words that should be capitalized in each of the following sentences. Do not include the words already capitalized.

EXAMPLE   **1.** The spanish explorer juan ponce de león landed in florida in 1513.
1. *Spanish, Juan, Ponce de León, Florida*

1. The area now known as florida was originally inhabited by native american peoples, including the apalachees, the creeks, and the seminoles.
2. The state is bordered on the north by alabama and georgia, on the east by the atlantic ocean, on the south by the straits of florida and the gulf of mexico, and on the west by alabama and the gulf of mexico.
3. The spanish founded st. augustine, the state's first permanent european settlement, in 1565, making it the oldest colonial city in the united states.
4. When spain ceded florida to the united states in 1821, the u.s. government demanded that the native peoples move west.
5. The strength and dignity of the seminole leader osceola, who led his people in the fight to retain

MECHANICS

their lands, are evident in this 1838 painting by george catlin.

6. Most of the seminoles were eventually deported to present-day oklahoma, but a few hundred fled to the everglades, a huge wilderness area in south florida that now includes everglades national park.

7. Founded in 1886, eatonville, florida, is the oldest incorporated african american town in the united states.

8. After the cuban revolution in the late 1950s, and again in the early 1980s, many cubans fled to miami.

9. Miami has also served as a major point of entry for haitian refugees who've braved the atlantic ocean in search of a better life.

10. Among the asians who've settled in the state are refugees from vietnam, many of whom make their living fishing along the northern coast of florida.

REVIEW B **Proofreading Paragraphs for Correct Capitalization**

Identify the words that should be capitalized in each sentence in the following paragraphs. Do not include the words already capitalized.

MECHANICS

EXAMPLE   [1]   Trivia games test your knowledge of subjects as diverse as american inventors, the korean war, and popular music.

    1.   *American, Korean War*

[1] Last saturday, may 18, my brother Ted and i finally won our first trivia match against our parents. [2] Some of the courses Ted is taking this semester are history, political science, and french; mine include world literature I and geography II. [3] We surged into the lead when our parents couldn't remember that the first u.s. satellite, *explorer I*, followed the u.s.s.r.'s *sputnik I* into space. [4] From my geography class I remembered that mount McKinley is the highest point and death valley is the lowest point on the north american continent.

[5] Our parents rallied for the lead by knowing that the boy on the cracker jack box is named jack and that his dog's name is bingo. [6] Then Ted came up with the fact that the steel framework of the statue of liberty was designed by the frenchman alexandre gustave eiffel, who also designed the eiffel tower in paris. [7] None of us knew that john wilkes booth was only twenty-six years old when he shot president lincoln at ford's theater on good friday in 1865. [8] Mom, who's a loyal democrat, knew that *engine 1401*—the southern railways locomotive that carried franklin d. roosevelt's body from warm springs, georgia, to washington, d.c.—can now be seen in the smithsonian institution.

[9] Ted and I lost some points because I didn't know that kleenex tissues were first used as gas-mask filters during world war I. [10] But Ted won the game for us by remembering that the white house was called the executive mansion before it was burned by the british during the war of 1812.

MECHANICS

PICTURE THIS

The year is 1850. After seeing this handbill, you and a friend decided to sign on as deckhands on the Mississippi River steamboat. Your friend, however, backed out at the

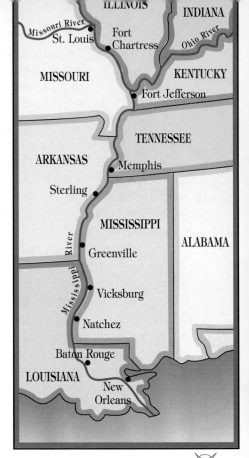

last minute. You've just completed your first trip down the river from St. Louis to New Orleans. Using this map, write a letter to your friend describing your experiences on the trip. Give reasons why your friend should (or should not) sign on for the next trip. In your letter, use a combined total of at least ten proper nouns and proper adjectives.

The Granger Collection, New York.

Subject: working as a deckhand on a steamboat

Audience: a friend

Purpose: to persuade

24e.   Capitalize titles.

(1) Capitalize the title of a person when it comes before a name.

EXAMPLES   **G**eneral Powell   **Dr.** Sakamoto   **P**resident Kennedy

Do not capitalize a title used alone or following a name, especially if the title is preceded by *a, an,* or *the.*

EXAMPLES   In 1987, Wilma Mankiller became the first woman elected **p**rincipal **c**hief of the Cherokee Nation of Oklahoma.
Who was **p**resident during World War II?
Ann Richards became the **g**overnor of Texas in 1991.

When a title is used without a person's name in direct address, it is usually capitalized.

EXAMPLES   **Ms. Mayor**, will you please test the microphone?
Do you intend to visit the disaster area, **Governor**?
Please be seated, **Sir** [or sir].

NOTE: For special emphasis or clarity, writers sometimes capitalize a title used alone or following a person's name.

EXAMPLES   The **Governor** firmly stated her opinion on the issue.
According to the **President**, America needs to strengthen its industrial base.

(2) Capitalize words showing family relationship when used with a person's name but *not* when preceded by a possessive.

EXAMPLES   **Aunt** Edith, **Uncle** Fred, **Grandmother** Bechtel,
my **b**rother, your **c**ousin Louise, Maria's **n**iece

(3) Capitalize the first and last words and all important words in titles and subtitles of books, periodicals, poems, stories, plays, historical documents, movies, radio and television programs, works of art, and musical compositions.

Unimportant words in a title include

- articles: *a, an, the*
- short prepositions (fewer than five letters): *of, to, in, for, from, with*
- coordinating conjunctions: *and, but, so, nor, or, yet, for*

MECHANICS

TYPE OF TITLE	EXAMPLES
Books	*Songs of the Tewa* *One of the Lucky Ones* *Silent Dancing: A Partial Remembrance of a Puerto Rican Childhood*
Periodicals	*U.S. News & World Report* *Chicago Sun-Times*

(continued)

TYPE OF TITLE	EXAMPLES
Poems	"Love Without Love" "I Like to See It Lap the Miles"
Stories	"The Man to Send Rain Clouds" "The Woman Who Had No Eye for Small Details"
Plays	*A Raisin in the Sun* *Life with Father* *Sunday in the Park with George*
Historical Documents	Treaty of Versailles Emancipation Proclamation Charter of the United Nations
Movies	*Lean on Me* *North by Northwest* *The Corn Is Green*
Radio and Television Programs	*War of the Worlds* *Face the Nation* *You Can't Do That on Television*
Works of Art	*Crossing the Brook* *Two Mexican Women and Child*
Musical Compositions	"Ebony and Ivory" *Pictures at an Exhibition* *Amahl and the Night Visitors*

MECHANICS

NOTE: The words *a, an,* and *the* written before a title are capitalized only when they are the first word of the title. They are usually not capitalized, however, at the beginning of the names of most magazines and newspapers.

EXAMPLES   Last summer, Joan read *The Outsiders* and *A Day in the Life of President Kennedy.*
Joan reads *The Atlantic Monthly* and the *Rocky Mountain News.*

REFERENCE NOTE: For information about which titles should be italicized and which should be placed in quotation marks, see pages 831–832 and 840.

(4) Capitalize names of religions and their followers, holy days and celebrations, holy writings, and specific deities.

TYPE OF NAME	EXAMPLES	
Religions and Followers	Judaism Buddhism Christianity	Muslim Taoist Mormon
Holy Days and Celebrations	Ash Wednesday Ramadan Yom Kippur	Hanukkah Potlatch Pentecost
Holy Writings	the Bible the Talmud the Koran	Rig-Veda Exodus Dead Sea Scrolls
Specific Deities	Allah God	Vishnu the Holy Spirit

The words *god* and *goddess* are not capitalized when they refer to the deities of ancient mythology. The names of specific mythological deities are capitalized, however.

EXAMPLE   **Ceres was the Roman goddess of grain.**

NOTE: Some writers capitalize all pronouns that refer to the Deity. Other writers capitalize such pronouns only to prevent confusion.

> EXAMPLE   Job wondered why the Lord allowed His servant to suffer.

MECHANICS

▶ REVIEW C   ## Correcting Sentences by Capitalizing Words

If the capitalization of a sentence is correct, write C. If not, write the correct form of each word that needs correcting.

1. At the hirshhorn museum in washington, d.c., we saw one of georgia o'keeffe's finest paintings, *cow's skull: red, white, and blue.*
2. In *people* magazine, Kim read about bill cosby's previous television series *the cosby show* and his new one, *cosby.*
3. When I visited grandma Sánchez at white sparrow Hospital, I read to her from jimmy santiago baca's *martín and meditations on the south valley.*
4. In 1908, mary baker eddy founded the *christian science monitor.*

5. My cousin Judy's favorite statue is *indian hunter* by paul manship.
6. I enjoyed reading annie dillard's *pilgrim at tinker creek*, particularly the chapter "the horns of the altar."
7. Prize-winning journalist carl t. rowan was the first african american to serve on the National Security council.
8. The president addressed the american people in a television news broadcast after he had met with the president of France.
9. Last week mayor johnson and the county commissioners attended the groundbreaking ceremony for the new hospital.
10. Jane White, president of our latin club, showed us a videotape of *julius caesar*.

▶ REVIEW D   **Proofreading Paragraphs for Correct Capitalization**

If the capitalization in a sentence is correct, write C. If not, write the correct form of each word that needs correcting.

EXAMPLE   [1] The energetic personality of montana's former state Senator from the Fiftieth District is obvious in this painting by Christopher Magadini.
   1. *Montana's, senator*

[1] Bill Yellowtail, jr., the first member of the crows to serve in the State Senate, represented an area hit hard by drought and a decline in the demand for beef. [2] Yellowtail, a democrat, ran for office to help save the Area's remaining small family farms and ranches. [3] A Rancher himself, he raises cattle in the Lodge Grass valley in Southeastern Montana with his Mother, his brother, and his sister.
[4] Yellowtail supplements his income from ranching by guiding fly-fishing trips on the Bighorn river. [5] In addition, he works as a Tour Guide on the Crow reservation and at the Custer battlefield national monument. [6] He has also served as a consultant for the Montana-wyoming Agriculture-Tourism Project, as a member of the

Board of Directors of the Nature Conservancy, and as the director of the Environmental protection agency.

[7] After graduating from Lodge Grass high school at the head of his class, Yellowtail attended dartmouth College in hanover, New Hampshire. [8] Although Dartmouth was founded to educate american Indians, Yellowtail was the first native american to enroll there in twenty years. [9] At first he was unprepared academically, but by the time he graduated in 1971, he was on the Dean's list. [10] Regarding his major subject, Geography, Yellowtail says, "the relationship between humanity and the environment is little understood; it's a Discipline we very much need today."

MECHANICS

WRITING APPLICATION

Using Capital Letters Correctly

Capital letters are signals. They let your readers know that you're starting a new sentence or that you're referring to a specific person, place, or thing. Notice how the use of capital letters affects the meaning in the following examples:

> To reach the old pioneer settlement, cross the little Yellow River and turn right at the sandy road exit.
> To reach the Old Pioneer Settlement, cross the Little Yellow River and turn right at the Sandy Road exit.

WRITING ACTIVITY

You've been asked to write a guidebook for a group of visitors from your town's sister city in Japan. Write an informative booklet that helps your visitors take a brief walking or driving tour through your town.

 Prewriting List the sights you'll include in your guidebook. (If you live in a small town, you may want to include some nearby points of interest. If yours is a large city, you'll have to limit the tour to only one part of town or only main sights.) For information on the town's history, you may want to check the local library.

 Writing As you write your first draft, keep in mind that this is your guests' first visit. Try to anticipate their questions without overloading them with details. If you'd like to, sketch a map of your tour with the various stops labeled.

 Evaluating and Revising Take a friend on a trial run of the tour. Is the route you've chosen a sensible one? Have you included enough information about each point of interest, and is the information correct? If you made a map, be sure to check it, too. Then add, delete, change, or rearrange items to make your guide book clearer and more interesting.

Proofreading and Publishing Proofread your guidebook carefully, paying special attention to the correct use of capital letters. Remember to proofread your map if you included one. Naturally, you'll also want to make sure that your grammar and usage are faultless for the visitors. After sharing your guidebook with your classmates, you could compile a larger guide to your town or city and give it to new students. You could also offer copies to the local chamber of commerce or historical society.

Review: Posttest

A. Capitalizing Sentences Correctly

For each of the following sentences, write the words that should be capitalized.

EXAMPLE   **1.** Renée searched everywhere in freeport, maine, until she found a gift at l. l. bean for her grandparents.
     1. *Freeport, Maine, L. L. Bean*

1. The title of her new television special, which airs next fall, is *one in a million.*
2. Both ernest hemingway and walt disney once worked for the *kansas city star.*
3. Every thanksgiving day before dinner, grandma penny sings "we praise thee, o god, our redeemer, creator," which was translated from the german by julia b. cady cory.
4. In 1982, colombian writer gabriel garcía márquez was awarded the nobel prize in literature.
5. The winner of the first kentucky derby, the annual race at churchill downs in louisville, was a horse named aristides.
6. In 1983, sally ride became the first american woman in space when the space shuttle *challenger* was launched from cape canaveral, florida.
7. One of the cities of the incas, machu picchu, lay hidden among the andes mountains in southern peru and was never discovered by the spanish conquerors.

8. Frederick douglass was the first african american member of the department of justice's u.s. marshals service.
9. If Beth passes english and history II, her parents will let her apply for a job at the 7-eleven store on forty-third street.
10. Our debate team argued in favor of pro-american economic policies as the best way to foster democracy in the developing countries of africa, asia, and south america.

B. Capitalizing a Paragraph Correctly

For each sentence in the following paragraph, write the words that should be capitalized.

EXAMPLE [1] Last summer we visited my uncle carlos, who lives in new york city.

    1. *Uncle Carlos, New York City*

[11] One of new york city's most popular tourist attractions is the empire state building. [12] The building, at fifth avenue and thirty-fourth street, attracts 2,500,000 visitors a year. [13] Among them are troops of boy scouts and girl scouts, who camp out on the eighty-sixth floor. [14] The building was financed by john jacob raskob, the founder of general motors. [15] It opened in 1931, during the great depression. [16] At the time, it was the tallest building on earth (1,250 feet), but it's since been overshadowed by the world trade center (1,350 feet) and by chicago's sears tower (1,450 feet). [17] The observatory on the one hundred and second floor accounts for much of the empire state building's continuing appeal; when the weather is clear, it provides a view of five states: new york, new jersey, connecticut, pennsylvania, and massachusetts. [18] On may 1, 1991, publicists threw a party to mark the building's sixtieth birthday. [19] One of those who attended was actress fay wray, who starred in the 1933 movie *king kong*, in which the building was featured. [20] Another attendee was jack brod, one of the original tenants, who proclaimed of the building, "it's got history woven into it."

SUMMARY STYLE REVIEW

Names of Persons

Mrs. Andrew D. McCall, Jr.	a family friend
Sean Jackson	the boy next door
Mr. Hank Bluehouse	a guidance counselor

Geographical Names

Kansas City	a city in Missouri
Cook County	a county in Illinois
Diego Garcia Island	an island in the Indian Ocean
Rocky Mountains	a mountain range
Arctic Ocean	on the ocean floor
Seventy-first Street	a busy street
Torreya State Park	a state park
in the West, South, Midwest	turning west, south, north

Organizations, Business Firms, Institutions, Government Bodies

Perfect Harmony Glee Club	a choral club
Head over Heels, Inc.	a gymnastics training center
Lane High School	an inner-city high school
Supreme Court	a federal court
Department of the Treasury	a department of government

Historical Events and Periods, Special Events, Calendar Items

the Vietnam War	a long war
the Ice Age	a prehistoric age
the World Series	a series of baseball games
Memorial Day	a national holiday
March, June, September, December	spring, summer, autumn, winter

Nationalities, Races, Religions

Australian	a nationality
Caucasian	a race
Christianity	a religion
God	myths about the Greek gods

(continued)

MECHANICS

MECHANICS

SUMMARY STYLE REVIEW *(continued)*

Brand Names

Chevrolet Blazer	an automobile
Amana	a refrigerator

Other Particular Places, Things, Events, Awards

Enterprise	an aircraft carrier
Silver Streak	a train
Discovery	a spacecraft
Bancroft Prize in History	an award
the Milky Way	a galaxy
Earth, Mercury, Neptune	here on earth
the Lincoln Memorial	a memorial in Washington
Junior Prom	a junior in high school
Medal of Freedom	a cherished medal

Specific Courses, Languages

Carpentry I	after carpentry class
Japanese	a foreign language
World History II	a history test

Titles

Mayor Feinstein	a mayor
the President of the United States	the president of the club
the Prince of Wales	a prince's hobby
Uncle Jim	her uncle
The Color Purple	a novel
the *Sacramento Bee*	a daily newspaper
Holy Bible	a religious book

25 PUNCTUATION

End Marks and Commas

Diagnostic Test

Correcting Sentences by Adding End Marks and Commas

Add end marks and commas where they are needed in the following sentences.

EXAMPLE   **1.** Well what do you want me to say
         1. *Well, what do you want me to say?*

1. Although scholars aren't certain about who was the first European printer to use movable type Johann Gutenberg is usually credited
2. The students who have signed up for the field trip may leave at noon but all others must attend classes
3. Gloria did you notice where I left my bowling ball and bowling shoes
4. Miriam Colón who was born in Puerto Rico founded the Puerto Rican Traveling Theatre.

MECHANICS

5. The Great Pyramid in Egypt was built sometime between 2600 and 2500 BC
6. Vendors sold T-shirts buttons caps and pennants to the sports fans outside the stadium
7. Listening to my friend's grandfather talk about the Mexican Revolution I realized that I'm proud to be Mexican American
8. The hikers munched on unsalted sunflower seeds and quenched their thirst with ice-cold refreshing spring water
9. Their address I think is 1042 Cleveland Ave Enid OK 73703
10. Marian Anderson a contralto was the first African American to become a permanent member of the Metropolitan Opera Company
11. Rita did not call me this morning nor did she call in the afternoon
12. We rushed to the airport stood in line bought our tickets and then heard that the flight would be delayed for three hours
13. Norm has had an incredible run of bad luck yet he still says that tomorrow will be a better day for he prides himself on being an optimist
14. The Ming vase wrapped in cotton and packed in a crate was delivered to the museum today
15. If we're late for practice again however Ms. Stubbs will kick us off the team
16. How lucky I was that my sister had taught me how to swim for I could have drowned when the boat tipped over
17. Early in the eighteenth century Chikamatsu Monzaemon wrote the first Japanese tragedies to focus on the lives of common ordinary people
18. Nowadays the Sioux generally speaking make their living as farmers and ranchers
19. Jan Matzeliger an inventor in Lynn Massachusetts revolutionized the shoe industry in 1883 with his machine that joined the top of a shoe to its sole
20. These four students should report to the auditorium after lunch: Bob Wilcox Amalia Gibson Cora Mall and Phil Assad Jr

In speaking, your tone of voice, your pauses, and your gestures and facial expressions help you express yourself. In writing, punctuation marks help you communicate these elements.

End Marks

End marks—periods, question marks, and exclamation points—indicate the purpose of a sentence. Periods are also used in many abbreviations.

 REFERENCE NOTE: For information on how sentences are classified according to purpose, see pages 565–566.

25a. A statement (*or* declarative sentence) is followed by a period.

EXAMPLES Margaret Walker's poems celebrate the trials and triumphs of African Americans.
Barb asked who could give her a ride home.

As the second example above shows, a declarative sentence containing an indirect question is followed by a period.

25b. A question (*or* interrogative sentence) is followed by a question mark.

EXAMPLES What score did you get on the road test?
Weren't you nervous?

A direct question should be followed by a question mark even if its word order is like that of a declarative sentence.

EXAMPLES You got what score on the road test?
You weren't nervous?

NOTE: Be sure to distinguish between a declarative sentence that contains an indirect question and an interrogative sentence, which asks a direct question.

INDIRECT QUESTION She asked me who nominated him.
[declarative]
DIRECT QUESTION Who nominated him? [interrogative]

MECHANICS

25c. An exclamation is followed by an exclamation point.

EXAMPLES   Great shot**!**
            Oh, no**!** Not again**!**

Declarative and interrogative sentences that express strong emotion may be followed by an exclamation point instead of a period or a question mark.

EXAMPLES   There you are**!**
            Why are you always late**!**

25d. An imperative sentence is followed by either a period or an exclamation point.

EXAMPLES   Open the door, please**.**
            Open the door**!**

An imperative sentence may be stated in the form of a question. However, since its purpose is to give a command or make a request, it should be followed by a period or an exclamation point.

EXAMPLES   May I have your attention, please**.**
            Will you pay attention**!**

> EXERCISE 1   **Correcting Sentences by Adding End Marks**

For each of the following paragraphs, write each word that should be followed by an end mark, and add the appropriate end mark. Then, if a sentence follows the end mark, write the first word of that sentence.

EXAMPLE   [1]   What striking costumes the musicians on the next
                  page are wearing they're members of *Campanas
                  de América,* a mariachi group in San Antonio,
                  Texas
           1.   *wearing! They're; Texas.*

[1] Have you ever heard mariachi music this lively, infectious music originated in central Mexico
[2] Before the nineteenth century, Mexican music was played by string ensembles or wind bands around 1800 the two types of groups merged the resulting sound came to be known as mariachi

[3] As social gatherings became larger, brass instruments such as cornets and trumpets were added adding the brasses made the music easier to hear above the sounds of dancing usually only the lyrics of the songs were written down younger players learned the melodies by ear did you know that some schools now offer courses in Mexican folk music and award academic credit for playing in a mariachi ensemble colleges, junior and senior high schools, and even elementary schools are incorporating mariachi music into the curriculum

[4] Now young mariachi players are studying music theory and writing their own mariachi music, sometimes adding instruments such as trombones, fluegelhorns, and accordions consequently, mariachi is changing some older players dislike the changes most people, however, applaud the music's new flexibility they ask how mariachi can grow if it doesn't change

[5] And growing is just what mariachi's doing it's becoming more popular each year in fact, the annual mariachi festival filled California's eighteen-thousand-seat Hollywood Bowl when the festival was launched in 1990 what an exciting event that must have been

25e. An abbreviation is usually followed by a period.

TYPE OF ABBREVIATION	EXAMPLES		
Personal Names	W.E.B. DuBois	Susan B. Anthony	
	W. H. Auden	N. Scott Momaday	
Organizations and Companies	Assn.	Corp.	Ltd.
	Co.	Inc.	Org.
Titles Used with Names	Mr.	Mrs.	Dr.
	Ms.	Jr.	Ph.D.
Time of Day	A.M.	P.M.	
Years	B.C. (written after the date)		
	A.D. (written before the date)		
Addresses	Ave.	St.	Pkwy.
	Blvd.	Rd.	P.O. Box
States	Calif.	Tex.	Mass.
	Ind.	Fla.	N.Y.

NOTE: Two-letter state codes are used only when the ZIP Code is included. Two-letter state codes are not followed by periods.

EXAMPLE   Nashville, TN 37201

When an abbreviation that ends with a period comes at the end of a statement, do not add another period as an end mark. *Do* add a question mark or an exclamation point if one is needed.

EXAMPLES   The history of Egypt dates back to before 3000 B.C.
When did she move to St. Louis, Mo.?

Many common abbreviations, especially for units of measurement, are often written without periods. However, you should use a period with the abbreviation *in.* (for *inch*) to prevent confusing it with the word *in*.

EXAMPLES   TV, OK, VCR, CD, DNA, NAACP, UN, IQ, YWCA, COBOL
mph, km, cm, ml, kg, hp, lb, rpm, cc, psi

NOTE: Most abbreviations are capitalized only if the words they stand for are capitalized. If you're not sure whether to use periods with an abbreviation or whether to capitalize it, look it up in a dictionary.

REVIEW A   **Using End Marks**

This chart shows the results of a 1990 *TV Guide* poll that asked people what types of TV shows they'd be willing to pay to see. Write five sentences expressing your reactions to the poll's results. Use each type of end mark—period, question mark, and exclamation point—at least once.

EXAMPLE   **1.** *Why didn't the poll ask about science fiction shows?*

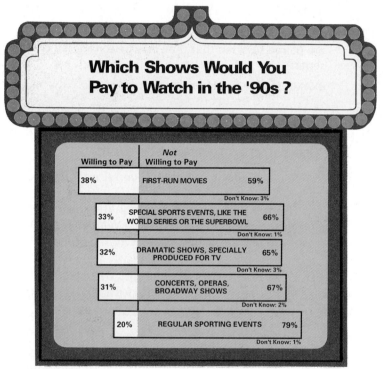

MECHANICS

Commas

Items in a Series

25f.   Use commas to separate items in a series.

EXAMPLES   The camp counselor distributed baseballs, bats, volleyballs, tennis rackets, and bandages. [words]

We have a government of the people, by the people, and for the people. [phrases]

I know I will pass the test if I take good notes, if I study hard, and if I get a good night's sleep. [clauses]

When the last two items in a series are joined by *and,* you may omit the comma before the *and* if the comma isn't needed to make the meaning clear.

CLEAR WITHOUT COMMA   The entertainers sang, danced and juggled.

NOT CLEAR WITHOUT COMMA   John, Sue and Mary went fishing. [Did John go fishing, or is he being addressed?]

CLEAR WITH COMMA   John, Sue, and Mary went fishing.

NOTE: Some words—such as *macaroni and cheese* and *law and order*—are paired so often that they may be considered one item in a series.

EXAMPLE   For lunch we could order a sandwich, macaroni and cheese, or soup.

(1) If all items in a series are joined by *and, or,* or *nor,* do not use commas to separate them.

EXAMPLES   We ran **and** walked **and** even limped to the finish line.
Neither poverty **nor** discrimination **nor** lack of encouragement prevented Alice Walker from becoming an accomplished writer.

(2) Independent clauses in a series are usually separated by semicolons. Short independent clauses, however, may be separated by commas.

EXAMPLES   To prepare for the race, we swam twenty-five laps in the pool; we jogged four miles around the lake; and we exercised with workout equipment.
We swam, we jogged, and we exercised.

 REFERENCE NOTE: Also see rule 25h on page 796.

25g.   Use a comma to separate two or more adjectives preceding a noun.

EXAMPLE   I've had a long, hectic, tiring day.

When the last adjective before a noun is thought of as part of the noun, omit the comma before the adjective.

EXAMPLE   I mailed the package at the main post office.
For lunch we had smooth, creamy broccoli soup.

MECHANICS

Compound nouns such as *post office* and *broccoli soup* are considered single units rather than two separate words.

You can use two tests to determine whether an adjective and a noun form a unit.

TEST 1: Insert the word *and* between the adjectives. If *and* fits sensibly between them, use a comma. In the first example above, *and* cannot be logically inserted: *main and post office.* In the second sentence, *and* sounds sensible between the first two adjectives (*smooth and creamy*) but not between the second and third (*creamy and broccoli*).

TEST 2: Change the order of the adjectives. If the order of the adjectives can be reversed sensibly, use a comma. *Creamy, smooth broccoli soup* makes sense, but *broccoli creamy soup* and *post main office* do not.

▶ EXERCISE 2　**Correcting Sentences by Adding Commas**

Write each word that should be followed by a comma, and then add the comma. If a comma may or may not be used, circle the word and the comma. If a sentence is correct, write C.

EXAMPLE　**1.** The singer wore a red vest blue shoes and white jeans.
1. *vest,(shoes,)*

1. I was late because my alarm clock didn't go off we were out of milk and the school bus had a flat tire.
2. The river overflowed again and filled our basement and our neighbors' basements.
3. Coriander cumin and saffron are three spices widely used in traditional Mexican cooking.
4. I took a flashlight a sleeping bag extra tennis shoes a pocket knife and a parka on our camping trip.
5. Magic Johnson Michael Jordan Larry Bird and Julius Erving have received Most Valuable Player Awards.
6. At the gymnastics meet Les performed on the parallel bars the rings and the high bar.
7. A little blond child in faded bluejeans emerged from the shrubbery to stare at the mail carrier.

8. Gwendolyn Brooks Toni Morrison and Alice Walker have each won a Pulitzer Prize for their writing.
9. Have you read any of the novels by Jane Austen or the Brontë sisters or Virginia Woolf?
10. With a quick powerful leap, the stuntman bounded over the burning balcony.

Independent Clauses

25h. Use a comma before *and, but, or, nor, for, so,* and *yet* when they join independent clauses.

EXAMPLES Patrick brought the sandwiches, and Cindy brought the potato salad.
We got there on time, but Jeff and María were late.

NOTE: Always use a comma before *yet, so,* or *for* joining independent clauses. The comma may be left out before *and, but, or,* and *nor* if the independent clauses are very short or if the sentence cannot be misunderstood.

EXAMPLE I applied for the job and I got it.

Don't confuse a compound sentence with a simple sentence that has a compound verb.

SIMPLE SENTENCE Bob brought charcoal and lighter fluid but forgot matches. [one independent clause with a compound verb]

COMPOUND SENTENCE Bob brought charcoal and lighter fluid, but he forgot matches. [two independent clauses]

☞ REFERENCE NOTE: For more information about simple sentences and compound sentences, see pages 610–611. For a discussion of compound subjects and compound verbs, see pages 467–468 and 554–555.

▶ EXERCISE 3 **Correcting Compound Sentences by Adding Commas**

If a comma should be used before the conjunction, write the word preceding the needed comma, the comma, and the conjunction. If a sentence is correct, write *C.*

MECHANICS

EXAMPLE   **1.** Uncle Phil carefully steered the boat through the narrow channel and Lynn began baiting the hooks.
      1. *channel, and*

1. All students must arrive on time for no one will be admitted late.
2. The movie review complimented all the performers but the leading actress received the strongest praise.
3. A few spectators tried to climb over the fence but the police ordered them back.
4. The Japanese actors in Kabuki plays do not speak but they pantomime lines chanted by narrators on the stage.
5. Most people today work fewer hours than their grandparents did yet for many there never seem to be enough hours in a day.
6. The cost of living is rising for consumers pay higher prices for gasoline and other products.
7. Our guide led and we followed closely.
8. When two groups of Hopis disagreed about running the town of Oraibi, they settled the matter with a tug of war and the losers moved away and founded the town of Hotavila.
9. She said she did not like the story in the science fiction magazine nor did she enjoy the illustrations.
10. High school graduates may go on to college or may begin working immediately.

Nonessential Clauses and Phrases

25i.   Use commas to set off nonessential clauses and nonessential participial phrases.

A *nonessential* (or *nonrestrictive*) clause or participial phrase is one containing information that isn't needed to understand the main idea of the sentence.

NONESSENTIAL CLAUSES   Emilia Ortiz, **who lives across the street from me,** won a scholarship to Stanford University.
     The capital of Massachusetts is Boston, **which is sometimes called the Athens of America.**

NONESSENTIAL PHRASES   Kelly**, waiting outside the stage door,** got the band leader's autograph.

Robert Hayden**, born in Detroit,** was educated at the University of Michigan and later became a distinguished professor there.

Each nonessential clause or phrase in the examples above can be left out without changing the main idea of the sentence.

EXAMPLES   Emilia Ortiz won a scholarship to Stanford University.

Boston is the capital of Massachusetts.

Kelly got the band leader's autograph.

Robert Hayden was educated at the University of Michigan and later became a distinguished professor there.

An *essential* (or *restrictive*) phrase or clause is one that can't be left out without changing the meaning of the sentence. Essential clauses and phrases are *not* set off by commas. Notice how leaving out the essential clause or phrase would change the meaning of each of the following sentences.

ESSENTIAL PHRASES   Students **planning to try out for a role in the play** should sign up no later than Friday afternoon.

Two poems **written by Lorna Dee Cervantes** are included in our literature book.

ESSENTIAL CLAUSES   The sophomores **who made the Honor Roll** were listed in the paper.

Library books **that are lost or damaged** must be paid for.

NOTE: Adjective clauses beginning with *that,* like the one in the example above, are nearly always essential.

Some clauses and participial phrases may be either essential or nonessential. The presence or absence of commas tells the reader how the clause or phrase relates to the main idea of the sentence.

NONESSENTIAL CLAUSE   Marla's sister**, who attends Stanford University,** sent her a sweatshirt. [Marla has only one sister. She sent the sweatshirt.]

ESSENTIAL CLAUSE Marla's sister **who attends Stanford University** sent her a sweatshirt. [Marla has more than one sister. The one at Stanford sent the sweatshirt.]

NONESSENTIAL PHRASE My former lab partner**,** **now living in Chicago,** visited me last week. [I have only one former lab partner. That person visited me last week.]

ESSENTIAL PHRASE My former lab partner **now living in Chicago** visited me last week. [I have more than one former lab partner. The one from Chicago visited me last week.]

☞ **REFERENCE NOTE:** See Chapter 18 for more information on clauses and pages 582–583 for more on participial phrases.

▶ EXERCISE 4   **Correcting Sentences by Adding Commas**

For each of the following sentences, write each word that should be followed by a comma, and place a comma after it. If a sentence is correct as it is written, write *C*.

EXAMPLE   **1.** Gigantic supermarkets like the one on the next page which offer a stunning variety of goods and services developed from much smaller stores that first opened in the nineteenth century.
     1. *page, services,*

1. The stores that became the world's first self-serve supermarkets were designed by Clarence Saunders.
2. Saunders who lived in Memphis, Tennessee named his stores Piggly Wiggly.
3. He got the idea for the name when he saw a fat pig wiggling under a fence.
4. The Piggly Wiggly store that Saunders developed had only one long aisle.
5. Customers who shopped there saw all the products before they came to the exit.
6. Albert Gerrard who noticed that people often had difficulty finding products opened his own grocery store.
7. All of the items that were for sale were arranged alphabetically.

MECHANICS

8. The name that Gerrard selected for his store was Alpha-Beta.
9. George Hartford who founded the Great Atlantic & Pacific Tea Company in 1859 nicknamed his stores A & P.
10. The model for today's huge supermarkets which was developed by Michael Cullen opened in an abandoned garage in Queens, New York, on August 30, 1930.

Introductory Elements

 25j. Use a comma after certain introductory elements.

(1) Use a comma after words such as *well, yes, no,* and *why* when they begin a sentence. Interjections such as *wow, yikes,* and *hey,* if not followed by an exclamation point, are also set off by commas.

EXAMPLES **No,** I haven't taken the exam yet.
Sure, I'll go with you.
Wow, look at that car!

(2) Use a comma after an introductory participial phrase.

EXAMPLES **Calling for a timeout,** the referee blew her whistle and signaled.
Exhausted after a three-mile swim, Diana emerged from the water.

MECHANICS

(3) Use a comma after two or more introductory prepositional phrases.

EXAMPLE **By the light of the harvest moon in September,** we went on an old-fashioned hayride.

A single introductory prepositional phrase does not require a comma unless the sentence could be misread or awkward to read without one.

EXAMPLES   In the book the writer develops a clever plot.
In the book, review pages 236–290.
In the book review, the critic praised the writer's clever plot.

(4) Use a comma after an introductory adverb clause.

An introductory adverb clause may appear at the beginning of a sentence or before any independent clause in the sentence.

EXAMPLES   **When you've gone to this school as long as we have,** you'll know your way around, too.
The first game of the season is Friday; **after we claim our first victory,** we'll celebrate at Darcy's Deli.

MECHANICS

▶ EXERCISE 5   **Correcting Sentences with Introductory Elements by Adding Commas**

If a sentence lacks a comma, write the word that should be followed by a comma, and place a comma after it. If a sentence is correct, write *C*.

EXAMPLE   **1.** Trying to reduce the amount of fat in their diets many Americans are eating less meat.
1. *diets,*

1. For many people in the world meat is not a daily food staple.
2. Serving as a main source of nutrition whole grains such as corn, oats, wheat, and rice feed millions.
3. In Mexico a favorite nutritious meal is a corn tortilla and beans.
4. Because the soybean is high in protein it has been a principal crop in Asian countries for more than five thousand years.

5. If you'd like more variety in your diet you may want to substitute unrefined whole grains for meat occasionally.

6. Offering healthful alternatives to meat whole grains contain nutrients such as vitamins, proteins, amino acids, and starches.

7. In the process of making spoilage-resistant products food manufacturers refine whole grains.

8. Refined for commercial use the grains lose most of their food value because the nutritious outer hulls are stripped away.

9. If you take time in the supermarket you should be able to find whole grains.

10. Since many cookbooks now include recipes for grain dishes you can learn to use grains in many tasty snacks and meals.

▶ REVIEW B   **Using Commas**

For each of the following sentences, write all the words that should be followed by a comma. Place a comma after each one. If a comma may or may not be used after a word, circle the word and the comma.

EXAMPLE   [1]   Throughout history around the world people have used weapons for hunting for fighting and for defending themselves from wild animals.

1.   *world, hunting,⟨fighting,⟩*

[1] Many weapons that were produced in early times were similar in appearance function and design. [2] The English word *weapon* is related to the Old English *wæpen* the Dutch *wapen* the German *Waffe* and an earlier common root. [3] Sticks stones and natural poisons such as the toxic sweat of these Central and South American frogs were probably the first weapons. [4] Among those varieties of weapons the stick thrown by hand became one of the most heavily specialized. [5] As you can see the dart the arrow the spear the lance and the javelin were all developed from the stick thrown by hand. [6] Another kind of weapon, the sling, was used all over the world for it was

easy to make and not too difficult to master. [7] According to the Biblical account, when the Hebrew king David was just a boy he killed the Philistine giant Goliath with a simple handmade sling like the one shown here. [8] An unusual weapon similar to the sling is the bola which is a cord or thong with heavy balls of stone or wood or metal at the ends. [9] In some parts of South America gauchos like this one still hunt with bolas which entangle the quarry without inflicting pain injury or death. [10] Over the centuries these simple weapons have been developed into highly sophisticated artillery like these missiles used in Operation Desert Storm.

MECHANICS

WRITING APPLICATION

Using Commas in Writing Instructions for a Game

When you talk, you punctuate your speech with pauses. When you write, you use commas to show where such pauses should occur. Commas, like pauses, indicate how parts of a sentence are related to one another. Making such relationships clear is especially important when you give directions. If commas are left out or used incorrectly, the result is an awkward or confusing sentence.

AWKWARD In the game players travel to Mars fly through the rings of Saturn and race back to Earth. [Because the sentence lacks commas, a reader may mistakenly run together *game players* or *Mars fly*.]

REVISED In the game, players travel to Mars, fly through the rings of Saturn, and race back to Earth.

CONFUSING The first player, who returns to Earth, wins the game. [The commas make it appear that the clause *who returns to Earth* is not essential—in other words, that the player who has the first turn always wins.]

REVISED The first player who returns to Earth wins the game.

 ## WRITING ACTIVITY

Create an educational board game or computer game, and write instructions explaining how to play it. In your game, include information from at least one of your school subjects, such as math, science, history, or a foreign language.

 Prewriting Choose a subject area that interests you. Then decide what the object of the game will be. Jot down notes about the number of players, the kinds of supplies or equipment each player will need, and other rules of the game. Give your game a catchy title, and then arrange the instructions in an order that will be easy for players to follow.

 Writing Keep in mind that your instructions will be the players' only source of information. Try to anticipate their questions, and aim for an informal, conversational tone, as if you were explaining the game in person.

 Evaluating and Revising Ask some of your friends to play the game. As you watch them, note any problems they have with understanding the instructions. Then add, delete, change, or rearrange information to make the instructions easier to understand and the game more fun to play.

Proofreading and Publishing Proofread your instructions carefully, paying special attention to your use of end marks and commas. Then input your instructions on a computer or photocopy them. You could offer copies of your game to your school's media center, to a local hospital, or to one of the agencies or organizations that serve your community.

Interrupters

 25k. Use commas to set off elements that interrupt a sentence.

(1) Appositives and appositive phrases are usually set off by commas.

An *appositive* is a noun or pronoun that follows another noun or pronoun to identify or explain it.

EXAMPLES   Nancy Landon Kassebaum, a **senator** from Kansas, was the principal speaker.
Do you know him, the **boy** wearing the blue shirt?

When you set off an appositive, be sure to include all the words that modify it.

EXAMPLES   I read *At Home in India*, **a book by Cynthia Bowles.**
Neil Armstrong, **the first person to walk on the moon,** took his historic step on July 20, 1969.

Sometimes an appositive is used to specify a particular person, place, thing, or idea. Such an appositive is called a *restrictive appositive.*

EXAMPLES   My brother **James** helped me. [The writer has more than one brother. The appositive *James* specifies which brother.]
Have you ever seen the movie ***Home Alone***? [The appositive *Home Alone* specifies the particular movie.]

☞ **REFERENCE NOTE:** See pages 590–591 for more information on appositives and appositive phrases.

 EXERCISE 6   **Correcting Sentences with Appositives and Appositive Phrases by Adding Commas**

Correctly punctuate the appositives in the following sentences. If a sentence is correct, write *C.*

1. Leonardo da Vinci's painting *Mona Lisa* is a prized possession of the Louvre in France.
2. The painting a portrait of a young Florentine woman is slightly cracked as a result of temperature changes.

MECHANICS

3. In 1911 an Italian house painter Vincenzo Peruggia stole the painting from its frame.
4. For two years the Paris police some of the world's cleverest detectives were baffled by the crime.
5. Since its recovery the painting one of the most valuable portraits in the world has been closely guarded.

(2) Words used in direct address are set off by commas.

EXAMPLES   **David,** please close the door.
Did you call me, **Mother**?
Yes, **Mr. Ramos,** I turned in my paper.

(3) Parenthetical expressions are set off by commas.

Parenthetical expressions are remarks that add incidental information or relate ideas to each other.

Commonly Used Parenthetical Expressions		
after all	however	nevertheless
at any rate	I believe	generally speaking
consequently	in fact	on the contrary
for example	that is	on the other hand
for instance	meanwhile	in the first place
of course	moreover	therefore

EXAMPLES   You are, **I hope,** planning to arrive on time.
Gwendolyn Brooks, **in fact,** is my favorite poet.

Some expressions may be used both parenthetically and not parenthetically.

EXAMPLE   Long-distance calls are a bargain, at any rate.
[parenthetical, meaning "in any case"]
Long-distance calls are a bargain at any rate.
[not parenthetical, meaning "at any cost"]

☞ REFERENCE NOTE: Parentheses and dashes are sometimes used to set off parenthetical expressions. See pages 862–864.

NOTE: A contrasting expression introduced by *not* or *yet* is parenthetical and should be set off by commas.

EXAMPLE   Emily Brontë, **not her sister Charlotte,** wrote *Wuthering Heights*.

MECHANICS

▶ REVIEW C

Correcting Sentences by Adding Commas

For each of the following sentences, write each word that should be followed by a comma, and place a comma after it.

EXAMPLE   [1] Artist Faith Ringgold painstakingly hand-letters her beautiful unique story quilts.
    1. *beautiful,*

[1] Continuing the ancient tradition of quilting Ringgold combines printed dyed and pieced fabric with acrylic paintings or photoetchings. [2] By placing the tradition in a new context the artist gives it new meaning.

[3] Ringgold whose earlier works include landscapes murals masks and soft sculptures began making story quilts in 1980. [4] Titled *Echoes of Harlem* the first one was a collaboration between the artist and her mother dress designer Willi Posey who learned quilting from her own grandmother who had learned it from her mother a slave.

[5] Most of Ringgold's story quilts are designed to be viewed as parts of a series not as separate pieces and many include portions of a narrative linking the works in the series. [6] This work *Double Dutch on the Golden Gate* lacks an accompanying text and is from the *Woman on a Bridge* series which includes five works. [7] Capturing the excitement of a childhood game it depicts a pastime cherished by generations of African Americans. [8] However the work speaks to more than a single culture and appeals to all people who recognize in it joyful moments from their childhood.

[9] Ringgold still lives and works in Harlem the section of New York City where she was born. [10] One of her story quilts which sell for $40,000 is in the permanent collection of the city's Guggenheim Museum a major gallery of modern art.

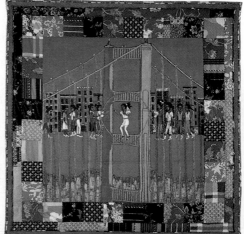

Faith Ringgold, *Double Dutch on the Golden Gate Bridge.* Acrylic, canvas, painted, dyed, pieced fabric, 68 1/2" × 68". © 1988 Faith Ringgold Inc. Private Collection.

MECHANICS

Conventional Situations

25l. Use commas in certain conventional situations.

(1) Use a comma to separate items in dates and addresses.

EXAMPLES   On Saturday, June 21, 1991, Robert moved to Miami
Beach, Florida, with his parents.
His new address is 814 Georgia Avenue, Miami Beach,
FL 33139.

Notice that no comma separates the month from the day,
the house number from the street name, or the ZIP Code
from the two-letter state code.

If the day is given before the month or if only the
month and the year are given, no comma is used.

EXAMPLES   The British forces at Pensacola Bay surrendered to
Bernardo de Gálvez on 10 May 1781.
The hottest month on record here was July 1962.

(2) Use a comma after the salutation of a friendly letter and after the closing of any letter.

EXAMPLES   Dear Marcus,   Dear Aunt Meg,
Affectionately yours,   Sincerely yours,

(3) Use a comma after a name followed by an abbreviation such as *Jr.*, *Sr.*, or *M.D.* and after the abbreviation when it is used in a sentence.

EXAMPLES   Elena Moreno, M.D.
Russell E. Davis, Jr., has been elected mayor.

PICTURE THIS

You're a writer for a company that prepares the closed
captions that hearing-impaired viewers see on their television screens. Write a page of dialogue that might be
shown with this scene from the *I Love Lucy* show, starring
Lucille Ball and Desi Arnaz. Use a variety of end marks,
and include commas where they are needed.

Subject: a scene from *I Love Lucy*
Audience: hearing-impaired viewers
Purpose: to entertain

Unnecessary Commas

25m. Do not use unnecessary commas.

Too many commas can be as confusing as too few. Don't use a comma unless a rule requires one or unless the meaning would be unclear without it.

CONFUSING   On Friday, after school, my friend, Rita, and I played badminton at her house until her dog, Ruffles, a frisky, golden retriever, joined us and ran off with the shuttlecock, clenched in its teeth.

CLEAR   On Friday after school, my friend Rita and I played badminton at her house until her dog Ruffles, a frisky golden retriever, joined us and ran off with the shuttlecock clenched in its teeth.

EXERCISE 7   **Correcting Sentences by Adding Commas**

For each of the following sentences, write each word that should be followed by a comma, and place the comma after it.

EXAMPLE **1.** On our way to Birmingham Alabama we stayed overnight in Chattanooga Tennessee.
        1. *Birmingham, Alabama, Chattanooga,*

1. On August 1 1991 we moved from Eureka California to 220 Tuxford Place Thousand Oaks California.
2. We left Tampa Florida on Monday June 15 and arrived in Albuquerque New Mexico on June 17.
3. The hotel on Gulfport Road was destroyed by fire on Tuesday March 13 1984.
4. My brother received a letter that started, "Dear John There's something I've been meaning to tell you."
5. We interviewed Franklin R. Thomas M.D. at his emergency clinic on Wilson Road.

▶ REVIEW D **Revising Paragraphs by Adding Commas**

For each sentence in the following paragraphs, write each word that should be followed by a comma, and place the comma after it. If a sentence is correct, write C. [Note: If a comma may or may not be used, circle the word and the comma.]

[1] As early as the sixth century B.C. plays were performed in this amphitheater the Theater of Dionysus in Athens Greece. [2] The Theater of Dionysus is located on the south slope of the Acropolis an elevated fortified section of Athens. [3] The plays presented in ancient Greece marked the beginning of drama in the Western world. [4] In fact the English word *theater* comes from the Greek word *theatron* which means "a place for seeing."

[5] Wearing masks to show which characters they were portraying the actors in ancient dramas often played several different roles. [6] In addition all roles including those of female characters were performed by men.

[7] Although records show that Greek playwrights wrote hundreds of tragedies fewer than thirty-five of these plays survive. [8] The earliest Greek dramatist Aeschylus wrote the *Oresteia* a powerful story of murder revenge and divine mercy. [9] Sophocles often regarded as the greatest dramatist of all time is credited with writing more than one hundred plays. [10] Among the surviving works of Aristophanes whom the ancient Greeks considered the greatest comic playwright are the three satires *The Clouds The Wasps* and *The Frogs.*

Review: Posttest

A. Correcting Sentences by Adding End Marks and Commas

Write the following sentences, adding end marks and commas where they are needed. [Note: If a comma may or may not be used, circle the comma.]

EXAMPLE   1. When is the bus coming or has it already left
　　　　　1. *When is the bus coming, or has it already left?*

1. On June 1 1992 I wrote to the Wisconsin Department of Development at 123 Washington Ave Madison WI 53702
2. Federico Peña mayor of Denver Colorado from 1983 to 1991 was born in Laredo Texas in 1947.
3. Wow Bill what a great save you made in last night's game
4. Water transports nutrients throughout the body aids in digestion and helps regulate body temperature
5. I M Pei who was born in China has designed many buildings in the United States for example the Dallas Texas City Hall and the Government Center in Boston Massachusetts
6. The chief crops grown in Trinidad one of the most prosperous islands in the Caribbean are sugar coffee cocoa citrus fruits and bananas
7. Did you know that Navajo Community College located in Tsaile Arizona was founded in 1968

8. If I finish my report if I do the laundry and if I promise to be home by eleven may I go to the concert
9. After staying up so late I was exhausted of course yet I couldn't fall asleep right away
10. In the mail last Wednesday a large heavy package addressed to Phyllis M Saunders M D was delivered to our house by mistake.

B. Correcting Paragraphs by Adding End Marks and Commas

For each sentence in the following paragraphs, add end marks and commas where they are needed. [Note: If a comma may or may not be used, circle the comma.]

EXAMPLE [1] As soon as I got home I called my best friend Stephanie to tell her about my vacation
1. *As soon as I got home, I called my best friend, Stephanie, to tell her about my vacation.*

[11] Stephanie have you ever visited Cody Wyoming [12] Well if you do be sure to stop by the Buffalo Bill Historical Center [13] Opened in 1927 in memory of William "Buffalo Bill" Cody an army scout who later had his own Wild West show the Center is actually four museums in one [14] Under one roof are the Buffalo Bill Museum the Whitney Gallery of Western Art the Winchester Arms Museum and the Plains Indian Museum

[15] All of the museums are interesting but the best one I believe is the Plains Indian Museum which has artifacts from Native American cowhands settlers and roving artists [16] Of all the treasures in the museum's collections the highlight is an exhibit on Tatanka Yotanka better known as Sitting Bull the mighty Sioux warrior holy man chief and statesman [17] The exhibit includes a dozen drawings that Sitting Bull who was born about 1831 and died in 1890 made while he was a prisoner at Fort Randall an army post in the Dakota Territory [18] Depicting some of his many battlefield conquests the drawings reveal his talent for design and composition

[19] Other displays show weapons clothing and accessories of the Cheyenne Shoshone Crow Arapaho Blackfeet and Gros Ventre peoples [20] What a journey back through time the museum offers

SUMMARY OF THE USES OF THE COMMA

25f Use commas to separate items in a series.

(1) If all items in a series are joined by *and*, *or*, or *nor*, do not use commas to separate them.

(2) Independent clauses in a series are usually separated by semicolons. Short independent clauses may be separated by commas.

25g Use commas to separate two or more adjectives preceding a noun.

25h Use a comma before *and*, *but*, *or*, *nor*, *for*, *so*, and *yet* when they join independent clauses.

25i Use commas to set off nonessential clauses and nonessential participial phrases.

25j Use commas after certain introductory elements.

(1) Use a comma after words such as *well*, *yes*, *no*, and *why* when they begin a sentence.

(2) Use a comma after an introductory participial phrase.

(3) Use a comma after two or more introductory prepositional phrases.

(4) Use a comma after an introductory adverb clause.

25k Use commas to set off elements that interrupt a sentence.

(1) Appositives and appositive phrases are usually set off by commas.

(2) Words used in direct address are set off by commas.

(3) Parenthetical expressions are set off by commas.

25l Use commas in certain conventional situations.

(1) Use a comma to separate items in dates and addresses.

(2) Use a comma after the salutation of a friendly letter and after the closing of any letter.

(3) Use a comma after a name followed by an abbreviation such as *Jr.*, *Sr.*, or *M.D.*

25m Do not use unnecessary commas.

MECHANICS

26 PUNCTUATION

Semicolons and Colons

Diagnostic Test

Correcting Sentences by Using Semicolons and Colons

Most of the following sentences have a comma or no punctuation mark where a semicolon or a colon should be used. Write the word preceding each error; then, add the needed punctuation mark. If a sentence is correct, write *C*.

EXAMPLE   **1.** No, the Arthurs are not home, they've left for work.
       1. *home;*

1. Native Americans inhabited North America long before any Europeans however, many Native Americans weren't recognized as citizens of the United States until 1924.
2. The meeting is scheduled for 3 30 this afternoon please don't be late.

3. The following committees will report at that time budget, membership, awards, and programs.
4. Every morning when I get up, I read a Bible verse this morning I read John 14 27.
5. We left some food out for the stray dog it looked so forlorn huddled in the doorway.
6. Our modern literature class has read these poems, "Incident" by Countee Cullen, "The Love Song of J. Alfred Prufrock" by T. S. Eliot, and "Ars Poetica" by Archibald MacLeish.
7. When she transferred to Barton Academy, Millie joined several clubs, helped in planning the Spring Carnival, and worked at a food bank for the needy nevertheless, it took her months to make some new friends.
8. While campaigning to become mayor of San Antonio, María Antonieta Berriozábal summed up her point of view in these words, "Our greatest resource is our people. We have to deal with business interests and human needs simultaneously."
9. Conrad Aiken was a correspondent for *The New Yorker* and also wrote essays and short stories he is best known, however, for his poetry.
10. The Bering Strait links the Arctic Ocean with the Bering Sea, both the strait and the sea are named for Vitus Bering, a Danish explorer.
11. S. I. Hayakawa made this statement "It is not true that we have only one life to live, if we can read, we can live as many more lives and as many kinds of lives as we wish."
12. The winners in the Douglas Fun Run last Saturday morning were Otis Williams, a sophomore, Janice Hicks, a senior, and Rodrigo Campas, a junior.
13. They opposed every motion that came before the meeting in addition, they said they would circulate petitions if any of the proposals were passed.
14. At first the children were afraid, believing that they were lost only after their teacher reassured them that she knew the way did they settle down.
15. This design will be applied to the following types of machines commercial, manufacturing, military, and agricultural.

16. Jennifer Lawson became programming chief of PBS in 1990 she is a former civil rights activist, film professor, and producer.
17. In addition to her coming-of-age short stories, Doris Lessing has written several novels, one of which is *African Laughter Four Visits to Zimbabwe,* based on her life in Africa.
18. In the past twelve years, Justin has lived in Tucson, Arizona Dallas, Texas, Shreveport, Louisiana, and Tulsa, Oklahoma.
19. For the golf tournament seasoned players were paired with players new to the game consequently, the experienced players were frustrated and the novices were confused.
20. When Hernando Cortés invaded Mexico in 1519, he burned his ships as a result, his troops were unable to return to Cuba.

Semicolons

26a. Use a semicolon between independent clauses in a sentence if they are not joined by *and, but, or, nor, for, so,* or *yet.*

EXAMPLE Everyone else in my family excels in a particular sport; I seem to be the only exception.

When the thoughts of two short sentences are very closely related, a semicolon can take the place of the period between them.

EXAMPLE The river is rising rapidly. It's expected to crest by noon. [two simple sentences]
The river is rising rapidly; it's expected to crest by noon.

26b. Use a semicolon between independent clauses joined by conjunctive adverbs or transitional expressions.

EXAMPLES   Leonor is planning to become an engineer**;** **however,**
she is also interested in commercial art.
Only two people registered for the pottery lessons**;** **as
a result,** the class was canceled.

Notice in the examples above that the conjunctive adverb
and the transitional expression are followed by commas.

Commonly Used Conjunctive Adverbs

accordingly	however	moreover
besides	indeed	nevertheless
consequently	instead	otherwise
furthermore	meanwhile	therefore

Commonly Used Transitional Expressions

as a result	for example	for instance	that is
in spite of	in conclusion	in other words	in fact

NOTE: When a conjunctive adverb or a transitional expression appears
within one of the clauses instead of *between* the clauses, it is
usually set off by commas. The two clauses are still separated by
a semicolon.

EXAMPLE   Ralph Ellison is best known for his 1952 novel,
Invisible Man **;** he has also**, however,** written short
stories and essays.

EXERCISE 1   Correcting Sentences by Adding Commas and Semicolons

For each of the following sentences, write all the words
that should be followed by a semicolon or a comma. Place
the needed punctuation mark after each one.

EXAMPLE   **1.** The clever carvings shown on the next page were
handmade in southern Mexico they're sold all over
the world.
    1. *Mexico;*

1. The carvings come from the Oaxaca (pronounced
wä hä′ kä) Valley in fact 90 percent of the two hundred families who make them live in three villages.

MECHANICS

2. Carving has been a tradition among Oaxacans for hundreds of years only recently however have the artists sold their work outside the valley.

3. In many families the fathers and older sons do the actual carving meanwhile the other members of the family sand and paint the figures.

4. The artists find inspiration for their creations in everyday life for example religion and nature are rich sources of ideas.

5. Even those carvers whose works have won world-wide acclaim have chosen to continue living in the valley their ties to their families and communities are very strong.

| **26c.** | A semicolon (rather than a comma) may be needed to separate independent clauses joined by a coordinating conjunction if commas appear within the clauses. |

CONFUSING   June sat with Tony, Pat, and me, and Josh sat with Flora, Zack, and Geraldo.

CLEAR   June sat with Tony, Pat and me; and Josh sat with Flora, Zack, and Geraldo.

CONFUSING   Searching for my house key, I found a dime, a nickel, and a penny, and, putting them into my wallet, I realized that my key had been in there all along.

CLEAR   Searching for my house key, I found a dime, a nickel, and a penny; and, putting them into my wallet, I realized that my key had been in there all along.

☞ REFERENCE NOTE: For information on using a comma to separate independent clauses joined by a coordinating conjunction, see page 796.

26d.   Use a semicolon between items in a series if the items contain commas.

EXAMPLES   There are three home stations for the Goodyear blimps: Carson, California; Akron, Ohio; and Pompano Beach, Florida.

You may turn in your book reports on Thursday, September 14; Friday, September 15; Monday, September 18; or Tuesday, September 19.

▶ REVIEW A   **Correcting Sentences by Adding Commas and Semicolons**

For each of the following sentences, write all the words that should be followed by a semicolon or a comma. Place the needed punctuation mark after each one. If a sentence is correct, write C.

EXAMPLE   **1.** The diagram on the next page shows the typical seating plan of a symphony orchestra the conductor occupies the podium.

1. *orchestra;*

1. All of the instruments in a symphony orchestra are divided into classes based on how they produce sound many musicians can play several instruments within a class.
2. The four classes are the stringed instruments, the woodwinds, the brasses, and the percussion instruments.
3. Woodwinds, which include the flute, the clarinet, and the saxophone, were once made solely of wood but today they may be made of metal or plastic instead.

MECHANICS

4. Some of the stringed instruments are played with a bow some are plucked with the fingers or with a pick and some are operated by means of a keyboard.

5. Most brass instruments, such as the trumpet, tuba, and cornet, have valves that regulate the pitch but the trombone has a sliding section for this purpose.

6. Kettledrums, or timpani, are percussion instruments that can be tuned to a specific pitch most other kinds of drums, the cymbals, and the triangle however cannot be tuned.

7. The conductor's job is to coordinate the sounds produced by these different instruments however this task is only one of a conductor's responsibilities.

8. Conductors must study the history and theory of music for many years furthermore they must be skilled at playing at least one instrument.

9. Many people think that a conductor just establishes and maintains the tempo of the music they don't realize that he or she also selects the music, interprets the composer's meaning, and brings out the best in each of the musicians.

10. The goal of every conductor is to lead a major orchestra such as one of those in London, England Mexico City, Mexico Boston, Massachusetts or Chicago, Illinois.

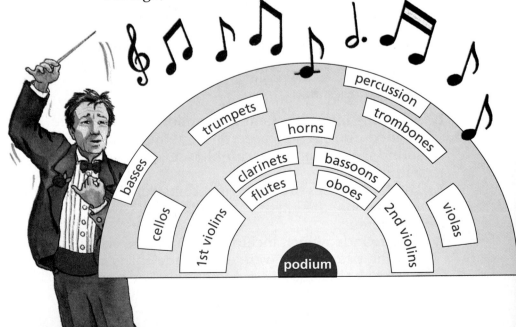

MECHANICS

Colons

26e. Use a colon to mean "note what follows."

(1) Use a colon before a list of items, especially after expressions such as *as follows* and *the following [items]*.

EXAMPLES   In Washington, D.C., we visited four important national sites**:** the White House, the Washington Monument, the Vietnam Veterans Memorial, and the Lincoln Memorial.

The only articles allowed in the examination area **are as follows:** pencils, compasses, rulers, and protractors.

During summer vacation, Juanita read biographies of **the following people:** John Ross, Annie Wauneka, and María Martínez-Cañas.

NOTE: Do not use a colon before a list that immediately follows a verb or a preposition.

INCORRECT   At the new amusement park we rode: the roller coaster, the Ferris wheel, the bumper cars, and the water slide.

CORRECT   At the amusement park we rode the roller coaster, the Ferris wheel, the bumper cars, and the water slide.

INCORRECT   Our family has lived in: California, Arizona, North Carolina, and Texas.

CORRECT   Our family has lived in California, Arizona, North Carolina, and Texas.

(2) Use a colon before a long, formal statement or quotation.

EXAMPLE   Thomas Paine's first pamphlet in the series *The American Crisis* starts with these famous words**:**

These are the times that try men's souls. The summer soldier and the sunshine patriot will, in this crisis, shrink from the service of their country; but he that stands it *now* deserves the love and thanks of man and woman.

 REFERENCE NOTE: See pages 838–839 for more information on using long quotations in a composition.

PICTURE THIS

The year is 1878. Responding to this poster, your family sold its home in Tennessee, and now you're on your way to Kansas with this wagon train. The land, the people, the chores—everything is different from the life you left behind. You've decided to keep a journal so that you'll always remember this difficult but exciting journey. Write a journal entry telling what happened today on the trail. In your entry, use at least three semicolons and two colons.

Subject: traveling to Kansas with a wagon train
Audience: you some time in the future
Purpose: to record

> **26f.** Use a colon in certain conventional situations.

(1) Use a colon between the hour and the minute.

EXAMPLES   6:15 P.M.   9:55 tomorrow morning

(2) Use a colon between chapter and verse in biblical references and between titles and subtitles.

EXAMPLES   Psalms 8**:**9   I Corinthians 13**:** 1–13
            Indian Oratory**:** A Collection of Famous Speeches

(3) Use a colon after the salutation of a business letter.

EXAMPLES   Dear Ms. Weinberg**:**   Dear Sales Manager**:**
            Dear Sir or Madam**:**   To Whom It May Concern**:**

NOTE: Use a comma after the salutation of a friendly letter.

         EXAMPLE   Dear Suzanne**,**

▶ EXERCISE 2   **Correcting Sentences by Adding Colons**

Correct the following sentences by adding colons where they are needed. If a sentence is correct, write C.

EXAMPLE   **1.** I began my acceptance speech as follows "Fellow students, thank you for your votes!"
           1. *follows:*

1. My little sister's favorite book is *The Great Kapok Tree A Tale of the Amazon Rain Forest* by Lynn Cherry.
2. Sometimes the paper comes at 6 15 A.M., but other times it doesn't hit the driveway until 7 00.
3. My little sister has several items embossed with Garfield's picture a poster, a nightgown, a notebook, and a clock.
4. In William Shakespeare's play *Julius Caesar,* the general Caesar says of courage
   Cowards die many times before their deaths,
   The valiant taste of death but once.
5. Sherry's favorite artists are Jacob Lawrence, Romare Bearden, and Margaret Burroughs.
6. The story of Moses and Pharaoh's daughter is told in Exodus 2 5–10.
7. The directions were as follows cover with plastic wrap, place in oven, and microwave for at least ten minutes.
8. I prefer my bicycle to a car for three reasons I don't pay for gasoline, I don't pay for insurance, and it's all mine.

MECHANICS

9. In Cuba, which is a Spanish-speaking country, most of the people are of Spanish, African, or Spanish-African descent.
10. Mr. Wise asked us to bring the following items to biology class a deciduous leaf, a coniferous needle or branch, and wax paper.

▶ REVIEW B **Correcting Sentences by Adding Semicolons and Colons**

For each numbered sentence in the following letter, write each word that should be followed by a semicolon or a colon. Place the needed punctuation mark after each word. [Note: A sentence may need more than one punctuation mark.]

EXAMPLE [1] Hampton University was founded in 1868 it was originally named Hampton Institute.
1. *1868;*

1238-C Landon Street
Kansas City, MO 64105
October 17, 1993

Director
George Foster Peabody Collection
Hampton University
Hampton, VA 23668

[1] Dear Sir or Madam

[2] The media coordinator at Central High School suggested that I write to you she explained that Hampton has an extensive collection of materials on African American history. [3] For my history class I am preparing an oral report on the August 28, 1963, March on Washington and, to make my report more interesting, I would like to display pictures of the march.

[4] I am particularly interested in pictures of the following speakers Floyd McKissick John Lewis Roy Wilkins and, of course, Martin Luther King, Jr. [5] I would also like pictures showing the size and diversity of the crowd for example, a shot of the marchers filling the area around the Reflecting Pool between the Lincoln Memorial and the

Washington Monument would be especially effective. [6] Either prints or slides will be useful however, I would prefer slides if they are available.

[7] My grandfather, who took part in the march, remembers it vividly in fact, he considers it one of the high points of his life. [8] He took several rolls of film himself that day unfortunately, the pictures were lost in a fire a few years ago.

[9] Please send me information on ordering copies of suitable pictures a stamped, self-addressed envelope is enclosed. [10] Thank you for your help I look forward to hearing from you.

Sincerely,

Jesse Fletcher

Jesse Fletcher

WRITING APPLICATION

Using Semicolons and Colons in a Business Letter

As you grow older, your knowledge and your thoughts expand and become more complex. To express what you know and think, you begin using longer, more complex sentences. When you write, semicolons and colons can help you make these sentences easier to understand. Compare the following examples.

IMMATURE	I'd like to visit three cities. The cities are in the Southwest. One is Santa Fe, New Mexico. One is Phoenix, Arizona. One is Los Angeles, California. I can't afford to. That's unfortunate.
MATURE	I'd like to visit three cities in the Southwest: Santa Fe, New Mexico; Phoenix, Arizona; and Los Angeles, California; unfortunately, however, I can't afford to.

▶ WRITING ACTIVITY

You have just won the grand prize in Blue Star Airlines' Fly-by-Night Sweepstakes. For one week, you can travel free to anywhere that Blue Star flies in the United States—just so long as your flights depart between 8 P.M. and 4 A.M. You can remain in one location for the whole week, or you can travel to as many places as you'd like. To use your prize, you must give Blue Star Airlines a detailed itinerary of your trip at least two weeks before you plan to take it. Write a letter to the airlines, giving the specific information needed to prepare your tickets. Use semicolons and colons to make your information easy to understand.

Prewriting   First, decide where you would most like to go. (If you plan to include more than one destination, remember that the trip is to last only one week from start to finish; be as realistic as you can about the travel time required.) Then, arrange the information in an order that will be easy for the ticket agent to understand.

Writing   As you write your first draft, remember that the accuracy and completeness of your letter could make the difference between an enjoyable trip and a disastrous one. Stick to the point, and try to make the information as clear as possible.

Evaluating and Revising   Put yourself in the ticket agent's place as you evaluate the letter. Have you included all the necessary flight information? Have you arranged the details in an order that's easy to understand? Add, delete, change, or rearrange information to make the letter clearer and more useful. Also make sure that you use the correct form for a business letter (see pages 973–977).

Proofreading   Proofread your letter carefully, paying special attention to your use of semicolons and colons. Check pages 822–823 to be sure that you have followed the rules for using colons in conventional situations. Also make sure that you have correctly spelled the names of the places you wish to visit.

Review: Posttest

Correcting Sentences by Adding Semicolons and Colons

For each of the following sentences, write the word preceding each punctuation error; then write the semicolon or colon needed. If a sentence is correct, write *C*.

EXAMPLE   **1.** Please bring the following items books, pencils, and newspapers.
1. *items:*

1. If you want to send fragile items through the mail, the post office recommends that you pack them in fiberboard containers use foam, plastic, or padding to cushion them and then seal the package carefully, reinforcing it with filament tape.
2. In 1904, Mary McLeod Bethune founded a school for girls in Daytona Beach, Florida that school is now Bethune-Cookman College.
3. Psalms 23 1–6 is one of the best-known passages in the Bible.
4. According to one of my main sources, *The Real McCoy The Life of an African-American Inventor,* an oilcan used in railroad maintenance gave rise to the popular expression "the real McCoy."
5. If I had a million dollars, I'd visit London, England Cairo, Egypt Buenos Aires, Argentina and Tokyo, Japan.
6. We have to write reports for gym class on one of the following athletes Jesse Owens, Sonja Henie, Jim Thorpe, Althea Gibson, or Babe Didrikson Zaharias.
7. Our neighbor's cocker spaniel barked on and off all night long as a result, I didn't sleep well.
8. Candice will take Sandra's place in tonight's performance unfortunately, Sandra sprained her ankle and cannot walk.
9. My aunt Pam loves to play backgammon and chess however, she rarely has time because she works at two jobs.

MECHANICS

10. Asia has both the highest and the lowest points on earth Mount Everest, the highest, soars 29,028 feet the Dead Sea, a salt lake, lies 1,300 feet below sea level.

11. Instructed to be prompt, we arrived at school at 7 15, but the doors were locked consequently, we had to wait until 7 30 to get in the building.

12. Indira Gandhi, who served for many years as the prime minister of India, grew up in the world of politics and government for her father, Jawaharlal Nehru was the first prime minister of India, from 1947 to 1964.

13. My friends Ruth and Cindy disagree about the role of fate in life Ruth believes that people can control their own destiny, but Cindy insists that people are simply pawns of fate.

14. I don't like to prepare outlines nevertheless, the highest grade I ever received was for a report that I wrote from an outline.

15. Mr. Kowalski has always regretted that he didn't learn to speak Polish when he was a child now he is taking conversational Polish.

16. The computer software industry is an enormous, growing business for instance, people can buy software for everything from balancing budgets to plotting biorhythm charts.

17. Every morning Lonnie rises at 5 00, jogs until 5 30, showers and eats breakfast by 6 15, and catches the 6 35 bus.

18. Red Cloud, leader of the Oglala Sioux, was a military genius he successfully defended Sioux lands against settlers who wanted to build a trail from Laramie, Wyoming, to Bozeman, Montana.

19. Gates of the Arctic National Park, which is located in northern Alaska, is known for its large populations of certain animals caribou, grizzly bears, moose, and wolves.

20. I have ridden bicycles, horses, and motorcycles and I have traveled in trains, buses, and planes someday I hope to ride in a hot-air balloon.

MECHANICS

27 PUNCTUATION

Italics and Quotation Marks

Diagnostic Test

Correcting Sentences by Adding Italics and Quotation Marks

Write each letter, word, title, or sentence that should be in italics (underlined) or in quotation marks. Then supply the needed underlining or quotation marks.

EXAMPLES
1. Can you tell me the way to Logan Street? she asked.
1. *"Can you tell me the way to Logan Street?"*
2. Takeda Izumo, Namiki Senryo, and Miyoshi Shoraku wrote the Kabuki play cycle known in English as The Treasury of the Loyal Retainers or as The League of the Loyal Ronin.
2. *The Treasury of the Loyal Retainers; The League of the Loyal Ronin*

1. Carlos Chávez, Mexican composer and conductor, wrote the symphony Sinfonía de Antígona in 1933.
2. We have subscribed to the Orlando Sentinel ever since we moved here.

3. Are you going to help me, he asked, or shall I look for someone else?

4. James Dickey wrote the novel Deliverance, which was made into a movie featuring the song Dueling Banjos.

5. In modern Spanish the letters that occur with the greatest frequency are a and s.

6. Clarita served a delicious appetizer called pulpo; when I asked her what it was, she told me that I'd just eaten octopus.

7. For our homework assignment we have to define ionization, electrolyte, quark, and neutrino.

8. During the Civil War, the Merrimack, on the Confederate side, and the Monitor, on the Union side, fought to a draw in the first battle between ironclad ships.

9. I never should have agreed to be on that committee, wailed Ellie. When I asked Mary to help, she said, Not on your life! Now I'm stuck doing all the work.

10. Where have you been, Ramón? asked Leroy. The bus leaves in three minutes.

11. Announcing the scholarship winners, the principal called the following students Elwood High's finest scholars: Daphne Johnson, Michael Lewis, Ruben Perez, and Winsie Chung.

12. One of my favorite TV shows, Disaster Chronicles, ran an episode called Volcanoes in Italy, which had some interesting facts I used in my report on ancient Rome.

13. Sam, who's originally from Boston, tends to drop the r's at the ends of words.

14. Politicians still quote Abraham Lincoln's phrase government of the people, by the people, for the people.

15. During lunch we discussed Ann Banks's magazine article Rafting with Kids.

16. Indians Today, the Real and the Unreal is the opening chapter in Vine Deloria's book Custer Died for Your Sins.

17. My mother has never liked the term baby boomer.

18. Many articles about Emily Dickinson's poems contain the term paradox.

19. When the players came onto the field, the fans shouted, Go for it!
20. Have you seen the sculpture Young Shadows, by Louise Nevelson?

Italics

Italics are printed letters that lean to the right, like this:

> *These words are printed in italics.*

When you are writing or typing, indicate italics by underlining. If your composition were printed, the type-setter would set the underlined words in italics. For instance, if you typed

> All sophomores in our school read <u>The Good Earth</u>, by Pearl Buck.

the sentence would be printed like this:

> All sophomores in our school read *The Good Earth,* by Pearl Buck.

NOTE: If you use a personal computer, you can probably code in italics to appear on the printout. Most word-processing software and many printers are capable of producing italic type.

27a. Use italics (underlining) for titles and subtitles of books, plays, films, periodicals, works of art, record albums, long musical compositions, television series, ships, aircraft, and so on.

TYPE OF TITLE	EXAMPLES	
Books	*Sophocles: The Oedipus Cycle*	*A Fire in My Hands* *Black Elk Speaks*
Plays	*A Raisin in the Sun*	*Julius Caesar*
Films	*Dances with Wolves*	*High Noon*

(continued)

TYPE OF TITLE	EXAMPLES	
Periodicals	*Ebony* *Kansas City Times*	*Women: A Journal of Liberation*
Works of Art	*The Three Musicians*	*Agrarian Leader Zapata*
Long Musical Compositions	*Peter and the Wolf*	*Black, Brown, and Beige*
Television Series	*All Creatures Great and Small*	*Soul Train* *The Wonder Years*
Ships, Trains	*Lusitania* *Flying Cloud*	*Orange Blossom Special*
Aircraft, Spacecraft	*June Bug*	*Pioneer 11*

NOTE: Italicize the title of a poem long enough to be published in a separate volume. Such poems are usually divided into titled or numbered sections, such as cantos, parts, or books. The titles of these sections are enclosed in quotation marks.

EXAMPLE   Longfellow's *Evangeline* opens with a section titled simply "Prelude."

The words *a, an,* and *the* before a title are italicized only when they are part of the title. They are not italicized (or capitalized) before the titles of newspapers unless they appear that way in the masthead of the publication.

EXAMPLES   John Hersey's *The Wall* recounts the destruction of the Jewish ghetto in Warsaw during World War II.
In Shakespeare's play *A Midsummer Night's Dream,* Bottom, a weaver, and his friends perform a play-within-a-play.
The article in *The Wall Street Journal* mentioned that among his other accomplishments, Frederick Douglass founded the *North Star,* a newspaper he published for seventeen years.

 REFERENCE NOTE: Use quotation marks, not italics, for chapter headings and the titles of magazine articles, short poems, short stories, short musical compositions, and single episodes of television series. See page 840 for this rule.

27b.   Use italics (underlining) for words, numerals, and letters referred to as such and for foreign words.

EXAMPLES   The first *o* in *zoology* has a long *o* sound.
On my old typewriter, the lowercase letter *l* was also used to type the numeral *1*.
Montana's state motto is *Oro y Plata,* the Spanish phrase for "gold and silver."

▶ EXERCISE 1   **Correcting Sentences by Adding Underlining (Italics)**

Identify all the words and word groups that should be italicized in the following sentences.

EXAMPLE   **1.** In 1988, Toni Morrison won the Pulitzer Prize for her novel Beloved.
    1. *Beloved*

1. Does the Vietnamese word chiao mean the same thing as the Spanish word hola?
2. The first full-length animated film, Walt Disney's Snow White and the Seven Dwarfs, used two million drawings.
3. Among the items that the Pilgrims brought with them on the Mayflower were apple seeds.
4. James Earle Fraser, best known for his painting End of the Trail, designed the U.S. buffalo nickel.
5. In the late eighteenth century, Edward Gibbon wrote the influential book History of the Decline and Fall of the Roman Empire.
6. In Voyage to the Bottom of the Sea, an old TV series, the submarine Seaview was commanded by Admiral Nelson.
7. Daktari is Swahili for the English word doctor.
8. The first U.S. space shuttle was named Columbia.
9. Richard Sears met Alvah Roebuck through an ad in the Chicago Daily News.
10. The three M's referred to in the company name 3M stand for the words Minnesota Mining and Manufacturing.

▶ EXERCISE 2   **Writing Sentences Containing Titles of Works**

You probably recognize at least some of the awards on the next page. Now you've been appointed to the nominating

MECHANICS

committee for a new award, the Golden Guppy, which will be presented for an outstanding work in each of these categories:

- a book
- a musical recording
- a television program
- a work of art (painting, sculpture, or some other form)
- a magazine

In a sentence or two, nominate a work in each category and explain why you think it should win one of the awards.

"Emmy" ® ATAS/NATAS

Quotation Marks

"Oscar" statuette © A.M.P.A.S.

27c. Use quotation marks to enclose a *direct quotation*—a person's exact words.

Do not use quotation marks for an *indirect quotation*.

DIRECT QUOTATION	Joan said, "My legs are sore from jogging." [Joan's exact words]
INDIRECT QUOTATION	Joan said that her legs were sore from jogging. [not Joan's exact words]

NOTE: Remember to place quotation marks at both the beginning and the end of a direct quotation.

INCORRECT	"I'm taking the road test tomorrow, said Reed.
CORRECT	"I'm taking the road test tomorrow," said Reed.

27d. A direct quotation begins with a capital letter.

EXAMPLE   Bianca asked, "When do we get our uniforms?"

NOTE: If a direct quotation is obviously only a fragment of a sentence and is not intended to stand alone, use a lowercase letter.

EXAMPLE Christine promised that she would be here "as soon as possible."

27e. When a quoted sentence is divided into two parts by an interrupting expression such as *he said,* the second part begins with a lowercase letter.

EXAMPLES "I hope," said Diego, "that it doesn't rain during the fiesta."
"I'm not sure," remarked Annette, "if I'll be able to attend the meeting."

If the second part of a divided quotation is a new sentence, a period (not a comma) follows the interrupting expression. The second part begins with a capital letter.

EXAMPLE "The date has been set," said Greg. "We can't change it now."

NOTE: An interrupting expression is not part of a quotation, so it should never be inside the quotation marks.

INCORRECT "Where, I inquired, have I seen you before?"
CORRECT "Where," I inquired, "have I seen you before?"

When two or more of the same speaker's sentences are quoted together, use only one set of quotation marks.

INCORRECT Tamisha suggested, "Let's donate the profits from the car wash to Project Day Care." "It provides help for many low-income working parents in this area."
CORRECT Tamisha suggested, "Let's donate the profits from the car wash to Project Day Care. It provides help for many low-income working parents in this area."

27f. A direct quotation is set off from the rest of the sentence by commas or by a question mark or an exclamation point.

EXAMPLES Mrs. Castaneda announced, "Remember that your research reports are due Monday," just as the bell rang.

MECHANICS

Elwyn asked, "On what date does the Ides of March fall?" when it was his turn to quiz the others in his study group.
"That's easy! It's March fifteenth!" Dot exclaimed.

27g. When used with quotation marks, other marks of punctuation are placed according to the following rules.

(1) Commas and periods are always placed inside the closing quotation marks.

EXAMPLE   "The concert tickets are sold out," Mary said, "and I had really hoped to go."

(2) Colons and semicolons are always placed outside the closing quotation marks.

EXAMPLES   The following students have been named "most likely to succeed": Corey Brown and Sally Ling.
Paka quoted a Cameroonian proverb, "By trying often, the monkey learns to jump from the tree"; it reminded me of the expression "If at first you don't succeed, try, try again."

(3) Question marks and exclamation points are placed inside the closing quotation marks if the quotation is a question or an exclamation. Otherwise, they are placed outside.

EXAMPLES   "What time is the game tomorrow?" Maria asked.
Why did you answer, "It doesn't matter"?

On the last lap Vicky said, "Do your best!"
Don't say, "I quit"!

EXERCISE 3   **Writing Sentences with Direct and Indirect Quotations**

Add quotation marks where they are needed in the following sentences. If a sentence is correct, write *C*.

EXAMPLE   **1.** When I saw this ad in the paper, I said to Grandmother Hsu, T'ai chi is Chinese, isn't it?
     1. *When I saw this ad in the paper, I said to Grandmother Hsu, "T'ai chi is Chinese, isn't it?"*

MECHANICS

1. She seemed pleased that I'd asked and replied, Yes, it's short for t'ai chi ch'uan.
2. She explained that t'ai chi ch'uan was developed in ancient China as a system of self-defense and as an aid to meditation.
3. But the ad says that it's for health and relaxation, I pointed out.
4. Yes, she said, it's that, too; it improves coordination and flexibility. In fact, in China people of all ages practice it.
5. You see, she went on, its postures and movements are all based on those of animals such as monkeys, birds, and snakes.
6. Snakes! I exclaimed.
7. Why do you twist your face so? Grandmother asked. If you observe a snake closely, you'll see how gracefully it moves.
8. That's true, I admitted.
9. Maybe, I said, thinking aloud, I'll check out this grand opening.
10. Imagine my surprise when Grandmother replied with a wide smile, I'll see you there. I'm one of the instructors.

MECHANICS

27h. When you write dialogue (a conversation), begin a new paragraph every time the speaker changes.

EXAMPLE A man of Merv, well known as the home of complicated thinkers, ran shouting one night through the city's streets. "Thief, Thief!" he cried.

The people surrounded him, and when he was a little calmer, asked: "Where was the thief?"

"In my house."

"Did you see him?"

"No."

"Was anything missing?"

"No."

"How do you know there was a thief then?"

"I was lying in bed when I remembered that thieves break into houses without a sound, and move very quietly. I could hear nothing, so I knew that there was a thief in the house, you fool!"

Niamat Khan, "The Thief"

27i. When a quoted passage consists of more than one paragraph, put quotation marks at the beginning of each paragraph and at the end of the entire passage. Do not put quotation marks after any paragraph but the last one in the passage.

EXAMPLE The saleswoman told my mother, "Now, this car is one of our hottest sellers. It has bucket seats, a CD player, and alloy wheels.

"It's also one of the safest cars on the road because of its heavy suspension and anti-lock brake system. It gets good mileage, too.

"All in all, I think this would be the perfect car for you."

NOTE: A long passage (not dialogue) quoted from a book or some other source is usually separated from the rest of the text in one of several ways. The entire passage may be either indented or set in smaller type. Sometimes the passage is single-spaced rather than double-spaced; however, Modern Language Association guidelines call for double-spacing. When a quoted passage is set off in one of these ways, no quotation marks are necessary.

EXAMPLE   The Sauk chief Black Hawk had this to say in his speech after his last battle against the whites:

> I fought hard. But your guns were well aimed. The bullets flew like birds in the air, and whizzed by our ears like the wind through the trees in winter. My warriors fell around me; it began to look dismal. I saw my evil day at hand. The sun rose dim on us in the morning, and at night it sank in a dark cloud, and looked like a ball of fire. That was the last sun that shone on Black Hawk. His heart is dead, and no longer beats quick in his bosom. He is now a prisoner to the white men; they will do with him as they wish. But he can stand torture, and is not afraid of death. He is no coward. Black Hawk is an Indian.

PICTURE THIS

It's 1870, somewhere on the plains of Nebraska. On your way back to camp, you and two friends stop to warm your hands at the chimney of this dugout built by a settler. One of your companions admires the comforts the dugout provides; the other scorns it because it can't be moved, as your own dwellings can. Write a short dialogue in which you side with one of your friends and the two of you try to convince your other friend to agree with you.

MECHANICS

Subject:
   dwellings
Audience:
   your
   companions
Purpose:
   to persuade

Tom Lovell, *The Hand Warmer.* National Cowboy Hall of Fame and Western Heritage Center, Oklahoma City, Oklahoma.

27j. Use quotation marks to enclose titles of articles, short stories, essays, poems, songs, individual episodes of TV series, and chapters and other parts of books and periodicals.

EXAMPLES   I chose to memorize "Pueblo Winter," by Bernice Zamora.
"The Unicorn in the Garden" is my favorite Thurber short story.
For tomorrow, read Chapter 8, "Twentieth-Century Playwrights."

☞ **REFERENCE NOTE:** Remember that the titles of long poems and long musical compositions are italicized, not enclosed in quotation marks. See the examples on page 832.

27k. Use quotation marks to enclose slang words, technical terms, and other unusual uses of words.

EXAMPLES   What's "in" one year is often "out" the following year.
The salesperson said that we should buy a "mouse" to operate the art software on our computer.

NOTE: It is best to avoid using slang words and technical terms whenever possible, except in dialogue, informal writing, technical writing, and other special contexts. If you're not sure whether a word is appropriate, look it up in a dictionary.

27l. Use single quotation marks to enclose a quotation within a quotation.

EXAMPLES   Ron said, "Dad yelled, 'No way!'"
Val asked, "Did you like my arrangement of 'America the Beautiful'?"

▶ REVIEW A

Correcting Sentences by Adding Underlining (Italics) or Quotation Marks

In the following sentences, write all the words that should be underlined (italicized) or placed in quotation marks, and add the appropriate markings.

MECHANICS

EXAMPLE   **1.** He read aloud The Tell-Tale Heart from The
Collected Stories of Edgar Allan Poe.
   1. *"The Tell-Tale Heart"; The Collected Stories of
Edgar Allan Poe*

1. Mr. Croce used the word denouement in discussing Rudolfo Anaya's novel Bless Me, Ultima.
2. By next Thursday I have to read the following works: The Medicine Bag, a short story by Virginia Driving Hawk Sneve; Crown of Shadows, a play by Rodolfo Usigli; and Daisy Bates: First Lady of Little Rock, an article by Lerone Bennett, Jr., in Ebony magazine.
3. Have you read this article, El Niño, Global Weather Disaster?
4. Karen asked me how many m's are in the word accommodate.
5. Oswald Rivera's 1990 novel Fire and Rain is about the Vietnam War.
6. My favorite plant is Saintpaulia ionantha, commonly called the African violet.
7. We had risotto alla milanese for dinner.
8. The short story Luke Baldwin's Vow deals with conflicts in values.
9. Wouldn't "Words and Music" be a good title for the new production by our drama club? Tom asked.
10. She crossed the t with such a flourish that she obliterated the letters above it.

REVIEW B

Correcting Sentences by Adding Underlining (Italics) and Quotation Marks

For each of the following sentences, add underlining (italics) or quotation marks where they are needed. If a sentence is correct, write *C*.

EXAMPLE   **1.** Look at this intriguing painting, said Marshall.
   1. *"Look at this intriguing painting,"* *said Marshall.*

1. He told us that he'd found the painting in Mexican American Artists, a book by Jacinto Quirate; the painting is in the chapter called The Third Decade.
2. The painting is by that man on the left, Emilio Aguirre, he explained, who titled it Alpha 1.

3. What do you see when you look at it? he asked.
4. You can't miss the Y on the left and the T on the right, he said.
5. But, he went on, can you make out the profile of a person sitting on the ground to the left of the T?
6. Laura said, Yes, the head is an O; but I objected, saying that it looked more like a Q to me.
7. I guess you're right, she said. Anyway, the G outlines the front of the body.
8. Ben asked, Is the little b on the big O supposed to be the person's glasses? And, he added, isn't that an M in the background, behind the T?
9. Look at this! exclaimed Marlene. If you turn the painting ninety degrees to the left, the body looks like a question mark.
10. Can you see why we all agreed when she said, Intriguing really is the word for Alpha 1?

WRITING APPLICATION

Writing an Interior Dialogue

Like many people, you probably carry on running conversations with yourself, especially when you have a decision to make. Expressing your ideas and feelings—even to yourself—can help you analyze a situation and arrive at a conclusion. Such interior conversations can involve two, three, four, or more points of view. If you were to write out one of these conversations, you would probably give each point of view a name and use quotation marks to reproduce the dialogue exactly.

▶ WRITING ACTIVITY

You're scheduled to give an oral report on a short story of your own choosing. Write an interior dialogue recording your thoughts as you decide which of two stories to use.

Prewriting   List the titles of several short stories you've read. Then choose the two that, for whatever reason, you feel most strongly about. Next, determine how you'll distinguish between your different points of view as you decide which story to choose. For example, you could use your first name for one side, your middle name for another, and other names for as many different points of view as you have.

Writing   Write down your thoughts as you consider the pros and cons about using the two stories. (You may want to skim both stories first, but remember, at this point you're not analyzing them, you're just deciding which one to use.) Keep writing until you reach a decision. Don't worry about grammar, mechanics, and usage, but do try to keep track of where you are in the decision-making process.

Evaluating and Revising   As you reread your dialogue, check whether your diction (word choice) and sentence structure sound authentic to you. Can you tell at all times which story you're referring to? Is it clear which one you decided to report on, and why? Revise your writing to make it express your thinking process more accurately.

MECHANICS

Proofreading and Publishing As you proofread, pay special attention to your use of quotation marks and to the capitalization and punctuation before and after them. Then, photocopy your dialogue or input it on a computer. You and your classmates could tape-record your dialogues or act them out for one another in person or on film. Then you could discuss your responses to writing an interior dialogue to help in decision making.

Correcting Sentences by Adding Italics or Quotation Marks

For each of the following sentences, add italics (underlining) or quotation marks where they are needed. If a sentence is correct, write C.

1. Why did you buy another sleeping bag? she asked.
2. In his surrender speech, Chief Joseph of the Nez Percé said that he would never fight again.
3. The dance company is performing Swan Lake, a ballet by Tchaikovsky.
4. Anita asked, Why did he say, I won't go to the game?
5. The Boston Cooking School Cookbook, now known as The Fannie Farmer Cookbook, was first published in 1891.
6. The first word my baby brother said was bird.
7. There's an article in this issue of Newsweek that I'd like you to read, said Joan.
8. Wendell B. Harris wrote, directed, and starred in the 1991 movie Chameleon Street.
9. Her street address has four 4's in it, said Rose. Did you know that?
10. Susan drove one hundred miles, he replied, to see you on your birthday.

11. My art teacher subscribes to Godzilla, a periodical about Asian artists working in New York City.
12. Please write to me, Joyce requested. I want to keep in touch with you.
13. In my report I wrote, One reviewer praised Dee Brown's book Bury My Heart at Wounded Knee in these words: an important and angry book; but I forgot to cite the New Republic magazine as the source of the quote.
14. As we ran down the street, Charles shouted, Faster! Faster!
15. Sally said, John just whispered, I'll be at the game tonight.
16. Our next history assignment is Chapter 14, Great Ideals in the Constitution.
17. Did you read the article The Costs of College Today?
18. My aunt asked, What did your friend mean when he said that you look rad in your new glasses?
19. The Novelist is in a collection of W. H. Auden's shorter poems.
20. You often use the French expression au revoir, said Hannah.

MECHANICS

28 PUNCTUATION

Apostrophes, Hyphens, Dashes, Parentheses

Diagnostic Test

A. Using Apostrophes and Hyphens Correctly

Add apostrophes and hyphens where they are needed in the following sentences. [Note: Some sentences contain more than one error.]

EXAMPLE **1. The childrens boots were lined up outside the door.**
    1. *children's*

1. The towns record on supporting youth projects has been good.
2. We hope to see some Aztec and Mayan ruins during our three week vacation in Mexico.
3. The police officer said that everyones house should be searched for the missing child.
4. Only fifty three people went to our ballet recital, and thirty of them were our relatives.
5. I bought four pairs of gloves as my two sisters birth day presents.

6. Judo, a Japanese martial art that is popular with both men and women, calls for strength, skill, and self discipline.
7. Christopher's writing is hard to read because his *a*s look like *o*s.
8. Were going on a field trip to the art museum to see the exhibit of post Victorian cartoons.
9. The womens basketball team, which is coached by an ex Laker, has run up quite an impressive string of victories.
10. Sampson and Smiths Bakery, which displays its pas tries in the window, is around the corner from my house.

B. Using Dashes and Parentheses Correctly

Add dashes or parentheses where they are needed in each of the following sentences. (Do not add commas or colons.)

EXAMPLE   **1.** The school's volunteers freshmen, sophomores, and juniors were honored during the assembly.
      1. *The school's volunteers—freshmen, sophomores, and juniors—were honored during the assembly.*

11. My cousins like many of Charlie Pride's songs his "Crystal Chandeliers" is their favorite.
12. When we met my chemistry teacher at the mall, my little sister's question "Why doesn't that man have any hair on his head?" embarrassed me so much I wanted to hide.
13. This report contains information about agriculture in three South American countries Brazil, Argentina, and Colombia.
14. Crystal's time for the fifty-yard dash the fastest time of anyone on the team qualified her for the regional track meet.
15. I read the wrong chapter for my history homework a disastrous mistake!
16. Mary Ellen Jefferson, a former district attorney, will speak at Thursday's assembly I'll have to miss gym class and will address the topic of student rights.

MECHANICS

17. Our newspaper, the *Sexton High Chronicle* it used to be called the *Weekly Warrior* won the highest award in the state.
18. Bessie Coleman I read an article about her was the first licensed African American pilot.
19. Rushing to catch the bus, I dropped my books in the mud I never should have overslept! and then lost the heel of my shoe.
20. He works nearly all day in his garden he retired last year and is always weeding, mulching, and pruning.

Apostrophes

Possessive Case

The possessive case of a noun or a pronoun shows ownership or relationship.

OWNERSHIP	**Jorge's** calculator has a solar battery. Where did she buy **her** bracelet?
RELATIONSHIP	**Pam's** aunt is a plumber. The mother birds had fed **their** young.

Many writers are not always sure about when an apostrophe should be used. Whenever you are in doubt about whether or not to use an apostrophe, try an "of" phrase in place of the word. If the "of" phrase makes sense, then an apostrophe is needed.

EXAMPLE: **yesterdays news** [Should there be an apostrophe in *yesterdays*?]
news "of yesterday" [Because this makes good sense, an apostrophe should be used.]
ANSWER: **yesterday's news**

Nouns in the Possessive Case

28a. To form the possessive case of a singular noun, add an apostrophe and an *s*.

EXAMPLES   Barbara's house   one boy's uniform
                a week's salary   that stereo's speakers

A proper name ending in *s* may add only an apostrophe if

- the name has two or more syllables
  and
- the addition of *s* after the apostrophe would make the name awkward to pronounce.

      EXAMPLES   Xerxes' army
                        Moses' law
                        Sophocles' plays

However, most proper names that end in *s* form the possessive case by adding an apostrophe and an *s*.

EXAMPLES   James's idea
                Dickens's stories
                Dr. Seuss's books

Singular common nouns ending in *s* need both the apostrophe *and* the *s* if the added *s* is pronounced as a separate syllable.

EXAMPLES   the princess's slipper
                my boss's orders
                a bus's wheels

28b.   To form the possessive case of a plural noun ending in *s*, add only the apostrophe.

EXAMPLES   cats' owners   cities' problems
                coaches' records   princesses' duties

The few plural nouns that do not end in *s* form the possessive case by adding an apostrophe and an *s*.

EXAMPLES   geese's migration   children's stories

☞ **REFERENCE NOTE:** For more examples of irregular nouns, see page 878.

NOTE: Don't use an apostrophe to form the *plural* of a noun.

          INCORRECT   The four horse's pulled the wagon
            CORRECT   The four horses pulled the wagon.

MECHANICS

EXERCISE 1 **Writing the Possessive Forms of Nouns**

Make four columns headed *Singular, Singular Possessive, Plural,* and *Plural Possessive.* Write those forms of each of the following words. If you don't know how to spell a plural form, check a dictionary.

	Singular	Singular Possessive	Plural	Plural Possessive
EXAMPLE				
1.	temple	temple's	temples	temples'

1. governor
2. secretary
3. bird
4. deer
5. woman
6. picture
7. pencil
8. class
9. chief
10. mouse

Pronouns in the Possessive Case

28c. Possessive personal pronouns and the relative pronoun *whose* do not require an apostrophe.

> ### Possessive Personal Pronouns
> my, mine   our, ours
> your, yours   their, theirs
> his, her, hers, its

My, your, her, its, our, and *their* are used before a noun. *Mine, yours, hers, ours,* and *theirs* are used as subjects, complements, or objects. *His* is used in both ways.

EXAMPLES   This is **my** desk. This desk is **mine.**
I borrowed **your** pencil. I borrowed a pencil of **yours.**
Her work is excellent. **Hers** is the best work.
Clara is **our** captain; Dena is **theirs.**

☞ REFERENCE NOTE: Don't confuse the possessive forms of pronouns with contractions, such as *whose* and *who's, its* and *it's, their* and *they're,* and *your* and *you're.* See pages 885, 889, and 890.

28d. Indefinite pronouns in the possessive case require an apostrophe and an *s.*

EXAMPLES   anyone**'s** choice   either**'s** idea

☞ REFERENCE NOTE: See page 517 for a list of indefinite pronouns.

MECHANICS

Compounds in the Possessive Case

28e. In compound words, names of organizations and business firms, and words showing joint possession, only the last word is possessive in form.

COMPOUND WORDS	someone **else's** problem sister-in-**law's** office
ORGANIZATIONS	board of **directors'** report Urban **League's** membership
BUSINESS FIRMS JOINT POSSESSION	Acosta and **Rivera's** law firm Bob and **Jim's** canoe Kimi and **Tanaki's** plan aunt and **uncle's** photograph

However, when one of the words showing joint possession is a pronoun, both words should be possessive in form.

EXAMPLE **Sean's** and her conversation

NOTE: To avoid forming a possessive that sounds awkward, use a phrase beginning with *of* instead.

> AWKWARD   the Samuel H. Scripps American Dance Festival Award's winner
> BETTER   the winner of the Samuel H. Scripps American Dance Festival Award

28f. When two or more persons possess something individually, each of their names is possessive in form.

EXAMPLES **Michael's** and **Lila's** wallets
Denise's and **Mark's** books

▶ EXERCISE 2   **Correcting Phrases by Adding Apostrophes**

Proofread the following phrases, adding apostrophes where they are needed. If a phrase is correct, write C.

MECHANICS

EXAMPLE   **1.** the cameras lens
           1. *the camera*'s lens

1. a weeks pay
2. Anns and my project
3. two pairs of tennis shoes
4. my father-in-laws boat
5. a good nights sleep

6. Socrates oration
7. Lynns and Mikes shoes
8. the seconds ticking by
9. the two balloonists feats
10. a citizens rights

EXERCISE 3   Correcting Paragraphs by Adding Apostrophes

For each sentence in the following paragraphs, write each word that should be in the possessive case, and add the missing apostrophe.

EXAMPLE   **[1]** Last week I followed my parents suggestion and enrolled in an amateur photography class offered by our citys art center.
        1. *parents'; city's*

[1] I shared my mom and dads exasperation when, once again, I spent a whole weeks allowance on disappointing pictures. [2] I had borrowed Uncle Freds expensive camera; but even with all that cameras extra features, my photographs looked like childrens smudged finger paintings.

[3] My pictures of Bob and Ruths wedding reception, our familys social event of the year, were destroyed when I fell into the pool with my camera. [4] Last summer I also took pictures during our weeklong visit to Arizonas famous Painted Desert. [5] Unfortunately, I did not understand enough about the suns strong light at midday, and most of my photographs had that washed-out look.

[6] My lifes most embarrassing moment occurred when I took a picture of my class for the schools yearbook and discovered that I had forgotten to put film in the camera. [7] Another time, I took my camera to Toms party but could not get anyones attention long enough to set up the shots that I wanted. [8] As a result, I gave up on people and tried to take my pets pictures; however, a dogs will and a parakeets wings are hard to control. [9] After all these bad experiences, I knew that I needed a professionals advice. [10] I'm pleased to report that during the very first

photography class, the instructor raised all the students confidence, including mine.

▶ EXERCISE 4 **Proofreading for Errors in Possessive Forms**

Most of the following sentences contain an incorrect possessive form. For each error, give the correct form of the word. If a sentence is correct, write *C*.

EXAMPLE **1.** The island nation of the Philippines bears the marks of both Spains and the United States occupations.
1. *Spain's; United States'*

1. The countrys national language is Pilipino, but its people also speak Spanish, English, and other regional languages.
2. Did you know that the yo-yos earliest use was as a weapon in the Philippine jungles?
3. My mothers boss was visiting the Philippines when Corazon Aquino became president in 1986.
4. He took this picture of Mrs. Aquino and some of her supporters dressed in yellow, the color identified with their campaign.

MECHANICS

LUZON

N
W ⊢ E
S

. Pinatubo ●
Manila ⊛

PHILIPPINE
SEA

VISAYAN
ISLANDS

TH
JA
A

ALAWAN

5. Tina's and Phil's plan to visit the Philippines was postponed when Mount Pinatubo erupted in 1991.
6. The Philippines capital and largest city is Manila, which is on the big island of Luzon.

7. Both Kim and Marta's lunches came with delicious Filipino custard.
8. It's anyones guess how many islands actually make up the Philippines, though there are certainly more than seven thousand islands.
9. The Spanish monarch who's soldiers named the Philippines was King Philip II.
10. Childrens pastimes in the Philippines include kite flying and swimming.

Contractions

28g. Use an apostrophe to show where letters, words, or numerals have been omitted in a contraction.

A *contraction* is a shortened form of a word, a figure, or a group of words. The apostrophes in contractions show where letters, words, or numerals have been left out.

Common Contractions	
who is .... who's	she will ...... she'll
there is .... there's	I am .... I'm
could have ..... could've	you are ..... you're
1993.............'93	we had........we'd
of the clock ..... o'clock	she has........she's
let us ....let's	Lisa is .... Lisa's

The adverb *not* is often shortened to *n't* and added to a verb without any change in the verb's spelling.

EXAMPLES
is not .... isn't	were not .... weren't
are not ...... aren't	has not .... hasn't
does not .... doesn't	have not .... haven't
do not .... don't	had not ...... hadn't
did not ...... didn't	would not .. wouldn't
was not ..... wasn't	should not .. shouldn't

EXCEPTIONS   cannot .... can't   will not .... won't

Make sure that you don't confuse contractions with possessive pronouns.

MECHANICS

CONTRACTIONS	POSSESSIVE PRONOUNS
Who's next? [who is]	**Whose** turn is next?
It's purring. [It is]	Listen to **its** purr.
You're late. [You are]	**Your** report is late.
There's a mule. [There is]	That mule is **theirs.**
They're healthy pets. [They are]	**Their** pets are healthy.

▶ EXERCISE 5   **Using Contractions**

You are learning how to draw these cartoon figures in action. Using these sketches as models, make five original drawings of characters in motion. Then write captions to go with your drawings. In your captions, use at least five of the following expressions correctly as contractions.

1. should not
2. they have
3. of the clock
4. they would

5. were not
6. she will
7. he is
8. let us

9. who is
10. does not

MECHANICS

Graceful fall

Running

Kicking

Awkward fall

Jumping

Back kick

Diving

Cartoons from *Drawing and Selling Cartoons* by Jack Markow, copyright © 1964 by Grosset & Dunlap, Inc. Reprinted by permission of Grosset & Dunlap, Inc.

▶ REVIEW A   **Correcting Sentences by Adding Apostrophes**

Identify each word that needs an apostrophe in the following sentences. Then insert the apostrophes correctly.

EXAMPLE   **1.** Werent you the one who said you didnt like
eggplant?
1. *Weren't; didn't*

1. Whos going to be at Leon and Joshs party?
2. Lets hide and see if theyll look for us.
3. I cant find the calamata olives and the feta cheese for the Greek salad.
4. Is her doctors appointment at nine oclock?
5. Cleve doesn't have time to mow both his and Rays lawns.
6. Thats the best idea youve had in two days.
7. Were lucky that that dogs barking didn't awaken them.
8. Im trying to follow Pauls map to Jeans house.
9. Its hailing; therefore, I dont think you should go skiing.
10. Elise couldnt remember the characteristics of the tiger in the Chinese zodiac.

▶ EXERCISE 6   **Recognizing the Correct Use of Apostrophes**

Choose the correct word in parentheses in each of the following sentences.

EXAMPLE   **1.** (*It's, Its*) never too late to learn something new.
1. *It's*

1. (*You're, Your*) sure that (*you're, your*) allowed to bring (*you're, your*) book to the exam?
2. (*Whose, Who's*) idea was (*you're, your*) trip to the National Civil Rights Museum in Memphis?
3. (*They're, Their*) trying to sell (*they're, their*) house.
4. (*It's, Its*) the best choice.
5. Do you know (*who's, whose*) responsible for (*they're, their*) confusion?
6. I hope the dog can find (*it's, its*) way home.
7. (*It's, Its*) Philip (*who's, whose*) always late.
8. Although (*it's, its*) been snowing all day, (*they're, their*) still planning to go.
9. (*Who's, Whose*) the designer of (*they're, their*) float for Galveston's Mardi Gras parade?
10. I know (*you're, your*) upset with the plan, but (*it's, its*) the only way to solve the problem.

PICTURE THIS

You are an art critic for *ARTnews* magazine. Write a short review of this modern sculpture. In your review, try to convince readers that *Geometric Mouse* either is or is not good art. In writing the review, rely on your own taste, as well as your understanding of art. Begin by stating your opinion of the sculpture, and then give reasons to support that opinion. Include five different contractions in your review. When you finish writing, compare your review with those of your classmates. Can your class agree on the artistic value of this work?

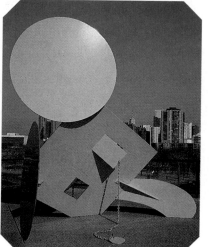

Walker Art Center, Minneapolis, Gift of Mr. and Mrs. Miles Q. Fiterman, 1991.

Subject: a sculpture
Audience: *ARTnews* readers
Purpose: to persuade

MECHANICS

Plurals

28h. Use an apostrophe and an *–s* to form the plurals of some letters, numerals, symbols, and some words referred to as words.

As a rule, only an *–s* is added to form the plurals of most letters and most words used as words.

EXAMPLES Make your uppercase *W*s higher so that they don't look like lowercase *w*s.
Mr. Carr suggested that I replace some of the *and*s in my paper with other words that are more exact.

However, in some cases both an apostrophe and an *–s* are added to prevent confusion.

EXAMPLES   There are four *s*'s and four *i*'s in *Mississippi.* [Without an apostrophe, the plural of *i* would look like the word *is.* Since an apostrophe and *s* are used to form the plural of one letter, an apostrophe and *s* are also used with the other letter for consistency.]

Mr. Carr suggested that I replace some of the *so*'s in my paper with other words that are more exact. [Without the apostrophe, the plural of *so* could be confused with the acronym *sos.*]

NOTE: Using both an apostrophe and an *s* is never wrong. If you have any doubt about whether or not to use the apostrophe, use it.

☞ REFERENCE NOTE: For more information about forming these kinds of plurals and the plurals of numerals, see pages 879–880.

▶ REVIEW B   **Correcting Sentences by Adding Apostrophes**

For each of the following sentences, write all the items needing apostrophes, and add the apostrophes.

EXAMPLE   **1.** You may agree with the school boards decision, but I dont.
1. *school board's; don't*

1. Arent you familiar with the expression "Threes a crowd"?
2. Youve forgotten that there are two *l*s in *llama.*
3. The countrys first African American on the Supreme Court was Justice Thurgood Marshall, who was appointed in 1967 and retired in 91.
4. Lewis Carrolls novel *Alices Adventures in Wonderland* was originally called *Alices Adventures Underground.*
5. Whos going to change the babies diapers?
6. After school were going to visit Pams brother; hes in St. Marys Hospital.
7. Rochelle thinks that shell be taking both biology and English this term.
8. Its been six weeks since I checked the cars oil and its tires.
9. Your story would be better if youd remove about thirty *verys.*
10. She learned the Hawaiian alphabets twelve letters, but Max didnt.

Hyphens

Word Division

28i. Use a hyphen to divide a word at the end of a line.

EXAMPLE Even with today's modern technology, scientists can ac‑count for only about 10 percent of the universe.

As the example shows, a word at the end of a line is always divided between syllables. If you're not sure about a word's syllables, check a dictionary. Also, keep in mind the following rules for dividing words.

(1) Do not divide one-syllable words.

INCORRECT After a long journey, the Spanish explorers reach‑ed their destination.

CORRECT After a long journey, the Spanish explorers reached their destination.

(2) Words containing double consonants should usually be divided between the double consonants.

EXAMPLES cor‑rect   begin‑ning

👉 REFERENCE NOTE: See the next subrule, 28i (3), for exceptions like *tell-ing* and *call-ing*.

(3) Words with a prefix or suffix can usually be divided between the prefix and the root or the root and the suffix.

EXAMPLES pro‑mote   peace‑ful   tell‑ing   de‑pend‑able

(4) If a word is already hyphenated, divide it only at the hyphen.

INCORRECT My stepsister Melissa plans to take a course in self-de‑fense.

CORRECT My stepsister Melissa plans to take a course in self‑defense.

INCORRECT Ms. Malamud always seems to have such a hap‑py-go-lucky attitude.

CORRECT Ms. Malamud always seems to have such a happy‑go-lucky attitude.

MECHANICS

(5) Do not divide a word so that one letter stands alone.

INCORRECT	In the gloomy twilight, we had caught a momentar-y glimpse of them.
CORRECT	In the gloomy twilight, we had caught a momen-tary glimpse of them.
INCORRECT	The other driver suddenly changed lanes to go a-round the line of cars.
CORRECT	The other driver suddenly changed lanes to go around the line of cars.

▶ EXERCISE 7 | **Using Hyphens to Divide Words at the Ends of Lines**

Write each of the following words, adding a hyphen where you would divide the word at the end of a line. If a word should *not* be divided, write *no hyphen*. If you are unsure where to divide a word, look it up in a dictionary.

EXAMPLE **1.** harmonious
1. *har-mo-ni-ous*

1. Olympic
2. algebra
3. toast
4. pemmican
5. drummer
6. alert
7. someone
8. Honduras
9. reservation
10. Johnny-come-lately

Compound Words

Some compound words are written as one single word (*blueberry*); some are hyphenated (*blue-collar*); and some are written as two or more words (*blue jay, Blue Ridge Mountains*).

Whenever you are not sure about the spelling of a compound word, look up the word in a recently published dictionary.

28j. Use a hyphen with compound numbers from *twenty-one* to *ninety-nine* and with fractions used as adjectives.

EXAMPLES twenty-seven students
a two-thirds majority [but *two thirds* of the class]

28k. Use a hyphen with the prefixes *ex–*, *self–*, and *all–*, with the suffix *–elect,* and with all prefixes before a proper noun or proper adjective.

EXAMPLES   ex-president   mid-December
               self-control   pro-American
               all-purpose   anti-Stalinist
               secretary-elect   pre-Civil War

28l. Hyphenate a compound adjective when it precedes the noun it modifies. Do not use a hyphen if one of the modifiers is an adverb ending in *–ly.*

EXAMPLES   a well-organized trip [But *The trip was well organized.*]
               an after-school job
               a perfectly good answer

NOTE: Some compound adjectives are always hyphenated, no matter whether they precede or follow the nouns they modify.

EXAMPLES   full-scale
               down-to-earth

If you have any doubt about whether a compound adjective is hyphenated or not, look up the word in a dictionary.

▶ EXERCISE 8   **Hyphenating Words Correctly**

For each of the following sentences, write and hyphenate the compound words that should be hyphenated.

EXAMPLE   **1.** The host of that late night show interviewed an expert on America's pre Civil War years.
           1. *late-night; pre-Civil War*

1. Ex students were not allowed at the festively decorated post prom party.
2. His self confidence faded when he forgot his well planned speech.
3. Twenty five students said they had never heard of the well traveled Overland Trail to California.
4. Two thirds of the class voted, but the proposal was defeated by a seven tenths majority.

5. Our new governor elect was once an all American football player.
6. In our last debate, some students were pro United Nations, but others were anti UN.
7. General Colin Powell, who is a former resident of the Bronx, spoke quite eloquently about the importance of self determination.
8. We all had to memorize a list of twenty five well known writers and their works.
9. You must turn in your reports by mid November.
10. Christopher's achievement test scores ranked in the eighty eighth percentile.

Dashes

Most parenthetical elements are set off by commas or parentheses.

EXAMPLES Felipe, **however,** had a better idea.
          Her suggestion **(that we serve fruit and cheese instead of junk food)** was approved unanimously.

Sometimes, though, such elements call for a sharper separation from the rest of the sentence. In such cases, dashes are used.

NOTE: On a typewriter or a computer, indicate a dash by typing two hyphens. Do not leave a space before, between, or after the hyphens.

28m. Use a dash to indicate an abrupt break in thought or speech or an unfinished statement or question.

EXAMPLES The party—I'm sorry I forgot to tell you—was not changed to next week.
          When Jiffy was born—he was the last puppy—we weren't sure he would survive.
          "Why—why won't you believe me?" Ronnie asked pleadingly.
          "What I meant was—" Vonda began as the doorbell rang.

MECHANICS

28n. Use a dash to mean *namely, that is, in other words,* and similar expressions that come before an explanation.

EXAMPLES Our family owns two vehicles—a station wagon and a pickup truck. [*namely*]
The weather was unseasonably warm—in the low eighties—which was a welcome change. [*that is*]

NOTE: Either the dash or a colon is acceptable in the first example above.

Parentheses

28o. Use parentheses to enclose material of minor importance in a sentence.

EXAMPLES The Pyramid of the Magician (I never thought I'd actually see it in person) rose majestically against the purple sky of Uxmal, in the Mexican Yucatán.
My grandmother (she's only fifty) swims three miles every day.

Material enclosed in parentheses may range from a single word to a short sentence. A short sentence in parentheses may stand by itself or may be included in the main sentence.

When punctuation marks belong with the parenthetical materials, place them inside the parentheses. When they belong with the sentence as a whole, place them outside the parentheses.

EXAMPLES Mark your answers with a lead pencil. (Do not use ink.) [The parenthetical sentence stands by itself.]
The child's question ("What inning is it?") tickled the rest of us watching the football game. [The parenthetical sentence is a quoted question included in the main sentence.]
When we reached Shaker Heights (it's just outside Cleveland), we met our cousins for dinner. [The parenthetical sentence is a statement included within the main sentence. Notice that no period is used at the end of a parenthetical declarative sentence included within another sentence.]

GUIDELINES FOR PUNCTUATING PARENTHETICAL MATERIAL

Commas, dashes, and parentheses are all used to enclose parenthetical material. In general, follow these guidelines for determining when to use the three different types of punctuation marks.

1. Remember that only material that can be omitted without changing the sentence's basic meaning is considered parenthetical.
2. Use commas to set off elements that are closely related to the rest of the sentence.
3. Use dashes to emphasize an abrupt change in thought.
4. Use parentheses to minimize the importance of the enclosed material.
5. Don't confuse your reader by using too many parenthetical elements.

EXAMPLES   We rehearsed for the show, a wonderful musical comedy.
We rehearsed for the show—the musical event of the year!
We rehearsed (at least those of us who managed to remember our lines did) for the show.

▶ EXERCISE 9   **Correcting Sentences by Using Dashes and Parentheses**

Write the following sentences, adding dashes and parentheses where they are needed. If a sentence is correct, write *C*.

EXAMPLE   1. The Oak Ridge Boys and Alabama I have every one of their albums have won many awards.
1. *The Oak Ridge Boys and Alabama (I have every one of their albums) have won many awards.*

1. "Yankee Doodle" it was the unofficial United States anthem at the time was played after the signing of the Treaty of Ghent.
2. Inspired by the view at the top of Pikes Peak, Katherine Lee Bates wrote the words to the song "America the Beautiful."

3. Gloria Estefan I love her songs! gave a concert here, and it was sold out.
4. There were three original members of the Sons of the Pioneers Roy Rogers his real name is Leonard Slye, Bob Nolan, and Tim Spencer.
5. Linda Ronstadt has recorded many different kinds of music, including rock, songs from the 1930s and '40s, and Mexican tunes.
6. The Beatles used several names Foreverly Brothers, the Cavemen, the Moondogs, and the Quarrymen before they settled on Beatles.
7. Bob Dylan's real name Robert Allen Zimmerman isn't commonly known.
8. Cathy agreed to listen to Mozart's concertos what a surprise! if her parents would listen to one of Paula Abdul's tapes.
9. Last night's concert was about average the beat was good, but the singers were uninspired.
10. Whitney Houston had a hit song Wouldn't Francis Scott Key be pleased? with her version of "The Star-Spangled Banner."

▶ REVIEW C **Proofreading for Errors in Punctuation**

Each of the following sentences contains at least one error in punctuation. Correct these errors by adding apostrophes, hyphens, dashes, or parentheses where they are needed.

EXAMPLE **1.** Dont you ever wonder I frequently do about who invented different kinds of machines and tools?
1. *Don't; —I frequently do—*

1. Both Trishs and Roberts reports the ones required for social studies were about the shoe industry.
2. Trish joked that she chose the subject because at least seventy five percent of the world's students wear shoes.
3. I thought the other report the one that Robert gave on the invention of the lasting machine was better written, though.
4. The lasting machine its many parts are numbered in the intricate patent drawing on the next page changed the shoe industrys future.

5. The machines inventor the distinguished looking young man pictured below was Jan Matzeliger.
6. He came to the United States from Dutch Guiana now Suriname in the 1870s and found work as a shoemakers apprentice.
7. Matzeliger wasnt happy with the amount of workers time that was spent putting shoes together.
8. Within ten years time, he perfected a machine that shaped leather for the upper shoe and attached it to the sole.
9. Matzeligers patent for this all important machine was granted in 1883.
10. The United Shoe Manufacturing Companys decision to buy the machine gave that company control of the United States shoe market.

No. 274,207.   J. E. MATZELIGER
LASTING MACHINE
PATENTED MAR. 20, 188

MECHANICS

WRITING APPLICATION

Using Dashes in Poetry

Have you ever noticed that many poems contain dashes? Poets use dashes not only to indicate sharp separations of thoughts but also to emphasize particular words or phrases. Notice how John Ciardi uses dashes in the following poem.

How Time Goes

How old am I? I really don't know,
  But I can tell you I have spent
My whole life—up to a minute ago—
  Being younger than I am now. I meant
To keep it that way, I suppose,
But that's how it is with time—it goes.

Which use of the dash in the poem signals a break in thought? Which use of the dash means *namely*?

▶ WRITING ACTIVITY

You've decided to enter a local poetry contest for high school students. The name of the contest is Poetry for Our Time, and all the poems have to reflect students' ideas about current subjects. For the contest, write a poem that uses at least four dashes.

Prewriting Start by making a list of some subjects that interest you. You might list abstract subjects, such as love and peace, or concrete ones, such as environmental or school issues. Choose a subject from your list, and then freewrite about it. List as many sensory details as you can to describe your subject. Then start grouping these details to create a loose structure for your poem. Before you begin writing your poem, decide on a rhyme scheme and rhythm.

Writing Use your freewriting notes to write your first draft. As you form your ideas into lines of poetry, keep in mind your rhyme scheme and rhythm pattern. Choose words carefully, paying attention both to their sound and to the images they create.

Evaluating and Revising Read your poem silently to be sure that it says what you want it to. Add, cut, or rearrange details to express your ideas more effectively. Then read your poem aloud and listen to the sound and rhythm of the words you've used. Make any changes that are necessary to create the rhyme scheme and rhythm you chose in your prewriting. Be sure that you've used at least four dashes in your poem.

MECHANICS

Proofreading and Publishing Now, check the spelling and punctuation in your poem. If you've typed your poem or input it on a keyboard, check to see that the spacing around hyphens and dashes is correct. You could publish your poem by submitting it to a school newspaper or literary magazine, or by reading it aloud to the class.

Review: Posttest

A. Correcting Sentences by Using Apostrophes and Hyphens

For each of the following sentences, write the word or words that should have an apostrophe or a hyphen, and add the appropriate punctuation mark. If a sentence is correct, write C.

EXAMPLE **1.** Michaels stamp collection contains thirty two rare stamps.
1. *Michael's; thirty-two*

1. Because of the sudden blizzard, the armies supplies were cut off.
2. Its frustrating when the car wont start because its battery is dead.
3. After hours of discussion, the decision is that we need a two thirds majority to pass new rules in the student council.
4. Even though Li moved here from Korea last year, shes making As in most of her classes.
5. If you go to the game on Saturday, whos going to watch the children?
6. Miranda had the flu this past week, and now she has five days worth of homework to do this weekend.
7. Rodney interviewed the treasurer elect of the Honor Society for the "Personality Profile" column in the school newspaper.

8. James Berry, who was born in Jamaica, wrote the well received collection of short stories *A Thief in the Village and Other Stories.*

9. One of my aunts favorite expressions is "Never let the sun set on your anger."

10. My brother in law Murray works at a resort in New Yorks Catskill Mountains.

11. If we return the tape recorder by five oclock, the store clerk said she would refund our deposit.

12. The alarm clock hasnt worked since the morning I knocked it off the night stand.

13. Last week, the senator presented as evidence the anti American pamphlets distributed by the terror ist group.

14. You have such a wonderful singing voice that Im sure youll get a part in the school musical.

15. Dont be alarmed, Brian; the red +s on your paper indicate correct answers.

B. Correcting Sentences by Using Dashes and Parentheses

Rewrite the following sentences, adding dashes or parentheses where they are needed. (Do not add commas or colons to these sentences.)

EXAMPLE **1.** The books on that table they are all nonfiction are on sale today.

    1. *The books on that table—they are all nonfiction—are on sale today.*

16. The discovery of gold at Sutter's Mill brought floods of people settlers, miners, prospectors, and merchants to California in their covered wagons.

17. The old white house on Tenth Street it was once a governor's mansion is a landmark in our town.

18. Answer the ten questions on this English quiz be careful, they're tricky! and then write a couplet or a limerick for extra credit.

19. My mom's Persian cookbook has a recipe I'm not making this up for eggplant pickles.

20. The Atacama Desert the driest region on the earth receives so little rain that it can barely be measured.

29 SPELLING

Improving Your Spelling

Good Spelling Habits

The following techniques can help you become a better speller.

1. *To learn the spelling of a word, pronounce the word, study it, and write it.*

   - First, pronounce the word.
   - Second, study the word, noting especially any parts that might be hard to remember.
   - Third, write the word from memory. Check your spelling.
   - If you misspelled the word, repeat the process.

2. *Use a dictionary.* Don't guess about correct spelling. Look up any words you misspell. In the dictionary, you can often find other, related words that may help you remember the correct spelling. For example, it may be easier to spell *denomination* after you see its kinship with the words *nominate* and *denominator*.

3. **Spell by syllables.** A *syllable* is a word part that can be pronounced by itself.

> EXAMPLES   **pul′•sate** [two syllables]
> **bul′•le•tin** [three syllables]
> **en•vi′•ron•ment** [four syllables]

4. **Pronounce words carefully.** If you say *suprise* instead of *surprise*, you'll likely misspell the word. When you look up the spelling of a word in a dictionary, notice how the word is pronounced. Knowing the correct pronunciation of a word will usually help you spell it correctly.

> EXAMPLES   **ath*l*etic** [not atha*l*etic]
> **es*c*ape** [not ex*c*ape]
> **heigh*t*** [not heigh*th*]

5. **Proofread for careless spelling errors.** Reread your writing carefully, correcting any mistakes and unclear letters.

6. **Keep a spelling notebook.** Divide each page into four columns:

> COLUMN 1   Correctly spell the word you missed. (Never enter a misspelled word.)
> COLUMN 2   Write the word again, dividing it into syllables and accenting the stressed syllable(s).
> COLUMN 3   Write the word a third time, circling the part(s) that cause you trouble.
> COLUMN 4   Jot down any comments that will help you remember the correct spelling.

MECHANICS

Correct Spelling	Syllables and Accents	Trouble Spot	Comments
February	Feb′•ru•ar•y	Feb(ru)ary	Pronounce correctly.
disapproval	dis′•ap•pro′val	di(sa)ppro(val)	Study rules 29d and 29f.

Spelling Rules

The following rules can help you remember how to spell many words.

ie and *ei*

29a. Write *ie* when the sound is long *e*, except after *c*.

EXAMPLES   chief, believe, niece, deceive, perceive, receipt
EXCEPTIONS   either, leisure, neither, seize, weird

29b. Write *ei* when the sound is not long *e*.

EXAMPLES   forfeit, freight, height, neighbor, veil, weigh
EXCEPTIONS   friend, mischief

–cede, –ceed, and *–sede*

29c. The only English word that ends in *–sede* is *supersede.* Only three words end in *–ceed: exceed, proceed,* and *succeed.* Most other words with this sound end in *–cede.*

EXAMPLES   concede, precede, recede

 EXERCISE 1   **Proofreading a Paragraph to Correct Spelling Errors**

Proofread the following paragraph, correcting the ten misspelled words.

[1] During the 1920s, one craze superceded another, each one weirder than the one that preceeded it. [2] Pictured on the next page is fifteen-year-old Avon Foreman, who acheived fame in Baltimore for his bizarre liesure-time activity. [3] In 1929, he spent ten days, ten hours, ten minutes, and ten seconds perched atop a hickory sapling, at a hieght of eighteen feet. [4] The people craning thier

necks to look up at him are just a few of the hundreds of freinds and neighbors from whom he recieved encouragement. [5] He even succeded in attracting the attention of the mayor, William F. Broening, who wrote to him that his "grit and stamina . . . show that the old pioneer spirit of early America is being kept alive by the youth of today." [6] Evidently the mayor beleived that Avon was indeed someone to look up to.

Adding Prefixes

29d. When a prefix is added to a word, the spelling of the original word remains the same.

EXAMPLES   mis + spell = **mis**spell   dis + advantage = **dis**advantage
                   un + likely = **un**likely   il + legible = **il**legible

Adding Suffixes

29e. When the suffix *–ly* or *–ness* is added to a word, the spelling of the original word usually remains the same.

EXAMPLES   nice + ly = nice**ly**   mean + ness = mean**ness**
                 usual + ly = usual**ly**   same + ness = same**ness**

EXCEPTIONS   1. Words ending in *y* usually change the *y* to *i* before *–ness* and *–ly*.
                steady—steadily, sloppy—sloppiness
           2. However, most one-syllable adjectives ending in *y* follow rule 29e.
                shy—shyness, dry—dryly

▶ EXERCISE 2   **Spelling Words with Prefixes and Suffixes**

Add the prefix or suffix given for each word, and spell the new word formed.

1. heavy + ness
2. dis + satisfied
3. il + legal
4. un + nerve
5. sincere + ly

6. ordinary + ly
7. im + mature
8. sudden + ness
9. special + ly
10. over + rate

29f.   Drop the final silent *e* before a suffix beginning with a vowel.

EXAMPLES   dine + ing = dining   safe + er = safer
            sense + ible = sensible   hope + ed = hoped
            use + able = usable   nice + est = nicest

EXCEPTIONS   1. Keep the final silent *e* in words ending in *ce* or *ge* before a suffix that begins with *a* or *o*.
                 servic**e**able, manag**e**able, advantag**e**ous
             2. To avoid confusion with other words, keep the final silent *e* in some words.
                 dyeing and dying   *singeing and singing*

29g.   Keep the final silent *e* before a suffix beginning with a consonant.

EXAMPLES   use + ful = useful
            advertise + ment = advertisement
EXCEPTIONS true + ly = truly
            argue + ment = argument
            judge + ment = judgment

▶ EXERCISE 3   **Spelling Words with Suffixes**

Add the suffix given for each word, and spell the new words formed.

1. courage + ous
2. nine + ty
3. advance + ing
4. hope + ful
5. approve + al

MECHANICS

29h. If the final *y* is preceded by a consonant, change the *y* to *i* before any suffix except one beginning with an *i*.

EXAMPLES   lively + ness = liveliness   rely + ed = relied
bury + al = burial   funny + er = funnier
study + ing = studying   hasty + est = hastiest

▶ EXERCISE 4   **Spelling Words with Suffixes**

Add the suffix given for each word, and spell the new words formed.

1. happy + est
2. marry + ing
3. delay + ed
4. shiny + er
5. beauty + ful
6. spy + ing
7. pity + ing
8. try + ed
9. pretty + ness
10. busy + ly

29i. Double the final consonant before a suffix that begins with a vowel only if the word

   1. has only one syllable or is accented on the last syllable

and

   2. ends in a *single* consonant preceded by a *single* vowel.

EXAMPLES   glad + est = gla**dd**est
[one-syllable word]
begin + ing = begi**nn**ing
[accent on the last syllable]

differ + ence = difference
[accent on the first syllable]
droop + ed = drooped
[single consonant preceded by a *double* vowel]

©John Caldwell 1986.

NOTE: In some words, the final consonant may or may not be doubled. Both spellings are acceptable.

   EXAMPLES   travel + ed = traveled *or* travelled
stencil + ing = stenciling *or* stencilling

MECHANICS

▶ EXERCISE 5   **Spelling Words with Suffixes**

Add the suffix given for each word, and spell the new words formed.

1. mad + er
2. propel + er
3. shovel + ing
4. refer + al
5. repel + ent

6. confer + ed
7. suffer + ance
8. hop + ing
9. shop + ed
10. remit + ance

▶ REVIEW A   **Proofreading a Paragraph to Correct Spelling Errors**

Proofread the following paragraph, correcting the misspelled word in each sentence.

[1] The Shawnee war chief Tecumseh was commited to the goal of uniting Native Americans. [2] He believed that unification was the only way to prevent white settlers from siezing and taking over the land that his people lived on. [3] Opposed to treaties that forced Native Americans to forfiet their land, Tecumseh believed that the land was owned by no one. [4] After much hard work, he succeded in convincing some midwestern Native American peoples to join together. [5] With his brother, known as the Shawnee Prophet, Tecumseh urged his people to preserve their traditional ways of liveing and not to surrender the land. [6] Tecumseh and the Shawnee Prophet (shown below) led thier followers in building Prophetstown at

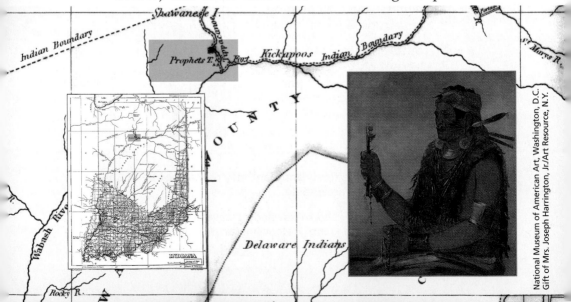

National Museum of American Art, Washington, D.C. Gift of Mrs. Joseph Harrington, Jr./Art Resource, N.Y.

MECHANICS

the location indicated on this map of Indiana. [7] In 1811, while Tecumseh was delivering a speech in a neighboring village, the governor of the Indiana Territory, William Henry Harrison, easly attacked Prophetstown. [8] Against Tecumseh's wishes, the Shawnee Prophet proceeded to counterattack, but he finally had to consede defeat in the Battle of Tippecanoe. [9] Overun by Harrison, Tecumseh's people scattered, leaving the town in ruins and bringing an end to twenty years of Tecumseh's work. [10] Tecumseh had planed to start over, but his death in 1813 at the Battle of the Thames ended all hopes of uniting the various Native American nations.

Forming Plurals of Nouns

29j. To form the plural of most English nouns, simply add *s*.

SINGULAR	dog	kite	pencil	video	organization
PLURAL	dogs	kites	pencils	videos	organizations

29k. To form the plurals of other nouns, follow these rules.

(1) If the noun ends in *s*, *x*, *z*, *sh*, or *ch*, add *es*.

SINGULAR	glass	waltz	suffix	bush	trench
PLURAL	glasses	waltzes	suffixes	bushes	trenches

NOTE: Proper nouns usually follow this rule, too.

EXAMPLES the Barneses, the Gómezes

(2) If the noun ends in *y* preceded by a consonant, change the *y* to *i* and add *es*.

SINGULAR	city	enemy	spy	penny
PLURAL	cities	enemies	spies	pennies

(3) If the noun ends in *y* preceded by a vowel, add *s*.

SINGULAR	alloy	turkey	essay	Sunday
PLURAL	alloys	turkeys	essays	Sundays

MECHANICS

(4) For some nouns ending in *f* or *fe,* add *s.* For others, change the *f* or *fe* to *v* and add *es.*

Add *s:*

SINGULAR	belief	roof	fife	cliff
PLURAL	beliefs	roofs	fifes	cliffs

Change *f* or *fe* to *v* and add *es:*

SINGULAR	wolf	thief	knife	leaf
PLURAL	wolves	thieves	knives	leaves

(5) If the noun ends in *o* preceded by a vowel, add *s.* If the noun ends in *o* preceded by a consonant, add *es.*

SINGULAR	patio	rodeo	tomato	hero
PLURAL	patios	rodeos	tomatoes	heroes

EXCEPTIONS   1. Nouns for musical terms that end in *o* preceded by a consonant form the plural by adding only *s.*

SINGULAR	alto	soprano	piano	solo
PLURAL	altos	sopranos	pianos	solos

2. A few other nouns that end in *o* preceded by a consonant form the plural by adding only *s.*

SINGULAR	photo	silo	taco
PLURAL	photos	silos	tacos

NOTE: In some cases, the plural of a word ending in *o* may be formed by adding either *s* or *es.*

SINGULAR	mosquito	cargo
PLURAL	mosquitos *or* mosquitoes	cargos or cargoes

(6) The plurals of some nouns are formed in irregular ways.

SINGULAR	child	ox	woman	tooth	mouse	foot
PLURAL	children	oxen	women	teeth	mice	feet

(7) Some nouns have the same form in both the singular and the plural.

SINGULAR AND PLURAL   Chinese   scissors   salmon   sheep

(8) For most compound nouns, make the main word plural.

The main word is the noun that is modified.

SINGULAR	editor in chief	son-in-law	looker-on	runner-up
PLURAL	editor**s** in chief	son**s**-in-law	looker**s**-on	runner**s**-up

The plurals of a few compound nouns are formed in irregular ways.

SINGULAR	drive-in	lean-to	two-year-old
PLURAL	drive-in**s**	lean-to**s**	two-year-old**s**

(9) Some nouns borrowed from other languages form their plurals as they do in the original language.

SINGULAR	PLURAL
alumnus [male]	alumn**i**
alumna [female]	alumn**ae**
vertebra	vertebr**ae**
parenthesis	parenthes**es**
datum	dat**a**

NOTE: A few nouns borrowed from other languages have two plural forms. Check a dictionary to find the preferred spelling of such plurals.

SINGULAR	formula	index
PLURAL	formul**ae** *or*	ind**ices** *or*
	formula**s** [preferred]	index**es** [preferred]

(10) To form the plurals of numerals, most capital letters, symbols, and words used as words, add either an –*s* or an apostrophe and an –*s*.

EXAMPLES   His *7*s [or *7*'s] look like *T*s [or *T*'s].
Do not write &s [or &'s] for *and*s [or *and*'s].
Phillis Wheatley wrote during the 1700s [or 1700's].

To prevent confusion, always use both an apostrophe and an –*s* to form the plurals of lowercase letters, certain capital letters, and some words used as words.

EXAMPLES   Mind your *p*'s and *q*'s.
His note is filled with *I*'s. [Without an apostrophe, the plural of the pronoun *I* would look like the word *Is*.]
Make sure that each one of your *her*'s has a clear antecedent. [Without the apostrophe, the plural of the word *her* could be confused with the possessive pronoun *hers*.]

MECHANICS

NOTE: In your reading, you may notice that some writers use an apostrophe and an *–s* to form the plurals of *all* capital letters and words used as words. Using both an apostrophe and an *–s* is never wrong. Therefore, if you have any doubt about whether or not to use an apostrophe, use it.

☞ REFERENCE NOTE: For more information on forming these kinds of plurals, see pages 857–858.

▶ EXERCISE 6   **Spelling the Plurals of Nouns**

Write the plural form of each of the following nouns.

1. girl	**5.** Japanese	**8.** self
2. valley	**6.** sister-in-law	**9.** loaf
3. sky	**7.** solo	**10.** hero
4. coach		

▶ EXERCISE 7   **Proofreading a Paragraph to Correct Spelling Errors**

Proofread the following paragraph, correcting the five misspelled words.

[1] This shoe repair shop in Bakersfield, California, is one of many businesses in citys across the United States whose shapes advertise the goods or services they offer. [2] Most of these eye-catching structurs, many of them originally drives-in, were built between the 1920s and the 1950s. [3] They appeal not only to childs but also to teenagers and adults who enjoy the offbeat. [4] Watch for restaurants and stores shaped like foods and other objects when you're traveling; photoes of them often make good souvenirs of a trip.

REVIEW B   **Applying Spelling Rules**

Explain the spelling of each of the following words.

1. crises
2. deceive
3. writing
4. believe

5. sopranos
6. misstep
7. meanness

8. noticeable
9. relief
10. countries

Spelling Numbers

29l.   Always spell out a number that begins a sentence.

EXAMPLE   **One hundred twelve** sea lions were spotted in the bay.

29m.   Within a sentence, spell out numbers that can be written in one or two words; use numerals for other numbers.

EXAMPLES   We drove **four hundred** miles in **seven** hours.
Edie weighs **110** pounds.

EXCEPTION   If you use some numbers that are written with one or two words and some written with more than two words, use numerals for all of them.
*The final vote was **201** to **90.***

29n.   Spell out numbers used to indicate order.

EXAMPLE   My brother placed **third** [not *3rd*] in the race.

EXCEPTION   Use numerals for dates when you include the name of the month.
*Cinco de Mayo is celebrated on May **5*** [not *5th*, but *the fifth of May* is also correct].

 REVIEW C   **Proofreading a Paragraph to Correct Spelling Errors**

Proofread the following paragraph, correcting the misspelled words.

[1] Last Saturday my mom's parents, Grandma and Grandpa Reyes, celebrated their fortyeth anniversary by repeating their wedding vows in a beautiful ceremony at

MECHANICS

St. Teresa's Church. [2] Since I have my learnner's permit now and it was light out when we went to the church, Mom let me drive. [3] My aunts and uncles on Mom's side of the family were there with their husbands and wifes. [4] In addition, all of my cousins except Ernesto, whom I'd been especially hopeing to see, attended the ceremony. [5] Unfortunately, the flights from Denver, where Ernesto goes to college, had been canceled because it had snowed heavyly there the night before. [6] Although I missed Ernesto, I enjoyed visiting with many of the 85 friends and family members who had come to the celebration. [7] Grandma and Grandpa had insisted that anniversary gifts were unecessary, but this time they were overruled. [8] You could tell that they were truely stunned when they opened the gift from their children. [9] Mom and her sisters and brothers had chiped in to buy them plane tickets to Mexico City, where they were born. [10] Everyone had such a good time that we've already started planing for Grandma and Grandpa's 50th anniversary.

Words Often Confused

affect	[verb] *to influence* How did that sad movie *affect* you?
effect	[verb] *to accomplish;* [noun] *consequence; result* Head Start centers can *effect* an improvement in the lives of underprivileged children. What *effect* did the rain have on the lawn?
all ready	*all are ready* We were *all ready* to leave.
already	*previously* We have *already* painted the sets.
all right	This is the only acceptable spelling. The spelling *alright* is not standard usage.

all together	*everyone in the same place* The players were *all together* in the gym.
altogether	*entirely* I'm not *altogether* convinced.
brake	[verb] *to slow down or stop;* [noun] *a device used to slow down or stop something* Georgia *braked* the speeding car. The worn *brakes* couldn't stop the car.
break	[verb] *to violate; to fracture;* [noun] *the fracture itself* Don't *break* the speed limit. The doctor says it isn't a bad *break*.
capital	correct spelling for all uses except when the word means *government building* What is the *capital* of Zimbabwe? You need *capital* to start a business. Begin every sentence with a *capital* letter. Do you believe in *capital* punishment?
capitol	*government building* We could see the *capitol* from our hotel.
choose	[verb, present tense] We *choose* partners today.
chose	[verb, past tense of *choose*] Each of us *chose* a partner.
coarse	*rough; crude* Burlap is a *coarse* fabric.
course	*a part of a meal; a program of study; a playing field;* also used with *of* to mean *naturally* or *certainly* She skipped the first *course* at dinner. The speech *course* helped my diction. A new golf *course* opened last week. Of *course*, you're always welcome.

MECHANICS

complement	[verb] *to make whole or complete;* [noun] *that which makes whole or complete* That scarf *complements* your outfit nicely. The *complement*, or full crew, is six hundred people.
compliment	[noun] *a courteous act; a flattering statement;* [verb] *to express these qualities* He received many *compliments* on his cooking. I *complimented* her on her success.
consul	[noun] *a representative of a foreign country* The Chinese *consul* returned to Beijing.
council	[noun] *a group charged with taking official actions*
councilor	[noun] *a member of such a group* Four of the *councilors* on the Security *Council* voted for the resolution.
counsel **counselor**	[noun] *advice;* [verb] *to advise* [noun] *an adviser* Sue followed her aunt's *counsel*. Sue's aunt *counseled* her to take judo lessons. Ask your guidance *counselor*.
des'ert	[noun] *a dry region* The car crossed the *desert* at night.
desert'	[verb] *to leave* The rats *deserted* the sinking ship.
dessert	[noun] *the last part of a meal* For *dessert* we had cheese and fruit.

▶ EXERCISE 8 **Distinguishing Between Words Often Confused**

Choose the correct word of the pair in parentheses.

1. The Epstein family was (*all together, altogether*) last week for the Hanukkah celebration.

2. The illness has had a strange (*affect, effect*) on everyone who has caught it.
3. My cousin knows the (*capitol, capital*) city of every state.
4. If you don't have your car's (*brakes, breaks*) inspected each year, you may be (*braking, breaking*) a state law.
5. The British (*council, consul*) (*counciled, counseled*) the reporter to leave the country.
6. After all his worry, everything turned out (*all right, alright*).
7. The two fast guards on our basketball team are (*complimented, complemented*) by our towering center.
8. The actors were (*all ready, already*) for the audition.
9. My uncle had either flan or sopapillas for (*desert, dessert*).
10. Did you (*choose, chose*) that topic for your essay?

formally	*in a formal manner* Do you plan to dress *formally* for the party?
formerly	*previously* This lake was *formerly* a valley.
hear	*to receive sound through the ears* Please speak up—I can't *hear* you.
here	*this place* Let's sit *here*.
its	[possessive form of *it*] The town hasn't raised *its* tax rate in years.
it's	[contraction of *it is* or *it has*] *It's* cold, and *it's* started to snow.
lead	[verb] *to go first* Who will *lead* the Juneteenth parade?
led	[verb, past tense of *lead*] He *led* us five miles out of the way.
lead	[noun, pronounced "led"] *a heavy metal; graphite in a pencil* A pencil *lead* is not made of *lead*.

MECHANICS

MECHANICS

loose [adjective, pronounced "loos"] *free, not connected tightly*
Put all your *loose* papers in a folder.
My little brother has two *loose* teeth.

lose [verb, pronounced "looz"] *to suffer loss*
Don't *lose* your tickets.

miner [noun] *worker in a mine*
The trapped *miners* were finally rescued.

minor [noun] *person under legal age;* [adjective] *of small importance*
The curfew applies only to *minors.*
He received *minor* injuries in the accident.

Rubes   By Leigh Rubin

Rubes by Leigh Rubin. By permission of Leigh Rubin and Creators Syndicate.

Miner surgery.

moral [adjective] *good;* [noun] *a lesson of conduct*
We admire a *moral* person.
The story's *moral* is "Look before you leap."

morale *mental condition, spirit*
After three defeats, the team's *morale* was low.

passed [verb, past tense of *pass*]
We *passed* our papers to the front.

past [noun] *the history of a person, group, or institution;* [adjective] *former;* [preposition] *farther on than*
Sitting Bull told his son Crow Foot many stories about the *past.*
Adele read the minutes of the *past* meeting.
The dog walked right *past* the cat.

▶ EXERCISE 9 **Distinguishing Between Words Often Confused**

Choose the correct word of the pair in parentheses.

1. Where did you (*here, hear*) that Kiowa legend?
2. If you (*lose, loose*) the directions, we'll never get there.
3. The mail from home improved the troops' (*moral, morale*).
4. The estate is being held in trust until the heir is no longer a (*minor, miner*).
5. My horse (*lead, led*) the parade.
6. In only a few minutes, the guest speaker will be (*hear, here*).
7. After he went on a diet, his clothes were too (*lose, loose*).
8. (*Formerly, Formally*), Gloria Estefan performed with the Miami Sound Machine.
9. (*Its, It's*) not every day that her parents let her use the car.
10. After taking French I twice, John (*passed, past*) the course.

▶ REVIEW D **Proofreading an Article to Correct Spelling Errors**

Proofread the following article, correcting the misspelled word or words in each sentence. If all words in a sentence are spelled correctly, write C.

NHS MEMBERS MEET GOVERNOR
by Cornelia Charnes, Staff Writer

[1] One of the advantages of living in the state capitol is having the opportunity to see state government up close. [2] Last Friday, twenty-seven members of our school's National Honor Society chapter toured the nearby capital building. [3] Tour guide Floyd Welty, who lead the group, outlined the workings of the government's three branches and pointed out many of the building's architectural features. [4] The students ate lunch in the underground cafeteria and even got to meet Governor (formally U.S. Senator) Iola Jones.

MECHANICS

[5] The group met Governor Jones just as they were already to leave the building. [6] Said student Botan Park, "Governor Jones shook hands with each of us and complimented us on being honor students. [7] Even though we're still miners, she told us, 'I want to here from you whenever you have a concern with my administration's policies.'" [8] "Of course," added student Elena Cruz, "its her first term as governor, and we'll be eligible to vote when she comes up for reelection."

[9] The group's sponsor, guidance councilor Diego Vargas, said, "I've been taking groups there for the passed ten years, but I've never met a governor before. [10] That had a big effect on me and on the students."

personal	*individual* The store manager gave us her *personal* attention.
personnel	*a group of people employed in the same place* The management added *personnel* to handle the increased workload.
principal	[noun] *head of a school;* [adjective] *main; most important* The *principal* of our school is Mr. Osaka. The *principal* export of Brazil is coffee.
principle	*a rule of conduct; a main fact* or *law* Her *principles* are very high. Martin Luther King, Jr., supported the *principle* of nonviolence.
quiet	*silent; still* I need complete *quiet* to study.
quite	*wholly; rather; very* Are you *quite* sure this is the right path?
shone	[past tense of *shine*] The stars *shone* brightly last night.
shown	[past participle of *show*] The slides were *shown* after dinner.

stationary	[adjective] *in a fixed position* Are these desks movable or *stationary?*
stationery	[noun] *writing paper* Purple *stationery* isn't appropriate for business letters.

than	[a conjunction, used for comparisons] She is smarter *than* I.
then	[an adverb or a conjunction] *at that time; next* I didn't know you *then.* We swam for an hour; *then* we ate.

their	[possessive of *they*] *Their* apartment has a view of the river.
there	[adverb] *in that place;* [expletive, used to fill out the meaning of a sentence] I haven't been *there* in a long time. *There* is too much pepper in my soup.
they're	[contraction of *they are*] *They're* reading a book by Virginia Driving Hawk Sneve.

MECHANICS

▶ EXERCISE 10 **Distinguishing Between Words Often Confused**

Select the correct word of the choices in parentheses.

1. I'm learning some of the (*principals, principles*) of physics.
2. The gold ring (*shone, shown*) with a warm glow.
3. He acts much older (*than, then*) he is.
4. The bookstore is having a big sale on (*stationery, stationary*).
5. You ask too many (*personnel, personal*) questions.
6. Soon after the strange uproar, all became (*quite, quiet*) again.
7. The *pad thai* they serve here is (*quite, quiet*) good.
8. Several Pueblo artists are displaying (*there, their, they're*) work.

9. If you see the (*principle, principal*) in the hall, tell her she's wanted in the main office.
10. (*Their, They're, There*) parents may not let them go.

---

to	[preposition; also part of the infinitive form of a verb] Please return these books *to* the library. He began *to* whistle.
too	[adverb] *also; more than enough* Rubén Blades is a musician and an attorney, *too.* You're *too* young to drive.
two	*one plus one* I will graduate in *two* years.
waist	*the midsection of the body* At the Japanese restaurant, the server wore an obi around her *waist.*
waste	[verb] *to use foolishly;* [noun] *a needless expense* *Waste* not; want not. Waiting in line is a *waste* of time.
weather	[noun] *conditions outdoors* The *weather* has been perfect all week.
whether	[subordinating conjunction; indicates alternative or doubt] They don't know *whether* or not they'll go.
who's	[contraction of *who is* or *who has*] *Who's* there? *Who's* been wearing my socks?
whose	[possessive of *who*] *Whose* book is this?
your	[possessive of *you*] *Your* coat is in the closet.
you're	[contraction of *you are*] *You're* never on time.

▶ EXERCISE 11 **Distinguishing Between Words Often Confused**

Select the correct word from the choices in parentheses.

1. Around his (*waste, waist*) he wore a handmade leather belt.
2. (*You're, Your*) mother made a delicious Korean dinner of *bulgogi* last night.
3. There was (*too, to, two*) much traffic on the road (*too, to, two*) enjoy the ride.
4. (*Whose, Who's*) going to use that ticket now?
5. It really doesn't matter (*whose, who's*) fault it is.
6. You, (*to, two, too*), can be a better speller if you try.
7. (*Weather, Whether*) it rains or not, we'll be there.
8. This is fine (*whether, weather*) for a softball game.
9. (*Your, You're*) sure Ms. Thompson wanted to see me?
10. I don't know (*whose, who's*) taller, Hakeem Olajuwon or Buck Williams.

▶ EXERCISE 12 **Proofreading a Paragraph to Correct Spelling Errors**

Proofread the following paragraph, correcting the misspelled words.

[1] The face on the postage stamp on the next page is that of Benjamin Banneker, considered too be the first African American man of science. [2] First issued on February 15, 1980, this stamp honors a man who's contributions in the areas of mathematics and astronomy are impressive. [3] Banneker grew up on a farm in Maryland in the 1700s, a time when life was particularly difficult for African American people weather they were slaves or not. [4] Although free, Banneker, to, faced prejudice and discrimination. [5] However, a neighbor who was interested in science gave some astronomy equipment too Banneker. [6] Banneker waisted no time in using it to determine when the sun and moon rose and set, when the brightest stars set, and when eclipses occurred. [7] All of this information was very helpful to a variety of people, including sailors who needed to chart courses and farmers who needed to know the whether. [8] Banneker compiled his data into an

MECHANICS

almanac, and after too or three attempts, he succeeded in getting his almanacs published each year for several years. [9] These popular books received widespread attention, and Benjamin Banneker became a symbol of what African Americans could do if their lives were not waisted in slavery. [10] If your someone who collects commemorative postage stamps, you'll likely want this one, which celebrates the achievements of this gifted scientist.

Benjamin Banneker

Black Heritage USA 15c

▶ REVIEW E Proofreading an Essay to Correct Spelling Errors

Proofread the following essay, correcting the misspelled words in each sentence. If all the words in a sentence are spelled correctly, write C.

[1] One of my most embarrassing moments occured the day I took the road test too get my driver's license. [2] Since one of the branches of the Motor Vehicle Department is near my dad's office, I met him their after school. [3] He tryed to calm me down by telling me that the world wouldn't end if I didn't pass the first time. [4] Still, my hands were shakeing noticably when I got behind the wheel.

[5] The examiner, Mrs. Ferro, was very patient. [6] She assured me that the coarse was a peice of cake and that she wouldn't ask me to do anything ilegal to try to trick me. [7] She said I'd be fine if I just proceded steadyly and didn't overeact to her instructions.

[8] Everything went surprisingly well until we reached the end of the course and Mrs. Ferro told me to stop the car and turn off the ignition. [9] I stopped, alright—I accidentaly slamed on the breaks so hard that we both went lurching forward against our seat belts. [10] Luckily, niether of us sustainned any injurys, and I succeeded in passing the test despite mistakeing the end of the course for the edge of a cliff.

100 Commonly Misspelled Words

ache	could	happiness	raise	tonight
again	country	having	read	too
always	dear	hear	ready	trouble
among	doctor	here	said	truly
answered	does	hoarse	says	Tuesday
any	done	hour	scene	two
been	don't	instead	seems	very
beginning	early	knew	separate	wear
believe	easy	know	shoes	Wednesday
break	enemy	laid	similar	week
built	enough	loose	since	where
business	every	lose	straight	whether
busy	existence	making	sugar	which
buy	February	meant	sure	whole
can't	finally	minute	tear	women
chief	forty	none	their	won't
choose	friend	often	there	would
color	grammar	once	though	write
coming	guess	piece	through	writing
cough	half	probably	tired	wrote

300 Spelling Words

absence	analyze	bulletin
absorption	angel	calendar
abundant	annual	category
acceptable	apparatus	changeable
accidentally	appearance	characteristic
accommodation	application	chemistry
accompaniment	appropriate	circumstance
accurate	approximately	civilization
accustomed	arousing	cocoon
achievement	arrangement	commencement
acquaintance	ascend	commissioner
actuality	association	committed
adequately	athlete	comparative
administration	bankruptcy	comparison
adolescent	basically	competition
aggressive	beneficial	conceivable
agriculture	benefited	confidential
amateur	bicycle	confirmation
ambassador	breathe	conscientious
analysis	brilliant	consciousness

MECHANICS

consequently
considerable
consistency
continuous
controlled
controversial
cordially
corps
correspondence
criticize

curiosity
curriculum
definition
delegate
denied
develop
difference
disastrous
disciple
dissatisfied

distinction
distinguished
dividend
dominant
dormitory
earnest
easily
ecstasy
eighth
eliminate

embroidery
endeavor
enormous
equipment
especially
essential
estimation
etiquette
exaggeration
examination

exceedingly
exceptional
excitable
executive
exercise
exhaustion
exhibition
expense
experience
extension

extraordinary
fallacy
fantasies
favorably
fiery
financial
foreigner
forfeit
fragile
fulfill

fundamentally
gasoline
gentleman
grammatically
grateful
guidance
gymnasium
handkerchief
heroic
hindrance

humorist
hygiene
hypocrisy
illustrate
imitation
immense
inability
incidentally
indispensable
influential

innocence
inquiry
institute
intellect
interference
interpretation
interruption
interval
irrelevant
irresistible

island
jealousy
journal
laborious
liability
lightning
likelihood
liveliest
locally
luxury

magnificence
maintenance
maneuver
mansion
martyr
maturity
medical
merchandise
merit
miniature

mischievous
missile
misspelled
monotony
mortgage
municipal
narrative
naturally
neighbor
noticeable

nuisance
obstacle
occasionally
occupy
odor
offensive
omitted
opinion
opposition
optimism

ordinary
organization
ornament
pageant
pamphlet
parachute
parallel
pastime
peaceable
peasant

peril
permanent
persistent
perspiration
pertain
phase
picnic
pigeon
playwright
pleasant

poison
politician
positively
possibility
practically
practice
precede
precisely
predominant
preferred

prejudice
preliminary
preparation
primitive
priority
prisoner
procedure
proceedings
procession
prominent

proposition
prosperous
prove
psychology
publicity
purposes
qualities
quantities
questionnaire
readily

reference
referring
regard
register
rehearsal
religious
remembrance
representative
requirement
resistance

resolution
responsibility
restaurant
ridiculous
satisfactorily
security
senator
sensibility
sheer
sheriff

significance
simile
situated
solution
sophomore
souvenir
specific
specimen
spiritual
strenuous

stretch
substantial
subtle
successful
sufficient
summarize
superintendent
suppress
surgeon
suspense

syllable
symbol
symphony
technique
temperature
tendency
tournament
traffic
twelfth
tying

tyranny
unanimous
undoubtedly
unforgettable
unpleasant
unusually
vacancies
varies
vengeance
villain

MECHANICS

30 CORRECTING COMMON ERRORS

Key Language Skills Review

This chapter reviews key skills and concepts that pose special problems for writers.

- Sentence Fragments and Run-on Sentences
- Subject-Verb and Pronoun-Antecedent Agreement
- Pronoun Forms
- Clear Pronoun Reference
- Verb Forms and Tenses
- Comparison of Modifiers
- Misplaced and Dangling Modifiers
- Capitalization
- Punctuation—Commas, Colons, Semicolons, Quotation Marks, and Apostrophes
- Spelling
- Standard Usage

Most of the exercises in this chapter follow the same format as the exercises found throughout the grammar, usage, and mechanics sections. You will notice, however, that two sets of review exercises are presented in standardized test formats. These exercises are designed to provide you with practice not only in solving usage and mechanics problems but also in dealing with these kinds of problems on such tests.

▶ EXERCISE 1   **Correcting Sentence Fragments and Run-on Sentences**

Each numbered item below is a sentence fragment, a run-on sentence, or a complete sentence. First, identify each by writing *F* for a fragment, *R* for a run-on, or *S* for a complete sentence. Then, correct each fragment and run-on.

EXAMPLE   **1.** Thunder roared and rumbled lightning flashed across the dark skies.
  1. *R—Thunder roared and rumbled, and lightning flashed across the dark skies.*

 1. Playing basketball with some of my friends who live in my grandmother's neighborhood.
 2. The largest province in Canada is Quebec, the capital of this province is Quebec City.
 3. Ruth tried out her new in-line skates today.
 4. The new movie about dinosaurs on Friday night.
 5. Radio waves travel at the speed of light they can go through many solid objects, including most buildings.
 6. Jeremy wants to ask Shelley to the dance, he doesn't know if she already has a date.
 7. Because my high school has a new athletic program for students with disabilities.
 8. The math problems in today's homework assignment were challenging there weren't many of them.
 9. Wasn't that an exciting and pleasant surprise?
10. Rabindranath Tagore wrote the national anthems of two countries, India and Bangladesh, I wonder if anyone else has written two national anthems.

▶ EXERCISE 2   **Correcting Sentence Fragments and Run-on Sentences**

Each numbered item below is a sentence fragment, a run-on sentence, or a complete sentence. First, identify each by writing *F* for a fragment, *R* for a run-on, or *S* for a complete sentence. Then, correct each fragment and run-on.

EXAMPLE   **1.** Nearly all cultures having traditional folk dances.
  1. *F—Nearly all cultures have traditional folk dances.*

 1. Most folk dances start as celebrations or rituals, such dances are often passed from generation to generation.

2. Certain dances to bring good fortune to the dancers.
3. Some cultures developed dances that they believed cured diseases and other afflictions, for instance, the tarantella developed in Italy as a ritual antidote for the bite of the tarantula.
4. Other dances celebrating birth, marriage, harvests, success in battle, and even death.
5. Over time, most folk dances change.
6. That some dances originally performed for religious or ritual purposes are now danced purely for recreation.
7. Anyone who knows the origins of "Ring-Around-the-Rosy"?
8. In the United States, square dancing may be the most popular kind of folk dance clogging is also widely enjoyed.
9. The do-si-do is a movement in square dancing in which two dancers start out facing one another, circle each other back-to-back, and then return to a facing position.
10. The term *do-si-do* from *dos à dos*, which is French for "back-to-back."

▶ EXERCISE 3 **Identifying Verbs That Agree with Their Subjects**

For each of the following sentences, choose the form of the verb in parentheses that agrees with the subject.

EXAMPLE 1. The cultural heritage of New Mexico's cities (*is, are*) reflected in their architecture, food, and customs.
1. *is*

1. Many of the travelers who visit New Mexico (*spend, spends*) time in Albuquerque.
2. The architecture of the buildings (*represent, represents*) various periods in the city's history.
3. (*Has, Have*) anyone here read about or been to Old Town in Albuquerque?
4. One of the books Adrienne read (*identify, identifies*) Old Town as the site of the city's original settlement, founded by Spanish settlers in 1706.
5. Arts, crafts, and food now (*fill, fills*) the shops around the Old Town Plaza.

6. Alexander's family (*has, have*) its annual reunion in Albuquerque.
7. Near Albuquerque (*is, are*) a number of American Indian reservations.
8. The pictures we took of the Rio Grande gorge (*give, gives*) you an idea of what the landscape is like in central New Mexico.
9. Neither Juan nor his parents (*was, were*) aware that near Albuquerque are mountains that often have snow on them.
10. Just east of the city (*lie, lies*) the Sandia Mountains.

▶ EXERCISE 4 **Proofreading Sentences for Correct Subject-Verb Agreement**

Most of the following sentences contain errors in subject-verb agreement. If a verb does not agree with its subject, write the subject and the correct form of the verb. If a sentence is correct, write *C*.

EXAMPLE **1.** Each of them repeat the chorus after the soloist finishes.
1. *Each repeats*

1. It seems that someone I know drop by every time I try to finish my work.
2. News of his accomplishments have spread in recent years.
3. Here's the articles about Buck Ramsey that Han said she would lend you.
4. The audience always sing along with the old songs.
5. The picture of Nanci, Lyle, and Michelle are on the bulletin board.
6. St. Elmo's fire, which has been seen around the masts of ships, the propellers and wingtips of planes, and even the horns of cattle, is an odd glow that at times accompanies a steady electric discharge.
7. Under some rocks in the woods were a small box.
8. Tornadoes that occur in the Northern Hemisphere whirls in a counterclockwise direction.
9. Has everybody signed up for a service project?
10. Singing and playing the guitar is also among Jan's talents.

▶ EXERCISE 5 **Using Pronouns That Agree with Their Antecedents**

Fill in the blanks in the following sentences by providing pronouns that agree with their antecedents.

EXAMPLE   **1.** One of the boys left _____ report card in the gym.
    1. *his*

1. Each member of the women's soccer team had played _____ best at the game.
2. Have all of the students in your biology class gotten seedlings for _____ experiments?
3. Nicholas or Quentin will demonstrate _____ favorite drawing technique in class today.
4. Mr. Williams told us that anyone who wants to go on the field trip should turn in _____ permission slip on Monday.
5. Each of the novels has _____ own significance in the trilogy.
6. If someone wants to use the computer in the library, _____ should do so this afternoon.
7. Neither Karen nor Susan has finished researching _____ topic.
8. Did one of the passengers leave _____ suitcase here?
9. If Ricky and Joe are ready at 7:45 A.M., _____ will be able to ride the bus to school.
10. Whenever we go hiking, everyone brings _____ own lunch and wears a comfortable pair of shoes.

▶ EXERCISE 6 **Proofreading Sentences for Correct Pronoun-Antecedent Agreement**

Most of the following sentences contain pronouns that do not agree with their antecedents. If a sentence contains an error, rewrite the sentence to correct the error. If a sentence is already correct, write *C*.

EXAMPLE   **1.** Almost everybody I know has their favorite comic strips.
    1. *Almost everybody I know has his or her favorite comic strips.*

1. Sara, one of my friends in art class, raised their hand and asked about the history of comic strips.

2. Ms. Seymour asked everyone to bring a sketchbook, their drawing pencils, and the Sunday comics to class so that we could begin designing a comic strip.
3. I think it was either Sara or Heather who showed me a copy of the *Calvin and Hobbes* collection *Scientific Progress Goes "Boink"* that they had bought at the mall.
4. The vivid color and elaborate artistry of a comic strip like *Prince Valiant* or *Calvin and Hobbes* often help to make them a popular Sunday strip.
5. About 100 million people in the United States spend some of his or her time each day reading comics.
6. Juan and Rob offered to bring in their collections of adventure comics from the 1940s; each of them will give his presentation on Thursday.
7. Are you familiar with Linus and Lucy Van Pelt and his or her friends Charlie Brown and Snoopy?
8. Joseph Pulitzer, one of the most famous newspaper publishers in the United States, introduced the first serialized comic strip in their paper in 1895.
9. The magazine-style comic book first appeared in the 1930s; they generally feature serialized stories about the same group of characters.
10. If anyone wants to learn more about the history of comics, they could research the topic at a library.

CORRECTING COMMON ERRORS

▶ EXERCISE 7 **Identifying Correct Forms of Pronouns**

Choose the correct pronoun in parentheses in each of the following sentences.

EXAMPLE   **1.** Jesse and (*I, me*) will compete at the track meet.
    1. *I*

1. No one else can climb the rope as fast as (*I, me*).
2. Didn't the police officer give (*them, they*) tickets for speeding in a school zone?
3. Both of the soloists in tonight's choir concert will be accompanied on piano by (*she, her*) and Paul.
4. Mr. Allen wondered (*who, whom*) had left him a gift.
5. The next president of the debate team will likely be (*she, her*).
6. Three volunteers—Hester, Kim, and (*I, me*)—will help paint the mural.

CORRECTING COMMON ERRORS

7. Are they two years younger than (*us, we*)?
8. Mrs. Murphy paid my sister and (*I, me*) ten dollars to shovel snow off her driveway.
9. "Aren't you going with Christy and (*him, he*) to the game?" Janet asked.
10. Carl Lewis and Michael Johnson are the two athletes (*who, whom*) I watched most closely during the 1996 Olympics.

▶ EXERCISE 8 **Rewriting Sentences to Correct Inexact Pronoun References**

Rewrite each of the following items to correct the inexact pronoun reference.

EXAMPLE **1.** Domingo first read about Tomás Rivera when he was in the school library.
    1. *When Domingo was in the school library, he read about Tomás Rivera for the first time.*

1. In the catalog, they tell about Tomás Rivera's novel, which is titled . . . *y no se lo tragó la tierra*.
2. As a boy, Rivera worked as a migrant field hand. That may partly explain why he wrote so vividly about migrant workers in . . . *y no se lo tragó la tierra*.
3. Rivera and his family worked long hours in the fields, and it interrupted his education.
4. In his novel, it focuses on a Mexican American family who work as migrant field hands.
5. The family follows crops and the work they provide; it means that they have to move often.
6. Rivera's novel is about the migrant workers' search for justice, which is inspiring.
7. After reading a novel by Tomás Rivera and stories by Reuben Sánchez, I decided to read more of his works.
8. Mandy talked to Adrianne about the development of the characters in Rivera's novel after she had read it.
9. In the biography I read about Rivera, it states that he became the first Mexican American chancellor in the University of California system.
10. After he told him that the film *And the Earth Did Not Swallow Him* was based on Rivera's novel, Todd and Rajiv went to the media center to check out the video.

▶ EXERCISE 9 **Writing the Forms of Irregular Verbs**

For each of the following sentences, fill in the blank with the correct past or past participle form of the verb in italics.

EXAMPLE **1.** *write* Joyce Carol Thomas ____ *Brown Honey in Broomwheat Tea.*
  1. *wrote*

1. *be* During the Cenozoic era, South America and North America ____ linked by a land bridge.
2. *speak* I had ____ to Jim before he left.
3. *bring* Kathy has ____ me her copy of *A Gathering of Flowers: Stories About Being Young in America.*
4. *give* Yesterday morning, Teresa ____ flowers to her grandmother.
5. *know* We ____ that the first czar of Russia was Ivan the Terrible.
6. *hear* Jonas had ____ that the picnic was postponed.
7. *choose* I wonder what subject Celeste ____ for her presentation.
8. *drive* My sister has ____ me to my ballet lessons every week this year.
9. *teach* Who ____ Jorge how to play the clarinet?
10. *ride* I once ____ a bus across Oklahoma.

▶ EXERCISE 10 **Proofreading Sentences for Correct Verb Forms**

Identify each incorrect verb form, and write the correct form. If a sentence is correct, write *C.*

EXAMPLE **1.** From the 1920s through the 1940s, people in the United States listened to radio programs and gone to the movies more than they do now.
  1. *gone—went*

1. The popularity of television brung about the end of many radio shows.
2. It has not took long for television to become one of the most popular mediums of entertainment in the United States.
3. I use to think television had always been around, but the first regular TV broadcasts in the United States didn't occur until 1939.

CORRECTING COMMON ERRORS

4. Demonstrations of television sets drawed big crowds at the New York World's Fair in 1939.
5. In 1941, when the United States begun fighting in World War II, television broadcasting was suspended, but it resumed in 1945.
6. The sales of television sets soared after World War II, and by 1951, telecasts reached viewers from coast to coast.
7. Color programs come along two years later, in 1953.
8. Of course, I've seen reruns of old black-and-white TV programs.
9. I also have heared some of the old radio shows from before the days of television.
10. Have you ever wondered about how television has changed the way people in the United States spend their leisure time?

▶ EXERCISE 11 **Revising a Paragraph to Make the Tenses of the Verbs Consistent**

Read the following paragraph, and decide whether to rewrite it in the present or past tense. Then, change some of the verb forms so that the verb tenses are consistent.

EXAMPLE   [1] The children were eager to hear a story, so I tell them the Navajo legend of Eagle Boy.
          1. *The children are eager to hear a story, so I am telling them the Navajo legend of Eagle Boy.*
                    or
             The children were eager to hear a story, so I told them the Navajo legend of Eagle Boy.

[1] A young Navajo boy who lives with his parents often dreamed of eagles flying overhead. [2] One day, Father Eagle flew down to the boy, caught hold of his shirt, and carries him to a nest high on a cliff. [3] Father and Mother Eagle feed the boy cornmeal and then took him to the eagle people at the top of the sky. [4] Eventually, the boy goes to the home of Eagle Chief, who told him to remain inside. [5] After Eagle Chief leaves, the boy becomes curious about an animal that he sees outside. [6] When the boy opens the door slightly to look more closely, Big Wind blew it completely open, pulling the boy outside, where the trickster

Coyote is waiting. [7] The boy, soon tricked into touching Coyote's fur, turns into a coyote himself. [8] When Eagle Chief returns home, he restored the boy to human form. [9] Afterward, Eagle Chief names him Eagle Boy and gave him an eagle feather. [10] Eagle Boy then returns home to his parents, and he eventually became a great medicine man.

▶ EXERCISE 12 **Proofreading for Correct Comparative and Superlative Forms**

Most of the following sentences contain an error in the use of the comparative or superlative form of a modifier. If a modifier is incorrect, give the correct form. If a sentence is correct, write *C*.

EXAMPLE **1.** The second time I made lasagna, I prepared it more quicklier.
1. *more quickly*

1. I planted lantana and petunias next to each other, but the lantana grew best because it could withstand heat and drought.
2. One of the more exciting field trips is scheduled for this fall.
3. I can't tell by this map which of the two mountain peaks is tallest.
4. Of the club's many members, he is less likely to run for president because he is so shy.
5. The more suspenseful part of the novel told of a storm that damaged the sails of the pirate ship and drove the ship off course.
6. Which is most fun for you, painting with watercolors or sketching?
7. Watching the two dogs digging in the ground, Carol laughed when the youngest one unearthed a small toy that had been buried.
8. The colorfulest sunset I have ever seen in Montana was near Billings.
9. Standing outside the theater, we all agreed that the movie was the least satisfying sequel that any of us had ever seen.
10. Of all the mailboxes in the neighborhood, ours is the more unusual.

▶ EXERCISE 13 **Proofreading Sentences for Correct Use of Modifiers**

Revise the following sentences to correct each error in the use of a modifier.

EXAMPLE   **1.** Daisies are often more easier to grow than orchids.
            1. *Daisies are often easier to grow than orchids.*

   1. Because they are nocturnal, flying squirrels are less likelier to be seen than other squirrels are.
   2. Raphael types faster than any student in our class.
   3. Fortunately, no one was injured bad when the boats collided.
   4. While elephants are the largest land mammals, blue whales are the most largest mammals of all.
   5. Tim is more creative than anyone I know.

▶ EXERCISE 14 **Correcting Misplaced Modifiers**

Each of the following sentences contains a misplaced modifier. Rewrite each sentence to correct the placement of the modifier.

EXAMPLE   **1.** Flying in close formation, the crowd watched the squadron of small biplanes.
            1. *The crowd watched the squadron of small biplanes flying in close formation.*

   1. Gathered into a heap, Nathan took a second look at the stalks of sugar cane.
   2. I always enjoy listening to stories about Grandma's childhood with my sister.
   3. We watched the sun rise from our front porch.
   4. Frank listened to music climbing the mountain.
   5. We watched a film about how comets are formed in science class.
   6. Late yesterday afternoon, I saw a deer going to check the mail.
   7. A fierce predator, the teeth of the *Tyrannosaurus rex* were about six inches long.
   8. They noticed a turtle on a log wading across the river.
   9. We learned that the bridge had once collapsed as we rode over it.
   10. Mr. Hall saw many earthworms planting his garden.

▶ EXERCISE 15 **Correcting Dangling Modifiers**

Each of the following sentences contains a dangling modifier. Rewrite each sentence so that the modifier clearly and sensibly modifies a word in the sentence.

EXAMPLE   **1.** Looking through the binoculars, the bird was brightly colored.
   1. *Looking through the binoculars, I saw that the bird was brightly colored.*

1. Well equipped and well rested, the ascent to the peak of the mountain took only a few hours.
2. The people below looked like ants peering down from the top of the Empire State Building.
3. Unable to print out the last two pages because of a power outage, Bob's report had to be turned in late.
4. While practicing the piano, the sheet of music fell off the music rack.
5. In addition to stretching to warm up, your running shoes should be laced tightly.
6. The telephone rang right after walking in the front door.
7. Determined to reach the finish line, the marathon seemed endless.
8. Looking overgrown and scraggly, the McKinneys decided to spend the weekend doing yardwork.
9. Studying fossilized oyster shells found in Kansas, it was hypothesized that a shallow sea once covered at least part of that state.
10. All alone, the woods were mysterious and silent.

▶ EXERCISE 16 **Correcting Double Negatives and Other Errors in Usage**

Eliminate the double negatives and other errors in usage in the following sentences. Although the sentences can be corrected in more than one way, you need to give only one revision.

EXAMPLE   **1.** Karen should of tried some of the chow mein.
   1. *Karen should have tried some of the chow mein.*

1. I went to the beach to look for driftwood but couldn't find none.

2. Just try and imagine a city without vehicles of any sort!
3. I would rather go to the beach this afternoon then stay indoors.
4. Our track team practiced until we weren't able to run no more.
5. The engine sounds like it is ready to fall out of the old truck.
6. We didn't want to see neither of the movies that were showing at the theater.
7. My little brother found a small toy inside of that box of cereal.
8. Joel drove a long ways across town just to trade one football card.
9. My science experiment didn't work as good as I had thought it would.
10. This long stretch of highway has hardly no curves in it.

▶ EXERCISE 17 **Correcting Errors in Usage**

Each of the following sentences contains a usage error. Identify and correct each error.

EXAMPLE   **1.** Young people with inventive minds had ought to be encouraged!
          1. *had ought—ought*

1. People between the ages of five and nineteen have discovered some new and important products and processes.
2. As a teenager, Jerrald Spencer used to take apart electronic devices to see what was inside of them.
3. In 1977, at age fifteen, Spencer got the idea for his first marketed invention, a type of an electronic toy.
4. That there toy led to a whole series of specialty toys sold in major department stores.
5. In 1895, the teenager Cathy Evans invented "tufting," an unique method of decorating bedspreads.
6. Her invention has had a marked affect on the carpet industry; in fact, most of the carpet manufactured today involves the process that Evans developed.
7. In 1922, eighteen-year-old Ralph Samuelson decided to try and ski on water.

8. He didn't think that skiing on water would be much harder then skiing on snow.
9. Like he had thought, after a number of tries the skis worked!
10. If you want to be an inventor, you won't succeed without you try.

▶ EXERCISE 18 **Proofreading Sentences to Correct Errors in Usage**

Each of the following sentences contains an error in English usage. Identify and correct each error.

EXAMPLE　**1.** The tour guide last summer learned us much about the Lincoln Memorial.
　　　　　　1. *learned—taught*

1. The memorial to President Abraham Lincoln, what was dedicated in 1922, has been a popular attraction ever since it opened.
2. Over the years, no less than 150 million people have visited the monument.
3. I was kind of amazed to hear that the memorial was built on what used to be marshland.
4. The architect Henry Bacon he designed the Lincoln Memorial.
5. I implied from our guide's talk that the Parthenon in Greece inspired Bacon's design.
6. It is not an allusion that the massive columns of both the Parthenon and the Lincoln Memorial tilt slightly inward.
7. The architects designed the columns this way because rows of perfectly straight columns give buildings the affect of bulging at the top.
8. I read where Daniel Chester French interviewed Lincoln's son Robert before sculpting the memorial's statue of Lincoln.
9. The 175-ton statue was carved in separate sections by the Piccirilli brothers, whose family had immigrated from Italy and settled in the United States.
10. The Gettysburg Address is inscribed on a wall inside of the memorial's hall.

CORRECTING COMMON ERRORS

Grammar and Usage Test: Section 1

DIRECTIONS   Read the paragraph below. For each numbered blank, select the word or group of words that best completes the sentence. Indicate your response by shading in the appropriate oval on your answer sheet.

EXAMPLE

_(1)_ you ever heard of sick building syndrome?

1. (A) Has
   (B) Have
   (C) Did
   (D) If
   (E) Hasn't

SAMPLE ANSWER   1. (A) ● (C) (D) (E)

In the 1980s, a number of health problems suffered by office workers _(1)_ for the first time as symptoms of an ailment called sick building syndrome. Besides fatigue and eye irritation, _(2)_ symptoms included headaches, sore throats, colds, and flu. Studies indicate that sick building syndrome, _(3)_ has caused a 30 percent rise in absenteeism in some businesses, can reduce productivity by as much as 40 percent. Problems resulting from this syndrome _(4)_ are caused by such pollutants as formaldehyde, benzene, and trichloroethylene. These substances, found in furniture, insulation, and paint, _(5)_ trapped in climate-controlled buildings. Even though such pollutants are so widespread, the situation _(6)_ hopeless. Research originally conducted to help astronauts _(7)_ to a simple solution—houseplants. Microorganisms in the roots of a potted plant _(8)_ remove harmful substances from the air. The _(9)_ plants include chrysanthemums, which remove benzene, and spider plants, which remove formaldehyde. In addition, both peace lilies and English ivy _(10)_ trichloroethylene.

---

1. (A) identified
   (B) was identified
   (C) were identified
   (D) being identified
   (E) was being identified

2. (A) these
   (B) them
   (C) these here
   (D) these kind of
   (E) them kind of

3. (A) this
   (B) which
   (C) who
   (D) what
   (E) it

4. (A) more likely
   (B) more liklier
   (C) liklier
   (D) most likely
   (E) most likliest

5. (A) becomes
    (B) becomed
    (C) becoming
    (D) become
    (E) are becoming

6. (A) is in no way
    (B) is not in no way
    (C) aren't in no way
    (D) it isn't hardly
    (E) isn't hardly

7. (A) have led
    (B) has led
    (C) has been leading
    (D) have been leading
    (E) leads

8. (A) they help
    (B) it helps
    (C) help
    (D) helps
    (E) is helping

9. (A) most useful
    (B) usefullest
    (C) most usefullest
    (D) more useful
    (E) more usefuller

10. (A) removes
    (B) they remove
    (C) removed
    (D) were removing
    (E) remove

Grammar and Usage Test: Section 2

DIRECTIONS   Either part or all of each of the following sentences is underlined. Using the rules of standard written English, choose the answer that most clearly expresses the meaning of the sentence. If there is no error, choose A. Indicate your response by shading in the appropriate oval on your answer sheet.

EXAMPLE

1. Has everyone chosen a topic for their essay?

    (A) chosen a topic for their
    (B) chose a topic for their
    (C) choosed a topic for their
    (D) chosen a topic for his or her
    (E) chosen a topic for his

SAMPLE ANSWER 1. (A) (B) (C) ● (E)

1. This evening less people will be driving cars to the parade because there is less space available for parking.

    (A) less people will be driving
    (B) fewer people will be driving
    (C) less people will have been driving
    (D) fewer people will have been driving
    (E) fewer people drive

2. In the 1936 Olympic Games, I read that Jesse Owens won four gold medals.

(A) In the 1936 Olympic Games, I read that Jesse Owens won four gold medals.
(B) In the 1936 Olympic Games, I read that four gold medals were won by Jesse Owens.
(C) I read where Jesse Owens won four gold medals in the 1936 Olympic Games.
(D) I read in the 1936 Olympic Games that Jesse Owens won four gold medals.
(E) I read that Jesse Owens won four gold medals in the 1936 Olympic Games.

3. In tennis, "love" is when a player has a score of zero.

(A) when a player has a score of zero
(B) where a player has a score of zero
(C) a score of zero
(D) scoring a zero
(E) that a player has a score of zero

4. I can't hardly remember a time when the temperature was lower than it is today.

(A) I can't hardly remember a time when the temperature was lower than it is today.
(B) I can't hardly remember a time when the temperature was lower then it is today.
(C) I can hardly remember a time when the temperature was more lower than it is today.
(D) I can hardly remember a time when the temperature was lower then it is today.
(E) I can hardly remember a time when the temperature was lower than it is today.

5. While running to the bus stop this morning, some books fell out of my backpack.

(A) While running to the bus stop this morning, some books fell out of my backpack.
(B) While running this morning, some books fell out of my backpack at the bus stop.
(C) While I was running to the bus stop this morning, some books fell out of my backpack.
(D) Some books fell out of my backpack while running to the bus stop this morning.
(E) I was running to the bus stop this morning while some of my books fell out of my backpack.

6. The first tennis match played at our school's spring tournament was <u>between she and I.</u>

   (A) between she and I
   (B) between her and I
   (C) between her and me
   (D) between she and me
   (E) among her and me

7. Raymond knows how to repair lawn mowers, <u>and he plans to make it his summer job.</u>

   (A) and he plans to make it his summer job
   (B) and he plans to make that his summer job
   (C) and that is his plan for a summer job
   (D) and he plans to make such repair work his summer job
   (E) which is his plan for a summer job

8. <u>Creole dishes, the origins of which can be traced to European, African, and Caribbean cooking.</u>

   (A) Creole dishes, the origins of which can be traced to European, African, and Caribbean cooking.
   (B) The origins of Creole dishes, which can be traced to European, African, and Caribbean cooking.
   (C) Tracing the origins of Creole dishes to European, African, and Caribbean cooking.
   (D) European, African, and Caribbean cooking, which are the origins of Creole dishes.
   (E) The origins of Creole dishes can be traced to European, African, and Caribbean cooking.

9. The coach <u>doesn't think that her and I</u> have practiced free throws enough today.

   (A) doesn't think that her and I
   (B) don't think that her and me
   (C) doesn't think that she and I
   (D) don't think that she and I
   (E) doesn't think that her and me

10. Some of the people <u>who are standing in line have all ready</u> bought their tickets.

   (A) who are standing in line have all ready
   (B) who are standing in line have already
   (C) whom are standing in line have all ready
   (D) whom are standing in line have already
   (E) that are standing in line have all ready

▶ EXERCISE 19 **Correcting Errors in Capitalization**

Each of the following groups of words contains at least one capitalization error. Correct the errors either by changing capital letters to lowercase letters or by changing lowercase letters to capital letters.

EXAMPLE   **1.** Robert Burns's poem "a red, red rose"
          1. Robert Burns's poem "A Red, Red Rose"

1. my aunt elizabeth
2. an interstate highway in the midwest
3. *the middle passage* by V. S. Naipaul
4. a red cross volunteer
5. west of sixty-fifth street
6. winter in denver
7. grandma's brother
8. senator Ann Greene
9. latin, art, and geometry II
10. a buddhist temple
11. the battle Of vicksburg
12. dr. l. f. livingstone
13. the book *a room with a view*
14. American indian pictographs
15. tickets to the world series
16. a xerox® photocopier
17. Father's day
18. A vietnamese festival
19. moons circling earth and mars
20. Grand teton national park

▶ EXERCISE 20 **Correcting Errors in Capitalization**

Each of the following sentences contains errors in capitalization. Correct the errors either by changing capital letters to lowercase letters or by changing lowercase letters to capital letters.

EXAMPLE   **1.** i recently read about oren lyons, an Influential onondaga chief.
      1. *I recently read about Oren Lyons, an influential Onondaga chief.*

1. The onondaga are an iroquois people.
2. Oren lyons's formal title is faith keeper of the turtle clan.

3. Before assuming this important position, mr. lyons was a successful commercial artist in new york city.
4. The iroquois tradition of having faith keepers dates back to hundreds of years before the pilgrims landed at plymouth rock.
5. Mr. lyons edits a publication called *daybreak*, which is dedicated to the seventh generation to come.
6. As faith keeper, mr. lyons is responsible for making decisions that will ensure that the earth is habitable for that future generation.
7. He also has many other responsibilities, including speaking before the united nations.
8. Mr. lyons, other members of the iroquois league, and a group of lakota sioux addressed the united nations in geneva, switzerland.
9. Faith keepers work to uphold the traditions of their people, as well as the principles of Democracy, community, and reverence for the Natural World.
10. To learn more about Mr. Lyons and other american indian leaders, look in *the encyclopedia of Native America*, which is a reference book I learned about in American History class.

▶ EXERCISE 21 **Proofreading Sentences for the Correct Use of Commas**

Each of the following sentences needs at least one comma. Write the word or numeral that comes before each missing comma, and add the comma.

EXAMPLE   1. The Green Club collects aluminum clear glass colored glass and paper for recycling.
   1. *aluminum, glass, glass,*

1. Orb weavers are spiders that create beautiful complex round webs.
2. On July 20 1969 the *Apollo 11* lunar module landed on the moon.
3. Cheeky the neighbor's dog that chewed up my athletic shoes is now kept in his own yard.
4. Oh when will I learn not to worry so much?
5. Italy in my opinion is the most beautiful country in the world.

6. The Perseids which are meteor showers that occur annually appear to come from the constellation Perseus.
7. I wasn't chosen for the track team but I am trying out for soccer next week.
8. The American painter Charles Russell who is famous for his scenes of life in the West is my favorite artist.
9. We had planned to climb the mountain but the trail was closed because mountain lions had been sighted in the area.
10. Tired of waiting for the movie to start the audience began to murmur and fidget.

▶ EXERCISE 22 **Using Commas Correctly**

Each of the following sentences needs at least one comma. Write the word or numeral that comes before each missing comma, and add the comma.

EXAMPLE   **1.** Tony have you ever heard of Dr. Percy L. Julian?
           1. *Tony,*

1. Julian born in Montgomery Alabama in 1899 grew up to become a renowned scientist.
2. After studying at DePauw University he graduated with highest honors; in fact he received a Phi Beta Kappa key and delivered the valedictory address.
3. Julian went on to Harvard where he earned a master's degree and then traveled to Austria to earn a Ph.D. at the University of Vienna.
4. As Ahmed says Dr. Julian must have been a brilliant man.
5. Dr. Julian taught at Howard University and at West Virginia University but his fame began after he went to work as a research chemist for Glidden a paint company in Chicago Illinois.
6. During World War II Dr. Julian created a firefighting foam which by the way was made out of soybean protein.
7. His achievements earned him the Spingarn Medal the NAACP's highest award.
8. Interested in developing other uses for soybeans Dr. Julian established Julian Laboratories and its subsidiaries.

9. In his lifetime he developed an inexpensive cortisone for arthritis sufferers drugs to relieve glaucoma drugs to help victims of rheumatic fever and many other helpful medicines.
10. Dr. Julian died in 1975 but his impressive achievements live on.

▶ EXERCISE 23 **Using Semicolons and Colons Correctly**

The following sentences need semicolons and colons. Write the word or numeral preceding and the word or numeral following the needed punctuation, and insert the proper punctuation. In some instances, you will need to replace commas with either semicolons or colons.

EXAMPLE   **1.** My brother likes to read adventure novels I prefer autobiographies of sports figures.
   1. *novels; I*

1. We signed up for field hockey, however, the heavy snow has prevented practice all month.
2. In art class, Joanna, Elaine, and Jim used acrylics and Todd, Tonya, and Jasper used oils.
3. We missed the 4 15 bus and had to wait an hour for the next one.
4. The movie Suzanne recommended was *Theremin An Electronic Odyssey.*
5. This airport has direct flights to Frankfurt, Germany, Rome, Italy, London, England, and Paris, France.
6. Our choir is singing a song based on Psalm 19 14.
7. Our neighborhood has fiestas for various holidays for example, we have a piñata party on Cinco de Mayo each year.
8. I walk to school every day with Darla, Gene, and Greg and Sven, Petra, and Arnold join us on the walk home.
9. I have several postcards that my stepsister sent me from towns with unusual names, for instance, here are ones from Cut and Shoot, Texas, and Truth or Consequences, New Mexico.
10. The Ecology Club has adopted the following projects this year setting out recycling bins, planting trees in the schoolyard, and adopting two miles of highway to keep clean.

▶ EXERCISE 24 **Punctuating Dialogue**

Add paragraph indentions, and insert quotation marks and other punctuation where needed in the following dialogue. You may need to change the capitalization of some words, too.

EXAMPLE   [1] Hey, Sarah, I hear you've become a vegetarian Colin said. Don't you ever get tired of eating nothing but vegetables?
[2] You've got some things to learn about vegetarians! Sarah said.

1.   *"Hey, Sarah, I hear you've become a vegetarian," Colin said. "Don't you ever get tired of eating nothing but vegetables?"*

2.   *"You've got some things to learn about vegetarians!" Sarah said.*

[1] So tell me Colin said, What exactly is a vegetarian? [2] Well, you already know that a vegetarian is someone who doesn't eat meat Sarah said But you don't seem to know what a vegetarian does eat. [3] Your mistake about a vegetarian diet is one that many people make. They think that a vegetarian eats only vegetables, but vegetarians eat quite a variety of foods. [4] Colin replied okay what else do vegetarians eat?

[5] Well, Sarah answered I eat whatever I want that isn't meat, and I try to eat healthful foods. I eat vegetables, of course, but also grains, breads, pastas, beans, nuts, soups, cereals, and fruit.

[6] Do you eat eggs and dairy products?

[7] Yes, Sarah replied I do, but some vegetarians don't. For instance, I sometimes eat quiche, cheese-and-vegetable enchiladas, and bowls of cereal with milk.

[8] Colin said, I guess you aren't having any trouble finding things to eat. I'm wondering, though, why you decided to become a vegetarian. [9] I just wanted to feel better. Studies show that being a vegetarian is very healthful Sarah said.

[10] Colin said I remember learning that people who don't eat meat are less likely to have heart disease than people who do eat meat and that a diet without any animal products is cholesterol free. I wonder if there are any other health benefits of vegetarianism.

▶ EXERCISE 25 **Punctuating and Capitalizing Quotations**

For each of the following sentences, insert quotation marks and other marks of punctuation where needed, and change lowercase letters to capital letters as necessary.

EXAMPLE   **1.** Should the U.S. flag be flown at the same level as or higher than a state flag asked Earl
          1. *"Should the U.S. flag be flown at the same level as or higher than a state flag?" asked Earl.*

1. Megan's note says, The electrician at the repair shop thinks that our VCR will be ready by 5:00 P.M.
2. Physical therapy Karen said is really strengthening my brother's legs.
3. Leiningen Versus the Ants, by Carl Stephenson, is a frightening short story Bob said.
4. Yes Laura Emilio replied you will want to plant the azaleas in partial sunlight.
5. Sean asked why did the judge shout Order in the court! just before she called a recess?
6. The following seniors will serve as ushers at the graduation ceremonies: Alexandra, Michael, and Jim, Mrs. Jackson said.
7. When she hit her finger with the hammer while she was repairing the roof, Hannah yelled that does it!
8. What I asked the doctor is the patella?
9. The song Long Distance Call was one of the hits of the Chicago blues singer Muddy Waters.
10. No! Paula exclaimed I didn't say to paint it green!

▶ EXERCISE 26 **Correcting Phrases and Clauses by Adding Apostrophes**

Proofread the following phrases and clauses, adding apostrophes where they are needed. If a phrase or a clause is correct, write C.

EXAMPLE   **1.** giving to United Ways fund
          1. *giving to United Way's fund*

1. somebodys hat
2. Are these Kims poems?
3. Judys and his show

4. Whos there?
5. both planes engines
6. The box was theirs.
7. How many *a*s are in *aardvark*?
8. womens shoes
9. Anya and Tonys team
10. hadnt finished
11. that canoes hull
12. no one elses parents
13. Its memory capacity is huge.
14. that clubs newsletter
15. Mr. Harriss Irish setter
16. neither ones fault
17. Howards and Marilyns tests
18. because Im sleepy
19. whose ring
20. Its going to rain.
21. the Sanchezes family reunion
22. one kings horses
23. Sams back already.
24. Dot your *i*s and cross your *t*s.
25. ten oclock

▶ EXERCISE 27 **Correcting Spelling Errors**

Each sentence contains two spelling errors. Find the errors, and rewrite the words correctly.

EXAMPLE   **1.** We forfieted the free vacation and enjoied our leisure time at home.
            1. *forfeited, enjoyed*

1. The poodle reacted in a wierd way, stareing straight ahead.
2. The pityful wailing of the lost kittens helped Stacy find them.
3. We traveled on the route that had been maped out for us and proceded at a steady pace.
4. They finally conceeded that the new system would cost a 3rd less to run than the old one did.
5. When the paper we had collected for recycling was wieghed, we were gratifyed to learn that the amount exceeded one ton.

6. All the puppys at the animal shelter were cute, but the 1st one they showed us was the one we decided to adopt.
7. 40 people signed up for the dance classes to learn waltzs and line dances.
8. Cleanlyness of the work space is especialy important when food is being handled.
9. My cousin drives 30 miles each way to her job at a nature preserve, where she takes care of the lions, tigers, and wolfs.
10. Both of the monkies are likely to throw tomatos at anyone standing nearby.

▶ EXERCISE 28 **Choosing Between Words Often Confused**

From each pair of words in parentheses, choose the word or words that will make the sentence correct.

EXAMPLE   **1.** (*You're, your*) endangering the pedestrians by skating too fast.
   1. *You're*

1. When I applied for work at the restaurant, I spoke with the (*personal, personnel*) manager.
2. It is a good idea to check the (*breaks, brakes*) on any vehicle before you start driving.
3. We had (*already, all ready*) opened the windows in the art room when Ms. Wong asked us to.
4. What theme do you think we should (*choose, chose*) for the prom?
5. Eleanor and Lupita said we could use (*they're, their*) binoculars when we go on the next field trip.
6. What (*effect, affect*) will all the rain have on the mown hay?
7. The elephant always returns to (*its, it's*) enclosure at feeding time.
8. Did the members of the (*counsel, council*) ever reach an agreement?
9. A (*lose, loose*) wing nut on the bracket for the spare tire caused a rattle in the trunk.
10. Use very fine, not (*course, coarse*), sandpaper for the finishing work on wood furniture or toys.

Mechanics Test: Section 1

DIRECTIONS   Each numbered item below contains an underlined group of words. Choose the answer that shows the correct capitalization, punctuation, and spelling of the underlined part. If there is no error, choose answer E (Correct as is). Indicate your response by shading in the appropriate oval on your answer sheet.

EXAMPLE

[1] <u>February 9 1998</u>

    (A) Febuary 9 1998
    (B) Febuary 9, 1998
    (C) February 9th 1998
    (D) February 9, 1998
    (E) Correct as is

SAMPLE ANSWER   1. (A) (B) (C) ● (E)

---

    327 Hickory Lane
[1] <u>Ankeny, Iowa, 50021</u>
    February 9, 1998

[2] <u>Susan Washington DVM</u>
    49-A Johnson Circle
    Des Moines, IA 50320

[3] <u>Dear Dr. Washington:</u>

Thank you for [4] <u>agreing to lead</u> the discussion at our club's next meeting. We members of [5] <u>Future Farmers of America</u> know how important the practice of veterinary medicine is to agriculture. [6] <u>39 students</u> have already signed up to attend. As I mentioned on the phone last [7] <u>week, our meeting will take place in Healy Lecture hall.</u> We will begin at [8] <u>3:00 PM,</u> and I will introduce you soon thereafter. We look forward to hearing [9] <u>your views on veterinary medicine,</u> and hope that you will stay for refreshments after the meeting.

[10] <u>yours sincerely,</u>

    Michael Yoder

    Michael Yoder
    Chapter President FFA
    Ankeny High School

1. (A) Ankeny, Ia. 50021
   (B) Ankeny, IA 50021
   (C) Ankeny IA, 50021
   (D) Ankeny I.A., 50021
   (E) Correct as is

2. (A) Susan Washington DVM.
   (B) Susan Washington, D.V.M.
   (C) Susan Washington, DVM
   (D) Susan Washington: DVM
   (E) Correct as is

3. (A) Dear Dr Washington:
   (B) Dear Dr. Washington,
   (C) Dear dr. Washington,
   (D) Dear Dr. Washington;
   (E) Correct as is

4. (A) agreing, to lead
   (B) agreing to led
   (C) agreeing to lead
   (D) agreeing too lead
   (E) Correct as is

5. (A) Future Farmers Of America
   (B) future farmers of america
   (C) future farmers of America
   (D) future Farmers of America
   (E) Correct as is

6. (A) Thirty nine students
   (B) Thirty-nine students
   (C) Thirty-Nine students
   (D) Thirty-nine students'
   (E) Correct as is

7. (A) week: our meeting will take place in Healy lecture hall
   (B) week: our meeting will take place in Healy Lecture Hall
   (C) week, our meeting will take place in Healy lecture hall
   (D) week, our meeting will take place in Healy Lecture Hall
   (E) Correct as is

8. (A) 3:00 PM
   (B) 3:00 PM.,
   (C) 3:00 P.M.
   (D) 3:00 P.M.,
   (E) Correct as is

9. (A) you're views on veterinary medicine,
   (B) you're views on veterinary medicine;
   (C) your views on veterinary medicine
   (D) your views on veterinary medicine:
   (E) Correct as is

10. (A) Yours sincerely,
    (B) Yours' sincerely,
    (C) Your's sincerely,
    (D) Yours sincerely:
    (E) Correct as is

Mechanics Test: Section 2

DIRECTIONS   Each of the following sentences contains an underlined word or group of words. Choose the answer that shows the correct capitalization, punctuation, and spelling of the underlined part. If there is no error, choose answer E (Correct as is). Indicate your response by shading in the appropriate oval on your answer sheet.

EXAMPLE

1. Please post these announcements for <u>the Columbus winter Carnival</u>.

   (A) the Columbus Winter Carnival
   (B) the columbus winter carnival
   (C) The Columbus Winter Carnival
   (D) the Columbus Winter carnival
   (E) Correct as is

SAMPLE ANSWER 1. ⬤ Ⓑ Ⓒ Ⓓ Ⓔ

1. "Can you tell us the <u>moral of the fable that we just read, Josh"?</u> asked Ms. Chen.

   (A) moral of the fable that we just read, Josh?"
   (B) morale of the fable that we just read, Josh?
   (C) moral of the fable that we just read," Josh?
   (D) moral of the fable that we just read, Josh?,"
   (E) Correct as is

2. We'll need <u>streamers balloons</u> and confetti to decorate for the baby shower.

   (A) Well, need streamers, balloons,
   (B) We'll need streamers, balloons,
   (C) We'll need: streamers, balloons,
   (D) We'll need streamers balloons,
   (E) Correct as is

3. <u>Dr. Martin Luther King, Jr.,</u> was awarded the Nobel Peace Prize in 1964.

   (A) Dr Martin Luther King, Jr.,
   (B) Dr. Martin Luther King Jr.,
   (C) Dr. Martin Luther King, Jr,
   (D) Dr. Martin Luther King, jr.,
   (E) Correct as is

4. Choose a free subscription to one of these <u>magazines *Time,*</u> *Newsweek,* or *Sports Illustrated.*

   (A) magazines, *Time,*
   (B) magazines; *Time,*
   (C) magazines: "Time,"
   (D) magazines: *Time,*
   (E) Correct as is

5. "Did Coach Sims really say, 'Run another <u>mile?'"</u> gasped Carla.

   (A) mile?"
   (B) mile,"
   (C) mile'?"
   (D) mile,'"
   (E) Correct as is

6. The <u>men's and womens</u> shoe departments and the housewares department are having sales now.

   (A) mens and women's
   (B) men's and women's
   (C) mens' and womens'
   (D) mens and womens
   (E) Correct as is

7. The bus driver <u>said "that we should be quiet."</u>

   (A) said, "That we should be quiet."
   (B) said "That we should be quiet."
   (C) said, that we should be quiet.
   (D) said that we should be quiet.
   (E) Correct as is

8. I've visited three state <u>capitals: Boise, Idaho, Tallahassee, Florida;</u> and Montpelier, Vermont.

   (A) capitals: Boise, Idaho, Tallahassee, Florida,
   (B) capitols: Boise, Idaho; Tallahassee, Florida;
   (C) capitols: Boise; Idaho; Tallahassee; Florida;
   (D) capitals: Boise, Idaho; Tallahassee, Florida;
   (E) Correct as is

9. Whether or not it rains will not <u>effect their plans</u> for this weekend.

   (A) Whether or not it rains will not affect their plans
   (B) Weather or not it rains will not affect their plans
   (C) Whether or not it rains will not affect they're plans
   (D) Whether or not it rains will not effect they're plans
   (E) Correct as is

10. <u>Its not John whose</u> left his papers in the library.

    (A) Its not John who's
    (B) It's not John whose
    (C) Its' not John who's
    (D) It's not John who's
    (E) Correct as is

PART THREE

RESOURCES

31 Speaking

32 Listening and Viewing

33 The Library/Media Center

34 The Dictionary

35 Vocabulary

36 Letters and Forms

37 Reading, Studying, and Test Taking

APPENDIX OF DIAGRAMING

GLOSSARY OF TERMS

GLOSSARY

31 SPEAKING

Skills and Strategies

A good speech requires careful thought and thorough preparation. To communicate effectively, you should think about your purpose, your topic, and your audience.

The Communication Cycle

Oral communication is a process that you take part in when you communicate your feelings or ideas to another person. In turn, this person responds to your message. This response is called *feedback.*

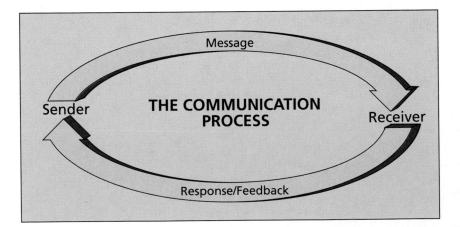

Nonverbal Communication

In addition to words (verbal signals), you communicate meaning with *nonverbal* (unspoken) signals. How you stand, move about, and gesture can communicate a variety of messages.

NONVERBAL SIGNALS	EXAMPLES
Gestures	thumbs up (approval, encouragement), shrugging (uncertainty), nodding head (yes), shaking head (disagreement)
Facial expressions	smiling, raising an eyebrow, smirking, frowning, grimacing, pouting, grinning, (meanings vary depending on context)
Body language	turning away (rejection), stroking the chin (puzzlement), crossing arms on chest (reluctance, uncertainty)
Sounds	laughing, groaning, giggling (meanings vary depending on context)

Speaking Informally

Speaking Impromptu

An *impromptu speech* is one you make on the spur of the moment. The ideas you express have not been prepared in advance. When an impromptu speech is required, consider the following suggestions.

1. *Consider your purpose.* Impromptu speeches are often informative (telling what you know about a subject) or persuasive (giving your opinion or trying to convince your listeners).
2. *Consider your topic.* Cover the main ideas and add details to support or explain your main points.
3. *Consider your audience.* Think about the specific speaking occasion and consider the interests and knowledge of the audience.

RESOURCES

Communicating Effectively

The most important part of speaking in many situations is to remember that you need to speak clearly and courteously. The following are situations in which you can work on your speaking skills. You will use these skills in similar situations in the workplace.

Speaking on the Telephone

1. Call people at a reasonable hour.
2. Identify yourself and state your purpose for calling.
3. Be polite and speak clearly.
4. Keep your call to an appropriate length.

Giving Instructions or Directions

1. Divide the information into clear, logical steps.
2. Give the steps in order.
3. Check to be sure your listeners understand all the steps.
4. If necessary, repeat the steps in the same order.

Making Introductions

1. Take the initiative; introduce yourself if no one else does.
2. When introducing others, identify them by name.
3. It is customary to address first
   - a person of higher status
   - an older person before a younger person
   - the person you know better

Speaking Formally

Preparing a Speech

When you are required to give a speech, you must choose a suitable subject and determine your purpose for speaking. You need to limit your subject to a manageable topic so that it can be adequately treated in your speech and so that it reflects a definite purpose.

PURPOSE	DESCRIPTION OF SPEECH	EXAMPLES OF SPEECH TITLES
To inform	gives facts *or* explains how to do something	Animals That Live on the Ocean Floor How to Avoid Snakebite
To persuade	attempts to change an opinion *or* attempts to get listeners to act	Senior Citizens Are Important to the Community You Should Eat a Low-fat Diet
To entertain	relates an amusing story or incident	My First Job as a Baby Sitter

Analyzing Your Audience

Your audience is the group of people who are going to listen to your speech. You will need to think about the needs, background, and interests of your audience if you expect them to understand and respond to your speech topic.

AUDIENCE CONSIDERATIONS		
QUESTIONS ABOUT AUDIENCE	EVALUATION	YOUR SPEECH WILL NEED
What does the audience already know about this subject?	very little	to provide background or details to better inform your listeners
	a little	to include some background details
	a lot	to focus on interesting aspects or issues
How interested will the audience be in this subject?	very interested	to maintain their interest
	somewhat interested	to focus on aspects that most interest them
	uninterested	to focus on persuading your listeners that this topic is important

RESOURCES

Gathering Material

After you've chosen a topic for your speech, you'll need to plan how you want to develop your topic. Then you'll need to brainstorm or do research to find material that supports your ideas or opinions. Try the following strategies for gathering interesting information.

1. *Explore your own background.* Ask yourself what you already know about the topic. Explore your own knowledge and experience.
2. *Observe.* Keep an eye out as you look through newspapers and periodicals for material related to your topic. Speeches or radio and television broadcasts may provide you with additional information.
3. *Read.* Go to the library. Use reference sources, magazines, and books to research your topic.
4. *Reflect.* Review the material you have gathered and take time to become familiar with it.

Organizing Speech Notes and Materials

The most effective type of speech to give is often an *extemporaneous speech.* An extemporaneous speech is one that is carefully developed and organized, but not memorized.

To develop an extemporaneous speech, you usually prepare a complete outline of your main points. Then use your outline to prepare note cards that can be used while delivering your speech to help you remember main ideas and supporting details.

Here are some suggestions for preparing your note cards.

1. Include one key idea (and possibly an example or detail) for each card.
2. Make a special note card for a quotation or a series of dates or statistics that you plan to read word for word.
3. Make a special note card to indicate when you plan to show a chart, diagram, graph, drawing, model, or other visual.
4. Number your completed cards to help you keep them in the appropriate order.

Speaking Expressively

Have you ever listened to a speaker who put you to sleep? You don't want that to happen to your audience. To speak expressively, you should practice using good verbal and nonverbal communication signals. Follow these suggestions.

1. *Stand confidently.* Be alert, be interested in what you're saying, and use natural gestures.
2. *Speak clearly.* Speak loudly enough so everyone in the audience can hear you. Pronounce your words slowly and carefully.
3. *Look at your audience as you speak.* Make direct eye contact as you focus on the faces of your listeners.
4. *Choose your words carefully.* Use specific rather than general words. Also, use vivid words that appeal to the senses to reinforce meaning.
5. *Use variety in speaking.* Vocal variety helps emphasize your message.
   - *Volume:* Speak loudly enough to be heard, but raise or lower your sound volume for emphasis.
   - *Pitch:* Use the rise and fall of your voice to emphasize various ideas and avoid a monotone.
   - *Stress:* Emphasize important words.
   - *Rate:* Speak at a comfortable, relaxed pace.

Giving Your Speech

Most speakers feel nervous before giving a speech. In fact, a little nervousness can help you by keeping you alert and focusing your energy. The following suggestions will help you avoid excessive nervousness.

1. *Relax.* Realize that your audience wants you to do well. They aren't waiting for you to make mistakes.
2. *Be prepared.* Organize and practice with your note cards and visual aids.
3. *Practice your speech.* Rehearse as if you're giving the actual presentation.
4. *Focus on your purpose.* Remember what you want to accomplish. Instead of focusing on yourself, think how your speech will affect your audience.

RESOURCES

Special Speaking Situations

Making an Announcement

The purpose of an announcement is to provide general information to an audience. Follow these suggestions for making an effective announcement.

1. When preparing your announcement, include all the necessary facts and add interesting details that will capture your listeners' attention.
2. Get your audience's attention and then announce your message slowly, clearly, and carefully.
3. Repeat information if necessary to be sure it is clear to your listeners.

Making an Introduction to a Presentation

An introduction is often given before a speaker's presentation or before a short performance. This type of an introduction focuses the audience's attention. It also provides listeners with important information about the speaker, the players, the subject, the dramatic work, or the author of the work being presented.

A good introduction fills in details that the audience might need to know before the main presentation begins. But don't provide too many details. A good introduction is short and to the point.

Group Discussions

Establishing a Purpose

Group discussions or cooperative learning groups work best when the group has a specific purpose to accomplish. This purpose may be

- to share ideas and cooperate in group learning
- to suggest solutions for solving a problem
- to make an evaluation, a recommendation, or a decision

To establish the purpose for the group, first decide what specific task the group needs to accomplish. Then the group can determine a plan of action, depending on how much time is allowed to reach this goal.

Assigning Roles for a Discussion

Each participant in a group discussion takes a role with specific responsibilities. Sometimes a group selects a chairperson who will help keep the discussion moving along smoothly. Another group member may be chosen to be secretary or reporter (recorder), with the responsibility of taking notes during the discussion.

Frequently, a group establishes an *agenda,* or outline of the order that they will follow in their discussion. Setting the agenda is often the responsibility of the chairperson, but the agenda may sometimes be agreed upon by all the members.

A Chairperson's Responsibilities

1. Announce the topic and establish the agenda.
2. Follow the agenda.
3. Encourage each member to participate.
4. Manage group conflict.

A Secretary's or Reporter's Responsibilities

1. Record significant information and developments.
2. Prepare a final report.

A Participant's Responsibilities

1. Take part in the discussion.
2. Cooperate and share information.
3. Listen carefully to others.
4. Be considerate.

Parliamentary Procedure

Groups such as clubs or committees often follow the principles of *parliamentary procedure* to make sure meetings are run smoothly and fairly.

RESOURCES

RULES OF PARLIAMENTARY PROCEDURE

The meeting follows a step-by-step agenda.

1. The chairperson calls the meeting to order.
2. The secretary reports details of the last meeting.
3. The treasurer makes a report.
4. Unresolved issues or actions are discussed.
5. New issues or proposed actions are discussed.
6. The chairperson ends the meeting.

The meeting has specific procedures for discussions.

1. Anyone wishing to speak must raise his or her hand until recognized by the chairperson.
2. A participant may introduce a motion by saying, "I move that . . ."
3. To support a motion or suggestion, a participant other than the one who made the motion must say, "I second the motion." If no one seconds it, the motion is then dropped.
4. If a motion is seconded, it is discussed by the group.
5. After discussion, the group votes on the motion. The chairperson usually votes only in case of a tie.

Oral Interpretation

Oral interpretation is like an acting performance. You use vocal techniques, facial expressions, body language, and gestures to indicate the meaning of the literary work you are interpreting.

Adapting Material

When you adapt material for an oral interpretation, you usually have a specific purpose, audience, and occasion in mind. Every situation has its own requirements. Be sure you have thought about factors such as the length of time for your presentation and your audience's interests. Most oral readings rely on the audience's imagination and not on props or costumes.

You will often need to make an abbreviated version, or *cutting,* of a work of fiction, nonfiction, a long poem, or a play. Here are some suggestions.

HOW TO MAKE A CUTTING

1. Follow the story line in time order.
2. Delete dialogue tags such as *she said softly.* Instead, use these clues to indicate how you should act when you interpret the character's words.
3. Take out any passages that don't contribute to the overall impression that you intend to create with your oral interpretation.

Presenting an Oral Interpretation

You may need to write an introduction to your interpretation to set the scene, tell something about the characters, give some background details about the author, or provide some necessary details about what has already taken place in the story.

To be effective in presenting an oral interpretation, you will need to prepare a reading script. A *reading script* is usually typed (double-spaced) and is marked to assist you in your interpretive reading. For example, you may underline words for emphasis or mark a slash (/) to indicate a pause.

COMPUTER NOTE: Use your word-processing program to prepare the script for your oral presentation. You can use bold, italic, or underline formatting to indicate presentation directions or notes to yourself. You can even change the type size and style for additional emphasis.

After you have developed a reading script, rehearse the material several different ways until you are satisfied that you have chosen the most effective manner of interpreting the passage.

RESOURCES

Use your voice in a manner that suits your presentation. Be sure to pronounce your words carefully. You can use your body and your voice to show that you are portraying different characters. Use body language and gestures to emphasize your meaning or to reveal traits of the major characters in the story as you act out what they say and do.

Review

EXERCISE 1 **Exploring Telephone Speaking Situations**

For each of the following situations, explain how you might handle the problem. What would you say to be polite but clear?

1. A caller is talking too long, and you need to get off the phone because your father wants to make a call.
2. You call the headquarters of a department store chain to complain about a billing error for a purchase that was charged at one of the chain's local stores.
3. You call a dentist's office at the last minute to reschedule an appointment.
4. You call a restaurant to make reservations for your family for dinner to celebrate your aunt's birthday.

EXERCISE 2 **Giving Directions**

Provide directions for each of the following situations. Make sure your directions are simple and easy to follow.

1. You are having a party Friday night. Explain to a classmate how to get from your school to your house.
2. A new student needs to know how to get from the cafeteria to the gymnasium.
3. Explain to a visitor how to get from your school to another school in the area. Be sure to point out any helpful landmarks.
4. Your aunt and uncle are visiting from another state. Give them directions to the post office nearest your house.

► EXERCISE 3 **Making Introductions**

In each of the following situations, explain what you would say.

1. You are at a party and the host doesn't seem to be around. Introduce yourself to another person who is standing alone.
2. You have an interview scheduled with Ms. Torres at the Youth Employment Center. Introduce yourself to the receptionist.
3. You are introducing your mother (or father or other relative) to your math teacher.
4. You are at your school's science fair with a friend from another school. Introduce your friend to your science teacher.

► EXERCISE 4 **Preparing and Giving a Speech**

Choose a topic for a three- to five-minute speech to give to your English class. Consider your audience and purpose when choosing your speech topic. First, gather appropriate material. Next, prepare note cards for your speech. Include one visual, such as a chart, diagram, time line, or drawing, and prepare a note card to indicate at what point in your speech you should pause to explain and incorporate this item. Finally, deliver your speech, using effective speaking techniques and appropriate nonverbal signals.

► EXERCISE 5 **Making an Announcement**

Write an announcement for one of the following events. Supply specific details wherever they are needed.

1. A car wash will be held by the sophomore class with the proceeds to benefit Special Olympics participants.
2. A special election will be held to choose the next student body president.
3. This year's sports award banquet has been scheduled. All students desiring to attend should bring the fee for tickets. Nominations for outstanding athletes in each school-sponsored sport are encouraged.

RESOURCES

4. Band members will hold a bake sale to raise money for the band's trip to compete in the state finals. You also want to encourage donations of baked goods and money from students who are not in the band.

▶ EXERCISE 6   **Introducing a Speaker**

Prepare and deliver in class an introduction for your state or national representative or senator, your mayor, your county commissioner, a school board member, or a famous person from history.

▶ EXERCISE 7   **Conducting a Group Discussion**

Select a group chairperson, and present a discussion about any of the following topics or one of your own choosing. Establish an agenda, and determine how much time you will have for your discussion.

1. Radio and television advertising
2. Comic books and their characters
3. Teenage crime
4. How to achieve a goal
5. The impact of the young voter
6. The ideal school
7. Choosing a career
8. Job opportunities in your city
9. Ways to prevent war
10. Our local environment

▶ EXERCISE 8   **Presenting an Oral Interpretation**

Select a portion of a short story, a scene from a play, or a section of a novel that contains a scene for one or two characters. Prepare a script for a five-minute oral interpretation to present to your classmates. Write a brief introduction that tells the title and author of the selection and gives enough background information about the characters and the setting so that your audience can understand the meaning of the scene.

32 LISTENING AND VIEWING

Strategies for Listening and Viewing

Listening and viewing are not the same as hearing and seeing. You constantly hear sounds and see images from potential sources of information, but you may not carefully listen to or look at very many of them. Listening and viewing are active processes that require you to think about what you hear and see.

If you use nonprint information as a resource for an assignment, you must be able to evaluate it and determine if it is suited to your purpose, just as you must do with print information. The listening and viewing strategies you learn in this chapter will help you do this.

Listening with a Purpose

You can become a more effective listener if you keep your purpose in mind as you listen. People hear things differently depending on what they are listening for. Common purposes for listening are

- for enjoyment or entertainment
- to gain information for personal, school, or workplace use
- to understand information or an explanation
- to evaluate or form an opinion

Listening for Information

Listening for Details

When you listen for information, you are listening for details that answer the six basic *5W-How?* questions: *Who? What? When? Where? Why?* and *How?*

For example, when you are asked to take messages on the telephone, you will need to listen to important details that the caller tells you, such as

- the caller's name
- the name of the person being called
- the caller's message
- the caller's telephone number

Using the LQ2R Method

The LQ2R study method is especially helpful when you are listening to a speaker who is giving information.

L *Listen* carefully to material as it is being presented. Focus your attention on the speaker.

Q *Question* yourself as you listen. Make a list, mentally or in your notes, of questions that occur to you.

R *Recite* in your own words the information as it is being presented. Summarize information in your mind, or jot down notes as you listen.

R *Relisten* as the speaker concludes the presentation. Major points may be reemphasized.

Listening to Instructions

Instructions are usually made up of a series of steps. When you listen to instructions, be sure you understand everything you are required to do.

1. *Listen for the order of steps.* Listen for words that tell you where each step ends and the next one begins, such as *first, second, next, then,* and *last.*

2. *Identify the number of steps in the process.* Take notes if the instructions are long and complicated.
3. *Visualize each step.* Imagine yourself actually performing each step. Try to get a mental image of what you should be doing at every step in the process.
4. *Review the steps when the speaker is finished.* Be sure you understand them.

Listening and Responding Politely

When you are listening and responding to a speaker, you are taking part in the communication cycle. Here's how to be more courteous and encouraging, both as a listener and as a responder.

1. Pay attention. Don't distract others.
2. Respect the speaker, and keep an open mind. Try to understand the speaker's point of view. Also, be aware of how your own point of view affects the way you evaluate the opinions and values of others.
3. Wait to hear the speaker's whole message before you make judgments or ask questions.
4. Ask appropriate questions loudly enough for all to hear. For better understanding, summarize or paraphrase the speaker's point you are questioning.
5. Use polite, effective language and gestures that are appropriate to the situation.

Conducting an Interview

An interview is a special listening situation. Most often an interview takes place between two people, an interviewer and the person being interviewed (called the *interviewee*). Follow these suggestions to conduct an effective interview.

Before the Interview

- Decide what information you really want to know.
- Make a list of questions. Make sure the questions are arranged in a logical order.
- Make an appointment and be prompt.

RESOURCES

During the Interview
- Give the interviewee time to answer the question.
- Pay attention, and ask questions if you're not sure you understand what the interviewee means.
- Ask permission to quote the person directly.
- Respect the interviewee's opinion. You can ask the other person to explain an opinion, but be polite, even if you disagree.
- Thank the person for allowing the interview.

After the Interview
- Check your notes to be sure they are clear.
- Summarize the interview while you still remember it.

 COMPUTER NOTE: Use your word-processing program's outlining feature to organize your prewriting or interview notes into an outline for the first draft of your paper.

Critical Listening

When you listen critically, you think carefully about what you hear. You can't remember every word a speaker says. But if you listen critically, you'll be able to find the parts of the speaker's message that are most important.

GUIDELINES FOR LISTENING CRITICALLY	
Find main ideas.	What are the most important points? Listen for clue words a speaker might use, such as *major, main, most important,* or similar words.
Identify significant details.	What dates, names, or facts does the speaker use to support the main points of the speech? What kinds of examples or explanations are used to support the main ideas?

(continued)

RESOURCES

GUIDELINES FOR LISTENING CRITICALLY *(continued)*	
Distinguish between facts and opinions.	A fact is a statement that can be proved to be true. An opinion is a belief or a judgment about something. It cannot be proved to be true.
Identify the order of organization.	What kind of order is the speaker using to arrange his or her presentation—time sequence, spatial order, order of importance?
Note comparisons and contrasts.	Are some details compared or contrasted with others?
Understand cause and effect.	Do some events that the speaker mentions relate to or affect others?
Predict outcomes and draw conclusions.	What can you reasonably conclude from the facts and evidence you have gathered from the speech?

☞ **REFERENCE NOTE:** For more information about interpreting and analyzing information, see pages 987–988.

Taking Lecture Notes

When you listen to a speaker, don't rely entirely on your memory. Take notes to help you remember information. You can take notes by writing the most important words or phrases the speaker says. Other note-taking techniques include paraphrasing and summarizing.

Paraphrasing. When you *paraphrase* material, you express the ideas of others in your own words. Translate complex terms or examples that the speaker uses into your own words, and write your paraphrase in your notes.

Summarizing. When you *summarize,* you condense material by restating it in fewer words. As you listen to the speaker, sum up the major points of the lecture. Write these statements in your lecture notes.

RESOURCES

Understanding the Impact of Mass Media

The *mass media* are forms of communication that affect you and millions of other people every day. The mass media include

- television
- radio
- newspapers
- magazines
- movies and videocassettes
- compact and laser discs
- the Internet

The mass media give you contact with the whole world. Today's mass media make all types of information available to just about everyone. Television, radio, and the Internet bring you information about world happenings almost instantly. Newspapers and magazines bring you detailed accounts and analyses of worldwide events within a short time of the occurrence.

Since the mass media distribute a great deal of information quickly, people often assume that the media's only purpose is to inform. However, the mass media also entertain. Today you can see and hear performances of your favorite music, television, and film stars, even if you never attend their performances in person. You can also tour great cities, view natural wonders, and visit historic landmarks without leaving home. When you view the media, you usually have a purpose in mind—to find information or to be entertained.

A primary goal of the broadcast and print media is to build a successful business and earn profits. Radio and television stations must find listeners and viewers. Magazines and newspapers must find readers. To do this, the media need your attention and loyalty.

The media produce programs designed to interest and entertain you so that you will continue watching, listening, or reading. Just as you have a purpose in watching or listening to the media, the media have their own purposes for you, their audience.

Both the media and the media audience have specific purposes and responsibilities. A media product may be intended by its creators to entertain you, to inform you, or to persuade you. Media products may also serve more than one purpose. For example, an editorial cartoon in a newspaper may entertain you, as well as persuade you to agree with the cartoonist's opinion.

THE MEDIA		
PURPOSE	MEANS	RESPONSIBILITIES
To attract a loyal audience To sell advertising time and increase profits	broadcasting, printing, and telecommunicating informative, entertaining, or persuasive presentations	presenting factual information in a truthful, fair, and unbiased manner striving for accuracy of information
THE AUDIENCE		
PURPOSE	MEANS	RESPONSIBILITIES
To receive information To be entertained	watching, reading, or listening to various media presentations	responding to the media actively through evaluating and assessing presentations choosing whether or not to watch, read, or listen to a presentation; or responding by writing letters or otherwise demonstrating an opinion

RESOURCES

Persuasive Techniques

Advertisers, politicians, and others frequently buy media time to sell their products or ideas. To convince you, they may use *persuasive techniques.* Knowing about persuasive techniques will help you evaluate the factors that are used in the media to influence you in various ways.

COMMON PERSUASIVE TECHNIQUES FOUND IN THE MEDIA	
Bandwagon	Those who use this technique urge you to "jump on the bandwagon" by suggesting that you should do or believe something because everyone (or everyone admirable or worthwhile) is doing it.
Testimonial	Experts or famous people sometimes give a personal "testimony" about a product or idea. However, the person offering the testimonial may not really know much about that particular product or idea.
"Plain folks"	Ordinary people (or people who pretend to be ordinary) are often used to persuade others. People tend to believe others who seem to be similar to themselves.
Emotional words	This technique uses words that appeal to your emotions rather than to your ability to reason.

Viewing for Information

Sources of Information

To use television programs and videos as sources of information for your writing, you must develop active viewing strategies. These strategies should reflect an awareness of both the persuasive techniques used by the media and the ultimate purposes of the media, which were discussed earlier in this chapter.

Since television programming is designed for many purposes, you must determine which kinds of programs are appropriate sources. If you are writing a research report about curfew laws for teenagers, for example, you might watch these types of programs for information.

- local or national news reports
- investigative news reports
- newsmagazines
- interviews or discussions

RESOURCES

Other kinds of television programming and videos that provide information include

- documentary or educational programs (history, biography, geography, science, nature)
- political speeches, debates, and town meetings
- trials or government hearings
- legislative sessions
- press conferences

When you use a television program or video as a source for a research report, take notes just as you would from a printed source. If you are going to quote any information, make sure you do so precisely. Be sure to list the source on your Works Cited list.

 REFERENCE NOTE: For information about documenting sources, see pages 416–418 and 428–429.

Evaluating What You See

Many viewers searching for information concentrate on just understanding what they see and hear. Critical viewers go a step further: They evaluate both the images and the spoken words.

Keep these questions in mind when you evaluate a television show or video for information:

1. How reliable and accurate is the information?
2. Who wrote the words being spoken? How knowledgeable or qualified is that person?
3. What kinds of images are shown? Have the images been selected to create an emotional impact?
4. Does the program present facts, opinions, or both? Does the factual information come from a first-hand report? statistics? a study? a survey? Is the source of information identified in the program or credits?
5. If the show presents experts, who are they, and what are their qualifications?
6. If the program presents a controversial issue, are both sides of the issue—or several different viewpoints—presented? Does the program show *bias* (a leaning or inclination toward one side of an issue) in any way?

What You Can Do

Knowing to ask the questions on the preceding page is an important step in becoming a critical viewer, but how can you find the answers to these questions?

1. *Watch the credits.* At the end of the program, a list of credits identifies the producer, the director, the writer, and the year the program was created. Experts may also be identified in the credits.
2. *Compare coverage.* Check the same story or issue in other programs and in other media. If every source reports basically the same facts, chances are the facts are accurate and unbiased.
3. *Make your views known.* Contact the director of programming at local television stations or national networks. Ask questions and make comments about the programs you watch. Some local TV stations offer viewers an opportunity to present their opinions on the air.
4. *Find out who's really who.* Read widely, and talk to adults to identify organizations, special-interest groups, and lobbyists, and to understand their positions.

Review

▶ EXERCISE 1 **Listening to Instructions**

Present instructions explaining how to do or make something, with the steps of the process listed in a specific order. Next, allow your classmates a chance to ask questions. Then, call on classmates to repeat your instructions to be sure that everyone understands all the steps.

▶ EXERCISE 2 **Listening Critically**

Take brief notes while listening to a short speech presented by your teacher in class. Then, answer the following questions about the speech.

1. What are the main ideas expressed in the speech?
2. What details are used to support the main points in the speech? Identify several supporting details.
3. Identify one fact and one opinion mentioned in the speech. What reasons does the speaker give that support this opinion?
4. What is the order of the speech's organization?
5. Draw a conclusion about the ideas presented in the speech. Was the speech convincing? Why or why not?

▶ EXERCISE 3   **Identifying Purpose in Mass Media**

Work in small groups to analyze a copy of a magazine or newspaper. List examples of regular features. Which are primarily for entertainment? for information? for persuasion? Prepare a brief report, and present it in class.

▶ EXERCISE 4   **Recognizing Persuasive Techniques**

Identify the persuasive technique used in each item.

1. "Join all the happy customers who buy our product."
2. "He's a greedy politician who will steal every taxpayer's money."
3. "As an Olympic champion, I can tell you this investment is solid gold."
4. "I'm just an 'average Joe,' but I know she's got the right stuff to be a great mayor."

▶ EXERCISE 5   **Viewing Critically for Information**

Work with a partner or small group to evaluate coverage of a specific news story. Each person should select a different channel and watch one national news report about the same national political event. Compare the different newscasts' coverage of the story by answering the following questions, and report your findings to the class.

1. Which newscast gave the most emphasis to the story?
2. Which report was easiest to understand? Which seemed most accurate? Support your choices with examples.
3. What images were shown with each story? Why do you think these images were chosen?

RESOURCES

33 THE LIBRARY/ MEDIA CENTER

Finding and Using Information

You can find the answers to a great number of questions by consulting the resources available in a library or media center. To take advantage of these resources, however, you must know how to find out what information sources your library contains and how the library's contents are arranged.

The libraries in schools and communities are similar to those in many businesses. If you understand the arrangement of your school or public library, you should be able to use the library in your workplace.

Classifying and Arranging Information

Libraries arrange books by classifying them according to the Dewey decimal or the Library of Congress system. These systems assign a number and letter code—a *call number*—to each book. The call number tells you how the book has been classified and where it can be found in the library.

Most school libraries use the Dewey decimal system. Using this system, works of nonfiction are assigned a number in one of ten subject categories.

Dewey Decimal Arrangement of Fiction

According to the *Dewey decimal system,* works of fiction are grouped in alphabetical order by their authors' last names. When a library has several novels by the same author, they are arranged alphabetically by the first word of their titles (not counting *A, An,* or *The*). Sometimes, collections of short stories are grouped separately.

Types of Card Catalogs

The *online catalog* is a computerized version of the card catalog. To find a catalog listing, type in an author's name, a title, or a subject on the library's computer. The computer then displays the results of your search request. When you select a title from the search results, information about the book, similar to this example, is shown.

MATERIAL:	Book
CALL NUMBER:	910.91432 THA
AUTHOR:	Thayer, Helen
TITLE:	Polar dream/Helen Thayer
PUBLICATION:	New York: Simon & Schuster, © 1993.
DESCRIPTION:	254 p., [8] p. of plates: col. ill., map; 25 cm.
ISBN:	0671793861
NOTES:	Foreword by Sir Edmund Hillary
SUBJECT:	Thayer, Helen—Journeys
SUBJECT:	Women explorers
SUBJECT:	North Pole

The *card catalog* is a cabinet of small drawers that contains cards. These cards list books by title, author, and subject. For each book in the library, there are at least two cards—a *title card* and an *author card*. If the book is nonfiction, there is a third card—a *subject card*. You can tell what type of card it is by what is printed on its top line. Occasionally, you may find *"see"* or *"see also"* cards. These are cross-reference cards that tell you where additional information on this subject may be found.

RESOURCES

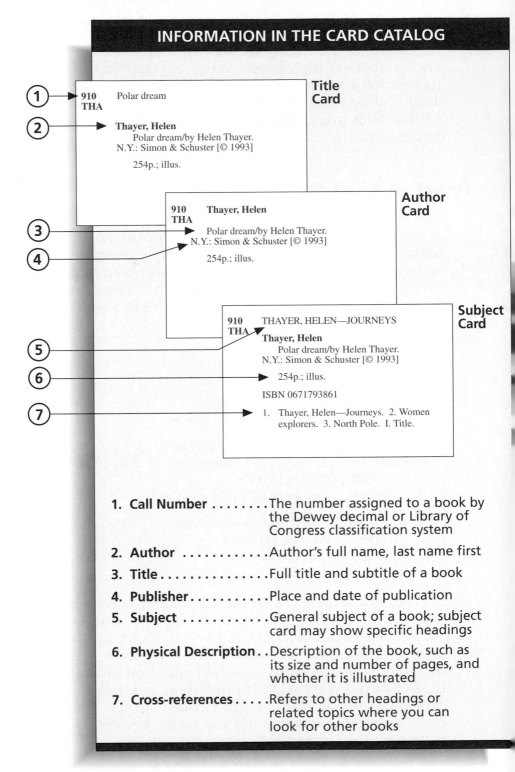

INFORMATION IN THE CARD CATALOG

Title Card

① 910 THA   Polar dream

② Thayer, Helen
    Polar dream/by Helen Thayer.
    N.Y.: Simon & Schuster [© 1993]

    254p.; illus.

Author Card

910 THA   Thayer, Helen

③ Polar dream/by Helen Thayer.
④ N.Y.: Simon & Schuster [© 1993]

    254p.; illus.

Subject Card

910 THA   THAYER, HELEN—JOURNEYS

⑤ Thayer, Helen
    Polar dream/by Helen Thayer.
    N.Y.: Simon & Schuster [© 1993]

⑥ 254p.; illus.

    ISBN 0671793861

⑦ 1. Thayer, Helen—Journeys. 2. Women
    explorers. 3. North Pole. I. Title.

1. **Call Number** . . . . The number assigned to a book by the Dewey decimal or Library of Congress classification system

2. **Author** . . . . Author's full name, last name first

3. **Title** . . . . Full title and subtitle of a book

4. **Publisher** . . . . Place and date of publication

5. **Subject** . . . . General subject of a book; subject card may show specific headings

6. **Physical Description** . . Description of the book, such as its size and number of pages, and whether it is illustrated

7. **Cross-references** . . . . . Refers to other headings or related topics where you can look for other books

Using Reference Materials

The *Readers' Guide*

To find a magazine article, use the *Readers' Guide to Periodical Literature*. The *Readers' Guide* indexes articles, poems, and stories from more than 150 magazines. Articles are listed alphabetically both by author and by subject. Use the key at the front of the *Readers' Guide* to find the meanings of the abbreviations used in the entries. Both the printed and the online versions of the *Readers' Guide* sometimes provide abstracts.

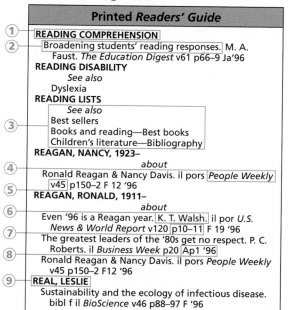

Printed *Readers' Guide*

① **READING COMPREHENSION**
② Broadening students' reading responses. M. A.
   Faust. *The Education Digest* v61 p66–9 Ja'96
READING DISABILITY
   See also
   Dyslexia
READING LISTS
      See also
③ Best sellers
   Books and reading—Best books
   Children's literature—Bibliography
REAGAN, NANCY, 1923–
④   *about*
   Ronald Reagan & Nancy Davis. il pors *People Weekly*
⑤ v45 p150–2 F 12 '96
REAGAN, RONALD, 1911–
⑥   *about*
   Even '96 is a Reagan year. K. T. Walsh. il por *U.S.*
⑦   *News & World Report* v120 p10–11 F 19 '96
   The greatest leaders of the '80s get no respect. P. C.
⑧   Roberts. il *Business Week* p20 Ap1 '96
   Ronald Reagan & Nancy Davis. il pors *People Weekly*
   v45 p150–2 F12 '96
⑨ **REAL, LESLIE**
   Sustainability and the ecology of infectious disease.
   bibl f il *BioScience* v46 p88–97 F '96

① Subject entry
② Title of article
③ Subject cross-reference
④ Name of magazine
⑤ Volume number of magazine
⑥ Author of article
⑦ Page references
⑧ Date of magazine
⑨ Author entry

Result of Online Search of *Readers' Guide*

AUTHOR:	Walsh, Kenneth T.
TITLE:	Even '96 is a Reagan year. (candidates striving to claim Reagan's mantle)
SOURCE:	U.S. News & World Report v. 120 (Feb. 19 '96) p. 10–11 il
STANDARD NO:	0041-5537
DATE:	1996
RECORD TYPE:	art
CONTENTS:	feature article
SUBJECT:	Reagan, Ronald, 1911–
	Republican Party (U.S.)
	Presidential candidates—1996.
	United States—History—1981–1989.

RESOURCES

Special Information Sources

The *vertical file* contains up-to-date materials such as pamphlets, newspaper clippings, and pictures.

Microforms are reduced-size pages from various publications. The two most common types are *microfilm* (a roll or reel of film) and *microfiche* (a sheet of film). A projector enlarges the images to a readable size.

Many libraries use computers to research reference sources. Some libraries are linked to **online databases.** These databases store all types of information. Libraries that are linked to the **Internet,** an international network of computers, have access to thousands of information sources. You search for a specific topic by typing a **keyword** or key phrase. Ask your librarian for help in wording your search requests and in using the Internet.

Reference Sources

There are many types of reference sources that you can use to find specific kinds of information.

REFERENCE SOURCES	
TYPE	DESCRIPTION

ENCYCLOPEDIAS
 	
Collier's Encyclopedia
Compton's Encyclopedia
The Encyclopedia Americana
The New Encyclopaedia
   Britannica
The World Book Multimedia
   Encyclopedia™
	■ multiple volumes
	■ articles arranged alphabetically by subject
	■ best source for general information
	■ may have index or annuals

GENERAL BIOGRAPHICAL
   REFERENCES
 	
Current Biography Yearbook
Dictionary of American
   Biography
Biography Index (database)
Webster's New Biographical
   Dictionary
	■ information about birth, nationality, and major accomplishments of prominent people

(continued)

RESOURCES

REFERENCE SOURCES *(continued)*

TYPE	DESCRIPTION
SPECIAL BIOGRAPHICAL REFERENCES *American Men & Women of Science* (database) *Mexican American Biographies* *Contemporary Authors* (series)	▪ information about people noted for accomplishments in a specific field or for membership in a specific group
ATLASES *Atlas of World Cultures* *National Geographic Atlas of the World*	▪ maps and geographical information
ALMANACS *The World Almanac and Book of Facts* *Information Please Almanac: Atlas & Yearbook*	▪ up-to-date information about current events, facts, statistics, and dates
SOURCES OF QUOTATIONS Bartlett's *Familiar Quotations* *Gale's Quotations: Who Said What?*™ (CD-ROM)	▪ famous quotations indexed or grouped by subject ▪ often tells author, source, and date
SOURCES OF SYNONYMS *Roget's International Thesaurus* *The New Roget's Thesaurus in Dictionary Form* *Webster's New Dictionary of Synonyms*	▪ lists of exact or more interesting words to express ideas
LITERATURE REFERENCE SOURCES *Granger's Index to Poetry* *Subject Index to Poetry* *Essay and General Literature Index* *Short Story Index* *Gale Literary Index CD-ROM*	▪ condensed information about various literary works

RESOURCES

Review

▶ EXERCISE 1 **Using Card Catalogs**

Use the card catalog or online catalog in your library to find the following information. If the information cannot be found, write "not in our library."

1. List the title of one book by each of the following authors.
   a. Marjorie Kinnan Rawlings
   b. Toni Cade Bambara

2. Find the title card for each of the following books. Give the author's full name.
   a. *The House on Mango Street*
   b. *Johnny Tremain*

3. Find a book on each of these subjects. List the title, author, and call number of each book.
   a. Inuits (or Eskimos)
   b. Martin Luther King, Jr.

▶ EXERCISE 2 **Using the *Readers' Guide***

In the *Readers' Guide*, find one entry listed for each of the following subjects. For each entry, give the title, author or authors (if given), magazine, date, and page numbers.

EXAMPLE Subject: water pollution
Readers' Guide entry: Our Polluted Runoff
J. G. Mitchell
il maps National Geographic
v189 p106–25 F '96

ANSWER *Title: "Our Polluted Runoff"*
Author: J. G. Mitchell
Magazine: National Geographic
Date: February 1996
Page Numbers: 106–125

1. games
2. artificial intelligence
3. African popular music
4. family
5. health

34 THE DICTIONARY

Types and Contents

Types of Dictionaries

There are many different types of dictionaries. They vary in the kinds of information they contain and in the arrangement of their contents. Some dictionaries contain terms and definitions used in a single occupation, such as computer programming. These dictionaries are designed to be used in the workplace.

TYPES OF DICTIONARIES		
TYPES OF DICTIONARIES	NUMBER OF ENTRIES	NUMBER OF PAGES
Unabridged *Webster's Third New International Dictionary, Unabridged*	460,000	2,662
College/Abridged *Merriam-Webster's Collegiate Dictionary,* Tenth Edition	160,000	1,600
Paperback *The Random House Dictionary*	74,000	1,054

A SAMPLE ENTRY

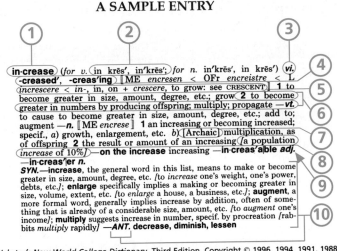

From *Webster's New World College Dictionary*, Third Edition. Copyright © 1996, 1994, 1991, 1988 by Simon & Schuster, Inc. Reprinted by permission of Macmillan USA, a Simon & Schuster Macmillan Company.

1. **Entry word.** The entry word shows how the word is spelled and how it is divided into syllables. The entry word may also show capitalization and provide alternate spellings.
2. **Pronunciation.** The pronunciation is shown using accent marks and other phonetic respellings or diacritical marks. A pronunciation key is provided as a guide to diacritical marks or phonetic symbols.
3. **Part-of-speech labels.** These labels (usually in abbreviated form) indicate how the entry word should be used in a sentence. Some words may be used as more than one part of speech. In this case, a part-of-speech label is given in front of each of the numbered (or lettered) series of definitions.
4. **Other forms.** These may show spellings of plural forms of nouns, tenses of verbs, or the comparative forms of adjectives and adverbs.
5. **Etymology.** The etymology is the origin and history of a word. It tells how the word (or its parts) came into English.
6. **Definitions.** If there is more than one meaning, definitions are numbered or lettered.
7. **Special usage labels.** These labels identify words that have special meaning or are used in special ways in certain situations.

8. **Examples.** Phrases or sentences may demonstrate how the defined word is to be used.
9. **Related word forms.** These are various forms of the entry word, usually created by adding suffixes or prefixes.
10. **Synonyms and antonyms.** Synonyms and antonyms may appear at the end of some word entries.

COMPUTER NOTE: Some spell-checking programs allow you to create a user dictionary and add the special terms you use often.

EXERCISE 1 **Looking Up the Spelling of Words**

Look up the following words in your dictionary and write any alternate spellings listed. If the word has only one spelling in your dictionary, write the word *single* as your answer.

EXAMPLE **1.** judgment
          1. *judgement*

1. encyclopedia
2. fledgling
3. theater
4. skeptic
5. yogurt

EXERCISE 2 **Dividing Words into Syllables**

Divide the following words into syllables. Check with the dictionary to see how well you have done.

1. ostentation
2. environment
3. conservation
4. particularize
5. distinction

EXERCISE 3 **Using the Pronunciation Key**

Pronounce each of the following words using the pronunciation key in your dictionary.

1. legerdemain
2. parquet
3. theocracy
4. indigent
5. Portuguese

RESOURCES

EXERCISE 4   **Identifying Part-of-Speech Labels**

Look up the following words in a dictionary and write the part-of-speech labels given for each of their meanings.

1. objective
2. dry
3. still

4. branch
5. no

EXERCISE 5   **Exploring the Etymology of Words**

Use a college or unabridged dictionary to find the etymology of the following words. For each word, tell what language the word came from.

1. rodeo
2. kindergarten
3. palm

4. tea
5. kayak

EXERCISE 6   **Finding Synonyms**

Come up with as many synonyms as you can for each of the following words. Then, using your dictionary, check your list and add to it.

1. famous
2. error
3. legal

4. old
5. beautiful

35 VOCABULARY

Learning and Using New Words

The larger your vocabulary, the more likely you are to be successful in high school, college, and the workplace. A good way to learn new words is by building your vocabulary as you read books, newspapers, and periodicals. You can also increase your vocabulary by analyzing how an unfamiliar term is used in context. And you can discover the meanings of words by learning how word parts are combined to form new words.

Creating a Word Bank

One good way to increase your vocabulary is to keep a word bank, or list, in a notebook. When you encounter an unfamiliar word, write the word and its definition in your notebook. Check your dictionary for the correct definition.

 COMPUTER NOTE: Create a vocabulary file on your computer. Add new words and definitions to the end of the file. Then, use the Sort command to arrange the words in alphabetical order. Review the words and their definitions frequently.

Using Context Clues

Sometimes you can figure out the meaning of a word by examining the context in which it is used.

HOW TO USE CONTEXT CLUES	
TYPE OF CLUE	EXPLANATION
Definitions and Restatements	Writers may sometimes restate a word in order to define it. ■ When Henry B. Gonzalez was elected to Congress, many of his Spanish-speaking *constituents,* the voters in his district, felt that he would fight for their rights.
Examples	Examples used in context may help reveal the meaning of an unfamiliar word. ■ The scientist was accused of several acts of *espionage,* such as photographing secret documents and taping private conversations.
Synonyms	Look for familiar words that may be synonyms of words you don't yet know. ■ The club's *coffers* were so low that the members had to ask for donations to refill the treasury.
Comparisons	An unknown word may be shown to be similar to a more common word. ■ As in so many polluted cities, the air in our community is sometimes too *contaminated* to breathe.
Contrast	An unfamiliar word may be contrasted to a more familiar word or phrase. ■ The team's uniforms were *immaculate* before the game, but by the end of the first quarter they were filthy.
Cause and Effect	Look for clues that indicate that an unfamiliar word is related to the cause or the result of an action, feeling, or idea. ■ Will Rogers was considered to be a *humanitarian* because he worked to improve people's lives.

Determining Meanings from the General Context

Context clues are not always obvious. Sometimes you have to read an entire passage to understand the meaning of an unfamiliar word. However, you can draw on what you already know about the subject of the passage as well as your own experiences. Your own knowledge and resources can frequently help you determine the meanings of many unfamiliar terms.

Choosing the Right Word

Sometimes context clues are not enough to help you figure out a word's meaning. At times, the best way to determine the meaning of an unfamiliar word is to look up the word in the dictionary.

Very few words in English have a single meaning. Most have several meanings that vary depending on the context in which the word appears. Therefore, when you're looking in a dictionary for the meaning of a word, read *all* the definitions given, keeping in mind the context in which you originally read or heard the word.

To help you, dictionaries often provide sample contexts. These are usually several words surrounding the word being defined. They help you see how the word generally appears in a sentence. When sample contexts are given, compare them with the original context in which the word occurred to make sure you've found the meaning that fits.

Synonyms are words that have the same or nearly the same meaning. Use a dictionary or thesaurus to make sure you understand the exact differences in meanings between synonyms.

It is also important to understand that two words may have the same *denotation,* or dictionary definition, but a different *connotation,* or emotional overtone. For example, the words *slender* and *skinny* both mean "thin." However, the word *slender* has a more positive connotation than *skinny,* which suggests a bony or gaunt appearance.

Using Word Parts

English words can be classified into two types: those that cannot be subdivided into parts, and those that can. Words that cannot be subdivided, like *maze, right,* and *leap,* are called **base words.** Words that can be subdivided, like *reception, quickly,* and *knowledge,* are made up of **word parts.** The three types of word parts are

- roots
- prefixes
- suffixes

Knowing the meanings of roots, prefixes, and suffixes can help you determine the meanings of many unfamiliar words.

Roots

The *root* is the foundation on which a word is built. It carries the word's core meaning, and it is the part to which prefixes and suffixes are added. For example, the root *–port–* means "carry." This root can be combined with various prefixes and suffixes to make new words such as *transportation, portable,* and *importer.* Here are some examples of words with roots, prefixes, and suffixes.

WORD	PREFIX	ROOT	SUFFIX
defective	de–	–fect–	–ive
unacceptable	un–	–accept–	–able
sympathy	sym–	–path–	–y
discouragement	dis–	–courage–	–ment

Some of the roots come from base words, such as *–accept–* in *unacceptable,* and are relatively easy to define. Other roots may be more difficult to define, such as those in *defective* (*–fect–,* "do, make") and *sympathy* (*–path–,* "feeling"). These roots and many others come from Greek and Latin. Becoming familiar with Greek and Latin roots and their meanings is an important step in improving your vocabulary.

COMMONLY USED ROOTS

ROOTS	MEANINGS	EXAMPLES
GREEK		
–anthrop–	human	anthropology, misanthrope
–chrono–	time	chronology, chronometer
–cycl–	circle, wheel	cyclone, bicycle
–dem–	people	demography, democracy
–graph–	write, writing	autograph, biography
–hydr–	water	hydrant, hydrate
–log, –logy	study, word	biology, monologue
–morph–	form	metamorphosis, polymorph
–phon–	sound	phonograph, symphony
LATIN		
–cis–	cut	decision, concise
–cred–	believe	incredible, discredit
–dic–, –dict–	say, speak	dictate, predict
–fac–, –fact–, –fec–, –fic–	do, make	deface, manufacture, defective, efficient
–fid–	belief, faith	confident, fidelity
–frag–, –fract–	break	fragment, fraction
–ject–	throw	eject, trajectory
–junct–	join	conjunction, juncture
–magn–	large, grand	magnate, magnificent
–mal–	bad	malice, dismal
–mit–, –miss–	send	missionary, transmit
–ped–	foot	biped, pedestrian
–pend–, –pens–	hang, weigh	pendant, pensive
–pon–, –pos–	place, put	exponent, position
–scrib–, –script–	write	inscribe, postscript
–solv–	to loosen, accomplish	solvent, resolve
–ven–, –vent–	come	convention, prevent
–vers–, –vert–	turn	reverse, convertible
–voc–, –vok–	call	vocal, provoke
–volv–	roll, turn around	revolve, evolve

RESOURCES

Prefixes

A *prefix* is a word part that is added before a root. The word that is created from a prefix and a root combines the meanings of both its parts.

COMMONLY USED PREFIXES		
PREFIXES	MEANINGS	EXAMPLES
GREEK		
anti–	against, opposing	antimissile, antisocial
hyper–	over, above	hyperactive, hyperventilate
mono–, mon–	one	monologue, monarch
para–	beside, beyond	parallel, parasail
psych–	mind	psychology, psychosomatic
LATIN AND FRENCH		
contra–	against	contraband, contraposition
de–	away, from, off, down	depart, deplane, descend
dif–, dis–	away, not, opposing	differ, dismount, dissent
ex–, e–, ef–	away from, out	excise, emigrate, efface
il–, im–, in–, ir–	not, in	illogical, impolite, incite, irrational
post–	after, following	postpaid, postwar
pre–	before	prejudge, preview
pro–	forward, favoring	proceed, pro-American
re–	back, backward, again	return, reflect, reforest
OLD ENGLISH		
be–	around, about	beset, behind
mis–	badly, not, wrongly	misbehave, misfire, mispronounce
un–	not, reverse of	untrue, unfold

☞ **REFERENCE NOTE:** For guidelines on spelling when adding prefixes, see page 873.

Suffixes

A *suffix* is a word part that is added to the end of a root. Often, adding or changing a suffix will also change the part of speech of a word, as seen in *operate/operation*.

COMMONLY USED SUFFIXES		
SUFFIXES	MEANINGS	EXAMPLES
GREEK, LATIN, AND FRENCH *NOUNS*		
–ance, –ence	act, condition	forbearance, excellence
–cy	state, condition	accuracy, normalcy
–er, –or	doing, actor	singer, conductor
–ion	action, result, state	union, fusion, dominion
–ism	act, practice of	baptism, socialism
–tude	quality, state	fortitude, magnitude
–ty, –y	quality, state, action	novelty, surety, jealousy
ADJECTIVES		
–able, –ible	able, likely to	washable, divisible
–ate	having, characteristic of	animate, collegiate
–ive	tending to, given to	reflective, pensive
–ous	marked by, full of	glorious, nervous
–ulent	full of, characterized by	turbulent, fraudulent
ADJECTIVES OR NOUNS		
–al	of, like, act of	proposal, autumnal
–ary	belonging to, one connected with	primary, adversary, auxiliary
–ent	doing, actor	confident, adherent
–ic	dealing with, caused by, person or thing showing	classic, choleric, workaholic
–ite	native, product of	Israelite, dynamite

(continued)

COMMONLY USED SUFFIXES *(continued)*		
SUFFIXES	MEANINGS	EXAMPLES

VERBS
–ate
 	
–ize
	become, cause, form
	cause to be,
	    subject to
		evaporate, irritate
		jeopardize,
		    realize

OLD ENGLISH ADJECTIVES OR ADVERBS –ly –ward	like, characteristic of in the direction of	friendly, cowardly backward, upward
VERBS –en	cause to be, become	deepen, darken

☞ **REFERENCE NOTE:** For guidelines on spelling when adding suffixes, see pages 873–875.

Review

 EXERCISE 1   **Using Context Clues to Find Meanings**

See how well you can figure out the meanings of words from the way they are used in a sentence. Write the letter of the definition that best fits each italicized word.

a. large structure   **e.** celebrity
b. coloring   **f.** lawmaker
c. amiable   **g.** worsening
d. profitable   **h.** emotional displays

1. Lars often uses *histrionics* such as wailing and crying to get his way.
2. Unlike our money-losing ventures, selling popcorn at soccer games has been a *lucrative* project for our club.
3. The towering *edifice,* like many buildings in New York, seems to reach to the clouds.

4. Because the empty building is *deteriorating* so rapidly, it will soon be beyond repair.

5. Former Congresswoman Barbara Jordan was one of the first African American women to become a *legislator*.

▶ EXERCISE 2 **Using the General Context to Determine Meaning**

For each italicized word, write your own definition or synonym. Then check the dictionary's definitions of each word. If you guessed incorrectly, check the context again to look for clues you might have missed.

Most jobs available to students are found in the service [1] *sector*, in places such as department stores and fast-food restaurants. This type of work is often [2] *menial* and [3] *monotonous*—regarded as servile and offering little or no variety. Federal laws [4] *curtail* the number of hours students under sixteen can work for pay, but some employers [5] *exploit* students by demanding that they work longer. Rather than disagree and lose their jobs, many students [6] *comply*. Working may also [7] *impede* learning, as time spent on the job [8] *encroaches* on time needed for homework. Even good students may find their grades [9] *degenerating* from A's to B's or from B's to C's or D's. In addition, officials [10] *cite* hazardous conditions in some workplaces, mentioning numerous injuries to young people who work around large or dangerous machines.

▶ EXERCISE 3 **Using Roots to Determine Meanings**

Use the list of commonly used roots on page 967 to identify the root or roots in the following words. Then, guess each word's meaning. Check your answers with a dictionary.

EXAMPLE **1.** vocation
       1. *–voc– (call);* vocation *means "a calling or summoning, especially in the sense of a chosen career"*

1. junction
2. contradiction
3. demographic

4. subvert
5. genealogy

RESOURCES

▶ EXERCISE 4   **Identifying Words with Prefixes**

Give an example of a word containing each of the following prefixes. (Do not use any of the words given as examples in this chapter.) Then, tell what each word means. Use a dictionary if necessary.

EXAMPLE   **1.** pre–
            1. *prehistoric—existing in times before written history*

1. hyper–   **4.** para–
2. dis–   **5.** be–
3. ex–

▶ EXERCISE 5   **Identifying Suffixes and Defining Words**

For each word, identify the suffix. Then, guess what the whole word means. Use a dictionary to check your answers.

EXAMPLE   **1.** privacy
            1. *–cy; the state or condition of being private*

1. depositor   **4.** militarism
2. leniency   **5.** activate
3. retractable

▶ EXERCISE 6   **Using Word Parts to Determine Meaning**

Identify the roots, prefixes, and suffixes in each of the following words. Then, try to guess what the words mean. Use a dictionary to check your answers.

EXAMPLE   **1.** anthropomorphous
            1. *–anthrop– (human); –morph– (form); –ous
            (marked by, given to)
            marked by human form or appearance*

1. emissary   **4.** revolver
2. hydrology   **5.** proponent
3. dependable

36 LETTERS AND FORMS

Style and Contents

You write letters for a variety of purposes. Clearly and concisely written letters will get results and create a favorable impression, whether you are writing them for personal use or as a workplace requirement. Following accepted business procedures and using the correct style will give your letters a professional look. You should also follow a few simple guidelines in completing printed forms.

The Appearance of a Business Letter

- Use white, unlined $8\frac{1}{2}$" × 11" paper.
- Type your letter if possible (single-spaced, leaving an extra line between paragraphs). Otherwise, neatly write the letter by hand, using black or blue ink. Avoid cross-outs, smudges, erasures, and inkblots. Check for typing errors and misspellings.
- Center your letter on the page with equal margins on the sides and at the top and bottom.
- Use only one side of the paper. If your letter won't fit on one page, leave a one-inch margin at the bottom of the first page and carry over at least two lines onto the second page.

Writing Business Letters

The Parts of a Business Letter

A business letter contains six parts:

(1) the heading
(2) the inside address
(3) the salutation
(4) the body
(5) the closing
(6) the signature

There are two common styles for arranging the parts of a business letter. For the *block form,* begin each of the parts of the letter at the left margin and don't indent any paragraphs. However, for the *modified block form,* align the heading, the closing, and your signature with an imaginary line down the center of the page. The other parts of the letter begin at the left margin. Paragraphs are indented.

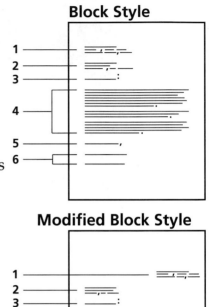

Block Style

Modified Block Style

The Heading.   The heading usually has three lines:

- your street address
- your city, state, and ZIP Code
- the date the letter was written

The Inside Address.   The inside address gives the name and address of the person you are writing. Use a courtesy title (such as *Mr., Ms., Mrs.,* or *Miss*) or a professional title (such as *Dr.* or *Professor*) in front of the person's name. After the person's name, include the person's business title. The name of the company or organization and the address follow.

The Salutation. The salutation is your greeting. If you are writing to a specific person, begin with *Dear*, followed by a courtesy title or a professional title and the person's name. End the salutation with a colon (*Dear Mr. Jones:*).

If you don't have the name of a specific person, you can use a general salutation, such as *Dear Sir or Madam* or *Ladies and Gentlemen.* You can also use a department or a position title, with or without the word *Dear*.

The Body. The body, or main part, of your letter contains your message. It begins beneath the salutation. If the body of your letter contains more than one paragraph, leave a blank line between paragraphs.

The Closing. The closing should end your letter courteously. There are several closings that are often used in business letters, such as *Sincerely yours, Yours truly,* or *Regards.* Capitalize only the first word.

The Signature. Your signature should be written in ink, directly below the closing. Type or print your name neatly below your signature.

GUIDELINES FOR THE CONTENTS OF A BUSINESS LETTER

There are a few simple guidelines to follow in writing business letters that get results.

- *Use a polite, respectful, professional tone.* A courteous letter will be much more effective than a rude, angry, or sarcastic one.
- *Use formal, standard English.* Avoid slang, contractions, and abbreviations. Informal language that might be acceptable in a personal conversation or letter is often inappropriate in a business letter.
- *Explain the purpose of your letter quickly and clearly.* Keep in mind that the person reading your letter is busy. Include only necessary details.
- *Include all necessary information.* Be sure your reader can understand why you wrote and what you are asking.

Types of Business Letters

Request or Order Letter

In a *request letter,* you're asking for something. You might request information about a product, or you might ask for someone's time or services. An *order letter* is a special kind of request letter asking for something specific, such as a free brochure advertised in a magazine. You might also write an order letter to purchase, by mail, a product for which you don't have a printed order form. In a request or order letter, the most important consideration is to be clear about exactly what you want.

19 Brookside Drive
Ithaca, NY 14850
September 2, 1998

Mr. Stuart Reinhardt, Manager
Rollerama Skating Rink
2008 Route 9
Ithaca, NY 14853

Dear Mr. Reinhardt:

Madison High School's sophomore class has voted to hold a class get-together at Rollerama. As class secretary, I am writing to ask if we could plan this event for Saturday, November 21, from 7:30 to 10:30 p.m. We expect about 85 students.

Could we rent the rink on the same terms you gave the senior class last spring? The sophomore class can guarantee a minimum attendance of 75 students. Students will pay at the door an admission price of $4.50. Skate rental will be a separate $2.00 charge.

Our class is looking forward to an enjoyable evening at Rollerama.

Yours truly,

Linda O'Connell

Linda O'Connell
Class Secretary
Madison High School
Class of '01

RESOURCES

When you are writing a request or order letter, remember the following points.

1. State your request clearly.
2. If you're asking someone to send you information, enclose a self-addressed, stamped envelope.
3. If you're asking someone to do something for you, make your request well in advance.
4. If you're ordering something, include all important information, such as the size, color, brand name, or any other specific information. If there are costs involved, add the amount correctly.

Complaint or Adjustment Letter

If you are dissatisfied with a service or product, you might wish to write a *complaint* or *adjustment letter.* The purpose of this type of letter is to identify what's wrong and how you think it should be corrected. Here is the body of a sample adjustment letter.

> I have noticed that there are only two litter cans in Edgemont Park. I think that the litter situation would improve if the Parks Department would get more litter cans for the park. I think these cans should be placed so that they are convenient to the field, the picnic area, and the creek. More people might pick up their litter if there were trash containers located close to where they are needed.
>
> Please give your attention to this suggestion. I think Edgemont Park is a wonderful neighborhood resource that should be kept clean for everyone in our community to enjoy.

RESOURCES

When you write a complaint or adjustment letter, remember these suggestions.

1. Register your complaint promptly.
2. Mention specifics. Necessary details might include the following:
   - how you were affected (lost time or money)
   - how you want the problem to be resolved
3. Keep the tone of your letter calm and courteous.

Appreciation or Commendation Letter

An *appreciation* or *commendation letter* is written to express your appreciation or to encourage a person, group, or organization to continue doing good work. When you write an appreciation or commendation letter, it is important to tell the person or organization exactly why you are pleased. Here is the body of a sample appreciation letter.

I am writing to congratulate all of you at WQBK on your change in format from oldies to Top 40.

Although I enjoy listening to oldies, I am more interested in hearing what musicians are recording today. Even my parents are getting tired of hearing nothing but '50s and '60s music.

I hope you succeed with your new format. I know my friends listen to your station, and sometimes my parents do, too. Good luck!

Letter of Application

The purpose of a *letter of application* is to provide a selection committee or possible employers with enough information about you so that they can make a decision about whether you are a good choice for a position, such as a scholarship or summer job. When you are writing a letter of application, remember the following points.

1. Identify the job or position you are applying for and tell how you heard about it.
2. Tell about yourself. Depending on the position you are applying for, you might include
   - your grade in school or grade-point average
   - your experience, or your activities, awards, and honors
   - personal qualities or characteristics that make you a good choice for the position
   - the date you can begin work

3. Offer to provide references. References are usually two or three responsible adults (generally not relatives) who can speak from experience about your character or qualifications and will give you a good recommendation. Be prepared to give the addresses and telephone numbers of your references when you are asked to provide them.

Here is a sample of an application letter.

1437 Windy Ridge Rd.
Milwaukee, WI 53224
January 23, 1998

Ms. Veronica Fong, Director
Spanish Student Exchange Program
P.O. Box 3001
New York, NY 10116

Dear Ms. Fong:

I am writing to apply for the summer exchange program to Barcelona, Spain, advertised in the January 14, 1998, edition of Student Voice.

I am a sophomore at Adams High School in Milwaukee, Wisconsin. My grade-point average is 3.3. I have studied Spanish for three years. Last semester I won an award for my translation work in this class.

I am aware of the responsibility this involves. I would feel privileged to gain a new understanding of the Spanish language and culture and, on my return, to share this information with others in my school and community.

I will gladly furnish references who can tell you more about my qualifications for this program.

Please let me know if there is any other information I need to give you before you can consider me as a candidate for this program.

Sincerely yours,

Brody Collins

Brody Collins

RESOURCES

Writing Informal or Personal Letters

Personal messages are often best expressed in the form of letters. Often a written message is more effective—and more appreciated—than a telephone call or other form of communication. The most common types of informal or personal letters are thank-you letters, invitations, and letters of regret. Personal letters are less formal than business letters and don't follow a rigid style.

Thank-you Letters. These are informal letters of appreciation that you send to tell someone that you appreciate his or her taking time, trouble, or expense on your behalf. Try to think of something about the person's effort or gift that made it special.

Invitations. An informal invitation should contain specific information about a planned event, such as the occasion, the time and place, and any other special details your guests might need to know.

Letters of Regret. Send a letter of regret if you have been invited somewhere but are unable to go. A written reply is especially appropriate if you were sent a written invitation with the letters *R.S.V.P.* (in French, these letters stand for "please reply").

Addressing an Envelope

Your return address (your name and complete address) goes in the top left-hand corner of an envelope. Just to the right of center, place the name and address of the person or organization to whom you are writing. The addressee's name and address should exactly match the inside address on your letter. Be sure to include correct ZIP Codes.

COMPUTER NOTE: Use your word-processing program to create a mailing list that will print the addresses from your letters onto labels or envelopes.

Completing Printed Forms

There are many types of printed forms, but there are certain common techniques that will help you fill out any form accurately and completely.

Read all of the directions carefully. Follow the instructions on the form exactly.

Type or write neatly, using a pen or pencil as directed. When you type or print your information on the form, avoid cross-outs or smudges if possible.

Proofread your completed form. Make sure you have given all the information requested on the form. Check for errors, and correct them neatly before you give the form to the appropriate person or mail it to the correct address.

Review

▶ EXERCISE 1 **Writing a Request Letter**

Choose one of the following situations to practice writing a request letter. Use your own return address and today's date, but make up any other information you need.

1. You are the president of a school club. Write a letter to a local business asking it to sponsor club members in a sports competition for a charity project.
2. You are working on a History Day project. Write a letter to your state historical society requesting information on early political campaigns or facts about the settlement of your region of the state.

RESOURCES

3. You want to buy a sweatshirt with the name of your favorite college. Write a letter to that school's bookstore requesting information about the item.

EXERCISE 2 Writing a Complaint or Adjustment Letter

Practice writing a letter of adjustment or complaint. Write a letter to your local town council complaining about a proposed curfew for teenagers. Be specific in suggesting alternate solutions to the problems that led the council to consider the curfew. Use your own return address, but make up any other information you need.

EXERCISE 3 Writing a Letter of Appreciation or Commendation

Practice writing a letter of appreciation or commendation. Write a letter to the author of a book you enjoyed. Explain how his or her writing has changed, inspired, or simply entertained you. Use your own return address, but make up any other information you need.

EXERCISE 4 Writing a Letter of Application

Practice writing a letter of application. Think about a part-time or summer job that you are interested in and for which you feel qualified. Use the classified ad section of a newspaper to find the name of an organization or company that might offer this kind of position. Write a letter of application that states your interest and qualifications.

EXERCISE 5 Writing a Thank-you Letter

Write a thank-you letter to someone you know. Express your appreciation for a specific comment, gift, or action.

EXERCISE 6 Addressing Business Envelopes

Draw a rectangular outline to represent an envelope. Then, address the envelope to Mahalia Hamlin, who lives at 32 Rio Seco, Albuquerque, New Mexico (ZIP Code 87120). Use your own return address.

RESOURCES

37 READING, STUDYING, AND TEST TAKING

Using Skills and Strategies

To be successful in your high-school studies, you need to develop skills and strategies for productive reading, efficient studying, and effective test taking. The methods you learn in this chapter will help you get better grades and complete your homework without last-minute agony. They will also help you succeed in college and in the workplace.

Planning a Study Routine

If you want to study effectively, you need to be committed to a realistic study schedule. Here are some suggestions.

1. *Know your assignments.* Keep an assignment planner or a calendar for recording your assignments and noting when they are due. Make sure you understand all the instructions for each assignment.
2. *Make a plan.* Break your big assignments into small steps. Make deadlines for completing each step.
3. *Concentrate when you study.* Set aside a specific time and place for studying. Then focus your attention solely on your assignment. Avoid distractions.

Strengthening Reading and Study Skills

Reading and Understanding

You will find it easier to keep focused and to remember what you read if you read with a purpose. Some common purposes for reading are

- to find specific details
- to find main ideas
- to understand and remember

When you need to deal with a variety of materials, adjust your rate of reading to suit your purpose.

READING RATES ACCORDING TO PURPOSE		
READING RATE	PURPOSE	EXAMPLE
Scanning	Reading for specific details	Searching a history chapter for the date on which a specific treaty was signed
Skimming	Reading for main points	Reviewing chapter headings in your health textbook the night before a quiz
Reading for mastery	Reading to understand and remember	Reading a new chapter in your science book before writing an outline

Writing to Learn

Your writing can be a very useful tool for learning. Writing helps you focus your thoughts, discover new ideas, record your observations, and plan your work. The following chart shows how you might use your writing as a method of learning.

TYPE OF WRITING	PURPOSE	EXAMPLE
Freewriting	To help you focus your thoughts	Writing to connect ideas from today's history lecture and yesterday's reading
Autobiographies	To help you examine and express ideas about important events in your life	Writing about the day you learned an important lesson
Diaries	To help you recall impressions and express your feelings	Writing about a person you admire and want to emulate
Journals and Learning Logs	To help you record your observations, descriptions, solutions, and questions	Writing to keep a record of the progress of a Spanish writing project
	To help you present a problem, analyze it, and propose a solution	Writing about the way you plan to organize a history project

Using Word-Processing Tools for Writing

A word processor or a computer word-processing program can help you plan, draft, and edit your writing. These tools can make every step of the writing process easier.

Prewriting. Typing is fast on a word processor. Revisions of rough notes or outlines can be made without retyping.

Writing First Drafts. You can revise as often as you want. If you like, you can use the printer to produce a hard copy (or printout) with each new revision.

Evaluating. The word processor lets you compare and evaluate different versions of your writing. Just save a copy of your document under a different name, and type your changes on this copy. Then, if you don't like the revisions, you still have the original.

Revising.   Changes can be typed in easily and a clean copy printed out without having to repeat steps.

Proofreading.   Some word processors offer a feature that checks your spelling. Some have features that evaluate sentence structure and punctuation.

Publishing.   Final revisions are easy to make on a word processor. After proofreading the last version, it's simple to print a final copy. You can even print multiple copies on your printer.

Using the SQ3R Reading Method

Francis Robinson, an educational psychologist, developed a method of reading called SQ3R. There are five steps to using this SQ3R method.

S   *Survey* the entire study assignment. Look at all of the headings, scan material in boldface and italics, and take note of the information in the charts, outlines, and summaries.

Q   *Question* yourself. What should you know after completing your reading? Make a list of questions that you want to be able to answer after finishing your reading.

R   *Read* the material section by section. Think of answers to your questions as you read.

R   *Recite* in your own words answers to each of the questions you have identified.

R   *Review* the material by rereading quickly, looking over your questions, and recalling the answers.

The SQ3R reading method can help you convert routine assignments into more interesting and active reading sessions. If you respond actively to what you read, it will be easier for you to recall what you have read.

 REFERENCE NOTE: For study techniques to help with listening skills, see page 942.

Interpreting and Analyzing What You Read

The information in every essay, article, or textbook chapter that you read is organized into a logical pattern in which the ideas are related to one another. If you interpret and analyze these relationships, you will find it easier to think critically about what you read.

Stated Main Idea.   When you are looking for the main idea, you want to find the most important point that the writer makes. When the main idea is stated, the author expresses the major point clearly and directly. A stated main idea can often be found in one specific sentence in a written passage.

Implied Main Idea.   The main idea is sometimes implied, or suggested, rather than directly stated. To find an implied main idea, you will need to analyze the relationship of the details you are given. Then decide what general meaning is expressed by these combined details.

HOW TO FIND THE MAIN IDEA

- Skim the passage. (What topic do all of the sentences have in common?)
- Identify the general topic. (What's the passage about?)
- Identify what the passage really says about the topic. (What is the message of the passage as a whole?)
- Sum up the meaning of the passage in one clear sentence.
- Check back over the passage. If you have correctly identified the main idea, the details will support it.

RESOURCES

☞ REFERENCE NOTE: For additional information on finding the main idea, whether stated or implied, see pages 67–69.

Reading to Find Relationships Among Details

To understand the meaning of a reading passage, you'll need to learn to identify details and understand how they are related to each other and to the main idea.

FINDING RELATIONSHIPS AMONG DETAILS	
Identify specific details.	What details answer specific questions such as *Who? What? When? Where? Why?* and *How?*
Distinguish between fact and opinion.	What information can be proved true (fact) or false? What statements express a personal belief or attitude (opinion)?
Identify similarities and differences.	Are there any details that are shown to be similar to or different from one another?
Understand cause and effect.	Is there an event that had an impact or effect on a later event?
Identify an order of organization.	In what kind of order are the details arranged—chronological order, spatial order, order of importance, or any other organizing pattern?

Reading Passage

On February 4, 1913, Rosa Parks was born in Tuskegee, Alabama. Her family later moved to Montgomery. Growing up, Ms. Parks saw the inequality in the treatment of African Americans in Montgomery. For instance, they had to sit in the back of a shoe store to try on shoes, even if every seat in the front of the store was vacant. Blacks also had to sit in the back section of buses or to stand if a white person wanted a seat. As an African American, Ms. Parks hated this injustice. In December of 1955, her feelings translated into action.

Sample Analysis

DETAIL: What are some places where African Americans encountered unfair treatment?
ANSWER: The passage cites examples from shoe stores and buses.

OPINION: How did Rosa Parks feel about the unfair treatment of blacks?
ANSWER: She hated the injustice of this treatment.

Ms. Parks was working at a tailor shop. One evening on the bus, wearily heading home, Ms. Parks refused to give up her seat to a white man. She was arrested for her refusal. After this incident, Ms. Parks decided to stop using the bus. She was soon joined in her boycott by thousands of African Americans in Montgomery. Many workers bravely risked their jobs by joining the boycott. Some white employers, however, preferred to give rides to their African American employees rather than do without their services.

The boycott lasted for 382 days and sparked the civil rights movement in America. The impact of this incident was like the first pebble of a landslide. Because she led the boycott, Ms. Parks was fired from her job and was harassed. She moved to Detroit in 1957 and was hired by Congressman John Conyers. She worked for him for more than twenty years. In 1987, she founded the Rosa and Raymond Parks Institute for Self Development.

Rosa Parks can be cited to refute those who say that the actions of one person cannot make a difference. Rosa Parks's actions took courage as well as faith that her demand for justice would not be in vain.

FACT: When did Rosa Parks refuse to be treated unfairly on the bus?
ANSWER: *She refused to give up her seat in December of 1955.*

SIMILARITY: How was the response of African Americans in Montgomery similar to the reaction of Rosa Parks?
ANSWER: *Many black people in Montgomery also refused to ride the bus.*

CAUSE AND EFFECT: What was the effect of this boycott?
ANSWER: *It encouraged other civil rights protests.*

ORDER: In the course of her life, where did Rosa Parks live?
ANSWER: *She was born in Tuskegee, Alabama; later, she lived and worked in Montgomery, Alabama; and finally, she worked for a congressman in Detroit, Michigan.*

RESOURCES

Applying Reasoning Skills to Your Reading

It's important to interpret and evaluate the evidence and facts that you gather from your reading. When you draw *conclusions* and make *inferences,* you come to a decision by evaluating, interpreting, and analyzing the facts and evidence.

For example, based on your analysis of the reading passage on pages 988–989, you might make the following conclusions or inferences about Rosa Parks.

> Many people shared Parks's hatred of the unequal treatment of African Americans. (Evidence: Thousands joined her in her boycott of the bus system—a protest that might have cost them their jobs.)

> Americans today benefit from Rosa Parks's act of courage. (Evidence: Rosa Parks's action marked the beginning of the civil rights movement, which had the goal of fairer treatment for all people, regardless of race, creed, or gender.)

A *valid* conclusion is a conclusion that is firmly grounded in facts, evidence, or logic. An *invalid* conclusion is one that doesn't follow reasonably or logically from the evidence. For example, it is invalid to conclude that Rosa Parks refused to give up her seat because of a sudden impulse. This conclusion is not consistent with facts stated in the reading passage about her lifelong hatred of the injustice in the treatment of black people.

When you draw conclusions and make inferences, you are doing what a detective does to solve a mystery.

HOW TO DRAW CONCLUSIONS OR MAKE INFERENCES	
Gather all the evidence.	What facts or details have you learned about the subject?
Evaluate the evidence.	Do you know enough to judge information without jumping to conclusions or making invalid assumptions?
Make reasonable connections.	Based on evidence you have gathered and evaluated, what connections can you make? What conclusions can you draw?

Reading Graphics and Illustrations

Many of your textbooks—as well as articles from newspapers and magazines—include diagrams, maps, graphs, and illustrations. Visuals such as these make information clear and easy to understand.

Paragraphs full of detailed information can be difficult to read and to remember. Graphs or diagrams are often much easier to understand. Graphics and illustrations help you understand the relationships between one set of facts and another. For example, the bar graph below shows the percentage of the U.S. population between ages five and seventeen from 1900 to 1980.

Percentage of U.S. Population Aged 5 to 17

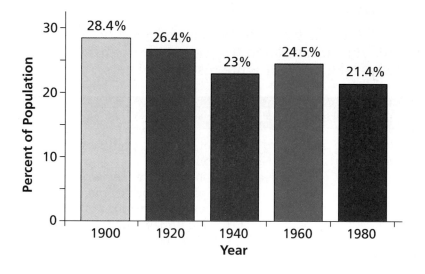

From this graph you can quickly compare the percentage of school-age children, measured in twenty-year periods, in the United States over the course of this century.

Suppose you were a television producer who was trying to decide whether to plan for an increase or decrease of programming for school-age children over the years after 2000. By looking at the graph, you could quickly see that the percentage of people of school age has shown an overall decrease over this century. You could reasonably assume that this trend would continue, and so you could plan for programming that focuses on other age groups.

Graphs such as the one above can help you make decisions more easily. They help you to see the relationship among items of data.

Applying Study and Reading Strategies

Various reading and study methods can be used to organize and handle information. Some of the most common are

- taking notes
- classifying
- organizing information visually
- outlining
- paraphrasing
- summarizing
- memorizing

Taking Notes

If you take careful notes when you read or listen to a lecture, your information will be better organized when you study, take tests, or write research papers.

HOW TO TAKE STUDY NOTES	
Recognize and record main points.	Set off main points as headings in your notes. ■ In a lecture, key words and phrases such as *major* or *most important* and similar clues may indicate key points. ■ In a textbook, chapter headings and subheadings are usually reliable clues about main ideas.
Summarize.	Don't write down every detail. Instead, summarize or abbreviate, using key words or phrases to note main ideas. Indent supporting points.
Note important examples.	Make notes of a few meaningful examples. They can help you remember the main ideas.

On page 993 are sample study notes that a careful student might make about the reading passage on pages 988–989. Note that the main points in the passage are identified and then arranged in groups. Each of these groups of main points is given a heading that identifies the key idea.

Rosa Parks

Biography

- African American, born Feb. 4, 1913—Tuskegee, Ala.
- grew up in Montgomery, Ala.
- despised injustice in treatment of blacks
- incident in Dec. 1955 started bus boycott
- fired from her tailoring job because of boycott
- hired by congressman in Michigan—worked for him for more than 20 years
- 1987—founded Rosa and Raymond Parks Inst. for Self Development

Examples of Inequality in Treatment

- had to sit at back of shoe stores
- had to sit at back of buses
- had to stand if white person wanted seat on bus

Details of Montgomery Bus Boycott

- Ms. Parks refused to give up seat to white man
- Ms. Parks arrested for her refusal
- Ms. Parks stopped using the bus
- thousands joined her boycott of bus system
- many risked jobs
- many employers gave rides instead of losing workers
- boycott lasted 382 days
- sparked American civil rights movement

RESOURCES

Classifying

Classification is organizing information by arranging items into categories. You use classification when you make an outline, deciding which supporting ideas fit together under a major heading. In order to group things, you need to identify relationships among them.

EXAMPLE   What do the following people have in common?
Dolly Madison, Bess Truman, Betty Ford, Barbara Bush

ANSWER   They are all former first ladies of the United States.

You also use classification when you identify patterns in data. For example, look at the relationship of the following items.

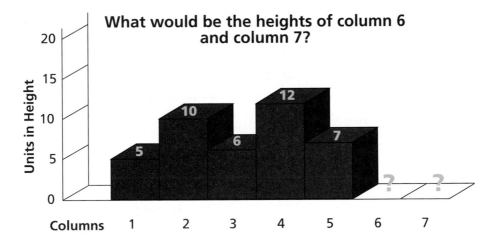

What would be the heights of column 6 and column 7?

ANSWER   The pattern is for even-numbered columns (columns 2 and 4) to be double the height of the columns that precede them (columns 1 and 3), while odd-numbered columns (1, 3, and 5) increase by one unit in height. The next column, column 6, should be double the height of column 5, or <u>fourteen units high</u>. Column 7 would then be <u>eight units high</u>.

Organizing Information Visually

Mapping, diagraming, and charting organize new information so that it is visually presented. This makes the information easier to understand.

For example, the passage that follows is full of literary terms. It contrasts two types of sonnets.

> A sonnet is defined as a poem containing fourteen lines, usually written in rhymed, iambic pentameter. Sonnets are generally classified into two types: the Petrarchan, or Italian, sonnet and the Shakespearean, or English, sonnet. Originating in Italy in the fourteenth century, the Petrarchan sonnet has two parts, an octave (eight lines) and a sestet (six lines). Often, the octave raises a poetic question that the sestet answers. This type of sonnet is usually rhymed *abba abba cdecde*. The second type of sonnet, the Shakespearean sonnet, consists of three stanzas of four lines each and a concluding couplet. This type of sonnet usually uses the rhyme scheme *abab cdcd efef gg*. Often the final rhyming couplet provides a statement that summarizes or concludes the poem by making an emphatic point about its theme.

It would be difficult to remember all the details in this reading passage. However, if you organize the information visually by mapping the details, you will find the information easier to remember.

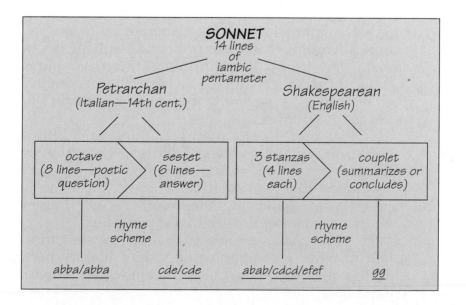

Outlining

An *outline* organizes ideas and information. When you make an outline, you identify the most important information and ideas in a passage. Then you group all these ideas into an organized pattern that shows their order and their relationship to one another.

Sometimes, however, as with lecture notes, you may want to use an informal outline form. This method of arranging notes allows you to organize information very quickly. (See an example in the study notes on page 993.)

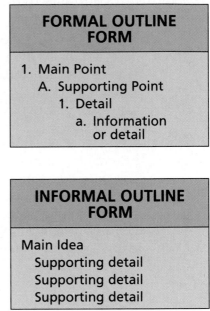

FORMAL OUTLINE FORM

1. Main Point
   A. Supporting Point
      1. Detail
         a. Information or detail

INFORMAL OUTLINE FORM

Main Idea
   Supporting detail
   Supporting detail
   Supporting detail

Paraphrasing

When you *paraphrase,* you restate someone else's ideas in your own words. Paraphrasing is a good way to check your understanding of what you read, especially if the original is written in poetic or elaborate language (such as complex wording in a poem or poetic language in a scene from a play by Shakespeare). A written paraphrase is usually approximately the same length as the original, so this technique is generally not used for very lengthy passages of writing.

As you read things that you think are difficult to understand, paraphrase what you read by putting these ideas into your own words in your study notes. Your paraphrased version might include dialect or slang expressions if you feel more comfortable with these than with the wording of the original expressions.

Or, in language arts classes, you may sometimes be asked to write a paraphrase of a short literary passage, such as a poem. Use the following guidelines to help you paraphrase.

HOW TO PARAPHRASE

1. Be sure you understand what the material means. Look up any unfamiliar words.
2. Identify the main idea of the selection. Keep it in mind while you write your paraphrase.
3. Identify the speaker in fictional material. (Is the poet or author speaking, or is it a narrator or a character?)
4. Write out your paraphrase in your own words, remembering to use complete sentences and traditional paragraph form.
5. Check to be sure that your paraphrase expresses the same idea as the original.

Here is an example of a poem to be paraphrased.

Sick Leave
by Po Chü-i[1] (translated by Arthur Waley)

Propped on pillows, not attending to business;
For two days I've lain behind locked doors.
I begin to think that those who hold office
Get no rest, except by falling ill!
For restful thoughts one does not need space;
The room where I lie is ten foot square.
By the western eaves, above the bamboo twigs,
From my couch I see the White Mountain rise.
But the clouds that hover on its far-distant peak
Bring shame to a face that is buried in the World's dust.

[1] Po Chü-i (pō′chōō′ē)

Following is one possible paraphrase of the poem.

A Chinese government official is home, sitting up in bed. He is thinking about all of his work that is not getting done. The official has been sick for two days, and he has apparently locked himself in his room to remain undisturbed. He states that he believes getting sick is probably the only way that people who have official responsibilities ever get any time off.

His room is very small, only ten feet by ten feet, but he comments that since all he is doing is resting and thinking, he does not need a large room. His room is on the west side of a house high enough to be above the growing bamboo. From his window, he can see the White Mountain rising above the clouds. He contemplates the contrast between the mountain, as it rises high above the pressures of life, and his own life, as it is burdened down by these pressures.

You will use paraphrasing when you write research reports. Remember, however, that you must cite your sources when you use someone else's ideas.

☞ REFERENCE NOTE: For more about paraphrasing in research reports, see pages 421–422.

Summarizing

A *summary* restates the main points of a passage in condensed form. A summary, or *précis*, helps you identify and remember the most important points of the material you are studying. When you write a summary, it is necessary for you to analyze the material in order to decide what is most important and should be included in the summary, and what can be left out.

RESOURCES

HOW TO SUMMARIZE

1. Skim the material and identify the main ideas.
2. Review the passage and look for supporting details.
3. Write a sentence in your own words about each main idea. Write approximately one sentence for each paragraph of the original.
4. Use your list of sentences to write your summary in standard paragraph form. Use transitional words between the ideas to show how the ideas are related.
5. Evaluate and revise your summary, checking to see if your summary covers key points. Make sure the reader can follow your ideas.

Here is a sample summary of the article on pages 402–404.

Astronomy was closer to religion than science, to many American Indian peoples. They believed the planets and the stars were gods. Since they thought these gods affected every aspect of human life, these early astronomers struggled to learn the exact patterns of the movements of heavenly bodies. Then they recorded their findings. In some places, calendars were made of wood, stone, or string. In others, astronomical observances were written on folded, booklike forms made of hide or bark. In some places, buildings and cities were aligned with planetary sightlines. The earth, too, was believed to be a sacred being. Certain routes were thought to be holy. Lines, such as the Nazca Lines in Peru, may also have had religious significance.

Memorizing

Frequent, short, focused sessions of practice are best when you are trying to memorize material. It is not very efficient to cram, because you will not retain the information well.

HOW TO MEMORIZE	
Condense the information, if possible.	If you're studying reading material, such as a chapter, passages can often be summarized or condensed.
Rehearse the material in several different ways.	Use several different senses. Copy or write the material so you can see it as well as touch it. Say it out loud so you can hear it.
Play memory games.	Make a word out of the initials of key terms or use other creative ways to make the information more memorable.

Improving Test-Taking Skills

Preparing Yourself

Your attitude is an important factor in doing well on a test. It's normal to feel nervous before a big test. However, you can channel this nervous energy productively if you concentrate on your test performance.

HOW TO PREPARE FOR A TEST

Analyze your preparedness. Decide early what you need to study most, then study thoroughly.

Focus on the test. During the test, as you read and answer the questions, concentrate on what you know, not anything else. Don't allow yourself to be distracted.

Make a commitment. Keep trying until you find the right study method for you.

Preparing for Standardized Tests

A *standardized test* is one in which your score is evaluated in comparison with a "standard" that is compiled from the scores of many other students nationwide who have taken the same test. There are two common kinds: achievement and aptitude tests.

Achievement tests are designed to measure how much you know about specific subjects, such as biology or Spanish. Aptitude tests evaluate your basic skills in various areas of study, such as reading comprehension or vocabulary skills.

Standardized tests often cover material you have learned during many years of study. To prepare for most standardized tests, it's best to improve your overall study habits: read often, write frequently, increase your vocabulary steadily, and use the study skills described earlier in this chapter. In addition, there are some short-term preparations you can make to improve your performance.

HOW TO PREPARE FOR STANDARDIZED TESTS

Learn what skills will be tested on the specific test you plan to take. Information booklets may be provided that tell about the types of questions and how the test is scored. Practice with these or with published study guides available through bookstores or libraries.

Know what materials you need for the test. For the test, you may need to bring specific materials, such as number 2 pencils or pens and a prepared examination booklet of lined paper for an essay answer.

Determine how this test scores answers. If there is no penalty for wrong answers, you should make your best guess on all questions possible. If wrong answers are penalized, make guesses only if you are fairly sure of your answer.

Objective Tests

Two basic types of tests are *objective* and *essay tests*. Certain strategies can help you with each type.

There are many types of objective tests. They may include multiple-choice, true/false, matching, reasoning or logic, or short-answer questions. Although they appear in many forms, all objective questions have one characteristic in common: There is usually only one correct answer.

HOW TO STUDY FOR OBJECTIVE TESTS

1. Review the study questions in your textbook, and skim class notes to identify important terms or facts.
2. Review the information in more than one form. For example, if you are responsible for knowing a list of important terms, test yourself on how well you can define each one of the terms without looking at your book or notes.
3. Practice and repeat factual information. Use flashcards to see if you can remember the correct terms. Identify difficult items and review them.

Adapt your study strategies to suit the specific type of objective test you will be taking. For example, if your test includes a map you'll have to label, test yourself by labeling a practice version.

Taking Different Kinds of Objective Tests

At the beginning of an objective test, scan the test quickly to count the number of test items. Then decide how to budget your time. For each type of objective test question, use the following specific, effective strategies.

Multiple-Choice Questions. Multiple-choice questions ask you to select a correct answer from among a given number of choices.

EXAMPLE **1.** After she was arrested for refusing to yield her seat on a bus, Rosa Parks
    Ⓐ decided to stop using the bus system.
    B was elected to Congress.
    C moved to Tuskegee, Alabama.
    D married Raymond Parks.

HOW TO ANSWER MULTIPLE-CHOICE QUESTIONS	
Read the initial statement carefully.	▪ Make sure you understand this statement before examining the choices. ▪ Look for qualifiers such as *not* or *always* since these—and other, similar terms—limit the answers.
Read all the answers before making a choice.	▪ Narrow the choices by eliminating incorrect answers. Some answers may be clearly wrong, while others may only be somewhat related to the correct answer. ▪ Seek the most correct choice. Some choices (such as "Both A and B" or "All of the above") affect your other choices.

True/False Questions. You are asked to determine whether a given statement is correct.

EXAMPLE   **1.** T Ⓕ The percentage of school-age children in the United States has increased over this century.

HOW TO ANSWER TRUE/FALSE QUESTIONS	
Read the statement carefully.	▪ If any part of the statement is false, the whole statement is false.
Check for qualifiers.	▪ Words such as *always* or *never* qualify or limit a statement. ▪ A statement is true only if it is wholly and always true.

Matching Questions. In matching questions, two lists are placed near each other so that you may match items on one list with those on the other.

Directions: Match the term in the left-hand column with its description in the right-hand column.

  <u>D</u> **1.** Shakespearean sonnet   **A** group of eight rhymed lines of a sonnet

  <u>C</u> **2.** couplet   **B** Italian sonnet

  <u>A</u> **3.** octave   **C** group of two rhymed lines in a sonnet

  <u>B</u> **4.** Petrarchan sonnet   **D** English sonnet

HOW TO ANSWER MATCHING QUESTIONS	
Read the directions carefully.	Sometimes answers may be used more than once.
Scan the columns and match items you know first.	You can gain more time to evaluate items you are less sure about.
Complete the matching process.	Make your best reasoned guess on remaining items.

RESOURCES

Reasoning or Logic Questions. Some questions (especially on standardized tests) may test your reasoning abilities more than they test your knowledge of a specific subject. These questions often ask you to identify the relationship between several items (such as words, pictures, or numbers), or they may ask you to predict what the next item in a series should be.

Reasoning questions might ask you to identify a pattern in a number sequence (for example: 3, 9, 27, 81—these are powers of the number 3). Or, you might be asked to predict the next item in a sequence of drawings.

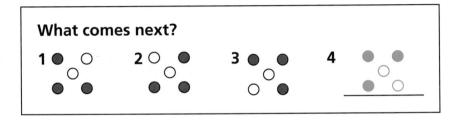

In this sequence of drawings, the two white dots are pointed outwards, moving counter-clockwise around the configuration of dots. Therefore, in the fourth frame the white dots should point toward the bottom right.

HOW TO ANSWER REASONING OR LOGIC QUESTIONS

Be sure you understand the instructions.	On standardized tests, reasoning or logic questions are usually multiple-choice. On some other tests, you may need to write a word or phrase, write out a number sequence, or draw your answer.
Analyze the relationship implied in the question.	Look at the question carefully to gather information about the relationship of the items.
Draw reasonable conclusions.	Evaluate the relationship of the items as a basis for your decision.

Analogy Questions. Analogy questions are special types of reasoning and logic questions that ask you to analyze the relationship between one pair of words and to identify or to supply a second pair of words that has the same relationship.

Analogy questions usually appear on standardized tests in multiple-choice form, but sometimes they appear as fill-in-the-blank questions.

EXAMPLE **1.** Directions: Select the appropriate pair of words to complete the analogy.

DRESS : CLOTHING :: _____

A wheel : car
B page : read
C bicycle : vehicle
D world : round

EXAMPLE **2.** Directions: Complete the following analogy.

SHOWER : CLEAN :: mud : _*dirty*_____

HOW TO ANSWER ANALOGY QUESTIONS	
Analyze the first pair of words.	Identify the relationship between the first two items. (In Example 1, a *dress* is a kind of *clothing;* this is an analogy of classification. See the Analogy Chart on pages 1006–1007.)
Express the analogy in sentence or question form.	Example 1 could be read as "A *dress* is a kind of *clothing,* just as . . . (what other pair of items among the choices given?)."
Find the best available choice to complete the analogy.	▪ If choices are given, select the pair of words with the same relationship between them as the first pair. ▪ If you must fill in a blank to complete an analogy, you may be asked to supply the final word. (Using Example 2, a *shower* makes you *clean.* What would *mud* make you? You would be *dirty.*)

RESOURCES

ANALOGY CHART		
TYPE	EXAMPLE	SOLUTION
Synonyms	ROUND : CIRCULAR :: strong : muscular	*Round* is similar in meaning to *circular,* just as *strong* is like *muscular.*
Antonyms	PATRIOT : TRAITOR :: loyal : unfaithful	A *patriot* is the opposite of a *traitor,* just as *loyal* means the opposite of *unfaithful.*
Cause	VIRUS : SICKNESS :: water : dampness	A *virus* causes *sickness,* just as *water* causes *dampness.*
Effect	TEARS : SORROW :: smiles : joy	*Tears* are the effect of *sorrow,* just as *smiles* are the effect of *joy.*
Part to Whole	DROPLETS : SEA :: grains : desert	*Droplets* (of water) make up a *sea,* just as *grains* (of sand) make up a *desert.*
Whole to Part	WALL : BRICKS :: deck : cards	A *wall* contains *bricks,* just as a *deck* contains *cards.*
Classification	BAGEL : BREAD :: pork : meat	A *bagel* is a type of *bread,* just as *pork* is a type of *meat.*
Characteristics	PUPPIES : FURRY :: fish : slippery	*Puppies* feel *furry,* just as *fish* feel *slippery.*
Degree	COLOSSAL : LARGE :: microscopic : small	*Colossal* means *very large,* just as *microscopic* means *very small.*
Use	DESK : STUDY :: bed : sleep	A *desk* is used to *study,* just as a *bed* is used to *sleep.*

(continued)

ANALOGY CHART *(continued)*		
TYPE	EXAMPLE	SOLUTION
Measure	BAROMETER : AIR PRESSURE :: scale : weight	A *barometer* is used to measure *air pressure*, just as a *scale* is used to measure *weight*.
Action to Performer	TEACHING : PROFESSOR :: cleaning : maid	*Teaching* is the action performed by a *professor*, just as *cleaning* is the action performed by a *maid*.
Performer to Action	AUTHOR : WRITE :: chef : cook	An *author's* profession is to *write*, just as a *chef's* profession is to *cook*.
Place	SPACE NEEDLE : SEATTLE :: Lincoln Memorial : Washington, D.C.	The *Space Needle* is in *Seattle*, just as the *Lincoln Memorial* is in *Washington, D.C.*

Short-Answer Questions. Answers to short-answer questions should show your knowledge of the subject. Like other objective questions, short-answer questions usually have only one correct answer. However, you do not have a choice of answers: You have to write out your response.

Some short-answer questions (such as a diagram, a map, or a fill-in-the-blank question) can be answered with one or a few words. In another type of short-answer question, you are asked a question and you must write a full response, usually one or two sentences in length.

EXAMPLE   Describe briefly the comparison made at the end of Po Chü-i's poem "Sick Leave."

ANSWER   *The speaker contrasts himself with the mountain he sees from his sickroom window. The mountain is above the world's cares, while he is buried beneath them.*

HOW TO RESPOND TO SHORT-ANSWER QUESTIONS	
Read the question carefully.	Some questions have more than one part, and you will have to include an answer to each part to receive full credit.
Plan your answer.	Briefly, decide what you need to include in the answer.
Be as specific as possible in your answers.	Give a full, exact answer.
Budget your time.	Begin by answering all of the questions you are certain about. Return later to the questions you are less sure about.

Essay Tests

Essay tests ask you to think critically about material you have learned and to express your understanding of that material in an organized way. You will be expected to write at least a full paragraph, if not several paragraphs, in answer.

HOW TO STUDY FOR ESSAY TESTS
1. Review your textbook carefully.
2. Make an outline, identifying main points and key details.
3. Make a practice set of possible questions on your own and practice writing out the answers.
4. Evaluate and revise your practice answers, checking your notes and textbook for accuracy and the writing chapters of this textbook for help in writing.

Taking Essay Tests

Before you start writing on an essay test, scan the questions quickly. Make sure you know how many answers you are expected to write. If you have a choice between several items, decide which one or ones you think you can answer best. Then plan how much time to spend on each answer, and stay on this schedule.

Read the question carefully. There may be several parts to the answer.

Pay attention to important terms in the question. Essay questions usually ask you to perform specific tasks. A verb expresses each one of these tasks. It helps to become familiar with each key verb. Each one identifies the tasks that you will need to accomplish in a good essay response.

ESSAY TEST QUESTIONS		
KEY VERB	**TASK**	**SAMPLE QUESTION**
argue	Take a viewpoint on an issue and give reasons to support this opinion.	Argue whether or not your school should require all students to participate in extra-curricular activities.
analyze	Take something apart to see how each part works.	Analyze the central character in Edgar Allan Poe's "The Tell-Tale Heart."
compare	Point out likenesses.	Compare George Washington Carver and Thomas Edison as inventors.
contrast	Point out differences.	Contrast the economic conditions in the South and in the North at the end of the Civil War.
define	Give specific details that make some-thing unique.	Define the term *colonialism* as it applies to America's early history.
demonstrate (also illustrate, present, show)	Provide examples to support a point.	Demonstrate that a line intersecting parallel lines produces equivalent angles.
describe	Give a picture in words.	Describe the eulogy scene in *Julius Caesar*.

(continued)

RESOURCES

ESSAY TEST QUESTIONS *(continued)*

KEY VERB	TASK	SAMPLE QUESTION
discuss	Examine in detail.	Discuss the term *manifest destiny.*
explain	Give reasons.	Explain why the United States entered World War II.
identify	Point out specific persons, places, things, or characteristics.	Identify the leaders of the Confederacy and their importance in the Civil War.
interpret	Give the meaning or significance of something.	Interpret the role of Cesar Chavez in organizing the farm labor movement.
list (also outline, trace)	Give all steps in order or all details about a subject.	List the events leading up to the Montgomery bus boycott.
summarize	Give a brief overview of the main points.	Summarize the plot of Bernard Malamud's short story "A Summer's Reading."

Take a moment to use prewriting strategies. After considering the key verbs in the question, make notes or a simple outline to help you decide what you want to say. Write the notes or outline on scratch paper.

Evaluate and revise as you write. You probably will not be able to redraft your whole essay. However, you can edit your essay to strengthen it.

QUALITIES OF A GOOD ESSAY ANSWER

- The essay is well organized.
- The main ideas and supporting points are clearly presented.
- The sentences are complete and well written.
- There are no distracting errors in spelling, punctuation, or grammar.

Review

▶ EXERCISE 1   **Choosing an Appropriate Reading Rate**

Identify the reading rate that best fits each of the given situations.

1. You are looking through a list of ZIP Codes to find the code for Scranton, Pennsylvania.
2. You are looking through a library book to see if it would be a good resource for a research paper on Pedro Menéndez de Avilés, founder of St. Augustine, Florida.
3. You have a 100-question, multiple-choice test tomorrow on a chapter in your science textbook that you have already read but need to review.
4. You are reading a chapter in your literature book for a class discussion tomorrow and a test in two weeks.
5. You are reading instructions on a standardized test to see how much time is allowed for a section of the test.

▶ EXERCISE 2   **Applying the SQ3R Reading Method**

Use the SQ3R method while reading a newspaper article or a chapter that you need to read for a class. List at least five questions that you might be asked on a test about the material and write brief answers to each one.

▶ EXERCISE 3   **Reading: Analyzing Details in a Passage**

Answer the following questions about the reading passage on pages 988–989.

1. Give two facts about Rosa Parks (other than those already noted in the sample analysis).
2. What was the reaction of other African Americans to Rosa Parks's actions?
3. What were the effects of the Montgomery bus boycott— good or bad—on Rosa Parks's life?
4. What is the impact of the Montgomery bus boycott compared to?
5. What order is used to arrange the details of the first three paragraphs of the passage?

RESOURCES

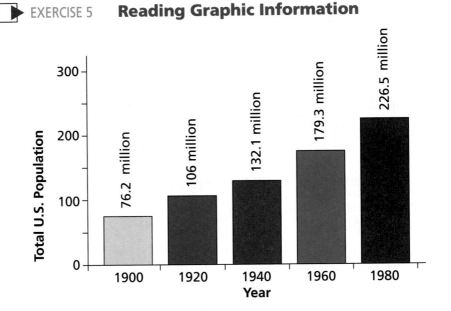

EXERCISE 4 **Reading: Drawing Conclusions and Making Inferences**

Using the reading passage on pages 988–989, identify the evidence or reasoning that you might use in order to make the following inferences or to draw the following conclusions.

1. Some people disagreed with Rosa Parks's refusal to obey the segregation laws.
2. Rosa Parks's job at the tailor shop was tiring.
3. People outside of Montgomery, Alabama, were aware of the bus boycott.
4. The services of many black employees were valued by their white employers.
5. Since a hero can be defined as someone who faces obstacles but manages to overcome them, Rosa Parks is a hero.

EXERCISE 5 **Reading Graphic Information**

Historical Summary of Total U.S. Population

Look at the graph above, and then compare its information with that of the graph on page 991. Review both graphs to answer the following questions.

1. Did the percentage of the population between the ages of five and seventeen increase or decrease between 1920 and 1940? By how much?
2. Did the percentage of the population between the ages of five and seventeen increase or decrease between 1940 and 1960? By how much?
3. Compare the percentage of the population between the ages of five and seventeen in the years 1960 and 1980. How much did this portion of the population increase or decrease?
4. Did the percentage of the population between the ages of five and seventeen increase or decrease between the years 1900 and 1980?

▶ EXERCISE 6   **Evaluating Graphic Information**

Study the numbers in the table below. Then follow the numbered instructions.

PERCENTAGE OF POPULATION ATTENDING HIGH SCHOOLS				
1900	1920	1940	1960	1980
3.3%	10.2%	26.0%	23.5%	32.9%

1. Using the graphs on page 991 and page 1012 as models, create a graph from the information in the table above.
2. Write a list of at least four conclusions you can draw from a point-by-point comparison of each of these three graphs. (You might look at your answers to Exercise 5 to suggest the type of questions you could ask.)
3. For each of the three graphs, make a prediction about the population figures for the year 2000.
4. Write a brief paragraph in which you discuss the observations and conclusions you have made. Cite specific information or identify evidence from the three graphs to support your findings.

RESOURCES

▶ EXERCISE 7   **Analyzing Your Note-Taking Method**

For one day, take notes in all of your classes by using the techniques suggested on pages 992–993. Write a paragraph comparing and contrasting your usual method and this new method. Be sure to address these points: How are the two methods similar? How are they different? Which works better? Why?

▶ EXERCISE 8   **Identifying Classifications**

For each of the following groups of items, describe the category.

1. telescope, binoculars, microscope, camera, periscope
2. T-bone, hamburger, filet mignon, pot roast, prime rib
3. 1, 2, 3, 5, 7, 11
4. television, movies, plays, concerts, musicals
5. albatross, pelican, sea gull, penguin, sandpiper
6. *The Adventures of Tom Sawyer, Adventures of Huckleberry Finn, The Innocents Abroad, The Prince and the Pauper*
7. 12, 23, 34, 45, 56, 67
8. butter, banana, blonde, canary, life raft
9. soccer, golf, tennis, field hockey, polo
10. tot, nun, deed, radar, pip

▶ EXERCISE 9   **Completing Analogies**

Consider the first relationship; then, write the word that best indicates the second relationship so that it parallels the first. There may be more than one correct answer.

EXAMPLE   **1.** CARPENTER : WOOD :: potter : _____
          1. *CARPENTER : WOOD :: potter : clay*

1. SHEEP : FLOCK :: cattle : ____
2. BOSTON : MASSACHUSETTS :: Reno : ____
3. DUCK : QUACK :: turkey : ____
4. OWL : WISE :: fox : ____
5. TROT : GALLOP :: jog : ____
6. LIZARD : REPTILE :: whale : ____
7. KEY : LOCK :: combination : ____
8. THUNDERSTORM : RAIN :: blizzard : ____
9. HAMMER : HIT :: saw : ____
10. ARTIST : PAINT :: weaver : ____

▶ EXERCISE 10   Reading: Applying Visual Organization

After reading the paragraph below, draw a visually organized representation of its contents. Then use your graphic to answer the numbered questions that follow the reading passage.

There are four layers of the atmosphere above the earth's surface. The lowest layer is the troposphere. This layer touches the earth's surface and extends to about seventeen kilometers above sea level. Within this layer are all the known living things, almost all the air and moisture, and almost all the weather conditions of our planet. The stratosphere extends from the upper limit of the troposphere to approximately fifty kilometers above sea level. This layer is important because it contains almost all the ozone in the atmosphere. Ozone protects the inhabitants of the earth from the harmful effect of the sun's rays. Since very little weather occurs in the stratosphere, airplane pilots like to fly there to avoid storms at low altitudes. The mesosphere extends from about fifty kilometers to about eighty kilometers above sea level. The mesosphere has greatly varying temperatures. At its lower level, it drops to about 0°C, but at its upper level it drops to about −100°C. Meteor trails, those hot gas streaks left behind by extraterrestrial debris, occur in the mesosphere. The thermosphere extends from approximately eighty kilometers above sea level into outer space. The upper limit of the thermosphere may extend to a thousand kilometers above sea level. In the upper limits of the thermosphere the air is especially thin. This is the region of the atmosphere where artificial satellites orbit the earth.

1. What is the temperature range of the mesosphere?
2. How many kilometers above sea level is the top of the thermosphere?
3. Why is the stratosphere important?
4. Which sphere has the least air?
5. Where in the atmosphere does most weather occur?

RESOURCES

▶ EXERCISE 11 **Reading: Paraphrasing a Poem**

Read the following excerpt from a poem by Percy Bysshe Shelley. Then write a paraphrase of the poem.

> *from* The Cloud
> *by Percy Bysshe Shelley*
>
> I bring fresh showers for the thirsting flowers,
>   From the seas and the streams;
> I bear light shade for the leaves when laid
>   In their noonday dreams.
> From my wings are shaken the dews that waken
>   The sweet buds every one,
> When rocked to rest on their mother's breast,
>   As she dances about the sun.
> I wield the flail of the lashing hail,
>   And whiten the green plains under,
> And then again I dissolve it in rain,
>   And laugh as I pass in thunder.

▶ EXERCISE 12 **Analyzing Essay Questions**

Identify the key verb that states the specific task in the following essay questions. Do not write an essay. Just state briefly what you would need to do to answer the question.

1. Compare the leadership abilities of Richard M. Nixon and John F. Kennedy, citing two specific crises.
2. Explain your beliefs about mandatory education.
3. Describe the events of a major earthquake.
4. Compare the characters of Romeo and Tybalt in *Romeo and Juliet.*
5. Trace the changes in the character of Pip in Charles Dickens's novel *Great Expectations.*
6. Show how the setting affects the action in the movie *The Third Man.*
7. List the steps in the water cycle, starting with rain.
8. Interpret the importance of the Bill of Rights to the American democratic system.
9. Analyze the economic conditions that helped cause the Civil War, including at least three factors.
10. Give the characteristics of a good mayoral candidate.

DIAGRAMING SENTENCES

A *sentence diagram* is a picture of how the parts of a sentence fit together and how the words in a sentence are related.

Subjects and Verbs (pages 546–555)

Every sentence diagram begins with a horizontal line intersected by a short vertical line, which divides the subject from the verb.

EXAMPLE   Alice Walker wrote *The Color Purple*.

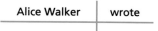

Understood Subjects (page 554)

EXAMPLE   Answer the phone, please.

Nouns of Direct Address (page 554)

EXAMPLE   Pass me the picante sauce, **Gina.**

Compound Subjects (page 554)

EXAMPLE   **Arturo** and **Patsy** are dancing the conga.

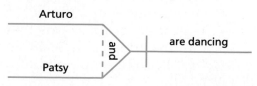

Compound Verbs (page 555)

EXAMPLE   Roger **swims** and **dives**.

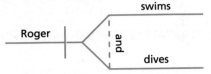

Here is how a compound verb is diagramed when the helping verb is not repeated.

EXAMPLE   Sally Ann **was reading** and **studying**.

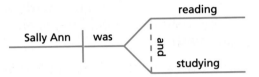

Compound Subjects and Compound Verbs
(pages 554–555)

EXAMPLE   **Kittens** and **puppies can play** together and **become** friends.

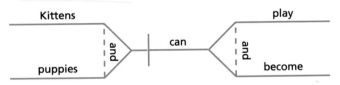

When the parts of a compound subject or a compound predicate are joined by a correlative conjunction, diagram the sentence this way:

EXAMPLE   **Both** Norma **and** Lisa will **not only** perform **but also** teach.

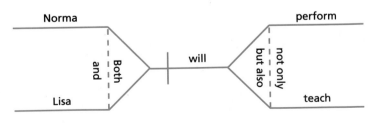

Modifiers (pages 518–521, 529–531, and 714–715)

Adjectives and Adverbs (pages 518–521 and 529–531)

Adjectives and adverbs are written on slanting lines beneath the words they modify.

EXAMPLE **The blue** car **quickly** swerved **left.**

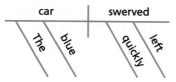

When an adverb modifies an adjective or an adverb, it is placed on a line connected to the word it modifies.

EXAMPLE The Neville Brothers performed **exceptionally** well.

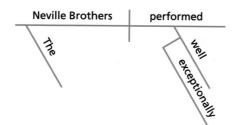

Here, There, and *Where* as Modifiers
(page 553)

EXAMPLES **Here** come the astronauts!

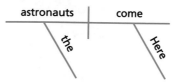

There goes the new Mohawk chief.

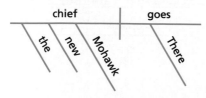

Where will the balloonists land?

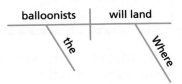

NOTE: Sometimes *there* begins a sentence but does not modify the verb. When used in this way, *there* is called an *expletive*. It is diagramed on a line by itself.

EXAMPLE   **There** are seven stars in the Pleiades.

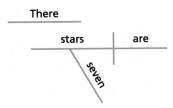

Subject Complements (page 560)

A subject complement is placed on the horizontal line with the simple subject and the verb. It comes after the verb. A line *slanting toward the subject* separates the subject complement from the verb.

Predicate Nominatives (page 560)

EXAMPLE   Some dogs are good **companions.**

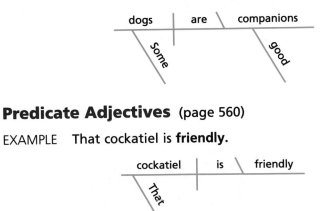

Predicate Adjectives (page 560)

EXAMPLE   That cockatiel is **friendly.**

cockatiel | is \ friendly

Compound Subject Complements (page 560)

EXAMPLE Martin Yan is both a **chef** and a **comedian.**

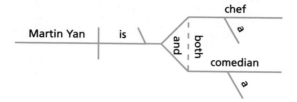

Objects (pages 562–563)

Direct Objects (page 562)

EXAMPLE Cathy led the **band.**

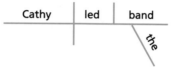

Notice that a vertical line separates the direct object from the verb.

Compound Direct Objects (page 563)

EXAMPLE We heard **cheers** and **whistles.**

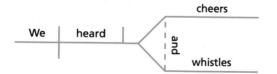

Indirect Objects (page 563)

The indirect object is diagramed on a horizontal line beneath the verb.

EXAMPLE They gave **her** a present.

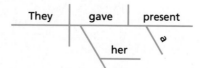

Compound Indirect Objects (page 563)

EXAMPLE   Mr. Stephens lent **Karen** and **Shanna** *The Fire Next Time.*

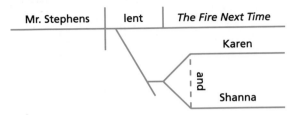

Phrases (pages 573–591)

Prepositional Phrases (pages 574–576)

The preposition is placed on a slanting line leading down from the word that the phrase modifies. The object of the preposition is placed on a horizontal line connected to the slanting line.

EXAMPLES   The steep slopes **of the mountains** are covered **with forests.** [adjective phrase modifying the subject; adverb phrase modifying the verb]

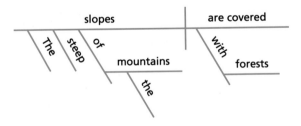

They sailed late **in the fall.** [adverb phrase modifying an adverb]

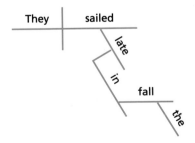

Nina read this Chinese folk tale **to Aaron and Joey.** [compound object of preposition]

Down the valley and **across the plain** wanders the river. [two phrases modifying the same word]

The princess lived **in a castle on the mountain.** [phrase modifying the object of another preposition]

Participles and Participial Phrases (pages 579–583)

EXAMPLES   I heard them **laughing.**

> **Waving her hat,** Sara flagged the train **speeding down the track.**

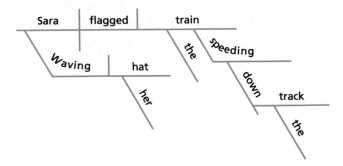

Gerunds and Gerund Phrases (pages 584–585)

EXAMPLES **Waiting** is not easy. [gerund used as subject]

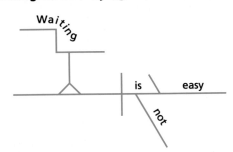

> **Waiting patiently for hours** is usually a sure means **of observing wild animals.** [gerund phrases used as subject and as object of a preposition]

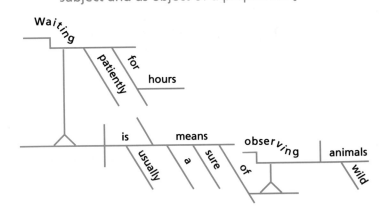

Infinitives and Infinitive Phrases (pages 586–588)

Infinitives and infinitive phrases used as modifiers are diagramed in the same way as prepositional phrases.

EXAMPLE **He plays to win.** [infinitive used as adverb]

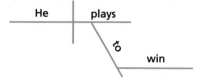

Infinitives and infinitive phrases used as nouns are diagramed as follows.

EXAMPLES **To choose the right career** takes careful consideration. [infinitive phrase used as subject]

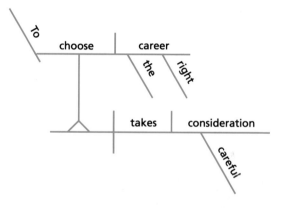

She is hoping to visit Morocco soon. [infinitive phrase used as direct object]

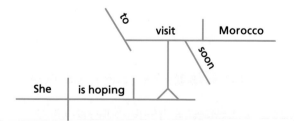

My brother watched **me prune the tree.** [infinitive with subject, *me*, and with *to* omitted]

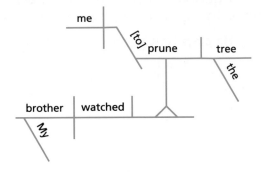

Appositives and Appositive Phrases (pages 590–591)

Place the appositive in parentheses after the word it identifies or explains.

EXAMPLES   My cousin **Bryan** is a carpenter.

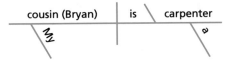

Mohammed Tahir, **our newest classmate,** comes from Yemen, **a country near Saudi Arabia.**

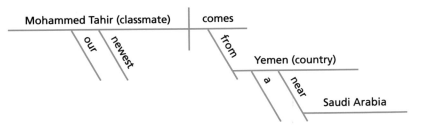

Subordinate Clauses (pages 598–606)

Adjective Clauses (pages 600–602)

An adjective clause is joined to the word it modifies by a broken line leading from the modified word to the relative pronoun.

EXAMPLES   The coat **that I wanted** was too expensive.

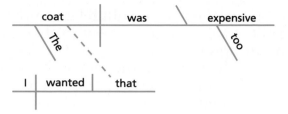

The box, **which contained the treasure,** was missing.

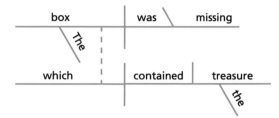

She is the woman **from whom we bought the used car.**

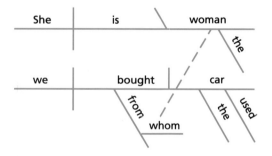

Adverb Clauses (pages 603–604)

Place the subordinating conjunction that introduces the adverb clause on a broken line leading from the verb in the adverb clause to the word the clause modifies.

EXAMPLE   **Before a hurricane strikes,** ample warning is given.

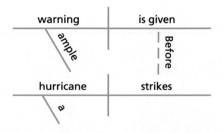

Noun Clauses (page 606)

Noun clauses often begin with relative pronouns, such as *that, what, who,* or *which.* These relative pronouns may have a function within the dependent clause or may simply connect the clause to the rest of the sentence. How a noun clause is diagramed depends on its use in the sentence and whether or not the relative pronoun has a specific function in the noun clause.

EXAMPLES   **What she said** convinced me. [The noun clause is used as the subject of the independent clause. *What* functions as the direct object in the noun clause.]

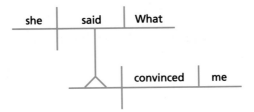

We know that you won the prize. [The noun clause is the direct object of the independent clause. *That* has no specific function in the noun clause.]

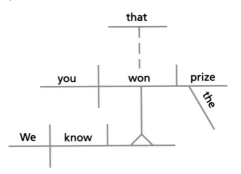

If the relative pronoun were omitted from the preceding sentence, the diagram would look like this.

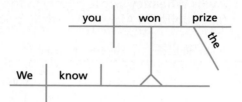

Sentences Classified According to Structure
(page 610)

Simple Sentences (page 610)

EXAMPLE   The Hudson is a historic waterway. [one independent clause]

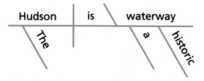

Compound Sentences (page 610)

EXAMPLE   A strange dog chased us, but the owner came to our rescue. [two independent clauses]

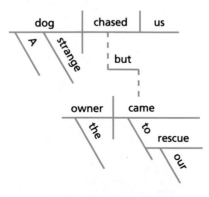

If the compound sentence has a semicolon and no conjunction, a straight broken line joins the two verbs.

EXAMPLE   Phillis Wheatley wrote poetry in the 1700s; she was the first published African American poet.

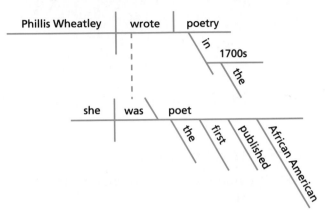

Notice that the compound adjective *African American* is written on one slanted line.

If the clauses of a compound sentence are joined by a semicolon and a conjunctive adverb (such as *consequently, therefore, nevertheless, however, moreover,* or *otherwise*), place the conjunctive adverb on a slanting line below the verb it modifies.

EXAMPLE   Dylan works part time after school; consequently, he can afford to buy a new bike.

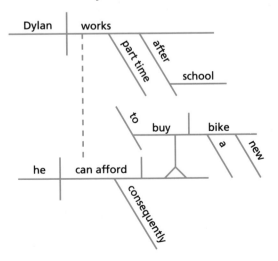

Complex Sentences (page 611)

EXAMPLE   **As night fell, the storm grew worse.** [one independent clause and one subordinate clause]

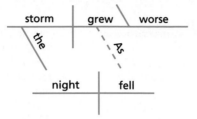

Compound-Complex Sentences (page 611)

EXAMPLE   **The room that Carrie painted had been white, but she changed the color.** [two independent clauses and one subordinate clause]

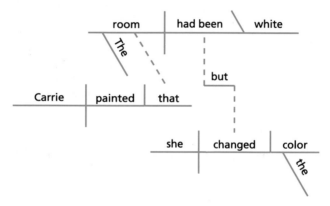

Glossary of Terms

A

Abstract noun Names an idea, a feeling, a quality, or a characteristic. (See page 515.)

Action verb Expresses physical or mental activity. (See page 524.)

Active voice The voice a verb is in when it expresses an action done *by* its subject. (See page 694.)

Adjective Modifies a noun or a pronoun. (See page 518.)

Adjective clause A subordinate clause that modifies a noun or a pronoun. (See page 600.)

Adjective phrase A prepositional phrase that modifies a noun or a pronoun. (See page 574.)

Adverb Modifies a verb, an adjective, or another adverb. (See page 529.)

Adverb clause A subordinate clause that modifies a verb, an adjective, or an adverb and tells *when, where, why, how,* or *to what extent.* (See page 603.)

Adverb phrase A prepositional phrase that modifies a verb, an adjective, or another adverb. (See page 576.)

Agreement The correspondence, or match, between grammatical forms. (See Chapter 19.)

Aim One of the four basic purposes, or reasons, for writing. (See page 7.)

Ambiguous reference Unclear phrasing that occurs when a pronoun can refer to either of two antecedents. (See page 669.)

Analyzing Looking at the parts of a whole and their relationships. (See pages 379 and 423.)

Anecdote An extended example, or story, used to support a main idea. (See pages 74 and 123.)

Antecedent The word to which a pronoun refers, usually preceding the pronoun and giving the pronoun its meaning. (See page 637.)

Appositive A noun or a pronoun placed beside another noun or pronoun to identify or explain it. (See pages 450 and 590.)

Appositive phrase Consists of an appositive and its modifiers. (See pages 450, 465, and 590.)

Article *A, an,* or *the,* the most frequently used adjectives. (See page 519.)

Audience The person(s) who reads or listens to what a writer or speaker says. (See pages 35 and 931.)

B

Base form The base form, or infinitive, is one of the four principal, or basic, parts of a verb. (See page 678.)

Base word A word that cannot be subdivided into parts. (See page 966.)

Block method A way of arranging details in a comparison/contrast essay by discussing all the features of the first subject, then the same features of the second subject in the same order. (See page 262.)

Body States and develops a composition's main points in one or more paragraphs. (See page 128.)

Brainstorming A technique for finding ideas by using free association: recording every idea about a subject that comes to mind, without stopping to evaluate any of the ideas. (See page 27.)

Business letter A formal letter in which a writer might request or order something, complain or seek the correction of a problem, or express appreciation for someone or something. (See Chapter 36.)

Call number A number and letter code a library assigns to a book, which tells how the book has been classified and where it has been placed on the shelves. (See page 952.)

Case The form of a noun or pronoun that shows how it is used in a sentence. (See page 649.)

Cause-and-effect essay A form of writing in which a writer examines and explains the reasons for a situation or event and its results. (See page 316.)

Chronological order A way of arranging ideas in a paragraph or composition according to when events happened. (See pages 39 and 82.)

Classification A strategy of development: looking at a subject as it relates to other subjects in a group. (See pages 97 and 994.)

Clause A group of words containing a verb and its subject, used as part of a sentence. (See pages 451 and 597.)

Cliché An overused, worn-out figure of speech. (See page 508.)

Climax The high point of a story plot; the tense or exciting scene that settles the main conflict. (See page 376.)

Clincher sentence The concluding sentence of a paragraph: pulls all the details together by restating or summarizing the main idea. (See page 76.)

Clustering A visual technique for finding writing ideas and gathering information: breaking a large subject into its smaller parts to create a visual map of one's thoughts. (See page 28.)

Coherence A quality achieved when all the ideas in a paragraph or composition are clearly arranged and connected. (See pages 82 and 128.)

Collective noun A noun that names a group of persons or things. (See page 629.)

Colloquialism An informal, colorful expression of conversational language. (See page 501.)

Comma splice A run-on sentence with only a comma to separate complete sentences. (See page 456.)

Common noun Names a member of a group of persons, places, or things; it is not capitalized. (See pages 515 and 764.)

Comparative degree The form a modifier takes when comparing two things. (See page 722.)

Comparison/Contrast essay A form of writing in which a writer discusses similarities or differences (or both) between two subjects. (See Chapter 7.)

Complement A word or group of words that completes the meaning of a predicate. (See page 557.)

Complex sentence Has one independent clause and at least one subordinate clause. (See pages 470 and 611.)

Compound-complex sentence Has two or more independent clauses and at least one subordinate clause. (See page 611.)

Compound sentence Has two or more independent clauses but no subordinate clauses. (See pages 468 and 610.)

Compound word Consists of two or more words used together as a single word. (See page 860.)

Compound subject Consists of two or more subjects that are joined by a conjunction and have the same verb. (See pages 554 and 627.)

Compound verb Consists of two or more verbs that are joined by a conjunction and have the same subject. (See page 555.)

Conclusion (1) Reinforces a main idea and brings a composition to a definite close. (See page 130.) **(2)** A decision or determination reached by reasoning from clearly expressed facts and evidence found in a reading passage or other materials. (See page 989.)

Concrete noun Names an object that can be perceived by the senses. (See page 515.)

Conflict The central problem a character faces in a story. (See pages 226 and 376.)

Conjugating Listing all forms of a verb in all tenses. (See page 684.)

Conjunctive adverb An adverb used as a connecting word between independent clauses in a compound sentence. (See page 457.)

Conjunction Joins words or groups of words. (See page 536.)

Connotation The emotional meanings suggested by or associated with a word. (See pages 504 and 965.)

Context The way a word is used in a reading passage. (See page 964.)

Contraction A shortened form of a word, a figure, or a group of words, written with an apostrophe to indicate where letters or numerals have been omitted. (See page 854.)

Coordinating conjunction Joins parallel words, phrases, or clauses. (See page 536.)

Correlative conjunctions Are used in pairs (*either . . . or, not only . . . but also,* and so on). (See page 536.)

Creative writing Aims at creating literature: stories, poems, songs, and plays. (See page 7.)

Critical analysis A form of writing in which a writer analyzes the ele-

ments, or parts, of a work such as a poem, a play, a novel, or a short story. (See Chapter 10.)

Dangling modifier A modifying word, phrase, or clause that does not clearly and sensibly modify a word or a group of words in a sentence. (See page 728.)

Declarative sentence Makes a statement and is followed by a period. (See page 565.)

Denotation The direct, plainly expressed meaning of a word— the meaning a dictionary lists. (See pages 504 and 965.)

Description A strategy of development: using sensory details and spatial order to describe individual features of a specific subject. (See pages 94 and 179.)

Dialect A distinct version or variety of a language used by a particular group of people; may be **ethnic** or **regional.** (See page 496.)

Dialogue The "talk," or conversation, in a story. (See page 229.)

Direct object A noun or pronoun that receives the action of the verb or shows the result of the action, answering the question *Whom?* or *What?* after a transitive verb. (See page 562.)

Direct quotation A reproduction of a person's exact words, enclosed in quotation marks. (See pages 427 and 834.)

Direct reference Connects ideas in a paragraph or composition by referring to a noun or pronoun used earlier. (See pages 88 and 128.)

Double comparison The use of both *−er* and *more* (*less*) or *−est* and *most* (*least*) to express the comparison forms of modifiers. (See page 724.)

Double negative The use of two negative words when one is sufficient. (See page 756.)

Double subject The use of an unnecessary pronoun after the subject of a sentence. (See page 744.)

Dramatic irony A device used by a writer to heighten readers' interest by letting the reader know something the main character in a story does not. (See page 378.)

Early plan An **informal** or **rough outline** for a composition in which a writer groups and orders information. (See page 117.)

Emotional appeal A strategy used to support a writer's opinion and to persuade an audience by appealing to readers' feelings. (See page 339.)

Emphasis The focus of a description, designed to create a specific impression for the reader. (See page 187.)

End marks Punctuation marks (periods, question marks, exclamation points) used to indicate the purpose of a sentence. (See page 789.)

Essay test Requires a student to think critically about material learned and to express his or her understanding of that material in an organized piece of writing. (See page 1008.)

Essential clause/Essential phrase Also called **restrictive:** is necessary to the meaning of a sentence; not set off by commas. (See page 798.)

Ethnic dialect A distinct version of a language used by people who share the same cultural heritage. (See page 498.)

Etymology The origin and history of a word. (See page 960.)

Euphemism An agreeable term that stands for a more direct, less pleasing one. (See page 505.)

Evaluating A stage in the writing process: making judgments about a composition's strengths and weaknesses in content, organization, and style. (See pages 6, 23, and 47.)

Evaluation A strategy of development: making judgments about a subject in an attempt to determine its value. (See page 100.)

Example A specific instance, or illustration, of a general idea. (See page 73.)

Exclamatory sentence Expresses strong feeling and is followed by an exclamation point. (See page 566.)

Expository writing *See* Informative writing.

Expressive writing Aims at expressing a writer's feelings and thoughts. (See page 7.)

Extemporaneous speech A speech for which a speaker researches and prepares notes, then delivers the rehearsed but not memorized speech. (See page 932.)

Fact Can be checked and proved to be true by concrete information. (See pages 71 and 337.)

Fallacy An error in logical thinking that may lead a writer into a false or oversimplified discussion of cause-and-effect relationships. (See page 316.)

Feedback The reaction of a receiver to the message given by a sender during the communication process. (See page 928.)

Figurative language Also called a **figure of speech:** a word or a group of words that has a meaning other than its literal one. (See pages 193 and 507.)

***5W-How?* questions** Questions (*Who? What? Where? When? Why? How?*) a writer uses to collect information about a subject. (See page 30.)

Foreshadowing A hint or suggestion of upcoming events in a story. (See page 377.)

Formal outline A highly structured, clearly labeled writing plan with a set pattern, using letters and numbers to label main headings and subheadings. (See page 118.)

Freewriting A technique for finding ideas: writing whatever thoughts occur, without regard to form. (See page 26.)

Fused sentence A run-on sentence with no punctuation separating the run-together sentences. (See page 456.)

General reference An error that occurs when a pronoun has no specific antecedent, but refers instead to a general idea. (See page 669.)

Gerund A verbal ending in *–ing,* used as a noun. (See page 584.)

Gerund phrase Consists of a gerund and its modifiers and complements. (See page 585.)

Idiom A word or phrase that means something different from its literal meaning. (See page 501.)

Imperative sentence Gives a command or makes a request and is followed by either a period or an exclamation point. (See page 565.)

Impromptu speech A short speech made on the spur of the moment, with little or no time for development or preparation of ideas. (See page 929.)

Indefinite pronoun A pronoun (*each, no one, anybody,* and so on) that does not refer to a specific person or thing. (See page 622.)

Independent clause Expresses a complete thought and can stand by itself as a sentence; also called a **main clause.** (See pages 451 and 597.)

Indirect object A noun or pronoun preceding a direct object that usually tells *to whom* or *for whom* (or *to what* or *for what*) the action of a transitive verb is performed. (See page 563.)

Indirect quotation A rewording or paraphrasing of something another person has said. (See page 834.)

Inference A decision or determination reached by reasoning from evidence that is hinted at or implied in a reading passage or other materials. (See page 989.)

Infinitive A verbal (verb form), usually preceded by *to,* used as a noun, an adjective, or an adverb. (See page 586.)

Infinitive phrase Consists of an infinitive and all of its modifiers and complements. (See page 587.)

Informative writing Aims at conveying information or explaining something. (See page 7.)

Interjection Expresses emotion and has no grammatical relation to the rest of the sentence. (See page 537.)

Interrogative sentence Asks a question and is followed by a question mark. (See page 566.)

Interview A special listening situation with the specific purpose of gathering information. (See page 943.)

Intransitive verb Expresses action (or tells something about the subject) without passing the action from a doer to a receiver. (See page 524.)

Introduction Begins a composition and should catch the reader's interest, set the composition's tone, and present the thesis statement. (See page 122.)

Invalid conclusion Is not reasonably or logically based on the available evidence. (See page 990.)

Irony A contrast between appearance or expectation and reality. (See page 378.)

Irregular verb Forms its past and past participle in some other way than by adding *–d* or *–ed*. (See page 679.)

Jargon Language that has a special meaning for a particular group of people; also wordy, puffed-up language called **gobbledygook.** (See page 506.)

Levels of usage The various forms of a language suitable for different situations. (See page 500.)

Linking verb Serves as a link between its subject and another word; may be a form of the verb *be.* (See page 525.)

Loaded words Words intended to provoke strong feeling, either positive or negative. (See page 505.)

Loanwords Words adopted from another language. (See page 487.)

Logical appeal A strategy used to support a writer's opinion and to persuade an audience by appealing to reason. (See page 337.)

Logical order A way of arranging details in a paragraph or composition according to what makes logical sense, such as grouping related ideas together. (See pages 39 and 84.)

Main idea The idea around which a paragraph or composition is organized. (See page 67.)

Mass media Forms of communication (television, radio, movies, newspapers and magazines) that reach a large audience daily. (See page 946.)

Metaphor A figure of speech directly comparing two things (without using the words *like* or *as*) by saying that something *is* something else. (See page 194.)

Misplaced modifier A word, phrase, or clause that makes a sentence awkward because it seems to modify the wrong word or group of words. (See page 730.)

Modifier A word, a phrase, or a clause that makes the meaning of another word more definite. (See pages 518 and 714.)

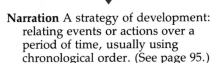

Narration A strategy of development: relating events or actions over a period of time, usually using chronological order. (See page 95.)

Nominative case The form a noun or pronoun takes as the subject or predicate nominative in a sentence. (See page 651.)

Nonessential clause/Nonessential phrase Also called **nonrestrictive:** adds information not necessary to the main idea in the sentence and is set off by commas. (See page 797.)

Nonverbal communication Sending a message—by gestures, facial expressions, and so on—without the use of verbal signals (words). (See page 929.)

Noun Names a person, place, thing, or idea. (See page 514.)

Noun clause A subordinate clause used as a noun. (See page 606.)

Noun of direct address Identifies the person spoken to or addressed in a sentence. (See page 554.)

Number The form of a word that indicates whether the word is singular or plural. (See page 618.)

Object A complement that does not refer to the subject. (See page 562.)

Objective case The form a noun or pronoun takes when used as a direct object, an indirect object, or the object of a preposition. (See page 655.)

Objective description Creates an accurate, thorough picture, using factual details without revealing a particular judgment or feeling about the subject. (See page 182.)

Objective test Requires a student to give a specific, limited response; may contain multiple-choice, true/false, matching, reasoning or logic, analogy, or short-answer questions. (See page 1001.)

Object of a preposition The noun or pronoun that ends a prepositional phrase. (See page 534.)

Opinion A belief or attitude. (See page 333.)

Oral interpretation An expressive presentation of a literary work to an audience, using vocal techniques, facial expressions, body language, and gestures. (See page 936.)

Order of importance A way of arranging details, in a paragraph or composition, from least to most important or from most to least important. (See pages 39 and 84.)

P

Parallel structure The use of the same form or part of speech to express equal, or parallel, ideas in a sentence. (See page 474.)

Paraphrase To restate someone else's ideas in different words. (See pages 421 and 945.)

Parenthetical expression A remark that adds incidental information or relates ideas. (See page 806.)

Parenthetical citation A form of documentation that places source information in parentheses at the end of a sentence in which someone else's word or ideas are used. (See page 428.)

Parliamentary procedure A plan for following a priority of actions: sometimes used by groups to keep meetings running smoothly. (See page 935.)

Participial phrase Consists of a participle and its complements and modifiers. (See pages 465 and 582.)

Participle A verbal (verb form) used as an adjective. (See pages 465 and 579.)

Passive voice The voice a verb is in when it expresses an action done *to* its subject. (See page 694.)

Personal letter An informal letter in which a writer might thank someone for something, invite someone to a particular event or occasion, or reply to an invitation he or she has received. (See Chapter 36.)

Personal narrative A form of writing in which an author explores and shares the meaning of an experience that was especially important to him or her. (See Chapter 4.)

Personification A figure of speech giving human characteristics to nonhuman things. (See page 194.)

Persuasive essay A form of writing in which a writer supports an opinion and tries to persuade an audience. (See Chapter 9.)

Persuasive writing Aims at persuading people to change their minds about something or to act in a certain way. (See page 7.)

Phrase A group of related words used as a single part of speech; does not contain both a predicate and its subject. (See pages 449 and 573.)

Plagiarism Using someone else's words or ideas without giving credit for them. (See page 422.)

Plot The series of events in a story that follow each other and cause each other to happen. (See pages 226 and 376.)

Point-by-point method A way of arranging details in a comparison/contrast essay by discussing one feature of the first subject, then the same feature of the second subject, repeating in the same order for all features. (See page 262.)

Point of view The vantage point, or position, from which a writer tells a story or describes a subject. (See pages 183 and 377.)

Possessive case The form a noun or pronoun takes when used to show ownership or relationship. (See page 848.)

Predicate The part of a sentence that says something about the subject. (See page 546.)

Predicate adjective An adjective in the predicate that describes the subject of a sentence or clause. (See page 560.)

Predicate nominative A noun or pronoun in the predicate that identifies or renames the subject of a sentence or clause. (See page 560.)

Prefix A word part added before a base or root word. (See page 968.)

Preposition Shows the relationship of a noun or a pronoun to some other word in a sentence. (See page 534.)

Prepositional phrase A group of words beginning with a preposition and ending with an object (a noun or a pronoun). (See pages 450, 465, and 574.)

Prewriting The first stage in the writing process: thinking and planning, deciding what to write about, collecting ideas and details, and making a plan for presenting ideas. (See pages 6 and 23.)

Principal parts of a verb A verb's forms—the *base form*, the *present participle*, the *past*, and the *past participle*—used to form the verb tenses. (See page 678.)

Progressive form of a verb Used in all six tenses to show continuing action; made up of a form of *be* plus the verb's present participle. (See page 686.)

Progress report A progress report is a form of writing that focuses on a project or activity, explains the writer's accomplishments or findings, and provides an overview of the project's standing. (See Chapter 8.)

Pronoun Is used in place of a noun or more than one noun. (See page 516.)

Proofreading A stage of the writing process: carefully reading a revised draft to correct mistakes in grammar, usage, and mechanics. (See pages 6, 23, and 55.)

Proper adjective An adjective formed from a proper noun. (See page 764.)

Proper noun Names a particular person, place, thing, or idea and is always capitalized. (See pages 515 and 764.)

Publishing The last stage of the writing process: making a final, clean copy of a paper and sharing it with an audience. (See pages 6, 23, and 57.)

Purpose A reason, or aim, for writing or speaking: to express yourself; to be creative; to entertain; to explain, inform, or explore; or to persuade. (See page 35.)

Regional dialect A distinct version of a language used by people in or from a particular geographical area. (See page 497.)

Regular verb Forms its past and past participle by adding *–d* or *–ed* to the infinitive. (See page 679.)

Relative pronoun A pronoun that relates an adjective clause to the word that the clause modifies, while also serving a function within the clause. (See page 601.)

Relevant features The specific details about a subject that are related to the main idea of a composition. (See page 260.)

Research report A form of writing in which a writer presents factual information discovered through exploration and research. (See Chapter 11.)

Revising A stage of the writing process: making changes in a composition's content, organization, and style in order to improve it. (See pages 6, 23, and 50.)

Root The base a word is built on, which carries the word's core meaning, but cannot stand alone. (See page 966.)

Run-on sentence Two or more complete sentences run together as one. (See page 456.)

S

Sensory details Precise bits of information observed, or collected, through any of the five senses—sight, sound, smell, touch, or taste. (See pages 71 and 191.)

Sentence A group of words that contains a subject and a verb and expresses a complete thought. (See pages 447 and 544.)

Sentence fragment A part of a sentence that does not express a complete thought. (See pages 446 and 545.)

Setting Where and when a story takes place; may provide background for understanding characters and events, establish the conflict, or create the mood in a story. (See pages 225 and 376.)

Simile A figure of speech comparing two basically unlike things, using the words *like* or *as*. (See page 194.)

Simple sentence Has one independent clause and no subordinate clauses but may have a compound subject, a compound verb, and any number of phrases. (See page 610.)

Situational irony A device used by the writer of a story: what is expected—by the character(s) and usually by the reader—is not what happens. (See page 378.)

Slang Informal language made up of newly coined words or of old words used in new ways. (See page 502.)

Source card An index card on which bibliographical information about a source for a research report is recorded. (See page 416.)

Spatial order A way of arranging details in a paragraph or composition according to how they are spaced—nearest to farthest, left to right, and so on. (See pages 39 and 83.)

Statistic A fact based on numbers. (See page 71.)

Story map A written plan of the essential elements of a story. (See page 228.)

Stringy sentence Has too many independent clauses strung together with coordinating conjunctions like *and* or *but*. (See page 475.)

Subject The part of a sentence that names the person or thing spoken about in the rest of the sentence. (See page 546.)

Subject complement A noun, pronoun, or adjective that follows a linking verb and describes or explains the subject. (See page 560.)

Subjective description Creates a selective picture, revealing the writer's thoughts and feelings about a subject. (See page 182.)

Subordinate clause Does not express a complete thought and cannot stand alone; also called a **dependent clause.** (See pages 452 and 598.)

Subordinating conjunction Introduces an adverb clause but does not serve a function in that clause. (See page 603.)

Suffix A word part added after a base or root word. (See page 969.)

Summarize To restate, in condensed form, the main points of a passage. (See pages 421 and 945.)

Superlative degree The form a modifier takes when comparing more than two things. (See page 722.)

Supporting sentences Give specific details or information to support the main idea. (See page 71.)

Suspense Unanswered questions in the plot development of a story that make a reader wonder what will happen next. (See page 227.)

Syllable A word part that can be pronounced by itself. (See page 871.)

Synonym A word that has a meaning similar to, but not exactly the same as, another word. (See pages 503 and 933.)

Tense The time indicated by the form of a verb: *present, present perfect, past, past perfect, future,* and *future perfect.* (See page 684.)

Theme The underlying meaning or message a writer wants to communicate to readers. (See page 378.)

Thesis statement Announces the limited topic of a composition and the main, or unifying, idea about that topic. (See pages 113 and 423.)

Time line A visual arrangement of information in chronological order. (See page 44.)

Tired word A word that has lost so much of its freshness and force through overuse that it has become worn-out and almost meaningless. (See page 507.)

Tone The feeling or attitude a writer conveys about a topic. (See pages 36 and 122.)

Topic sentence Expresses the main idea of a paragraph. (See page 68.)

Transitional expression A word or phrase that indicates relationships between ideas in a paragraph or composition. (See pages 89 and 129.)

Transitive verb Expresses an action directed toward a person or thing named in a sentence. (See page 524.)

Understood subject The unstated subject *you* in a request or a command. (See page 554.)

Unity A quality achieved when all the sentences or paragraphs in a composition work together as a unit to express or support one main idea. (See pages 77 and 128.)

Valid conclusion Is firmly grounded in facts, evidence, or logic. (See page 990.)

Verb Expresses an action or a state of being. (See page 524.)

Verbal irony A device used by the author of a story: what a character says is not what is meant. (See page 378.)

Verbals A word (participle, gerund, or infinitive) formed from a verb, but used as another part of speech. (See pages 449 and 579.)

Verbal phrase Consists of a verbal and its modifiers and complements. (See page 449.)

Verb phrase Consists of a main verb preceded by at least one **helping verb** (also called an **auxiliary verb**). (See page 527.)

Voice Writing in a way that sounds like oneself, using language to sound as natural and distinctive as possible. (See page 36.)

Weak reference Unclear phrasing that occurs when a pronoun refers to a suggested, but not clearly stated, word or idea. (See page 670.)

"What if?" questions A creative thinking technique used to help a writer draw upon his or her imagination to explore ideas for writing. (See page 34.)

Word bank A writer's storehouse of words to be used in writing. (See pages 192 and 963.)

Works Cited A list of all the print and nonprint sources used in a research report; the term **bibliography** means that only print sources were used. (See page 429.)

Writer's journal A written record of a person's experiences and observations, feelings and opinions, ideas and questions. (See page 25.)

Writing A stage in the writing process: putting ideas into words, following a plan that organizes the ideas. (See pages 6, 23, and 45.)

Writing process The series of stages, or steps, that a writer goes through to develop ideas and to communicate them clearly in a piece of writing. (See pages 6 and 22.)

Glossary

This glossary is a short dictionary of words found in the professional writing models in this textbook. The words are defined according to their meanings in the context of the writing models.

Pronunciation Key

Symbol	Key Words	Symbol	Key Words
a	asp, fat, parrot	b	bed, fable, dub, ebb
ā	ape, date, play, break, fail	d	dip, beadle, had, dodder
ä	ah, car, father, cot	f	fall, after, off, phone
e	elf, ten, berry	g	get, haggle, dog
ē	even, meet, money, flea, grieve	h	he, ahead, hotel
i	is, hit, mirror	j	joy, agile, badge
ī	ice, bite, high, sky	k	kill, tackle, bake, coat, quick
ō	open, tone, go, boat	l	let, yellow, ball
ô	all, horn, law, oar	m	met, camel, trim, summer
ᴏᴏ	look, pull, moor, wolf	n	not, flannel, ton
ᴏ̄ᴏ	ooze, tool, crew, rule	p	put, apple, tap
yᴏᴏ	use, cute, few	r	red, port, dear, purr
yᴏᴏ	cure, globule	s	sell, castle, pass, nice
oi	oil, point, toy	t	top, cattle, hat
ou	out, crowd, plow	v	vat, hovel, have
u	up, cut, color, flood	w	will, always, swear, quick
ʉr	urn, fur, deter, irk	y	yet, onion, yard
ə	a in ago	z	zebra, dazzle, haze, rise
	e in agent	ch	chin, catcher, arch, nature
	i in sanity	sh	she, cushion, dash, machine
	o in comply	th	thin, nothing, truth
	u in focus	*th*	then, father, lathe
ər	perhaps, murder	zh	azure, leisure, beige
		ŋ	ring, anger, drink

Abbreviation Key

adj.	adjective	*pl.*	plural
adv.	adverb	*prep.*	preposition
conj.	conjunction	*vi.*	intransitive verb
n.	noun	*vt.*	transitive verb

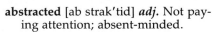

abstracted [ab strak'tid] *adj.* Not paying attention; absent-minded.

adjacent [ə jā'sənt] *adj.* Next to or beside.

anna [än'ə] *n.* A former unit of money in India, equal to 1/16 of a rupee.

aquiline [ak'wə līn'] *adj.* Curved.

assimilate [ə sim'ə lāt'] *vt.* To absorb.

auspicious [ôs pish'əs] *adj.* Successful and deserving of respect.

befuddled [bē fud''ld] *adj.* Confused.

buffoonery [bə fōōn'ə rē] *n.* Clowning around.

careworn [ker'wôrn'] *adj.* Visibly exhausted by worrying.

chauvinist [shō'vin ist] *adj.* Characterized by an unthinking loyalty toward a particular behavior.

cheroot [she rōōt'] *n.* A square-tipped cigar.

contrivance [kən trī'vəns] *n.* A plan or device designed to produce a specific, intended result.

cowrie shell [kou'rē shel'] *n.* A shiny, bright-colored seashell once used as money in India.

curb [kurb] *vt.* To limit or restrain.

din [din] *n.* Loud and continuous noise.

dissipate [dis'ə pāt'] *vi.* To gradually disappear.

draw [drô] *n.* A deep ditch formed by rainwater drainage.

effigy [ef'i jē] *n.* Representation.

electrodynamics [ē lek'trō dī nam'iks] *n.* The science of electricity and magnetic forces.

embolden [em bōl'dən] *vt.* To make bold.

émigré [em'i grā'] *n.* A person who has moved from his or her native country to live in another.

endue [en dōō'] *vt.* To give desirable qualities to.

eradicate [ē rad'i kāt'] *vt.* To do away with; to remove.

execute [ek'si kyōōt'] *vt.* To make or create.

exhilaration [eg zil'ə rā'shən] *n.* Happy excitement.

expertise [ek'spər tēz'] *n.* Highly qualified knowledge or skill.

gnome [nōm] *n.* A mythological dwarf.

gulch [gulch] *n.* A deep, narrow riverbed.

guru [gōō'rōō'] *n.* A respected spiritual leader.

harbor [här'bər] *vt.* To keep in mind and remember frequently.

humor [hyōō'mər] *n.* Moisture.

hydrocarbon [hī'drō kär'bən] *n.* A poisonous chemical compound made of hydrogen and carbon.

hypothesis [hī päth'ə sis] *n.* A theory to be proved.

icon [ī′kän′] *n.* A symbol or easily recognized image.

illustrious [i lus′trē əs] *n.* Well-known and greatly respected.

imbue [im byoo′] *vt.* To give ideas or feelings to.

impetuous [im pech′oo əs] *adj.* Impulsive; acting without prior thought.

implication [im′pli kā′shən] *n.* An unstated but expected result of an action or event.

incredulous [in krej′oo ləs] *adj.* Not believing.

indifferent [in dif′ər ənt] *adj.* Uncaring; unaware.

inferences [in′fər əns əz] *n., pl.* Conclusions or opinions derived by reasoning.

jaggery [jag′ər ē] *n.* A dark-colored sugar made from palm-tree sap.

lorry [lôr′ē] *n.* A type of truck.

malevolent [mə lev′ə lənt] *adj.* Evil.

malicious [mə lish′əs] *adj.* Wishing harm.

maxim [maks′im] *n.* A statement generally accepted as true.

mesmerize [mez′mər īz′] *vt.* To capture the attention as if by magic; to hypnotize.

notoriously [nō tôr′ē əs lē] *adv.* In a well-known and undesirable manner.

ode [ōd] *n.* A long poem with short lines, usually in a specific rhyme pattern; it commonly expresses emotion in a formal manner.

ordnance [ôrd′nəns] *n.* Weapons, ammunition, parts, etc.

palmyra writing [pal mī′rə rīt′iŋ] *n.* Ancient writing on strips of the leaves of a palmyra palm tree.

paraphernalia [par′ə fər nāl′yə] *n.* A group of articles used for a specific purpose; tools or equipment.

parochial [pə rō′kē əl] *adj.* Narrow-minded; limited in the way one sees the world.

pie [pī] *n.* A former unit of money in India, equal to 1/192 of a rupee.

piqued [pēkt] *adj.* Irritated or displeased.

pontoon [pän toon′] *n.* A floating support for a temporary bridge.

porous [pôr′əs] *adj.* Having tiny holes to absorb moisture.

precipice [pres′i pis] *n.* A steep cliff.

prerequisite [pri rek′wə zit] *adj.* Required beforehand.

procure [prō kyoor′] *vt.* To find and get.

proselytize [präs′ə li tīz′] *vi.* To argue in a persuasive manner.

purgatory [pur′gə tôr′ē] *n.* Temporary punishment.

rupee [roo′pē] *n.* The basic unit of money in India.

S

saffron [saf′rən] *adj.* Orange-yellow.

scant [skant] *adj.* Limited in amount or quantity; not enough.

scapegrace [skāp′grās′] *n.* An unprincipled person; a rascal.

searing [sir′iŋ] *adj.* Causing a feeling of being marked or changed by an experience.

serried [ser′ēd] *adj.* In a tight formation, as soldiers.

siege [sēj] *n.* An attack in which the enemy is encircled and fired upon.

sodden [säd″n] *adj.* Soaked.

spare [sper] *adj.* Minimal; using few words to describe.

stark [stärk] *adj.* Not softened; realistic.

stipulated [stip′yo͞o lāt′id] *adj.* Specific; set.

strut [strut] *n.* A metal brace to stiffen the leg.

subterranean [sub′tə rā′nē ən] *adj.* Underground.

succulence [suk′yo͞o ləns] *n.* Juiciness.

T

tabular [tab′yo͞o lər] *adj.* Arranged in a table.

tapestry [tap′əs trē] *n.* A cloth or rug with designs and pictures.

tendency [ten′dən sē] *adj.* Relating to a habitual action.

tram [tram] *n.* A streetcar.

trapezoid [trap′i zoid] *n.* A figure similar to a rectangle but with only two sides parallel.

V

vermilion [vər mil′yən] *n.* Bright red paint.

vigor [vig′ər] *n.* Energy.

vociferousness [vō sif′ər əs nis] *n.* Loud, continuous talk.

volition [vō lish′ən] *n.* Exercise of the will; deliberate decision.

Index

A

A, an, 519, 738–39
Abbreviations
    addresses, 792
    capitalizing, 765, 792
    organizations, 792
    personal names, 792
    punctuating, 792
    states, 792
    time of day, 792
    titles used with names, 792
    units of measure, 792
    years, 792
Abstract noun, defined, 515
Accept, except, 739
Action verb
    defined, 524–25
    distinguished from linking verb, 715
    and objects, 562
    in personal narrative, 166
Active listening and viewing, 941
Active reading, 369
Active voice, 694–96
Add, as revision technique, 50–51, 53
Addresses
    abbreviations with, 792
    commas with, 808
    hyphenated street numbers, 768
Addressing envelopes, 980–81
Adjective, 518–21
    articles, 519
    commas and, 794–95
    comparison of, 719–25
    compound, 765, 861
    defined, 518
    diagramed, 1019
    distinguished from pronoun, 520
    nouns used as, 521
    placement of, 519
    predicate, 560
    proper, capitalizing, 764–79
Adjective clause, 600–602
    beginning with *that,* 798
    and combining sentences, 470–71
    comma and, 471
    defined, 600
    diagramed, 1026–27

essential, nonessential, 600–601
    placement of, 600
    relative adverb, 602
    relative pronoun, 601
Adjective phrase
    defined, 574
    placement of, 575
Adjustment letter, 977
Adverb, 529–31
    comparison of, 719–25
    conjunctive, 817
    defined, 529
    diagramed, 1019
    distinguished from preposition, 535
    modifying adjectives, 530
    modifying other adverbs, 531
    modifying verbs, 529
    relative, 602
Adverb clause, 603–604
    and combining sentences, 452, 471
    comma and, 471
    defined, 603
    diagramed, 1027
    introductory, 471, 603, 801
    placement of, 452
    subordinating conjunction, 471,
        603–604
Adverb phrase
    defined, 576
    placement of, 576
Advertising, 359, 509
Affect, effect, 739, 882
Affixes. *See* Prefixes; Suffixes.
Agenda, in group discussion, 935
Agreement, number, 618–34, 619,
        637–39
Agreement, pronoun-antecedent,
        637–39
    collective noun, as antecedent, 629
    compound antecedents, 639
    gender, 637–39
    indefinite pronouns, 638–39
    number, 637–39
    personal pronouns, 637–38
Agreement, subject-verb, 619–34
    collective nouns, 628–29
    and combining sentences, 468
    compound subjects, 627
    contractions, 631, 633

every or *many a*, 632–33
indefinite pronouns, 622–23
and intervening words or phrases,
620, 632
nouns plural in form with singular
meaning, 633
number, 619
plural subjects, 619
predicate nominative, agreement
not with, 631
singular subjects, 619
subject following verb, 631
title of work of art, music,
literature, as subject, 633
words stating amount, 632
Aims for writing
creative, 7, 22
expressive, 7, 22
informative, 7, 22
persuasive, 7, 22
All ready, already, 882
All right, 882
All the farther, all the faster, 739
All together, altogether, 883
Allusion, illusion, 739
Almanacs, 957
Ambiguous reference, pronoun, 669
American Childhood, An, 156–58
American English, 493–94
"America's Ancient Skywatchers,"
402–404
Among, between, 740
An, a, 519, 738–39
Analogy chart, 1006–1007
Analogy questions, 1005–1007
And etc., 739
Anecdote, 74, 123
Angelou, Maya, 448, 764
Anglo-Saxon, 486
Anne of Green Gables, 83
Announcement, as speaking
situation, 934
Antecedent
agreement with pronoun, 637–39
defined, 637
Antecedent-pronoun agreement.
See Agreement, pronoun-antecedent.
Antonyms, in dictionaries, 961
Anywheres, 740
Apostrophe
contractions, 854–55
indefinite pronouns, 850
plurals, 857–58, 879–80
possessive case, 848–51

Application letter, 978–79
Appositive, 590–91
defined, 450, 590, 664, 805
diagramed, 1026
pronoun as, 664
punctuating, 591, 805
restrictive, 805
Appositive phrase, 590–91
and combining sentences, 465–66
defined, 450, 590
diagramed, 1026
placement of, 465–66, 590
punctuating, 466, 591, 805
as sentence fragment, 450
Appreciation letter, 978
Arbetter, Sandra R., 123
Arrangement of library/media center,
952–53
Arranging ideas/information, 39–44
block method, 262–64
classifying information, 43
comparison/contrast essay, 260–64
critical analysis, 383
order, choosing type of, 39–40
personal narrative, 154
point-by-point method, 262–64
visuals used in, 43–44, 300, 990–91
Art, 443–44
Articles, 519, 738
As, like, 747
As follows, colon with, 821
As if, like, 747
Asking questions, 30
As though, like, 747
"Astrologer's Day, An," 370–75
At, 740
Atlases, 957
Attacking the person, 340
Audience
analyzing, 36–38
in communication process, 5
comparison/contrast essay, 258–59
critical analysis, 381
description, 182
personal narrative, 147
persuasive essay, 333, 335
research paper, 410
short story, 223
speech preparation, 931
writing process, 35
Author card, 953
Autobiography, 441
as study skill, 985
Auxiliary verb. *See* Helping verb.

Background information, in
introduction, 125
Bad, badly, 716
Baker, Sherry, 126
Ballard, Robert D., 79
Bandwagon, 948
Baseball: An Illustrated History, 74
Base form, as principal part, 678
Base word, 966
Battle of Hastings, 487
Be
  forms of, 526
  as helping verb, 527
  as linking verb, 525–26
  and passive voice, 694
  and progressive form, 686
"Bean Eaters, The," 396
Beat, principal parts of, 680
Begin, principal parts of, 680
Behind the Headlines, 98
Being as, being that, 740
Bend, principal parts of, 680
Beside, besides, 740
*Best, Worst, and Most Unusual: Horror
  Films, The,* 364–67
Between, among, 740
Bibliography. *See* Works Cited.
Bibliography cards. *See* Source cards.
Biographical references, 956–57
Black Elk Speaks, 140–42
Blair, Gwenda, 124
Block method, comparison/contrast
  writing, 262–64
Blow, principal parts of, 680
Blue Highways, 193
Body, 128–29
  business letter, 975
  coherence, 128–29
  comparison/contrast essay, 266
  critical analysis, 384
  defined, 128
  direct references, 128
  personal narrative, 155
  persuasive essay, 350
  progress report, 303
  research paper, 426
  transitional expressions, 129
  unity, 128
Body language, 929
Borrowed words. *See* Loanwords.
Bosveld, Jane, 343–46

Brainstorming, 27, 61, 148
Brake, break, 883
Break, principal parts of, 680
Bring, principal parts of, 680
Bring, take, 741
Brooks, Gwendolyn, 11–13, 396
Brown, Christy, 290–92
Browser's Dictionary, A, 40
Burn, principal parts of, 679
Burns, Ken, 74
Burst, principal parts of, 680
Business letters
  appearance of, 973
  block form, 974
  guidelines for contents of, 975
  modified block form, 974
  parts of, 974–75
  types of, 976–79
Bust, busted, 741

Call number, 952
Call to action, in conclusion, 131
Calvino, Italo, 231–35
"Can Bicycles Save the World?,"
  343–46
Capital, capitol, 883
Capitalization
  abbreviations, 765, 792
  brand names of business products,
    772
  common nouns, 764–65
  direct quotation, 834–35
  first word in sentence, line of
    poetry, 764
  geographical names, 767–68
  historical events and periods, 771
  holidays, calendar items, 771
  hyphenated number, 768
  interjection *O,* 764
  names consisting of more than one
    word, 765
  names of persons, 765
  nationalities, races, and peoples, 772
  organizations, businesses, etc.,
    770–71
  pronoun *I,* 764
  proper adjectives, 764–79
  proper nouns, 764–79
  quotations, 763

religions and their followers, holy days, writings, 778–79
school subjects, 773
ships, monuments, awards, planets, 772–73
special events, 771
specific deities, 778–79
summary style review, 785–86
titles and subtitles of books, poems, periodicals, stories, plays, etc., 777–78
titles of movies, television programs, works of art, musical compositions, 777–78
titles of persons, 776–77
of words showing family relationship, 777
Capitol, capital, 883
Card catalog, 953–54
Carlson, Robert B., 402–404
Case forms of pronouns, 649–58
defined, 649
nominative case, 649, 651–53
objective case, 649, 655–58
possessive case, 649
Cause and effect
false, 340
progress report, 316
narration, 96
and vocabulary, 964
Cause-and-effect essay
evaluating and revising, 318
prewriting, 318
progress report, 316–18
proofreading and publishing, 318
Cause-and-effect explanations, 316–18
Caxton, William, 491
"CD & Videodisc Players," 398–99
–cede, –ceed, and *–sede,* spelling rule for, 872
Characters
as literary elements, 377
short story, 225–26, 229, 235
Charts, 43–44, 150
Chaucer, Geoffrey, 489
Chollar, Susan, 316–17
Choose, chose, 883
Choose, principal parts of, 680
Choppy sentences, 461–62
Chronological order, 82–83, 117
arranging ideas, 39
critical analysis, 383
description, 189–90
personal narrative, 154

progress report, 301
short story, 227
Ciardi, John, 40
Circular reasoning, 341
Citations, parenthetical, 428–29
Classification, strategy of, 93, 97–99, 117–18
comparing and contrasting, 99
comparison/contrast essay, 257
defining, 98–99
dividing, 98
as study skill, 994
Classification system, in library/media center, 952–53
Clause. *See also* Independent clause; Subordinate clause.
adjective clause, 470–71, 600–602
adverb clause, 471, 603–604
defined, 451, 597
essential (restrictive), 600–601, 798–99
independent, 597–98
infinitive, 587
nonessential (nonrestrictive), 600–601, 797–99
noun clause, 472, 606
placement, 732
punctuating, 600–601
subordinate, 451–54, 598–606
"Clean Fun at Riverhead," 79–80
Cliché, 196, 508
Climax, as literary element, 376
Clincher sentence, 76
Closing, business letter, 808, 975
Clustering, 28–29
Coarse, course, 883
Coherence, 82–90, 128–29
connections between ideas, 88–90
defined, 128
direct references, 88, 128
order of ideas, 82–85
transitional expressions, 89–90, 129
Collective nouns, agreement of, 628–29
Colloquialisms, defined, 501
Colon, 821–23
in conventional situations, 822–23
before list of items, 821
before long, formal statement or quotation, 821
not before list following verb or preposition, 821
and quotation marks, 836
after salutation of business letter, 823
Combining sentences, 461–72

with adjective clause, 470–71
with adverb clause, 452, 471
and agreement of subject and verb, 468
with complex sentence, 470–72
with compound sentence, 468–69
with compound subject and compound verb, 467–68
inserting phrases, 465–66
inserting words, 462–63
with noun clause, 472
Come, principal parts of, 680
Comma, 793–809
adjective clause, 471
adjectives preceding noun, 794–95
adverb clause, 471, 603
appositive phrase, 465–66, 805
compound noun, 795
compound sentence, 469, 794, 796
conjunctive adverb, 817
in conventional situations, 808
direct address, 806
interjection, 537, 800
interrupters, 805–806
introductory elements, 800–801
items in series, 793–95
letter salutations and closings, 808
after name followed by abbreviation, 808
nonessential clauses, phrases, 797–99
parenthetical expressions, 806, 864
and quotation marks, 835–36
summary of use, 813
transitional expression, 817
unnecessary use of, 809
verbal phrase, 728
Comma splice, 456
Commendation letter, 978
Common noun, 515, 764–65
Communication, 5, 928–33
Communication cycle, 928
Community resources, for research paper, 415
Comparative degree of comparison, 279, 719–21, 722–25
Comparing and contrasting
in classification, 99
figures of speech, 195
vocabulary, 964
Comparison/contrast essay, 256–81
arranging information, 260–64
audience, 258–59
block method, 262–64

body, 266
choosing subjects, 256
classification, 257
conclusion, 266–67
elements of, 266–67
evaluating and revising, 274–75
framework, 271–73
gathering information, 260–64
introduction, 266
point-by-point method, 262–64
prewriting, 256–65
proofreading and publishing, 278–81
purpose, 258–59
relevant features, 260–61
thesis statement, 265
Writer's Model, 271–73
writing a first draft, 266–73
Comparison of modifiers, 719–25
comparative degree, 279, 720–25
double comparison, 724
irregular, 721–22
positive degree, 720–22
regular comparison, 720–21
superlative degree, 720–25
Complaint letter, 977
Complement, 557–63
compound, 558
defined, 557
direct object, 562
and independent clause, 558
indirect object, 563
never in prepositional phrase, 558
predicate adjective, 560
predicate nominative, 560
subject complement, 560
Complement, compliment, 884
Complete predicate, 547
Complete subject, 547
Complex sentence
and combining sentences, 470–72
defined, 611
diagramed, 1031
Composition, 112–34
body, 128–29
coherence, 128–29
conclusion, 130–33
direct references, 128
early plan, 117–18
formal outline, 118
framework, 134
grouping information, 117
informative, 135–37
introduction, 122–26

order, types of, 117
point of view, 134
thesis statement, 113–14
title, 133
transitional expressions, 129
unity, 128
Writer's Model, 120–21
Compound adjective, 765, 861
Compound-complex sentence
defined, 611
diagramed, 1031
Compound direct object, 563, 656, 1021
Compound indirect object, 563, 656, 1022
Compound noun, 515, 521, 548, 795
Compound numbers, hyphen with, 860
Compound preposition, 535, 620
Compound sentence
and combining sentences, 468–69
comma and, 469
conjunctive adverb, 457, 469
coordinating conjunction, 457, 469
defined, 468–69, 610–11
diagramed, 1029–30
distinguished from simple sentence
with compound elements, 796
punctuating, 457
revising run-on sentences, 456–57
semicolon and, 469
Compound subject
and combining sentences, 467–68
defined, 554, 627
diagramed, 1017
personal pronouns as, 651
Compound subject complement,
diagramed, 1021
Compound verb
and combining sentences, 467–68
defined, 555
diagramed, 1018
and helping verb, 555
Compound words, 851, 860–61
Computers. *See also* Internet; World
Wide Web.
brainstorming with, 61
collaboration over network, 115, 274
Cut and Paste commands, 483
Find command, 351
formatting screenplays, 230
formatting type, 508, 937
grammar checker, 447
mailing lists, 981
making corrections, 45
making tables, 302

multiple-window feature, using, 383
outlining feature, 944
Save command, 97
Sort command, 963
spell-checking programs, 961
storing files, 147
word-processing program, 985
Conclusion of a composition
comparison/contrast essay, 266–67
composition, 130–33
critical analysis, 384
personal narrative, 155
persuasive essay, 350
progress report, 303
research paper, 426
techniques for writing, 130–33
Conclusions, drawing, 989–90
Concrete noun, defined, 515
Conflict, in story, 226–27, 376
Conjunction
coordinating, 457, 467, 469, 536, 597
correlative, 536
defined, 536
subordinating, 471, 603–604
Conjunctive adverb
and compound sentence, 457, 469, 598
list of, 817
punctuating, 816–17
Connections between ideas. *See*
Direct references; Transitional
expressions.
Connotation, 339, 504, 965
Consistency of tense, 692
Consul, council, councilor, counsel, counselor, 884
Content, evaluating, 47
Context, reading, 964–65
Contractions, 854–55
adverb *not,* 854
and agreement of subject and
verb, 631
defined, 854
distinguished from possessive
forms of pronouns, 850, 854–55
list of, 854
Contrast, and vocabulary, 964
Conversation. *See* Dialogue.
Coordinating conjunction
and compound sentence, 457, 469
and compound subjects or verbs, 467
defined, 536
Correlative conjunction, 536
Could of, 742

Council, councilor, counsel, counselor, consul, 884
Courlander, Harold, 321–22
Course, coarse, 883
Creative writing, 7, 11–13, 22, 220. *See also* Short story.
Critical analysis, 369–92
  audience, 381
  body, 384
  characters, 377
  climax, 376
  conclusion, 384
  conflict, 376
  elements, 376–78
  evaluating and revising, 387–89
  foreshadowing, 377–78
  introduction, 384
  irony, 378
  literary elements, 376–78, 383
  main idea, 381–82
  mood, 377
  order, types of, 383
  paraphrasing, 382
  planning, 381–83
  plot, 376
  point of view, 377
  prewriting, 369–83
  proofreading and publishing, 390–92
  purpose, 368, 381
  quotations from story, 382
  setting, 376–77
  summarizing, 382
  supporting your ideas, 382–83
  theme, 378
  thesis statement, 381
  topic, 381
  Writer's Model, 385–86
  writing a first draft, 384–86
Critical listening, 944–45
Critical review, 393–95
Critical Thinking
  Analyzing a Short Story, 379–80
  Analyzing Accomplishments, 299
  Analyzing Point of View, 223–24
  Analyzing Purpose and Audience, 36–38
  Analyzing Topic, 423–24
  Arranging Information, 40
  Classifying Information, 43
  Classifying Objects and Ideas, 257
  Evaluating, 49
  Evaluating Reasoning, 340–41
  Interpreting Meaning, 152
  Making Comparisons, 195
Cross-reference cards, 953
Crum, Mason, 94
Cut, as revision technique, 50–51, 53

Dangling modifier, 728
Dashes, 862–63
  abrupt break in thought or speech, 862
  to mean *namely, that is, in other words,* 863
  parenthetical elements, 862
  unfinished statement or question, 862
Database, 957
"Date with Dracula," 176–78
Da Vinci, Leonardo, 326–29
Deckert, R. A., 110
Declarative sentence
  defined, 565
  punctuating, 565, 789, 790
Defining, as classification, 98–99
Definite article, 519
Definition. *See also* Meaning of a word.
  in dictionaries, 960
  extended, 282–84
  and vocabulary, 964
Degrees of comparison, 279
Demonstrative pronoun, list of, 517
Denotation, 339, 504, 965
  of titles, 390
Dependent clause. *See* Subordinate clause.
Description, strategy of, 93–94, 181–206
  audience, 182
  details, 186–90
  in developing paragraph, 94
  emphasis, 187
  evaluating and revising, 200–202
  figurative language, 193–96
  narration, 209–10
  objective, 182
  point of view, 183
  prewriting, 181–90
  proofreading and publishing, 204–206
  purpose, 181
  sensory word bank, 192–93
  subject for, 179–83

subjective, 182–83
tone, 183
Writer's Model, 198–99
writing a first draft, 191–99
Descriptive language, 191–96
Desert, dessert, 884
Details
  anecdotes, 74
  brainstorming, 148
  and charts, 150
  critical analysis, 383, 389
  description, 186–90
  examples, 73
  facts, 71, 72
  figures of speech, 193–94
  freewriting, 148
  imagining, 187
  listening for, 942
  observing directly, 186
  organizing, 154, 189–90
  in paragraph, 71
  people, places, events, 149
  personal narrative, 148–51
  recalling, 148–51, 186
  recognizing relationships among,
    987–88
  researching, 187
  sensory, 31, 71, 149, 191, 192–93, 202
  statistics, 71–72
  thoughts and emotions, 150
Development of a paragraph, 93–101
Dewey decimal classification system
  fiction, 953
  nonfiction, 952–53
Diagraming, 1017–31
  adjective and adverb, 1019
  adjective clause, 1026–27
  adverb clause, 1027
  appositive, appositive phrase, 1026
  complex sentence, 1031
  compound-complex sentence, 1031
  compound direct object, 1021
  compound indirect object, 1022
  compound sentence, 1029–30
  compound subject, 1017–18
  compound subject complement, 1021
  compound verb, 1018
  direct object, 1021
  gerund, gerund phrase, 1024
  here, there, where, as modifiers,
    1019–20
  indirect object, 1021
  infinitive and infinitive phrase,
    1025–26

noun clause, 1028–29
noun of direct address, 1017
participle, participial phrases,
  1023–24
predicate adjective, 1020
predicate nominative, 1020
prepositional phrase, 1022–23
simple sentence, 1029
subject, 1017–18
understood subject, 1017
verb, 1017–18
Dialects
  defined, 496
  ethnic, 498
  and origins of languages, 485
  regional, 497
Dialogue
  personal narrative, 149
  punctuating, 241
  and quotation marks, 838
  short story, 229
Diary, as study skill, 985
Dictionaries
  as aid to spelling, 870
  antonyms, 961
  definitions, 282, 960
  entry word, 960
  etymology, 960
  examples, 961
  paperback, 959
  part-of-speech labels, 960
  pronunciation, 960
  related word forms, 961
  sample entry, 960
  synonyms, 961
  types of, 959
  usage labels, 960
  word forms, 960
Dillard, Annie, 156–58
Direct address, noun of, 554, 806
Direct object, 562–63
  compound, 563
  defined, 562, 655
  diagramed, 1021
  never in prepositional phrase, 562
  pronoun, objective case, 655
Direct quotations, 427, 834–40
Direct references, 88, 128
Directions, 930
Discover, invent, 743
Discussion. *See* Group discussion.
Dive, principal parts of, 680
Divided quotation, 835
Dividing, as classification, 98

Do, principal parts of, 678, 680
Do Animals Dream?, 99
Documenting research sources, 428–29
Don't, doesn't, 633, 743
Double comparison, 724
Double negative, 756
Double subject, 744
Dramatic irony, 378
Draw, principal parts of, 680
Drawing conclusions, 989–90
Drink, principal parts of, 680
Drive, principal parts of, 680

"Eagle-Feather Fan, The," 287
Early plan, 117–18
    grouping information, 117
    ordering information, 117
    research paper, 420–21
Eat, principal parts of, 680
Ebert, Roger, 37
Effect. *See* Cause and effect;
    Cause-and-effect essay.
Effect, affect, 739, 882
Egan, Timothy, 131
ei and *ie,* spelling rule, 872
Either-or reasoning, 341
Elkington, John, 72
Else, other, 724
Emigrate, immigrate, 743
Emotional appeals
    advertising, 359
    loaded words, 359
    persuasive essay, 339
Emphasis, in description, 187
Encyclopedias, 956
End marks, 789–92
English, Betty Lou, 98
English language
    changes in, 495
    cliché, 508
    colloquialisms, 501
    connotation, 504
    denotation, 504
    dialects, 485, 496–98
    dictionaries, 492
    euphemisms, 505
    figures of speech, 193–94, 286–87,
        507
    formal, informal, 500–502
    gobbledygook, 506
    idiom, 501
    jargon, 506
    levels of usage, 500
    loaded words, 505
    loanwords, 487, 488, 492, 494
    meaning of a word, 503–506
    Middle English, 487–89
    Modern English, 490–92
    nonstandard, 499, 738
    Old English, 486–87
    slang, 502
    standard, 498–99, 738
    synonyms, 503
    thesaurus, 503
    tired word, 507
    usage, 496–501
Entry word, 960
Envelope, addressing, 980–81
–er, –est, 720–21
*Ernie's War: The Best of Ernie Pyle's
    World War II Dispatches,* 209–10
Eshugbayi, Ezekiel A., 321–22
Essay tests, 285–86, 1008–10
    evaluating and revising, 1010
    prewriting, 1010
    qualities of good answer, 1010
    study methods, 1008
Essential clause, phrase, 600–601, 798
Ethnic dialect, 498
Etymology, 960
Euphemisms, 505
Evaluating and revising
    comparison/contrast essay, 274–75
    content, 47
    critical analysis, 387–89
    description, 200–202
    essay tests, 1010
    guidelines for, 48–49, 53
    organization, 47
    peer evaluation, 47–48
    personal narrative, 163–66
    persuasive essay, 351–54
    progress report, 310–11
    of reading, 989–90
    research paper, 436–38
    self-evaluation, 47
    short story, 239
    style, 47
    word processor used in, 985–86
    writing process, 6, 22–23, 47–53
Evaluation, strategy of, 93, 100–101
    criteria for, 441
    in developing paragraph, 100–101
    and judgment, 441

Events, sequence of, 692
Everywheres, 740
Evidence
    critical analysis, 382–83
    expert opinion, 338
    fact, 337
    as logical appeal, 337–38
Examples
    defined, 73
    in dictionaries, 961
    in introduction, 123
    in paragraph, 73
    and vocabulary, 964
Except, accept, 739
Exclamation point, 790
    interjection, 537
    and quotation marks, 835–36
Exclamatory sentence
    defined, 566
    punctuating, 566, 790
Experience, meaning of, 151, 152
Expert opinion, 338
Explanatory writing, 319–20. *See also*
    Progress report.
Expletive, 553
Exploring the Titanic, 79
Exposition. *See* Comparison/contrast
    essay; Critical analysis; Informative
    writing; Progress report; Research
    paper.
Expressions, interrupting, 835
Expressive paragraph, 102–103
Expressive writing, 7, 10, 22, 144. *See
    also* Personal narrative.
Extemporaneous speech, 932

F

Fable, 247
Facial expressions, 929
Fact
    defined, 71, 333, 337
    in introduction, 124
    in paragraph, 71–72
    persuasive essay, 337
    in supporting sentences, 71–72
Fall, principal parts of, 680
False cause and effect, 316, 340
Features, relevant, 260–61
Feedback, 928
Fewer, less, 743
Fiction, arrangement of, 953
Figurative language

cliché, 196, 508
    defined, 507
    metaphor, 194, 286–87
    mixed, 507
    personification, 194
    simile, 194
Figures of speech. *See* Figurative
    language.
Final comment, in conclusion, 131
"Financial Folklore," 125
Fire in My Hands, A, 18–20
First draft. *See* Writing a first draft.
First-person point of view
    in description, 183
    as literary element, 377
    personal narrative, 147
    short story, 224
First-person pronoun, 517, 649
Fisher, Lawrence M., 113
5W-How? questions, 30, 942
Fly, principal parts of, 680
Focused freewriting, 26
Focused listening, 33
Focused reading, 32
Folktales, 320–23
Follensbee, Billie, 421, 422, 434
Footnotes, 428
"For Young and Old, a Pocket
    Paradise," 123, 132
Foreshadowing, as literary element,
    377–78
Formal composition, 134
Formal English, 500
Formal outline, 118, 425
Formal research paper, 406
Formal speaking, 930–34
    extemporaneous speech, 932
    giving speech, 933
    introduction to presentation, 934
    making announcement, 934
    preparing speech, 930–33
Formally, formerly, 885
Forms, completing, 981
4 *R's*, 415
Fractions used as adjectives, 860
Fragment. *See* Sentence fragment.
Free verse poem, 207–208
Freewriting, 26
    for details, 148
    as study skill, 985
Freeze, principal parts of, 680
Fused sentence, 456
Future perfect tense, uses of, 689
Future tense, uses of, 688–89

G

Gallant, Roy A., 98–99
Garbage! Where It Comes From, Where It Goes, 73
Gender, agreement of pronoun and antecedent, 637–39
Generalization, hasty, 340
General reference, pronoun, 669
"Genuine Mexican Plug, A," 76
Gerund, 584
    defined, 584
    diagramed, 1024
Gerund phrase, 585
    defined, 585
    diagramed, 1024
Gestures, 929
Give, principal parts of, 680
Go, principal parts of, 680
Gobbledygook, 506
Going Green, 72
Good, well, 717, 743–44
Goodman, Ellen, 351
Gordon, John Steele, 125
Graphics, 300, 990–91. *See also* Visuals.
Group discussion, 934–36
    agenda, 935
    assigning roles, 935
    parliamentary procedure, 935–36
    purpose, 934–35
Grouping information, 117. *See also* Arranging ideas/information.
Gullah, 94

H

Had of, 742
Had ought, hadn't ought, 744
Hadingham, Evan, 73
Hadingham, Janet, 73
Hailes, Julia, 72
Hamilton, Edith, 95
Hardly, scarcely, 756
Hayes, Helen, 84
"Hayes: 'There Is So Much to Do,'" 84
He, she, they, as double subject, 744
Heading, business letter, 974
Hear, here, 885
Hear, principal parts of, 680
Heat-Moon, William Least, 193
Helping verb
    agreement with subject, 619

and compound verb, 555
    list of, 527
    and passive voice, 694
Hemingway, Ernest, 163
Here, there, 553, 631
Here, there, where, as modifiers, diagramed, 1019–20
Hill, Douglas, 72
His or her construction, 638
Historical present tense, 688
"Home," 11–13
Homonyms, 882–90
Hyphen, 859–61
    compound adjective, 861
    compound numbers, 860
    compound words, 860–61
    fractions used as adjectives, 860
    prefixes, 861
    suffix, 861
    word division at end of line, 859–60

I

I Know Why the Caged Bird Sings, 448
Ideas for writing. *See also* Arranging ideas/information; Main idea; Order of ideas.
    brainstorming, 27
    clustering, 28–29
    5W-How? questions, 30
    focused freewriting, 26
    focused listening, 33
    focused reading, 32
    freewriting, 26
    imagining, 34
    looping, 26
    prewriting techniques, 24
    sensory details, 31
    webbing, 28–29
    "What if?" questions, 34
    writer's journal, 25
Idiom, 501
ie and *ei*, spelling rule for, 872
Illusion, allusion, 739
Illustrations, 990–91. *See also* Visuals.
Imagining, 34, 187
Immigrate, emigrate, 743
Imperative sentence
    defined, 565
    punctuating, 565, 790
Implied main idea, and supporting sentences, 78–79
Imply, infer, 744

Impromptu speech, 929
Indefinite article, 519, 738–39
Indefinite pronoun
  agreement with verb, 622–23
  defined, 622
  list of, 517
Indefinite reference pronoun, 670
Independent clause, 597–98
  commas and, 794, 796
  and complement, 558
  conjunctive adverb, 598
  coordinating conjunctions, 597
  defined, 451, 597
  semicolon and, 597, 794, 816–19
Indirect object, 563
  compound, 563, 656
  defined, 563, 656
  diagramed, 1021
  distinguished from prepositional
    phrase, 563
  pronoun, objective case, 655–56
Indirect question, 789
Indirect quotation, 834
Inexact reference, pronoun, 668–70
Infer, imply, 744
Inference, 989–90
Infinitive
  diagramed, 1025–26
  distinguished from prepositional
    phrase, 586
  with *to* omitted, 588
  as verbal, 586
Infinitive clause, 587
Infinitive phrase, 587, 1025–26
Informal composition, 134
Informal English, 500–502
  colloquialisms, 501
  formal English compared with,
    500–502
  idiom, 501
  slang, 502
Informal outline. *See* Early plan.
Informal research paper, 406
Informal speaking, 929–30
  instructions, directions, 930
  social situations, 930
  telephone, 930
Informal tone, 147
Information. *See also* Details; Fact.
  arrangement of, in library/media
    center, 952–53
  background, in introduction, 125
  comparison/contrast essay, 260–64
  interpreting and analyzing, 987–89
  listening for, 942–44

progress report, 297–302
  viewing for, 948–50
Information sources
  card catalog, 414
  CD-ROMs, 414
  community resources, 415
  evaluating, 4 *R*'s, 415
  librarian, 414
  National Newspaper Index, 414
  nonprint sources, 414
  online catalog, 414
  *Readers' Guide to Periodical
    Literature,* 414
  reference books, 414
  research paper, 414–19
  selecting topic, 408–409
  source cards, 416–19
  vertical file, 414
  World Wide Web/online services, 415
Informative writing, 7, 8, 22, 135–37,
  255.
    See also Comparison/contrast essay;
    Critical analysis; Progress report;
    Research paper.
Inside, 747
Inside address, business letter, 974
Instructions, 930, 942–43
Interjection
  defined, 537
  punctuating, 537, 800
Interjection *O,* distinguished from *oh,* 764
Internet, 406, 956
Interpretation, 152
Interrogative pronoun, 517
Interrogative sentence
  defined, 566
  punctuating, 566, 789, 790
Interrupters, 805–806, 835
Intervening phrases, subject-verb
  agreement, 620
Interview, conducting, 943–44
Intransitive verb, 524–25
Introduction, 122–26
  anecdote, 123
  background information, 125
  comparison/contrast essay, 266
  and conclusion, 131
  critical analysis, 384
  personal narrative, 155
  persuasive essay, 350
  progress report, 303
  question in, 123
  reader's interest, 122
  research paper, 426
  setting scene, 125

startling fact, 124
techniques for writing, 123–26
thesis statement, 122, 126
tone, 122
Introduction to presentation, 934
Introductory elements, commas and,
603, 800–801
Invalid conclusions, 990
Invent, discover, 743
Invitations, 980
Irony
dramatic, 378
as literary element, 378
situational, 378
verbal, 378
Irregular comparison of modifiers,
721–22
Irregular verbs, 679–81
Italics (underlining), 831–33
foreign words, 832–33
and personal computer, 831
titles of books, plays, films,
etc., 390
titles and subtitles of books, plays,
films, etc., 831–32
words, letters, figures, 832–33
Items in series
and colon, 821
and comma, 793–95
and semicolon, 819
as sentence fragment, 454
Its, it's, 885

"Japanese Americans: Home at Last," 68
Jargon, 506
Journal
as study skill, 985
writer's, 25
"Juan's Place," 124
Judgment, and evaluation, 441
Jurmain, Suzanne, 77–78

K

Kael, Pauline, 393–94
Keyword, 956
Khan, Niamat, 838
Kind, sort, type, 746
Kind of, sort of, 746
Kind of a, sort of a, 746
King, Coretta Scott, 360–61

Kingston, Maxine Hong, 82–83
Know, principal parts of, 680

L

Language, in communication process,
5. *See also* English language.
Language skills, review of, 896–925
Lay, lie, 697–98
Lay, principal parts of, 698
Lead, led, 885
Leap, principal parts of, 679
Learn, teach, 746
Learning log, as study skill, 985
Least, less, 721
Leave, let, 747
Leave, principal parts of, 680
"Leiningen Versus the Ants," 88
Leopold, Aldo, 172–73
Less, fewer, 743
Let, principal parts of, 680
Letter of regret, 980
"Letter to the Duke of Milan, A,"
326–29
Letter to the editor, 357–58
Letters. *See* Business letters; Personal
letters.
Levels of usage, 500
Librarian, as resource for research
paper, 414
Library/media center, 952–57
arrangement of fiction, 953
arrangement of nonfiction, 952–53
call number, 952
card catalog, 414, 953–54
Dewey decimal classification
system, 952–53
Library of Congress classification
system, 952
online catalog, 414
reference materials, 414, 955–57
Lie, lay, 697–98
Lie, principal parts of, 698
Like, as, 747
Like, as if, as though, 747
Limited topic, 113
Linking verb
defined, 525
distinguished from action verb, 715
list of, 526, 715
and modifiers, 715
and subject complement, 560
Listening and viewing, 941–50
active, 941

conducting an interview, 943–44
critical listening, 944–45
for details, 942
5W-How? questions, 942
focused, 33
for information, 942–44, 948–50
to instructions, 942–43
LQ2R study method, 942
note taking, 945
Literary elements, 229–30, 376–78
character, 377
development of, 381–82
foreshadowing, 377–78
functions of, 382
irony, 378
mood, 377
narrator, 377
plot, 376
point of view, 377
setting, 376–77
theme, 378
Literary present tense, 688
Literary writing, 11–13, 220. *See also*
Short story.
Literature. *See also* Critical analysis;
Short story.
comparison, 286–87
folktales, 320–23
purposes for writing about, 368
reference books, 957
responding to, 396–97
Loaded words, 359, 505
Loanwords, 487, 488, 492, 494
Logical appeals, 337–38
evidence, 337–38
expert opinion, 338
fact, 333, 337
reasons, 337
Logical order
arranging ideas, 39
and paragraph coherence, 84–85
progress report, 301
London English, 491–92
Looping, 26
Loose, lose, 886
Low, David, 96
LQ2R study method, 942
–ly, –ness, spelling rule for, 873

INDEX

M

Main clause. *See* Independent clause.

Main idea
in conclusion, 130
critical analysis, 381–82
identifying, 987
implied, 78–79
of paragraph, 67
stated, 77–79
thesis statement, 113
unity, 77–78
Main verb, 603
Making Connections
Brainstorming with a Computer, 61
Cause and Effect in Literature:
Folktales, 320–23
Combining Description with
Narration, 209–10
Comparison Across the
Curriculum: Literature,
286–87
Creating Research Sources: Public
Opinion Polls, 444–45
Critical Analysis Across the
Curriculum, 398–99
Description Across the Curriculum:
Objective Description in Science,
210–11
Enter a Contest, 483
Fill in the Missing Pieces, 460
Persuasion Across the Curriculum:
Advertising and Persuasion, 359
Process Explanations, 319–20
Research Across the Curriculum:
The Visual Arts, 443–44
Responding to Literature, 396–97
Self-Expression Across the
Curriculum: Science, 172
Short Story Writing Across the
Curriculum: History, 247
Speaking and Listening: Creating a
Fable, 247
Speaking and Listening: Public
Speaking and Persuasion, 360–61
Test Taking: Writing for an Essay
Test Question, 285–86
Writing a Paragraph That Is
Creative, 106–107
Writing a Paragraph to Express
Yourself, 102–103
Writing a Paragraph to Inform,
103–104
Writing a Paragraph to Persuade,
104–105
Writing a Travel Ad, 509
Writing an Informative

Composition, 135–37
Makower, Joel, 72
Mann, Charles, 124
Manuscript form, guidelines for, 59
Mass media, 946–48
  audience, 947
  defined, 946
  impact of, 946–48
  persuasive techniques of,
    947–48
Matching questions, 1003
McLarey, Myra, 250–53
Meaning of a word
  cliché, 508
  connotation, 339, 504, 965
  context, 964–65
  denotation, 339, 504, 965
  dictionary definition, 960
  euphemisms, 505
  gobbledygook, 506
  jargon, 506
  loaded words, 505
  mixed figure of speech, 507
  synonyms, 503
  thesaurus, 503
  tired word, 507
  and vocabulary, 964
Meaning of experience, 151–52
Memorizing, as study skill, 999
Metaphor, 194, 286–87
Microforms, 956
Middle English, 487–89
Might of, 742
Miner, minor, 886
Misplaced modifiers, 730, 732
Mixed figure of speech, 507
MLA format for source credit, 419,
    428–29
Modern English, 490–92
Modern Utopia, A, 169–70
Modifiers. *See also* Adjective; Adverb.
  bad, badly, 716
  clause, 732
  comparative degree, 720–22, 722–25
  comparison of, 719–25
  dangling, 728
  defined, 518, 714
  diagramed, 1019–20
  forms of, 714–17
  irregular comparison, 721–22
  and linking verbs, 715
  phrase, 730
  placement of, 730–32
  positive degree, 720–22

regular comparison, 720–21
  slow, slowly, 717
  superlative degree, 720–25
  well, good, 717
Momaday, N. Scott, 287
Moncrief: My Journey to the NBA, 250–53
Moncrief, Sidney, 250–53
Montgomery, Lucy Maud, 83
Mood, as literary element, 377
Moore, Darrell, 364–67
Moral, morale, 886
More, most, 721
Morrison, Daniel D., 176–78
Multiple-choice questions, 1002
"Mushrooms in the City," 231–35
Must of, 742
My Left Foot, 290–92
My Life with Martin Luther King, Jr.,
    360–61
Mythology, 95

N

Narayan, R. K., 370–75
Narration, strategy of, 93, 95–96. *See
    also* Creative writing; Expressive
    writing.
  cause-and-effect explanation, 96
  description, 209–10
  in developing paragraph, 95–96
  process explanation, 95–96
  telling a story, 95
Narrator
  limited, 224
  as literary element, 377
  omniscient, 224
  in short story, 223–24
  third-person omniscient, 377
National Newspaper Index, 414
Negative construction, and agreement
    of subject and verb, 620
Neihardt, John G., 140–42
"Neil Armstrong's Famous First
    Words," 131–32
–ness, –ly, spelling rule for, 873
Nisei Daughter, 64–65, 67
Nominative case, 649, 651–53. *See also*
    Predicate nominative; Pronoun;
    Subject of sentence.
Nonessential clause, phrase, 600–601,
    797
Nonrestrictive clause, phrase. *See*
    Nonessential clause, phrase.

Nonstandard English, 499, 738
Nonverbal communication, 929, 933
Note cards
    for research paper, 422
    for speech preparation, 932
Note taking
    direct quotations, 421
    key words, 422
    listening skills, 944–45
    note cards, 422
    paraphrasing, 421, 945
    for research paper, 421–23
    as study skill, 992–93
    summarizing, 421, 945
"Nothing Happened," 96
Noun
    abstract, 515
    collective, 629
    common, 515, 764–65
    compound, 515, 795
    concrete, 515
    defined, 514
    of direct address, 554, 1017
    forming plural, 877–80
    in possessive case, 848–49
    proper, 515, 764–79
    used as adjective, 521
Noun clause
    and combining sentences, 472
    defined, 606
    diagramed, 1028–29
    introductory words, 606
Nowheres, 740
Number. *See also* Plurals.
    agreement in, 618, 619–34, 637–39
    defined, 618
    plural, 618
    singular, 618
Numbers, 860, 881

O

Object of a preposition
    compound, 574
    defined, 534, 574, 658
    pronoun, objective case, 658
Object of a verb, 524. *See also* Direct
    object; Indirect object.
Objective case
    direct object, 655–56
    indirect object, 655–56
    object of a preposition, 658
    personal pronouns, 649, 655–58

Objective description, 182, 210–11
Objective tests, 1001–1008
    analogy questions, 1005–1007
    matching questions, 1003
    multiple-choice questions, 1002
    reasoning or logic questions, 1004
    short-answer questions, 1007–1008
    study methods, 1001
    true/false questions, 1003
Of, 747
Off, 747
Old English, 486–87, 968, 970
"Olmec Heads: A Product of the
    Americas," 421, 422, 434
On Being a Writer, 351
Once Upon A Horse, 77–78
*Once Upon a Time . . . When We Were
    Colored*, 37
Online catalog, 953
Online database, 956
Opinion
    defined, 333
    emotional appeals to support, 339
    expert, 338
    logical appeals to support, 337–38
    statement of, 333
    supporting, critical analysis, 382–83
    supporting, persuasive essay,
        337–39
Oral interpretation, 936–37
Order letter, 976–77
Order of ideas, 117
    chronological order, 39, 82–83, 117,
        189–90, 301
    classification, 117
    logical order, 39, 84–85, 301
    order of importance, 39, 84, 117,
        189–90
    and paragraph coherence, 82–85
    research paper, 426
    spatial order, 39, 83, 117, 189–90
Order of importance, 117
    arranging ideas, 39
    critical analysis, 383
    description, 189–90
    and paragraph coherence, 84
Organization, and evaluating, 47
Other, else, 724
Ought to of, 742
Outline, 117–18
    defined, 996
    formal, 118, 425
    informal, 117
    research paper, 424–25

sentence, 118
  speech preparation, 932
  as study skill, 996
  topic, 118
Outlining, with computers, 61
Outside, 747
Oversimplifying, 316

P

Paragraph, 67–101
  anecdotes, 74
  classification, 97–99
  clincher sentence, 76
  coherence, 82–90
  description, 94
  direct references, 88
  evaluation, 100–101
  facts and statistics, 71–72
  implied main idea, 78–79
  main idea, 67, 77–78
  narration, 95–96
  sensory details, 71
  sequence of events, 79–80
  supporting sentences, 71–74
  topic sentence, 68–69
  transitional expressions, 89–90
  unity, 77–80
Parallel structure, 474
Paraphrasing
  critical analysis, 382, 389
  defined, 996
  how to, 997
  for note taking, 421, 945
  as study skill, 996–98
Parentheses, 863–64
  material of minor importance, 863
  parenthetical elements, 864
  punctuating within, 863
Parenthetical citations, 428–29
Parenthetical expressions
  defined, 806
  list of, 806
  punctuating, 806, 862, 864
Parliamentary procedure, 935–36
Participial phrase, 582–83
  and combining sentences, 465
  defined, 465, 582
  diagramed, 1023–24
  introductory, punctuating, 800
  placement of, 465
Participle
  defined, 465, 579

diagramed, 1023–24
  past participle, 580
  present participle, 580
  as principal part of verb, 678–81
  and sensory details, 202
  as verbal, 579–80
Part-of-speech labels, 960
Parts of speech
  adjectives, 518–21
  adverbs, 529–31
  conjunctions, 536
  determined by use, 538
  interjections, 537
  nouns, 514–15
  prepositions, 534–35
  pronouns, 516–18
  summary chart, 542
  verbs, 524–27
Passed, past, 886
Passive voice
  and *be*, 694
  conjugation of verb *pay*, 694–95
  defined, 694
  and helping verbs, 694
  and past participle, 694
  use of, 696
Past participle
  and passive voice, 694
  as principal part of verb, 678–81
  as verbal, 579–80
Past perfect tense, uses of, 689
Past tense
  as principal part, 678
  uses of, 688
Pay, conjugation of in passive voice, 694–95
Pearl, The, 90
Peer evaluation, 47–48
Period
  after abbreviation, 792
  at end of sentence, 789
  and quotation marks, 836
Personal, personnel, 888
Personal letters
  invitations, 980
  letters of regret, 980
  thank-you letters, 980
Personal narrative, 145–68
  action verbs, 166
  audience, 147
  body, 155
  chronological order, 154
  conclusion, 155
  details, recalling, 148–51

dialogue, 149
evaluating and revising, 163–66
informal tone, 147
introduction, 155
meaning of experience, 151–52
point of view, 147
prewriting, 145–54
proofreading and publishing, 167
purpose, 147
structure, 155–62
tone, 147
Writer's Model, 159–61
writing a first draft, 155–62
Personal pronoun
case forms, 649–58
list of, 517
possessive, 850
Personification, 194
Persuasion
advertising, 359
public speaking, 360–61
Persuasive essay, 332–56
audience, 333, 335
basic elements of, 343–47
body, 350
conclusion, 350
evaluating and revising, 351–54
evidence, 337–38
expert opinion, 338
fact, 333, 337
framework, 348–50
introduction, 350
logical appeals, 337–38
opinion statement, 333
opposing opinions, 333
prewriting, 332–41
proofreading and publishing,
355–56
purpose, 335
reasons, 337
supporting your opinion, 337–39
tone, 335
topic, 332–34
Writer's Model, 347–49
writing a first draft, 343–50
Persuasive techniques, 947–48
bandwagon, 948
emotional words, 948
of mass media, 947–48
"plain folks," 948
testimonial, 948
Persuasive writing, 7, 9, 22, 330. *See
also* Persuasive essay.
Petry, Ann, 196–98

Phrase
adjective, 574–75
adverb, 576
appositive, 590–91
defined, 449, 573–74
gerund, 585
infinitive, 587–88
participial, 582–83
prepositional, 534, 574–76
and varying sentence beginnings,
479
verb, 527, 548
verbal, 579–88
Picture This
adverbs, 532
agreement of subject and verb, 626
appositives and appositive phrases,
591–92
commas, 808–809
contractions, 857
dialogue, 839
end marks, 808–809
personal pronouns, 659–60
proper nouns and adjectives,
775–76
semicolons and colons, 822
sentence structure, 612–13
subject and predicate, 557
usage, 758–59
verb tense, 691
"Pioneers Underfoot," 126
Plagiarizing, 422
Plimpton, George, 131–32
Plot
climax, 376
conflict, 226–27, 376
as literary element, 376
order of events, 227
suspense, 227
Plurals
compound nouns, 878–79
irregular, 878
letters, numerals, symbols, words
referred to as words, 857–58,
879–80
nouns borrowed from other
languages, 879
regular, 877
Po Chü-i, 997
Poetry, 60, 207–208
Point-by-point method of comparison/
contrast writing, 262–64
Point of view, 134
description, 183

first-person, 147, 183, 224, 296, 377
  limited narrator, 224
  as literary element, 377
  omniscient narrator, 224
  second-person, 134
  short story, 223–24
  third-person, 134, 183, 224, 377
Pope, Joyce, 99
Portfolio, 58, 107, 137, 167, 171, 205,
  208, 242, 246, 280, 284, 314, 318, 355,
  358, 391, 395, 439, 442
Positive degree of comparison, 279,
  720–22
Possessive case
  and apostrophe, 848–51
  compound words, 851
  individual possession, 851
  joint possession, 851
  nouns, 848–49
  organizations, businesses, 851
  personal pronouns, 649–50
  plural, 849
  pronouns, distinguished from
    contractions, 850, 854–55
  singular, 848–49
Précis, 998
Predicate, 546–57. *See also* Verb.
  complete, 547
  defined, 546
  simple, 548–49
Predicate adjective, 560, 1020
Predicate nominative, 560
  agreement of subject and verb, 631
  defined, 653
  diagramed, 1020
  pronoun as, 653
Predictably, comparison of, 721
Prefixes
  defined, 968
  and hyphen, 861
  list of, 968
  spelling rule for, 873
  as word parts, 966, 968
Preposition, 534–35
  compound, 535, 620
  defined, 534
  distinguished from adverb, 535
  list of, 535
  object of, 534, 574
Prepositional phrase, 534
  adjective phrase, 574–75
  adverb phrase, 576
  and combining sentences, 465
  defined, 450, 550, 574

  diagramed, 1022–23
  distinguished from indirect object,
    563
  distinguished from infinitive, 574
  never contains complement, 558,
    562
  never contains subject, 550–51, 620
  object of, 574
  punctuating, 801
  as sentence fragment, 450
Present participle, 580
  as principal part of verb, 678–81
  and progressive form, 686
  as verbal, 579–80
Present perfect tense, uses of, 689
Present tense, 688
Prewriting
  comparison/contrast essay, 256–65
  critical analysis, 369–83
  description, 181–90
  essay tests, 1010
  personal narrative, 145–54
  persuasive essay, 332–41
  progress report, 294–302
  research paper, 407–25
  short story, 221–28
  word processor used in, 985
  writing process, 6, 22–23, 24–44
Principal, principle, 888
Principal parts of verbs, 678–81
Private Lives of the Stars, 98–99
Process explanation, 319–20. *See also*
  Cause and effect.
  in narration, 95–96
Progress report, 294–315
  addressing problems, 300
  audience, 295
  body, 303
  cause-and-effect explanation,
    316–18
  choosing subjects, 294–95
  conclusion, 303
  evaluating and revising, 310–11
  format, 301–302
  framework, 308
  gathering information, 297–300
  introduction, 303
  organizing information, 301–302
  oversimplifying, 316
  point of view, 296
  prewriting, 294–302
  proofreading and publishing, 313–15
  purpose, 295
  showing progress, 294

tone, 296
using graphics to present
    information, 300
Writer's Model, 307–308
writing a first draft, 303–309
Progressive form of verb, 686
Pronoun. *See also* Reference, pronoun.
    agreement with antecedent, 637–39
    as appositive, 664–65
    case forms, 649–58
    and collective noun, 629
    defined, 516
    demonstrative, 517
    distinguished from adjective, 520
    first person, 296
    gender, 638
    in incomplete constructions, 668
    indefinite, 517
    interrogative, 517
    nominative case, 649, 651–53
    number, 637
    objective case, 649, 655–58
    personal, 517
    personal narrative, 147
    possessive case, 850
    possessive confused with
        contractions, 850, 854–55
    reflexive and intensive, 517
    relative, 517
    third-person singular, 638
    unnecessary, double subject, 744
    usage, 649–70
    who, whom, 661–63
Pronoun-antecedent agreement. *See*
    Agreement, pronoun-antecedent.
Pronunciation
    and dictionaries, 960
    history of, 490
Proofreading and publishing
    comparison/contrast essay, 278–81
    critical analysis, 390–92
    description, 204–206
    guidelines for manuscript form, 59
    guidelines for proofreading, 56
    personal narrative, 167
    persuasive essay, 355–56
    progress report, 313–15
    research paper, 439
    short story, 241
    symbols for revising and
        proofreading, 60
    word processor used in, 986
    writing process, 6, 22–23, 55–60
Proper adjective

capitalizing, 764–79
    defined, 764–65
Proper noun
    capitalizing, 764–79
    defined, 515, 764–65
"Psychological Benefits of Exercise,
    The," 316–17
Public speaking. *See* Speaking.
Publishing. *See* Proofreading and
    publishing.
Punctuation
    apostrophe, 848–58
    colon, 821–23
    comma, 793–809
    dashes, 862–63
    end marks, 789–92
    hyphen, 859–61
    italics (underlining), 831–33
    parentheses, 863–64
    quotation marks, 834–40
    semicolon, 816–19
Purpose
    analyzing, 36–38
    comparison/contrast essay, 258–59
    critical analysis, 381
    description, 181
    group discussion, 934–35
    listening and viewing, 941
    personal narrative, 147
    persuasive essay, 335
    progress report, 295
    research paper, 410
    short story, 223
    writing process, 35
Purposes for writing
    creative, 7, 22
    expressive, 7, 22
    informative, 7, 22
    persuasive, 7, 22
Pyle, Ernie, 209–10

Q

"Quasi-Humans," 110
Questioning programs, 61
Question mark
    as end mark, 789
    and quotation marks, 835–36
Questions. *See also* Interrogative
    sentence; Tests.
    agreement of subject and verb, 631
    asking, 30
    essay test, 285–86

5W-How?, 30, 942
indirect, 789
in introduction, 123
research, 412
"What if?," 34, 221
Quiet, quite, 888
Quotation marks, 834–40
and colons, 836
and commas, 835–36
dialogue, 838
direct quotation, 834–40
and exclamation points, 835–36
and interrupting expressions, 835
and periods, 836
and question marks, 835–36
quotation within a quotation, 840
and semicolons, 836
slang words, technical terms, 840
titles of articles, short stories,
essays, poems, etc., 390, 832, 840
Quotations
capitalizing, 763
and colon, 821
in conclusion, 132
critical analysis, 382, 389
direct, 427, 834–40
indirect, 834
for note taking, 421
reference books, 957
research paper, 427

R

Raise, principal parts of, 704
Raise, rise, 704
Readers' Guide to Periodical Literature, 955
Reading
active, 369
focused, 32
purposes of, 984
as study skill, 984–99
Reading skills
graphics and illustrations, 990–91
interpreting and analyzing, 987–89
reasoning skills and, 989–90
relationships among details, 987–89
Reasoning
evaluating, 340–41
false cause and effect, 340
faulty, attacking the person, 340
faulty, circular, 341
faulty, either-or, 341
faulty, hasty generalization, 340

as study skill, 989–90
Reasoning or logic questions, 1004
Reasons
as logical appeals, 337
statements disguised as, 340–41
Receive, principal parts of, 679
Reference, pronoun
ambiguous reference, 669
general reference, 669
indefinite reference, 670
inexact reference, 668–70
weak reference, 670
Reference materials. *See also*
Information sources.
almanacs, 957
atlases, 957
biographical references, 956–57
database, 956
encyclopedias, 956
general, 414
literature reference books, 957
microforms, 956
National Newspaper Index, 414
quotation books, 957
*Readers' Guide to Periodical
Literature,* 955
specialized, 414
thesaurus, 957
vertical file, 956
References, direct, 128
Reflecting on Your Writing
answering questions, 137
comparison/contrast essay, 280
description, 205
details, 171
essays, 167
paragraphs, 107
persuasive essay, 355
portfolio, 58
progress report, 314
short story, 242, 391
Reflexive and intensive pronoun, 517
Regional dialects, 497
Regular comparison of modifiers,
720–21
Regular verbs, 679
Relative adverb, and adjective clause,
602
Relative pronoun
and adjective clause, 601
list of, 517, 601
number, 639
understood, 601–602
Relevant features, 260–61

Reorder, as revision technique, 50–51, 53
Replace, as revision technique, 50–51, 53
Request letter, 976–77
Research paper, 407–40
   audience, 410
   body, 426
   conclusion, 426
   early plan, 420–21
   evaluating and revising, 436–38
   formal, informal, 406
   formal outline, 424–25
   introduction, 426
   MLA format, 419, 428–29
   note taking, 421–23
   organizing information, 420–26
   prewriting, 407–25
   proofreading and publishing, 439
   purpose, 410
   research questions, 412
   source cards, 416–19
   source credit, 427–29
   sources, 414–19
   thesis statement, 423, 426
   tone, 410
   topic, 408–13
   Works Cited, 429
   Writer's Model, 430–35
   writing a first draft, 426–35
Restatements, and vocabulary, 964
Restrictive appositive, 805
Restrictive clause, phrase. *See* Essential
   clause, phrase.
Revising
   comparison/contrast essay, 274–75
   critical analysis, 387–89
   description, 200–202
   essay tests, 1010
   personal narrative, 163–66
   persuasive essay, 351–54
   progress report, 310–11
   research paper, 436–38
   short story, 239
   symbols for revising and
      proofreading, 60
   techniques of add, cut, replace,
      reorder, 50–53
   word processor used in, 986
   writing process, 6, 22–23, 47–53
Ride, principal parts of, 680
Riding the Iron Rooster, 71
Ring, principal parts of, 680
Rise, principal parts of, 704
Rise, raise, 704
Robinson, Francis, 986

*Rock of Ages: The Rolling Stone History
   of Rock & Roll*, 84–85
Roots, 966–67
Run, principal parts of, 680
Run-on sentence
   comma splice, 456
   defined, 456
   fused sentence, 456
   revising, 456–58

Salinas, Marta, 214–18
Salutation, business letter, 975
Scarcely, hardly, 756
"Scholarship Jacket, The," 214–19
"School for Homeless Children: A Rare
   Experience," 131
Second-person point of view, 134
Second-person pronoun, 517, 649
Secter, Bob, 267–70
–sede, –cede, and *–ceed*, spelling rule
   for, 872
See, principal parts of, 681
"Seeds in the bank could stave off
   disaster on the farm," 125
Self– (prefix), 861
Self-evaluation, 47
Sell, principal parts of, 680
Semicolon, 816–19
   compound sentence, 469
   conjunctive adverb, 816–17
   independent clauses, 597, 794,
      816–19
   items in series containing
      commas, 819
   and quotation marks, 836
Sensory details
   description, 94, 191–93, 202
   in paragraph, 71
   and participles, 202
   personal narrative, 149
   words, 191–93
   in writing process, 31
Sentence. *See also* Run-on sentence;
      Sentence fragment; Sentence
      parts.
   adjective placement in, 519
   base, 558
   beginning with *there* or *here*, 553
   beginnings, varying, 478–79
   classified by purpose, 565–66
   classified by structure, 610–11

clincher, 76
combining, 461–72
complements, 557–63
complex, 470–72, 611
compound, 468–69, 610–11
compound-complex, 611
declarative, 565, 789
defined, 544
diagramed, 1017–31
exclamatory, 566
imperative, 565, 790
interrogative, 566, 789
punctuating, 789–90
question, 553
simple, 610
supporting, 71–74
topic, 68–69
Sentence base, 558
Sentence fragment, 446–54
   appositive phrase, 450
   defined, 446, 545
   identifying, 447
   phrase fragment, 449–50
   prepositional phrase, 450
   series of items, 454
   subordinate clause fragment,
     451–52
   used for effect, 448
   verbal phrase, 449–50
Sentence outline, 118
Sentence parts
   complements, 557–63
   predicate, 546–57
   subject, 546–57
Sentence style, 474–81
   parallel structure, 474
   stringy sentences, 475–76
   varying beginnings, 478–79
   varying length, 354
   varying structure, 481
   wordy sentences, 477
Sequence of events
   and paragraph unity, 79–80
   short story, 227
   and verb tense, 692
Series of items
   punctuating, 793–95, 819, 821
   as sentence fragment, 454
Set, principal parts of, 701
Set, sit, 700–701
Setting
   in introduction, 125
   as literary element, 376–77
   short story, 225–26, 235

She, they, he, 744
Shell, Ellen Ruppel, 125
Shone, shown, 888
Short-answer questions, 1007–1008
Short story, 221–43, 369–92
   audience, 223
   characters, 225–26, 229, 235, 377
   chronological order, 227
   conflict, 226–27, 235
   dialogue, 229, 241
   elements of, 229–30, 376–78
   evaluating and revising, 239
   foreshadowing, 377–78
   framework, 236–38
   ideas for writing, 221–22
   irony, 378
   mood, 377
   narrator, 223–24
   plot, 226–27, 376
   point of view, 223–24, 377
   prewriting, 221–28
   proofreading and publishing, 241
   purpose, 223
   responding to, 230–35, 369–75
   setting, 225–26, 235, 376–77
   story map, 228
   suspense, 227
   theme, 378
   tone, 223
   "What if?" questions, 221
   Writer's Model, 236–38
   writing a first draft, 229–38
Should of, 742
Shown, shone, 888
"Sick Leave," 997
Signature, business letter, 975
Simile, 194
Simple predicate, 548–49. *See also* Verb.
Simple sentence
   defined, 610
   diagramed, 1029
   distinguished from compound
     sentence, 796
Simple subject, defined, 548
Sing, principal parts of, 681
Single quotation marks, 840
Single-word modifier, and varying
   sentence beginnings, 479
Sit, principal parts of, 701
Sit, set, 700–701
Situational irony, 378
Sky Dance, 172–73
Slang, 502, 840
Sleep, principal parts of, 681

Slow, slowly, 717
So, overuse of, 469
Social introductions, 930
Some, somewhat, 749
Somewheres, 740
Sone, Monica, 64–65, 67
Sort, type, kind, 746
Sort of, kind of, 746
Sort of a, kind of a, 746
Soto, Gary, 18–20
Sounds, as nonverbal communication, 929
Source cards, 416–19
Source credit
    within body of paper, 428–29
    footnotes, 428
    guidelines, 428–29
    MLA format, 428–29
    parenthetical citations, 428–29
    research paper, 428–29
    Works Cited, 429
Spatial order, 83, 117
    arranging ideas, 39
    description, 94, 189–90
    and paragraph coherence, 83
Speak, principal parts of, 681
Speaking. *See also* Speech preparation.
    communication cycle, 928
    extemporaneous speech, 932
    formal, 930–34
    giving speech, 933
    group discussion, 934–36
    impromptu speech, 929
    informal, 929–30
    introduction to presentation, 934
    making announcement, 934
    nonverbal communication, 929
    oral interpretation, 936–37
    social situations, 930
    speech preparation, 930–33
Speech preparation
    audience, 931
    note cards, 932
    organizing notes and materials, 932
    outline, 932
    selecting a topic, 930–31
    speaking expressively, 933
Spelling
    –cede, –ceed, and *–sede,* 872
    ie and *ei,* 872
    –ly, –ness, 873
    numbers, 881
    plurals of nouns, 877–80
    prefixes, 873

    rules for, 872–81
    suffixes, 873–75
    techniques for good spelling, 870–71
    words commonly misspelled, list of, 893
    words often confused, 882–90
SQ3R study method, 986
Standard English, 498–502, 738
Standardized tests, 1000–1001
State-of-being verb. *See* Linking verb.
Stationary, stationery, 889
Statistics, 71–72
Steal, principal parts of, 681
Steinbeck, John, 90
Stephenson, Carl, 88
Stocker, Sharon, 130–31
Stokes, Geoffrey, 84–85
Story. *See* Short story.
Story map, 228
Strategies for writing, 93
    classification, 93, 97–99
    description, 93, 94
    evaluation, 93, 100–101
    narration, 93, 95–96
Street, The, 196–98
"Stretchbreak: Good-Morning Wake-Up Stretch," 130–31
Stringy sentences, 475–76
Study skills, 984–99. *See also* Reading.
    analyzing graphics and illustrations, 990–91
    analyzing information, 987–89
    classification, 994
    conclusions, drawing, 989–90
    inferences, 989–90
    main idea, 987
    memorizing, 999
    note taking, 992–93
    organizing visually, 994–95
    outlining, 996
    paraphrasing, 996–98
    reading and understanding, 984–99
    reasoning skills, 989–90
    recognizing relationships, 987–88
    SQ3R method, 986
    study methods, 992–99
    study routine, 983
    summarizing, 998–99
    word processor use, 985–86
    writing to learn, 984–85
Style, in writing, 47, 474–81
Subject card, 953
Subject complement
    defined, 560

diagramed, 1020–21
and linking verb, 560
placement of, 560
predicate adjective, 560
predicate nominative, 560
Subjective description, 182–83
Subject of a composition
choosing, 407
in communication process, 5
comparison/contrast essay, 256
description, 181
limiting, 408–409
research paper, 407–13
Subject of a progress report, 294–95
choosing, 294–95
Subject of sentence, 546–57
agreement with verb, 619–34
complete, 547
compound, 554, 627
defined, 546
diagramed, 1017–18
double, 744
finding, 549–51, 553, 620
nominative case, 651–53
simple, 548
understood, 554
Subject-verb agreement. *See*
Agreement, subject-verb.
Subordinate clause, 598–606
adjective clause, 600–602
adverb clause, 603–604
complement, 558, 599
defined, 598
diagramed, 1026–27
noun clause, 606
placement of, 452
as sentence fragment, 451–52
and varying sentence beginnings, 479
who, whom, 661–62
Subordinating conjunction, 471, 603–604
Suffixes
defined, 969
hyphens and, 861
list of, 969–70
spelling rules for, 873–75
as word parts, 966
Summarizing, 945, 998–99
defined, 998
how to, 998
for note taking, 421, 945
as study skill, 998–99
as support for analysis, 382, 389
Summary, in conclusion, 130–31
Superlative degree of comparison, 279,

720–25
Supporting sentences
and implied main idea, 78–79
in paragraph, 71–74
and paragraph unity, 77–78
Swim, principal parts of, 681
Syllable
as aid to spelling, 871
defined, 871
division at end of line, 859–60
Symbols for revising and proofreading, 60
Synonyms
and dictionary, 961
and meaning of a word, 503
reference books, 957
and vocabulary, 964
Syntax. *See* Clause; Complement;
Phrase; Predicate; Sentence; Subject
of sentence.

T

Take, bring, 741
Take, principal parts of, 681
Taking notes. *See* Note taking.
Talk
conjugation of, 685–86
principal parts of, 685
Teach, learn, 746
Teach, principal parts of, 681
Technical terms, 840
Telephone communication, 930
Teltsch, Kathleen, 123, 132
Tense, 684–92
conjugation of verb *talk,* 685–86
conjugation of verb *throw,* 686–87
consistency of, 692
defined, 684
progressive form, 686
and sequence of events, 692
Tests, 1000–10
analogy questions, 1005–1007
essay test questions, 1008–10
matching questions, 1003
multiple-choice questions, 1002
objective tests, 1001–1008
preparing for, 1000
reasoning or logic questions,
1004
short-answer questions, 1007–1008
standardized, 1000–1001
true/false questions, 1003
Than, then, 750, 889

Thank-you letter, 980
That, who, which, 751
That there, this here, 750
The, 519
Their, there, they're, 889
Them, 750
Theme, as literary element, 378
There, here, 553, 631
Theroux, Paul, 71
Thesaurus, 503, 957
Thesaurus, computer programs, 61
Thesis statement, 113–14
    comparison/contrast essay, 265
    critical analysis, 381
    defined, 113
    in introduction, 122, 126
    and limited topic, 113
    and main idea, 113
    research paper, 423, 426
    revising, 114
    writing, 113–14
They, she, he, 744
"Thief, The," 838
Think, principal parts of, 681
Third-person point of view
    in composition, 134
    in description, 183
    limited, 377
    as literary element, 377
    narrator in short story, 224
    omniscient narrator, 377
Third-person pronoun, 517, 649
"Thirsty California Is Trying
    Desalination, A," 113
This here, that there, 750
Throw, conjugation of, 686–87
Throw, principal parts of, 681, 686
Time line, 44
Time order. *See* Chronological order.
"Time Out! Is Baseball Finnished?,"
    267–70
Tired words, 507
Title card, 953
Titles
    agreement of subject and verb, 633
    of composition, 133
    denoting, 390
    italics (underlining), 831–32
    quotation marks, 832, 840
To, too, two, 890
Tone
    description, 183
    introduction, 122
    personal narrative, 147

persuasive essay, 335
progress report, 296
research paper, 410
short story, 223
writing process, 36
Topic
    critical analysis, 381
    and information sources, 408–409
    personal narrative, 145–46
    persuasive essay, 332–34
    research paper, 408–409
Topic outline, 118
Topic sentence, 68–69
    importance of, 69
    location of, 68
    in a paragraph, 68–69
    unity, 77–78
"Tornadoes Damage School," 244–45
Toth, Susan Allen, 96
Transitional expressions, 89–90, 129
    list of, 817
    and paragraph coherence, 89–90
    punctuating, 816–17
Transitive verb, 524
True/false questions, 1003
Try and, 750
Tucker, Ken, 84–85
"Tumbleweed," 207
Twain, Mark, 76
Two, to, too, 890
Type, kind, sort, 746

Underlining (italics). *See* Italics
    (underlining).
Understood subject and dangling
    modifier, 728
    defined, 554
    diagramed, 1017
Unity, 77–80, 128
    defined, 128
    in paragraph, 77–80
Unless, without, 751
Usage, 738–56. *See also* Agreement;
    English language; Modifiers;
    Pronoun; Verb.
Usage labels, 960

Valid conclusions, 990

Variety in sentence beginnings, 478–79
Variety in sentence structure, 481
Verb, 524–27
  action, 524–25
  active voice, 694–96
  agreement with subject, 619–34
  compound, 555
  defined, 524
  diagramed, 1017–18
  helping, 527, 555, 694
  intransitive, 524–25
  irregular verbs, 679–81
  lie, lay, 697–98
  linking, 525–26
  main, 603
  object of, 524
  passive voice, 694–96
  principal parts, 678–81
  regular verbs, 679
  rise, raise, 704
  simple predicate, 548–49
  sit, set, 700–701
  tense, 684–92
  transitive, 524
  verb phrase, 527
Verb phrase, 527, 548
Verb-subject agreement. *See* Agreement, subject-verb.
Verbal, 579–88
  defined, 449, 579
  gerund, 584
  infinitive, 586
  participle, 579–80
Verbal irony, 378
Verbal phrase, 579–88
  and comma, 728
  gerund phrase, 585
  infinitive phrase, 587
  participial phrase, 582–83
  placement of, 450
  as sentence fragment, 449–50
Vertical file, 956
Viewing. *See* Listening and viewing.
Visuals
  charts, 43–44
  to present information, 300
  as study skill, 990–91, 994–95
  time line, 44
Vocabulary, 963–65. *See also* Word parts.
  cause and effect, 964
  choosing right word, 965
  connotation, 965
  context, 964–65
  denotation, 965
  and dictionary, 965
  restatements, 964
  synonyms, 964, 965
  thesaurus, 965
  word bank, 963
Voice
  of verbs, 694–96
  in writing process, 36

W

Wagoner, David, 207
Waist, waste, 890
Walk, principal parts of, 678
Ward, Ed, 84–85
Ward, Geoffrey C., 74
Way, ways, 750
Weak reference, pronoun, 670
Weather, whether, 890
Webbing, 28–29
Well, good, 717, 743–44
Wells, H. G., 169–70
What, 750
"What if?" questions, 34, 221
"What's Your Type? Introverts and Extroverts," 123
When, where, 750
Where, 750, 751
Where . . . at, 740
Which, that, who, 751
Who, whom, 661–63
Who's, whose, 850, 890
"Why No One Lends His Beauty," 321–22
"Winterblossom Garden," 96
Without, unless, 751
Wolfe, Tom, 79–80
Woman Warrior: Memoirs of a Girlhood Among Ghosts, The, 82–83
"Woman Work," 764
Word-association computer programs, 61
Word bank, 192–93, 963
Word division, rules of, 859–60
Word forms, 960
Word parts, 966–70. *See also* Vocabulary.
  base word, 966
  prefix, 966, 968
  root, 966–67
  suffix, 966, 969–70
Word-processing tools, in writing

process, 985–86. *See also* Computers.
Words
  changing form of, 462–63
  choosing right word, 965
  compound, 851, 860–61
  dividing at end of line, 859–60
  foreign, 832–33
  hyphenated, 860–61
  often confused (spelling), 882–90
  sensory, 191–93
  spelling list, 893–95
  technical, 840
Wordy sentences, 477
Work, principal parts of, 679
Workplace skills. *See also* Listening
    and viewing.
  addressing an envelope, 980
  business letters, 973–79
  completing printed forms, 981
  group discussions, 934–35
  introducing a presentation, 934
  making an announcement, 934
  making speeches, 930–34
  oral interpretation, 936–37
  parliamentary procedure, 935–36
  progress report, 303
  speaking informally, 929–30
  writing to explain: exposition, 288
  writing a travel ad, 509
Works Cited, 416, 429
World Wide Web, 407, 408. *See also*
    Internet.
  search engines for, 61
Would of, 742
Write, principal parts of, 681
Writer's journal, 25
Writers, in communication process, 5
Writers on Writing, 163
Writing a final draft, word processor
    used in, 986
Writing a first draft
  comparison/contrast essay, 266–73
  critical analysis, 384–86
  description, 191–99
  personal narrative, 155–62
  persuasive essay, 343–50
  progress report, 303–309
  research paper, 426–35
  short story, 229–38
  word processor used in, 985
  writing process, 6, 22–23, 45–46
Writing Application
  adjectives, 521–22
  agreement, 644–45
  capitalization, 782–83

commas, 803–804
comparative and superlative
    degrees of comparison, 726–27
dashes, 866–68
interior dialogue, 843–44
prepositional phrase, 578–79
pronouns, 671–72
semicolons and colons in a business
    letter, 825–26
Standard English, 752–53
subordination, 608–609
varied sentences, 567–68
verb tense, 706–707
Writing process, 22–60. *See also*
    Audience; Evaluating and
    revising; Prewriting;
    Proofreading and publishing;
    Revising; Writing a first draft.
  audience, 35
  evaluating and revising, 6, 23,
    47–53
  ideas for, 24–34
  prewriting, 6, 23, 24–44
  proofreading and publishing, 6, 23,
    55–60
  purpose, 35
  tone, 36
  voice, 36
  writing a first draft, 6, 23, 45–46
Writing Workshop
  Book Report That Evaluates, A,
    441–42
  Critical Review, A, 393–95
  Extended Definition, An, 282–84
  Free Verse Poem, A, 207–208
  Imagining a Utopia, 169–71
  Letter to the Editor, A, 357–58
  News Story, A, 244–46
  Writing a Cause-and-Effect Essay,
    316–18

You, as understood subject, 554
Your, you're, 890

Zich, Arthur, 68

Acknowledgments

For permission to reprint copyrighted material, grateful acknowledgment is made to the following sources:

Emily R. Alling: Adapted from "Letter to the Editor" by Emily R. Alling from *Newsweek,* July 30, 1990.

Allyn & Bacon: From *The Elements of Style* by William Strunk, Jr. Copyright 1918, © 1959, 1979 by William Strunk, Jr. All rights reserved.

American Heritage: From "The Business of America: Financial Folklore" by John Steele Gordon from *American Heritage,* vol. 42, no. 1, February/March 1991. Copyright © 1991 by American Heritage, a Division of Forbes, Inc.

Andrews & McMeel: From a movie review of *Once Upon A Time . . . When We Were Colored* from *Roger Ebert's Video Companion* by Roger Ebert. Copyright © 1996 by Roger Ebert. All rights reserved.

Atheneum Books for Young Readers, an imprint of Simon & Schuster Children's Publishing Division: From "The Sun: The Star We Know Best" from *Private Lives of the Stars* by Roy A. Gallant. Copyright © 1986 by Roy A. Gallant.

The Atlanta Committee for the Olympic Games: From "Employment Impacts" from *The Economic Impact on the State of Georgia of Hosting the 1996 Olympic Games.*

Margaret Atwood: Quotation by Margaret Atwood.

August House, Inc.: From *Moncrief: My Journey to the NBA* by Sidney Moncrief with Myra McLarey. Copyright © 1990 by Sidney A. Moncrief.

Bilingual Press/Editorial Bilingüe, Arizona State University, Tempe, AZ: "The Scholarship Jacket" by Marta Salinas from *Nosotras: Latina Literature Today,* edited by María del Carmen Boza, Beverly Silva, and Carmen Valle. Copyright © 1986 by Bilingual Press/Editorial Bilingüe.

Stanley Bing: From "The Most Beautiful Girl in the World" by Stanley Bing from *Esquire,* January 1990. Copyright © 1990 by Esquire.

Gwenda Blair and Charles Mann: From "Juan's Place" by Charles Mann and Gwenda Blair from *GEO,* vol. 6, no. 7, July 1984. Copyright © 1984 by Knapp Communications Corporation.

Gwendolyn Brooks: "The Bean Eaters" from *Blacks* by Gwendolyn Brooks. Copyright © 1991 by Gwendolyn Brooks. Published by Third World Press, Chicago. "Home" from *Maud Martha* by Gwendolyn Brooks. Copyright © 1993 by Gwendolyn Brooks. Published by Third World Press, Chicago.

James Chiles: From "To break the unbreakable codes" by James R. Chiles from *Smithsonian,* vol. 18, no. 3, June 1987. Copyright © 1987 by James Chiles.

Michael D. Coe: From "Olmec and Maya: A Study in Relationships" by Michael D. Coe from *The Origins of Maya Civilization,* edited by Richard E. W. Adams.

Consumers Digest® Inc.: From "CD & Videodisc Players" from *Consumers Digest,* vol. 34, no. 6, November/December 1995. Copyright © 1995 by Consumers Digest Inc.

Estate of Harold Courlander: "Why No One Lends His Beauty" from *Olode: The Hunter and Other Tales* by Harold Courlander with Ezekiel A. Eshugbayi. Copyright © 1968 by Harold Courlander.

Gary N. DaSilva: Quotation by Neil Simon from "Up from Success" from *Newsweek,* February 2, 1970. Copyright © 1970 by Neil Simon.

Delacorte Press/Seymour Lawrence, a division of Bantam Doubleday Dell Publishing Group, Inc.: From "Where Have You Gone, Charming Billy?" from *Going After Cacciato* by Tim O'Brien. Copyright © 1975, 1976, 1977, 1978 by Tim O'Brien.

Betty Lou English: From "Covering the News" from *Behind the Headlines at a Big City Paper* by Betty Lou English. Copyright © 1985 by Betty Lou English.

Farrar, Straus & Giroux, Inc.: From "Clean Fun at Riverhead" from *The Kandy-Kolored Tangerine Flake Streamline Baby* by Tom Wolfe. Copyright © 1965 and renewed © 1993 by Thomas K. Wolfe, Jr.

Billie Follensbee: From "Olmec Heads: A Product of the Americas" by Billie Follensbee, September 4, 1996. Copyright © 1996 by Billie Follensbee.

Stephen Foster: *Agayuh* chart by Harry A. Moneyhun.

Harcourt Brace & Company: From "Mushrooms in the City" from *Marcovaldo, or the Seasons in the City* by Italo Calvino. Copyright © 1963 by Giulio Einaudi editore s.p.a., Torino; English translation copyright © 1983 by Harcourt Brace & Company and Martin Secker & Warburg Ltd. From *The Name of the Rose* by Umberto Eco. Copyright © 1980 by Gruppo Editoriale Fabbri-Bompiani, Sonzogno, S.p.A.; English translation copyright © 1983 by Harcourt Brace & Company and Martin Secker & Warburg Ltd.

HarperCollins Publishers, Inc.: From *A Browser's Dictionary* by John Ciardi. Copyright © 1980 by John Ciardi. From *An American Childhood* by Annie Dillard. Copyright © 1987 by Annie Dillard. From *Voices from the Civil War: A Documentary History of the Great American Conflict*, edited by Milton Meltzer. Copyright © 1989 by Milton Meltzer.

Henry Holt and Company, Inc.: From *My Life with Martin Luther King, Jr.* by Coretta Scott King. Copyright © 1969, 1993 by Coretta Scott King.

Houghton Mifflin Company: From "How Time Goes" from *Doodle Soup* by John Ciardi. Copyright © 1985 by Myra J. Ciardi. All rights reserved. From *The Street* by Ann Petry. Copyright 1946 and renewed © 1974 by Ann Petry. All rights reserved.

Alfred A. Knopf, Inc.: From "The Faith of Fifty Million People: 1910–1920" from *Baseball: An Illustrated History*, narrative by Geoffrey C. Ward, based on documentary film script by Geoffrey C. Ward and Ken Burns. Copyright © 1994 by Baseball Film Project, Inc. From "White Tigers" from *Memoirs of a Girlhood Among Ghosts* by Maxine Hong Kingston. Copyright © 1975, 1976 by Maxine Hong Kingston.

The Ledger, a New York Times Co. Newspaper: From "Two tornadoes damage airport, Miami school" (Retitled: "Tornadoes Damage School") from *The Ledger,* January 16, 1991. Copyright © 1991 by The Lakeland Ledger Publishing Company.

Elmore Leonard: Quotation by Elmore Leonard from *Newsweek*, April 22, 1985. Copyright © 1985 by Newsweek, Inc.

Little, Brown and Company: From *Mythology* by Edith Hamilton. Copyright 1942 by Edith Hamilton; copyright renewed © 1969 by Dorian Fielding Reid and Doris Fielding Reid. From *Blue Highways: A Journey into America* by William Least Heat Moon. Copyright © 1982 by William Least Heat Moon. From *Nisei Daughter* by Monica Sone. Copyright 1953 and renewed © 1981 by Monica Sone. From *Blooming: A Small-Town Girlhood* by Susan Allen Toth. Copyright © 1978, 1981 by Susan Allen Toth.

Los Angeles Times Syndicate: From "Time Out! Is Baseball Finnished?" by Bob Secter from *The Miami Herald,* August 3, 1990. Copyright © 1990 by Los Angeles Times Syndicate.

W. W. Norton & Company, Inc.: From the Editors' Introduction to "The Origin of Diseases" by Mourning Dove (Hum-ishu-ma) from *The Norton Anthology of Literature by Women: The Tradition in English,* edited by Sandra M. Gilbert and Susan Gubar. Copyright © 1985 by Sandra M. Gilbert and Susan Gubar.

The Octagon Press Ltd.: From "The Thief" from *Caravan of Dreams* by Idries Shah. Copyright © 1968 by Idries Shah.

Omni Publications International, Ltd.: "Can Bicycles Save the World?" by Jane Bosveld from "Continuum" from *Omni,* vol. 11, no. 5, February 1989. Copyright © 1989 by Omni Publications International, Ltd. From "Pioneers Underfoot" by Sherry Baker from "Continuum" from *Omni,* vol. 12, no. 1, October 1989. Copyright © 1989 by Omni Publications International, Ltd. From "Quasi-Humans" by R. A. Deckert from *Omni,* vol. 12, no. 5, February 1990. Copyright © 1990 by Omni Publications International, Ltd.

Oxford University Press, Inc.: From "Sky Dance" from *A Sand County Almanac: And Sketches Here and There* by Aldo Leopold. Copyright © 1949, 1977 by Oxford University Press, Inc.

PREVENTION Magazine: From "stretchBREAK GOOD MORNING WAKE-UP STRETCH" by Sharon Stocker from *PREVENTION,* vol. 28, no. 2, February 1996, p. 56. Copyright © 1996 by Rodale Press, Inc. All rights reserved. For subscription information call 1-800-666-2503.

The Progressive, 409 East Main Street, Madison, WI 53703: From "We Need Power, Program, and Progress" by Jesse L. Jackson from *The Progressive,* vol. 54, no. 11, November 1990. Copyright © 1990 by The Progressive, Inc.

Publications International, Ltd.: "Frankenstein" (review) from *The Best, Worst, and Most Unusual: Horror Films* by Darrell Moore. Copyright © 1983 by Publications International, Ltd.

The Putnam Publishing Group: From "The Slow Train to Langxiang: Number 295" from *Riding the Iron Rooster* by Paul Theroux. Copyright © 1988 by Cape Cod Scriveners Co.

Random House, Inc.: From "Woman Work" from *And I Still Rise* by Maya Angelou. Copyright © 1978 by Maya Angelou. Quotation by John Gardner from "North Africa: November 1942–June 1943" from *Ernie's War: The Best of Ernie Pyle's World War II Dispatches,* edited with a biographical essay by David Nichols. Copyright © 1986 by David Nichols.

Reed Consumer Books Ltd.: From *My Left Foot* by Christy Brown. Copyright © 1954 by Christy Brown.

Reprint Management Services™: From "The Psychological Benefits of Exercise" by Susan Chollar from *American Health,* vol. xiv, no. 5, June 1995. Copyright © 1995 by American Health.

St. Martin's Press Incorporated: From *Sassafrass, Cypress & Indigo* by Ntozake Shange. Copyright © 1982 by Ntozake Shange.

Scholastic, Inc.: From "Foreword" from *A Fire in My Hands: A Book of Poems* by Gary Soto. Copyright © 1990 by Scholastic, Inc.

Ellen Ruppel Shell: From "Seeds in the bank could stave off disaster on the farm" by Ellen Ruppel Shell from *Smithsonian,* January 1990. Copyright © 1990 by Ellen Ruppel Shell.

Simon & Schuster Books for Young Readers, an imprint of Simon & Schuster Children's Publishing Division: From *Garbage! Where It Comes From, Where It Goes* by Evan & Janet Hadingham. Copyright © 1990 by Evan and Janet Hadingham, and WGBH Educational Foundation.

Simon & Schuster: From "Leonardo da Vinci Asks the Duke of Milan for a Job" from *A Treasury of the World's Great Letters*, edited by M. Lincoln Schuster. Copyright © 1940, 1968 by Simon & Schuster, Inc. From "It's Only Make Believe" from *Rock of Ages: The Rolling Stone History of Rock & Roll* by Ed Ward, Geoffrey Stokes, and Ken Tucker. Copyright © 1986 by Rolling Stone Press.

Sports Illustrated: From "A Yen for Baseball Cards" by Rick Wolff from *Sports Illustrated*, March 4, 1991. Copyright © 1991 by Time Inc. All rights reserved.

Carl Stephenson (Ann Elmo Agency, Inc.): From "Leiningen Versus the Ants" by Carl Stephenson from *Esquire*, vol. 10, no. 6, December 1938. Copyright © 1938 by Carl Stephenson.

Time Inc.: From "The Surprises of the Mail" by Shana Alexander from *Life*, June 30, 1967. Copyright © 1967 by Time Inc. From "Reopening the Gateway to America" by Doris G. Kinney from *Life*, vol. 13, no. 11, September 1990. Copyright © 1990 by Time Inc.

United Press International, Inc.: From "Hayes: 'There Is So Much to Do'" by Helen Hayes.

University of Nebraska Press: From "Grandmother's Land" from *Black Elk Speaks: Being the Life Story of a Holy Man of the Oglala Sioux* by John G. Neihardt. Copyright 1932, © 1959, 1972 by John G. Neihardt; copyright renewed © 1961 by the John G. Neihardt Trust.

Viking Penguin, a division of Penguin Books USA Inc.: Quotation by James Baldwin from "On Revising: Self-Evaluation" from *The Writer's Chapbook*, edited by George Plimpton. Copyright © 1989 by The Paris Review. From *Going Green: A Kid's Handbook to Saving the Planet* by John Elkington, Julia Hailes, Douglas Hill, and Joel Makower. Text copyright © 1990 by John Elkington, Julia Hailes, Douglas Hill, and Viking Penguin, a division of Penguin Books USA Inc. From *The Pearl* by John Steinbeck. Copyright 1945 by John Steinbeck; copyright renewed © 1973 by Elaine Steinbeck, Thom Steinbeck and John Steinbeck IV. From *Golden Lilies* by Kwei-li, adapted and with a foreword by Eileen Goudge Zhang Qing. Copyright © 1990 by Eileen Goudge.

David Wagoner: "Tumbleweed" from *Collected Poems 1956–1976* by David Wagoner. Copyright © 1976 by David Wagoner.

Wallace Literary Agency, Inc.: "An Astrologer's Day" from *Malgudi Days* by R. K. Narayan. Copyright © 1972, 1975, 1978, 1980, 1981, 1982 by R. K. Narayan. Published by Viking Press, 1982.

Weekly Reader Corporation: From "What's Your Type? Introverts and Extroverts" by Sandra R. Arbetter from *Current Health 2*, March 1991. Copyright © 1991 by Weekly Reader Corporation.

The H. W. Wilson Company: Entry for "Reading Comprehension" to "Real, Leslie" from *Readers' Guide to Periodical Literature,* vol. 96, no. 3, May 1996. Copyright © 1996 by The H. W. Wilson Company.

Jon Winokur: Quotations by Anne Bernays, Anthony Burgess, Truman Capote, Willa Cather, Ernest Hemingway, and Toni Morrison from *Writers on Writing,* selected and compiled by Jon Winokur. Copyright © 1986, 1989, 1990 by Jon Winokur.

PHOTO CREDITS

Abbreviations used: (t) top, (c) center, (b) bottom, (l) left, (r) right, (bckgd) background, (bdr) border.

COVER: Ralph J. Brunke Photography.

TABLE OF CONTENTS: Page vi, NASA; vii, Karen Kasmauski; viii, Don Klumpp/The Image Bank; ix, National Anthropological Archives/ Smithsonian Institution; x, ©Fred Bavendam/ Peter Arnold, Inc.; xi, James Newberry; xii(all), Carol Boone; xiv(b), Rob Nelson/Black Star; xv, Everett Collection; xvi(t), Fridmar Damm/Leo de Wys; xvi(b), Donne Bryant/DDB Stock Photo; xvii, Robert Foothorap; xx, Smithsonian Institution; xxi, Richard T. Nowitz; xxiii(l)(c), Craig Aurness/Westlight; xxiii(r), Burke/Triolo; xxiv(tl), W. K. Fletcher/ Photo Researchers; xxiv(tr), Ray Coleman/Photo Researchers; xxiv(bl)(br), Kjell B. Sandved/Photo Researchers; xxv(tl), Lawrence Migdale/Photo Researchers; xxv(tr), Doug Wechsler; xxv(bl), J. H. Carmichael/ Photo Researchers; xxv(br), Fletcher & Bayliss/ Photo Researchers; xxvi(all), Courtesy of McAllen International Museum, HRW photos by Eric Beggs; xxix, Vicki Ragan; xxxi, xxxiii, xxxiv, James Newberry; xxxvii(l), Carolyn Soto; xxxvii(c), Photo by John Montre, Courtesy of HarperCollins.

CHAPTER 0: Page 4, Jeffrey Sylvester/FPG International; 5, Diana Walker/Gamma Liaison; 6, P. Cantor/SuperStock; 7, Rivera Collection/ SuperStock; 14(l), R. Dahlquist/SuperStock; 14(b), Manley/SuperStock; 14(r), L. Manning/ Westlight; 15(tl), Robert Landau/Westlight; 15(tr), A. Butera/SuperStock; 15(bl), Steve Vidler/Leo de Wys; 15(br), Carroll Seghers II/Leo de Wys.

CHAPTER 1: Page 19, Carolyn Soto; 19(bckgd), Gary R. Zahm/Bruce Coleman; 20(all), Gary R. Zahm/Bruce Coleman; 27, Cindy Lewis; 28(l), SuperStock; 28(r), G. Seghers/Photo Researchers; 32(all), Stanley Schoenberger/Grant Heilman; 33(l), Jeff Apoian/Nawrocki Stock Photo; 33(r), Patrick Hagan/Bruce Coleman; 37, Republic Entertainment/ Shooting Star; 38, Peter Menzel/ Stock Boston; 40, William Nawrocki/Nawrocki Stock Photo; 41, D'Arcy McNickle Center for the History of the American Indian, The Newberry Library; 42, Jacques Chenet/Woodfin Camp &

Associates; 44, NASA; 45, David Madison/Bruce Coleman; 46, HRW photo by Eric Beggs; 48, Frank Siteman/Stock Boston; 54(l), Figaro Magazine/Gamma Liaison; 54(r), Giannoni/Sipa Press; 57, Courtesy of General Motors.

CHAPTER 2: Page 69, U.S. Signal Corps (Brady Collection), National Archives; 70, Reuters/ Bettmann Newsphoto; 72, HRW photo by Dennis Fagan; 73, Bernard Wolff/Photo Researchers; 74, Brown Brothers; 75, Robert Kristofik/The Image Bank; 78, SuperStock; 80, David York/The Stock Shop; 81(t), Shooting Star; 81(b), T. Rosenthal/ SuperStock; 85, Photoworld/FPG International; 86(all), Culver Pictures; 87, National Archives; 94, Karen Kasmauski; 99, Kitagaw II/SuperStock; 101, Paramount/Shooting Star; 105(inset), © S. J. Krasemann/Peter Arnold; 105, Images Unlimited/ The Image Bank.

CHAPTER 3: Page 110, C. Orrico/SuperStock; 111(l), Richard Himelsen/Medichrome/The Stock Shop; 111(c), Journalism Services; 111(r), C. Orrico/ SuperStock; 114, John Kelly/The Image Bank; 116, Rex Weyler/Greenpeace; 119, R. Kresge/ SuperStock; 121(tl), Tom Haug/The Stock Shop; 121(tr), Dann Coffey/The Image Bank; 121(b), HRW photo by Eric Beggs; 124, Peter Menzel; 126, Culver Pictures; 127, Hans Wendler/The Image Bank; 129, 130, Park Street; 132(l), NASA; 132(r), Culver Pictures; 133, Don Klumpp/The Image Bank; 135, The President's Council on Physical Fitness and Sports; 137, Park Street.

CHAPTER 4: Page 141, National Anthropological Archives/Smithsonian Institution; 145, Eric Beggs; 149, Lance Schriner; 153, James Newberry; 156, Photo by John Montre, Courtesy of Harper-Collins; 157, Robert Dunne/Photo Researchers; 160(all), David Madison; 170, Reprinted with permission from Popular Science Magazine, ©1930, Times Mirror Magazines, Distributed by Los Angeles Times Syndicate.

CHAPTER 5: Page 177, The Kobal Collection/SuperStock; 178, Dan Morrison; 184, George Archibald, Courtesy of International Crane Foundation; 186, George Tiedemann/ Sports Illustrated; 188, Park Street; 189, James

Newberry; 190(t), Peter & George Bowater/The Image Bank; 190(c), Mark Stephenson/Westlight; 190(b), Myrleen Ferguson Cate/PhotoEdit; 191, ©Fred Bavendam/Peter Arnold; 194, Harald Sund/The Image Bank; 195, Michael Pasdzior/The Image Bank; 204, James Newberry; 209, Brown Brothers; 211(l), Wolfgang Bayer/Bruce Coleman; 211(r), Bob Burch/Bruce Coleman.

CHAPTER 6: Page 238, James Newberry; 245, Roy Britt/Weatherstock; 246, HRW photo by Henry Friedman.

CHAPTER 7: Page 251, Manny Millan/Sports Illustrated; 252, Rick Rickman/Duomo; 253, Focus On Sports; 254, Brian Drake/Sportschrome East/West; 256(l), Tri-Star/Shooting Star; 256(r), © MGM, courtesy of Herb Bridges/HRW photo by Eric Beggs; 259(t), Culver Pictures; 259(b), Brian Lovell/Nawrocki Stock Photo; 264(l), New York Public Library; 267, Markku Ulander/Lehtikuva Oy; 269(all), Pressfoto; 272, Johnny Johnson/Tony Stone Images; 273, Carol Boone; 278, James Newberry; 281(l), HRW photo by Eric Beggs; 281(r), Shelby Thorner/David Madison; 283(tl), Carol Boone; 283(tc), Michal Heron/Woodfin Camp & Associates; 283(tr), (bl), (br), Carol Boone; 287, Panhandle-Plains Museum, Photo by Scott Hyde.

CHAPTER 8: Page 291, The Kobal Collection Granada/Miramax; 295, Gay Bumgarner/Tony Stone Images; 298, D. Young-Wolff/PhotoEdit; 299, HRW photo by Peter Van Steen; 308(l), Bettmann Archive; 308(r), Culver Pictures; 315, HRW photo by Peter Van Steen; 317, Mark Lewis/Tony Stone Images.

CHAPTER 9: Page 326, SuperStock; 327(l), AKG/London; 327(r), Bridgeman Collection/SuperStock; 328, AKG/London; 329, Scala/Art Resource; 332(t), Michael Baytoff/Black Star; 332(b), Bill Curtsinger/Photo Researchers; 338, Stephen Frisch/Stock Boston; 344, Bruce Forster/Tony Stone Images; 346, Jeffrey M. Spielman/The Image Bank; 348, Nick Gunderson/Tony Stone Images; 349, R. L. Kaylin/Tony Stone Images; 353, M. Keller/SuperStock; 360, HRW photo by Lance Schriner; 361, Rob Nelson/Black Star.

CHAPTER 10: Page 364, 365, Everett Collection; 366, Nawrocki Stock Photo; 376(l), Jonathan T. Wright/Photographers Aspen; 376(r), D. Palais/SuperStock; 380, Dover Publications; 394, Everett Collection; 395, Skrebneski/The Dial Magazine/The Everett Collection; 397, Park Street.

CHAPTER 11: Page 403, SuperStock; 404(all), Georg Gerster/Comstock, Inc.; 405, Cornell Capa/Magnum Photos; 413, James Newberry; 430, 431, Donne Bryant/DDB Stock Photo; 433, Fridmar Damm/Leo de Wys; 435, Donne Bryant/DDB Stock Photo; 443(all), AKG/London; 445, James Newberry.

CHAPTER 12: Page 451, Gerry Ellis/Ellis Nature Photography; 453(inset), Library of Congress; 455, Didier Givois/Vandystadt/Photo Researchers; 457(l), G. Desteinheil/SuperStock; 457(r), Joe Cavanaugh/DDB Stock Photo; 459(all), Lee Boltin/Lee Boltin Picture Library; 460, Duomo.

CHAPTER 13: Page 462, Courtesy of the Steinhart Aquarium/Tom McHugh/Photo Researchers; 466, Paul Conklin/PhotoEdit; 470, Robert Foothorap; 475, S. Vidler/SuperStock; 480, Rivera Collection/SuperStock; 482, Lance Schriner.

CHAPTER 14: Page 491, Culver Pictures; 493, Historical Picture Service/Stock Montage; 509(all), SuperStock.

CHAPTER 15: Page 516(all), Tom Jimison; 520, Smithsonian Institution; 527, Walter Rawlings/Robert Harding Picture Library; 529, Four by Five/SuperStock; 532, Martha Swope ©Time Inc.; 540(tl), Eric Beggs; 540(cl), Luis Castaneda, Inc./The Image Bank; 540(cr), Robert Harding Picture Library; 540(tr), Guido Alberto Rossi/The Image Bank; 540(bl), M. Bruce/Lightwave; 540(br), Robert Harding Picture Library.

CHAPTER 16: Page 546, Nebraska State Historical Society; 549, Richard Laird/FPG International; 551, Richard T. Nowitz; 556(tl), (cr), (tr), (bl), Culver Pictures; 556(cl), HRW photo by Rodney Jones; 556(br), HRW photo by Eric Beggs; 557, Scala/Art Resource, NY; 559, M. Richards/PhotoEdit; 564, HRW photo by Eric Beggs; 567(l), Phil Degginger/Color-Pic; 567(r), Steve McCutcheon/Alaska Pictorial Service; 569, Ron Watts/Westlight.

CHAPTER 17: Page 577, Photo courtesy of the National Broadcasting Company; 583, Culver Pictures; 589, David Frazier; 591, Kent & Donna Dannen; 593, SuperStock.

CHAPTER 18: Page 599, Kennedy/TexaStock; 605(t), Alain Dejean/Sygma; 605(b), Ron Behrmann; 612(l)(c), Craig Aurness/Westlight; 612(r), Burke/Triolo.

CHAPTER 19: Page 625, NASA; 626, Russ Kinne/Comstock, Inc.; 630, Adam J. Stoltman/Duomo; 635, Courtesy, Peabody Essex Museum, Salem, MA, Photo by Mark Sexton; 637(tl), W. K. Fletcher/Photo Researchers; 637(tr)(c), Kjell B. Sandved/Photo Researchers; 637(cl), Fletcher & Bayliss/Photo Researchers; 637(c), Ray Coleman/Photo Researchers; 637(cr), Doug Wechsler; 637(bl), J. H. Carmichael/Photo Researchers; 637(br), Lawrence Migdale/Photo Researchers; 640, George Skene/Orlando Sentinel; 643(all), Circus World Museum, Baraboo, Wisconsin.

CHAPTER 20: Page 650(r), Tate Gallery, London/Art Resource, NY; 650(c), People's Republic of Congo, Northeast Region, Mahongwe

Ethnic Group, Mask, Musee Barbier-Mueller, Geneva; 653(tl)(tr)(br), Marcus Castro/Mercury Pictures; 653(bl), Curtis Norman; 655, Park Street; 660, Jo Browne/Mick Smee/Tony Stone Images; 667(l), Jeffrey W. Myers/Stock Boston; 667(c), Bernard Giani/Agence Vandystadt/Photo Researchers; 667(r), Richard Hutchings/Photo Researchers; 674, Kerrick James.

CHAPTER 21: Page 683, Hampton University Museum, Hampton, Virginia; 684, Bob Sebree; 691, Wide World Photos; 702, HRW photo by Art Commercial Studios.

CHAPTER 22: Page 716(all), Courtesy of McAllen International Museum/HRW photo by Eric Beggs; 719, Caroline Wood/Tony Stone Images; 723(l), The Bettmann Archive; 723(r), Chad Slattery/Tony Stone Images; 726(all), Courtesy of School of American Research, Indian Arts Research Center; 731, Joseph A. DiChello.

CHAPTER 23: Page 742(l), Historical Photograph Collection, Washington State University Libraries; 742(r), Okanogan County Historical Society; 759(l)(r), Photo by Charles Nes, Courtesy of Ya-Ya, Inc.; 759(c), Leo Touchet.

CHAPTER 24: Page 766(l), Gordon Parks, Jr.; 766(br), John Dominis; 772, Walter Bibikow/The Image Bank; 781, Christopher Magadini/HRW photo by Eric Beggs.

CHAPTER 25: Page 791, Al Rendon; 800(l), Fernando Bueno/The Image Bank; 800(r), Peter Mauss/Esto; 802(t), Bill McMackins/Unicorn Stock Photo; 802(bl), Tom McHugh/Photo Researchers; 802(br), Gary Retherford/Photo Researchers; 803(l), HRW photo by Eric Beggs; 803(r), Courtesy of Raytheon; 809, Photoworld/FPG International; 810, Arthur Hustwitt/Leo de Wys.

CHAPTER 26: Page 818(all), Vicki Ragan; 822(l), Kansas State Historical Society; 822(r), Courtesy of the Union Pacific Railroad.

CHAPTER 27: Page 834(l), Park Street; 834(cr), Four by Five/SuperStock; 842, Courtesy of Emilio Aguirre/HRW photo by Eric Beggs.

CHAPTER 28: Page 853(t), Christopher Morris/Black Star; 853(b), Paul Conklin; 866(l), Courtesy of United Shoe Manufacturing Corp.

CHAPTER 29: Page 873, UPI/Bettmann; 876(l), Library of Congress; 880, John Margolies/ESTO; 892, HRW Collection.

ILLUSTRATION CREDITS

Pierre Babasin—475, 480, 482

Brian Battles—564, 959

Kate Beetle—221

Linda Blackwell—21, 107, 112, 162, 167, 180, 274, 323, 358, 389, 426

Keith Bowden—466, 497, 559, 577

Stephen Brayfield—87, 193, 225, 621, 803

Rondi Collette—xxii, 26, 76, 81, 455, 485, 490, 608, 612, 657, 810, 820

Chris Ellison—371, 372, 374

Richard Erickson—xxi, 200, 242, 487, 525, 551, 589

Janice Fried—83, 145

Tom Gianni—72, 73, 80, 124, 149, 723, 731

John Hanley—451, 549

Tom Herzberg—197

Mary Jones—501, 508

Linda Kelen—xix, 43, 97, 230, 356, 456, 488, 496

Susan Kemnitz—11, 13, 122 & 123, 206, 232, 235

Rich Lo—xiii, xvii, 50, 209, 323, 430, 435, 470, 523, 625, 626, 749, 880

Pamela Paulsrud—64, 65, 66, 67

Precision Graphics—653, 776, 853

Doug Schneider—91, 99, 182

Jack Scott—222, 489, 746

Steve Shock—30, 92

Theresa Smith—215, 216, 219

Troy Thomas—464

Nancy Tucker—88, 409, 447, 457, 729